The Process of Financial Planning

Developing a Financial Plan, Second Edition

Ruth H. Lytton • John E. Grable • Derek D. Klock

National Underwriter Academic Series

ISBN 978-0-936362-98-1

THE NATIONAL UNDERWRITER COMPANY

Copyright © 2006, 2013
The National Underwriter Company
5081 Olympic Blvd.
Erlanger, KY 41018

Second Edition

Printed in the United States of America

PREFACE

The growth of financial planning from 1969 to the present day represents a phenomenal trend that has influenced the delivery of financial products and services as well as the financial and personal lives of countless Americans—and others—as the profession of financial planning has spread around the world. Globally, the increase in the number of financial planning professionals outpaces that in the United States. In its purest sense, financial planning can make clients' dreams come true. But regardless of the significant contributions of financial planning professionals, financial planning is, in the second decade of the 21st century, plagued by disillusionment and disagreement among those affiliated with the profession, the American public, and the various groups that stand ready to regulate or set standards for ethical practice. No doubt financial planning will continue to evolve over the next 40-plus years just as it has to date. We can only guess that the evolution will continue in response to marketplace changes (i.e., economic, financial, legal, tax, regulatory), changes in financial products, demographic and social changes among consumers, and other factors that we cannot begin to anticipate.

Although there may be disagreement, debate, and worry about the future of financial planning as concurrently conceptualized and practiced, one fact remains true—as it did when the first edition of this book was published; namely, the growth in financial planning as a professional endeavor is manifest on college and university campuses in the United States and worldwide. The discipline of financial planning is being defined, in part, by educators and researchers working with practitioners and students to describe the financial planning process and to develop practice models that are theoretically and scientifically based. The growth in student enrollment in financial planning certificate and degree programs has created the need for a text that explains the financial planning process, the factors associated with writing a financial plan, and the integration of the process with emerging ethical and regulatory standards that govern the profession. *The Process of Financial Planning, Second Edition*, was written to meet this need.

HISTORY

The tools, procedures, and techniques presented in this book originated and were tested at Kansas State University and Virginia Tech for more than a decade. Before the publication of the first edition, we, the authors, would individually provide information, forms, and lecture material to students and hope that each student could distill the information at a high enough cognitive level to write comprehensive financial plans. It did not take long to determine that there must be a better (i.e., systematic) way to teach aspiring planners and others interested in learning about financial planning. This led us to combine notes and materials into what became the first edition of this text.

We look back with satisfaction at the success of this combination of materials. During the period beginning in 2000 and ending in 2011, teams of undergraduate students from Kansas State University and Virginia Tech used the methods and forms presented in this book to compete in and win several national collegiate financial planning competitions. Even more exciting, many of our colleagues around the country started to use this and our other book to help their students achieve success in national competitions—and more importantly, in their careers. Ultimately, we are most proud of the numerous students who have used these materials and gone on to pursue successful careers delivering financial planning and other financial products and services to clients.

PURPOSE

The purpose of *The Process of Financial Planning, Second Edition*, is fourfold. The first objective is to base the financial planning process on foundational concepts central to everyday practice: the ethical, legal, and regulatory environment; planner-client communication; and planner-client decision making. The second—and primary—objective is to offer a more in-depth and multidisciplinary explanation of what we call the *systematic process of financial planning*, which can be used to ground the practice of financial planning and the education of future professionals. Ideally the process described in this text can serve as a framework for the practice of financial planning regardless of an advisor's business model or method of compensation. The third objective is to integrate the systematic process of financial planning with the CFP Board of Standards, Inc., *Standards of Professional Conduct*, so that all students—those who aspire to CFP® certification and those who do not—gain an understanding of the dominant ethical practice challenges facing financial planning practitioners. The fourth objective is to provide an explanation of the components of a model financial plan, whether comprehensive or modular, to document and guide the process for advisor and client.

The myriad factors that affect the delivery of financial planning, as well as the need for personalized product and service delivery, provide a unique professional challenge. Central to the profession is the six-step process proffered by the CFP Board of Standards, Inc., which many authors have explained or adapted. But our experience as educators, practitioners, and observers of financial planning suggested that there was and remains a need for a more definitive explanation. When it was published, the first edition of this text was alone in fully describing and explaining the six-step process of financial planning by introducing a systematic process.

This edition of the book expands on the earlier work by further describing and explaining the systematic method. It has also been updated to include regulatory changes that have affected and will continue to affect the way financial planning is practiced in the United States. Further, material has been added to help students and faculty meet the learning objectives related to client communication as outlined by the CFP Board of Standards, Inc., and other designation and certification organizations. It is also important to note that the materials presented have been written to partially meet course requirements for the capstone Financial Plan Development course described in the CFP Board of Standards, Inc., model curriculum guidelines[1] for all registered personal financial planning programs at colleges and universities. Several objectives were used to guide the revision of *The Process of Financial Planning, Second Edition*, including:

- Updating financial planning impact and characteristic statistics;

- Revising ethical, legal, and regulatory provisions that affect financial planners;

- Developing more concise definitions and descriptions of the process of financial planning;

- Summarizing more completely the systematic processes associated with plan development, implementation, and monitoring; and

- Updating samples of plan documents and planning forms to illustrate their use with clients.

ASSUMPTIONS AND INTENTIONS UNDERLYING CONTENT

When first published in 2006, *The Process of Financial Planning* was unique because it was the only text to fully describe the process of financial planning beyond a few descriptors associated with each step of the process. The text was also the only source of key disclosure documents (e.g., sample client contracts, vision and mission statements, privacy statements) and examples of graphic and textual content for crafting a well-written financial plan. Furthermore, the original edition was among a limited number of sources in which a student who had never seen a financial plan—but was asked to write a plan—could find outlines, forms, and examples, including a complete sample section on education planning from a comprehensive plan.

Before the publication of *The Process of Financial Planning*, students tasked with writing a financial plan were never quite sure how to integrate, develop, and craft a plan based on multiple discrete analyses. The book addressed many of the conceptual and practical aspects of developing and writing either a modular or comprehensive plan. This edition of the text has been further refined to meet the needs of students learning both the process of financial planning and the tasks associated with writing and communicating a plan to clients.

The following points comprise key assumptions underlying the presentation of material in this book:

- This is a companion book to *A Case Approach to Financial Planning, Second Edition, (2013)* by John Grable, Derek Klock, and Ruth Lytton and published by The National Underwriter Company. As the foundational text for the *Case* book, *The Process of Financial Planning, Second Edition,* explores the systematic financial planning process and how it can be used as a model for developing comprehensive financial plans. This book provides a running narrative about the experiences of the Kims and their financial planner, Jane, as they progress from initial client meeting to an ongoing planner-client relationship. Following the process elaborated in this book, *A Case Approach to Financial Planning, Second Edition,* illustrates how the systematic financial planning process is applied in each of the core content planning areas on which a comprehensive or modular plan is based. The *Case* book provides multiple cases for the application of the systematic methodology, including a running case narrative that students can use as a "practice client" to execute the methods learned in this text.

- This book, is intended for use in either mid–level or capstone courses in the financial planning programs of colleges and universities. It is appropriate for use at the undergraduate, graduate, and certificate levels. At the undergraduate level, some programs incorporate the text into their first advanced financial planning class. This use of the book provides students with direct information about the process of financial planning and the regulatory environment early in their academic careers. The text has also been used effectively in capstone courses, which typically entail writing a financial plan, because it can be very beneficial when undertaking the writing process. Most often, the text has been used at the undergraduate and graduate levels in case-based plan development classes, in conjunction with *The Case Approach to Financial Planning*.

- The text is not intended for use as a CFP® comprehensive examination study guide. Although content related to process, ethics, laws, and regulations (including CFP Board expectations for ethical conduct) and the elements of communication in the planning process is useful to those studying for the CFP® examination, the material is intended to be more broadly descriptive of the financial planning profession.

- The book *is* intended to present timely and accurate information; however, it is designed for educational purposes only. Although the information—especially regarding the ethics, laws, and regulations of financial planning and CFP Board expectations for ethical conduct—has been reviewed by the authors and others, some material could be affected by changes in the tax law, court findings, or the future interpretation of rules, regulations, or CFP Board expectations for conduct. Thus, the accuracy and completeness of the information, data, and opinions provided in this book are in no way guaranteed. The authors specifically disclaim any personal, joint, or corporate (profit and nonprofit) liability for loss or risk incurred as a consequence of the content of this book.

FEATURES

Readers will find *The Process of Financial Planning, Second Edition,* unique in its focus and approach. It has several important features that enhance student learning. The pedagogical features of the book are described below.

Core Chapters

The Process of Financial Planning, Second Edition, consists of four sections of nine chapters and four major appendices. It begins with a broad overview of the profession of financial planning by answering the key questions, "What is financial planning?" and "What ethics, laws, and regulations control the practice of financial planning?" The second part of the book reviews important planner-client communication tools and decision-making processes. The third section examines each step of the systematic financial planning process, from framing the planner-client relationship to implementing and monitoring financial planning products and services. The discussion of each step is followed by an explanation of the *Code of Ethics* principles, the *Rules of Conduct*, and the *Practice Standards* that comprise CFP Board expectations for ethical conduct integrated into each step. The fourth part of the book considers the requirements for explaining planning recommendations and motivating a client to take action. The book concludes with appendices including a risk-tolerance assessment, a client intake form, financial planning benchmarks, and a sample financial plan section/chapter. The major parts of the book and their content include:

Part I—The Profession of Financial Planning

1. *What Is Financial Planning?* This chapter describes the historical development of financial planning as a profession. Compensation methods, key stakeholders, and the role of comprehensive planning in serving clients are introduced in this chapter.

2. *Ethics, Law, and Regulation: How Standards Affect the Plan, the Process, and the Profession.* This chapter offers a comprehensive review of ethical issues related to the practice of financial planning. Historical and regulatory frameworks are also introduced. Fiduciary standards are discussed. Procedures associated with registration and certification as a practitioner of financial planning are summarized. Most importantly, this chapter provides examples of disclosure and contract documentation that can be adapted for use when developing a financial plan.

Part II—Fundamental Tools for Financial Planning

3. *Client Communication.* This chapter explains why financial planning requires a mix of technical, counseling, and coaching skills. Examples showing how to reduce client stress, increase client trust, and establish and maintain long-lasting planner-client relationships are provided. This chapter reviews baseline communication skills, the significance of information processing styles when working with clients, and the role of marketing and social media.

4. *Decision Making.* This chapter describes and applies a general model of decision making to the financial planning process and how decision-making rules can be applied to help clients make important financial decisions. Behavioral finance concepts are introduced, as are threats to the decision-making process. The chapter concludes with a summary of how uncertainty, intuition, and habits influence decision making.

Part III—The Systematic Process of Financial Planning

5. *The Systematic Financial Planning Process: An Overview.* This chapter identifies and explains the six steps of the systematic financial planning process. The concept of professional judgment is introduced using the criteria of stakeholders, setting, problem framing and resolution, and standards of practice. The difference between the goal orientation and the cash flow orientation to planning is discussed.

6. *Framing the Relationship, the Situation, and the Goals.* This chapter reviews the fundamental outcomes associated with the first two steps of the systematic financial planning process. It details the types of data and documentation that should be collected from clients as well as the disclosure documentation planners should provide clients. How data can be collected using forms and

interviews and the role of life planning in the discovery process are described. A goal-ranking form is introduced as a mechanism to promote effective goal-oriented financial planning.

7. *Analyzing the Situation and Developing a Plan.* This chapter shows how client data can be analyzed in relation to the planning process. The discussion focuses on identifying the information—including assumptions—used to analyze client data, and understanding the products and strategies available to meet planning needs. This chapter includes several examples of how a planner can explain, apply, and defend recommendations when the cost of funding all recommendations exceeds the discretionary cash flow available. It concludes with a description of how a financial plan is developed and presented. Forms used in the systematic process of financial planning are incorporated, as are CFP Board standards for ethical conduct.

8. *Implementing and Monitoring the Plan.* This chapter examines the importance of implementation and monitoring to build and sustain planner-client relationships. It describes what is meant by implementation and the significance of motivation in encouraging clients to implement recommendations. The chapter concludes with a discussion of the key aspects of ongoing plan monitoring. Forms used in the systematic process of financial planning are incorporated, as are the CFP Board standards of ethical conduct. This chapter explains how the planning process is not a linear progression but rather a recursive process.

Part IV—The Product of Financial Planning

9. *Developing a Financial Planning Product: Writing a Financial Plan.* This chapter introduces readers to the process of writing a financial plan, whether modular or comprehensive. Issues related to writing style, voice, information processing style, and client communication preferences are introduced and discussed. Fundamental guidelines for crafting a well-written plan are identified and applied, and the purpose of each plan component is explained. An outline for writing a plan is provided and disclosure documents are explained.

Part V—Appendices

This part of the text provides four important documents for use throughout the planning process. Appendix A provides a financial risk-tolerance measure for use when assessing a client's willingness to take on financial risk. A client intake form for collecting both quantitative and attitudinal client data is provided in Appendix B. In easy-to-use tables, Appendix C offers common financial planning benchmarks to assess a client's situation. Finally, in Appendix D, a sample plan section—Education Planning—is presented to show those who have never seen a complete financial plan how to develop a section or chapter.

Process to Practice —A Continuing Narrative

Although working through the systematic financial planning process successfully can be a rewarding experience, sometimes the process can seem far removed from reality. *The Process of Financial Planning, Second Edition,* attempts to bridge the gap between theory and practice by providing a real-life example. A retrospective story, told from the perspective of the Kims, a young professional couple with an 8-year-old daughter named Azalea, and their financial planner, Jane, is featured in each chapter in Part III. Each vignette recounts their experiences from the perspectives of the Kims and Jane as another means to explore, define, and illustrate the steps of the financial planning process. The vignettes incorporate the forms recommended as part of the systematic financial planning process as they apply to the Kims' situation. Finally, the Education Chapter of the Kims' comprehensive plan is shown in Appendix D as an example for students to read and for instructors' to use to critique and gauge reader response— either as a student assignment or for in-class discussion.

Fillable Forms

The systematic financial planning process promotes the repeated use of planning forms and procedures to guide and document the planning process. Some financial planners, instructors, and students find the systematic tools and techniques useful for framing a protocol to "attack" the issues presented by a client's situation. Because the approach is methodical and repeatable, the forms on the Web site are fillable so students and instructors can download and complete them. They are exact duplicates of many of the forms and exhibits shown in the chapters, including the client intake form in Appendix B, all of which can be completed electronically. The fillable forms needed to complete text activities can be found on the student website at: http://pro. nuco.com/booksupplements/NUCollege-ProcessBook2e.

End-of-chapter Resources and Review Questions

Each chapter lists additional resources to supplement the educational experience or use as the basis of student assignments. Short essay questions are offered as a way to assess key learning objectives and content mastery of each chapter.

Instructor's Resources

The answers to all end-of-chapter questions are provided in a separate instructor's manual. The instructor's manual provides model answers for each chapter. Recommended teaching techniques and/or students projects are also listed. PowerPoint slides for each chapter are available on the Web site (www.nucollege. com), as is a test bank for assessing student mastery of content.

Summary

When the first edition was published, we fully expected the book to foster disagreement over the explanations and examples offered. To our surprise, we did not receive as much criticism as anticipated. Instead, we think that we were able to encourage dialogue that is continuing to help shape both the process and practice of financial planning—and that will benefit students, practitioners, and most importantly, the clients they serve. We encourage you to join the dialogue and help shape the future course and continuing evolution of financial planning.

Ruth H. Lytton, Ph.D.

John E. Grable, Ph.D., CFP®, RFC

Derek D. Klock, M.B.A

---

1. More information about the model curriculum can be found at www.cfp.net/teamup/model_curriculum.asp#top.

ABOUT THE AUTHORS

RUTH H. LYTTON, PH.D.

Professor, Financial Planning, Virginia Tech

Ruth Lytton is the Director of the CFP Board of Standards, Inc.–Registered undergraduate programs at Virginia Tech. In addition to serving as program director, she provides student services (e.g., academic/career advising, internship supervision, and job placement coaching) and teaches several courses. Dr. Lytton has received various student association, university, and national professional association awards for her contributions as a teacher, researcher, and career/academic advisor, including the College of Human Resources Certificate of Teaching Excellence, the North American Colleges and Teachers of Agriculture (NACTA) Teaching Award of Merit, the College of Human Resources and Education Excellence in Undergraduate Student Advising Award, the Virginia Tech Award for Excellence in Career Advising, and the Association for Financial Counseling, Planning, Education (AFCPE) Mary Ellen Edmondson Educator of the Year Award.

To date, more than 5,000 students have taken her introductory personal finance course. She is coauthor of two financial planning books as well as the student study guide, instructor's manual, and other print and Internet resources for multiple editions of a leading personal finance textbook. She is an academic member of the National Association of Personal Financial Advisors (NAPFA) and the Financial Planning Association (FPA). In 2009 she was awarded the John H. Cecil Lifetime Service Award from the Central Virginia Chapter of the FPA, and in 2012 she was selected as a national FPA Heart of Financial Planning Award recipient. Dr. Lytton also serves as an advisory editor for the *Journal of Behavioral & Experimental Finance* of the Social Science Research Network's (SSRN). She previously served as editor of the *Journal of Personal Finance* and currently serves on its editorial board. Dr. Lytton received her B.S., M.S., and Ph.D. degrees from Virginia Tech. Honorary memberships include Phi Upsilon Omicron, Phi Sigma Society, Kappa Omicron Nu, Phi Kappa Phi, and Golden Key National Honor Society.

JOHN E. GRABLE, PH.D., CFP®, RFC

Professor and Athletic Association Endowed Professor of Family Financial Planning

University of Georgia

John Grable received his undergraduate degree in economics and business from the University of Nevada, an M.B.A from Clarkson University, and a Ph.D. from Virginia Tech. He teaches and conducts research in the CFP Board of Standards, Inc. undergraduate and graduate programs at the University of Georgia. Before entering the academic profession, he worked as a pension/benefits administrator and later as a registered investment advisor in an asset management firm. Dr. Grable served as founding editor of the *Journal of Personal Finance*, a peer-reviewed research journal, and he is currently coeditor of the *Journal of Financial Therapy*. His research interests include financial risk-tolerance assessment, financial planning help-seeking behavior, and financial therapy/counseling. He has been the recipient of several research and publication awards and grants, and is active in promoting the link between research and financial planning practice; he has published numerous refereed papers, coauthored two financial planning textbooks, and co-edited a financial planning and counseling scales book on this topic.

Dr. Grable has served on the board of directors of the International Association of Registered Financial Consultants (IARFC), as Treasurer and President of the American Council on Consumer Interests (ACCI), and as Treasurer for the Financial Therapy Association. He also served on the Research Advisory Council of the Take Charge America Institute (TCAI) for Consumer Education and Research at the University of Arizona. He is the recipient of the prestigious Cato Award for Distinguished Journalism in the Field of Financial Services, the IARFC Founders Award, the Dawley-Scholer Award for Faculty Excellence in Student Development, and the ACCI Mid-career Award.

DEREK D. KLOCK, M.B.A.

Assistant Professor of Practice, Pamplin College of Business, Virginia Tech

Derek Klock is an award-winning faculty member at Virginia Tech. During his six-year tenure with the Department of Finance, he has won both departmental and university awards for his teaching and career-advisory efforts, including the Herakovich Undergraduate Teaching Excellence Award and the Virginia Tech Award for Excellence in Career Advising. Mr. Klock serves as the Coordinator of the Pamplin Finance CFP Program and also serves as career advisor for the more than 500 undergraduate Finance majors. He is also co-advisor to the student-led, fixed-income, investment group BASIS, which manages approximately $5 million for the Virginia Tech Foundation. He has developed print and Internet financial education tools, including co-developing personal financial planning educational software packages for top-ranking collegiate-level textbooks, and he is the coauthor of two financial planning books.

Mr. Klock serves the financial planning industry as a consultant to the *NextGen* initiative of *Investment News* and has previously served as a board member for IARFC and as a reviewer for the *Journal of Personal Finance*. He received both his bachelor's degree and M.B.A. from Virginia Tech. Before returning to the Pamplin College of Business to pursue his M.B.A., he worked in the banking and brokerage industry for nearly five years. Since leaving banking, Mr. Klock has worked as an independent financial advisor and consultant. He has previously held the Virginia State Life and Health Agents License, and NASD (now FINRA) Series 6, 7, and 63 licenses as well as the registered financial consultant (RFC) designation. Mr. Klock also served the nation in the military, where he was twice decorated for meritorious achievement during his service as a drill sergeant.

ABOUT THE PEER REVIEWER

Corey Franco, in 2008, founded Cross Creek Capital Management, LLC, a private wealth management firm located in Teaneck, New Jersey. Currently Mr. Franco is President and Chief Compliance Officer. His 14-year career in investment advisory services and compliance issues has comprised a variety of roles, including director and chief compliance officer of independent investment advisers, providing solutions that address regulatory challenges and support strategic business growth. Mr. Franco's focus is translating regulatory requirements into procedures and controls, managing conflicts of interest, resolving information barrier issues, and conducting personnel training. He is currently also a compliance consultant to a number of independent advisory and broker-dealer clients. He can be contacted at cfranco@crosscreekfinancial.com or at (973) 632-4577.

ACKNOWLEDGMENTS

This book would not have been possible without the contributions of numerous Virginia Tech and Kansas State University students and alumni who helped us learn about financial planning; too many financial planning professionals to name who shared their experiences; anonymous reviewers who challenged us to make the manuscript stronger; and the editors at National Underwriter who showed unwavering confidence in the original book concept and supported the project through countless delays and obstacles.

The second edition would not have been possible without the tireless work of our editor, Jane Garwood. Little did she know what she was tackling when she first met us. We will forever be grateful for her unflagging encouragement and patience, as well as her editing talents and professionalism. Thanks also go to Kathy Flanagan, Rebecca von Gillern, Diana Reitz, Rick Kravitz, and Gerry Centrowitz for fully supporting this book from revision through publication.

Whether named or unnamed, everyone who contributed to this book furthered the overarching mission of financial planning—to make clients' dreams come true—in their own lives and, for those with the resources, changed the lives of others. They also contributed to our mission to firmly establish financial planning as a recognized field of study with a growing body of academic work. Ideally, the process described in this text can serve as a framework for the education of planners and the ethical practice of financial planning regardless of an advisor's business model or method of compensation. Thanks to all for their assistance.

We also want to recognize the important contributions of the following:

- Pinnacle Advisory Group, Inc., of Columbia, Maryland, for allowing us to include its privacy policy and investment management agreement as models for students.

- Ed Morrow of Financial Planning Consultants in Middletown, Ohio for allowing us to include PracticeBuilder financial forms for the client engagement letter and the client plan acceptance letter as models for students.

- Cory Franco, for allowing us to include his example of the ADV Brochure receipt letter as a model for students, and for his expertise in reviewing Chapter 2: Ethics, Law, and Regulation: How Standards Affect the Plan, the Process, and the Profession.

- The CFP Board of Standards, Inc. for allowing us to include many excerpts from the *Standards of Professional Conduct* to make it easier for students to read and study the ethical conduct standards.

Ruth H. Lytton
John E. Grable
Derek D. Klock

ABBREVIATIONS COMMONLY USED IN FINANCIAL PLANNING

Accredited Investment Fiduciary®— AIF®

Alternative Minimum Tax—AMT

American Institute of Certified Public Accounts—AICPA

Assets under management—AUM

Central Registration Depository— CRD®

Certificate of deposit—CD

Certified Financial Planner Board of Standards, Inc.—CFP Board

Certified Financial Planner® Certification Examination—CFP® exam

Certified Financial Planner—CFP®

Certified investment management analyst—CIMA

Certified investment management consultant— CIMC (No longer awarded)

Charitable remainder annuity trust—CRAT

Charitable remainder unitrust—CRUT

Chartered financial analyst—CFA

Chartered financial consultant—ChFC

Chartered investment counselor—CIC

Chartered life underwriter—CLU

Chief compliance officer—CCO

Consolidated Omnibus Budget Reconciliation Act—COBRA

Continuing education—CE

Coverdell education savings account—Coverdell ESA or CESA

Discretionary cash flow—DCF

Employee Retirement Income Security Act of 1974—ERISA

Enrolled agent—EA

Errors and omissions insurance— E&O insurance

Exchange traded fund—ETF

Federal Deposit Insurance Corporation—FDIC

Federal Trade Commission—FTC

Financial Industry Regulatory Authority—FINRA

Financial Planning Association—FPA

Flexible spending account—FSA

Government Accountability Office—GAO

Gramm-Leach-Bliley Act—GLBA

Grantor retained annuity trust—GRAT

Grantor retained unitrust—GRUT

Guaranteed auto protection insurance—GAP insurance

Health Insurance Portability and Accountability Act of 1996—HIPAA

Health savings account—HSA

High-deductible health plan—HDHP

Homeowners policy—HO policy

Incentive stock option—ISO

Individual retirement arrangement—IRA

Investment adviser public disclosure—IAPD

Investment advisor representative—IAR

Investment Advisor Registration Depository —IARD

Investment policy statement—IPS

Internal Revenue Code—IRC

Internal Revenue Code § 529—§ 529 plan

Internal Revenue Service—IRS

Irrevocable life insurance trust—ILIT

Joint tenancy with right of survivorship—JTWROS

Long-term care—LTC

Million Dollar Round Table—MDRT

Minimum required distribution—MRD

Municipal Securities Rulemaking Board—MSRB

National Association of Insurance Commissioners— NAIC

National Association of Personal Financial Advisors—NAPFA

National Association of Securities Dealers—NASD

Nonqualified stock option—NQSO

North American Securities Administrators Association—NASAA

Payable on death—POD

Personal automobile policy—PAP

Personal financial specialist—PFS

Qualified personal residence trust— QPRT

Qualified terminable interest property trust—QTIP trust

Real estate investment trust—REIT

Registered investment advisor—RIA

Required minimum distribution—RMD

Securities and Exchange Commission—SEC

Securities Industry and Financial Markets Association—SIFMA

Securities Investor Protection Corporation—SIPC

Self-regulatory organization—SRO

Spousal lifetime access trust—SLAT

Tenancy/tenants by the entirety—TBE

Tenancy/tenants in common—TIC

Transferable on death—TOD

Uniform Gift to Minors Act account—UGMA account

Uniform Prudent Investor Act—UPIA

Uniform Transfers to Minors Act account—UTMA account

Variable universal life—VUL

SUMMARY TABLE OF CONTENTS

The fillable forms needed to complete text activities can be found on the student website at: http://pro.nuco.com/booksupplements/NUCollege-ProcessBook2e.

DETAILED TABLE OF CONTENTS

Part IV: The Product of Financial Planning

Part V: Appendices

PART I: The Profession of Financial Planning

Chapter 1

What Is Financial Planning?

Learning Objectives

1. Review the historical development of financial planning as a professional career.

2. Recognize examples of financial planning membership and certification organizations as well as the designations, credentials, and registrations offered.

3. Describe the traits of successful financial planners.

4. Explain the terms *financial planning*, *life planning*, and *financial therapy*.

5. Identify the reasons why consumers seek financial planning.

6. Differentiate between a comprehensive and a targeted, or modular, financial plan.

7. Identify why someone might consider a career in financial planning.

8. Describe the different employment channels and business models for financial planning products and services.

9. Identify Financial Industry Regulatory Authority (FINRA) and Securities and Exchange Commission (SEC) requirements for employment as a registered representative, registered principal, or registered investment adviser.

10. Explain the different methods of compensation commonly used by financial planners.

11. Describe career options for those with a financial planning education.

Key Terms

Annual retainer

Assets under management (AUM)

Boutique firms

Certified Financial Planner Board of
  Standards, Inc.

Certified Financial Planner (CFP®)
  certificant

Certification

Coalition for Financial Planning

Commission

Comprehensive financial planning

Dodd-Frank Wall Street Reform and
  Consumer Protection Act of 2010

Dually registered advisors

Ensemble firms

Entrepreneur

Fee-based

Fee-only

Fee-offset

Fiduciary

Financial counselors

Financial Industry Regulatory Authority
  (FINRA)

Financial planning

Financial Planning Association (FPA)

Financial planning process

Financial Planning Standards Board, Ltd.

Financial planning services

Financial Therapy Association

Goal

Hourly fees

Investment adviser representative

Life planning

National Association of Personal Financial
  Advisors (NAPFA)

Objective

Principal

Professional practice standards

Registered investment adviser (RIA)

Registered representative (registered rep)

Securities and Exchange Commission
  (SEC)

Suitability

Targeted, or modular, financial plan

A BRIEF HISTORY OF FINANCIAL PLANNING

The history of financial planning reads, in many ways, like a fast-paced dramatic novel. Imagine a small group of individuals meeting in an airport hotel in Chicago in the late 1960s. This group envisions a new service that will dramatically alter the financial landscape, change the way personal finance is taught in colleges and universities, and alter consumer laws and regulations. After the meeting this small group continues to come together and invite new members. Fast forward 40 years and their dream has become a financial reality—a multibillion-dollar profession considered by many to be one of the top career choices in the new millennium. The process of financial planning, as practiced today in its multiple forms, has its roots in this story. Because the profession is new and in a state of continual change, it is important for those studying the planning process to understand the historical development of the profession.

Financial planning has been called the "first broad-scope service profession to emerge in recent years."[1] Its history can be traced to a meeting in 1969 that led to the founding a year later of the International Association of Financial Planners (IAFP) trade association. The name was later changed to the International Association for Financial Planning (IAFP), but the objective of bringing together professionals representing the variety of specialized financial products and services remained the same. The premise that integrated the group was an emphasis on *service* and not *sales*, although it was the latter that served as the association's and practitioners' foundation. Loren Dunton and James Johnson are credited with organizing the 1969 meeting of 13, and they were instrumental in the development of the IAFP and the College for Financial Planning (originally called the International College for Financial Counseling).[2] The early group envisioned The College for Financial Planning as providing the education and certification to become a financial planner.

Before 1969, only a handful of people practiced what might be considered a kind of financial planning. Nearly all financial services professionals at that time were engaged in stock, bond, or insurance sales. Some practitioners sold products door-to-door, and others sold from storefront locations to individuals or more broadly to companies and their employees. Very few firms used a process to (a) establish a relationship with the client, (b) gather broad-based financial data, (c) examine the data to develop a plan, (d) recommend and implement a solution that included product sales, and (e) monitor a client's situation into the future. The idea of hiring an individual or firm to serve a client as a comprehensive financial planner was something that few practitioners or consumers envisioned at the time.

It did not take long for consumers to realize that there was more involved in achieving financial success than purchasing a product or talking with a financial advisor periodically. Success was more attainable if a professional advisor was hired to help establish goals and objectives and then to develop a comprehensive financial plan to fulfill those aspirations. The 1969 meeting also helped practitioners realize that a process could be used for financial planning both to improve clients' financial well-being and to enhance planners' career and income opportunities by offering greater income stability and allowing practitioners to create a business that could be sold at retirement. Neither of these outcomes was widely available to salespersons prior to 1969.

With the goal of integrated services—the birth of comprehensive financial planning—came the need for education and the establishment of the College for Financial Planning in 1971. Designation of the first 42 **Certified Financial Planner (CFP®) certificants** occurred in 1973.[3] Today, there are more than 64,000 CFP® certificants.[4] Although not without discord and competition from other professional designations that have emerged, the CFP® certification is nevertheless recognized as the premiere designation or consumer standard for qualified financial planners in the United States and internationally.

In 1985, the College for Financial Planning became an independent entity with an educational mission, and the **Certified Financial Planner Board of Standards, Inc.** (CFP Board) was formed to administer the **certification**—a declaration that an individual has met predetermined professional competencies—and to register academic programs that offer education leading to a certificate or a Bachelor's or graduate degree (M.S. or Ph.D.) focused on financial planning. In 1987, the first 20 universities were approved to offer registered educational programs. By 1992, the modular, or topical, examination schedule was replaced with a 10-hour comprehensive, integrated exam. In 2007 a Bachelor's degree became a required element of earning CFP® certification.

The recent pass rate for the exam has averaged less than 60%, which bears witness to the rigor of the preparation and examination process.[5] In describing the certification, the CFP Board asserts that

> a professional certification, like the CFP® certification, is awarded to someone who passes an examination tied not to a particular course or series of courses, but rather to someone who meets professional standards based on broad industry knowledge often called a practice analysis, independent of any training courses or course providers... The purpose of a certification examination is to evaluate a person's mastery of the knowledge, skills, or competencies required for certification, and the examination typically takes place after the participant has had the opportunity to acquire the required knowledge, skills, or competencies.[6]

However, the road from where financial planning began, with only 42 CFP® certificants, to where financial planning is today has not always been a smooth one. Early adopters of the term *financial planning* were dominated by advisors whose primary objective was selling products and assisting clients with tax-avoidance strategies. The use of tax shelters, annuity products, limited partnerships, and hard asset investing captured the attention of financial planners and their clients through the 1970s and early 1980s. Only after significant tax law changes in 1986 and the substantial reduction in inflation of the mid-1980s did the focus of financial planning turn toward a more holistic and comprehensive view of a client's financial affairs.

The 1990s witnessed record numbers of people entering the field of financial planning. Much of the growth was attributable to the robust economy and rising securities prices of the last decade of the 20th century. From that growth emerged a unified organization, the **Financial Planning Association (FPA)**, which was established to develop and promote the financial planning profession. The FPA was formed in 2000 from the merger of the Institute of Certified Financial Planners (ICFP), an organization of CFP® certificants established by 36 of the initial 42 program graduates, and the original integrative trade association formed in 1970, the International Association for Financial Planning (IAFP). The FPA, with more than 25,000 members, has positioned itself as the "heart of financial planning" with the intent of representing the profession and consumers served without regard to business model or method of compensation.[7]

Although the CFP Board and FPA tend to dominate many aspects of the profession, other organizations play an important role in shaping the way financial planning is emerging as a profession. For example, the growth of fee-only financial planning as an alternative to the commission-based sales-oriented model from which financial planning originated resulted in the **National Association of Personal Financial Advisors (NAPFA)** becoming the preeminent organization of comprehensive fee-only financial planners. Currently, NAPFA has approximately 1,500 members and affiliates.[8] In December 2008 the CFP Board, the FPA, and NAPFA formed the **Coalition for Financial Planning** to provide the financial planning profession with a unified voice to promote a fiduciary standard for the delivery of financial planning services and to advocate for more uniform regulation of those who provide financial planning. The Coalition contributed to the **Dodd-Frank Wall Street Reform and Consumer Protection Act of 2010** (typically referred to as *Dodd-Frank*) and represented the financial planning profession in the studies and subsequent rulings that resulted from the legislation and that continue to impact the future of financial planning services and advice.

That meeting in 1969 literally changed forever the face of financial services in the United States, and eventually worldwide. In 2004, the **Financial Planning Standards Board, Ltd.,** became an independent group to foster professional standards and ethical practice among financial planners globally. In 2008, the number of CFP professionals outside the United States (59,676) exceeded the number in the United States (58,830), the birthplace of financial planning.[9]

The diversity of professionals, services, products, and consumers served under the broad umbrella of financial planning has resulted in the widespread growth of membership and certification organizations. Today, a wide range of professional associations promotes research to enhance the body of knowledge about financial planning, professional development regarding the best client and management practices, and networking opportunities for those who provide financial planning products and services. Table 1.1 presents a partial listing of membership organizations active in the United States and Canada. The Financial Industry Regulatory Authority, Inc., (FINRA, discussed later in this chapter) lists more than 100 professional certifications and designations that planners or advisors can earn to differentiate themselves.[10] (For a complete list see http://apps.finra.org/DataDirectory/1/prodesignations.aspx/.) However, only a small number of these are members of the Institute for Credentialing Excellence within the National Commission for Certifying Agencies as of 2011.[11] Table 1.2 presents a select directory of the most widely recognized professional designations, credentials, and registrations. The information in both tables points to the diversity of specialties and richness of the training and ongoing continuing education available to enhance career prospects and enable planners to serve their clients better.

Table 1.1 Select Listing of Financial Planning Membership Organizations

AFS	Academy of Financial Services	www.academyfinancial.org/
ACAT	Accreditation Council for Accountancy and Taxation	www.acatcredentials.org/
ABA	American Bankers Association	www.aba.com/
ABA	American Bar Association	www.americanbar.org/
AICPA	American Institute of Certified Public Accountants (Personal Financial Specialist)	www.aicpa.org/
ARIA	American Risk and Insurance Association	www.aria.org/
AALU	Association for Advanced Life Underwriting	www.aalu.org/
AFCPE	Association for Financial Counseling and Planning Education	www.afcpe.org/
CAIFA	Canadian Association of Insurance and Financial Advisors	www.advocis.ca/
CFA Institute	Certified Financial Analyst Institute	www.cfainstitute.org/
CIFP	Canadian Institute of Financial Planning	www.cifps.ca/
CIMA	Chartered Institute of Management Accountants	www.cimaglobal.com/
FAAC	Financial Advisors Association of Canada	www.advocis.ca/
FPA	Financial Planning Association	www.fpanet.org/
FMA	Financial Management Association International	www.fma.org/
FTA	Financial Therapy Association	www.financialtherapyassociation.org/
GAMA	International General Agents and Managers Association	www.gamaweb.com/
IBF	Institute of Business and Finance	www.icfs.com/
ICFE	Institute of Consumer Financial Education	www.financial-education-icfe.org/
IIAA	Independent Insurance Agents and Brokers of America	www.iiaba.net/
IAQFP	International Association of Qualified Financial Planners	www.iaqfp.org/
IARFC	International Association of Registered Financial Consultants	www.iarfc.org/
IFP	Institute of Financial Planning	www.financialplanning.org.uk/
InFRE	International Foundation for Retirement Education	www.infre.org/
IMCA	Investment Management Consultants Association	www.imca.org/
IDFA	Institute for Divorce Financial Analysts	www.institutedfa.com/
MDRT	Million Dollar Round Table	www.mdrt.org/
NAEA	National Association of Enrolled Agents	www.naea.org/

NAEPC	National Association of Estate Planners and Councils	www.naepc.org/
NAFEP	National Association of Financial and Estate Planning	www.nafep.com/
NAIFA	National Association of Insurance and Financial Advisors	www.naifa.org/
NAPFA	National Association of Personal Financial Advisors	www.napfa.org/
NAPIA	National Association of Professional Insurance Agents	www.pianet.com/
NICCP	National Institute of Certified College Planners	www.niccp.com/
NICEP	National Institute of Certified Estate Planners	www.nicep.org/
RFPI	Registered Financial Planners Institute	www.rfpi.com/
SCSA	Society of Certified Senior Advisors	www.csa.us/
SFSP	Society of Financial Service Professionals	www.financialpro.org/

Table 1.2 Select Professional Designations, Credentials, and Licenses

Acronym	Title	Granting Organization	Web Site
AAMS	Accredited Asset Management Specialist	College for Financial Planning	www.cffp.edu
AI®	Accredited Investment	fi360, Inc. Fiduciary®	www.fi360.com/
CASL	Chartered Advisor of Senior Living	The American College	www.theamericancollege.edu
CDP	Certified Divorce Financial Analyst	Institute for Divorce Financial Analysts	www.institutedfa.com
CFA	Chartered Financial Analyst	Certified Financial Analyst Institute	www.cfainstitute.org
CFP®	Certified Financial Planner	Certified Financial Planner Board of Standards, Inc.	www.cfpboard.org
ChFC	Chartered Financial Consultant	The American College	www.theamericancollege.edu
CLU	Chartered Life Underwriter	The American College	www.theamericancollege.edu
CIMA	Certified Investment Management Analyst	Investment Management Consultants Association	www.imca.org
CPA	Certified Public Accountant	American Institute of Certified Public Accountants	www.aicpa.org
CRC	Certified Retirement Counselor	International Foundation for Retirement Education	www.infre.org

EA	Enrolled Agent	Internal Revenue Service	www.irs.gov
PFS	Personal Financial Specialist	American Institute of Certified Public Accountants	www.aicpa.org
REBC®	Registered Employee Benefits Consultant	The American College	www.theamericancollege.edu
RFA/ RFC	Registered Financial Associate or Consultant	International Association of Registered Financial Consultants	www.iarfc.org
RLP®	Registered Life Planning	Kinder Institute of Life Planning	www.kinderinstitute.com/
RP	Registered Paraplanner	College for Financial Planning	www.cffp.edu

* RIA, or Registered Investment Advisor, is not a professional designation, credential or license, although it is often mistaken for one. The term cannot be used after a professional's name. Registration as an RIA with the Securities and Exchange Commission or state securities regulator(s) is discussed later in this chapter and also in Chapter 2.

As the profession of financial planning moves forward in the new millennium, financial planners have had to retrench as a result of several unexpected economic shocks, not the least of which was the market decline following the Internet stock bubble in the early 2000s and the credit and housing crises that culminated in broad international market declines beginning in 2008. Greater regulatory scrutiny of financial services firms and providers has influenced how financial planners shape their practice models. Financial planning practitioners, policy makers, and regulators continue to debate the role of financial planning, the need for regulation, and the standards that should be applied to those practicing financial planning. The next decade promises to be one of challenge and progress. One thing that is unlikely to change is the continued evolution of financial planning from an emphasis on product sales or transactions toward a more service-oriented, consultative process of helping clients define and achieve life-fulfilling financial goals.

Consumers want to work with financial planning professionals who can deliver value for their lives. In an FPA survey of consumers before the 2008 recession, the responses from those who were actively working with a planner and those who were not were markedly different. Among those working with a planner, 74% were more likely to feel prepared for changing market conditions, whereas only 54% of those who were "self-directing" expressed the same sentiment. More of those working with planners (82%) than those working alone (57%) were likely to feel confident when coping with the financial impact of unexpected events.[12]

Financial planning, as a service, is not inexpensive in terms of time, money, and/or personal vulnerability. Before engaging the services of a financial planner, consumers demand that the benefits outweigh the costs of hiring a planner. Furthermore, both clients and planners want the planning relationship to be pleasant. For the process to succeed, clients must share their hopes and dreams for the future. They should trust the planner to guide their financial situation expertly through the best and worst events that life and the economy can present. As such, it is important for financial planners to be skilled in both "hard" and "soft" planning applications.

Examples of hard planning skills include being able to quickly and accurately evaluate a person's financial situation, calculate projections using time value of money calculations, and provide advice on financial planning products and services. Soft planning skills are those that promote implementation through communication techniques, trust-building exercises, and relationship management. In fact, in surveys of planners over three years, they ranked people/communication skills as the primary factor contributing to their success.[13]

In a recent survey of consumers, when asked to identify the 10 most important factors for choosing a financial planner, traits such as trustworthiness, listening skills, interest in meeting needs rather than product sales, proven performance, and expertise were at the top of the list. Other traits included professionalism, allowing clients to choose the degree of control over decisions, reasonable costs, technological competence, and professional accreditation.[14] As this list illustrates, it is the combination of skills—not a focus on one or two attributes—that consumers find appealing when choosing a financial planner.

Individuals seriously considering entry into the financial planning profession ought to ask themselves if they have, or can attain, these client-identified traits. If the answer to this question is yes, the chance for success in the profession is significantly enhanced. There must also be a commitment to continuing professional development and lifelong learning. Furthermore, dedication to the principles of ethical practice and continuing education will almost certainly help resolve the nagging question of whether financial planning is truly a profession. Many consider financial planning to be a profession in its infancy, and others question whether financial planning is a profession at all. A focus on product and service delivery, not just product sales, is central to the debate.

Many continue to believe that salesmanship should be a primary characteristic of new entrants to the practice of financial planning; however, the ability to foster strong client relationships and technical competence top the list of planner- and client-identified traits. Although the ability to close a sale can be an aspect of relationship management and technical expertise, this personal attribute is not, in and of itself, sufficient to be successful as a financial planning professional. Characteristics such as trustworthiness, problem-solving abilities, and listening skills are necessary aspects of professionalism. These types of characteristics contribute to professional success, whether one is promoting an idea (e.g., a change in household spending to yield savings) or a product (e.g., investment or insurance). Unmistakably, financial planning has grown from a small group of individuals in 1969 to what it is today—a multibillion-dollar service industry that is evolving into a profession focused on better meeting the needs of all consumers.

WHAT IS FINANCIAL PLANNING?

No national standards define what is meant by the term *financial planning*. However, there have been attempts to create a common definition. According to the CFP Board: "**Financial planning** denotes the process of determining whether and how an individual can meet life goals through the proper management of financial resources. Financial planning integrates the financial planning process with the financial planning subject areas."[15] Specifically, the **financial planning process** entails six steps, according to the *CFP Board's Standards of Professional Conduct*.[16] These include:

1. establishing and defining the client-planner relationship;

2. gathering client data, including goals;

3. analyzing and evaluating the client's financial status;

4. developing and presenting financial planning recommendations and/or alternatives;

5. implementing the financial planning recommendations; and

6. monitoring the financial planning recommendations.

Furthermore, these six steps serve as the foundation for the Standards of Professional Conduct or **professional practice standards,** first promulgated by the CFP Board in 1995 through its self-regulatory function to establish a level of professional practice among CFP Board certificants. These steps and the accompanying standards were developed to establish identifiable practice methods to promote professionalism among planners and to increase the value of financial planning relationships for consumers.

Others have defined financial planning much more broadly than the CFP Board. Some practical definitions of financial planning follow:

1. Creating order out of chaos.

2. A deliberate and continuing process by which a sufficient amount of capital is accumulated and conserved and adequate levels of income are attained to accomplish the financial and personal objectives of the client.

3. The development and implementation of coordinated plans for the achievement of a client's overall financial objectives.

4. Income tax planning, retirement planning, estate planning, investment and asset allocation planning, and risk management planning.[17]

It is important to note that both the CFP Board definition and the practical definitions of financial planning are *general* in nature. Someone can follow the process, for instance, without writing a comprehensive financial plan—or any plan, for that matter. The CFP Board asserts that the determination of whether a certificant is providing financial planning, or material elements of financial planning, can be based on consideration of the following factors:

- The client's understanding and intent when engaging the certificant;

- The degree to which multiple financial planning subject areas arc involved;

- The comprehensiveness of data gathering; and

- The breadth and depth of recommendations.

But the CFP Board also asserts that financial planning can occur even if material elements are not provided simultaneously, are provided over a period of time, or are provided as distinct subject areas. Whereas the nuances of this definition may not be apparent to the student or the novice planner, these distinctions will be more evident in discussions of the employment options (typically referred to as *channels*), business models, and regulation of financial planning later in this chapter and in Chapter 2.

For the purposes of this text, **comprehensive financial planning** is defined as the process of helping clients achieve multiple financial goals and objectives through the application and integration of synergistic personal finance strategies. Financial planners and their clients often use the terms goal and objective interchangeably. However, there is a difference between these concepts. A **goal** is a global statement of a client's personal or financial purpose, and an **objective** is a more definite financial target that supports a goal.[18] Goals tend to be broader and more encompassing than objectives. For example, in support of the goal of funding $1.5 million for retirement, the objective might be accumulating $250,000 in a Roth IRA. But the process of arriving at these definitive and quantifiable statements might begin with a client's generalized statements, such as:

- "I want a comfortable retirement."

- "I want to be able to spend time with my grandchildren, who are scattered halfway across the country."

- "I want the freedom to do _____ as long as I'm healthy."

From such broad statements of life goals and dreams the interchange between planner and client—and ultimately the process of financial planning—begins.

An increasing number of financial planners are beginning to recognize the potential significance of a broader exploration of a client's life goals, dreams, and aspirations, and they are choosing to expand, or integrate, financial planning with **life planning**. A review of the literature on life planning reveals concepts such as the exploration of attitudes toward life and money: the emotional, experiential, and spiritual concerns that influence life choices and the use of money; the "soft" issues surrounding money; and the significance or legacy of the individual that supersedes a focus on net worth or assets. In essence, life planning offers the planner and client a richer foundation for asset-focused financial planning by more broadly exploring the *person* for whom the planning is being conducted. Stated another way, attention to life planning reminds the client and planner to build a financial plan grounded in the life—past, present, and future—of the client. Life planning is not psychological self-help or relationship counseling; it is a guided exploration of what is most meaningful in the client's life relative to money.

A new professional association was created in 2010 to unite practitioners from different professional backgrounds who are interested in financial therapy, the integration of cognitive, emotional, behavioral, relational, and economic issues that promote financial health among consumers. The **Financial Therapy Association** (FTA) publishes the *Journal of Financial Therapy* and sponsors an annual conference where financial planners, financial counselors, psychologists, marriage and family therapists, social workers, and others gather to discuss life planning issues, as well as establish standards of practice. The growth of the FTA exemplifies the expanding role of financial planning beyond a product or service emphasis into a holistic approach to helping clients manage the financial and relational aspects of their lives.

Regardless of the planner-client commitment to a broader personal exploration of the role of money in a client's life, the central purpose of financial planning is to position the client to achieve financial goals and objectives. Accordingly, the financial planning process typically involves a review of at least seven broad areas in a client's financial life:

1. current financial position;

2. income taxes;

3. risk management;

4. retirement;

5. investments;

6. estate planning; and

7. education planning and other special needs issues.

It is important to note that these are broad categories of inquiry. Often, comprehensive financial planning results in a written plan delivered to a client that addresses each of these core topics. Whereas baseline analysis should be conducted for every client, the scope of planning services must be tailored to the individual planner-client situation. For example, client financial concerns communicated to planners and reported in a 2011 survey typically included the following, ranked according to their importance to clients:[19]

1. Health care costs

2. Retirement funding

3. Tax burden

4. Investment/asset growth

5. Outliving assets

6. Managing money

7. Amount of personal debt

8. Estate planning

9. Funding education costs

10. Long-term care funding

11. Potential for job loss/downsizing

In a 2009 CFP Board national survey of consumers, 35% or more ranked the following as the most important financial planning issues in their lives: [20]

1. Generating current income

2. Providing health insurance coverage

3. Managing/reducing current debt

4. Building a retirement fund

5. Building an emergency fund

6. Preparing for future medical needs (your or others, e.g., parents)

7. Managing retirement income

8. Providing life insurance coverage

Comprehensive financial planning practitioners typically review *all* areas of a client's financial situation before making a recommendation on any single topic. Rather than focus on one service or product line, a comprehensive financial planner incorporates multiple products and service recommendations into a plan designed to enhance a client's total financial wellness. Comprehensive financial planners believe that this approach offers clients the best opportunity to meet short- and long-term financial goals and objectives, rather than attempting to build a lifetime plan in a piecemeal manner using services and products gathered over time from different advisors.

Nonetheless, some clients' needs may be met most effectively by a single-focus, **targeted**, or **modular financial plan**. The two help-seeking lists of client issues make it clear that an opportunity exists for those interested in writing modular plans. These lists point to the need for planners who can create targeted financial solutions to meet specific client needs. This helps explain why the practice of financial planning is so diverse.

According to the College for Financial Planning 2011 *Survey of Trends in the Financial Planning Industry*, planners continue to report relatively strong demand for separate investment, college education funding, tax, estate, elder care, and insurance plans, although the demand for these types of plans appears to have leveled off at levels similar to those reported in 2006 and 2007. Investment plans, in particular, were most popular among consumers each year the question was included in the survey from 2005 to 2011.[21] Investment and other targeted plans concentrate analyses and recommendation development on specific areas. Although broad questions about a client's financial situation might be considered, a comprehensive analysis of the seven financial areas generally is not conducted.

However, other financial planners are conducting comprehensive reviews of a client's financial situation and writing financial plans—especially comprehensive plans. According to results reported from the same survey, in 2011 55% of all financial planners indicated preparing between 1 and 19 plans, compared to only 18% who indicated never writing a comprehensive plan.[22] When the number of comprehensive plans prepared in 2008 and 2011 is compared to those reported in 2005 to 2007, the numbers remained similar or only slightly lower, except for planners who produced the largest number of plans. Those reportedly producing 50 or more plans in a year increased from 4% in 2007 to 10% in 2011.[23] This increase supports the need for comprehensive financial planning services in the marketplace, and the need for individuals who can synthesize multiple client wishes into a single detailed plan for the future. The ability to evaluate a client's comprehensive financial situation, combined with the skill to write a financial plan that details the current situation and supplies procedures to implement and monitor recommendations, represents traits that are in demand by both employers and consumers.

Societal trends (e.g., the aging of the Baby Boomers, a reduction in employer-provided pensions, the downturn in real estate prices), the complexity and uncertainty of the financial marketplace, and the time-starved lives of Americans contribute to the demand and the diverse market opportunities for financial planning services. Financial planners serve markets ranging from middle America to the ultrawealthy. In fact, there are financial planning opportunities whenever services and products are appropriately matched to the geographic and demographic profile of the clients to be served. Unlike **financial counselors**—sometimes called debt counselors, who work with clients as they react to stressful financial situations and attempt to recover from too much accumulated debt —financial planners typically work with clients in a proactive, future-oriented manner. Debt management could be an issue for a household seeking financial planning, but financial mediation is typically not a primary concern of financial planning clientele.

WHY CONSIDER A CAREER IN FINANCIAL PLANNING?

As a career option, financial planning is perennially ranked as one of the top professional choices in the United States and Canada. For example, in 2006, *Money* magazine and Salary.com ranked a career as a financial advisor third on their list of the 50 best jobs in America based on salary, job prospects, and career characteristics.[24] In 2011, CareerCast.com ranked a career as a financial advisor fifth on its list of the 10 best jobs for 2012 based on work environment, stress, physical demands, and hiring outlook.[25] While in the same year, *Money/CNN* ranked a career as a financial advisor as third on their list of the 10 best jobs in fast-growing fields in America based on personal satisfaction, benefit to society, low stress, and flexibility.[26]

Several other reasons help explain this popularity. First, financial planning is a helping-relationship career. Financial planners strive to help their clients achieve personal and financial success; as a result, the career offers the reward of personal fulfillment. Second, financial planning offers significant earnings potential and job security. In May 2010, according to the Bureau of Labor Statistics, the median annual salary for financial advisors was $64,750, with the bottom 10% of planners earning less than $32,660, and the top 10% earning more than $166,400.[27] In 2011, the College for Financial Planning reported that the mean gross income for financial planners was $190,922—a figure far above the national average.[28]

The aging of financial planners is another factor that makes financial planning attractive as a career, especially for those still in college. As of 2011–2012, the majority of all practicing financial planners are over the age of 50.[29] Many of these planners are business owners who will most likely be transitioning out of the business over the next 15 years. A common theme discussed in trade publications involves how to pass ownership of planning firms to younger employees, what is known as *succession planning*. Young planning professionals today have a unique opportunity to help shape the profession and direct the way planning firms are owned and managed in the future. In fact, in 2012 the Bureau of Labor Statistics projected a 32% 10-year job growth rate in personal financial advisors between 2010 and 2020, much faster than all occupations, which are projected to grow at 14%.[30]

In some respects, the field of financial planning tends to be recession proof. Consumers often need more financial advice and counsel when faced with financial threats and stress. This means that the demand for financial planning services is strong even when the economy is in recession. When the economy is strong, consumers increasingly turn to financial planners as well, as a means to secure a better financial future. This bodes well for those interested in financial planning as a career. Undergraduate or graduate students who are studying financial planning in collegiate programs, and those making a career change after completing a certificate program, are in a unique position to benefit from employment opportunities in the financial planning profession.

Data in Figure 1.1 underscore the reality that financial planners provide services beyond what might typically be considered comprehensive financial planning. In a 2011 survey of CFP® certificants and recent graduates of the College for Financial Planning, 63% of respondents classified their daily activities as "financial planning."[31] However, the multiple affiliations reported by those responding to the annual *Survey of Trends in the Financial Planning Industry* illustrate that the professional practices and business models of financial planners are actually quite diverse.

At the time of the study, nearly 40% were affiliated with the investment planning industry. Almost an equal number, 36%, considered their field of employment to be securities. Insurance affiliations comprised 24%, with the remainder identified as banking (9%), accounting/tax (3%), real estate (1%), and other affiliations (7%). In the survey, it was possible for a planner to indicate multiple affiliations. An interesting trend is that more financial planners appear to be listing multiple professional connections, but the majority identify with financial planning—a continuing trend over the 2005, 2007, and 2011 surveys. Those working in the field seem to be embracing a comprehensive approach to practice, as described by the CFP Board definition of financial planning and the six-step process, despite the fact that the delivery of financial planning services and products occurs through a variety of venues and business models.

Figure 1.1 Industry Affiliations for Respondents with the CFP® Credential

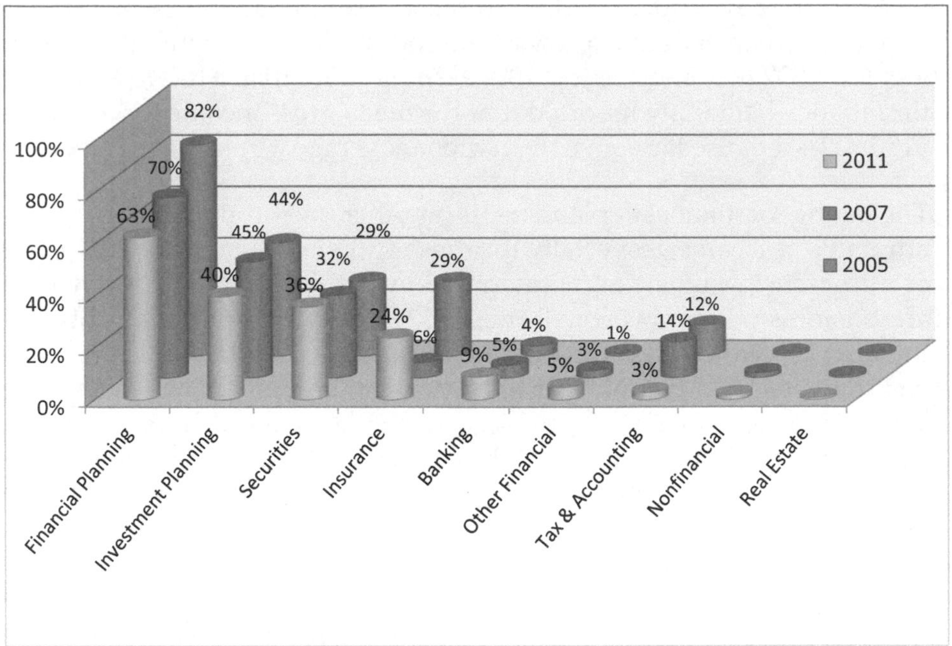

Note: Numbers do not aggregate to 100 because of multiple affiliations reported by planners and rounding. Data for 2009 were unavailable because the industry affiliation question was not included in the 2009 survey.

Source: College for Financial Planning, 2007 *Survey of Trends in the Financial Planning Industry*. Available at http://www.cffpinfo. com/pdfs/2007SOT.pdf, p. 5. Also *2011 Survey of Trends in the Financial Planning Industry*. Available at http://www.cffpinfo.com/pdfs/2011SOT.pdf, p. 4.

Understanding the variety of venues and business models, often referred to as *channels*, for the delivery of financial planning services and products can be challenging for students, novice planners, and consumers. Despite the perennial ranking of financial planning as a top professional career choice, discerning the career paths and characteristics of each channel can be daunting because the entry requirements, methods of compensation, and standards of client care when conducting business can vary. As illustrated in Figure 1.2, based on data from 2000 to 2004, providers of financial planning services, advice, and products can represent five distinct channels:

1. Brokerage firms (independent, regional, and wirehouse);

2. Insurance companies;

3. Banks (as both financial advisors and bank trust officers);

4. Registered investment advisory firms (or advisory firms that function alone or in combination with law or accounting services); and

5. Family (multifamily or single-family) office firms.

Before discussing channels and entry requirements, methods of compensation, and standards of client care, a clarification of brokerage firms may be helpful. The brokerage industry is characterized by *brokers* who buy and sell securities, and by *broker-dealers* that also maintain an inventory of securities that brokers can sell. Brokers are individual investment professionals, whereas a broker-dealer is a firm that may be *brokering* trades or *dealing* (i.e., buying and selling) for its own inventory of securities.

The term *wirehouse* refers to the largest national firms; it originated from the communication system that the main office of a firm used to communicate prices, transactions, and other research to branch offices spread across the country. The next-largest brokerage firms are typically referred to as *regionals*, because the firms originally focused their inventory of securities and services on a specific region of the country, but they may now be serving the entire United States. Finally independent brokerage firms, or broker-dealers, mentioned above, are stand-alone operations that offer a range of securities and services. Regional and independent firms may operate as unique firms, whereas other investment product companies, insurance companies, and banks might operate a broker-dealer as a subsidiary. In addition to simply offering a platform for buying and selling securities, the broker-dealer might also provide a range of products and services (i.e., software platforms, regulatory compliance services, brand recogntion and marketing) that attracts financial advisors to affiliate with it. Examples of such brokerage, or broker-dealer, firms are shown later in Table 1.5.

Figure 1.2 Financial Advisors by Channel

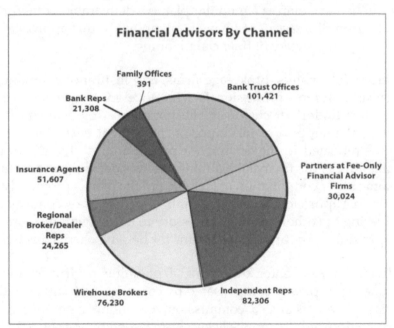

Note: Another source indicated that there were 350,000 CPAs, 60,000 wirehouse brokers, 50,000 independent reps, 50,000 regional broker/dealer reps, 15,000 partners at fee-only financial advisor firms, and 3,000 pension consultants; another source indicated that there are 500,000 financial advisors across all channels.

Source: 2/04 Registered Representative; 11/24/03 Cerulli Edge; 2/9/00 Prima Capital Meeting (Watson); 1/00 Prima FA, CPA, & FO Interviews; 12/10/99 Prima Capital Conversation (McColl); Tiburon Research & Analysis.

Source: Drucker, D. J. "Chasing the Wrong Clients?" *Financial Advisor*, 6. Available at http://www.fa-mag.com/component/content/article/1268.html?issue=62&magazineID=1&Itemid=27

Figure reprinted with permission of Tiburon Strategic Advisors.

Another characteristic that can define the difference in channels is the target market served. For example, mulitfamily and single-family office firms provide integrated financial planning, wealth management, legal, and accounting services, as well as other services, to wealthy clients, typically defined as those with a net worth of $20 million or more. Registered investment advisory firms typically set minimum investment asset requirements (e.g., $500,000 to $5 million or more of investment assets) to differentiate among clients served, as well as the products or services that the market demands. Banks, through financial advisors affiliated with a broker-dealer, serve middle-income America with mutual fund, security, or insurance products (depending on the bank), and trust department services might target more affluent clients of the bank. Addtionally, some brokerage firms, insurance companies, banks, and registered investment advisory firms are targeting products and services to the mass affluent, U.S. households with between $100,000 and $1 million of investable assets.

Central to understanding the practice of financial planning is awareness of the demarcation that divides *and* integrates financial planning channels and business models. The delivery of **financial planning services**—the collaboration of planner and client to identify goals and develop, implement, and monitor recommendations—can be completely detached from the products required for the plan's implementation. For example, insurance, investment, retirement, or other ancillary financial planning products are fundamental building blocks of plan implementation. In its truest sense, a comprehensive plan or a modular plan is a deliverable, sometimes salable, *product* that results from the *service* of financial planning. In this approach the planner's primary focus is on the *service* of financial planning.

Alternatively, banks, brokerage firms, and insurance companies can have a cadre of financial planning professionals who develop comprehensive financial plans based on a "fact finder" or customer questionnaire administered by an advisor or product provider in support of insurance or investment *product* sales. Upon completion, the plan is returned to the advisor for presentation to the client. In some instances, the availability of the financial planning services depends on account holdings, net worth, or some other combination of factors, and the plan is provided as a free service or for a fee. In this approach, financial planning services are secondary to the primary focus of delivering the other products necessary to implement the plan. Nevertheless, the plan can provide a comprehensive means for helping clients reach their goals.

Individuals who enter the financial planning profession through a sales-oriented channel are typically compensated by **commission** (with or without salary). Financial advisors who receive a commission for selling insurance or investment products must be licensed. Insurance licenses are issued by the state(s) in which the agent does business and are differentiated by the type of product sold (e.g., life, health, long-term care, property and casualty). Investment professionals, known as **registered representatives,** who represent a broker-dealer when making a security transaction with the public, and who only provide advice incidental to the sale, must be licensed with the **Financial Industry Regulatory Authority (FINRA),** or what was known prior to 2007 as the National Association of Security Dealers (NASD). The FINRA exams commonly required for entry and advancement are shown in Table 1.3. To advance into the role of **principal**, a manager who supervises registered representatives, additional FINRA exams are required as outlined in Table 1.4. FINRA-registered financial advisors can be employed by brokerage firms, insurance companies, or banks; the requirement for insurance licenses or FINRA licenses is determined by the products sold. In 2012, FINRA is responsible for overseeing nearly 4,450 brokerage firms, 161,065 branch offices, and 629,755 registered securities representatives.[32]

Table 1.3 Entry-Level (Registered Rep) FINRA Licensing Exams

Series Number	Series Title
6	Investment Company Products/Variable Contracts Representative Exam This exam qualifies an individual to sell only investment company securities, variable annuities, and variable life insurance mutual funds.
7	General Securities Representative Examination This exam qualifies a representative to sell any type of security. This exam covers information contained on exams 6, 22, 42, 52, and 62.*
11	Assistant Representative—Order-Processing Exam This exam qualifies an individual associated with a FINRA member firm to accept unsolicited telephone orders and give quotes to customers.
52	Municipal Securities Representative This exam qualifies an individual to sell only municipal securities of qualifying government issuers.
55	Equity Trader Limited Representative The exam qualifies an individual to trade equity and convertible debt securities on a principal or agency basis. Only for those persons holding the FINRA Series 7, 17, 37, 38, or 62 license.
63	Uniform Securities Agent State Law Examination This exam qualifies individuals to sell securities across state lines. These laws are sometimes called "Blue Sky" laws.
65	Uniform Investment Adviser Law Examination This exam qualifies a representative to act as an investment adviser and receive a fee.
66	Uniform Combined State Law Examination This exam qualifies an individual to be both an "agent" of a broker-dealer and an "investment adviser" representative in each state. Only for persons holding the FINRA Series 7 license.
86/87	Research Analyst Qualification Examination/Analysis and Regulations Modules This exam qualifies an individual to produce written or electronic communications that analyze equity securities or individual companies/industry sectors, and provide reasonably sufficient information upon which to base investment decisions. Only for persons holding the FINRA Series 7, 17, 37, or 38 license.

*The FINRA Series 22, 42, and 62 are little-used limited representative examinations, for representing Direct Participation Programs, Options, and Corporate Securities, respectively.

Source: FINRA. Adapted from FINRA Administered Qualification Examinations. Available at http://www.finra.org/Industry/Compliance/Registration/QualificationsExams/RegisteredReps/Qualifications/p011096.

Table 1.4 Advanced-Level (Principal) FINRA Licensing Exams

Series Number	Series Title
4	Registered Options Principal Examination This exam qualifies an individual to manage supervising option sales personnel or individuals supervising options compliance. Only for persons holding the FINRA Series 7 or for persons holding the FINRA Series 62 license with 42, 17, 37 or 38 license
9/10	General Securities Sales Supervisor/Options Module and General Module This exam qualifies an individual to register as principals to supervise sales activities in corporate, municipal, and options securities; investment company products; variable contracts and direct participation programs. Only for persons holding the FINRA Series 7 license. This exam covers information from the 4, 24, and 53 exams.
23	General Securities Principal Sales Supervisor Module This exam qualifies an individual to be an officer, partner, or supervisor of sales personnel with a FINRA member firm. Only for persons holding the FINRA Series 8, 9/10, or 12 license.
24	General Securities Principal Examination This exam qualifies an individual to be an officer, partner or supervisor of sales personnel with a FINRA member firm. Only for persons holding the FINRA Series 7, 17, 37, 38, 62, 79 or 82 licenses.
26	Investment Company Products/Variable Contracts Principal This exam qualifies an individual to supervise the sale of investment company securities and variable contracts. Only for persons holding the FINRA Series 6 or 7 license.
27	Financial and Operations Principal This exam qualifies an individual to be a financial officer of a FINRA member firm.
53	Municipal Securities Principal Examination This exam qualifies an individual to be an officer, partner, or supervisor of a municipal securities dealer. Only for persons holding the FINRA Series 52 or 7 (if passed prior to 11/7/11) license.

Source: FINRA. Adapted from FINRA Administered Qualification Examinations. Available at http://www.finra.org/Industry/Compliance/Registration/QualificationsExams/RegisteredReps/Qualifications/p011096.

The basis for distinguishing the need for FINRA licensure from **Securities and Exchange Commission (SEC)** registration is whether advice is the *primary* aspect of the client-planner relationship. Those who provide investment advice can be registered with the SEC or a state securities office in the states where their clients reside. Although the rules leave some room for interpretation (e.g., the existence of a state investment adviser statute, the number of states where an adviser has client accounts, the number of accounts per state, and the amount of assets under management), generally $100 million of assets under management is the dividing line between registering with the state where the business is located or with the SEC.

Advisers with their "home" or principal office in New York and Wyoming must register with the SEC because New York does not conduct examinations for advisers' business practices and Wyoming does not regulate advisers. Advisers with clients in 15 or more states are exempt from the $100 million minimum and can register with the SEC.

Professionals who are compensated for providing advice, whether or not a product sale results from that advice, must register with the SEC or equivalent state board as a **registered investment adviser (RIA)**. A professional who works for an RIA is typically referred to as an **investment adviser representative (IAR).** Most states (with certain exceptions like Minnesota, New York, and Wyoming) require registration of the IARs affiliated with firms located within the state. Additionally, if a state-registered RIA is working with more than five clients in any state, registration with that state is also required, but four states, Nebraska, New Hampshire, Louisiana, and Texas, require advisers to register with the state if any clients are served within the state. SEC-registered advisers must only "notice file" (i.e., submit paperwork and pay a fee) in states where they have a business office or have more than five clients living, but they are not required to complete the individual state registration process.

Independent financial planners who operate as RIAs often practice in solo firms or in small-to-large group practices referred to as **ensemble firms** because of the variety of professionals (e.g., tax, insurance, aging issues, legal, retirement, executive compensation, business ownership) working together as a group. Small practices, composed of planners and support staff, are sometimes referred to as **boutique firms**, an analogy drawn from retailing because of the specialized products and services offered to a niche market. Table 1.5 profiles the primary financial advisory industry channels in 2010. Registered representatives associated with a wirehouse or one of the other broker-dealer channels represent almost 90% of 320,378 total advisors. Representatives with independent, insurance, and bank broker-dealers attract fewer clients with investable assets over $2 million; but this client group represents 11.1% of clients served by the financial advisory industry.

Table 1.5 Profile of Advisor Channels, 2010

	Number of Advisors	Assets under Management (AUM in billions of $)	Percentage of Clients with Investable Assets Greater than $2 million	Key Products Offered	Select Examples of Companies in Each Channel
Wirehouses	50,742	$4,777.6	15.1%	Individual securities, separate accounts	• Merrill Lynch • Morgan Stanley Smith Barney • Wells Fargo Advisors • UBS
Bank broker/ dealers (B/Ds)	14,986	$464.2	6.1%	Mutual funds, fixed and variable annuities	• JP Morgan Chase • Wells Fargo PNC Financial • SunTrust
Insurance B/Ds	89,121	$429.0	6.2%	Mutual funds, fixed and variable annuities	• Primerica • Allstate Financial • Lincoln Financial • MetLife Securities
Regional B/Ds	34,359	$1,649.6	13.6%	Mutual funds, individual securities, separate accounts	• Edward Jones • Waddell & Reed • RBC Wealth Mgmt. • Stifel, Nicolaus & Co.
Independent B/Ds (IBDs)	97,792	$1,731.9	2.8%	Mutual funds, fixed and variable annuities	• LPL • Ameriprise • H. D. Vest • Raymond James
Registered investment advisors (RIAs)	20,605	$1,298.4	14.8%	Mutual funds, individual securities, exchange-traded funds (EFTs)	
Dually registered advisors (Both IBDs and RIAs)	12,773	$813.1	13.0%	Mutual funds, individual securities, exchange-traded funds (EFTs)	
Total financial advisory industry	320,378	$11,163.8	11.1%		

Source: Cerulli Associates. (2012). The Cerulli Edge © Advisor Edition, 34, p.16.

Points of professional entry, as well as requirements for employment or advancement, also characterize a firm's business model and method of compensation. Financial planners are typically compensated by one or more of the methods listed in Table 1.6, which also loosely parallel financial planning channels and business models. As noted in that table, almost half of the respondents to the *2011 Financial Plan Development and Fees* study conducted by the FPA reported some type of commission revenue.[33] Note that whenever product sales are involved, applicable state insurance and FINRA licensing requirements must be met. It is also important to note that methods of compensation have changed and are likely to continue to change as the profession of financial planning continues to mature and to broaden the client markets served.

Table 1.6 How Financial Planners Are Compensated

Method of Compensation	Example[1,2]	Reported Usage by Practice and Mean Fee[2]
Commission	Varies with the product (investment or insurance), but typically provides a commission at the time of the sale (referred to as a load) and for many products a trailing commission would continue for a specific time or indefinitely.	46%
Flat fee, per plan	Less than $1,000 to $5,000 or more for preparation and delivery of a financial plan; less than $500 to $1,500 or more for a modular plan.	46%, $1,077 per plan
Flat fee, annual retainer	Flat fee of $1,000 to $5,000 or more provides year-round access to a planner and may include plan preparation.	34%, $4,938 annually
By the hour	$100 to $300 or more per hour to work on specific client projects.	47%, $201 per hour
Assets under Management (AUM)	Annual fee for assets actively managed by the planner (typically a sliding scale such as less than 0.50% to 2.49% inversely related to the dollar value of assets managed).	82%, 1.07%
Fee-based/ Fee plus commissions	Plan preparation fee is charged in addition to AUM or other fee structure for investment management services or commissions earned on sales of financial products (e.g., investments, insurance).	
Fee-offset[3]	Charge $3,000, for example, for a comprehensive plan, but use commissions earned on plan implementation (e.g., products sold) to offset the initial planning fee.	
Net worth and income fee	Charge of a percentage of net worth and income, such as 1% of annual adjusted gross income and .0.50% of net worth, with the percentage charged on net worth declining as net worth increases.[4]	

1. R. Powell, "How Much Are Consumers Paying for Financial Plans?" Practice Solutions Magazine, September/ October 2005, 3.

2. R. King, "Fees for financial Planning Services: What Planners Charge." Practice Solutions Magazine, January/February 2012, http://www.fpanet.org/professionals/PracticeManagment/PracticeSolutionsMagazine/JanuaryFebruary2012/FeesforFinancialPlanningServices/. Percentages do not total 100 because of the reporting of multiple methods of compensation.

3. Proper disclosure and explanation are very important because of possible FINRA ramifications and confusion with the illegal practice of rebating. For more information, see Chapter 2, Ethics, Laws, and Regulations.

4. D. Maxey, "How to Pay your Financial Advisor," The Wall Street Journal, December 12, 2011, R8.

Commissions for investment and insurance products are a longstanding source of revenue and they can take many forms as these examples, based on broad industry practices, illustrate. For security trades (e.g., stocks, bonds, and exchange-traded funds) a commission is paid at the time of sale based on the amount of the transaction and the type of brokerage services used, whereas the sale of mutual funds can yield a commission (front-end or back-end) and potentially a trailing commission as well as other marketing fees. Insurance products are typically sold with similar commission structures of a one-time and continuing payment or trail. For example, an annuity could generate a 5% or 6% commission of the amount invested, often with no trail, and a long-term care policy might yield a 25% to 40% commission on the initial premium with a 10% to 20% trail on future premiums. Life insurance products can provide a 20% to 35% commission on the first-year premium, followed by a 5% to10% trail for the first five years, then perhaps 2% for the next 10 or 15 years, and then the trail ends. Other life insurance companies might pay a first-year commission of 80% to 90% of the first year premium and then no subsequent trails. Or a lower first-year commission with a higher trail over a longer period of time might be paid for a life insurance product, such as 15% of the first year premium and a 10% trail for the life of the policy. Finally, it should be noted that insurance commission structures vary widely by company, product line (e.g., life or property and casualty insurance), and product type (e.g. term or variable universal life insurance). Similarly, investment product commissions vary by company, product, and a variety of related fees.

For financial planners who are registered as RIAs with the SEC or state in which they practice (or the states where their clients live) a full range of financial planning services can be offered or coordinated with wealth management or other services, depending on the size of the firm and client capacity. In this case a constant stream of firm revenue can be generated through planning fees or fees for investment management services. Some firms charge **hourly fees**, or a flat fee, such as an **annual retainer** or per plan fee, depending on the planning services sought or the scope of the work to be done. An hourly fee might be charged for a targeted plan or consultation on a particular issue whereas a plan fee would provide for a modular or comprehensive plan. For an annual retainer a client might receive a comprehensive plan, implementation and monitoring services, and access to a planner throughout the year.

As shown in Table 1.6, the majority of planners, as represented in the 2011 FPA study, charge for planning, implementing and monitoring services, and access to a planner through a fee based on **assets under management (AUM)**. Some firms charge a planning fee for the plan in addition to fees for investment services (typically AUM) to determine client charges. As reported in the study, half of the advisers who charged an AUM fee charged between 1% and 1.25%, with a mean or average fee of 1.07%.[34] Because the AUM fee is tied directly to market performance, there is an incentive for planners to protect and increase a client's assets. However, during extreme market downturns, the significant loss of revenue challenged some planning and advisory firms to consider other revenue methods.

A variation that considers a combination of factors such as net worth, income range, or other factors with or without AUM is growing in popularity. This method can benefit the planner with a more secure income stream, but it also offers an incentive to serve a market that might not otherwise be cost-effective to serve under an AUM model. For example, consider a young medical or other type of professional who has a relatively small net worth, high income, and the potential to contribute to wealth accumulation. Initially charging this client a planning or wealth management fee based on net worth and/or income would benefit the client and the firm until the asset growth warrants moving the client to the AUM model.

Firms that choose hourly, retainer, or AUM-based methods of compensation can represent themselves to the public as **fee-only** firms only if no commission-based products are sold directly to clients. Should products be required to implement the plan, fee-only firms typically refer clients to no-load providers or other financial product providers who can meet clients' product needs. NAPFA defines a fee-only planner as

> ...one who, in all circumstances, is compensated solely by the client, with neither the advisor nor any related party receiving compensation that is contingent on the purchase or sale of a financial product. A NAPFA member or affiliate may not receive commissions, rebates, finder's fees, bonuses or any form of compensation from others as a result of a client's implementation of the individual's planning recommendations.[35]

Furthermore, many states mandate a license or other requirements based on experience, education, and/or examination to be eligible to offer fee-based insurance advice as an alternative to commission-based insurance sales.

Depending on the compensation philosophy, some firms use a combination of *planning fees and commissions* to determine client charges. This is referred to as **fee-based** planning. Because a commission is involved, fee-based compensation is not offered by firms that are fee-only. However, some firms use both fee and commission approaches to provide planners the latitude to choose the most cost-effective approach for clients, particularly if the commission-based approach would be more cost effective for a smaller portfolio or a household with a modest net worth. As noted in Table 1.5, advisors using this business model represented a small segment—less than 5%—of the financial advisory industry in 2010.[36] But fee-based, or hybrid, firms are increasing rapidly. These advisors are known as **dually registered advisors**, because they are affiliated with an independent broker-dealer for the commission product sales and with the state or SEC to charge fees as a registered investment advisory service. A variation on this approach is the **fee-offset** method, where commissions generated by the sale of products used in the plan implementation reduce the charge initially assessed for the financial plan.

The differences in methods of compensation are at the core of the debate over business models and the standard of care for serving clients. In effect, the profession is split philosophically over the competing ideas of fiduciary status, which is *required* of planners registered as RIAs with the SEC or states, compared to following a suitability standard, which is the requirement for brokers or those licensed through FINRA. Essentially, federal law requires investment adviser representatives (IARs) to act in the best interest of the client and requires registered representatives (RRs) to act in the best interest of their employer.

Loosely defined, to act as a **fiduciary** means that a professional advisor has entered a relationship built on trust, confidence, and responsibility and, as the result of ethical, professional, or legal duty, will act for the benefit of the other party. A fiduciary relationship is defined by a professional's actions. In a legal sense, as generally defined by the SEC and the American Bar Association, fiduciaries have a responsibility to manage another person's or entity's financial, business, or property assets with care and without considering their own interests. NAPFA membership requires allegiance to a fiduciary oath. The FPA, in its Standard of Care, lists as the first two tenets, "put the client's best interests first" and "act with due care and utmost good faith."[37] In recognition of the diversity of professional activities in which a CFP certificant might engage, the CFP Board of Standards maintains essentially two standards. For those offering financial planning services, the care of a fiduciary is expected. For those involved in other professional activity, the expectation is a high duty of care, but not that of a fiduciary. Specifically, in Rule 1, Defining the Relationship with the Prospective Client or Client, the CFP Board *Rules of Conduct* 1.4 states

> A certificant shall at all times place the interest of the client ahead of his or her own. When the certificant provides financial planning or material elements of financial planning, the certificant owes to the client the duty of care of a fiduciary as defined by CFP Board.[38]

Suitability refers to the recommendation of products and services that appropriately match a client's financial limitations and investment objectives, based on the client's investment profile. Specifically, FINRA in 2012 issued a rule that states:

> A customer's investment profile includes, but is not limited to, the customer's age, other investments, financial situation and needs, tax status, investment objectives, investment experience, investment time horizon, liquidity needs, risk tolerance, and any other information the customer may disclose. . . in connection with such recommendation.[39]

In other words, the suitability standard of care requires that the investment product recommended be suitable, or appropriate, for the client's situation as defined by the investment profile. Although the recommended product *could* be in the client's best interest and the advisor *could* have undivided loyalty to the client, the fact that these are not requirements of the suitability standard is a matter of concern. Although ethical and fair dealing in the recommendation and sale of insurance products is an assumed standard of care in the marketplace, the application of a suitability standard applies only to the sale of annuities. The Dodd-Frank Wall Street Reform and Consumer Protection Act of 2010 requires all 50 states to comply with the Suitability in Annuity Transactions Model Regulation (National Assocation of Insurance Commissioners 2010) by June 16, 2013. Among other things, the model requires insurance companies to monitor annuity sales closely to ensure that the product sold is good for the buyer, and it requires training for agents who sell annuities to help clients make a good decision about the purchase.

Some planners assert that anyone involved in the delivery of financial products and services in a client-planner relationship is a fiduciary, and therefore must act in the best interest of the *client*. Others argue that in some employment situations, the professional has a fiduciary responsibility first to the *employer* to promote products and meet sales goals that must be fulfilled in concert with meeting the client's interests. The availability of sales incentives and commissions can bias the delivery of financial products and services, making it impossible for a salesperson to meet a fiduciary standard.

This bias, or conflict of interest, is not unique to the sales model, however. Recommendations can also be influenced within a fiduciary relationship by decisions that could change the asset structure from which the financial planner's income is derived. For example, consider a situation where a financial planner is paid on an AUM basis. If a client wishes to contribute a large sum to a charity or invest assets in a managed portfolio, the adviser faces a potential conflict of interest. If the recommendation is made to invest in the portfolio, the adviser's income could increase; on the other hand, a recommendation to reduce the portfolio to make a charitable gift or pay off the mortgage could result in a decrease in adviser income. This creates a potential conflict of interest. In fact, any method of compensation has the potential for conflict of interest, although most would agree that a commission-based model offers the most latitude and therefore perhaps the greatest potential for abuse.

Regardless of the type of financial planning undertaken, an understanding of the standard of care and the potential for client litigation should inform all planning activities. Documenting all planning work is key to the client standard of care, whether fiduciary or suitability. Any source that documents a situation analysis, whether for a modular or comprehensive plan, protects the advisor. Without a plan in hand, a client can more easily assert that an advisor acted without adequately evaluating the client's situation. Increasingly, financial planners are encouraged to use written financial plans or suitability analysis documents (in fact, FINRA and the SEC require some documentation) when working with clients because doing so limits a firm's and an advisor's liability exposure. A written financial plan, whether comprehensive or targeted to a specific client need, is one of the single best methods available to avoid future disputes over recommendations or product selection. Drafting a plan obliges a planner to systematically complete and document each step in the process. Delivering a written plan also ensures that a client gives explicit approval of the strategies presented.

As noted earlier, understanding the variety of venues and business models—often referred to as *channels*—for the delivery of financial planning services and products can be challenging for students, novice planners, and consumers. Table 1.7 summarizes the typical employment opportunities and career paths available, noting also compensation methods and levels as well as mandatory and optional education and licensing requirements. The channel, or place of employment and range of securities or services offered, determines entry requirements as well as the method of compensation. For example as shown in Table 1.7, retail sales of mutual funds in a bank or insurance environment entail only a Series 6 exam, not a Series 7, because stocks or other securities may not be represented. The same is true for state insurance licenses, where the licenses needed depend on the products being represented.

In some cases, a firm might specialize in a particular product, such as long-term care insurance. Also of note, assistants or paraplanners employed with multiproduct financial planning firms (e.g., Ameriprise or Waddell & Reed) could be subject to the same licensing requirements as advisors. The need for licensure is determined primarily by whether the assistant or paraplanner facilitates financial product transactions. Requirements for financial planners to register as RIAs in one or more states or with the SEC vary, but the Series 65 exam or an industry designation is typically required.

Table 1.7 Employment Opportunity Comparisons for Financial Services Students

Entry-Level Position in This Type of Firm or Sector	Job Opportunities	Career Advancement	Compensation Method	First-Year Compensation	Long-Term Compensation	Required Education and Licensing	Optional Education and Licensing
Brokerage firm							
Client services/sales assistant	4	1	S+B	$	$$	11	BA+7+63
Retail broker	3	1	C	$	$$$$	7+63+65	BA
Institutional broker/trader	2	4	S+C	$$	$$$$$	7+63+65	BA
Education and outreach	2	3	S+B	$$	$$$	BA	M+7+63+CFP
Analyst	2	3	S+B	$$$	$$$$	BA+86+CFA	M+87
Management	1	3	S+B	$$	$$$	BA+7+63+65	M+10+24+CFP
Insurance firm							
Retail sales	5	1	C	$	$$$$	6 or 7+63	65
Institutional sales	2	3	C+B	$$$	$$$$$	6 or 7+63	65
Management	1	3	S+B+C	$$$	$$$$	6 or 7+65	BA+10+26
Financial planning firm							
Paraplanner	4	4	S+C	$	$$	7+63	BA+65
Financial planner	3	3	C	$$	$$$$	BA+7+63+65+CFP	M
Fee-only planning firm							
Paraplanner	3	4	S+B	$	$$	BA or 65	BA
Financial Planner	1	3	S+B	$$	$$$$	BA+RIA+CFP	M, MBA
Mutual fund firm							
Client services	5	5	S	$$	$$$	6 or 7+63	BA+65
Internal sales	1	5	C+S	$$$	$$$$	6 or 7+63	BA
Wholesaler	1	3	C	$$$	$$$$$	BA+7+63	
Education and outreach	2	4	S+B	$$	$$$$	BA+7	M+CFP
Human resources	2	2	S	$$	$$$	BA	M
Analyst	2	5	S+B	$$$	$$$$$	BA+86+CFA	M+7+87
Accounting	5	2	S	$$	$$$	BA	M+7
Banking firm							
Customer relations	4	4	S	$	$$		BA+6+63
Bank management	2	3	S	$$	$$$	BA	M+6+63
Trust management	2	3	S	$$	$$$	BA	CFP+CFA
Securities sales	5	2	C	$$	$$$$	BA+7+63	M+65+CFP
Financial counseling firm							
Counselor	2	2	S	$	$$	BA	AFC
Manager	1	1	S	$	$$$	BA	M+CFC
Consulting firms							
General consultant	3	5	S+B	$$$	$$$$	BA	M
Benefits consultant	2	5	S+B	$$$	$$$$	BA	M

Key:

Opportunity: 1 = Low; 3 = Average; 5 = High

Compensation method: B = Bonus; C = Commission; S = Salary

Compensation amount: $ = Low Salary; $$$ = Average Salary; $$$$$ = High Salary

Education: BA = Bachelor's degree; M = Master's degree; CFP = Certified financial planner certification; CFA = Certified financial analyst; AFC = Accredited financial counselor: RIA = SEC and/or state securities registered investment adviser:

FINRA Licenses: 6, 7, 10, 11, 24, 26, 63, 65, 86, 87

FINRA Note: For persons holding the FINRA Series 7 license, the FINRA Series 66 license substitutes for both the Series 63 and Series 65.

Source: Grable, J. E., R. H. Lytton, and J. Cantrell. "Financial services employment opportunities: Beyond product sales." *Proceedings of the Association for Financial Counseling and Planning Education,* (2001): 132–142.

As financial planning continues to evolve, the dissension over business models and compensation can be viewed as yet another opportunity for those entering the profession. Although opinions vary, a primary characteristic of success in financial planning is the ability to look at the world with an entrepreneurial perspective and to see income as the by-product of providing a useful service. While the French origin of **entrepreneur** means to undertake or begin anew, what may be more important than the actions of an entrepreneur are the traits they exhibit. Many entrepreneurs are innovative risk takers who enjoy developing or transforming products, services, or delivery methods. These are the same characteristics exhibited by many financial planners in the financial services profession. Individuals who are willing to endure the financial challenges of establishing, growing, or merging a business are generally well rewarded—for themselves financially and for their clients through a legacy provided by the financial planning firm that can serve families for generations in the future. The challenge for the future lies in the continued development of product and service delivery models grounded in the process of financial planning that can effectively serve a broader range of consumers and the life transitions they face.

CHAPTER SUMMARY

In response to the question, "What is financial planning?" this chapter introduced the notion that financial planning is a profession, a process, and a product. Although arguments can be made to counter these assertions, it is important to consider the broader view. Professions are characterized by intensive training, specialized knowledge, and/or concentrated academic study. Professionals, by default, abide by a strict code of ethics and adhere to a policy of continuing education. The history of financial planning supports the claim of professionalism.

Financial planning attracts professionals from a variety of disciplines, designations, credentials, and licensures, nearly all of whom embrace the process of financial planning and developing the required integrative and specialized tools and techniques to work successfully with clients. Consistent with this diversity is the variety of business models and compensation methods used by practitioners and firms; these are also grounded in the process of financial planning. The process of financial planning, summarized in the six steps offered in *CFP Board's Standards of Professional Conduct*, serves to integrate the products and services offered by financial planners in response to the seven broad categories of inquiry within a client's financial life. As such, financial planning can be defined as a deliverable product or service, ranging from the service of exploring life and financial planning issues, to the product, encompassing discrete financial products, to a modular or comprehensive financial plan. Understanding these concepts will help students and novice planners match their skills, interests, and personalities to the appropriate career path in this multifaceted career field, which nearly everyone involved with career assessment agrees offers abundant opportunity not only for the professionals in the field, but more importantly, for the families and individuals they serve.

Learning Outcomes

1. This chapter briefly reviews the historical development of financial planning as it originated in the late 1960s and developed through the first decade of the 21st century. The role of professional designations and certifications is examined, and the current debate regarding fiduciary versus suitability standards is discussed.

2. As highlighted in this chapter, numerous financial planning membership and certification organizations, as well as designations, credentials, and registrations are available to those in the field of financial planning. Although various valuable and prestigious certifications characterize a specialization in financial planning, the CFP® certification—administered by the Certified Financial Planner Board of Standards, Inc.—is generally considered the premier professional certification. Today, more than 64,000 CFP® professionals work in the United States.

3. The demand for financial planning services among the general public is forecast to grow in the future. When polled, consumers indicate they want financial planners to exhibit several important traits, including: trustworthiness, listening skills, the ability to solve problems and achieve performance expectations, technical expertise, professionalism, and technological competence. Consumers also have a strong desire to work with professionals who are accredited or certified.

4. How financial planning services are delivered to the public differs dramatically based on the practice philosophy of each financial planner. Financial planning is a process-oriented service (and sometimes product) that helps clients reach their life goals through the management of financial resources. Some advisors have extended this definition to include the management of other personal and household resources. For example, life planning practitioners and financial therapists look not only at a client's financial resources but also at the cognitive, emotional, behavioral, relational, and economic aspects of a client's situation. Financial life planning integrates financial planning and life planning by exploring how a client's attitudes, beliefs, and values as well as emotional, experiential, and spiritual issues influence the use of money and a meaningful life for the client. Financial therapists combine their expertise in traditional psychotherapy or treating emotional or behavioral disorders with specialized knowledge about the factors that influence financial behavior. Those who practice more holistic planning feel that they can provide meaningful guidance and a plan grounded in the past, present, and future of a client's life.

5. Demographic trends in the United States suggest that the demand for financial planning services will continue to grow over the next 10 to 15 years. Growth projections bode well for the employment prospects of people interested in financial planning as a career. For those considering entering the financial planning field it is important to understand the typical reasons that consumers seek financial planning services. Primary help-seeking questions revolve around the following topics: (a) investment planning; (b) education funding; (c) tax planning; (d) estate planning; (e) insurance planning; (f) elder care; (g) retirement funding; (h) longevity planning; and (i) managing personal debt.

6. When first conceptualized, the process of financial planning was defined to include the writing and delivery of a comprehensive plan. Comprehensive financial plans include a detailed analysis of the seven key financial aspects relevant to most clients' lives: (1) financial situation; (2) taxation; (3) insurance; (4) retirement; (5) investments; (6) estate; and (7) special needs. Although many financial planners still draft comprehensive plans for clients, a growing number of advisors have adopted the use of targeted, or modular, financial plans. As the name suggests, a modular plan typically has a single or limited focus, such as providing specific guidance on investment issues, retirement planning goals, or some other client-directed topic. Neither approach to financial planning is better or worse than the other; what is most important is that the written plan matches each client's needs, desires, and objectives.

7. Financial planning is perennially ranked among the top five career choices in the United States. Two reasons help explain why financial planning might appeal to someone in college or someone considering a career change. First, as a profession based on building a helping relationship, financial planning allows advisors to help others while gaining personal fulfillment. Second, financial planning typically pays well while providing those with entrepreneurial skills the opportunity to build a practice that can ultimately be sold in retirement.

8. Although the nuances surrounding the delivery of financial products versus financial services and planning advice range from distinct to subtle differences, the perceptions affect both financial professionals and consumers. In fact, the differences in some cases have been upheld by legislative and regulatory mandate. Moreover, these differences often fuel the debate over which standard of care providers of financial planning products and services are expected to offer clients and the array of compensation methods used. Typical employment channels within the broker-dealer model include wirehouses and banks, as well as insurance, independent, and regional broker-dealers. More limited opportunities are available in bank trust departments and single- or multifamily office practices. Finally, state- and SEC-registered investment advisory offices offer a range of wealth management and financial planning products and services.

9. Generally, financial planners are regulated either by the Financial Industry Regulatory Authority (FINRA), the Securities and Exchange Commission (SEC), or the state where a business is located. Planners who receive a commission on the sales of securities, in any form, are known as *registered representatives*, who must obtain a license as administered by FINRA. A registered principal is a manager who supervises registered representatives. A series of other licenses are required to be a principal in a firm. Additionally, a distinct license is needed for those who earn a commission on the sale of insurance products. Generally, insurance licenses are issued by the state in which an advisor conducts business. Financial planners who provide investment advice for a fee must register either with the SEC or the state(s) in which they conduct business. Advisers with more than $100 million in assets under management must register with the SEC.

10. Financial planners and financial planning firms commonly use several methods of compensation. Commissions were once the dominant form of compensation. Today, commission-based advisors are no longer in the majority; an increasing number are paid based on a combination of fees and commissions. Different approaches include fee-based and

fee-offset planning services. A growing segment of the profession charges clients on a fee-only basis. These financial planners do not receive commissions of any kind. Examples of a fee-only approach include charging a percentage based on assets under management, charging an hourly rate, or applying an annual retainer fee for services.

11. Employment opportunities are extensive for trained financial planners. Qualified college graduates will find many opportunities to begin a career at financial planning, brokerage, and insurance firms. A growing segment of the financial planning marketplace can be found in fee-only registered investment advisory firms. Typically, these companies are composed of a few employees and an owner, but the size can vary widely depending on the number of clients served or assets managed. Other firms that hire individuals with a background in financial planning include mutual fund companies, banks, and to a more limited extent, financial counseling and consulting firms.

Chapter Resources

Brandon, Jr., E. D. and H. O. Welch. *The History of Financial Planning, The Transformation of Financial Services*. John Wiley & Sons., Inc., Hoboken, NJ.

Certified Financial Planner Board of Standards, Inc. (www.cfp.net).

Consumer resources related to financial planning (http://www.fpanet.org/docs/assets/9-15-06Englishhow.pdf).

Financial Planning Association (www.fpanet.org).

Financial Planning Standards Board, Ltd. (http://www.fpsb.org/).

Financial Therapy Association (www.financialtherapyassociation.org).

International Association of Registered Financial Consultants (www.iarfc.org).

National Association of Personal Financial Advisors (www.napfa.org).

Profile of financial planning practitioners (http://www.fpanet.org/docs/assets/929DBE6C-1D09-67A1-7A769D7720054E6B/2011FPADemographicPortrait.pdf).

For more information on RIA registration, see Advisor Guidance (http://www.advisorguidance.com/index.html) or RIA Investment Consultants (http://www.ria-compliance-consultants.com/).

Select industry publications:

Financial Services Review

Journal of Financial Counseling and Planning

Journal of Financial Planning

Journal of Financial Service Professionals

Journal of Financial Therapy

Journal of Personal Finance

Financial Planning magazine

Investment Advisor magazine

Registered Rep magazine

InvestmentNews

Discussion Questions

1. How has the practice of financial planning changed since 1969?

2. Why are so many membership organizations, designations and credentials, and licenses available to financial advisors? For each of these three categories, identify and explain two examples.

3. What are the goals of the Financial Planning Association (FPA) and how has it positioned itself rather than the Financial Planning Coalition as "the heart of financial planning"?

4. Describe the six-step process that serves as the foundation of the professional practice standards promulgated by the CFP Board of Standards, Inc., through its self-regulatory function. What is the purpose of these professional practice standards?

5. Describe the difference between a goal and an objective. How does each relate to life planning, financial planning, or the suitability of a product?

6. Which seven core content areas should be included in a comprehensive financial plan? How might life planning or financial therapy expand an advisor's perspective or understanding of a client's goals and objectives?

7. Describe the differences and similarities between a targeted, or modular, financial plan and a comprehensive financial plan.

8. Why is financial planning ranked as one of the top career choices?

9. Describe the differences between fee-only and commission-based financial advisors. Explain the various ways that financial advisors can be compensated.

10. What does it mean to act as a fiduciary? How does the standard of care for a client potentially change according to employment channel?

Notes

1. Rattiner, J. H., *Getting Started as a Financial Planner* (Princeton, NJ: Bloomberg Press, 2000).

2. Brandon, Jr., E. D. and H. O. Welch, *The History of Financial Planning, the Transformation of Financial Services* (Hoboken, NJ: John Wiley & Sons, 2009).

3. Brandon and Welch, *History of Financial Planning*, 17.

4. Certified Financial Planner Board of Standards, Inc., *CFP® Certificant Profile*. Available at http://www.cfp.net/media/profile.asp.

5. Certified Financial Planner Board of Standards, Inc. *CFP® Certification Exam Statistics*. Available at http://www.cfp.net/media/survey.asp?id=9.

6. Certified Financial Planner Board of Standards, Inc., "CEO's Report," *CFP Board Report*, September 3, 2009,   http://www.cfp.net/certificants/boardreport_7_2009.asp#2.

7. Financial Planning Association, *Demographic Portrait: You Belong at FPA*. Available at http://www.fpanet.org/docs/assets/929DBE6C-1D09-67A1-7A769D7720054E6B/2011FPADemographicPortrait.pdf.

8. National Association of Personal Financial Advisors, *History of NAFPA*. Available at http://www.napfa.org/about/HistoryofNAPFA.asp.

9. Brandon and Welch, *History of Financial Planning*, 121.

10. FINRA, *Understanding Professional Designations*. Available at http://apps.finra.org/DataDirectory/1/prodesignations.aspx.

11. A complete listing can be found at http://www.credentialingexcellence.org/ICEMembersByOrganizationlistedbyOccupation/tabid/241/Default.aspx

12. FPA, *FPA Experts and Survey Cite Reliance on Long-term Plans for Consumers*. Available at http://www.fpanet.org/professionals/PressRoom/PressReleases/FPAExpertsandSurveyCiteRelianceonPlansforConsumers.

13. College for Financial Planning, *2011 Survey of Trends in the Financial Planning Industry* (Denver, CO: College for Financial Planning, 2011), 32. Available at http://www.cffpinfo.com/pdfs/2011SOT.pdf. Also College for Financial Planning, *2009 Survey of Trends in the Financial Planning Industry* (Denver, CO: College for Financial Planning, 2009), 21. Available at http://www.cffpinfo.com/pdfs/2009SOT.pdf.

14. CFP Board, *CFP Board's 2004 Consumer Survey*. Available at http://www.cfp.net/media/survey.asp?id=4, p. 12.

15. CFP Board, *CFP Board's Standards of Professional Conduct*. Available at http://www.cfp.net/Downloads/2010Standards.pdf, p. 4.

16. CFP Board, *Standards of Professional Conduct*, 5.

17. Leimberg, S. R., M. J. Satinsky, R. T. LeClair, and R. J. Doyle, *The Tools and Techniques of Financial Planning* (Erlanger, KY: The National Underwriter Co., 2002).

18. For simplicity, references to clients throughout the text typically appear in the singular form. Readers are encouraged to remember that a client can be an individual, couple, multigenerational family, or legal entity (e.g., trust, estate, business).

19. College for Financial Planning, *2011 Survey of Trends*, 21.

20. CFP Board, *2009 National Consumer Survey on Personal Finance*. Available at http://www.cfp.net/downloads/CFP_Board_2009_National_Consumer_Survey.pdf, p. 8.

21. College for Financial Planning, *2011 Survey of Trends*, 17–18.

22. College for Financial Planning, *2011 Survey of Trends*, 13.

23. College for Financial Planning, *2011 Survey of Trends*, 13. Also College for Financial Planning, *2007 Survey of Trends in the Financial Planning Industry* (Denver, CO: College for Financial Planning, 2007), 14. Available at http://www.cffpinfo.com/pdfs/2007SOT.pdf.

24. T. Kalwarski, D. Mosher, J. Paskin, and D. Rosato, "The 50 Best Jobs in America," *Money*, May 2006, 35.

25. CareerCast.com .The 10 Best Jobs of 2012: 5 - Financial Planner. Available at http://www.careercast.com/content/10-best-jobs-2012-5-financial-planner/.

26. Jessica Dickler, Anne C. Lee, and Greg Swiatek, *Best Jobs in America: Best Jobs for Fast Growth*. Available at http://money.cnn.com/magazines/moneymag/best-jobs/2011/fast-growing-jobs/3.html.

27. Bureau of Labor Statistics, U.S. Department of Labor, *Occupational Outlook Handbook, 2012-13 Edition*, Personal Financial Advisors, Available at http://www.bls.gov/ooh/business-and-financial/personal-financial-advisors.htm

28. College for Financial Planning, *2011 Survey of Trends*, 6.

29. M. Branham, "Rising tides: State of Succession Planning," *Risk Business* (A supplement to *Investment Advisor* magazine), 2012, (January) 13–16.

30. Bureau of Labor Statistics, U.S. Department of Labor, *Occupational Outlook Handbook, 2012–13 Edition*, Personal Financial Advisors. Available at http://www.bls.gov/ooh/business-and-financial/personal-financial-advisors.htm.

31. College for Financial Planning, *2011 Survey of Trends*, 4.

32. FINRA, *About the Financial Industry Regulatory Authority*. Available at http://www.finra.org/AboutFINRA/

33. R. King, "Fees for Financial Planning Services: What Planners Charge." *Practice Solutions Magazine*, (January/February2012), http://www.fpanet.org/professionals/PracticeManagement/PracticeSolutionsMagazine/JanuaryFebruary2012/FeesforFinancialPlanningServices/.

34. R. King, "Fees for Financial Planning Services."

35. National Association of Personal Financial Advisors, FAQ, Consumer Services FAQ. Available at: http://www.napfa.org/faq/index.asp.

36. Cerulli Associates, "1Q 2012," *The Cerulli Edge© Advisor Edition* 34 (2012): 16.

37. FPA, *Standard of Care*. Available at http://www.fpanet.org/professionals/AboutFPA/Organization/StandardofCare/.

38. CFP Board, *Standards of Professional Conduct*.

39. FINRA, "2111. Suitability," FINRA Manual. Available at http://finra.complinet.com/en/display/display.html?rbid=2403&record_id=13390&element_id=9859&highlight=2111.

Chapter 2

Ethics, Laws and Regulations: How Standards Affect the Plan, the Process, and the Profession

Learning Objectives

1. Describe the two approaches used to define ethical behavior.

2. Understand the role of significant legislative actions in shaping the delivery of financial products and services.

3. Explain the role of the SEC, NASAA, and state regulators for registering, examining, and setting practice standards for financial advisers.

4. Explain the role of FINRA, as a self-regulatory organization, for registering, examining, and setting practice standards for registered representatives.

5. Compare and contrast investment adviser representatives and registered representatives.

6. Understand the dual role of Form ADV for adviser registration and disclosure to potential and current clients.

7. Describe the role of NAIC and the requirements to be licensed to sell insurance.

8. Explain the responsibility of a fiduciary and the legislative history on which that responsibility is based.

9. Explain how a financial professional may be subject to ethical conduct standards established by a professional organization, the CFP Board, and/or state or federal regulatory authorities.

10. Summarize the basic expectations of the SEC, FINRA and NAIC for advertising to the public.

11. Explain the importance of adviser disclosure when working with potential and current clients.

12. Summarize the basic FINRA regulatory expectations for the use of social media.

Learning Objectives

13. Understand the importance of careful archiving and reporting when managing client assets.

14. Describe the various continuing education requirements and understand their benefits.

15. Explain how financial professionals protect themselves from client allegations of wrongdoing.

16. Describe the FINRA arbitration and mediation processes.

17. Explain how professional organizations contribute to the delivery of financial planning products and services to clients.

Key Terms

Arbitration

Banking Act of 1933 (Glass-Steagall Act)

Blue sky laws

Central Registration Repository®

Certification

Certified Financial Planner (CFP®)

CFP Board *Code of Ethics*

Chartered Financial Analyst (CFA)

Chartered Financial Consultant (ChFC)

Chartered Life Underwriter (CLU)

Chief compliance officer

Continuing education

Custody

Deontological ethics

Descriptive ethics

Designation

Employee Retirement Income Security Act (ERISA)

Errors and omissions (E&O) insurance

Ethics

Fidelity bond

Fiduciary

Fiduciary liability insurance

Financial Industry Regulatory Authority (FINRA)

Financial Planning Association (FPA)

Financial Privacy Rule

Financial Services Modernization Act of 1999 (Gramm-Leach-Bliley Act)

Form ADV

Form U4

Gramm-Leach-Bliley Act (GLBA)

Investment Adviser Registration Depository (IARD)

Investment Adviser Public Disclosure (IAPD)

Investment Advisers Act of 1940

Investment Adviser Representative (IAR)

Investment discretion

Legal Tender Act of 1862

Maloney Act of 1938

Mediation

Million Dollar Roundtable

Model Prudent Man Rule Statute

Municipal Securities Rulemaking Board (MSRB)

NAPFA Fiduciary Oath

NAPFA-registered Financial Advisor

National Association of Insurance Commissioners (NAIC)

National Association of Personal Financial Advisors (NAPFA)

National Association of Securities Dealers (NASD)

National Banking Act of 1863

National Banking Act of 1864

National Securities Markets Improvement
Act of 1996

Normative ethics

North American Securities Administrators
Association (NASAA)

Personal Financial Specialist (PFS)

Practice standard

Quasi-certification

Rebating

Registered Investment Adviser (RIA)

Registered representative

Rule 1120

Safeguards Rule

Securities Act of 1933 (Paper Act)

Securities and Exchange Commission
(SEC)

Securities Exchange Act of 1934 (People's
Act)

Securities Investor Protection Act of 1970

Self-regulatory Organization (SRO)

Selling away

Series 65 Examination

Teleological ethics

Uniform Investment Adviser Law
Examination

Uniform Prudent Investor Act (UPIA)

Uniform Securities Act of 1956

Values

Wall Street Reform and Consumer
Protection Act of 2010 (Dodd-Frank
Act)

Web CRD

THE ETHICAL FOUNDATIONS OF FINANCIAL PLANNING

Financial planners confront ethical choices in almost every aspect of their business. Consider the situation where an advisor recommends a product that has not been approved by the firm's broker-dealer. The advisor argues that the product is more suitable for the client than any from the "approved product list." Does this action violate ethical and regulatory standards? How about a situation where an insurance agent uses commissions earned on the sale of life insurance to offset fees associated with writing a financial plan? Is this ethical?

These are only two examples of how a financial planner can innocently cross the line into unethical conduct. The first case is called **selling away**, and it is a violation of Rule 3040, established by the **Financial Industry Regulatory Authority (FINRA)**, a self-regulating organization that oversees stockbroker activities.[1] This rule requires FINRA-regulated representatives to obtain written approval from their firms before they sell any security. Although the advice may have been in the best interest of the client, the action still violates the rule, which is in place to ensure that clients are sold only products that meet the standards of the planner's broker-dealer. Selling away can subject a broker-dealer to claims of product unsuitability, unnecessary fees, and regulatory sanctions.

The second case is an example of **rebating**, which is defined as an agent discounting or waiving a commission to induce a client to purchase a security or insurance product. The essence of the situation described above is that the insurance agent was attempting to coerce the client into purchasing another product by offering a discount on either the service or the product. Rebating is unethical and, in most states, illegal because it might cause a planner to sell products that are not in the client's best interest to increase the planner's income or entice a client to engage in additional services. Rebating can be a violation of FINRA Rule 2420,[2] as well as numerous state insurance regulations.

As these two examples illustrate, the line that separates legal and ethical financial planning actions from those that are unethical and sometimes illegal is at times hard to distinguish. To fully understand how ethics, standards, regulations, and laws influence the daily life of financial planners, it is first necessary to define certain key terms. To begin with, it is essential to understand what the term **ethics** really means. According to Hansen, Rossberg, and Cramer, "ethics are suggested standards of conduct based on an agreed-upon set of values," where **values** are preferred attitudes and behaviors.[3] The study of ethics has its foundation in Western moral philosophy. Viewed from the perspective of philosophers such as Aristotle, Locke, Kant, and Hume, ethics can be categorized as either teleological or deontological.[4]

A **teleological** or consequential approach to ethics is based on relativism, where actions are deemed to be right or wrong based on the consequences of the actions. Sometimes this is referred to as situational ethics. Acting in one's own interest is ethical from a teleological perspective so long as another party is not hurt or put at a disadvantage. Ethics from a **deontological** approach are based on absolutism, the concept of universally accepted rights and wrongs. The ethical perspective that enslavement is wrong is based on the notion that this action is intrinsically wrong at all times, regardless of the outcomes or consequences. Ethical codes used by financial planners tend to be based on a deontological foundation; however, everyone should be able to recognize that very few situations are universal in intent and outcome. In other words, right and wrong actions are predetermined, and prescribed proceedings will ensue against a violator regardless of the outcome, but mitigating circumstances might affect the severity of the sanction or punishment. This ethical framework provides the only foundation for practice management standards used in the industry today, but in practice the application of ethical values tends to be more fluid.

A **practice standard** is defined as a behavior that is deemed acceptable by a certain segment of society or society as a whole and is typically codified in a code of ethics or statement of standard practices. For the financial planning industry, practice standards reflect **normative ethics**, as defined by the governing bodies (e.g., FINRA) membership organizations (e.g., FPA and NAPFA), and groups offering certifications or designations (e.g., CFP Board, CIMA, and Fi360) within the financial planning industry. Examples of this codification of ethics and practice standards are shown throughout this chapter and others. A normative standard signals what a financial planner should do in a given situation. Standards serve as benchmarks for ethical behavior. "Stealing from clients is wrong" is an example of a normative standard.

Although nearly all financial planning rules and regulations have a deontological ethical foundation, where practitioners and regulators have pre-established which activities are acceptable and which are not, many other situations are judgment calls, meaning that a more teleological approach is warranted. To that end, practice standards or ethics can also be **descriptive**, where actions are "right" or "wrong" based on their outcomes (i.e., relativism). For a practice standard to come into existence and be enforced, certain groups of people must agree on what is inherently right and wrong. This means that normative standards must be practiced. Although it is unnecessary for all practitioners and regulators to agree with a standard, standards cannot be enforced if behaviors are evaluated solely on relative outcomes.

Adding to the complexity of the application of practice standards and ethical professional conduct is the variety of channels for delivering the financial planning services and products introduced in Chapter 1. The differences between registered representatives and investment adviser representatives were introduced, including differences in the expected standard of client care, method of compensation, qualifications, and regulation. In effect, the profession is split philosophically over the competing ideas of the fiduciary status required of planners registered with the SEC or with state securities regulators as RIAs compared to following a suitability standard, which is the requirement for brokers or those registered through FINRA.

Chapter 1 provided a glimpse into this situation; this chapter attempts to add depth and breadth to that understanding based on a brief history of the federal regulatory environment. Although some content may seem redundant, together Chapters 1 and 2 are designed to provide a richer—although by no means exhaustive—understanding of how financial planning products and services are delivered. Be assured that what follows is, at best, a summary of the vast amount of information available on these topics. Specifically, this chapter reviews (1) the regulatory efforts of the SEC, states, and SROs as they pertain to financial professionals; (2) the fiduciary rules and expectations for ethical conduct; (3) select examples of communication requirements; (4) select examples of professional practice expectations; and (5) information on the primary professional organizations and their contributions to financial planning.

FEDERAL REGULATIONS: A HISTORICAL PERSPECTIVE

Once society started basing transactions on a monetary value rather than a use value, financial regulation became necessary. Throughout most of history humans traded goods and services in a barter system that did not employ a medium of exchange such as money. However, beginning in the 1700s in France and then in the 1800s in the United States, a money-based system of payment developed.

Pre-Depression System (1862–1933): The Rise of the Financial System

The modern system in the United States was developed primarily to help the U.S. government pay its financial obligations after the Civil War had depleted most of its gold and silver reserves. Although the United States had previously chartered the First and Second Banks of the United States for similar purposes after the Revolutionary War and the War of 1812, respectively, not until the **Legal Tender Act of 1862** and the **National Banking Acts of 1863** and **1864** was the current version of the monetary system created.

From 1862 until 1933 the national banking system was fairly unregulated. As a practical matter, only very rich industrialists and the U.S. government accessed the system as a means of trade. In fact, one magnate, J.P. Morgan, nearly single-handedly saved the U.S. financial system after a series of financial panics leading up to 1907—a panic created by perceived illiquidity in New York City banks that resulted in many bank runs. This action served as the impetus for the creation of the Federal Reserve System in 1913 by Congressional act. The Federal Reserve Act created the Federal Reserve Bank, and its primary mandate was the regulation of the banking system and the administration of national-level monetary policy.

However, it would take more than one person's actions to save the system from the Great Depression. The lack of laws, rules, regulations, and general standards of practice validated the saying "caveat emptor" (i.e., let the buyer beware). The lack of standards meant that frauds and rip-offs were almost as common as legitimate investment and financial advice activities. Only during the aftermath of the stock market crash of October 1929 and the ensuing economic collapse did policy makers, legitimate investment advisers, and citizens band together to enact legislation to protect consumers against illegal, unethical, and fraudulent securities schemes. In effect, these early acts of regulation helped codify the ethical standards that dominate today's financial planning profession.

Post-Depression System (1933–1999): The Separation of the Financial Systems

Five landmark pieces of legislation passed between 1933 and 1940 vastly changed the landscape of banking and investing for almost the next 70 years. The first major piece of federal legislation, passed in response to the debacle of the Great Depression, was the **Banking Act of 1933**, also known as the **Glass-Steagall Act**. This legislation contributed stability and confidence to the U.S. financial system with two key outcomes. First, it established the Federal Deposit Insurance Corporation (FDIC), which insured bank customers' deposits against bank failure. Second—and probably more famously—it separated traditional commercial banking from the newer investment banking. In other words, banks were now prohibited from using bank assets to speculate in the yet-to-be regulated securities market.

The second major piece of legislation was the **Securities Act of 1933**, also known as the **Paper Act**. This law required full disclosure of any new security offered for sale to investors. This legislation required new securities to be registered with the Federal Trade Commission (FTC), which was the first step in national-level market regulation. From 1911 to 1933, security issuance had been regulated at the individual state level under the "blue sky laws" until 1919 when the **North American Securities Administrators Association (NASAA)** was established to coordinate the efforts.[5] (NASAA and state-level regulation are discussed later in the chapter.)

The **Securities Exchange Act of 1934**, also known as the **People's Act**, was another major step forward in establishing ethical standards in the practice of corporate and personal finance. The 1934 act was responsible for creating the **Securities and Exchange Commission (SEC)**, established specifically to regulate the national securities markets so that the investing public would have greater trust in the market system. Under the 1934 act, publicly traded companies were required to provide investors with more information, including quarterly and annual reports. The 1934 act was strengthened further by the **Maloney Act of 1938**. This Act of Congress added § 15A to the Securities Exchange Act of 1934, which allowed for the establishment of registered securities associations to promote self-regulation of the securities industry. The primary outcome of the Maloney Act was the establishment of the **National Association of Securities Dealers (NASD)** in 1939 as the first self-regulatory organization (SRO). The NASD was the predecessor of FINRA, which was formed in 2007.

By the late 1930s all securities markets in the United States were under federal regulation. Stock brokers and others who earned a commission on the purchase and sale of securities were also regulated through NASD, with SEC oversight. However, it was still possible for those who only charged a fee for service, rather than a commission based on the product sold, to avoid federal regulation. Up to that point, there were no practice standards for individuals who marketed investment adviser services for a fee. This changed in 1940 with the passage of the **Investment Advisers Act of 1940**.[6] The Investment Advisers Act has had the greatest impact on the way financial planning had been and is currently practiced. It initially set the stage for all individuals who provide investment advice for a fee to be registered with the SEC. However, the Act left the regulation of broker-dealers in the hands of the NASD, which had been established the year before as an SRO. This marked the beginning of the two-party system that still exists today, where "brokers" who are allowed to advise incidental to a sale are regulated by FINRA, and "advisers" are regulated by the SEC or the state securities regulators.

Legislation and regulation, however, were just getting started. Several events in the 1940s helped codify the new legislative landscape, including the adoption of a Uniform Practice Code by the NASD in 1941, the adoption of SEC Rule 10b-5 in 1948 prohibiting insider trading, and individual broker registration by the NASD in 1946. However, the next landmark legislation did not occur until the passage of the **Uniform Securities Act of 1956**. This act and its 1985, 1988, and 2002 revisions provided model legislation that could be adopted by individual states to assist the regulation efforts of the SEC.

The 1970s was another busy time for securities market regulators. The **Securities Investor Protection Act of 1970** provided insurance to investors against fraudulent activities on the part of the investor's broker-dealer, similar to the FDIC. However, this did not insure investors against losses caused by market volatility or poor investment decisions. In 1974 Congress passed the **Employee Retirement Income Security Act (ERISA)**, the federal regulatory scheme for corporate pension trusts. This legislation also required investment professionals to follow the Uniform Prudent Investors Act (UPIA), discussed later in this chapter, through the prudence standard of ERISA. The Supreme Court of the United States has said, "ERISA's legislative history confirms that the Act's fiduciary responsibility provisions 'codify and make applicable to [ERISA] fiduciaries certain principles developed in the evolution of the law of trusts.'"[7]

This enhanced investor protection by setting minimum standards for private company pension and health care plans. These protections were subsequently modified in 1985 by the Consolidated Omnibus Budget Reconciliation Act (COBRA) and in 1996 by the Health Insurance Portability and Accountability Act (HIPAA). However, although ERISA also intended the fiduciary standard of care, a 1975 Department of Labor (DOL) ruling narrowed the statutory definition, which diluted the meaning of fiduciary as it pertains to advice about retirement plans. At the time of publication, the DOL was in the process of reviewing its definition of a fiduciary and working to more closely define the type and scope of financial planning work covered under ERISA.

Another important Congressional undertaking was the creation of the **Municipal Securities Rulemaking Board (MSRB)** in 1975 and the subsequent adoption of the Uniform Practice Rules in 1976. These actions initiated the regulation of the municipal securities markets in a manner more consistent with the regulation of the private company stock and bonds markets that began in the 1930s.

Modern financial planning was developing during the 1970s. But not until the 1980s did NASAA (the group of state securities regulators formed in 1919) in conjunction with the SEC work together to promote more uniform regulation of investment advisers under both federal and state law. Together they issued "releases" to interpret and define the Investment Advisers Act of 1940. A notable one, SEC Release IA-1092, was issued in 1987; it further defined the requirements for being an investment adviser and considered those requirements relative to others practicing as financial planners; **investment adviser representatives (IARs)**; pension consultants; and sports, entertainment, or other representatives who provided financial advisory services.

In that same year, 1987, NASAA issued model uniform rules for investment adviser firms and investment adviser representatives to establish a system of requirements for initial registration. The rules established minimum financial requirements and recordkeeping protocols and instituted new standardized exams, the Series 63 and Series 65 exams, which became prerequisites to registration. These rules catalyzed the standards by which the profession still practices today. In fact, NASAA periodically issues new model rules to establish requirements for investment advisers and their actions. For more information and a list of rules, see http://www.nasaa.org/1325/adopted-model-rules/.

Legislation passed in 1996 brought about two landmark changes in the business practices of financial advisers and investment advisers. Congress amended the

Investment Advisers Act of 1940 with the Investment Advisers Supervision Coordination Act of 1996, which was a part of the National Securities Market Improvement Act. Prior to the Coordination Act, the Investment Advisers Act of 1940 required that generally all firms and professionals acting as investment advisers for compensation (three exceptions were sited) must register with the SEC. The Coordination Act, which went into effect in 1987, established coordination between the states and the SEC for the registration and supervision of advisers based on the standard of $25 million of assets under management (AUM).

Those managing less—the smaller advisers—were to be registered with and supervised by their state regulatory agency, unless the advisers' business was located in a state that did not require registration. If that was the case, then the adviser would register with the SEC. SEC-registered investment advisers were also required to file a copy of any and all filings made with the SEC with the states in which they were doing business, strictly for notification purposes. Hence, these state filings are called "Notice Filings," which were discussed in Chapter 1.

The second landmark change resulting from the Coordination Act was the requirement that the SEC establish a readily accessible electronic system to (1) register investment advisers, resulting in the Investment Adviser Registration Depository (IARD), and (2) respond to public inquiries about investment advisers IARs and their disciplinary information, which led to the **Investment Adviser Public Disclosure (IAPD)** to make the information accessible to the investing public.

Modern System (1999–Present): The Reintegration of the Financial Systems

After nearly 70 years of financial markets' separation into traditional banking and investment-banking related activities, Glass-Steagall was repealed in 1999 by the **Financial Services Modernization Act**, also referred to as the **Gramm-Leach-Bliley Act (GLBA)**. This act removed the structural barriers, created by §§ 20 and 21 of the Banking Act of 1933, to banks owning broker-dealers. It also provided for SEC regulation over securities business conducted by banks, adding to the already complex situation of bank regulation. This brought about widespread change in financial services by eliminating the legal barriers between the securities, insurance, and banking industries and allowed the blurring of lines that earlier had demarcated product delivery. For example, insurance companies could offer banking products and banks could offer insurance products.

Another major component of this legislation was the development of privacy laws and regulations. The GLBA gives eight federal agencies and the states authority to administer and enforce the **Financial Privacy Rule** and the **Safeguards Rule**. These two regulations apply to "financial institutions," which include not only banks, securities firms, and insurance companies, but also companies providing many other types of financial products and services to consumers. Among these services are lending, brokering, or servicing any type of consumer loan; transferring or safeguarding money; preparing individual tax returns; providing financial advice or credit counseling; providing residential real estate settlement services; collecting consumer debts; and an array of other activities.

Section 504 of the GLBA requires the SEC and other organizations to adopt rules implementing notice requirements and restrictions on a financial institution's ability to disclose nonpublic personal information about consumers.[8] Under this Act, financial institutions must provide their customers with notice of their privacy policies and practices and must not disclose nonpublic personal information about a consumer to nonaffiliated third parties without proper disclosure and consent.

In 2000 NASAA created a more robust Series 65 for persons wishing to become financial advisers to ensure that the investing public would receive competent advice. This new exam added components on financial products and strategies to the original regulation information. This greatly expanded the coverage of the exam to test economics, investment products and strategies, and ethics.[9] However, for brokers already holding the Series 7 and having already passed an exam that covered much of the financial product information on the new Series 65, the NASAA created the Series 66 exam, which combines the state regulations component of the Series 63 and the federal regulations and ethics component of the Series 65 without all of the product and strategy components of Series 7.

Also in 2000, Rule 10b-5, which had its foundation in the Securities Exchange Act of 1934, was amended by Rule10b5-1 to more clearly define the purchase or sale of securities that constitute trading "on the basis of" material nonpublic information. This is better known as insider trading.

In 1999, the NASD launched the Web-based licensing and regulation system, **Web CRD**, for the registration of broker-dealers and their representatives. The system is now known as the **Central Registration Depository (CRD®)**. The public disclosure BrokerCheck system, which contains information about brokerage firms and registered representatives of brokerage firms, was also made available. According to FINRA, Web CRD currently includes the registration records of more than 6,800 registered broker-dealers and the qualification, employment, and disclosure histories of more than 660,000 active registered individuals.[10] Subsequently the NASD developed and initiated, in collaboration with NASAA and the SEC, a similar electronic reporting system for investment advisers and adviser firms, although NASD, now FINRA, has no regulatory authority over investment advisers.

Effective 2001, the **Investment Adviser Registration Depository (IARD)** was initiated to streamline the registration of financial advisers and adviser firms, regulatory review, the annual registration renewal process, and the public disclosure of investment adviser and adviser firm employment and disciplinary histories. The latter objective resulted in the **Investment Adviser Public Disclosure (IAPD)**, an electronic database that provides information about current and some former investment adviser representatives (IARs), investment adviser firms registered with the SEC and/or state securities regulators, and exempt reporting advisers (e.g., fund managers) who file reports with the SEC and/or state securities regulators. According to FINRA, the IAPD currently includes professional background information on approximately 441,000 current and former IARs and 45,700 current and former investment adviser firms.[11] IAPD also links to the FINRA BrokerCheck.

FINRA was created in 2007 by merging the NASD and the regulation, enforcement, and arbitration functions of the New York Stock Exchange. But the most recent sweeping development in financial regulation was the passage of the **Wall Street Reform and Consumer Protection Act of 2010**, usually referred to as the **Dodd-Frank Act**. Named after Chris Dodd (Democrat from Connecticut) and Barney Frank (Democrat from Massachusetts), the Dodd-Frank Act does and will provide the most sweeping financial regulatory reform since the Great Depression.

Dodd-Frank Summary Pertaining to Investment Advisers

Although Dodd-Frank will effect many rule changes in investment banking, investment adviser registration, hedge funds, and private equity, Title IX—Investor Protections and Improvements to the Regulation of Securities will have the most impact on investment advisers' practices in serving clients. Subtitle A increases investor protection by providing oversight with respect to the relationship between customers and broker-dealers and investment advisers. As a result of the creation of a standard of care, there are two noteworthy outcomes. First is the creation of the Office of the Investor Advocate.[12] Second is the ability of the SEC to impose regulations requiring a fiduciary duty of broker-dealers, proposed under § 913.[13]

Although it will not be legislated until after an SEC review study, this represents a long-term break from the original "suitability requirement" imposed by the Securities Exchange Act of 1934 that will bring broker-dealer registered representatives closer to the fiduciary standard set forth for investment advisers by the Investment Advisers Act of 1940. In support of this change is § 914, which requested a study on the enhancement of investment adviser examinations and the expansion of enforcement resources. As the result of a request for additional funding in support of greater enforcement, Representative Spencer Bachus, Chairman of the House Committee on Financial Services, sponsored a bill in September 2011 asking that Congress establish one or more SROs, with an SRO under FINRA a likely alternative. (The outcome of this potential legislation is unknown as of publication.) One potential outcome is the legislation of an investment adviser SRO under the SEC funded by adviser user fees, as proffered by Congresswoman Maxine Waters.

Another implication of Dodd-Frank is the change to small and mid-sized investment advisers that would no longer register with the SEC, but with the state regulatory authority. Before Dodd-Frank, which increased the SEC registration threshold from $25 million to $100 million in AUM, investment advisers with less than $25 million in AUM generally registered with the appropriate state regulator(s).[14]

One item noteworthy because it did not come out of the Dodd-Frank regulation is that, pursuant to § 919C, the U.S. General Accountability Office (GAO) was to study and make a recommendation on the effectiveness of current regulation on persons who hold themselves out as financial planners.[15] The GAO determined that an additional layer of regulation specific to financial planners was unwarranted, but it did recommend more robust enforcement of existing laws and encouraged additional collaboration between the SEC and state regulators in matters involving financial planners.

REGULATION OF FINANCIAL PROFESSIONALS

The primary role of the SEC, NASAA, and FINRA is to provide regulatory oversight of those who provide investment advice and products to consumers by registering, licensing, examining, and setting practice standards for individual practitioners. Having gained some historical perspective on the legislative history of these organizations, attention can now turn to reviewing them and some of the functions they serve in regulating providers of investment products and services.

Federal Regulation

The Investment Advisers Act of 1940 created two new terms for professionals who provide investment advice for a fee—the **registered investment adviser (RIA)** and **investment adviser representative (IAR)**. The definition of an investment adviser as established in the Investment Advisers Act of 1940 states that an investment adviser is:

> any person who, for compensation, engages in the business of advising others, either directly or through publications or writings, as to the value of securities or as to the advisability of investing in, purchasing, or selling securities, or who, for compensation and as part of a regular business, issues or promulgates analyses or reports concerning securities.[16]

SEC Release IA-1092 is recognized as establishing the "three-pronged approach" to determining whether a person is an investment adviser and therefore subject to registration and examination requirements. The requirements for a person or firm include the following three tests:

1. Provides advice or analysis on securities either by making direct or indirect recommendations to clients or by providing reports or opinions on securities or securities markets;

2. Engages in a regular business of providing advice on securities; and

3. Receives compensation in any form for the advice provided.[17]

A basis for the second test is how the individual or adviser firm advertises, promotes, or holds itself out as providing investment advice. The other two are more obvious, although Release 1092 offers a lengthy discussion of the nuances for interpreting each test. For more information, see http://www.sec.gov/rules/interp/1987/ia-1092.pdf.

An IAR is defined as an individual who performs services on behalf of or works for an RIA. It may be possible for a person to be both an RIA and IAR. This would be true, for example, if the person is the sole owner of a corporation registered as an RIA. The owner then needs to be registered as an IAR. The SEC prohibits practitioners registered as investment advisers from using the initials "RIA" as a marketing or certification mark.

The Investment Advisers Act of 1940 required all advisers to register with the SEC until the amendment of 1996, which established the coordination between state-level and SEC-level registration. Starting in 1997, advisers with AUM of less than $25 million were required to register with their state securities regulator, and those with assets of greater than $25 million were allowed to register directly with the SEC.

The Dodd-Frank Act raised the threshold for SEC registration to $100 million by creating a new category of advisers called mid-sized advisers in addition to the "small" advisers managing less than $25 million. A mid-sized adviser, which generally may not register with the Commission (some exceptions apply) and is subject to state registration, is defined as an adviser that:

- Manages between $25 million and $100 million for its clients;

- Is required to be registered in the state where it maintains its principal office and place of business; and

- Would be subject to examination by that state, if required to register.

As a result of this amendment to the Investment Advisers Act, by mid-2012 approximately 3,200 of the 11,500 currently registered advisers will have switched from registration with the SEC to registration with the states.[18] Mid-size advisers in New York, Minnesota, and Wyoming remain registered with the SEC, because these states either do not register (Minnesota and Wyoming) or do not examine (New York) registered advisers. Advisers with clients in more than 15 states register with the SEC, but must "notice file" in all states, as required by individual state rules.

It is sometimes possible to provide investment advice for a fee but not be required to register as an investment adviser. Exceptions to adviser registration may include, but are not limited to: (1) banks and bank holding companies; (2) lawyers, accountants, engineers, or teachers whose investment advice is solely incidental to their business; (3) publishers of newspapers, news magazines, and business or financial publications of general and regular circulation; and (4) persons whose advice is limited to direct obligations of the U.S. government.[19] Advisers whose only clients are insurance companies or charitable organizations are exempt from registration. Advisers who had fewer than 15 total clients in the previous 12 months, do not hold themselves out publicly as investment advisers, and do not advise a registered investment company or business development company may also be exempt from registration. Advisers who advise on securities not listed on national exchanges and limit their services to clients living in the same state as the business location can also qualify for an exemption. In general, however, anyone not included in these exceptions who advises others for compensation must register. Federal and state law imposes severe penalties for failure to register, including cease-and-desist orders, injunctions, fines, and imprisonment.

There is much "examination" in the financial planning industry, so understanding the context of the word is key to understanding which meaning is intended. In one sense of the word, examination is used to mean the initial or ongoing testing of knowledge; but in another sense, it means a review of records and advisers' work products. The term audit is also used. An adviser's examination, or audit, would be conducted by the applicable federal (e.g., SEC or FINRA) or state regulator. For a list of state regulators, visit http://www.nasaa.org/about-us/contact-us/contact-your-regulator/. According to NASAA, a survey of state regulators identified the top five problems identified in audits as issues with Form ADV, the Uniform Application for Investment Advisers Registration disclosure (discussed later in this chapter); custody of client assets; poorly maintained books and records; advertising; and poorly maintained financial records.[20]

State Regulation

As mentioned earlier, individual state regulation of securities and investment advisers predates the creation of the federal SEC by more than two decades. Regulation of securities offerings, the licensing of broker-dealers and their agents, and the registration of investment advisers by individual states are governed by what is known as **blue sky laws**. The term *blue sky* refers to speculative schemes that have no more substance than so many feet of blue sky.[21] In most states, a registered representative must pass—minimally—the Series 63: Uniform Securities Agent State Law Examination to satisfy state registration requirements.

The first modern blue sky law was adopted by the state of Kansas in 1911. The Kansas law served as a nationwide model for state securities regulation. As a result of this pioneering work, the North American Securities Administrators Association (NASAA) was organized in the state of Kansas in 1919. Currently, NASAA membership consists of 67 state, provincial, and territorial securities administrators in 50 states, the District of Columbia, the United States Virgin Islands, Puerto Rico, Canada, and Mexico. NASAA moved its Corporate Office from Topeka to Washington, D.C., in 1987.

NASAA serves the financial profession and its client-investors by:

1. Licensing stockbrokers, investment adviser firms, and securities firms that conduct business in the state.

2. Registering certain securities offered to the states' investors.

3. Investigating investor complaints and potential cases of investment fraud.

4. Enforcing state securities laws by fining, penalizing, providing restitution to investors, prosecuting white-collar criminals, and imposing legally binding conduct remedies designed to correct specific problems.

5. Examining brokerage and investment adviser firms to ensure compliance with securities laws and maintenance of accurate records of client accounts.[22]

It also advocates for securities-related regulations and laws, educates investors, and reviews securities that are not exempt from state law. Model rules proposed by NASAA may be adopted by state securities regulators or enacted through state legislative action. Although NASAA itself is not a regulatory entity, its members have regulatory authority as securities administrators, directors, or commissioners. To review the list of security regulators by state, see the NASAA Web page at http://www.nasaa.org/about-us/contact-us/contact-your-regulator.

Although each state implements its own securities regulations, the **National Securities Markets Improvement Act of 1996**, along with the aforementioned Uniform Securities Act, provides for greater coordination among individual state regulators and the SEC and enhances the efficiency of regulation. This Act served to amend the Investment Company Act of 1940 to enhance investor protection and attempted to reduce the regulatory burden by harmonizing laws across states and eliminating inconsistencies between state and federal regulations.

Self-regulatory Organization (SRO) Regulation

The Maloney Act of 1938 made it possible for broker-dealers and other organizations involved in the financial services industry to band together to create one or more **self-regulatory organizations (SROs)**. As the name implies, SROs are managed and funded by fees paid by firms that participate in a particular segment of securities markets. The primary purpose of an SRO is to provide consumers with protection against fraud while providing a mechanism to enforce the rules and standards developed by the SRO. All SROs allowed by the Maloney Act of 1938 are subject to SEC oversight.

A person licensed with FINRA is known as a *registered representative* (or *registered rep)*. A **registered representative** is a person associated with a broker-dealer firm who is engaged in the investment banking or securities business. This definition can include those working in a solicitation role and those who are engaged in the training of persons associated with a broker-dealer. (Note, however, that anyone acting in a training or supervisory role would also have to pass an additional licensing exam, e.g., the General Securities Principal Exam, or Series 24).

Registered representatives are affiliated with broker-dealer firms and to be eligible for a license must be sponsored by a broker-dealer. The typical registered representative engages in arm's length transactions with clients by executing customer orders to purchase and sell securities. As such, registered representatives are required to hold either a Series 6: Investment Company Products/Variable Contracts Limited Representative license and/or a Series 7: General Securities Representative FINRA license. (Additionally, they must pass the Series 63: Uniform Securities Agent State Law Examination to meet state registration requirements.)

The difference between an RIA and a registered representative can sometimes be confusing. RIAs typically charge a fee for their advice. Registered representatives execute transactions for a commission. In general, financial planners who provide investment advice to others, are self-employed and state- or SEC-registered as an RIA (or affiliated with an RIA), or are members of a firm must be registered with the SEC or licensed with FINRA. In some cases, a financial planner must be registered and licensed with both regulatory agencies. Table 2.1 provides a comparison of investment adviser representatives and registered representatives.

FINRA is, by far, the most powerful SRO with an interest in financial service activities. FINRA oversees the activities of more than 4,405 brokerage firms, approximately 162,780 branch offices, and nearly 629,865 registered securities representatives or stock brokers.[23] FINRA licenses individuals to sell securities, admits firms to the industry, writes rules to govern stockbroker and firm activities, conducts regulatory and ethical compliance examinations, and disciplines those who fail to comply with the rules. FINRA also oversees and regulates equity, corporate bond, futures, and options trading. In addition, FINRA operates the largest securities dispute resolution forum; more than 6,000 arbitration and 500 mediation cases are filed every year.[24]

Table 2.1 Investment Adviser and Registered Representatives Compared

	Investment Adviser Representative (IAR)	**Registered Representative (RR)**
Purpose	Provides individually tailored and continuous investment advice and/or manages securities portfolios on a discretionary or nondiscretionary basis.	Provides recommendations, incidental only to the sale of securities, and executes transactions, often only on a nondiscretionary basis.
Primary service	Develops and implements an investment plan based on all investment and asset information provided by the client.	Conducts investment research, processes orders/trades, and manages investment activity in the client's investment account.
Firm registration	Affiliated with an advisory firm registered with the SEC or the state(s).	Affiliated with a brokerage firm registered with FINRA and the state(s).
Examination and licensing requirement	No examination process required if firm is registered with the SEC. State-specific test such as Series 65 examination (or Series 66 and 7, in most states) and license generally required unless waived for current certification such as the CFP, CIC, ChFC, or PFS in most states.	Must successfully complete examination process administered by FINRA, usually Series 6 (limited securities) or 7 (general securities) exams to be licensed by FINRA and the states to sell securities.
Standard of care*	Fiduciary duty to the client, including: • placing the best interests of the client first; • treating all clients impartially and fairly (undivided loyalty and utmost good faith); • making suitable recommendations matched to the client's goals, needs, and financial situation; • exercising care to provide full and truthful disclosures of fees and conflicts of interest; and • providing client-specific recommendations based on factual analysis consistent with practice standards.	Suitability requirement for the client, including: • satisfying the three tests of general product suitability, customer-specific suitability, and frequency suitability; • treating all clients fairly and honestly; and • disclosing material information about recommendations.

*The CFP Board, or others, may have higher ethical conduct standards than required by securities laws.

Note: In a hybrid firm, representatives of the brokerage firm may be dually licensed to provide both advisory and brokerage services. Some broker-dealers permit affiliated representatives to also register as separate advisory firms to provide independent financial planning services or advice for a fee.

As part of its efforts to educate and protect consumers, FINRA operates BrokerCheck, which is marketed as the first tool that investors should consider when deciding about a relationship with a financial services firm or professional. Through BrokerCheck, available online or by a toll-free number or email, investors can:

- Search for information about brokerage firms and brokers.

- Search for information about investment adviser firms and representatives.

- Obtain some background reports.

- Link to investor educational resources.

Recall that BrokerCheck links professional background information from the CRD® system for FINRA-regulated firms and brokers (i.e., RRs) and data from the IAPD database for IARs and investment adviser firms. This enables investors to easily conduct research on professionals from both groups—brokerages and investment advisers. Additionally, both BrokerCheck and the IADP sites can be accessed from the SEC Web site at http://www.sec.gov/answers/crd.htm.

To promote professional competency, a securities license is required of anyone who sells securities for a commission. As first discussed in Chapter 1, numerous licenses are available and each allows a specific kind of activity. Table 2.2 lists the most commonly held securities licenses that can be obtained through NASAA and FINRA.[25]

Table 2.2 Common Securities Licenses and Testing Formats

Securities License			Testing Format	
Series Name	Series Number	Administering Organization	Testing Time	Question (Type and Number)
Investment Company Products/Variable Contracts Limited Representative	6	FINRA	2 hours and 15 minutes	100 multiple-choice questions
General Securities Representative	7	FINRA	6 hours total; 3 hours for each of two parts	250 multiple-choice questions; two parts of 125 questions each
General Securities Sales Supervisor	9 and 10 (Series 7 required)	FINRA	5 hours and 30 minutes total; 1:30 (Series 9) and 4:00 (Series 10)	200 multiple-choice questions; 55 questions (Series 9) and 145 questions (Series 10)
Compliance Officer	14	FINRA	3 hours	110 multiple-choice questions
General Sales Principal	24 (Series 7, 17, 62, 79, or 82 required)	FINRA	3 hours and 30 minutes	150 multiple-choice questions

Investment Company Products/Variable Contracts Limited Principal	26 (Series 6 or 7 required)	FINRA	2 hours and 30 minutes	110 multiple-choice questions
Uniform Securities Agent State Law Examination	63	NASAA	1 hour and 15 minutes	65 multiple-choice questions
Uniform Investment Adviser Law Examination	65	NASAA	3 hours	130 multiple-choice questions
Uniform Combined State Law Examination	66 (Series 7 required)	NASAA	2 hours and 30 minutes	100 multiple-choice questions
Research Analyst	86 and 87 (Series 7 or 17 required)	FINRA	5 hours and 30 minutes total; 4 hours (Series 86) and 1.5 hours (Series 87)	150 multiple-choice questions; 100 questions (Series 86) and 50 questions (Series 87)

A complete list of registration exams is available on the FINRA Web site at http://www.finra.org/industry/compliance/registration/qualificationsexams/registeredreps/p011051.

Table 2.3 lists some of the largest SROs in the United States. Notable in its absence is an SRO for the financial planning profession. Currently, no SRO exists to provide self-regulation to those who specifically practice financial planning. Recall from Dodd-Frank that although a study was commissioned under § 919C for the GAO to review the need for an SRO for financial planning, the result was that there was not a specific need and that '"more robust enforcement" of current laws could strengthen oversight'.[26]

Table 2.3 U.S. Self-regulatory Organizations (SROs)

SRO Name	Acronym	Industry Members
Financial Industry Regulatory Authority	FINRA	Broker-dealers
American Stock Exchange	AMEX	Securities firms
Chicago Board Options Exchange	CBOE	Options trading firms
Municipal Securities Rulemaking Board	MSRB	Municipal bond dealers
National Futures Association	NFA	Derivative trading firms
New York Stock Exchange	NYSE	Securities firms
Options Clearing Corporation	OCC	Options trading firms

Adviser Registration

Pursuant to the Advisers Act of 1940 as well as later amendments, investment advisers (i.e., the firms) must register with either the SEC or a state securities regulator, depending on the amount of client AUM. Although the SEC does not register individual representatives of investment adviser firms separately, many states do—consistent with the objective of the Investment Advisers Act of 1940 to identify individuals functioning as investment advisers.

The main document in the registration process is **Form ADV**, the **Uniform Application for Investment Advisers Registration**. Sections 203 and 204 of the Advisers Act of 1940 authorize the SEC to collect the information required by Form ADV; f iling the form is mandatory. This two-part form is used to register advisers with the SEC and with state security authorities. Once investment advisers registration is granted, the Form ADV must be amended at least annually and whenever material changes occur.

Part 1 asks for information about the adviser's business, the persons who own or control the advisory firm, and whether the adviser or its employees have been sanctioned for violating securities-related or other laws. Part 1 is organized in a check-the-box, fill-in-the-blank format. In 2001, RIAs were required to register with their home state or the SEC electronically through the automated IARD system. Once an IARD account is established, Form ADV Part 1 can be accessed, completed, and updated. If filed with the SEC, the adviser will be notified within 45 days after receipt of Form ADV whether the registration has been accepted or rejected. The SEC and individual states rely on Part 1 to identify which investment advisers warrant more immediate examination or who might pose a risk to clients or the general public.

In July 2010, the SEC unanimously agreed to amend the Part 2 requirement, adopting a "plain English" standard for the verbiage of this written disclosure statement or the brochure(s). Part 2A and Part 2B brochures provide information for customers in a narrative format and must address the adviser's business practices, advisory personnel, including services and investment strategies, fees, and conflicts of interest. Items that must be addressed in Part 2A include:

- The education and business background of management and key advisory personnel;

- Certifications information;

- Advisory services offered;

- Annual updates to material change;

- Fees and compensation charged;

- Types of clients

- Methods of analysis;

- Types of investment risk and investment strategies;

- Descriptions of firm legal problems and any disciplinary actions;

- Conflicts of interest and affiliations;

- Brief, concise summary of its Code of Ethics;

- Brokerage practices;

- Client account review procedures;

- Adviser arrangements and other compensation;

- Custody disclosure and procedures;

- Investment discretion information;

- Proxy voting procedures as under Rule 206(4)-6; and

- Financial information.[27]

Items that must be addressed in Part 2B include:

- Advisory personnel information;

- Background and experience;

- Disciplinary information;

- Outside business activities;

- Additional compensation;

- Supervision procedures; and

- Disciplinary events and bankruptcy petition information.[28]

Part 2A and Part 2B must be given to clients and potential clients as a disclosure brochure. The Investment Advisers Act of 1940 requires the delivery of a copy of Part 2A and Part 2B or a brochure(s) containing comparable information to prospective clients and it must be offered annually to all clients. These brochure(s) are the primary disclosure document that investment advisers provide their clients.

Although the IARD electronic filing system was designed to facilitate registration and oversight of advisers by regulators, it serves as a very useful tool for consumer education and protection. Before hiring an investment adviser's representative, financial planner or advisory firm, investors are encouraged to examine both parts of Form ADV and then ask for an explanation of any of the activities of the adviser and adviser representative that may remain unclear. Once filed, all parts of Form ADV are available to the public on the IAPD Web site.

Each state has its own unique laws involving the registration of investment adviser firms (RIAs) and investment adviser representatives (IARs). In general, however, states require advisory firms to complete a Form ADV and IARs to obtain a passing score on a competency examination, pay a fee, and provide a bond, especially if the adviser takes custody of client assets. Table 2.4 shows each state's examination requirement for registration as an investment adviser. It does not attempt to provide details on every state regarding pertinent administrative codes, statutes, or regulations. For additional registration information see the NASAA link http://www.nasaa.org/ industry-resources/investment-advisers/ia-switch-resources/state-investment-adviser-registration-information/ or consult the individual state regulatory authority http://www.nasaa.org/about-us/contact-us/contact-your-regulator/.

Table 2.4 State Investment Adviser and IAR Examination Requirements

State	State Examination Requirements for Investment Advisers and Investment Adviser Representatives	Wavier Granted for Current Certification
Alabama	Series 65 (or Series 66 & 7)	CFP, CIC, ChFC, PFS, CFA
Alaska	Series 65 (or Series 66 & 7)	CFP, CIC, ChFC, PFS, CFA
Arizona	Series 65 (or Series 66 & 7 or Series 66 & 2)	CFP, CIC, ChFC, PFS, CFA
Arkansas	Series 65 (or Series 66 & 7)	CFP, CIC, ChFC, PFS, CFA
California	Series 65 (or Series 66 & 7)	CFP, CIC, ChFC, PFS, CFA
Colorado	Series 65 (or Series 66 & 7)	CFP, CIC, ChFC, PFS, CFA, CIMC, CIMA
Connecticut	Series 65 (or Series 66)	CFP, CIC, ChFC, PFS, CFA, CLU
Delaware	Series 65 (or Series 66 & 7)	CFP, CIC, ChFC, PFS, CFA
District of Columbia	Series 65 (or Series 66 & 7)	CFP, CIC, ChFC, PFS, CFA
Florida	Series 65 (or Series 66 & 7)	CFP, CIC, ChFC, PFS, CFA
Georgia	Series 65 (or Series 66 & 7 or Series 65 & 6 & 22 or Series 65 & 7 or Series 65 & 2)	CFP, CIC, ChFC, PFS, CFA
Hawaii	Series 65 (or Series 66 & 7)	CFP, CIC, ChFC, PFS, CFA
Idaho	Series 65 (or Series 66 & 7)	CFP, CIC, ChFC, PFS, CFA
Illinois	Series 65 (or Series 66 & 7)	CFP, CIC, ChFC, PFS, CFA
Indiana	Series 65 (or Series 66 & 7)	CFP, CIC, ChFC, PFS, CFA
Iowa	Series 65 (or Series 66 & 7)	CFP, CIC, ChFC, PFS, CFA
Kansas	Series 65 (or Series 66 & 7)	CFP, CIC, ChFC, PFS, CFA
Kentucky	Series 65 (or Series 66 & 7)	CFP, CIC, ChFC, PFS, CFA
Louisiana	Series 65 (or Series 66 & 7)	CFP, CIC, ChFC, PFS, CFA
Maine	Series 65 (or Series 66 & 7)	CFP, CIC, ChFC, PFS, CFA
Maryland	Series 65 (or Series 66 & 7)	CFP, CIC, ChFC, PFS, CFA
Massachusetts	Series 65 (or Series 66 & 7)	CFP, CIC, ChFC, PFS, CFA
Michigan	Series 65 (or Series 66)	CFP, CIC, ChFC, PFS, CFA
Minnesota	Series 65 (or Series 66)	CFP, CIC, ChFC, PFS, CFA
Mississippi	Series 65 (or Series 66 & 7)	CFP, CIC, ChFC, PFS, CFA
Missouri	Series 65 (or Series 66 & 7)	Waivers are granted at the discretion of the Commissioner of the Missouri Securities Division.
Montana	Series 65 (or Series 66 or 24)	CFP, CIC, ChFC, PFS, CFA
Nevada	Series 65 (or Series 66 & 7)	CFP, CIC, ChFC, PFS, CFA

Nebraska	Series 65 (or Series 66 & 7)	CFP, CIC, ChFC, PFS, CFA
New Hampshire	Series 65 (or Series 66 & 7)	CFP, CIC, ChFC, PFS, CFA
New Jersey	Series 65 (or Series 66 & 7)	CFP, CIC, ChFC, PFS, CFA
New Mexico	Series 65 (or Series 66 & 7)	CFP, CIC, ChFC, PFS, CFA
New York	Series 65 (or Series 66 & 7)	CFP, CIC, ChFC, PFS, CFA
North Carolina	Series 65 (or Series 66 & 7)	CFP, CIC, ChFC, PFS, CFA
North Dakota	Series 65 (or Series 66 & 7)	CFP, CIC, ChFC, PFS, CFA
Ohio	Series 65 (or Series 66 & 7)	CFP, CIC, ChFC, PFS, CFA
Oklahoma	Series 65 (or Series 66 & 7)	CFP, CIC, ChFC, PFS, CFA
Oregon	Series 65 (or Series 66 & 7)	CFP, CIC, ChFC, PFS, CFA
Pennsylvania	Series 65 (or Series 66 & 7)	CFP, CIC, ChFC, PFS, CFA
Rhode Island	Series 65 (or Series 66 & 7)	CFP, CIC, ChFC, PFS, CFA
South Carolina	Series 65 (or Series 66 & 7)	CFP, CIC, ChFC, PFS, CFA
South Dakota	Series 65 (or Series 66 & 7)	CFP, CIC, ChFC, PFS, CFA
Tennessee	Series 65 (or Series 66 & 7)	CFP, CIC, ChFC, PFS, CFA
Texas	Series 65 (or Series 66 & 7 or 63 & 7)	CFP, CIC, ChFC, PFS, CFA
Utah	Series 65 (or Series 66 & 7)	CFP, CIC, ChFC, PFS, CFA
Vermont	Series 65 (or Series 66 & 7)	CFP, CIC, ChFC, PFS, CFA
Virginia	Series 65 (or Series 66 & 7)	CFP, CIC, ChFC, PFS, CFA
Washington	Series 65 (or Series 66 & 7)	CFP, CIC, ChFC, PFS, CFA
West Virginia	Series 65 (or Series 66 & 7)	CFP, CIC, ChFC, PFS, CFA
Wisconsin	Series 65 (or Series 66 & 7)	CFP, CIC, ChFC, PFS, CFA
Wyoming	Does not register investment adviser or investment adviser representatives	Not Applicable

Source: Adapted and updated from K. C. Garrett and J. E. Grable, "State Investment Advisor Representative Examination and Waiver Requirements," *Journal of Personal Finance* 6, no. 1 (2007): pp. 38–43. Used with permission.

As shown, most states require an investment adviser to pass a **Series 65 examination**, also known as the **Uniform Investment Adviser Law Examination**. This test, administered by NASAA, ensures that those who hold themselves out to be investment advisers have a sound understanding of securities laws, rules, and regulations. If the individual currently holds and maintains in good standing the Certified Financial Planner (CFP), Chartered Financial Analyst (CFA), Personal Financial Specialist (PFS), Charter Financial Consultant (ChFC) or Chartered Investment Counselor (CIC) credential, most state securities regulators will waive the requirement for successfully completing the Series 65 examination to register as an IAR. However, if an individual is no longer in good standing with the certifying organization, most state securities regulators will require the successful completion of the Series 65 examination before continuing any further activities as an IAR. Most state securities regulators require an individual to take the Series 65 examination if it has been two years since the individual has been registered as an IAR in any jurisdiction. FINRA defines a jurisdiction as any state, the District of Columbia, the Commonwealth of Puerto Rico, the U.S. Virgin Islands, or any subdivision or regulatory body thereof.[29] If an individual has successfully completed and currently maintains both the Series 66 and the Series 7 licenses with a FINRA-registered securities broker-dealer, most state securities regulators will not require the completion of the Series 65 examination. Investment adviser firms must also determine in which jurisdictions their advisory representatives must register, but this is a separate issue from exam and waiver requirements.

In addition, a **Form U4**, Uniform Application for Securities Industry Registration or Transfer, application must be filed for each investment adviser representative that provides services on behalf of an adviser firm. To apply for registration as an IAR, one must file the Form U4 through FINRA IARD and pay the associated registration fees to the applicable state securities regulator(s). An example of Form U4 is available on the FINRA Web site at http://www.finra.org.

The registration for an advisor working with a broker-dealer or selling investments for commission is similar to that for an IAR. As explained earlier in this chapter and in Chapter 1, a number of FINRA-administered exams must be completed to work in different capacities in the securities industry. Minimal qualifications are the Series 6 or Series 7 exam, and the Series 63 exam required for state registration. Broker-dealers also use Form U4 to register licensed personnel with SROs or state regulatory authorities. Financial professionals must file a Form U4 upon being hired by a FINRA member firm when acting as a registered representative or when engaging in the securities industry as a FINRA-licensed member.

Recall from Chapter 1 that fee-based advisory firms offer services for a fee and can also sell securities for commissions to have the freedom to match compensation method to client needs. These dually registered, or hybrid, firms are registered and regulated as advisory firms (registered with the state security regulator or the SEC) and as FINRA member broker-dealer firms.

Financial planners who use insurance products to implement recommendations also fall under state regulatory authority. The **National Association of Insurance Commissioners (NAIC)** is the national organization of state insurance regulators that develops uniform insurance regulations and agent examinations. NAIC was created in 1871 to provide regulatory oversight of insurance companies operating in more than one state. Authority was then given to NAIC and state regulators to provide more comprehensive consumer protection by requiring anyone selling life, health, or property insurance to be licensed in their respective states of operation.

Table 2.5 lists the most common types of insurance licenses held by financial planners who use insurance products. Eight licenses require an examination and six licenses require registration with a state regulator. Note that it is possible to obtain a combined license that covers life, accident and health, property and allied lines, and casualty and allied lines insurance. If this combined license is not obtained, a financial planner will be required to take individual examinations to obtain each license separately.

Table 2.5 Common Types of Insurance Licenses

Licenses That Require an Examination	Licenses That Do Not Require an Examination
Life	Variable contracts*
Accident and health	Travel
Property and allied lines	Auto club
Casualty and allied lines	Viatical settlements
Personal lines	Reinsurance intermediary
Crop	Excess lines
Title	
Bail bond	

*Financial planners who sell variable contracts must be licensed through FINRA and have a life agent license.

To obtain an insurance agent's license, a person must meet the following eight criteria:

1. Be at least 18 years of age;

2. Submit a NAIC Uniform Application to the state insurance regulator;

3. Submit an application fee;

4. Notify the state regulator if an insurance license is held in another state;

5. Provide evidence of Series 6 or Series 7 FINRA registration if selling variable contracts;

6. Pass a licensing examination;

7. Secure an insurance company certification showing where business will be transacted; and

8. Meet ongoing continuing education requirements.

FIDUCIARY RULES

A **fiduciary** is anyone who provides financial services and acts in a position of trust on behalf of, or for the benefit of, a third party.[30] Titles signaling a fiduciary capacity include trustee, executor, administrator, registrar of stocks and bonds, transfer agent, guardian, assignee, receiver, or custodian, but generally a financial planning fiduciary is anyone who provides specific recommendations regarding securities, is paid to provide ongoing financial advice, or works with unsophisticated clients who rely on the adviser's advice. A financial planner becomes a fiduciary when the advice given to a client becomes comprehensive and continuous.[31]

Determining who is a fiduciary and what responsibilities fiduciaries have when working with clients has a long history in the United States. Fiduciary standards, also known as prudence standards, can be traced back to a landmark lawsuit in 1830.[32] The ruling stated that trustees should "observe how men of prudence, discretion and intelligence manage their own affairs, not in regard to speculation, but in regard to the permanent disposition of their funds, considering the probable income, as well as the probable safety of the capital to be invested." This became the foundation of the **Model Prudent Man Rule Statute**, which was adopted in 1942.

The "prudent man" standard is based on the following statement: "The trustee shall observe the standards in dealing with the trust assets that would be observed by a prudent man dealing with the property of another ..." In 1959 the prudent man rule was reissued to include the following statement: "In making investments of trust funds the trustee is under a duty to the beneficiary ... to make such investments and only such investments as a prudent man would make of his own property having in view the preservation of the estate and the amount and regularity of the income to be derived ...."[33]

The **Uniform Prudent Investor Act (UPIA)**, as adopted in 1994, was a further update of the prudent man statute. Although the Act is primarily concerned with the management of trust and foundation assets, most states apply it much more broadly. As such, any financial planner who is also a fiduciary will find that the act is applicable. Investment professionals who advise charities and pensions also fall under the scope of the UPIA, which specifically states that, "In making investments of trust funds the trustee of a charitable trust is under a duty similar to that of the trustee of a private trust." The UPIA also applies to executors, conservators, and guardians of property. The UPIA has five fundamental components:

1. The standard of prudence is applied to any investment as part of the total portfolio rather than to individual investments. In the trust setting, the term portfolio embraces all trust assets.

2. The trade-off in all investing between risk and return is identified as the fiduciary's central consideration.

3. All categorical restrictions on types of investments have been abrogated; the trustee can invest in anything that plays an appropriate role in achieving the risk/return objectives of the trust and that meets the other requirements of prudent investing.

4. The long-familiar requirement that fiduciaries diversify investments has been integrated into the definition of prudent investing.

5. The much-criticized former rule of trust law forbidding a trustee to delegate investment and management functions has been reversed. Delegation is now permitted, subject to safeguards.

The UPIA requires a trustee to follow the following strict rules when making investments:

1. A trustee shall invest and manage trust assets as a prudent investor would, by considering the purposes, terms, distribution requirements, and other circumstances of the trust. In satisfying this standard, the trustee shall exercise reasonable care, skill, and caution.

2. A trustee's investment and management decisions respecting individual assets must be evaluated not in isolation but in the context of the trust portfolio as a whole and as a part of an overall investment strategy having risk and return objectives reasonably suited to the trust.

3. Among circumstances that a trustee shall consider in investing and managing trust assets are such of the following as are relevant to the trust or its beneficiaries:

   a. General economic conditions;

   b. The possible effect of inflation or deflation;

   c. The expected tax consequences of investment decisions or strategies;

   d. The role that each investment or course of action plays within the overall trust portfolio, which may include financial assets, interests in closely held enterprises, tangible and intangible personal property, and real property;

   e. The expected total return from income and the appreciation of capital;

   f. Other resources of the beneficiaries;

   g. Needs for liquidity, regularity of income, and preservation or appreciation of capital; and

   h. An asset's special relationship or special value, if any, to the purposes of the trust or to one or more of the beneficiaries.

4. A trustee shall make a reasonable effort to verify facts relevant to the investment and management of trust assets.

5. A trustee may invest in any kind of property or type of investment consistent with the standards of the UPIA.

6. A trustee who has special skills or expertise, or is named trustee in reliance upon the trustee's representation that the trustee has special skills or expertise, has a duty to use those special skills or that expertise.

The effect of the UPIA on financial planners is potentially significant. It requires anyone who falls under the scope of the act to act in the best interest of the client. Specific duties include being objective, monitoring investments, investigating investments, diversifying portfolios, maintaining loyalty to the client, remaining impartial, reducing costs to maximize portfolio efficiency, and maintaining regulatory compliance. These are the minimum requirements a prudent person would expect of a financial planner.

The antifraud provisions of the Investment Advisers Act of 1940, § 206, clearly imply that investment advisers must act as fiduciaries when dealing with clients. Because of this, investment advisers may also fall within the scope of the UPIA. The SEC states that fiduciaries must:

1. Hold the client's interests above all other matters.

2. Use the highest standards of care when working with clients.

3. Avoid conflicts of interest.

4. If conflicts of interest cannot be avoided, be diligent in disclosing such information to all interested parties.

5. Disclose compensation methods.

6. Ensure client confidentiality.

7. Select broker-dealers based on their ability to provide the best execution of trades for accounts where the adviser has authority to select the broker-dealer.

8. Make recommendations based on a reasonable inquiry into a client's investment objectives, financial situation, and other factors.

The burden of proof regarding a breach of fiduciary duty always lies with the adviser. Financial planners individually, as well as the firms they work for, can be held financially liable for a breach of fiduciary duty. In some cases, a financial planner can also face criminal charges for a fiduciary mistake. Section 206 of the Investment Advisers Act of 1940 applies to *all* firms and persons meeting the definition of investment adviser, whether registered with the SEC, a state securities authority, or not at all.

The fiduciary standards through the antifraud provisions required by the SEC and similar guidelines at the state level apply to all RIAs and IARs. Although at the time of publication the SEC exempts broker-dealers and broker-dealer representatives from fiduciary and ethics rules, future changes may result from § 913 of Dodd-Frank. Section 913 mandated study and possible regulatory efforts to create a uniform fiduciary standard. Stockbrokers at the time of this publication are required to meet only three standards when working with clients. First, FINRA requires a broker to know a client's investment goals and objectives. Second, investment recommendations must be suitable to meet the client's objectives. (For more information on the definition of suitability, see Chapter 1.) Third, trades must be made correctly. Based on these standards, stockbrokers currently are not considered fiduciaries. On the other hand, financial planners are almost always considered fiduciaries. Under SEC rules, *stockbrokers cannot call themselves financial planners.* They may, however, use terms such as *financial consultant* or *wealth manager.*

ETHICAL REQUIREMENTS FOR FINANCIAL PLANNERS

Whether ethical actions are considered based on relative or absolute measures, most people associate ethics with a set of principles or values. This is fundamentally true for financial planners. Although grounded in ethical principles, expectations of ethical conduct have been promulgated by various groups associated with financial planning, and in some cases the expectations of ethical conduct or what might be thought of as practice standards have been legislated. This discussion follows that same progression, from the foundation of ethical principles to business practice expectations enforceable by sanctions.

Principles of Ethical Conduct

Almost all professional financial services organizations require their members to abide by a code of ethics. The same is true for many financial planning designations that also support an ethical code. NAPFA, the nation's largest fee-only financial planning organization, states that members "uphold the highest standards of care in the industry" by supporting and practicing the following eight principles: objectivity, competence, professionalism, full disclosure, fairness and suitability, regulatory compliance, integrity and honesty, and confidentiality.[34] Each principle is more fully explained, such as the following example of full disclosure:

> NAPFA members shall fully describe method of compensation and potential conflicts of interest to clients and also specify the total cost of investments.[35]

The FPA has adopted the CFP Board *Code of Ethics*. This sharing of ethics statements is unique, however. Although the CFP Board has established the standard for ethics, the CFP Board's principles, or their interpretation of the principles in the context of financial planning, are by no means universally accepted or used.

The CFP Board *Code of Ethics* consists of seven principles, as shown in Exhibit 2.1 with specific explanations related to each principle. The CFP Board describes the principles of integrity, objectivity, competence, fairness, confidentiality, professionalism, and diligence as "general statements establishing the ethical and professional ideals certificants and registrants are expected to display in professional activities."[36]

Other organizations typically have statements of ethics that are general in nature, such as the term *integrity*, which is common to NAPFA, FPA, and CFP® professionals as well as holders of the CPA and CFA credentials. But each organization explains the principle in the context of its professional practice. This approach results in a set of general principles or values that can be promoted, but it also provides a foundation for the establishment of ethical professional practice standards that can be promulgated and controlled via sanctions. In fact, the Board states that

> The Principles form the basis of CFP Board's *Rules of Conduct, Practice Standards and Disciplinary Rules*, and these documents together reflect CFP Board's recognition of certificants' and registrants' responsibilities to the public, clients, colleagues and employers.[37]

Exhibit 2.1 CFP Board Code of Ethics and Professional Responsibility

Code of Ethics and Professional Responsibility

CFP Board adopted the *Code of Ethics* to establish the highest principles and standards. These Principles are general statements expressing the ethical and professional ideals certificants and registrants are expected to display in their professional activities. As such, the Principles are aspirational in character and provide a source of guidance for certificants and registrants. The Principles form the basis of CFP Board's *Rules of Conduct, Practice Standards and Disciplinary Rules,* and these documents together reflect CFP Board's recognition of certificants' and registrants' responsibilities to the public, clients, colleagues and employers.

Principle 1 – Integrity: Provide professional services with integrity.

Integrity demands honesty and candor which must not be subordinated to personal gain and advantage. Certificants are placed in positions of trust by clients, and the ultimate source of that trust is the certificant's personal integrity. Allowance can be made for innocent error and legitimate differences of opinion, but integrity cannot co-exist with deceit or subordination of one's principles.

Principle 2 – Objectivity: Provide professional services objectively.

Objectivity requires intellectual honesty and impartiality. Regardless of the particular service rendered or the capacity in which a certificant functions, certificants should protect the integrity of their work, maintain objectivity and avoid subordination of their judgment.

Principle 3 – Competence: Maintain the knowledge and skill necessary to provide professional services competently.

Competence means attaining and maintaining an adequate level of knowledge and skill, and application of that knowledge and skill in providing services to clients. Competence also includes the wisdom to recognize the limitations of that knowledge and when consultation with other professionals is appropriate or referral to other professionals necessary. Certificants make a continuing commitment to learning and professional improvement.

Principle 4 – Fairness: Be fair and reasonable in all professional relationships. Disclose conflicts of interest.

Fairness requires impartiality, intellectual honesty and disclosure of material conflicts of interest. It involves a subordination of one's own feelings, prejudices and desires so as to achieve a proper balance of conflicting interests. Fairness is treating others in the same fashion that you would want to be treated.

Principle 5 – Confidentiality: Protect the confidentiality of all client information.

Confidentiality means ensuring that information is accessible only to those authorized to have access. A relationship of trust and confidence with the client can only be built upon the understanding that the client's information will remain confidential.

Principle 6 – Professionalism: Act in a manner that demonstrates exemplary professional conduct.

Professionalism requires behaving with dignity and courtesy to clients, fellow professionals, and others in business-related activities. Certificants cooperate with fellow certificants to enhance and maintain the profession's public image and improve the quality of services.

Principle 7 – Diligence: Provide professional services diligently.

Diligence is the provision of services in a reasonably prompt and thorough manner, including the proper planning for, and supervision of, the rendering of professional services.

Source: CFP Board of Standards, Inc., *CFP Board's Standards of Professional Conduct.* Available at http://www.cfp. net/Downloads/2010Standards.pdf, pp. 6–7. Used with permission.

It is important that students and novice financial planners understand the ethical standards of conduct established by the CFP Board for certified financial planners.

CFP Board Standards of Ethical Conduct

The CFP Board distinguishes between certificants who are currently certified by the Board and **registrants** who have previously been certified by the Board and are eligible to resume use of the marks without having to pass the current certification examination. Registrants are subject to the *Standards of Professional Conduct* for activities conducted as certificants; therefore, the activity could be investigated later as a registrant.

The *Standards of Professional Conduct* are based on the *Code of Ethics and Professional Responsibility*, the *Rules of Conduct and Financial Planning Practice Standards*. The CFP Board, in describing the *Code of Ethics and Professional Responsibility*, states that the "principles are general statements expressing the ethical and professional ideals certificants and registrants are expected to display in their professional activities. As such, the Principles are aspirational in character but are intended to provide a source of guidance for CFP Board certificants and registrants."[38]

The *Rules of Conduct*, which set the high standards and level of professionalism expected, "govern all those who have the right to use the CFP® marks, whether or not the marks are actually used."[39] Despite these statements, the Board does not declare that the *Rules of Conduct* are globally applicable, similar to the exceptions applied with the *Practice Standards*. The Board states that

> The universe of activities engaged in by a certificant is diverse, and a certificant may perform all, some or none of the typical services provided by financial planning professionals. Some Rules may not be applicable to a certificant's specific activity. As a result, when considering the Rules of Conduct, the certificant must determine whether a specific Rule is applicable to those services.[40]

The Board further clarifies that a certificant can be compliant with the rules based on actions performed by the certificant's employer. The six *Rules of Conduct* include:

1. Defining the Relationship with the Prospective Client or Clients

2. Information Disclosed to Prospective Client or Clients

3. Prospective Client and Client Information and Property

4. Obligations to Prospective Clients and Clients

5. Obligations to Employers

6. Obligations to the CFP Board

Each of the *Practice Standards* establishes expected practices related to each of the six steps within the financial planning process. (For a review of these steps, see Chapter 1.) Specifically, the Board noted that the *Practice Standards* were intended to establish norms of practice, advance professionalism, and enhance the value of the financial planning process. The Board further states that

> Compliance with the *Practice Standards* is mandatory for certificants whose services include financial planning or material elements of financial planning, but all financial planning professionals are encouraged to use the *Practice Standards* when performing financial planning tasks or activities addressed by a *Practice Standard*. The *Practice Standards* are designed to provide certificants with a framework for the professional practice of financial planning.[41]

Whereas the *Practice Standards* may not be applicable to all of a certificant's professional activities, the *Code of Ethics and Professional Responsibility* are globally applicable to certificants and registrants.

Additionally, the CFP Board relates the individual *Practice Standards* with the most applicable individual *Codes of Ethics* and *Rules of Conduct* in the explanation of each Practice Standard in the *Standards of Professional Conduct*. The integration of these guidelines is more fully discussed in Chapters 6, 7, and 8, following the explanation of each step in the systematic financial planning process. As background for this discussion, it is important to consider the CFP Board explanation of whether a certificant is providing financial planning or material elements of financial planning and is, therefore, subject to the *Rules of Conduct* or *Practice Standards*. As explained in Chapter 1, providing financial planning (i.e., integrating the financial planning process with the financial planning subject areas) or material elements of financial planning may be based on the following factors:

- The client's understanding and intent when engaging the certificant;

- The degree to which multiple financial planning subject areas are involved;

- The comprehensiveness of data gathering; and

- The breadth and depth of the recommendations.[42]

But the CFP Board also asserts that financial planning can occur even if material elements are not provided simultaneously, a written plan is not provided, parts are provided over a period of time, or they are provided as distinct subject areas.

In combination, the *Code of Ethics and Professional Responsibility*, the *Rules of Conduct*, and the *Financial Planning Practice Standards* constitute what the Board refers to as its *Standards of Professional Conduct*. Jointly referred to as the Standards, these documents represent the standards of ethical conduct for CFP® professionals. The Board enforces the Standards through the *Disciplinary and Ethics Commission*, as established by the *Disciplinary Rules and Procedures* (referred to as the *Disciplinary Rules*). Violations of the Standards can result in a range of disciplinary actions ranging from a private letter of censure to revocation of the right to use the CFP® marks.

At the time of publication of this book, the CFP Board was considering standard sanction guidelines to direct disciplinary procedures and promote consistency in the sanctions imposed for similar offenses. As a certifying and standard-setting body, the Standards promulgated by the Board are not a basis for legal liability to any third party. However the Standards do serve as a basis for protecting the interests of financial planning clients and the public, as well as CFP practitioners and their employers.

SEC Standards of Ethical Conduct

The SEC, most state securities agencies, and financial services professional organizations require financial planners to abide by a code of ethics. Rule 204A-1 amended the Investment Advisers Act of 1940 so that every adviser must have a code of ethics that sets forth the standards of conduct expected of advisory personnel. The focus of the rule was to reduce conflicts of interest between advisers and clients by requiring RIAs and RIA representatives to report personal securities transactions, including purchases and sales in any mutual fund managed by an adviser. At a minimum, under this rule a code of ethics must include the following the following requirements:

- that standards of business conduct that reflect a firm's fiduciary duty be written;

- that the chief compliance officer and supervised persons comply with federal securities laws;

- that all access persons (i.e., supervised persons with access to nonpublic client information about securities transactions or who make recommendations about securities), including new hires, annually report and have reviewed all personal investment holdings per the specified guidelines;

- that all access persons quarterly report and have reviewed all personal investment transactions per the specified guidelines;

- that an adviser's approval be obtained before an RIA representative (i.e. supervised person) invests in an initial public offering or private placement;

- that any violation of the code of ethics be promptly reported internally;

- that receipt of the code of ethics by all RIA representatives (i.e. supervised persons) be documented and that employees receive adequate training on the principles and procedures of the code;

- that all of a firm's employees receive subsequent amendments to the code;

- that the adviser keep copies of the code, records of violations of the code, and actions taken as a result of any violation of the code; and

- that advisers describe their code of ethics in Form ADV Part 2A and provide a copy to clients.[43]

The SEC adopted two additional rules to further refine how a firm's code of ethics should be written, reviewed, and enforced. Rules 206(4)-7 and 204-2 require all registered RIAs to adopt written policies and procedures, perform annual reviews, and maintain accurate books and records for testing policies and procedures and to designate a chief compliance officer to oversee and enforce these policies and procedures. Written policies and procedures must include the following 11 points:

1. Identification of supervisory guidelines and procedures, conflicts of interest and risks facing the RIA;

2. Description of the portfolio management process used by the RIA, including allocation practices, consistency of investment objectives, proxy voting, disclosures made by the investment adviser, and any applicable regulatory restrictions;

3. Description of trading practices, including best execution obligations, use of soft dollars, and allocation of aggregated trades;

4. Description of the policies for proprietary trading of the RIA and RIA representatives (i.e. supervised persons);

5. Policy on the accuracy of disclosures made to clients, including account statements and advertisements;

6. Policy on safeguarding clients' assets;

7. Description of the books and records maintained by the RIA, security of books and records, and protection of information from alteration or untimely destruction;

8. Description of marketing policies, including the use of solicitors;

9. Processes to value client holdings and calculation of fees;

10. Description of safeguards for the privacy of client records and information; and

11. Disaster recovery and business continuity plan.[44]

The rules also require an annual review of policies and procedures. RIAs must maintain documentation of annual reviews and of actions taken to rectify any deficiencies. The role of the **chief compliance officer** is to administer compliance policies and procedures. The SEC requires a compliance officer to be competent and knowledgeable about the Investment Advisers Act of 1940, and to be in a position to take full responsibility and authority for developing and enforcing appropriate policies and procedures. In 2010, the SEC passed Rule 206(4)-5, which among other requirements established another ethics requirement for recording all employee political contributions and approving select employee political contributions.[45]

Although the SEC's ethics requirements are commendable, it is important to note that they apply only to RIAs and RIA representatives registered at the federal level, and in certain cases, also when they are adopted at the state level. Stockbrokers, insurance agents, and other financial advisers are exempt from these ethical guidelines. Professional organizations help fill this ethics void by establishing, maintaining, and enforcing ethical standards within the profession.

The CFP Board has made the greatest strides in defining and formalizing a code of ethics for financial planning practitioners. The process of defining financial planning ethics and standards began in 1985. At that time, the CFP Board undertook the task of defining competency in financial planning. From this assignment emerged the CFP Board's *Code of Ethics and Professional Responsibility*. Ten years later, in 1995, the CFP Board created a Board of Practice Standards, which was charged with the responsibility of drafting financial planning standards. The *Standards of Professional Conduct* continue to evolve, with the most recent update in 2009. For more information about expectations for ethical conduct or the *Disciplinary Rules* see *The Standards of Professional Conduct* available at http://www.cfp.net/Downloads/2010Standards.pdf or http://www.cfp.net/learn/ethics.asp#intro.

RULES GOVERNING COMMUNICATION

Special consideration must be given to all communication from financial professionals to the public regardless of whether the recipient of the communication is a client. The rationale for this is that an implied level of knowledge is imputed to a person who is credentialed or licensed to practice a certain type of business. How a financial professional (e.g., RIA, registered rep, insurance agent) conducts business dictates the guidelines and regulations for public communication and advertising. As might be expected, there also are guidelines and regulations regarding communication with a client; these are often referred to as *required disclosure documents*. Finally, social media have created a new challenge for financial professionals, i.e., determining effective and acceptable uses. Each of these three broad areas is briefly considered for major requirements.

Advertising and Marketing

"The Advertising Rule"—Rule 206(4)-1 under the Investment Advisers Act of 1940 (and its amendments)—establishes advertising practices for SEC-registered advisers. An "advertisement" includes any communication addressed to more than one person that offers any investment advisory service with regard to securities, including both written publications (such as a Web site, newsletter, or marketing brochure) and oral communications (such as an announcement made on radio or television).

Advertising may not be false or misleading or include untrue statements. Specifically prohibited are testimonials from clients about their experience or endorsements of the adviser; the use of past specific recommendations that were profitable, unless the adviser includes a list of all recommendations made during a minimum of the past year; the representation that any graph, chart, or formula could be used to make decisions regarding which securities to buy or sell; and advertisements stating that any report, analysis, or service is free, unless it really is free and without any obligations.

Similar restrictions regarding client communication with the public are established in FINRA Rule 2210. Accordingly, communication must:

- Be based on principles of fair dealing and not omit material information, particularly risk disclosure;

- Not make exaggerated, unwarranted, or misleading claims;

- Give the investor a sound basis for evaluating the facts in regard to any particular security, type of security, industry or service;

- Not contain predictions or projections of investment results; and

- Identify the name of the member firm.[46]

FINRA also defines advertising very broadly. Anything that is likely to make its way into the hands of a consumer is considered advertising. This includes newspapers, radio and television ads, signs and billboard messages, and voice recordings. The key to whether information will be considered advertising is the level of control the purveyor of the information has over who receives it. In the preceding examples, the purveyor or publisher of the information has no control over who sees and reads the advertisement.

FINRA also regulates sales literature, which is defined as any written communication distributed to customers or the general public upon request, meaning that the publisher has some control over who is receiving the information. This type of communication includes research reports, form letters, and educational seminar materials. In any case, whether the communication is classified as advertising or sales literature, FINRA requires the materials to be approved by the registered principal of a FINRA member firm before distribution.[47]

All broker-dealer advertising, including electronic advertising, must be filed with FINRA. The exception is prospectuses and other similar documents used in conjunction with offering securities that have already been filed with the SEC. In addition to the approval and filing process, written communication pieces must be kept on file by the issuing party for a period of not less than three years from the initial use date, and they must include the names of the people who prepared and approved their use.

Of course, when it comes to the last word concerning public communication for the purposes of solicitation or facilitation of financial transactions, look to the SEC. According to the SEC it is unlawful for any person to use the mail or any other form of interstate commerce (including telephone and email) to employ manipulative or deceptive practices in conjunction with the purchase or sale of any security.

Regulations do not stop with written communication; both telephonic and electronic communication are also regulated. Most SROs and other membership organizations also control telephone communication in accordance with the Telephone Consumer Protection Act of 1991. This act, as administered by the Federal Communication Commission (FCC), protects consumers from unwanted telephone calls for the purposes of soliciting business. Specifically, it limits the hours that a person can be called (8:00 a.m.to 9:00 p.m. local time), and it requires the maintenance of a "Do Not

Call" list. However, exceptions exist for parties with an already-established working relationship and where the recipient of the call has given prior permission.

For electronic communication, the SEC, FCC, and Federal Trade Commission (FTC) have banded together to attempt to control the amount and content of email communication and solicitation. The SEC requires that email communications between broker-dealers or other financial intermediaries and their clients or the general public be archived. The SEC's authority to enact this requirement is grounded in the Securities Exchange Act of 1934. Rules 17a-3 and 17a-4 of this act require financial intermediaries to create, and preserve in an easily accessible manner, a comprehensive record of each securities transaction they effect and of their securities business in general for a period of at least three years for the purpose of monitoring compliance with applicable securities laws and financial responsibility standards. In 1997, the SEC amended paragraph (f) of Rule 17a-4 to allow broker-dealers to store records electronically in a non-rewriteable, nonerasable format.[48]

For practicing insurance agents, NAIC defines advertising as any material designed to create public interest in a product or induce the public to purchase, increase, modify, reinstate, borrow from, surrender, replace, or retain a policy.[49] Advertising under this broad definition includes everything from business cards to brochures and any other communication used to enhance sales. The language used in such advertising pieces must be clear, easily understood, and not worded in such a way as to mislead the reader or misrepresent the product. Though NAIC is working on nationalizing some of these requirements, currently individual states control the maintenance schedule of advertising files that must be maintained by agents and insurance companies. Duration requirements range from two to three years on the lower end to as much a seven to 10 years on the upper end.

Client Disclosures

Full client disclosure is a very important component of ethical professional conduct that can generally be summarized in four categories: (1) disclosures about the advisory firm and representatives; (2) disclosures about the engagement or contractual agreement; (3) disclosures about the protection of client data and the sharing of data with other parties; and (4) disclosures about investment management policies in an investment policy statement. Although some of this information was mentioned earlier in this chapter and will be considered again in Chapter 6 relative to the financial planning process and in Chapter 9 relative to the components of a financial plan, this discussion considers disclosures relative to regulatory requirements. Investment policy statements are not mandated; therefore this disclosure is not considered.

Stockbrokers are currently exempt from most disclosure rules. Brokers need only disclose that brokerage accounts are different from managed advisory accounts, and that the broker may receive incentive income from third parties. FINRA has proposed a regulation to require fuller broker disclosure, FINRA Regulatory Notice 10-54, Concept Proposal to Require a Disclosure Statement for Retail Investors at or Before Commencing a Business Relationship. More information can be found at http://www.finra.org. Additionally, comments in response to this proposed regulation from the wirehouses, banks, and other sources can be found on the Internet.

The SEC and most state regulatory agencies require that all RIAs distribute Part 2 of Form ADV to prospective clients before or at the time an advisory agreement is executed. Rule 204-3(b) under the Investment Advisers Act (and subsequent amendments) and similar state rules establish this requirement, as well as the ongoing fiduciary obligation to inform clients and to deliver a brochure to each client annually. Clients must be informed annually of material changes in ADV Part 2, and a summary of the material changes or a copy of the updated brochure must be delivered within 120 days of the end of the adviser's fiscal year. If the client consents, the annual update can be delivered electronically. The SEC has published interpretive guidance on delivering documents electronically, which can be found at www.sec.gov/rules/concept/33-7288.txt. Material impacts (i.e., disciplinary information) to the adviser or advisory firm must be shared during the year with clients on an interim amendment. The most recent copy of an investment adviser's Form ADV and any amendments are available at the IAPD Web site for either state- or SEC-registered advisers. Exhibit 2.2 is an example of a letter of confirmation that can be used to document that required information was delivered to and received by clients.

Exhibit 2.2 Brochure Receipt Letter

Mr. and Mrs. Robert T. Sample
103 West Lake Avenue
Montclair, NJ 07042

Dear Bob and Laura:

Annually or when we have any change to (1) our business or personnel, (2) the services we offer, or (3) material information that could affect our advisory relationship we must deliver to you the latest version of our "firm brochure," as part of our ongoing obligations. This brochure has been prepared to include a summary of material changes either as an interim statement or annual amendment.

Additionally, if when reading our firm brochure or our reporting of any material changes questions should arise, we are available to review the brochure with you and answer any questions you may have.

We are happy to deliver these communications electronically, if in the future you would prefer to receive brochure amendments by this means. You may reach our compliance staff at compliancepersonnel@company.com

Please acknowledge your receipt below:

By: _____ Date: _____

Please return this letter to us, as we are required to keep a copy in our file.

Sincerely,

For any reason, you do wish to make an adjustment to your account or further discuss your managed account, please contact your Financial Advisor.

Source: Corey Franco, Compliance Consultant, Teaneck, NJ, ©2012. Used with permission.

It is also important to obtain a client's written agreement regarding financial planning and investment management services before gathering data or making a recommendation. Although this seems like common sense, the Investment Advisers Act of 1940 does not require that a contract be in writing, although state laws require that contracts between state-registered investment advisers and clients be in writing. A sample financial planning agreement provided by the FPA for pro bono financial planning services is shown in Appendix 2A. An example of an advisory firm investment management agreement is shown in Appendix 2B. Both illustrate how planning and investment management contracts can be structured to meet the needs of a financial planner or investment adviser while also disclosing the parameters of professional service that comply with the Investment Advisers Act of 1940, the Uniform Securities Act, and other SEC rulings, all of which establish requirements for investment adviser contracts.

The CFP Board *Practice Standards* outline exactly what disclosures must be made when providing financial planning services and other professional services. The CFP Board of Standards offers several sample disclosures, including:

- Form OPS, Disclosure Form for Other Professional Services;

- Form FPD, Disclosure Form for Financial Planning Services; and

- Form PDA, Written Agreement and Disclosure Form for Financial Planning Services.

These forms can be found on the CFP Board Web site at http://www.cfp.net/aboutus/standards.asp. Consistent with other regulatory requirements, these sample documents are designed to meet the *Standards of Professional Conduct* for CFP® professionals by informing clients about the professional and providing an explanation of the services offered, potential conflicts of interest that might influence the professional, and a full explanation of the costs associated with the services and/or products to be delivered.

The Gramm-Leach-Bliley Act, also known as GLBA, requires the SEC and other organizations to adopt rules implementing notice requirements and restrictions on a financial institution's ability to disclose nonpublic personal information about consumers.[50] In accordance with § 504 of the GLBA, the SEC adopted Regulation S-P. Recall that GLBA requires financial institutions to provide customers notice of its privacy policies and practices and must not disclose nonpublic personal information about consumers to nonaffiliated third parties without proper disclosure and consent. As it relates to brokers, planners, and other investment professionals, Regulation S-P states that, as a general rule, the initial privacy notice must be given to a customer or proposed customer no later than when a registered adviser provides each client with a written disclosure statement or investment advisory contract. Exhibit 2.3 provides a sample privacy statement and the information to include.

Exhibit 2.3 Sample Privacy Statement

Our Privacy Policy

Our relationship with you is our most important asset. We understand that you have entrusted us with your private financial information, and we do everything we can to maintain that trust.

This notice is being provided to you in accordance with the Securities and Exchange Commission's rule regarding the privacy of consumer financial information ("Regulation S-P"). Please take the time to read and understand the privacy policies and procedures that we have implemented to safeguard your nonpublic personal information.*

We collect personal information to do financial planning and to perform our investment management responsibilities.

1. **We do not sell your personal information to anyone.**

2. **We do not disclose any nonpublic information about our customers or former customers to anyone, except as permitted by law.**

   In accordance with Section 248.13 of Regulation S-P, in limited circumstances where we believe in good faith that disclosure is required or permitted by law, we may disclose all of the information we collect, as described above, to certain nonaffiliated third parties such as attorneys, accountants, auditors and persons or entities that are assessing our compliance with industry standards. We enter into contractual agreements with all nonaffiliated third parties that prohibit such third parties from disclosing or using the information other than to carry out the purposes for which we disclose the information.

   Outside of this exception, we will not share your personal information with third parties unless you have specifically asked us to do so.

   We collect personal information in the normal course of business in order to provide planning and investment management services.

   New client information. We collect information that you provide to us when you become a client. The information we collect includes name(s), address, phone number, email address, Social Security number(s), and other information about your investing and financial planning needs.

3. **We protect the confidentiality and security of your personal information.**

   We restrict access to personal information to our staff and for business purposes only.

   We maintain physical, electronic, and procedural safeguards to guard your personal information.

4. **We continue to evaluate our efforts to protect personal information and make every effort to keep your personal information accurate and up to date.**

   If you identify any inaccuracy in your personal information, or you need to make a change to that information, please contact us so that we may promptly update our records.

5. **We will provide notice of changes in our information sharing practices.**

   If, at any time in the future, it is necessary to disclose any of your personal information in a way that is inconsistent with this policy, we will give you advance notice of the proposed change so that you will have the opportunity to opt out of such disclosure.

* Nonpublic personal information means personally identifiable information and any list, description or other grouping of consumers that is derived using any personally identifiable financial information that is not publicly available.

One of the best ways to avoid the claim of professional misconduct is to run a financial planning practice using the highest level of professional ethical standards. Abiding by a code of ethics is a good starting point. Using disclosure and practice management standards as they apply to fiduciaries, regardless of how one is paid or what type of planning one does, is another way to reduce the possibility of errors and omissions claims. Exhibit 2.4 offers a comprehensive yet likely not exhaustive listing of the items a financial planner ought to disclose to prospective and current clients, as applicable to the financial planners' business model. It may be similar in content to Form ADV, if one is required of the adviser, but it is broader in scope to include items that might be disclosed, as other federal or state regulators require. These items must be disclosed to, received by, and confirmed in writing by a client prior to implementing recommendations—or in some cases, before consummating a professional relationship.

Exhibit 2.4 Client Disclosure Summary Checklist

Disclosure Item	Document Given to Client		
	Yes	No	Date
Name and address of firm			
Listing of services provided			
Custody of assets			
Discretionary authority over assets managed			
Listing of licenses			
Listing of certifications and designations			
Listing of professional membership organizations			
Listing of other professional associations			
Educational background			
Number of years of practice experience			
Listing of all disciplinary actions			
Listing of all legal actions			
Conflicts of interest			
Method of compensation			
Sources of compensation			
Delivery of code of ethics			
Delivery of applicable brochures			
Signature for client's receipt of disclosure items			

Regulation of Social Media Communication

There have been no enforcement actions by regulators for the improper use of social media in the securities industry...yet. The SEC, through Advisers Act Rule 206(4)-7, and FINRA, through Rule 2210, require a social media policy, describing who is allowed to use social media for business purposes, how it will be used, and a description of disciplinary actions that will be taken in the event social media are used in a way that violates company policy. The SEC has stipulated that the use of social media must comply with all applicable parts of Section 17 of the Securities Act of 1933 pertaining to adviser communication and all other applicable legislation.[51]

Firms must adopt policies and procedures reasonably designed to ensure that employees who participate in social media sites for business purposes are appropriately supervised. Employees must receive the necessary training to engage in social media communication, ensuring that they do not pose undue risks to investors or their company. Firms must have usage guidelines and content standards, as a well as a general policy prohibiting any employee from engaging in business communications in a social media site that are not subject to the firm's supervision. This social media policy must be in place before a financial adviser representative uses social media. The compliance procedures of a firm should also consider without limitations the reputation and validity of the source of information when utilizing social media. Also, the firm is responsible for monitoring and enforcing actions against any representatives who violate these policies. Furthermore, firms are encouraged to be thoughtful about privacy settings to thwart the efforts of those who might threaten the firm's secure use of social media. Firms can avoid liability by appropriate disciplinary action of the representative in violation and proper handling, such as reporting the acts immediately to the appropriate regulatory authorities.[52]

Compliance is focused primarily on outbound communication, so compliance issues do not arise from "the mere fact that you have a [social media] account used to listen and learn."[53] For some advisers, listening and learning is all they require of social media, and they are happy to participate in these sites without communicating outwardly. Other advisers, who choose to have a voice in their social media communities, require annual training and should avail themselves of resources that help them create and maintain their social media policies. Several program providers are available to advisers to ensure their social media policies are appropriate for their level of usage. Financial planners can choose the policy most appropriate for their business from the options these companies provide, which focus on the compliance and regulatory issues associated with social media.

> Every firm that intends to communicate, or permit its associated persons to communicate, through social media sites must first ensure that it can retain records of those communications as required by Rules 17a-3 and 17a-4 under the Securities Exchange Act of 1934 and NASD Rule 3110. SEC and FINRA rules require that for record retention purposes, the content of the communication is determinative and a broker-dealer must retain those electronic communications that relate to its 'business as such.'[54]

Also, under NASD Rules 2210 and 2211, firms must retain all communications for a period of three years from the date of last use.

Suitability Responsibilities

FINRA Rule 2310 (suitability) requires firms to make reasonable efforts to obtain certain information from the customer, and to have reasonable grounds for believing that a recommendation is suitable for a customer based on financial situation and needs. Furthermore, the rule requires a broker-dealer to determine that a recommendation is suitable for every investor for whom it is made. If a broker-dealer—or anyone else whose business is regulated by FINRA—communicates a recommendation via a social media platform that is viewed by multiple investors, then Rule 2310 may be violated if the recommendation is not suitable for every investor.

For example, a broker dealer might communicate in a blog or other social media outlet that she recommends that investors roll over their traditional IRA to a Roth IRA because of anticipated increases in the marginal tax brackets. This is a seemingly innocent and reasonable recommendation if there were reasonable grounds to believe that an 85-year-old widower would not act on this information and make the Roth conversion. Therefore, this seemingly sound recommendation could be a violation because the advice might not be suitable for all investors viewing the recommendation.[55]

Electronic Forums (Real-time vs. Static Communication)

In reference to social media sites, which consist of both static and real-time interactive communications, the registered principal of a firm must approve all static content on a social networking site established by the firm before it is posted, because FINRA considers static postings to constitute "advertisements" under Rule 2210. Therefore, Web communications that meet the definition of advertisements, sales literature, or independently prepared reprints set forth in FINRA Rule 2210(a) must be approved in writing before use by a registered principal of the broker-dealer. Or if a firm sponsors a blog, a principal must approve it before any posts are made.

However, if a blog is used to engage in real-time interactive communications, FINRA considers the blog an interactive electronic forum that does not require prior principal approval. Also, FINRA generally does not treat posts by customers or other third parties as the firm's communication with the public subject to Rule 2210. However, under certain circumstances, third-party posts may be attributed to the firm if the firm has (1) involved itself in the preparation of the content, known as the "entanglement theory" or (2) has explicitly or implicitly endorsed or approved the content, known as the "adoption theory."[56] These theories traditionally have applied to third-party content hyperlinked to a firm's Web site, but the same would apply to the firm's social media sites. Any procedures a firm adopts, however, must be reasonably designed to ensure that interactive electronic communications do not violate FINRA or SEC rules.

Social media usage among both the public and advisers continues to expand. Advisers who have taken advantage of social media are finding it beneficial in their practice for generating new clients, communicating with existing clients, and providing a means to demonstrate their professionalism and expertise. Although the SEC and FINRA have set forth regulations and compliance issues pertaining to social media, the benefits outweigh the costs when properly used. Additional information about the use of social media can be found on the FINRA Web site referenced in the chapter resources.

PROFESSIONAL PRACTICE ISSUES

As this chapter indicates, ethical standards have a wide-ranging impact on the way financial planners work with clients. The ethical foundations of financial planning directly influence the way client data are gathered, how they are used, and how specific recommendations are implemented. Opportunities exist at every step of the financial planning process to cross the line from an ethical approach to one shaded by questionable standards. Federal, state, and organizational regulators stand ready to enforce rules and standards, but these entities can do so only after a prohibited act has taken place.

To a large extent, financial planners are responsible for monitoring their own actions to ensure that ethical standards are not violated. In fact, planners must take great care to protect consumers while at the same time taking steps to improve their practice methods to limit potential fiduciary and ethical standard liabilities. Following are several brief examples and explanations of requirements designed to protect both clients and planners, and more importantly, to enhance the profession of financial planning.

Managing Client Assets

Investment advisers are required to maintain practice management and client records for at least five years. At a minimum, investment advisers must retain the following documents:

- Receipts and disbursement journals;

- A general ledger;

- Order memoranda;

- Bank records;

- Bills and statements;

- Financial statements;

- Written communications and agreements (including electronic transmissions);

- A list of discretionary accounts;

- Advertising;

- The personal transactions of representatives and principals; and

- Client records:

  - Powers granted by clients,

  - Disclosure statements,

  - Solicitors' disclosure statements,

  - Performance claims,

  - Customer information forms and suitability information, and

  - Written supervisory procedures.

If an adviser has custody over client assets, the required disclosures, and archiving and reporting of client account information increases dramatically. **Custody** is defined as having direct or indirect access to, or a legal responsibility for, a client's funds or securities. Generally, independent investment advisers are advised against taking custody of client assets. If an adviser is also a custodian, the adviser must prove that client assets are safeguarded. The role of the adviser as custodian must also be disclosed to clients. Furthermore, the custodian must submit to random audits by an independent accountant. Custodians must maintain and keep the following documents, in addition to the ones previously listed:

- Journals of securities transactions and movements;

- Separate client ledgers;

- Copies of confirmations;

- Records showing each client's interest in a security; and

- Client purchases and sales history.

Rule 206(4)-2, known as the "Custody Rule," underwent significant amendments that advisers had to implement by March 12, 2010. The amendments represented a push toward more stringent controls over client assets and increased responsibilities for advisers and others deemed to have custody of those client assets. The new rules are complex and require significant compliance resources and expenditures to avoid SEC penalties and sanctions. The staff of the SEC has also updated its frequently asked questions (FAQs) to address some, but certainly not all, interpretive issues raised by the amended rule. The SEC FAQs are available at http://www.sec.gov/divisions/investment/custody_faq_030510.htm.

Many financial professionals have **investment discretion** over client assets. According to § 35 of the Securities and Exchange Act of 1934, financial professionals have investment discretion if they (1) are authorized to determine the disposition of assets (e.g., which securities should be purchased or sold) by or for the account of another person, or (2) make decisions regarding the account even if another person has responsibility for the investment decisions, or (3) otherwise exercises such influence with respect to the purchase and sale of securities in the account of another person.[57]

Although a custodial relationship must be disclosed to a client before taking possession of an asset, discretionary investment management, or "trading authority," must be agreed to and typically requested by the client before any trading can begin. In other words, there is a very fine line between the two: custody means that a financial professional has physical possession of an asset but must follow the directions of the client regarding its disposition; *discretion* means that the financial profession can determine the disposition of an asset but probably does not have possession of it. In both instances, however, the financial adviser has greater fiduciary responsibility and disclosure requirements; and according to CFP Board *Rule of Conduct* 3.4, "A certificant shall clearly identify the assets, if any, over which the certificant will take custody, exercise investment discretion, or exercise supervision."[58]

Continuing Education

One of the first and best ways to ensure that a planner is continuing to act in accordance with the multitude of industry regulations is by participating in and taking seriously the continuing education requirements imposed by the various governing bodies and membership organizations. All credentialing and designating organizations require their members to stay current in the profession via **continuing education (CE)**. (Ancillary service providers, such as insurance agents, accountants, and lawyers also spend a great deal of time ensuring that they meet state-required minimums for CE for their respective licensures.) Current CFP Board rules direct that all CFP® certificants complete at least 30 hours of CE every two years, of which two hours must be from an approved program on CFP Board's *Standards of Professional Conduct*. The remaining 28 hours can be from one or more of the accepted subject topics. Some organizations, like NAPFA, have more stringent CE requirements. NAPFA requires that 60 hours of approved CE be completed every two years. But to be best in the profession for service, product delivery, and compliance, a financial planning professional should count on spending much more time than the required minimum in class, regardless of whether the class counts for CE credit.

For FINRA and registered representatives, in 1995 the SEC created CE requirements consisting of two parts—the regulatory element and the firm element, known together as **Rule 1120**. The regulatory element requires regular participation in computer-based training on topics including licensure and registration, communication with the public, product suitability, and professional conduct. This training program must be completed within 120 days of the second anniversary of a representative's registration approval date and every three years thereafter. The firm element requires that a broker-dealer establish a formal training program to keep employees up to date on job- and product-related subjects.

What happens if a financial planner or investment representative fails to comply with the CE requirement of an organizational or regulating body? Failure to comply with the regulatory element of the FINRA requirement results in a registered representative's registration being deemed inactive until all program requirements are fulfilled. Similar to the individual punishment for FINRA, NAPFA requires that a member who becomes "CE deficient" must relinquish all benefits of and reference to membership in the organization, and the CFP Board of Standards will not renew the certificant's CFP certification, thereby precluding any use of the CFP marks. Thus, penalties are severe if not monetary. However, the organization for which the financial professional works also bears responsibility and is subject to penalties. According to a 1996 press release, NASD [now FINRA] censured and fined Citicorp Securities, Inc., $25,000 and ordered it to comply with an undertaking to pay $300,000 for violating FINRA's CE requirements—and this was for only 19 employees.[59]

Professional Liability Insurance

Maybe even more important than keeping up to date with CE is protecting one's financial planning practice and livelihood in the event of a mistake that leads to a lawsuit. Financial planners operate in an environment conducive to litigation. In some cases, a financial planner may be required to provide a bond or insurance to protect clients, and although it is not required, a growing number of planners are turning to **errors and omissions (E&O) insurance** to protect themselves against claims from clients. E&O insurance affords protection against claims arising out of the actions, errors, or omissions of a planner, or any other covered person for whom the financial planner is legally liable, in the rendering of professional services. However, E&O insurance does not cover acts of fraud.

In some cases, the SEC or state securities regulators require financial planners to post a **fidelity bond**. This is most often the case when a financial planner has custodial power of a client's assets. Financial planners who fall under the reach of ERISA also must post a bond. Fidelity (fiduciary) bonds cover dishonest acts by a financial planner. E&O insurance, on the other hand, provides advisers with coverage against losses due to any actual or alleged negligent act, error, or omission committed in the scope of performing their professional services. E&O insurance protects a financial planner's business, corporation, business officers, directors, and employees from claims arising out of acts, errors, or omissions in rendering or failing to render professional services. **Fiduciary liability insurance** is a subcategory of E&O insurance. This type of insurance provides additional coverage against claims arising from fiduciary breaches. Before purchasing E&O insurance, advisers should consider coverage in relation to the following factors:

1. Will the insurance cover prior acts? Prior acts coverage protects a planner from claims of practice error that may have occurred before taking out the E&O coverage. Prior acts coverage can be acquired for an extra premium.

2. Will all legal expense be paid? Some policies include legal expenses as part of the maximum liability limit of the policy. If, for instance, the liability plus legal fees exceed the policy limit, the planner will be responsible for paying the excess. Some policies, on the other hand, pay legal expenses above the policy liability limit.

3. Where is the policy in force? Planners who do business in several states or in Mexico or Canada should determine whether there are restrictions on where E&O coverage applies.

4. What is covered? Financial planners who perform other services, such as tax preparation, need to determine whether these ancillary services are covered in a basic E&O policy. Sometimes professional activities related to limited partnerships, private placements, syndicated investments, and real estate investments are excluded from E&O policies.

However, sometimes, no matter how diligent a financial planner is, something goes wrong. What happens? Well, it depends.

Regulation, Arbitration, and Litigation

Finally, the best method to avoid claims of misconduct, errors, and omissions is to know the applicable laws related to one's profession, to disclose any and all items that might be considered a conflict of interest with clients, and to avoid actions that might be deemed unethical, illegal, or in violation of accepted practice standards. In general terms, offenses commonly regarded as misconduct on the part of financial professionals can be grouped into the following six categories:

1. Breach of duty or contract, failure to perform;

2. Unsuitability, overconcentration;

3. Unauthorized trading, excessive trading;

4. Misrepresentation, omission, or failure to disclose;

5. Fraud, theft, embezzlement, commingling, misappropriation; and

6. Failure to supervise, failure to follow instructions.

Exhibit 2.5 provides a list of some of the most common actions financial advisers engage in that later lead to claims of misconduct; the best practice is to avoid all of these. The exhibit is not intended to be exhaustive or categorically definitive, but only to serve as a general guide to help students and novice planners recognize the most common types of infractions.

Exhibit 2.5 Client Disclosure Summary Checklist

Financial Advisor or Registered Representative Action
Unsuitability
Making a recommendation about something in which one is has no expertise
Engaging in activities designed to deceive clients (a.k.a. manipulation and fraud)
Failing to perform due diligence
Creating or failing to offer advice against concentrated investment positions
Trading
Charging excessive commissions or unreasonable fees
Trading securities based on information not publicly available (a.k.a. insider trading)
Actively trading a client's account to maximize commission income (a.k.a. churning)
Misrepresentation/failure to disclose
Referring to insurance as an investment
Misrepresenting material facts
Failing to deliver disclosure information to all clients on a yearly basis
Failing to disclose conflicts of interest
Failing to disclose investment risks
Failing to disclose to all customers the availability of fee discounts
Paying someone for a client referral when a written agreement does not exist between the adviser and person making the referral and this information has not been disclosed to the client and confirmed by written receipt (a.k.a. paying for referral)
Taking non-cash forms of compensation without full disclosure. Examples include receiving trips, vacations, golf outings, clothing, and other materials (i.e., soft-dollar transactions)
Hiding fees

Fraud

Borrowing money from or lending money to clients

Any activity that acts as a fraud or is deceitful to clients

Stealing from clients or firm

Commingling personal assets with client assets

Profit splitting with clients

Using a network marketing scheme to increase planner income from the recruitment of new salespersons (i.e., pyramid scheme)

Creating a fraudulent investor where early investors are paid back with investments made by later investors (i.e., Ponzi scheme)

Failure to supervise

Refunding insurance premiums, in any way, to a client or third party (i.e., rebating)

Failure to supervise employees

Recommending an investment that has not been pre-approved by a registered representative's broker-dealer (i.e., selling away)

According to FINRA Rule 3080, and as disclosed on Form U4, any FINRA member is "agreeing to arbitrate any dispute, claim or controversy that may arise between you and your firm, or a customer, or any other person, that is required to be arbitrated under the rules of the self-regulatory organizations with which you are registering."[60] However, although this ruling compels the *professional* to seek resolution through arbitration, it does not compel a client to follow the same process.

To level the playing field, almost all investment contracts and brokerage account applications require clients to pursue actions against advisers through an arbitration process. **Arbitration** is a dispute resolution process that takes the place of traditional court system lawsuits. The arbitration process involves putting a case before a trained expert who imposes a final solution to resolve a conflict. In such cases, the parties agree that the arbitrator's solution is bilaterally binding and is based on facts, evidence, and law. In simpler or less egregious cases, clients and planners might use meditation. **Mediation** involves working with a trained conflict resolution expert to help the parties reach an agreement that both parties approve. Unlike arbitration, a mediator's solution is not binding and the outcome is based on the needs of the parties.

The arbitration process begins with the claimant, usually a client, filing a Statement of Claim and a Submission Agreement with FINRA. Although the fees associated with arbitration might be thousands of dollars, it is normally less expensive for client and adviser than pursuing remuneration in the court system. Once a claim has been filed, a very court-like process ensues. Next, a response in the form of an Answers Statement is filed by the financial professional. In this statement, the professional in question provides relevant facts and can file counterclaims against the client as part of the defense. Then, from a list provided, the parties choose a panel of arbitrators to hear the case. A telephone conference is then held to schedule the date of the hearing and to resolve other preliminary issues. Once a hearing location has been determined and the discovery process completed (the discovery process is the collection and sharing of evidence), the hearing begins. Hearings typically are scheduled for two days during which the arbitrators and parties meet in person. At the conclusion, the three-member arbitration panel deliberates for up to 30 days. At the end of deliberations, the panel renders its verdict, called an award, to which the parties previously pledged acceptance. More information is available on the FINRA Web site at http://www. finra.org/ArbitrationAndMediation/Arbitration/.

Mediation follows a similar but less formal process; a case may be referred from arbitration or go directly to mediation. Parties choose the mediator, who has no authority to decide the case but works with the parties to explore the issues and reach a mutually satisfying outcome. The exchange of information is voluntary and more limited; the objective is to facilitate a resolution. Both joint and individual meetings are held between the parties and their counsel. Mediation is a lower-cost, confidential alternative that is settled only with the approval of the parties. More information is available at http://www.finra.org/ArbitrationAndMediation/Mediation/. Significantly fewer cases are filed for mediation. In 2010–11, only 4,466 new cases were filed, or an average of more than 2,200 cases per year.[61]

From 1997 until 2011, FINRA (and its predecessor organization, NASD) received slightly more than 90,000 arbitration cases, or an average of 6,000 arbitration filings per year. However, in the six years during and immediately following market downturns (2001–2004, and 2008–2009) the average exceeded 7,300 filing per year, whereas the remaining 11 years saw an average of only about 5,300 cases filed annually.[62] Additionally, as represented in Table 2.6, the number of controversies filed for arbitration jumped from slightly more than 12,000 in 2008 to more than 22,000 in 2009.[63] Table 2.6 also reports the categories of allegations subject to arbitration, although as noted, individual cases can include multiple allegations. Therefore, although the threat of arbitration should not overwhelm a financial planner's thought processes, it should serve as a reminder to do the best possible job for each client. For more information about arbitration procedures, view the FINRA *Code of Arbitration Procedure* on the FINRA Web site.[64]

Table 2.6 Types of FINRA Arbitration Cases by Year (2008–2011)

Type of Controversy	2008 Total	2008 %*	2009 Total	2009 %*	2010 Total	2010 %*	2011 Total	2011 %*
Margin calls	64	0.5	128	0.6	83	0.5	80	0.5
Churning	212	1.8	306	1.4	270	1.5	236	1.6
Unauthorized trading	248	2.1	478	2.1	397	2.2	288	2.0
Failure to supervise	1,029	8.5	2,691	12.0	2,372	13.4	2,007	13.7
Negligence	1,602	13.3	3,405	15.2	2,698	15.3	2,249	15.3
Omission of facts	1,201	10.0	2,453	11.0	1,941	11.0	1,603	10.9
Breach of contract	1,658	13.8	2,802	12.5	2,184	12.4	1,904	13.0
Breach of fiduciary duty	2,836	23.6	4,206	18.8	3,162	17.9	2,589	17.6
Unsuitability	1,181	9.8	2,473	11.1	1,974	11.2	1,619	11.0
Misrepresentation	2,005	16.7	3,408	15.2	2,601	14.7	2,102	14.3
Online trading	3	0.0	0	0.0	0	0.0	0	0.0
Total controveries claimed**	12,039		22,350		17,682		14,677	

* Percentages may not add up to 100 due to rounding.
** Each case filed can include multiple types of controversy.

If a case involves violations of FINRA rules or federal securities laws, rules, and/ or regulations, FINRA takes disciplinary actions against firms or individuals. These cases can result in the censure, fining, suspension, or barring of a professional or organization found in violation. At one end of the spectrum, censuring involves publicly admonishing a financial professional; at the other end is barring, where a professional can be permanently prohibited from working in the financial industry. In 2012, the FINRA National Adjudicatory Council handed down a penalty that barred two persons from the securities industry, fined the firm $1 million, and required that restitution of more than $1,600,000 be paid to their customers.[65] In the most serious cases—those involving criminal offenses such as fraud, embezzlement, extortion, or theft—the SEC or other authority can turn the case over to the appropriate state or federal court for resolution, because the SEC cannot incarcerate individuals for offenses.

The penalties for acting in an unethical or illegal manner can be very severe, as they should be, considering the level of trust and responsibility bestowed on financial professionals. However, by adhering to laws and regulations, placing the client's welfare first, and documenting every aspect of the client/planner relationship, most financial professionals will never have to worry about defending their actions to either an arbitration panel or a court of law.

PROFESSIONAL ORGANIZATIONS: WHAT ROLE DO THEY PLAY?

Professional organizations differ from regulatory entities in that participation in a professional organization is voluntary. People join professional organizations for a number of reasons, including continuing education, the opportunity to use a designation or certification, and camaraderie with other professionals committed to serving clients successfully. Professional financial services organizations can be classified into one of four types: (1) credentialing organizations; (2) quasi-credentialing organizations; (3) designation organizations; and (4) membership organizations. FINRA lists more than 100 professional certifications and designations that planners or advisers can earn to distinguish themselves.[66] For a complete list, see http://apps. finra.org/DataDirectory/1/prodesignations.aspx/.

A **certification** organization validates that a financial planner has met a minimum qualification and level of knowledge. Certification is generally granted only after a practitioner has met stringent criteria based on experience and received a passing score on a knowledge competency examination. Although participation in a certification organization is voluntary, the right to use a certification mark is restricted only to those who maintain good standing with the certifying body. Almost all certification organizations require members to maintain their knowledge through CE. One of the oldest financial services certification organizations is the American College, which was founded in 1927 to provide education and certification to those in the insurance industry. The American College created—and to this day maintains—the **Chartered Life Underwriter (CLU)** certification. It also certifies financial planners through its **Chartered Financial Consultant (ChFC)** certification.

The certification organization most closely associated with the financial planning profession is the Certified Financial Planner Board of Standards, Inc. (CFP Board). The CFP Board was established in 1985 to "benefit the public by establishing and enforcing education, examination, experience and ethics requirements for CFP® certificants."[67] To obtain the right to use the CFP® mark, a financial planner must meet five requirements:

1. Before applying for the CFP® Certification Examination, one must complete education requirements established by the CFP Board in one of three ways:

    a. Complete a CFP Board-registered Education Program from one of more than 300 academic programs at colleges and universities.

    b. Apply for challenge status. Academic degrees and credentials that fulfill these educational requirements include:

        *   Certified Public Accountant (CPA)—inactive license acceptable;

        *   Licensed attorney—inactive license acceptable;

        *   Chartered Financial Analyst® (CFA®);

        *   Doctor of Business Administration;

        *   Chartered Financial Consultant (ChFC);

        *   Ph.D. in business or economics; or

        *   Chartered Life Underwriter (CLU).

    c. Request a transcript review. Certain industry credentials recognized by the CFP Board, or the successful completion of upper-division-level college courses, may satisfy some or all of the education requirements established by the CFP Board.

    d. Beginning in 2012, complete a financial plan development course as a part of the education program for those beginning enrollment after January 1, 2012, or for those sitting for the exam under "Challenge" status for March 2012 or later administration.

    e. Complete a bachelor's degree, in any field of study or program. The bachelor's degree requirement is a condition of initial certification; it is not a requirement to be eligible to take the CFP® Certification Examination.

2. Pass the CFP® Certification Examination. The examination tests a candidate's ability to apply financial planning knowledge to client situations. The 10-hour exam is divided into three sessions. It is comprehensive, and all questions are multiple choice. The exam is administered three times a year—generally on the third Friday and Saturday of March, July, and November. There is currently a $595 examination fee.

3. Meet an experience requirement. At least three years of qualifying full-time work experience are required for certification. Qualifying experience includes work that can be categorized into one of the six primary elements of the personal financial planning process. Experience can be gained in a number

of ways including working on any portion of the financial planning process, supervising others who do planning, or teaching financial planning.

Effective September 1, 2012, the experience requirement can be met through two years full-time, or the equivalent part-time (2,000 equals one year full-time) experience focused exclusively on "personal delivery of all or part of the personal financial planning process to a client," with direct supervision by a CFP® professional, and documented qualifying experience in all six primary elements of the personal financial planning process.

Two other changes to the experience requirement effective in 2012 include (1) the elimination of the requirement that six months of experience must have been gained within 12 months of an individual's reporting of experience to CFP Board, and (2) allowing individuals to submit experience to CFP Board for review prior to passing the CFP® exam. Credit will be granted only for experience completed within 10 years before and five years after successful completion of the CFP® exam.

4. Pass the CFP Board's *Fitness Standards for Candidates and Registrants* (available at http://www.cfp.net/become/fitness.asp), which describes conduct that will or may bar an individual from being certified, such as having filed one personal or business bankruptcy within five years of completing the CFP® Certification Application. After candidates have met the education, examination, and work experience requirements, they must disclose past or pending litigation or agency proceedings and agree to abide by CFP Board's *Code of Ethics and Professional Responsibility* and *Financial Planning Practice Standards*. A background check will also be conducted. Finally, a candidate must adhere to the CFP Board of Standards, Inc., *Code of Ethics and Professional Responsibility* and acknowledge CFP Board's right to enforce its standards through its *Disciplinary Rules and Procedures*.

5. Pay certification fees. A one-time, nonrefundable initial certification application fee of $100 for the background checks and an annual certification fee of $325 will be charged.

For more information, see the CFP Board Web site at http://www.cfp.net/become/Steps.asp.

Another highly regarded certification is the **Chartered Financial Analyst (CFA)** certification offered by the CFA Institute (formerly known as the Association for Investment Management and Research [AIMR]). Those holding a CFA certification must pass three examinations administered by the CFA Institute. This professional certification is an appropriate designation for people most interested in investment management and financial analyst work. The CFA study materials do not encompass the full range of financial planning. Those with a CFA designation must have three years of experience working in an investment decision-making capability, join the CFA Institute, and abide by its code of ethics.

There are several quasi-certification organizations that serve the interests of financial planners. **Quasi-certifications** are those that are based on a planner showing proof of completing another recognized certification or proving attainment of education through an accredited college or university. The American Institute of Certified Public Accounts (AICPA) allows CPAs who specialize in financial planning the opportunity to obtain the **Personal Financial Specialist (PFS)** designation. This certificate requires CPAs to have at least 250 hours of experience per year in personal financial planning. The examination requirement, necessary for all certifications, is fulfilled by completing the CPA education requirement.

Designation organizations make up another category of professional organizations. To obtain a designation, a person simply needs to meet the standards established by the designation granting board. Designations differ from certifications in that one need not pass an examination to obtain one, although this is not universally true because some designations do require an examination. The College for Financial Planning markets itself as the "financial designation resource" and offers eight different designations, all of which require an end-of-course exam. For more information see http://cffpdesignations.com/.

Membership organizations make up the last important category of professional financial services organizations. Membership organizations are voluntary associations of individuals with shared interests, practice management techniques, and practice management objectives. Generally, membership organizations do not offer certifications or designations. The **Financial Planning Association (FPA)** is the largest financial planning membership organization in the United States. Anyone can join the FPA by paying an annual fee and agreeing to abide by the organization's code of ethics. Thus, members need not be financial planners. Some membership organizations are voluntary but open only by invitation. The **Million Dollar Roundtable** is an example of a membership group that has significant restrictions on who can join the organization based on insurance sales performance.

Some organizations do not fit neatly into any one category. The **National Association of Personal Financial Advisors (NAPFA)** is such an example. NAPFA is an organization established to further the cause of fee-only financial planning. NAPFA has several categories of membership, and in general, anyone who pays a membership fee and agrees to abide by the group's code of ethics can join. To be a **NAPFA-registered Financial Advisor**, one must meet several additional standards, which makes the organization more like a quasi-credentialing organization than a pure membership organization. Full NAPFA members must agree to be bound by the NAPFA Code of Ethics, Fiduciary Oath, and Standards of Membership and Affiliation. Additionally, members must meet the following standards:

- A bachelor's degree, in any discipline, from an accredited institution of higher learning.

- The CFP credential or the CPA/PFS, provided the applicant attained the credential by taking the comprehensive exam offered by the CFP Board or the AICPA.

- A minimum of 60 hours of approved continuing education every two years, including 32 core hours with a minimum of five credit hours in each of the core areas: Insurance and Risk Management, Investments, Income Tax Planning, Retirement Planning and Employee Benefits, Estate Planning and

Communication and Counseling, and a minimum of two hours in the Ethics of Financial Planning. The remaining 28 hours can be earned in either seven electives or five core areas.

- Offer comprehensive financial planning services to consumers. This means offering or supervising others who offer client consultation in all areas of comprehensive financial planning. This requirement does not imply that every client must receive comprehensive financial planning services, but only that the member make such services available to clients. NAPFA defines comprehensive financial planning advice as requiring consideration of each of the following areas for clients: income tax, cash flow, retirement planning, estate planning, investments, risk management, and any special needs planning. NAPFA-registered Financial Advisors are required to attest to the continuing availability of comprehensive services with each annual membership renewal.

- Applicants for NAPFA-registered Financial Advisor status have three ways to satisfy the peer review requirement. First, an applicant can submit a case documenting client service completed within the previous 12 months that profiles the client, summarizes the recommendations and implementation, and shows evidence of an integrated approach across all core areas. The second option is the submission of a comprehensive financial plan, which must have been prepared within the previous 12 months and profile the client, summarize the recommendations and implementation, show evidence of an integrated approach across all core areas, and make an offer of periodic review. The work must be the applicant's original work, or work completed under the supervision of the applicant. A third offer has essentially the same requirements as the second, except that the plan is created from the fact pattern provided by NAPFA associated with an actual client case or a fictitious case. In either option, the applicant must address all of the following core factors: income tax; cash flow; retirement planning; estate planning; investments; risk management; and any special needs planning. Additionally all three options should follow the current NAPFA peer review checklist. If a plan is submitted, it must apply a comprehensive approach to advisory services and include the collection and assessment of all relevant data from the client; the identification of client goals; the identification of client financial problems; the provision of recommendations; and the provision of assistance with implementing the recommendations.

- An individual must have had at least 36 months of experience being engaged primarily in the provision of comprehensive financial planning services. This experience must have been attained within the past 60 months and must include the most recent 12 months.

The NAPFA code of ethics was discussed earlier in this chapter, and the **NAPFA Fiduciary Oath**, which all members must sign, is as follows:

The adviser shall exercise his/her best efforts to act in good faith and in the best interests of the client. The adviser shall provide written disclosure to the client prior to the engagement of the adviser, and thereafter throughout the term of the engagement, of any conflicts of interest, which will or reasonably may compromise the impartiality or independence of the adviser.

The adviser, or any party in which the adviser has a financial interest, does not receive any compensation or other remuneration that is contingent on any client's purchase or sale of a financial product. The adviser does not receive a fee or other compensation from another party based on the referral of a client or the client's business.

What the Fiduciary Oath means to you, the client:

- I shall always act in good faith and with candor.

- I shall be proactive in my disclosure of any conflicts of interest that may impact you.

- I shall not accept any referral fees or compensation that is contingent upon the purchase or sale of a financial product.

For more information, see the most recent *NAPFA Policies and Procedures Manual*, available at http://www.napfa.org/about/FiduciaryOath.asp.

The proliferation of designations and the importance of protecting consumers from unscrupulous business practices resulted in regulations regarding approved uses. For example, the College for Financial Planning offers a page (http://cffpdesignations. com/Designation/Regulation) listing the NASAA and NAIC model rules as well individual state regulations regarding the use of designations. FINRA offers guidance on the use of designations in FINRA Regulatory Notice 07-43 (http://www.finra.org/Industry/Regulation/Notices/2007/P036815), and also offers information on the states that have enacted regulations or legislation or issued special notices regarding the use of professional designations by registered representatives and investment adviser representatives. For more information see the NAPFA Web site (http://www.finra.org/investors/protectyourself/beforeyouinvest/p120759).

CHAPTER SUMMARY

The primary requirement for all professions is that people affiliated with or who hold themselves out as a members of the profession conduct business in an ethical manner. Although this is a fairly innocuous statement, adhering to all of the rules, regulations, and professional standards of a member's chosen profession can be a daunting task. This is especially true in financial planning. Before the 1930s, *caveat emptor* was the byword that guided financial transactions in the United States. However, as a result of the financial instability of the Great Depression, numerous Congressional Acts were passed that began to regulate the financial industry and its participants. Though much has changed in the nearly 80 years since those first acts were passed—the Glass-Steagall Act of 1933 was passed and subsequently repealed by the Gramm-Leach-Bliley Financial Modernization Act of 1999, the Prudent Man Statute of 1942 was adopted and then amended by the Uniform Prudent Investor Act of 1994—the financial planning profession must still abide by this legal foundation.

However, today's financial planning environment is as much the product of its current representatives as it is its original legal foundation. Many different credentialing and membership organizations have developed practice standards and codes of ethics to help direct and guide the profession. Although these standards are not more important than the laws on which they are based, clients can most readily hold their planning professional accountable to these standards. Therefore, it is incumbent on all professionals, regardless of their chosen business model, to understand the ethical and legal requirements of the financial planning profession and the ramifications of failing to follow those standards.

Learning Outcomes

1. A teleological or consequential approach to ethics is based on relativism, where actions are deemed to be right or wrong according to the consequences of the actions. Sometimes this is referred to as *situational ethics*. Acting in one's own interest is ethical from a teleological perspective as long as another party is not hurt or put at a disadvantage. Ethics from a deontological approach are based on absolutism, or the concept of a universally accepted right and wrong.

2. The Federal regulatory framework has developed over the course of 150 years, since the beginning of the modern monetary system in the 1860s. However, much of the basis of financial planning regulation stems from the Great Depression and the Maloney Act of 1938 and the Investment Advisers Act of 1940. These two acts, along with the Uniform Prudent Investors Act of 1994, have laid much of the groundwork for both the fiduciary standard and the suitability standard that are applied to registered investment advisers and registered representatives, respectively. Glass-Steagall was repealed in 1999 by the Financial Services Modernization Act, also referred to as the Gramm-Leach-Bliley Act, which brought about widespread change in financial services by eliminating the legal barriers among the securities, insurance, and banking industries; it also mandated requirements for keeping client data private and safe. Dodd-Frank, in 2010, brought about significant changes with potentially higher-impact oversight and supervision to come.

3. If meeting the definition of an investment adviser, the firm or in some cases the individual must register with the state where the business is located or with the SEC, as determined by the amount of assets under management—whether more or less than $100 million. Both the SEC and NASAA establish rulings that determine business standards; the NASAA model rulings were adopted by the states. In some instances the states expect state-registered advisory firms to meet many of the same standards required by the SEC. Both the states and the SEC require advisers to file Form ADV to register, contributing to a professional history that is then disclosed to the public through the IAPD. Examination occurs through SEC or state audits of the advisers' books and records of business. The SEC registers firms, as do the states, but most states also register individuals or investment adviser representatives (IARs).

4. The primary purpose of a self-regulatory organization (SRO) is to provide consumers with protection against fraud while providing a mechanism to establish and enforce rules and standards developed by the SRO. As established by the Maloney Act of 1938, all SROs are subject to SEC oversight, which explains why broker-dealers and registered representatives

(registered reps) are subject to FINRA and SEC rulings that set practice standards. SROs are managed and funded by firms participating in a particular segment of the securities markets. Registered reps, or brokers, register with FINRA by submitting a Form U4, thereby contributing to a professional history that is then disclosed to the public through BrokerCheck. Examination occurs through FINRA audits of a broker's books and records of business.

5.   The difference between an investment adviser representative (IAR) employed with an RIA (as regulated by the SEC or applicable state regulatory agency) and a registered representative (as registered by FINRA) is that investment advisers typically charge a fee for their advice, whereas registered representatives execute transactions for a commission. In general, financial planners who provide investment advice to others and are not exempt from registration generally must be registered with the SEC or state regulators or licensed with FINRA. In some cases, a financial professional may be registered and licensed with both regulatory agencies, for example, when functioning as a hybrid or as a dually registered firm doing business for both commissions and fees.

   The other big difference, beyond that of compensation structure, is the standard of care. As a fiduciary, an RIA must place the client's interest above his or her own and not favor one client over another. Additionally, extensive disclosure requirements regarding conflicts of interest and the qualifications required of an IAR working for an RIA are usually not necessary for registered reps acting only to fulfill a suitability requirement for recommendations. A similarity between IARs and registered reps is that, to give advice or sell securities, both generally must pass exams administered by NASAA or FINRA.

6.   Pursuant to the Advisers Act and its amendments, the main document in the registration process is Form ADV. Part 1 asks for information about an adviser's business, the persons who own or control the advisory firm, and whether the adviser or certain personnel have been sanctioned for violating securities laws or other laws. The SEC and the individual states rely on Part 1 to identify which investment advisers warrant more immediate examination or might pose a risk to clients or the general public. Part 2 is a plain-English written disclosure statement or brochure that provides information about an adviser's business practices, fees, and conflicts of interest. Items include education, certifications, types of investments offered, fees charged for different services, methods of analysis, investment strategies, and descriptions of any legal problems in the history of the firm. Part 2 must be given to clients and potential clients as a disclosure statement, and updates must be delivered to clients on an interim basis (as required by disclosure of disciplinary information) and/or annually. Form ADV is available to the public through the IAPD.

7.   NAIC serves as a state-level regulatory component of the financial industry. As the national organization of state insurance regulators, NAIC develops uniform insurance regulations and agent examinations. NAIC and state regulators provide comprehensive consumer protection by requiring anyone selling life, health, or property insurance to be licensed in their respective states of operation. Eight licenses require an examination and six licenses require registration with a state regulator, although some combined licenses are available. Licensing to sell insurance requires being 18 years of age, filing an application and fee, passing an examination(s), filing a certification for the location of business transactions, and meet continuing education requirements. If variable contracts are to be sold, proof of a FINRA Series 6 or Series 7 license is required.

8. A fiduciary is responsible to preserve and protect the trust of a third party, often unsophisticated in dealing with the product or service, for whom the fiduciary, acting as an adviser, trustee, executor, guardian, or custodian provides advice. Fiduciary, or prudence, standards are on record as early as 1830 and were the foundation for the "prudent man" rule of 1942. The passage of the Uniform Prudent Investor Act (UPIA) in 1994 focused primarily on trust and foundation assets. But most states apply it more broadly with the expectation that a professional will objectively and impartially investigate, select, diversify, and manage investments paying heed to costs and compliance. The antifraud provisions of the Investment Advisers Act of 1940, § 206, clearly imply that investment advisers must act as fiduciaries. In fact, § 206 applies to all firms and persons meeting the definition of investment adviser, whether registered with the SEC, a state securities authority, or not at all. The SEC exempts broker-dealers and broker-dealer representatives from fiduciary rules; although at the time of publication changes were possible as a result of a Dodd-Frank mandated study and possible regulatory efforts.

9. Ethical requirements may be based on a set of ideals or formalized as business practices and standards that carry enforcement sanctions. Ethical requirements for financial planning practitioners that are CFP certificants or registrants include adherence to the CFP Board *Standards of Professional Conduct*, for which violations are handled through the *Disciplinary Rules and Procedures*. The CFP Board *Code of Ethics*, also adopted by the FPA, consists of seven principles including integrity, objectivity, competence, fairness, confidentiality, professionalism, and diligence. For financial planners who are not CFPs, but who may be holders of other professional certifications or designations or members of one or more of the other financial planning membership organizations, other codes of conduct or ethics may apply. For example, NAPFA requires its members to adhere to the Fiduciary Oath, which requires acting in good faith, disclosing any conflicts of interest, and not accepting any compensation based on the sale of a financial product. The SEC and state securities agencies require financial planners to abide by a code of ethics based on amendments to the Investment Advisers Act of 1940. Stockbrokers, insurance agents, and other financial advisers are exempt from these ethical guidelines. Professional organizations help fill this ethics void by establishing, maintaining, and enforcing ethical standards within the profession.

10. The SEC, FINRA, and NAIC have established broad definitions of advertising, but all require that public communications follow guidelines to ensure that the message is not misleading or untrue. The SEC defines advertisements as including both written and oral communication and it has specific guidelines for the content of a message; client testimonials are forbidden. For practicing registered representatives, FINRA has oversight of most public communication. Anything that is likely to make its way into the hands of a consumer is considered advertising; this includes newspapers, radio and television ads, signs and billboard messages, and voice recordings. In other words, the purveyor of the information may not have any control over who has access to the information.

    FINRA also defines another form of written communication with the public as sales literature, which is defined as any written communication distributed to customers or the general public upon request. This is different from advertising because the publisher has some control over who is receiving the information. Sales literature includes research reports, form letters, and educational seminar materials.

For practicing insurance agents, NAIC defines advertising as any material designed to create public interest in a product, or induce the public to take action on (i.e., modify, borrow from, or cancel) an existing or new policy. Requirements for archiving all communications range from as little as two or three years to as much a seven to 10 years.

11. Financial advisory firms and investment adviser's representatives provide disclosures to current and potential clients. The SEC and most state regulatory agencies require that Form ADV Part 2, which provides information about the firm and representatives, be given to potential clients prior to or at the signing of the engagement, and any updates must be made available at least annually to clients. The most recent copy of an investment adviser's Form ADV, which serves to inform clients before engaging an adviser, is available at the IAPD Web site for either state- or SEC-registered advisers. The scope of the engagement, costs, conflicts of interest, and other information should be clearly explained in the agreement or contract.

    The Investment Adviser's Act of 1940 and its amendments do not require a written contract, but this act, the Uniform Securities Act, and other SEC rulings establish requirements for investment adviser contracts. To assist those offering financial planning and other professional services, the CFP Board offers sample disclosure agreements that comport with CFP Board ethical professional conduct. Because of their accessibility on the CFP Board Web site, they are also a disclosure resource for the public. The Gramm-Leach-Bliley Act and SEC Regulation S-P establish standards for client privacy policies and practices, as well as disclosure to nonaffiliated third parties. Investment policy statements describe investment management policies, and although recommended, they are not required client disclosures.

12. Basic FINRA compliance is focused primarily on outbound communication, because using social media to gain information about what others are saying or reporting is not a compliance issue. Social media offer significant potential or little return on investment, depending on an adviser's point of view. However, static content or blog postings as Web-based communication must meet the requirements of advertisements, sales literature, or independently prepared reprints set forth in FINRA Rule 2210(a) and be approved in writing by a registered principal of the broker-dealer before use.

    In the case of real-time interactive communications, FINRA does not require prior principal approval, but pursuant to FINRA Rule 2310, broker-dealers must determine that a recommendation is suitable for every investor to whom it is made; therefore, recommendations via a social media platform, which may be viewed by multiple investors, could be problematic if the recommendation is not suitable for every investor who could potentially review the post.

13. Careful archiving and reporting when managing client assets is critical for financial advisers. A firm's financial activities when handling client accounts, as well as written (including electronic) communications and agreements must be documented. All advertising must be archived, per the rules, and records of all supervised person's personal investment transactions must be kept. Required information must also be maintained and accurate when keeping books and records. For example, information about client accounts, documents regarding powers granted by the client, performance claims made to the client, suitability documentation, and supervisory procedures for actions of the investment adviser representative must be maintained. Taking custody of an account by assuming actual responsibility for the funds, as opposed to having the funds held by a third-party custodian,

requires increased recordkeeping and compliance. Adviser discretion to act on a client's behalf in regard to the account must be clearly documented. For custody and discretion, the CFP Board requires certificants to clearly identify the assets in question.

14. It is a significant accomplishment to achieve an educational standard for entering a career as a financial professional, but over the course of a career, products, rules, regulations, and best practices change. Therefore, it is very important that financial professionals continue to learn and grow as the profession changes. Current CFP Board rules direct that all CFP® certificants complete at least 30 hours of continuing education every two years; two hours must be from a CFP Board-approved program on the Standards of Professional Conduct. NAPFA requires that 60 hours of CE be completed every two years, specifying education across the core subject areas. The FINRA requirements for registered reps consist of two parts—the regulatory element and the firm element, known together as Rule 1120; requirements are established in three year cycles.

15. Financial professionals protect themselves from client allegations of wrongdoing by purchasing errors and omissions (E&O) insurance, including the subcategory of fiduciary liability insurance to protect against allegations of failing to act as a fiduciary, and by posting a fidelity bond. E&O insurance protects against claims resulting from the actions, errors, or omissions of a planner, or any other covered person for whom the financial planner is legally liable, while providing professional services. E&O insurance does not protect against fraudulent actions.

16. All FINRA members agree to arbitration rather than to seek legal action to settle client disputes; most investment and brokerage account contracts require clients to do the same. The FINRA arbitration process breaks down into seven basic steps: filing the claim, answering the claim, selecting the panel of arbitrators, holding prehearing conferences, conducting discovery, holding the hearings, and deciding the outcome. The outcome, which the parties initially agreed to accept, is the responsibility of the three-member arbitration panel.

    Mediation is a lower-cost, confidential, more informal process in which the mediator and the parties strive to reach a mutually satisfying outcome. It, too, follows a several-step process, but the exchange of information is voluntary and more limited. Significantly fewer cases are filed for mediation than for arbitration.

17. Professional organizations contribute to the delivery of financial planning products and services to clients by offering designations or certifications, continuing education, a forum for camaraderie with other professionals, and in some cases an advocacy voice for the profession. All of these efforts serve to enhance the profession and promote successful client service regardless of whether the professional organization's primary objective is to offer a credential, a designation, or membership.

    A certification organization validates that a financial planner has met a minimum level of qualification and knowledge. Certification is generally granted only after a practitioner has met stringent criteria based on experience and earned a passing score on a knowledge-based competency examination. Comparatively, a designation organization requires only that a practitioner meet the standards established by the designation-granting board, although some designations do require an exam. Membership organizations may offer camaraderie, continuing education, and perhaps a voice of advocacy for the profession.

Not all organizations align with these broad categories; for example, NAPFA is a quasi-credentialing, membership, and advocacy organization.

Chapter Resources

Advisor Guidance (http://www.advisorguidance.com/).

Certified Financial Planner Board of Standards (CFP Board) (http://www.cfpboard.org/).

Certified Financial Planner Board of Standards, *Standards of Professional Conduct* (http://www.cfp.net/Downloads/2010Standards.pdf).

Certified Financial Planner Board of Standards, continuing education requirements (http://www.cfp.net/certificants/ce.asp).

Financial Industry Regulatory Authority (FINRA) (www.finra.org/).

FINRA, registration and licensing information (http://www.finra.org/industry/compliance/registration/qualificationsexams/registeredreps/p011051).

FINRA, continuing education requirements (http://www.finra.org/Industry/Compliance/ContinuingEducation/).

FINRA, arbitration and mediation information (http://www.finra.org/ArbitrationAndMediation/FINRADisputeResolution/MoreonFINRADisputeResolution/Publications/).

FINRA, Guide to Public Communication (http://www.finra.org/industry/issues/advertising/p006118).

FINRA, Guide to Relevant Adviser Disclosure for Registration (http://www.iard.com/firm_users_man.asp).

FINRA, BrokerCheck (http://www.finra.org/Investors/ToolsCalculators/BrokerCheck/).

Financial Planning Association (FPA) (http://www.fpanet.org/).

National Association of Insurance Commissioners (NAIC) (www.naic.org).

National Association of Personal Financial Advisors (NAPFA) (www.napfa.org).

North American Securities Administrators Association (NASAA) (www.nasaa.org).

NASAA Investor Bill of Rights (http://www.nasaa.org/2715/investor-bill-of-rights/).

RIA Compliance Consultants (http://www.ria-compliance-consultants.com/).

Regulatory Compliance Association (https://www.rcaonline.org/).

Securities and Exchange Commission (SEC) (http://www.sec.gov/).

SEC, Information for new investment advisers (http://www.sec.gov/divisions/investment/advoverview.htm).

SEC, arbitration process (http://www.sec.gov/answers/arbproc.htm).

Establishing an Investment Adviser Registration Depository (IARD) with the SEC (http://www.sec.gov/divisions/investment/iard/setup.shtml).

SEC, Investment Adviser Public Disclosure (IAPD) (http://www.adviserinfo.sec.gov/IAPD/Content/IapdMain/iapd_SiteMap.aspx).

SEC, Rules under the Investment Adviser Act of 1940 (http://www.sec.gov/rules/extra/iarules.htm#20643).

Securities Industry and Financial Markets Association (SIFMA) (http://www.sifma.org/).

SIFMA Investor Bill of Rights (http://www.sifma.org/education/consumer-resources/investor-bill-of-rights/).

Thomson Reuters Governance, Risk and Compliance—Accelus (http://accelus.thomsonreuters.com/).

Discussion Questions

1. How do teleological and deontological approaches to ethics differ? Why do you believe that financial planning standards are grounded in a deontological approach to ethics? What could be the potential problems that arise from a more consequential or teleological approach?

2. Use the following CFP Board definition of a client to answer questions a through c below:

   > ...denotes a person, persons, or entity who engages a certificant and for whom professional services are rendered. Where the services of the certificant are provided to an entity (corporation, trust, partnership, estate, etc.), the client is the entity acting through its legally authorized representative.[68]

   a. If a CFP® certificant was at a party and was overheard by someone he or she did not know talking about the sale of a stock, and the person acts on the information, would the CFP® Board consider the person to be the financial planner's client? Why or why not?

   b. Must a person pay for services to be considered a client under this definition?

   c. Are all financial planners required to use this definition of *client*?

3. Define a practice standard, and based on a review of the chapter, site a practice standard established by the SEC, FINRA, NAPFA, the CFP Board, NASAA, and NAIC. For each, identify to whom the practice standard applies.

4. Which was legislated first, selling financial products for a commission or selling financial advice for a fee? Which legislation regulated which form of business?

5. Was financial security regulation first undertaken at the state or federal level? Which organization first took the lead in regulating financial securities? What services does this organization provide for the industry today?

6. What was the purpose of the Glass-Steagall and the Gramm-Leach-Bliley acts? What important changes and requirements resulted from each?

7. How did the Coordination Act and the Dodd-Frank legislation change the registration and examination of registered investment advisory firms?

8. What may be the most important outcome of the Dodd-Frank legislation as it pertains to the fiduciary standard?

9. Provide three examples of how adviser registration requirements and consumer or investor/client disclosure requirements are interrelated.

10. Describe the licensing, registration, and standard-of-care differences between a registered representative employed with a broker-dealer and an investment adviser representative employed with a registered investment adviser.

11. Briefly summarize the similarities and differences between registering with the state regulatory authority, the SEC, and FINRA.

12. What is a Form U4? What important practice standard is agreed to when submitting a Form U4?

13. In practical terms, what does it mean to be a fiduciary? How do the five fundamental components of the Uniform Prudent Investor Act serve to define the standard of care when one acts in a fiduciary capacity?

14. List and briefly describe the eight SEC fiduciary requirements. How do the requirements on conflicts of interest, compensation, confidentiality, and recommendations matched to client needs correlate with or match other practice standards, disclosures, or principles?

15. Describe in your own words how the CFP Board *Code of Ethics and Professional Responsibility* differs from the *Rules of Conduct* and the *Financial Planning Practice Standards*. What is the relationship between the *Standards of Professional Conduct* and the *Disciplinary Rules* and *Procedures*?

16. What guidelines control advertising by professionals who provide financial advice, investments, or insurance to the public? How do these guidelines correlate with communication through social media?

17. Review the list of practice management and client records that investment advisers must retain. Select five examples and explain the purpose or significance of the information for each. How do the requirements change when an adviser has custody or investment discretion?

18. It is often said that financial professionals must be committed to lifelong learning. How do certifications, designations, and continuing education serve to enhance the profession of financial planning and distinguish professionals?

19. Briefly explain the differences between dealing with client-adviser controversies or allegaions and allegations of adviser-securities rule or law violations.

20. Compare and contrast the requirements to become a Certified Financial Planner® and a NAPFA-registered Financial Advisor.

Notes

1. FINRA, "Private Securities Transactions of an Associated Person," *FINRA Manual*, NASD Rule 3040. Available at http://finra.complinet.com/en/display/display.html?rbid=2403&record_id=4405&element_id=3727&highlight=3040#r4405.

2. FINRA, "Dealing with Non-Members," *FINRA Manual*, NASD Rule 2420. Available at http://finra.complinet.com/en/display/display.html?rbid=2403&record_id=4333&element_id=3656&highlight=2420#r4333.

3. J. C. Hansen, R. H. Rossberg, and S. H. Cramer, *Counseling Theory and Process* (Boston: Allyn and Bacon, 1994), 362.

4. J. White and S. Taft, "Frameworks for Teaching and Learning Business Ethics within the Global Context: Background of Ethical Theories," *Journal of Management Education* 28 (2004): 463–477.

5. A. Westbrook, "Blue Sky Laws for 100 Years: Introduction to the Special Issue on Corporate and Blue Sky Law," *Washburn Law Journal* 50, no. 3 (2011).

6. Based on the Investment Advisers Act of 1940, all references to advisers in this chapter–the firm or the individual functioning as either a state- or SEC-registered investment adviser—use the term *adviser*. Throughout the remainder of the book, the term *advisor* is used to reference financial professionals, both investment advisers and those registered with FINRA, acting in the capacity of providing financial planning products and/or services.

7. *Firestone Tire & Rubber Co.* v. *Bruch*, 489 UNITED STATES 101, 110–11 (1989).

8. 15 U.S.C. Chapter 94, Subchapter I § 6801. As found on the Cornell University Law School Web site at http://www.law.cornell.edu/uscode/text/15/6801.

9. NASAA, *New Investment Advisers Must Take "Competency Exam" Starting Jan. 1.* Available at http://www.nasaa.org/8188/new-investment-advisers-must-take-competency-exam-starting-jan-1/.

10. FINRA, *Central Registration Depository (CRD®).* Available at http://www.finra.org/industry/compliance/registration/crd/.

11. FINRA, *FINRA BrokerCheck® - Research Brokers, Brokerage Firms, Investment Adviser Representatives and Investment Adviser Firms.* Available at http://www.finra.org/Investors/ToolsCalculators/BrokerCheck/.

12. 111th Congress of the United States of America. Dodd-Frank Wall Street Reform and Consumer Protection Act. Title IX, § 915. Available at http://www.sec.gov/about/laws/wallstreetreform-cpa.pdf, p. 455.

13. Dodd-Frank, § 913.

14. Dodd-Frank, Title IV, § 410, Para. 2, Subpara B., p. 202.

15. Dodd-Frank, Title IX, § 919C, Subsection a, p. 464.

16. Investment Advisers Act of 1940, § 202, p. 3. Available at www.sec.gov/about/laws/iaa40.pdf.

17. SEC, *Applicability of the Investment Advisers Act to Financial Planners, Pension Consultants, and Other Persons Who Provide Investment Advisory Services as a Component of Other Financial Services.* Available at www.sec.gov/rules/interp/1987/ia-1092.pdf.

18. SEC, SEC *Adopts Dodd-Frank Act Amendments to Investment Advisers Act.* Available at http://www.sec.gov/news/press/2011/2011-133.htm.

19. SEC, *General Information on the Regulation of Investment Advisers.* Available at http://www.sec.gov/divisions/investment/iaregulation/memoia.htm.

20. NASAA, *Investment Adviser Guide, Audits.* Available at http://www.nasaa.org/industry-resources/investment-advisers/investment-adviser-guide/.

21. The first use of the term is found in a written opinion by Justice McKenna of the United States Supreme Court in 1917. Justice McKenna wrote, "The name that is given to the law indicates the evil at which it is aimed, that is, to use the language of a cited case, speculative schemes which have no more basis than so many feet of 'blue sky'; or, as stated by counsel in another case, 'to stop the sale of stock in fly-by-night concerns, visionary oil wells, distant gold mines and other like fraudulent exploitations.' Even if the descriptions be regarded as rhetorical, the existence of evil is indicated, and a belief of its detriment; and we shall not pause to do more than state that the prevention of deception is within the competency of government and that the appreciation of the consequences of it is not open for our review." *Hall* v. *Geiger-Jones Co..*, 242 UNITED STATES 539 (1917).

22. From the North American Securities Administrators Association Web site. Available at http://www.nasaa.org/about-us/our-role/.

23. FINRA, *About the Financial Industry Regulatory Authority.* Available at http://www.finra.org/aboutfinra/.

24. FINRA, *FINRA Dispute Resolution Arbitration, Mediation and the Neutrals Who Serve.* Available at http://www.finra.org/web/groups/arbitrationmediation/@arbmed/@fdr/documents/arbmed/p124105.pdf.

25. For additional license information visit http://www.finra.org/industry/compliance/registration/qualificationsexams/registeredreps/p011051.

26. *FI360 Executive Summary of the GAO Study Report to Congress.* Available at http://www.fi360.com/main/pdf/GAOstudy_executivesummary_011811.pdf.

27. SEC, Form ADV (Paper Version), Uniform Application for Investment Adviser Registration, Part 2A of Form ADV: Firm Brochure. Available at http://www.sec.gov/about/forms/formadv-part2.pdf, pp. 1–10.

28. SEC, Form ADV (Paper Version), Uniform Application for Investment Adviser Registration, Part 2B of Form ADV: Brochure Supplement. Available at http://www.sec.gov/about/forms/formadv-part2.pdf, pp. 1–4.

29. Form U4 Explanation of Terms. Available at http://www.finra.org/web/groups/industry/@ip/@comp/@regis/documents/appsupportdocs/p116979.pdf, p. 2.

30. D. B Trone, W. R. Allbright, and P. R. Taylor, *The Management of Investment Decisions* (New York: McGraw-Hill, 1996), p. 20.

31. See "Don Trone on the Fiduciary State of Mind," in *Voice, Journal of Financial Planning* (February, 2005): 10–14.

32. *Harvard College* v. *Amory*, 26 Mass. (9 Pick.) 446 (1830).

33. Restatement of Trusts 2d § 227 (1959).

34. NAPFA, *2011 Policies and Procedures Manual, Section 10.10 Code of Ethics.* Available at http://www.napfa.org/UserFiles/File/National/NAPFAPolicyandProceduresJune2011Final.pdf#xml=http://www.napfa.org/search/index.asp?cmd=pdfhits&DocId=222&Index=D%3a%5cComponenets%5cNapfa%5cdtSearchIndexes%5cnapfaFull&HitCount=50&hits=8+9+15+1d+29+3b+3c+34c+3c3+3ea+5d6+695+e21+f87+1024+1083+119a+119e+11c0+12ae+12b1+12b2+12c9+12ca

+1309+131a+1562+1970+1b75+1dcc+1dd3+1e24+24b0+2519+251a+2fa7+324b+325e+3277+3283+32b8+3a37+3cf3+3cf 5+3cf6+418b+419d+444e+4454+4455+&hc=3225&req=2011+policy+and+procedures+manual.

35. NAPFA, *2011 Policies and Procedures.*

36. Certified Financial Planner Board of Standards, Inc., *CFP Board's Standards of Professional Conduct.* Available at http://www.cfp.net/Downloads/2010Standards.pdf, p. 6. Also available at http://www.cfp.net/learn/codeofethics.asp.

37. CFP Board, *Standards of Professional Conduct*, p. 2. Available at http://www.cfp.net/learn/ethics.asp#intro.

38. CFP Board, *Standards of Professional Conduct*, p. 6. Available at http://www.cfp.net/learn/codeofethics.asp.

39. CFP Board, *Standards of Professional Conduct*, p. 8. Also available at http://www.cfp.net/learn/rulesofconduct.asp.

40. CFP Board, *Standards of Professional Conduct*, p. 8. Available at http://www.cfp.net/learn/rulesofconduct.asp.

41. CFP Board, *Standards of Professional Conduct*, p. 14. Also available at http://www.cfp.net/learn/standards.asp.

42. CFP Board, *Standards of Professional Conduct*, p. 4. Also available at: http://www.cfp.net/learn/terminology.asp.

43. U.S. SEC, *Investment Adviser Codes of Ethics.* Available at http://www.sec.gov/rules/final/ia-2256.htm#P108_25376 Or see U. S. SEC. *Rule 204A-1 — Investment Adviser Codes of Ethics.* Also available at http://taft.law.uc.edu/CCL/InvAdvRls/rule204A-1.html.

44. U.S. SEC, *Final Rule: Compliance Programs of Investment Companies and Investment Advisers.* Available at http://www.sec.gov/rules/final/ia-2204.htm.

45. U.S. SEC, *Political Contributions by Certain Investment Advisers.* Available at http://www.sec.gov/rules/final/2010/ia-3043.pdf.

46. FINRA, "Communication with the Public," *FINRA Manual,* Section 2210 Section (c)(8)(d)(1). Available at http://finra.complinet.com/en/display/display_main.html?rbid=2403&element_id=3617.

47. FINRA, "Communication with the Public," *FINRA Manual,* Section 2210 Section (a) and Section (b). Available at http://finra.complinet.com/en/display/display_main.html?rbid=2403&element_id=3617.

48. SEC, SEC *Interpretation: Electronic Storage of Broker-Dealer Records.* Available at http://www.sec.gov/rules/interp/34-47806.htm.

49. National Association of Insurance Commissioners, *Interstate Insurance Product Regulation Compact* (2003), p. 692-2. Available at http://www.insurancecompact.org/documents/compact_statute.pdf.

50. 15 USC § 6801—Protection of Nonpublic Personal Information. Title 15, Chapter 94, Subchapter I § 6801. As found on the Cornell University Law School Web site at http://www.law.cornell.edu/uscode/text/15/6801.

51. SEC, Securities Exchange Commission National Examination Risk Alert. Investment Adviser Use of Social Media (2012) Vol. II, Issue 1, p. 2. Available at http://www.sec.gov/about/offices/ocie/riskalert-socialmedia.pdf.

52. FINRA, *"Guidance on Blogs and Social Networking Web Sites," FINRA Regulatory Notice 10-06* (January 2010). Available at http://www.finra.org/Industry/Regulation/Notices/2010/P120760.

53. Michael E. Kitces, "How Advisors Are Using Social Media (With No Compliance Headaches!)," *Advisor One* 27 (2012). Available at http://www.advisorone.com/2012/02/27/how-advisors-are-using-social-media-with-no-compli?page=3.

54. FINRA, Regulatory Notice 10-06 (January 2010). Available at http://www.finra.org/Industry/Regulation/Notices/2010/P120760, p. 3.

55. FINRA, "Recommendation to Customers (Suitability)," Rule 2310. Available at http://finra.complinet.com/en/display/display_main.html?rbid=2403&element_id=3638.

56. FINRA Regulatory Notice 10-06, *Social Media Web Sites: Guidance on Blogs and Social Networking Web Sites.* (January 2010). Available at http://www.finra.org/web/groups/industry/@ip/@reg/@notice/documents/notices/p120779.pdf, pp. 7–8.

57. U.S. Securities Exchange Act of 1934. *Section 3 – Definitions and Application.* Available at http://taft.law.uc.edu/CCL/34Act/sec3.html#a.35.

58. CFP Board, *Standards of Professional Conduct, Rule 3.4,* p. 10. Also available at http://www.cfp.net/learn/rulesofconduct.asp#3.

59. FINRA Press Release. Available at http://www.finra.org/Newsroom/NewsReleases/1996/P010578.

60. *Finance Industry Regulatory Authority Compliance Handbook,* NASD Rule 3080 Arbitration Disclosure Statement. Available at http://finra.complinet.com/en/display/display.html?rbid=2403&record_id=4409&element_id=3731&highlight=3080#r4409.

61. FINRA, *Dispute Resolution Statistics: Summary Arbitration Statistics May 2012.* Available at http://www.finra.org/ArbitrationAndMediation/FINRADisputeResolution/AdditionalResources/Statistics/.

62. FINRA, *Dispute Resolution Statistics: Arbitration Cases Filed*. Available at http://www.finra.org/ArbitrationAndMediation/FINRADisputeResolution/AdditionalResources/Statistics/.

63. FINRA, *Dispute Resolution Statistics: Arbitration Cases Served by Controversy Involved*. Available at http://www.finra.org/ArbitrationAndMediation/FINRADisputeResolution/AdditionalResources/Statistics/.

64. FINRA *Code of Arbitration Procedure*. Available on-line at http://www.finra.org/arbitrationandmediation/arbitration/rules/codeofarbitrationprocedure/.

65. FINRA News Release (June 2012); as found at http://www.finra.org/Newsroom/NewsReleases/2012/P126718.

66. FINRA, Understanding Professional Designations. Available at http://apps.finra.org/DataDirectory/1/prodesignations.aspx.

67. CFP Board, *Standards of Professional Conduct*. Available at http//www.cfp.net/Downloads/2010Standards.pdf, p. 2. Also available at http://www.cfp.net/learn/ethics.asp#intro.

68. CFP Board, *Standards of Professional Conduct*, p. 4. Also available at http://www.cfp.net/learn/terminology.asp.

Letter of Engagement in Pro Bono Financial Planning

USING THE LETTER OF ENGAGEMENT IN
PRO BONO FINANCIAL PLANNING

A letter of engagement, or client agreement, is a standard part of any financial planner's practice.   A letter of engagement is no less of an important tool in a *pro bono* relationship.

The *Pro Bono* Letter of Engagement has three major purposes:
1) It establishes the scope of the *pro bono* engagement;
2) It documents the client's agreement to release the planner, the chapter and FPA from liability;
3) It helps planners and chapters track the number of *pro bono* clients served and hours spent.

The letter of engagement must be signed by the planner and the client. The planner may delegate underlying tasks involved to others, including allied professionals, candidates for CFP certification and paraplanners, but retains ultimate responsibility for the engagement.

SCOPE

The letter outlines a "mini plan" process for use when working with *pro bono* clients. The mini plan consists of three basic steps: 1) gathering data and setting goals, 2) data review and clarification, 3) plan presentation and discussion. It is in fact the basic financial planning process with the important exception of implementation and monitoring. The mini-plan is meant to help *pro bono* clients and partner organizations understand what is involved in a client-centered financial planning engagement, and to help set an end-point to the engagement. The amount of work required will depend on the case – the three steps might require three meetings or just one – and it is up to the planner and client to determine what services are to be provided.

The meetings may be conducted in person or electronically, although most will likely be conducted in person.

LIABILITY

The letter requests the client to agree to hold FPA, the chapter and the planner harmless from any loss, damage, cost or liability arising from the engagement. The planner may wish to supplement the FPA *pro bono* engagement letter with his or her own firm's letter   (with the fee set at zero, of course) if that letter is preferable to the planner, the planner's firm and/or the planner's liability insurance coverage.

TRACKING

In addition to furnishing the client with a signed copy of this Letter of Engagement, copies should be forwarded to the appropriate FPA chapter contact, often the *pro bono* director or chapter executive, and to the sponsoring non-profit organization. Upon completion of the engagement, Appendix A should be filled out and copies provided to the client, FPA chapter and the partner organization. The chapter and partner organization can then keep a record of engagements and track the number of clients served and hours provided by *pro bono* planners.

Questions regarding the letter of engagement should be sent to the chapter's *pro bono* director, or to the FPA *Pro Bono* Services Department at fpaprobono@fpanet.org, or 800-282-7526.

LETTER OF ENGAGEMENT
FOR *PRO BONO* FINANCIAL PLANNING SERVICES

1) We, the undersigned planner and *pro bono* recipient (herein referred to as "you" or "client"), acknowledge that we are entering into a limited *pro bono* financial planning engagement for which the planner will receive no compensation, directly or indirectly, for services provided.

2) The scope of this engagement is to provide to you general financial planning advice and consultation. A basic *pro bono* engagement generally consists of three steps: 1) gathering data and setting goals, 2) data review and clarification, 3) plan presentation and discussion, including a financial statement, assessment of risk, and any tax implications. These steps may be covered in one meeting or multiple meetings. They may be conducted in-person, over the telephone, or via electronic communications.

3) The planner may delegate the services provided within this engagement to another qualified professional. If so, the undersigned planner remains responsible for all work.

4) The scope of this *pro bono* engagement is not intended to be a long-term or ongoing relationship. This engagement does not provide for implementation of the advice by the planner or monitoring any action taken by you. You are responsible for making all decisions and may pursue other options to implement your financial plan. The engagement will terminate upon the completion of the *pro bono* financial planning process described above, or by written notice of either the planner or you.

5) The planner will receive no compensation for this engagement. Furthermore, the planner is prohibited from charging for additional services not anticipated but provided during the period of engagement.

6) The planner will not pursue an ongoing financial planning business relationship unless initiated solely by you. If you request such a relationship, and the planner agrees to provide services for compensation, you and the planner shall check and sign the release contained in Appendix A and enter into a new and separate agreement for financial planning services, with the *pro bono* engagement terminated prior to execution of the business agreement.

7) The planner is a member of the Financial Planning Association® and will abide by FPA's Code of Ethics and *Pro Bono* Guidelines, and if applicable by the Certified Financial Planner Board of Standards' *Code of Ethics and Professional Responsibility* and *Financial Planning Practice Standards*.

8) The planner will comply with all regulatory, professional and ethical obligations, including but not limited to any imposed by the Securities and Exchange Commission (SEC) and banking, state securities and insurance authorities. The planner affirms that all professional licenses and certifications held by the planner are in good standing, and that the planner has not at any time been censored, convicted or otherwise found by competent authority to be guilty of any fraudulent activity or professional misconduct.

9) Neither FPA, its affiliated chapters, nor its officers, members or staff assume responsibility or liability for the accuracy or appropriateness of the advice given by the planner. By accepting assistance, you acknowledge and agree that FPA and affiliated chapter do not purport to provide or hold out as providing any financial advice to the participant and that FPA, nor any of its directors, officers, employees, agents or members, has any professional or business relationship with, or has or assumes any responsibility or liability for the accuracy or appropriateness of any advice or assistance provided by the planner. You acknowledge that you must make an independent judgment regarding a particular planner's qualifications and suitability for your particular needs and circumstances.

10) All personal financial advice and assistance provided by the planner is provided solely by the individual financial planner. The planner is solely responsible for his or her professional advice and services. Both the planner and you agree to hold FPA as well as its directors, officers, employees, agents or members, and affiliated chapter harmless from any loss, damage, cost or liability in any way arising from such advice, acts or omissions.

11) You understand that the responsibility for financial planning decisions are your own and that you are under no obligation to follow, either wholly or in part, any recommendation or suggestion provided by the planner. By accepting assistance, you agree to hold the planner and the planner's firm harmless from any loss, damage, cost or liabi   lity in any way arising from such advice, acts or omissions.

12) Should any concern arise regarding this advisory relationship, it is agreed that the parties will consult with each other to resolve such issues. Any unresolved issue shall then be submitted to non-binding mediation under the Commercial Mediation Rules of the American Arbitration Association. Any dispute still unresolved may then be submitted to binding arbitration under the Securities Industry Arbitration Rules of the American Arbitration Association.

_____ / _____   _____ / _____
(Pro Bono Planner signature)   (Date)   (Pro Bono Client signature)   (Date)

_____   _____

_____   _____

_____   _____

_____   _____
(Print name, address and telephone number)   (Print name, address and telephone number)

Copies of this engagement letter are to be provided to: 1) the pro bono client; 2) the pro bono planner; 3) the sponsoring organization; and 4) the FPA chapter.

LETTER OF ENGAGEMENT FOR
PRO BONO FINANCIAL PLANNING SERVICES
Appendix A

Pro Bono Advisory Services Provided (check all that apply):

____ Review of client's goals and objectives
____ Review of spending patterns and bill payments and/or creation of a spending plan
____ Review of debts and/or creation of a debt management plan
____ Review of medical, disability, life, property, casualty or other insurance, including information about benefits, settlements and claims administration
____ Review of savings and investment goals and plans
____ Review of tax issues
____ Review of estate issues
____ Review of financial benefits for which the client and his or her family may be eligible
____ Consulting with other allied professionals such as accountants, attorneys and insurance professionals
____ Other (specify) _____

Time Allocated to Pro Bono Engagement: _____ hours.

Next Step (check all that apply):

☒ Client has elected to implement some or all of the recommendations on his/her own.
☒ Client has been referred to PlannerSearch on the Financial Planning Association's website at www.FPAnet.org.
☒ Client has received referrals to allied professionals (accountants, attorneys, insurance professionals) or agencies (credit counseling, housing counseling).
☒ Client has inquired about a business relationship with the *pro bono* planner on a compensation basis and under a separate agreement. Client has received the brochure *How a Financial Planner Can Help You...and How to Choose the Right One* available from FPA and been referred to PlannerSearch. The *pro bono* engagement will terminate prior to execution of any other agreement with the planner.
☒ Other _____

Notes: _____

_____

_____

Signed: _____ Date: _____
(*Pro Bono* financial planner)

Signed: _____ Date: _____
(*Pro Bono* client)

At the conclusion of the pro bono engagement, copies of this appendix are to be provided to: 1) the pro bono client; 2) the pro bono financial planner; 3) the sponsoring organization; and 4) the FPA chapter.

Investment Management Agreement

This Agreement sets forth the Investment Advisory engagement entered into by and between <The Firm>, a duly registered advisor and

_____ (Client)

SERVICES OF <THE FIRM>: <The Firm> shall provide investment management to the Client. Client appoints <The Firm> as the investment manager of those assets designated to be held in the managed investment portfolio.

TRADING AUTHORIZATION AND ESTABLISHMENT OF ACCOUNTS: Client hereby constitutes and appoints <The Firm> as its true and lawful agent for the selection of securities to be bought and sold and the amount of securities to be bought and sold that <The Firm> deems, in its sole and unrestricted discretion and judgment, to be consistent with Client's investment policy and to take all actions necessary for the execution of any purchase or sale of securities. <The Firm> is granted authority to collect advisory fees from clients account, remit checks, wire funds, and otherwise make disbursements of funds held in clients account to 1) banks, other broker-dealers, investment companies, or financial institutions to or for credit to an account of identical registration; or 2) to client at their address of record. Client retains the right to make deposits or withdrawals from his/her account at any time, however, Client is requested to notify <The Firm> of each withdrawal or deposit before it occurs. The term "securities" herein means stocks, bonds, notes, or any other types of instruments defined as a security under federal securities law.

BASIS OF ADVICE: Client acknowledges that <The Firm> obtains information from a wide variety of publicly available sources and that <The Firm> has no sources, and does not claim to have, sources of inside or private information. The recommendations developed by <The Firm> are based upon the professional judgment of <The Firm> and its individual professional counselors and on information received from Client and neither <The Firm> nor its individual counselors can guarantee the results of any recommendation. Client at all times can elect unilaterally to follow or ignore completely, or in part, any information, recommendation or counsel given by <The Firm> under this Agreement. <The Firm> is not responsible for tax reporting of gains and losses. Client should keep trade confirmations, account statements, or other correspondence supplied by the custodian (Custodian) for this purpose.

INVESTMENT POLICY: The managed investment portfolio is to be managed according to the risk parameters as set by the Client. An investment policy with more detailed risk parameters will be agreed upon specifically by the Client after completion of the financial plan. <The Firm> will not make discretionary investments on behalf of the Client until an Investment Policy Statement is complete. If the Client wishes to change the Investment Policy Statement at any time, Client must provide written instructions to <The Firm>.

LIABILITY OF <THE FIRM>: The Client agrees that <The Firm> will not be liable for any recommendation, act or omission, including but not limited to any error in judgment, with respect to the managed investment portfolio, so long as such recommendation, act or omission does not constitute a breach of fiduciary duty to the Client. Nothing contained herein shall in any way constitute a waiver or limitation of any rights which the Client may have under applicable federal or state securities laws. <The Firm> shall not be liable for complying with any directive or instruction of the Client that is received verbally. <The Firm> shall not be liable for any act or omission of any Custodian, broker or other third party with respect to the managed investment portfolio.

SERVICES TO OTHER CLIENTS: Client understands and agrees that <The Firm> performs investment advisory services for other clients. Client agrees that <The Firm> may give advice or take action in the performance of its duties with respect to any of its other clients, or for <The Firm> and/or its employees' own accounts, which may differ from advice given to or action taken on behalf of Client. <The Firm> is not obligated to buy, sell or recommend for Client any security or other investment that <The Firm> or its employees may buy, sell or recommend for any other Client or for their own accounts.

COMPENSATION: Fees for investment management are computed based on the attached fee schedule. Management fees are based upon a percentage of the assets under management and are payable in advance four (4) times per year: January, April, July, and October. The first payment is due and payable when the account is opened and will be assessed pro rata if the account is opened other than the first day of the month when billing occurs. Fees for subsequent billing periods will be assessed based on the value of the portfolio as of the last business day of the previous billing period. Client agrees to the fee schedule as attached and authorizes the Custodian to deduct these fees from the Client's account.

TRANSACTION COSTS: All transaction costs with respect to the managed portfolio shall be paid by the Client.

LEGAL AND ACCOUNTING SERVICES: It is understood and agreed that <The Firm> and its employees are not qualified to, and will not, render any legal or accounting advice nor prepare any legal or accounting documents for the implementation of Client's financial and investment plan. Client agrees that his/her personal attorney and/or CPA shall be solely responsible for the rendering and/or preparation of the following: (i) all legal and accounting advice; (ii) all legal and accounting opinions and determinations; and (iii) all legal and accounting documents.

PROXY: <The Firm>'s stated policy is that clients shall maintain all proxy voting authority over all securities managed by the company. On rare occasions we may share our thoughts regarding a proxy vote, if we deem a communication beneficial to assisting our clients.

CONFLICT OF INTEREST DISCLOSURE STATEMENTS: <The Firm> is an investment advisor registered with the Securities and Exchange Commission under the Investment Advisors Act of 1940. <The Firm> has delivered information providing disclosures regarding its background and business practices. The Client acknowledges receipt of such information.

In the course of services to Client, an advisor/employee may receive other commissions, consideration and fees from insurance carriers. In the event an employee of <The Firm> is acting in the capacity of registered representative, he/she shall disclose any fees or commissions as required by existing federal and state securities laws and regulations.

REPRESENTATIONS BY CLIENT: Client represents that the terms herein do not violate any obligation by which Client is bound, whether arising by contract, operation of law or otherwise, and that, if required: (i) this contract has been duly authorized by appropriate action and is binding upon Client in accordance with its terms; and (ii) the Client will deliver to <The Firm> such evidence of such authority as it may reasonably require, whether by way of a certified resolution, trust agreement, or otherwise. A trustee or other fiduciary entering into this Agreement represents that the proposed investment objective designated by Client in the Investment Policy Statement is within the scope of policies authorized by the governing instrument.

ARBITRATION: Any dispute, controversy or claim, including but not limited to, any claim relating to errors and omissions arising out of, or relating to, this Agreement, the breach thereof, or the purchase or sale of any security, the handling of funds or any other matter relating to the handling of Client's account, shall be settled by arbitration in accordance with the Code of Commercial Arbitration of the American Arbitration Association, and judgment upon the award rendered by the arbitrator(s) may be entered in any court having jurisdiction thereof. Client understands that this agreement to arbitrate does not constitute a waiver of the right to seek a judicial hearing or other forum where such waiver would be void under the federal and state securities laws. Arbitration is final and binding on the parties.

MISCELLANEOUS PROVISIONS: The Agreement shall be governed by the laws of the State of Maryland and in compliance with the Federal Securities Laws, including the Investment Advisors Act of 1940 and any regulations promulgated there under. The Agreement shall inure to the benefit of any successor of <The Firm> and shall be binding upon the successors and assigns of Client. <The Firm> shall not assign this Agreement without written consent of the Client. <The Firm> will notify Client of any change in the legal ownership of <The Firm> within a reasonable time after such change. This Agreement shall not become effective until accepted by <The Firm> as evidenced by the signature of an authorized representative below. No modification or amendment to this Agreement shall be effective unless made in writing and signed by Client and an authorized representative of <The Firm>. The parties hereto acknowledge and agree that this Agreement alone constitutes the final written expression of the parties with respect to all matters contained herein, and the parties further acknowledge and agree that there are no prior or contemporaneous agreements different or distinct from those contained herein, and all such prior and contemporaneous agreements, if any, are merged herein, and this Agreement alone constitutes the final understanding between parties. Client certifies that he or she has read this Agreement and understands its terms in its entirety before executing it.

TERM OF AGREEMENT AND TERMINATION: This Agreement shall be valid for one (1) year from the effective date and will be automatically renewed annually for one (1) year terms. However, either party may terminate this Agreement at any time by giving <u>written</u> notice to the current address of each party. Upon termination, <The Firm> will not liquidate the account(s) unless Client provides written instructions to the contrary. Termination of this Agreement shall not affect any liability for <The Firm> resulting from sales or exchanges initiated prior to receiving written notice of such revocation. Transactions in progress will be completed in the normal course of business. Upon termination, Client shall receive a pro-rata refund of that portion of any prepaid advisory fees that have yet to be earned. Such refund will be calculated from the date of receipt of the written termination notice or other agreed upon date.

SEVERABILITY: It is understood by the parties hereto that if any term, provision, duty, obligation or undertaking herein contained is held by the courts to be unenforceable or illegal or in conflict with the applicable state law, the validity of the remaining portions shall not be affected, and the rights and obligations of the parties shall be construed and enforced as if such invalid or unenforceable provision was not contained herein.

NOTICE: All written notices required hereunder shall be deemed effective when received by <The Firm> at its office at 2222 Street Address, Suite 103, City, State 89502 or by the Client at the address of record. Each party shall be entitled to presume the correctness of such address until notified in writing to the contrary.

CONFIDENTIALITY: Except as otherwise agreed in writing or as required by law, <The Firm> will exercise the highest degree of due diligence and care with respect to keeping confidential all Client information. However, by signing this Agreement, Client authorizes <The Firm> to give a copy of this Agreement to any broker, dealer or other party to a transaction for the account, or the Custodian as evidence of <The Firm>'s limited power of attorney and authority to act on Client's behalf. In addition, Client grants Advisor authority to discuss, disclose and provide confidential Client information to outside attorneys, auditors, consultants and any other professional advisors retained by <The Firm> to assist in the management of this Agreement and Client's account. It is <The Firm>'s policy to make available Client's account information to Client's spouse. A Client may restrict such availability to his/her spouse by notifying <The Firm> in writing.

PRIVACY: In compliance with the Securities and Exchange Commission's Regulation S-P (Privacy of Consumer Financial Information), which was adopted to comply with Section 504 of the Gramm-Leach-Bliley Act (the "G-L-B Act"), <The Firm> has disclosed to Client its policies and procedures regarding the use and safekeeping of personal information, including, if applicable, how such Client may avoid ("opt out" of) having his/her information shared. By signing below, Client acknowledges that Client has read and understands <The Firm>'s privacy policy.

ACKNOWLEDGMENT OF RECEIPT OF BROCHURE AND FORM ADV PART II: Client hereby acknowledge(s) that he/she has received and has had an opportunity to read <The Firm>'s Form ADV Part II as required by Rule 204-3 of the Investment Advisors Act of 1940. Notwithstanding anything to the contrary herein, Client shall have the right to terminate this Agreement within five (5) business days of the effective date of this Agreement at no financial cost.

Date	Client	Print Name

Date	Client	Print Name

Date	Advisor	Print Name

ASSET MANAGEMENT FEE SCHEDULE

Management fees are based upon a percentage of the assets under management and are invoiced and paid pro-rata in January, April, July and October.

The ongoing management fees based upon assets are as follows:

• First $500,000	1.30% annually
• Next $1,000,000 ($500,001 - $1,500,000)	0.85% annually
• Next $1,000,000 ($1,500,001 - $2,500,000)	0.80% annually
• Next $1,000,000 ($2,500,001 - $3,500,000)	0.75% annually
• Next $1,500,000 ($3,500,001 - $5,000,000)	0.70% annually
• Above $5,000,000	0.60% annually

Examples:

1) Clients with $650,000 in assets under management (AUM) will be charged annually 1.30% of the first $500K, plus 0.85% on the next $150K.

2) Clients with $2,750,000 AUM are billed 1.30% on the first $500K, plus 0.85% on the next $1M, 0.80% of the next $1M, plus 0.75% of the remaining $250K.

3) Clients with $6,250,000 AUM are billed 1.30% on the first $500K, plus 0.85% on the next $1M, 0.80% of the next $1M, plus 0.75% of the next $1M, plus 0.70% of the next $1.5M, plus 0.60% of the remaining $1.25M.

_____	_____	_____
Date	Client	Print Name
_____	_____	_____
Date	Client	Print Name
_____	_____	_____
Date	Advisor	Print Name

Management fees are paid in advance at the beginning of each billing period. They are assessed based upon the account asset value(s) on the last business day of the previous billing period. When an account is established, the management fee is charged for the remainder of the current billing period and is based upon the initial contributions. This schedule is effective March 1, 2009.

Rev. 5-17-2012

PART II: Fundamental Tools for Financial Planning

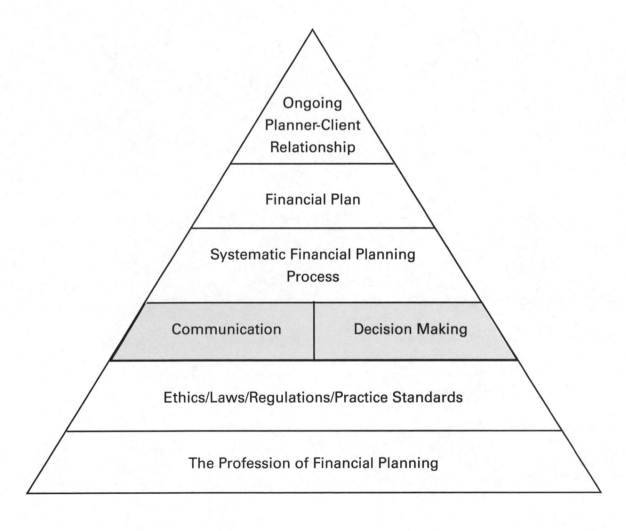

Client Communication

Learning Objectives

1. Explain why financial planning requires a mix of technical and counseling skills.

2. Describe how verbal, nonverbal, and paralanguage cues contribute to communication.

3. Explain how office privacy, image, and control influence planner-client communication.

4. Explain the role of experiential maps, heuristics, money scripts, and emotions in the communication process.

5. Identify the three preferred information processing styles for learning and communicating.

6. Explain and demonstrate the use of active listening, clarification techniques, questioning, and silence.

7. Explain how different communication techniques can be used to better understand or modify client objections or resistance.

8. Identify and explain how ongoing communication efforts are used for planner marketing.

Key Terms

Active listening	Marketing
Attending	Mirroring
Auditory communicator/learner	Money script
Body language	Paralanguage
Communication	Paraphrasing
Congruence	Prospecting
Content	Rate
Direct marketing	Restating
Drip marketing	Servicing
Experiential map	Space
Heuristic	Summarizing
Indirect marketing	Tone
Kinesthetic communicator/learner	Visual communicator/learner
Level-I probe	Volume
Level-II probe	

FINANCIAL PLANNER: TECHNICIAN, COUNSELOR, OR COACH?

Financial planning is built on a sound technical knowledge of a range of financial products and services coupled with the quantitative skills necessary to analyze a client's situation. In essence, a financial planner diagnoses a client's financial issues or problems and then recommends the products or strategies with the greatest probability of meeting those needs. This perspective of financial planner as technician neglects the critical role of the client—the whole person, not just the person's financial issues—as the foundation of the financial planning process. In fact, it is communication and the evolving planner-client relationship that contextualize the client's reasons for seeking financial planning assistance. Both client and planner must recognize a client's attitudes, feelings, and emotions about money as well as how those attitudes, feelings, or emotions can affect financial action or inaction.[1] Change may be necessary to accomplish the client's goals, but changing attitudes and behaviors involves incremental steps rather than a command for action. Moreover, it is often the changes that life presents—expected and unexpected—that clients are attempting to prepare for or respond to.

Chapter 1 presented a list of the 10 most important factors identified by consumers when choosing a financial planner. A review of these traits confirms the perception that a financial planner is a blend of counselor and technical expert who can solve problems *with* the client, but not necessarily *for* the client. In other words, the client wants to be involved. Although multiple theories and approaches to counseling abound, Geis provided a seminal definition of counseling when he asserted that it:

> [I]s an activity in which a person who is trained and experienced in the psychological theory and practice of understanding and changing human behavior seeks to influence, mainly but not exclusively by the techniques of talking, the perceptions, thinking, feelings, emotions and actions of one or more counselees, with the intention of producing short- and/or long-range changes in the counselee and/or in his reality situation which are more self-benefiting and self-actualizing and less self-defeating and self-inhibiting, with regard to what the counselee and/or counselor define as the counselee's self-interest as it relates to his personality and/or his reality problems.[2]

Given this definition, it is evident that financial planners are not counselors. Few financial planners have academic training in personality assessment, psychotherapy, or behavioral change theory—although attention to these applications in financial planning is on the rise. In fact, some firms have added, formally as a part of the planner's team or informally through referrals, financial therapists with this expertise to serve clients better. But these apparent differences should not suggest that the traits associated with successful counseling are completely inapplicable to financial planning. In fact, the opposite is true. The way in which a counselor achieves communication breakthroughs with a client should be similar to the method by which a financial planner optimizes communication with clients.

Both counselors and planners focus on getting to know a client and increasing the client's self-awareness. Increasingly, as planners incorporate life planning into their discovery process with clients, planners are exploring with clients their healthy and unhealthy relationship with money. From this perspective, the financial planning process might include attention to changes in attitudes or behaviors that could reduce "self-defeating and self-inhibiting" practices.[3] Although specialized training and licensed tools to guide planner-client interaction are available to facilitate the incorporation of life planning strategies into the financial planning process (for more information, see Chapter 6), communication and trust-building skills are the foundation. Furthermore, Kinder and Galvan assert that coaching and life planning are not therapy that considers a client's deep-seated psychological problems.[4] In fact, the traits associated with successful counselors are easily adaptable to financial planning, as shown in Table 3.1, and should be characteristics of accomplished financial planners' client interactions.

Table 3.1 Important Financial Planner Communication Traits

Trait	Example
Regards clients as persons of worth	Unconditional acceptance of the client and the client's past actions
Nonpossessive warmth	Reflects genuine concern for the client with overtones of personal caring while at the same time fostering client independence and professional boundaries
Competence and confidence	Presents an image that highlights personal strengths and professionalism through appearance and communication methods
Sincerity and openness	Displays sincere openness and respect for the client as an individual
Empathy and understanding	Strives to fully understand and respect the client's paradigms and share the client's concerns
Sensitivity	Acknowledges the importance of the client's emotional as well as financial needs and respects personal values, morals, and ethics
Objectivity	Provides neutral, suitable advice in the best interest of the client
Flexibility	Is willing to explore new planning strategies and to adapt previous recommendations to new client, market, or economic situations
High intelligence	Values the role of continuing professional education and lifelong learning
Absence of emotional disturbance or instability	Avoids biases or moods that might distort or disrupt the planner-client relationship or the client's financial situation
Absence of disruptive personal values	Screens religious, political, social, philosophical, and personal differences when values are not shared by client, or works only with clients who share personal views
Personal style	Uses body language, humor, stories, and emotion comfortably when working with clients
Miscellaneous aspects	Presents a congruent message consistent with age, gender, appearance, and habits

Table based on Geis, H. J. (1973). "Toward a Comprehensive Framework Unifying All Systems of Counseling," In John Vriend (ed.). Counseling Effectively in Groups. Englewood Cliffs, NJ: Educational Technology Publications. Page 10-31.

Financial planners are almost always better serving in the roles of counselor, educator, and coach rather than as authoritative expert or financial technician. Counselors ask probing questions. Educators inform and offer new insights from which others can make sound decisions that reflect both fact and emotions, but that limit irrational responses. Athletic coaches promote success through disciplined actions, perseverance, and motivation, although the same may be true of those who provide executive, life, or career coaching services. In fact the International Coach Foundation defines coaching as "partnering with clients in a thought-provoking and creative process that inspires them to maximize their personal and professional potential."[5]

Although this definition, like the definition of counseling, may seem unrelated to financial planning, research on nonfinancial issues reveals otherwise. Survey results from approximately 1,400 planners revealed that approximately 25% of contact with clients was devoted to nonfinancial issues. The top five nonfinancial issues that clients raised with planners were personal life goals; physical health; job/career/profession; the death of someone close to the client; and conflict with children.[6] Certainly these issues reflect the "personal and professional" lives, borrowing from the coaching definition, of those planning clients who were, at some level, seeking their financial advisor's assistance through their financial planning partnership.

Authoritative expert planners focus on facts and presuppose what is right or wrong for a client's financial situation. But a truly effective financial planner brings together—either individually or through the combined efforts of a team of professionals—the roles of technician, counselor, educator, and coach to best serve the client. An effective financial planner has personality and communication traits similar to successful professionals in other helping careers. A great counselor or planner is open to a client's needs. Effective counselors blend empathy, compassion, and warmth with professional expertise. Planners must demonstrate similar qualities as they help prepare clients and their families financially for the unknown, but at some level that preparation might also include coping skills. In these roles, planners have the opportunity to share in the joy of dreams that come true as well as the disappointments and despair that life brings. Ongoing client communication is the mechanism that makes this possible.

Perfecting the craft of effective client communication is built on training, practice, and experience that go far beyond the very basic review presented in this chapter. Some of the skills may be easily recognized, and others may seem awkward and typically not practiced in everyday conversation. Perhaps Evans, Hearn, Uhlemann, and Ivey phrased it best, asserting on the first page of their book, *Essential Interviewing*, that

> Participating in a conversation differs from interviewing, in that interviewing has a purpose—to gather information, set goals, and/or solve problems and resolve issues. It focuses on a client's story, needs, and/or goals.[7]

Certainly that definition reflects the emerging expectations for financial planners and life planners —and corroborates the need for an advisor to master the interviewing skills needed for both advisor and client to *hear* the client's story. A thorough grounding in the communication skills necessary to initiate and foster long-term planner-client relationships is fundamental to the process of financial planning.

THE MULTIFACETED ASPECTS OF CLIENT COMMUNICATION

Communication, in its broadest sense, is defined as the exchange of information between two or more parties. Verbal, nonverbal, and **paralanguage** cues contribute to communication. Tone, rate, and volume of speech are sometimes referred to as paralanguage. Although it is important to individually consider the meaning or message sent in each of these different modes of communication, in reality attention to all three will likely yield the most accurate interpretation.

Communication goes well beyond a person's words or verbalizations. In fact, the message sent by the combination of nonverbal and paralanguage cues is particularly important. Experts suggest that less than 10% of communication is truly conveyed by the verbal message. Overreliance on the specific words used to relay information, referred to as the **content** of communication, can be misleading. Although content is important, the manner in which the words are delivered may be more important. Understanding paralanguage or other nonverbal communication is important to interpreting a client's feelings or emotions. For example, a client may state "This is huge!" but the true meaning of the phrase will be communicated through the paralanguage, not the words. If the phrase is said loudly with a frown, the meaning will be interpreted differently than if it is said loudly with a smile and a "high five" gesture.

Emotions or feelings can often be interpreted through another example of a nonverbal cue, a client's **body language**. Body language typically refers to an individual's facial expressions, gestures, body positioning, or movements as well as the use of space between parties. A client who sits leaning slightly back in the chair with arms folded across his or her chest is sending a message of reluctance, skepticism, and/or annoyance. On the other hand, a client who sits forward taking notes while the planner describes the recommendation outcome is sending another message, one of engagement and interest. Body language that enhances the communication process includes leaning forward to hear, presenting an image of active engagement with the other person, avoiding overly expressive facial movements, and minimizing nervous or distracting mannerisms.

Gender, ethnic, or cultural differences must also be accounted for in nonverbal communication. Women tend to display more nonverbal cues than men, especially cues that suggest affirmation or support for the speaker, regardless of the actual level of agreement. Consistent with this message, women typically display more direct eye contact than men. Also the **volume** of conversation between men and women can vary dramatically. Tonal and volume differences can also come into play when a planner and client share different ethnic backgrounds. What one person considers yelling, for instance, may be another person's form of normal expression. In the Northeastern United States, people talk considerably faster than residents of the South or Midwest. It is possible for an otherwise friendly and caring planner from the East to be considered rude or pushy in the Midwest. It is also possible for someone from the South to be considered less confident, capable, or sophisticated to someone in New York City.

In terms of body proximity, most North Americans like to maintain distance between each other (at least one arm's length distance or three to four feet) while talking. Sitting too close or touching may make some clients uncomfortable. For example, in the United States it is common to provide those with who you are in close contact sufficient personal **space**. This is not the case in some other countries where "personal space" is a foreign concept. Spatial differences are less of a factor between women than they are with men. Men, for instance, are not as comfortable making physical contact in emotional situations.

According to Sommers-Flanagan and Sommers-Flanagan, non-Hispanic Whites prefer to maintain eye contact throughout an interview or meeting session. Native Americans, African-Americans, and Asians, on the other hand, prefer less eye contact. Native American groups display different listening habits than Whites in that asking questions is not a common indicator of listening or engagement and neither is direct eye contact.[8] Eye-to-eye contact between two men is appropriate in a Middle Eastern culture, but it is not permitted between a man and a woman except for a brief time, if at all. In many Middle Eastern cultures, intense eye contact between men is meant to convey honesty, sincerity, and trust. General rules suggest that a planner maintain eye contact when listening and less contact when speaking. In the United States, increased eye contact is associated with sincerity, self-confidence, friendliness, and maturity, and less eye contact suggests a lack of confidence, defensiveness, indifference, coldness, or immaturity.

Despite these generalizations about implicit cultural messages, planners must also become aware of their own strategies with clients. For example, too much direct eye contact can make a client uncomfortable, and so can too much time looking down at the floor or at notes. It is important to practice natural and comfortable eye contact. Some professionals accomplish this by looking at a person's face, or a particular facial feature, so as to avoid intense eye contact.

It is important for planners to assess the congruence or consistency of their own as well as their client's communication. **Congruence** refers to the consistency between *how* something is said and *what* is said. For example, a client could say "I think this will work," to reflect uncertainty with the effectiveness of a strategy. On the other hand, a different client might use the same phrase to express strong agreement with the planner's recommendation. Again, the client's **tone**, paralanguage, and body language can tell an astute planner much about the client's state of mind. The nonverbal message is often assumed to be the most accurate when the messages are incongruent. Rather than make assumptions, the more effective communicator will—with sensitivity—explore the discrepancy, or comment on it by saying, "Your words say this will work, but *you* don't seem to be fully convinced." The effective interpretation and use of communication strategies, in this case openly and cautiously confronting the client, is central to promoting a trusting environment for the planner-client relationship.

The synergistic combination of verbal and nonverbal cues, including eye contact, constitutes **attending,** or attentiveness, a very important component of effective communication. Attending behavior typically focuses on maintaining comfortable *eye contact*, a comfortable *distance* between speakers, and a relaxed but comfortable *posture* with *gestures* used appropriately to punctuate the message. All of these should be culturally appropriate. The planner's verbal responses should be congruent with those of the client. Tone of voice and rate of speech as well as the content of the response should match the client's. Effective verbal attending behavior requires the listener to "stay with the conversation," by asking questions or making comments that directly fit the topic or context of the speaker's message; nonverbal cues and facial expressions should also be congruent. An advisor should not interrupt the client or add new meanings or explanations to the client's message. Recommended verbal statements include simple confirmations, such as "I see what you mean," "I understand," or the restatement of a word or phrase used by the speaker. Attending behavior reinforces, supports, and encourages the client to continue talking about experiences, ideas, or feelings. Attending behavior validates the client and sends the message that the speaker and the topic are important—a significant contributor to building trust.

Despite the significance of attending skills for promoting communication, Sommers-Flanagan and Sommers-Flanagan observe that some typical attending behaviors can become obnoxious if overused. They cite repetitive head nods and "uh huh" or other vocalizations; intense eye contact; selective repetition of the client's last words; or too much mirroring (i.e., body positioning and gestures that match the client's actions) as examples of successful strategies that, if misused, may not have the desired effect of conveying genuine interest in the client. These habits may be distracting to clients or lead them to feel as if the advisor is attempting to over-analyze, intimidate, or manipulate them.[9]

Messages to Clients

Messages beyond the explicit content of spoken words are constantly being sent and received by financial planners and their clients. Consider the initial planner-client meeting. This engagement provides a unique opportunity to present an image to the client that will define the working relationship from that moment forward. First impressions are very important. How a client perceives a financial planner affects current and future interactions as well how they frame their communication approach. It is important for financial planners to take an unbiased look at the type of image they present. Unless a client perceives the environment as safe, comfortable, and representative of the firm, the client could misinterpret a planner's qualifications, skills, and abilities. Sommers-Flanagan and Sommers-Flanagan note that physical factors directly influence communication interactions.[10] They suggest that three elements should be present to make an interview setting effective: (a) privacy; (b) image; and (c) control.

Clients are often hesitant to reveal emotional and financial information with people they consider strangers. There are cultural and social prohibitions against talking about money. The client is also vulnerable, perhaps having to admit and acknowledge financial mistakes, poor judgment, or a lack of knowledge or experience. Clients often share information not previously shared with a spouse or partner or viewpoints that differ from the spouse or partner's. For this reason, attention to the privacy and sensitivity of the planner-client relationship should be reflected in the design of the office environment.

Viewed strategically, the purpose of client meeting spaces is to send a message of competence, order, diligence, professionalism, and confidentiality. Regardless of office design, it is important that the office or room where an interview occurs offer soundproofing so that clients cannot hear others nor be heard in adjacent spaces. Other planning personnel should exhibit care in the types of conversations or sharing of client information that can be overhead in the office. It may be appropriate to provide a private exit or meeting facility for clients, especially if the office is busy and the work being done is confidential or for highly visible members of the community who desire privacy. Recall from Chapter 2 that confidentiality is often a principle of ethical conduct, and that safeguards to maintain the privacy and security of client information are mandated practice standards for financial professionals.

Traditionally, financial planners have taken their office design cues from the banking industry. This explains why many financial planning and private banking offices are decorated with dark, heavy, traditional-looking furniture and fixtures. The look of dark cherry or mahogany with subdued lighting, for example, is thought to create a mood of confidence, trust, and stability, as well as signaling that the financial planner is a successful practitioner. Some clients prefer this type of office environment, but other clients have a preference for a more informal setting or the uncluttered look of a modern office environment. Assuming that an office provides optimal privacy, it is important for clients to feel comfortable with the image an office conveys. Just as when counselors from other helping professions work with clients, it is essential for financial planners to cultivate a feeling of trust.

One of the best ways to do this is by designing the office and client meeting spaces to effectively balance professional formality with casual comfort. Focusing on ways to reduce client stress is an effective method for increasing comfort and trust. Although not as widely applied in financial planning settings as it should be, a customary financial therapy technique involves removing physical barriers between a planner and the client. Traditionally, financial planners have met with clients, especially during initial client prospecting meetings, around a small office or larger conference table. The planner usually sits on one side of the table, and the client sits across from the planner. Although this meeting arrangement is quite common, this approach tends to increase client stress levels. The table acts as a barrier between planner and client. Clients often sense barriers as limiting open communication. Research has revealed a directly negative association between client stress and the perceived trustworthiness of the financial planner.[11]

One way to reduce client stress is to remove barriers between financial planners and their clients.[12] Figure 3.1 illustrates a possible meeting room arrangement. The openness between planner and client makes this meeting environment effective in reducing client stress. Typically, the client sits on the couch. Note how the couch is positioned so the client's view cannot be distracted by windows. The financial planner, on the other hand, has a sweeping view of the room. The advisor might place a small clock on the table next to the couch as way to monitor the meeting time without making it obvious to the client. Also, the office space should contain live green plants and tasteful lamps and wall hangings.

Figure 3.1 Client Meeting Area Designed to Reduce Client Stress

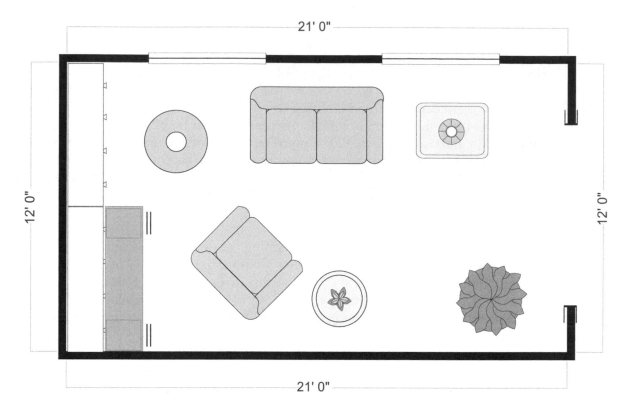

Some financial planners may look at Figure 3.1 and worry that they will not be able to show financial projections, use a computer or calculator, or have clients complete forms if they are sitting in a comfortable chair without a table. For some advisors, these may be valid points; however, if the goal of the meeting is to engage a client, promote client trust, and improve the likelihood of plan implementation, this type of meeting space can be very effective. For example, rather than illustrating planning recommendations using physical plans, charts, and figures, it might be possible to incorporate a flat-screen monitor on the wall facing the couch. In this way the planner can illustrate strategies and planning outcomes in a way that engages the client through an interactive communication process.

Although every planner needs to create a work space that maximizes performance, there are a few simple ways to communicate trust and professionalism to clients that do not interfere with a planner's work needs. It goes almost without saying, but the office environment should be neat, clean, and organized. Questions to ask include:

- Is the space aesthetically pleasing and well maintained?

- Are important diplomas and certificates framed and prominently displayed? Displaying too many professional, personal, or family accomplishments can send the wrong message to clients.

- Is a variety of refreshments (if offered) available?

- Is the financial planning staff professional, courteous, and knowledgeable?

As these questions indicate, there are many ways a financial planner can design an office environment to provide privacy and comfort—and project the desired professionalism to clients.

Control deals with creating an atmosphere that suggests competence, confidence, and leadership on the part of the professional. The arrangement should make data collection, communication, and interaction with the client and other staff, as appropriate, efficient and effective. An image of control can facilitate client acceptance of planning strategies and recommendations For example, as discussed above, it is possible to create an authoritative relationship by maintaining a barrier (e.g., a desk or other piece of office furniture) between the client and planner. If a table is needed, a more open relationship can be established by using a round or oval table. If used, the planner should position his or her chair at an angle, as shown in Figure 3.2.

Figure 3.2 Seating Arrangement when Meeting around a Table

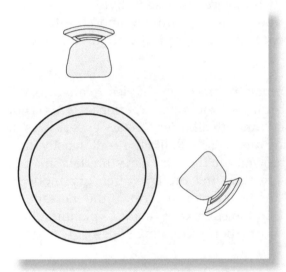

Control means that a financial planner has created an environment that offers privacy and comfort, and one that allows the planner to manage the information flow, the tempo of the interview, and the overall client experience. Sommers-Flanagan and Sommers-Flanagan report that seating arrangements can be used to control the setting, or context, of an interview.[13] They recommend that a client and advisor be seated at 90- to 150-degree angles from each other during interviews and client meetings. A 120-degree angle is sometimes preferred because this allows a planner to make eye contact with a client without having to look at the client all the time. Control issues extend as far as to where to place a clock in an office. Preferably, when seated, a client should not be able to see the clock; however, the planner should be able to see it without the client noticing. This control factor allows a planner to pace the flow of the meeting and manage time more effectively.

Preparing for a client meeting goes beyond managing the physical office environment. The way a financial planner dresses communicates a great deal about the firm and its practice management style. For example, some very successful firms have adopted a business casual policy for work. The work of the planners may be exceptional, but they have decided that promoting a comfortable environment for meeting and working with clients is more important than dressing in more formal and traditional business attire. Other planners feel that making a forceful first impression warrants wearing a suit every day. This rule is particularly true of those seeking to work with clients who expect their financial planner to exhibit outward success. It is important to remember that not all clients will appreciate a planner's personal or professional style. It is more important to work with clients who appreciate and are comfortable with the planner's business model than to attempt to be all things to all clients.

Developing a unified and consistent communication strategy is extremely important to attracting and retaining clients. Factors such as the appearance, demeanor, and verbal and nonverbal communication style of the planner and other office personnel, as well as the office environment, all contribute to the total impression the firm conveys to current and prospective clients. Planners who proceed with a client meeting without addressing these and other communication issues are taking a leap of faith that their message, both personal and professional, will be received and understood by clients. Some firms take great pride in the personalized service that clients always experience—from the moment they walk into the office and are greeted to the telephone and other avenues of client communication and interaction.

Assessing a Client's Information Processing and Communication Style

Through verbal, nonverbal, and paralanguage clues, clients divulge their preferred method of communicating and processing information. It is up to the planner to receive and interpret these signals and, to the extent possible, tailor communication appropriately to the client. The literature on information processing and learning styles is extensive. Fundamental to that study is the premise that individuals use three primary modes for learning and communication—**visual**, **auditory**, and **kinesthetic**—and that most individuals display a preference, although typically all three styles are used.

For simplicity's sake, consider these information processing styles relative to the primary sensory inputs: eyes; ears; and physical and emotional experiences. This is not to suggest that experiences are not processed through all three sensory experiences in addition to smell and taste. In fact, activating one sense will likely result in activation of the other senses, just as triggering a significant life memory can stimulate images, smells, or sounds. By recognizing and activating the preferred sensory mode, a message is more likely to be received and the listener, or receiver of the message, is more likely to feel validated or recognized. In the context of financial planning, it is easy to see how important recognition of information processing styles can be to the planner-client relationship.

Visual learners rely on their eyes and thus prefer to watch others complete a task or skill. They find figures, graphs, charts, videos, and PowerPoint presentations very effective. Those with a visual preference favor learning and communicating by reading and taking notes, and favor an organized and sequenced presentation of information. People who prefer this style of communication tend to read the entire plan, prospectus, or annual report and may take detailed notes during meetings. They are also likely to be quiet during a formal presentation of information, such as when a planner presents or explains the financial plan.

Auditory communicators rely on what they hear and may not directly observe the speaker or pay attention to the visual displays of information. Note taking is unlikely, although auditory learners are often quite talkative. They prefer lectures or the interaction of discussion and question-and-answer sessions. In general, a client who prefers the auditory method of communication would rather talk to the planner than read the plan.

A kinesthetic communicator prefers involvement in the learning process, such as touching, feeling, or manipulating something. Kinesthetic processing can involve affective, or emotional, reactions or physical actions—either of which engage the learner in the experience. Mental imagery through drawing pictures, brief descriptive writing tasks, or responding to projections about feelings (e.g., "How would you feel if you could not fund half of your child's college costs?") are sometimes used by planners to more fully involve kinesthetic learners and to tap into emotional issues or personality traits that affect financial goals or actions.

The physical aspect of kinesthetic processing involves direct action and activities. Kinesthetic clients would find reading a comprehensive plan tedious and not very helpful, while interacting with computer or Internet-based financial planning applications or calculators could be very insightful. They might prefer to simply jump in and address financial issues as they arise. Their approach to learning is more haphazard or random rather than organized and sequential like visual learners'. A planner might misinterpret fidgeting during plan presentation as a lack of interest or commitment, while it is really an indicator of the need to be involved. Role plays and games are preferred learning methods for this type of learner. Table 3.2 compares the three learning and communication styles.

Table 3.2 Information Processing and Communication Style Comparisons

Learning and Communication Preference	Visual	Auditory	Kinesthetic
Learns by listening		√	
Learns by watching others	√		
Learns by reading	√		
Learns by taking notes and writing	√		
Learns by doing			√
Makes decisions after conducting thorough research	√		
Makes decisions after listening to proposals		√	
Makes decisions based on life experiences			√

Although it is important to remember that most people have a preferred, or more effective, information processing style, some do not. Furthermore, everyone adapts to obtain information in a variety of ways. For example, someone who is primarily an auditory learner may also like to see data and conclusions presented visually. If one communication approach does not seem to be working, a financial planner should use another or multiple communication techniques. In such cases, the planner should attempt another type of communication or combine more than one style. Table 3.3 shows a sampling of words commonly used to indicate a person's preferred communication style.

Table 3.3 Words Associated with Communication Styles

Word or Phrase Reflecting Communication Style	Example	Visual	Auditory	Kinesthetic
Show	Show me what you mean.	√		
See	I see what you are saying.	√		
Look	Let me look it over.	√		
Perspective	That is an interesting perspective.	√		
Note	I need to make a note of that.	√		
Study	I would like to study those documents.	√		
Hear	I hear what you are saying.		√	
Sounds	That sounds like a great plan.		√	
Say	I understand what you are saying.		√	
Touch base	Let's touch base in a month.			√
Feel	I feel very good about this decision.			√
Handle	Can you handle the implementation?			√
Tie, found, follow	That certainly helps to tie things together. But I found her explanation harder to follow.			√

Effective communication strategies can provide a richer understanding of the client's experiential map and emotions that influence financial decision making and actions. This information is useful to the planner, but it may be even more useful to the client, who may never have had an opportunity to consider some of these life-influencing factors. As a part of the financial planning relationship, planners can help clients understand, adjust, expand, or revise their experiential maps and deeply held heuristic-based beliefs, or—if change is not to occur—to accept the consequences of the choice. This can happen by exploring the source of the heuristic or through education or new experiences that expand the client's perspective. It is important to recognize that clients act on the basis of the information they have; expanding that information might expand their options and empower them to choose new ones.

Opportunities abound for planner-client communication throughout the financial planning relationship. Direct exchange can occur during the discovery process or initial interview meetings between the client and planner, the actual narrative of the plan, the planner's presentation of the plan to the client, or the planner's explanation of how the planning process will improve the client's life, and the client's emotional responses that may arise from these exchanges. Indirect opportunities can occur through the Web site, client newsletters, periodic account updates or quarterly reports, or other informal means of communication, which increasingly involve social media. In other words, there are many opportunities for exchange and influence via various modes of communication. Planners who recognize a client's money scripts, experiential maps, and heuristics, and who incorporate multiple information processing styles in their various forms of client communication, significantly increase the likelihood that their message will be heard, understood, and acted upon.

A BASIC TOOL BOX FOR PLANNER-CLIENT COMMUNICATION

A financial planner must be knowledgeable of the advantages, disadvantages, and appropriate uses of a variety of financial products and strategies—what might be referred to as the financial "tools of the trade." It is equally important—many would argue more important—to have a tool box of communication strategies. Effective use of those strategies enables a planner to gain a window into the client's world and empower the client to share the view.

Clients and planners, like everyone else, view the world differently. Too often, people assume that their view is correct and shared by others. In fact, everyone has, in effect, an **experiential map**, which is used to help explain and define the world around them. Experiential maps are based, in part, on heuristics. A **heuristic** is a cognitive shortcut that can be used to simplify a difficult decision. (For more information on heuristics, see Chapter 4.) Thus, an experiential map is based on the notion that individuals do what is best for them using past experience and knowledge as their guide.

Habits are one example of a heuristic, while strongly held beliefs or conclusions can also represent heuristics. If someone, for instance, has consistently lost money buying and selling stock, there may be a strongly held heuristic that says stock equals loss. This person's experiential map suggests that investing in stocks is imprudent and fruitless, whereas the planner, with greater knowledge and experience of market trends, knows that this heuristic is not true. A financial planner who works with this kind of client runs the risk of miscommunication and perhaps an unsatisfying planner-client relationship, because both parties may struggle to change the view of the other.

Similar to the concepts of heuristics and experiential maps are **money scripts**, or what Klontz, Kahler, and Klontz describe as unconscious beliefs about money, formed in childhood, typically unexplored as adults, and only partially true.[14] Yet these money scripts, expressed through beliefs, attitudes, and expectations, influence client behavior. If a client's beliefs, attitudes, and expectations are not thoroughly explored, a planner may draw incorrect conclusions about the client's willingness to implement recommendations or to accept the professional judgment of the planner. Furthermore, without an understanding of these seemingly unrecognized factors that can directly and indirectly influence a client's behavior, change may be impossible.

Thus, a significant contribution of the advisor-client relationship is inquiry, or planner-guided discovery. Students and novice planners often assume that the purpose of this discovery is for the planner to gain information about the client, and this is a secondary purpose. But the primary objective is to increase a client's self-awareness through a better understanding of developmental or cultural experiences that shape the individual and provide a context for life decisions—including those involving money.

Just as a planner must recognize the advantages, disadvantages, and appropriate uses of each of the financial tools of the trade, the same is true of the tool box of communication strategies. Communication is used to initiate, build, foster, maintain, and enrich the planner-client relationship. Basic tools of communication focus on effective strategies for listening, clarifying, questioning, and using silence. Learning to use a variety of communication tools makes the process more interesting and less predictable and provides the fuel for a planning relationship that promotes action and, when necessary, change.

Listening

Two important ratios should serve as the foundation of any discussion on listening. First, people have two ears and two eyes but only one mouth. That ratio of 4:1 should guide most communication. Second, the typical **rate** of speaking and listening ranges from 125 to 400 words per minute, but most people think at a rate of 1,000 to 3,000 words per minute. Without a concerted effort, boredom or faster-paced thinking will drown out the spoken words and listening will give way to hearing. Hearing, however, is not listening, although the two are often confused. Real listening, or **active listening**, involves the ears as well as the face, the body, the mind, and the heart. The total engagement of the listener makes active listening a learned skill built on discipline and self-control that permits the listener to ignore mental "self-talk" and truly focus on the speaker.

Similar to the concept of attending, active listening involves both verbal and nonverbal communication. Active listening does not require agreement; however, through a combination of facial expressions, posture, and gestures the planner communicates understanding, interest, acceptance and empathy—even if the planner's initial response is to disagree. These physical efforts, involving face and body, support active listening. By truly focusing on the client, a planner is better equipped to combine other communication strategies to help the client explore and amplify the experiential map, heuristics, money scripts, or feelings surrounding an issue. It is important that the planner avoid interrupting the speaker, or prejudging the situation and finishing the client's sentences. Instead, the planner can be most helpful by helping the client explore a topic systematically. These efforts engage the planner's mind in listening. An open mind is necessary, as is a concerted effort to limit environmental distractions or other mental self-talk that diverts attention from the client.

By engaging the heart when listening, a planner is challenged to be empathetic and to fully assume the client's perspective —even when their viewpoints diverge. For example, why would a client with significant wealth and an annual salary of $250,000 strongly assert that he has no intention of paying for four years of college education for his children? The planner's role is not to agree or to change the client's attitudes and feelings; instead, the planner's role is to use communication techniques to explore the surrounding issues in an effort to inform the planning process. Furthermore, it may be necessary to act as mediator, as when the planner negotiates a discussion between a husband, who refuses four years of total funding, and the wife, who does not want the child to be constrained by a job during college or debt after college. Empathetically exploring and assuming the client's perspective leads to better understanding and acceptance of the client's feelings, values, and beliefs— by both the planner and the spouse, partner, or extended family in the case of multigenerational planning. Acceptance, not personal agreement, precludes judgment that could negatively affect or destroy the relationship with the client or within the family.

Attention to the spoken as well as the emotional message is a hallmark of active listening. But not every planner-client exchange requires empathetic listening. Straightforward exchanges regarding factual or quantitative issues (e.g., the client's family, health, employment, or financial status) are unlikely to have emotional overtones, although a planner should be sensitive to verbal or nonverbal messages that suggest that a topic is potentially emotional or stressful. However, the discussion of qualitative issues (e.g., the client's personal and social dimensions, including goals, personality, interests, attitudes, and values) will likely require the planner to assume the role of active listener. In other situations, the emotions will be apparent and the obvious reason for the communication.

Individuals, be they clients or prospective clients, tend to seek the help of financial planners when one or more of five emotions is present: (1) anger; (2) anxiety; (3) fear; (4) disappointment; and (5) enthusiasm.[15] Dealing with what Weisinger calls emotionally charged clients is one of the most challenging aspects of being a financial planner. Although it is often easy to tell whether someone is emotionally charged (e.g., they tell you they are angry or fearful), sometimes the only way to know is to evaluate the way in which the person is communicating. Clues to emotionality include facial expressions and paralanguage (i.e., the rate, tone, and volume of speech). Table 3.4 illustrates communication clues that indicate whether a person is emotionally stressed.

Table 3.4 Communication Clues of Emotional Stress

Clue	Indicator of Emotional Stress
Tone of voice	✓ Higher than normal pitch
Volume of voice	✓ Raised ✓ Very low
Rate of speech	✓ Faster than normal ✓ Slower than normal
Facial expression	✓ Frown ✓ Pursed lips ✓ Tears
Body gestures	✓ Arms folded across chest ✓ Use of index finger to point at advisor ✓ Covering face with hands

In the end, the best strategy is to simply be quiet and listen—whether working with emotionally charged clients or clients who are trying to explore and identify emotional triggers within their experiential maps or money scripts. In other words, practice active listening. Rather than push forward in awkward situations or attempt to change the topic, the most effective financial planners allow clients to talk. A planner can use communication strategies to interpret and steer a conversation or systematically explore an issue, but in almost all cases, it is best to allow the client to talk freely and openly.

Clarification

Many types of verbal communication strategies can be used when working with clients, but five stand out as particularly useful. Each of these strategies signals to the client that the planner is listening, but moreover that the planner is taking an active role in the communication process. Restating, paraphrasing, summarizing, reflecting emotions, and mirroring are related in that the skills are used to reflect content, emotion, or both through verbal and nonverbal communication. Although clarification of content is important to the planner to ensure accurate understanding of the message, clarification of content also confirms that the advisor is interested and gives the client permission to continue. Using the client's name in statements reflecting content or emotion is a recommended practice that shows sensitivity and promotes trust.

Sometimes an effective strategy involves **restating** a client comment. With restatement, the planner repeats the main or primary thought of a message in a condensed or more direct way. If a client states that

> "I want to save money for my child's college expenses, but I don't see how I can do that and save for retirement at the same time,"

it may be appropriate to restate the comment back to the client. A restatement might include remarking that,

> "You would like to save for college and retirement ... and it would be helpful if a solution could be found to accomplish both."

The motto with restatement is, "Use the speaker's words." It is important to avoid sounding like a parrot while still accomplishing the central objectives of fully engaging the client in communication and clarifying the message. It is important to acknowledge that the restatement is more for the client's benefit than the advisor's, because the topics explored—either individually or with couples, partners, or other family members—may not have been discussed or the personal views may not have been expressed previously.

The second strategy involves **paraphrasing**, or restating a client's comment, suggestion, or concern. With paraphrasing, the motto is, "Use your own words." To paraphrase, reword the basic message in a concise and simple statement. Then check for a nonverbal or verbal cue from the client about the accuracy of the interpretation. Suppose a client says that

"I'm just not sure what to do. I know that I need to be saving for Omar's education, but the account balance in my 401(k) seems pitifully small."

A paraphrase approach would have the planner state

"You're concerned about accomplishing the two goals of funding education and retirement."

If the paraphrase is accurate, as an indication that both the client and advisor understood the client is likely to respond with "Yes!" or "That's exactly what I think (or feel)...." If the client is presenting a mixed or double message, perhaps about the commitment to increased savings for goals *and* a reluctance to review lifestyle issues to increase cash flow, a paraphrased statement offers the planner an opportunity to reflect the discrepancy and better gauge the client's response.

In other cases it is may be appropriate for the planner to **summarize** the client's comments, or to ask the client to summarize or identify major issues. Summaries can be made after an extended discussion between client and planner, following longer remarks, or after unrelated comments by the client. Summarizing focuses on the main ideas but integrates them into a more cohesive reflection of the discussion. Summaries are used to indicate movement or progress, as from one discussion subject to another or from one session to another. Summaries can occur naturally at the end of a meeting or at the beginning of a new session. In the latter case, the previous meeting would generally be summarized, or perhaps the results of that meeting would be summarized relative to the actions taken subsequently by the planner or client. For example,

"At our previous meeting we discussed your wishes for the distribution of your estate and agreed to.... In addition you were going to draft a list of all personal property that you would like to distribute to your children and grandchildren. Let's begin our meeting by reviewing that list. Then, we'll review our other plans in preparation for the meeting with the estate attorney later this week."

A summary at the end of the meeting can also be used as the foundation for identifying tasks, responsibilities, or behaviors to be completed by the planner or client. A summary at the end of the meeting can also be used to focus attention on unfinished business or unresolved dilemmas that require the client's consideration or discussion with others.

With practice, restating, paraphrasing, and summarizing can become useful tools for client interviews and discovery sessions, despite the fact that aside from summarizing, the skills may initially feel unnatural. A more advanced skill, both in terms of practice and effective use with clients, involves reflecting emotions instead of, or in conjunction with, only the message content. As technicians, planners and other professionals are often criticized for focusing too much on the content or rational dimension of the message and ignoring the emotional, presumably irrational dimension of the message.

This is true for several reasons. Cultural and gender biases influence the decision, because some cultures, such as Asians or Asian Americans, discourage emotional displays and value the restraint of feelings.[16] Women are typically believed to be more emotional and more sensitive to emotional messages then men. There is also the sheer difficulty of recognizing and "naming" the feelings or emotional state of another individual, beyond the obvious demonstrations of anger, sadness, or happiness. Empathy, or truly trying as a listener to put oneself in the speaker's world, may not be a natural response, but with awareness and practice it can be achieved. The following are examples of reflection of emotion:

"Sounds like you feel _____."

"I guess you must feel _____."

"You sound _____."

A typical response to practicing the reflection of feelings is, "What if I'm wrong?" Although sensitivity to another is always a concern, whether the reflection is right or wrong it demonstrates to the client a sincere and genuine desire to understand the client's perspective. Therefore, this strategy promotes a stronger relationship. Another outcome is to help the client to identify, accept and explore feelings. This can be accomplished regardless of accuracy, because the client has an opportunity to correct the advisor. Advisors are cautioned that reflecting feelings should be used for all feelings, whether positive, negative, or uncertain, and that time must be allowed for both advisor and client to deal with the ensuing emotions and discussion. This is true even if the emotions are directed toward the advisor.

Some planners use a mirroring technique to enhance planner-client communication. **Mirroring** refers to reflecting both the client's verbal and nonverbal communication. The advisor's choice of words is one example of mirroring. A knowledgeable client may use very specific or technical language, whereas less knowledgeable clients may try to make associations between more familiar concepts and the ones presented to them in the plan. The planner should "match" the client's language, just as the planner might match a client's more formal or relaxed posture. However, excessive mirroring can be distracting, and if the planner's attempts are too overt the client may find the technique offensive. This communication strategy is another example of building a connection with the client by establishing quite clearly that the planner is indeed listening to the client.

Mastering these clarification techniques, as well as other strategies recommended in this chapter, enhances planner-client communication, but more importantly it contributes to a stronger planner-client relationship. Use of these techniques also accomplishes the following goals:

- Communicates empathy, understanding, acceptance, warmth, and a willingness to develop a personal but professional relationship with the client;

- Fosters mutual trust and collaboration, which can facilitate decision making as well as the framing of goals and objectives and the selection of recommendations and suggest methods for implementing and monitoring the plan;

- Supports continued exploration of a topic, issue, emotion or goal, which typically encourages the speaker to add detail through more introspection;

- Expands the planner's knowledge and understanding of a client's experiential map, heuristics, money scripts, or emotions;

- Establishes a feedback loop between client and planner; and

- Encourages continuation of the discussion and promotes the planner-client relationship.

It is also important to note that all of these strategies promote working *with* the client and not *for* the client. This is an important distinction for several reasons. First, long-term planning relationships are built on trust and an attitude of shared responsibility. This can be accomplished only if the client is comfortable with fully sharing the information needed, and doing so honestly and without regard for socially acceptable or expected answers. Second, it is important that clients accept responsibility for the decisions and actions that affect their financial future. Third, an attitude of collaboration and shared responsibility makes it easier for an advisor to manage the client's expectations and to fully acknowledge that the plan was built on sound judgment but that the outcomes cannot be predicted or guaranteed by the planner. Intellectually that statement cannot be disputed, but the emotional distress of a major market loss can change that perspective.

Prospective financial planning clients are often categorized as delegators, validators, and self-directed or do-it-yourselfers. In fact the latter group rarely becomes financial planning clients because they rely on their own knowledge and ability to make decisions and coordinate the products or services of other professionals, as needed. If they do become financial planning clients, the relationship may be difficult because the client may be hesitant to accept or follow the plan. Validators are do-it-yourselfers who want an advisor to give a second opinion, evaluate and confirm the plan of action chosen, or occasionally provide advice. Delegators are ideal clients because they engage in the financial planning process but are willing, because of a lack of time, interest, or knowledge, to relinquish control to an advisor who is authorized to act with or without the client's consent (i.e., to give the advisor discretion) to implement the plan.

Communication strategies that promote working with the client are important when initially ascertaining the client's needs and screening for whether the client is a good match for the planner's firm; when working collaboratively with the client during the planning process; and also when sustaining a long-term planner-client relationship through life's challenges. In other words, identifying the do-it-yourselfers and wishing them success is a valuable investment, as is the skill to guide a client deftly through financial and nonfinancial issues.

Obtaining Information through Questioning

Questions are a staple of everyday conversation, but they must be used carefully in a planning situation. Too many questions can hinder the relationship; responsibility for the entire process shifts to the planner because of the implicit message that the planner is "in charge" and will ask what is necessary. In the worst case, too many questions become more like an interrogation with the technical expert in search of a quick resolution. Planners are cautioned not to use questions as an alternative for making a statement, such as

> "Wouldn't you agree that making periodic contributions to a § 529 plan is the best alternative?"

Although, on the one hand, the question may be meant to solicit the client's involvement in decision making, on the other hand the question is a safer position for the planner than clearly stating

> "Opening and funding a § 529 plan with periodic contributions is the best alternative for your situation."

Care also must be taken to avoid questions that have no apparent answer or appear to be insulting, such as

> "Why didn't you sign up for the insurance at work?"

Whereas the intent of the question may have been sincere exploration of the factors that led to that decision, the question can have an accusatory tone. Better options might be

> "Could you tell me more about your decision not to sign up for the insurance at work?" *or*

> "What factors contributed to your decision not to sign up for the insurance at work?"

Finally, planners must be careful not to ask questions that solicit the socially acceptable answer from the client, but not the client's true feelings or behaviors. Because of cultural, ethnic, and societal expectations surrounding money and its use, planners must be particularly careful that the planner-client relationship is honest and trustworthy; communication techniques, especially questions, are critical to establishing that rapport. Typically, two types of probing questions, what Pulvino and Pulvino refer to as level-I probes and level-II probes, are helpful when seeking information.[17] Both types of question are similar in that each type may begin with interrogatives, such as who, what, when, where, why, or how. However, the scope and intent of the question and the typical response elicited can be quite different.

A **level-I probe** is a question used to obtain factual client information. Answers to level-I probes are verifiable and often limited to providing "yes" or "no" responses or giving replies based on data or other known facts. For this reason, this type of question is commonly referred to as a "closed-end" question. Questions that begin with "Do," "Did," "When," and "Where" typically generate level-I responses. Variations focus on *you*, such as "Did you," "Are you," "Have you," or "Could you." While a level-I probe is a useful tool during initial client data gathering, responses to level-I probes are less useful for understanding a client's motives for maintaining or changing a financial situation. However, level-I probes can be helpful to limit the responses of a client who is very talkative or a client whose excessive responses limit others' participation (e.g., spouse, partner, or others).

Level-II probes are used to delve deeper into a client's knowledge and attitudes. A level-II probe is the most effective method for obtaining information from a client about feelings, emotions, or reactions to a goal or some other aspect of the planning process. Also known as "open-ended" questions, level-II probes invite exploration. One way to solicit level-II responses is to ask questions that begin with "What," "When," "Where," "How," and "Why." Level-II probes can be very useful in determining a client's personal and financial goals and objectives or when significant life events have brought about changes that could affect the client's financial situation or planning efforts.

However, planners are cautioned about careful use of "why" questions, which may not be as effective as questions that begin with "what" or "how." "Why" questions can become tedious, and accusatory, and they are simply difficult to answer; whereas questions phrased more carefully encourage clarification, expansion, or focus—all of which serve to better inform the planning process for both planner and client. Another caution is also warranted. According to Evans, Hearn, Uhlemann, and Ivey, asking questions is more common to the European American culture, and other cultural groups find direct questions intrusive and somewhat disrespectful. A more indirect approach, such as a discussion of the issues in question, is more effective for gathering information.[18]

Silence

Although questioning may be a staple of normal conversation, silence is not. Silence can be golden (or so the old adage says), but most people are uncomfortable with it. Sometimes, however, silence can be an effective tool to help a client continue processing and discussing a difficult, emotional, or important topic. This may be true because people do not like to sit in silence, so they tend to continue talking. Or the discussion may have truly allowed the individual the time and opportunity—perhaps for the first time—to fully consider a topic and the silence is simply an extension of that reflection or introspection.

Allowing silence, for perhaps 5 to 10 seconds, is a way to encourage a client to provide more detailed information about a situation or to resolve an important issue without additional questions or comments. Furthermore, silence benefits the planner by allowing time for careful attention to nonverbal cues, reflection on the client's message, or the crafting of clarification statements or questions to continue the exploration. Most important is not to interrupt naturally occurring silence, but to foster it through nonverbal messages such as gestures (head nodding), comfortable eye contact, simple vocalizations ("um-hum," "yes") or the restatement of a key word. The use of silence as a communication technique can be a challenge, but the benefits are well worth the effort to become comfortable with the uncomfortable.

Putting It All Together

Rattiner stresses five important attributes for effective planner communication.[19] First, good communicators are genuine and allow clients to see the real person, not just the planner. Second, good communicators listen with empathy and use paraphrasing to convey understanding. All good planners tune into their clients' needs and goals, spoken or otherwise. These planners attempt to understand the different communication styles that clients use to send messages. Third, the best planners display a positive attitude at all times. The planner is always looking for positive outcomes, which often requires shifting a client's focus away from apparent weaknesses to hidden strengths. In other words, they see the glass half full and not always half empty. Fourth, a great communicator is also able to establish rapport with a client. This does not mean that the planner is necessarily charismatic. If a planner is genuine, it is natural to communicate in a caring and empathetic way. Fifth, good communicators ask open-ended questions that help clients convey information, analyze the situation, and develop an appropriate course of action. But in the end, some of the best advice may simply be to "shut up and listen." Remember the ratio: one mouth, but two ears and two eyes.

ONGOING PLANNER-CLIENT COMMUNICATION

The communication skills that support personal, or face-to-face, communication can serve as an important foundation for other dimensions of planner-client communication. These skills are critical to the formative work that the planner and client must complete as part of the planning process. In addition, planners must master the other communication skills necessary to initiate and manage client relationships. Specifically, three areas of planner communication should not be overlooked and are worthy of continued study and skill development.

First is responding effectively to client resistance or objections. Granted, this type of communication will most likely occur face-to-face, and some of the same skills of active listening, clarification, questioning, and silence are applicable. However, this dimension of planner-client communication warrants special consideration because of its significance. For many planners and clients, "closing the deal" has a negative connotation, but failure to close the deal can have far-reaching implications for both.

Second is the rapidly expanding use of electronic communication through email, Web sites, webinars, videoconferencing, and social media, which combine the characteristics of personal communication and in some cases more impersonal marketing efforts. Financial advisors, using a variety of electronic communication and social media platforms, can give themselves the best opportunity to connect with their current clients and a wide array of prospective clients. Some of the major social media platforms include LinkedIn, Facebook, Twitter, and various blogs.

Third is marketing, which can be just as intimidating as a client's rejection of a plan or recommendation. But as overwhelming as these communication challenges may appear, the good news is that there is a wealth of expert wisdom to guide the student or novice planner beyond the brief summaries that follow.

Resistance and Objections

The financial salesperson may not be a good counselor; nor is the counselor likely to be a good salesperson. But one fact is unavoidable: financial planners *must market and sell products, services, or both*. When it comes right down to it, the primary role of a financial planner is to help clients optimize their financial situation to meet short- and long-term personal and financial goals. But that will not happen unless the planner can effectively provide products and/or services at a price that is satisfactory to the client and that will sustain the planner's business in the long term. This is true whether the advisor is an independent planner or the salaried employee of a larger company. Central to the business relationship is the ability to prepare and present the plan in a way that cements the planner-client relationship.

One of the best ways to ensure client implementation of recommendations is to use a combination of communication strategies and effective follow up. Listening and nonverbal affirmations do not mean that the client is willing to implement recommendations. If a client presents objections or resistance, it is important to listen quietly and hear the client out. There is no need to jump to defend a recommendation until the client has voiced all objections. Communication techniques such as paraphrasing and summarizing can then be used to isolate the client's reservations. When isolating the issues it is prudent to focus on one objection at a time, but in no way should the planner willingly accept a client's objection without first attempting to fully understand its emotional and intellectual underpinnings. Active listening, clarification techniques, and level-II probes may be useful for both planner and client to fully amplify any objections.

An objection may be driven by the client's experiential map, heuristics, money script, or a broad range of emotions. Objections can also be based on a client's comfort level, which may need to be modified if financial objectives are to be met. Client education might be one approach; however, most important is for the planner to fully acknowledge, respect, and demonstrate understanding of the client's position. Replacing the planner's arguments, rationales, and facts with empathetic listening for the client's view can be an important step. It is said that good communicators and good salespeople are good listeners. Helping the client explore the emotions that underlie an objection as well as the emotions that make the goal or objective important is likely to be more productive than using a purely factual or logical tactic.

Focusing on the benefits of a recommendation or some possible middle ground for accomplishing the goal can also help the client weigh the risks and rewards of the recommendation more fully. On first consideration, a client's reasons for not buying life insurance (e.g., my spouse will remarry or my in-laws will help out) may be humorous or simply evasive. But there may be a need for the client to fully acknowledge the sad reality of what life might be like without insurance to replace lost income. At this juncture the difference between salesperson and counselor or coach may become most evident.

If a trustworthy, genuine relationship has been forged as the foundation of the planning process, it will ground the comparison of risks and rewards. "Pulling the heart strings," or questioning the client regarding their feelings or self-assessment if not prepared for an untimely death by purchasing life insurance could be viewed as sincere concern or simply good salesmanship—contingent on the planner-client relationship. Furthermore, a planner's genuine concern and courage to confront the client could lead to a compromise recommendation acceptable to the client, but that still provides some level of goal achievement or client protection advocated by the advisor.

Finally, it is important to keep the dialogue open to fully explore the client's inaction or confusion. Sometimes the process of presenting to a client is quick and easy; at other times, however, explaining the complexities of a financial proposal can take time. In addition to other communication attributes, patience can strengthen the communication process. It is essential to be patient with clients as they work through the rational, emotional, and financial aspects of a plan. Rather than rush a client to make a rash decision that may later be reversed, it is often better to patiently work with a client to answer questions and create an environment of trust, which will lead to greater client commitment. For more information on presenting a financial plan to clients, see Chapter 9.

Electronic Communication

Electronic communication has dramatically changed the way financial planners interact with current and prospective clients. Although keeping abreast of the rapidly changing opportunities this medium presents and their usefulness to individual planners, everyone seems to agree on one thing: planners must adopt technologies that enhance communication to remain competitive. Client newsletters can be made available by mail, email, or online. Tools such as email, Twitter, and blogs allow for more frequent communication. This can ensure that clients are kept up to date and offered informative content, but the easy access can offer planners a quick and effective means to allay clients' fears and avoid panic responses to market activity or quick tips.

Electronic communication is not only efficient, it is also less expensive, which can translate into reduced fees for clients. Billing and reporting can be done using email or password protected Web sites, and clients can make use of private Web pages and electronic vaults to organize and store their records. There are drawbacks to technology, however. Planners lose communication clues with electronic communication, but videoconferencing and periodic meetings or telephone conversations offer alternatives for more personal dialogue.

Social media also have the potential to change the way that advisors prepare for client meetings. Although client relationship management software is a valuable tool for tracking client data and client interactions, it is no longer the sole source of client information. Planners have access to many more details about a client's life simply by looking at their client's social profile pages, such as Facebook or LinkedIn or by following Twitter to learn about a client's interests. Information posted on a Facebook page about family news or a new interest or hobby could suggest new planning needs that a planner should prepare to discuss. Likewise, a LinkedIn update on a professional change could prompt the need for planning for a change in retirement strategies or other employee benefits. Although these sources can help planners be more proactive in serving clients and adapting their plans to changing life events, planners must use discretion when incorporating such information into meetings. Clients choose to be open with the information placed on such social networking pages; thus, it is important to use this information, not more private information generated from search engines, to connect with a client.

Marketing: Initiating and Managing the Planner-Client Relationship

Multiple modes of communication are particularly important when marketing a planning practice. **Marketing** involves identifying the need for a product or service and then determining how to deliver that product or service responsively to consumers. Marketing for financial planners can be thought of in two ways: **prospecting** and **servicing**. Ideally, both should elicit action from the recipient. When prospecting for clients, a financial planner's primary goal is to enhance visibility and name recognition while informing potential clients of available services. Servicing (also known as relationship marketing) involves nurturing or expanding existing relationships through periodic communication.

In financial planning, such communication might range from periodic account reporting to educational newsletters, or articles about a special or shared interest, or cards acknowledging a client's life event. From a client's perspective, all communication should be of some value to them and add value to the relationship; otherwise, the communication will be viewed as just another piece of junk mail, spam, or random solicitation. Although both prospecting and servicing are important, continuing communication with existing clients can result in the most beneficial marketing strategy of all: "word of mouth" or client referrals.

Table 3.5 shows a sampling of publications, forms, and actions that financial planners use to market a practice. Each requires written, verbal, or a combination of both communication skills to be effective. For example, a well-written, informative article or newsletter sent to current clients to educate them could also be shared with potential clients and will enhance the planner's credibility. By cross-linking social media sites, an article, news, or commentary, once launched on Facebook, could result in a status update on LinkedIn and a new tweet on Twitter. **Drip marketing**—defined as a continuous, recurring, or ongoing flow of letters, cards, articles, newsletters, or other marketing items that are being replaced by Twitter and blog postings—can be used for both prospecting and servicing. Because of the continuous attention, prospective clients could become clients. Thus, well-designed, client-appropriate drip marketing efforts can further solidify the planner-client relationship.

Marketing can also be categorized as direct or indirect marketing. **Direct marketing** (e.g., telephone calls, direct mailings, targeted seminars), or what FINRA typically refers to as "sales literature" because the message is targeted to a particular closed group of recipients, should have a personal touch because each recipient would like to feel as if the communication was meant just for them. Whether a planner has said something to them, handed them something, or mailed something to them, clients want to feel that they received something "special." **Indirect marketing** (e.g., Web sites, newspaper columns, television advertisements, mass media, article postings on Facebook or LinkedIn, or other networking sites), or what FINRA normally considers "advertising" because the message is spread broadly to an uncontrolled audience, typically has a more formal or general viewpoint. Although some tailoring is possible, a planner would want to generate widespread appeal.

Some planners expand their expertise and time by purchasing one or more marketing items from, or outsourcing their marketing efforts to, specialized providers.

Independent companies also offer social media marketing management for financial professionals. Other planners might choose not to use certain strategies, or they may find that some strategies simply are ineffective or no longer necessary as their reputation and referral network expands.

For planners who are not independent, some marketing materials might be provided by the parent company or other product providers. For example, Morgan Stanley has been recognized for its leadership in allowing its 17,000-plus advisors access to LinkedIn and Twitter for branding and as a news source, with certain restrictions. Because of the regulation of materials posted online, Morgan Stanley has prepared preapproved content and, for busy market days, preapproved research Tweets.[20] In all instances, marketing materials should be reviewed for accuracy, broad-based demographic appeal (unless a specific market segment is being targeted), and compliance-related issues. More information about the compliance and/or regulatory issues surrounding communication with the public is provided in Chapter 2.

Table 3.5 Financial Planning Marketing Strategies

Marketing Item	Communication Skill	Prospecting/ Servicing	Direct/Indirect
In-person			
Speeches	Oral and written	Prospecting	Direct
Community service or pro bono work	Oral and written	Both	Indirect
Telephone	Oral	Both	Direct
Periodic meetings with clients	Oral	Servicing	Direct
Seminars	Oral and written	Both	Direct
Trade show or other community business forum	Oral and written	Both	Indirect
Electronic			
Web-based videos	Written and oral	Both	Indirect
Email updates	Written	Servicing	Direct
Web sites	Written	Both	Indirect
CDs, videos, and DVDs	Written and oral	Both	Direct
LinkedIn account	Written	Prospecting	Indirect
Blogs/Tweets	Written	Both	Direct
Radio and TV shows	Oral	Prospecting	Indirect
Print			
Books	Written	Prospecting	Indirect
Professional, trade, or other articles	Written	Prospecting	Indirect
Cards of congratulations or recognition of other personal events	Written	Servicing	Direct
Brochures	Written	Servicing	Both
Newsletters	Written	Prospecting	Both
Drip marketing	Written	Servicing	Direct
Direct mail marketing	Written	Both	Direct
Print and on-air advertising	Written and oral	Prospecting	Indirect
Newspaper columns	Written	Prospecting	Indirect
Press releases	Written	Prospecting	Indirect

CHAPTER SUMMARY

The planner, office, client documents, marketing strategies, and even what is not said when using silence—in person or through social media—*communicate* to clients and potential clients. Considered from this broad perspective, it is easier to understand the complexity and significance of communication in the totality of the planner-client relationship. Attention to interpersonal communication strategies (e.g., the use of active listening, clarification, questioning, and silence) allows for an exchange of information, but more importantly it builds planner-client trust and rapport. Awareness of the importance of information-processing styles should influence oral and written client communication as well as marketing strategies and Web site design. Mastering the fundamental concepts introduced in this chapter will enable students and novice advisors to enhance their client relationships and establish a foundation for continued learning about the multifaceted application of communication to the process and practice of financial planning.

Learning Outcomes

1. Financial planning is built on sound technical knowledge of a range of financial products and services coupled with the quantitative skills necessary to analyze a client's situation. However, this perspective of financial planner as technician neglects the critical role of the client—the whole person, not merely the client's financial issues—as the foundation of the financial planning process. But the apparent differences between technician and counselor should not suggest that the traits associated with successful counseling are inapplicable to financial planning. In fact, the opposite is true. The way a counselor achieves communication breakthroughs with a client should be similar to how a financial planner optimizes communication with clients. Few financial planners have academic training in personality assessment, psychotherapy, or behavioral change theory—although attention to these applications within financial planning is on the rise. Increasingly, as planners incorporate life planning into their discovery process with clients, planners are incorporating more communication strategies to explore with clients their healthy and unhealthy relationship with money.

2. Communication goes well beyond a person's words. Relying solely or too much on the *words* used to relay information, the *content* of communication, can be misleading or even destructive to the message. Although content is important, the manner in which the words are delivered may be more important; therefore, body language and paralanguage are both crucial to the entire message being delivered and received. Body language that enhances the communication process, such as leaning forward to hear, creates the impression of active engagement with the other person. Additionally, the tone, rate, and volume of speech—paralanguage—are also extremely important cues that can contribute to or detract from the effectiveness of a planner's message. The ability to deliver a message with all forms of communication congruent is of paramount importance to effective communication and engendering client trust.

3. According to Sommers-Flanagan and Sommers-Flanagan, privacy, image, and control should be present in an interviewing environment because of the sensitive nature of the discussion between planner and client. Privacy is very important because clients must

feel relaxed about sharing very intimate details of their financial and personal lives. But in addition to privacy, creating an image of success, stability, and caring will also make the client feel more at ease with a planner. A blend of formal and comfortable has been shown to create the most relaxing yet trustworthy environment.

Finally a planner needs to convey confidence and an ability to control the environment. Control means that a financial planner has created an environment that offers privacy and comfort, and one that allows the planner to manage the information flow, the tempo of the interview, and the client's overall experience. The arrangement of the office should make data collection, communication, and interaction with the client and other staff, as appropriate, efficient and effective. An image of control can also facilitate client acceptance of planning strategies and recommendations.

4. There is a theory that individuals use three primary modes for learning and communication— visual, auditory, and kinesthetic—and that most individuals display a preference, although all three styles typically are used. Visual learners rely on their eyes and thus prefer to watch others complete a task or skill. They find figures, graphs, charts, videos, and PowerPoint presentations very effective. Auditory communicators rely on what they hear and may not directly observe the speaker or pay attention to the visual displays of information. Note taking is unlikely, although auditory learners are often quite talkative. A kinesthetic communicator prefers involvement in the learning process, such as touching, feeling, or manipulating something. Kinesthetic processing can involve affective, or emotional, reactions or physical actions—either of which engage the learner in the experience.

5. Planners and their clients are going to view the world differently and it should never be assumed that one view is correct and shared by others because everyone has an experiential map to explain and define the world around them. Experiential maps are based, in part, on cognitive shortcuts that can be used to simplify a difficult decision: heuristics. Thus, the experiential map is based on the notion that individuals do what is best for them using past experience and knowledge as their guide. Habits are one example of a heuristic and strongly held beliefs or conclusions represent another. Money scripts, or unconscious beliefs about money that are formed in childhood, also influence client behavior.

If a client's beliefs, attitudes, and expectations are not thoroughly explored, the planner may draw incorrect conclusions about the client's willingness to implement recommendations or accept the professional judgment of the planner. Furthermore, without an understanding of these seemingly unrecognized factors that can directly and indirectly influence a client's behavior, change may be impossible.

6. Active listening involves both verbal and nonverbal communication. Although active listening does not require agreement, through a combination of facial expressions, posture, and gestures a planner communicates understanding, interest, acceptance, and empathy— even if the planner's initial response is disagreement. These physical efforts, involving *heart*, *face*, and *body*, support active listening.

Five types of clarification techniques stand out as particularly useful: restating, paraphrasing, summarizing, reflecting emotion, and mirroring. Each of these strategies signals to the client that a planner is listening, but moreover that the planner is taking an active role in the communication process. With restatement, the main or primary thought of the message is repeated using the client's words. The second strategy involves paraphrasing, or rephrasing a client's comment, suggestion, or concern using the planner's words. Summarizing focuses on the main ideas, but serves to integrate them into a more cohesive reflection of the discussion. Summaries are used to indicate movement or progress, as from one discussion subject to another or from one session to another. Reflection of emotion or naming the client's feelings is a less natural, more advanced skill, but a powerful contributor to effective communication. Mirroring refers to reflecting both the client's verbal and nonverbal communication. The advisor's choice of words matched to the terminology used by the client is an example of mirroring.

Questions are a staple of everyday conversation, but they must be used carefully in a planning situation. Excessive use of questions can hinder the relationship; responsibility for the entire process shifts to the planner because of the implicit message that the planner is "in charge" and will ask what is necessary. Planners should gain experience using both level-I and level-II probes to fully collect client data and understand the client situation.

Sometimes, silence can be an effective tool to help a client continue processing and discussing a difficult, emotional, or important topic. Allowing silence is a way to encourage the client to provide more detailed information about a situation or to resolve an important issue without additional questions or comments.

7. Clients' objections are often the result of their experiential map, heuristics, money script, or broad range of emotions, but they can also stem from a client's comfort level. It is most important for a planner to fully acknowledge, respect, and demonstrate understanding of the client's position. Replacing arguments, rationales, and facts with empathetic listening for the client's view can be paramount. It is important to keep the dialogue open to fully explore a client's inaction or confusion. Sometimes the process of presenting to a client is quick and easy; at other times, however, explaining the complexities of a financial proposal can take time. In addition to other communication attributes, patience can strengthen the communication process.

8. It is important to use multiple modes of communication when marketing a planning practice. Marketing, both prospecting and servicing, involves identifying the need for a product or service and then determining how to deliver that product or service responsively to consumers. In financial planning, such communication might range from periodic account reporting to educational newsletters (print or online) or social media. From a client's perspective, all communication should be of some value to them and add value to the relationship.

Chapter Resources

The Financial Life Planning Institute (http://www.flpinc.com/).

Kay, Michael F. *The Business of Life: An "Inside-Out" Approach to Building a More Successful Financial Planning Practice*. Sunnyvale, CA: AdvisorPress, 2010.

Kinder, G. *Seven Stages of Money Maturity: Understanding the Spirit and Value of Money in your Life*. New York: Dell Publishing, 2000.

Kinder, G., and S. Galvan. *Lighting the Torch: The Kinder Method™ of Life Planning*. Denver, CO: FPA Press, 2006.

The Kinder Institute of Life Planning (http://www.kinderinstitute.com/index.html).

Klontz, B., R. Kahler, and T. Klontz. *Facilitating Financial Health: Tools for Financial Planners, Coaches, and Therapists*. Cincinnati, OH: National Underwriter Company, 2008.

Money Quotient® Putting Money in the Context of Life™ (http://moneyquotient.org/).

Parisse, A., and D. Richman. *Questions Great Financial Advisors Ask…and Investors Need to Know*. Chicago, Kaplan Publishing, 2006.

West, S., and M Anthony. *Your Client's Story: Know Your Clients and the Rest Will Follow*. Chicago, Kaplan Publishing, 2005.

Discussion Questions

1. Explain the convergence of roles required to be a financial planner.

2. What messages can eye contact convey? Why might this sometimes be misleading or incongruent?

3. How does attending improve a communicator's ability to read verbal and nonverbal messages?

4. Develop a list of methods for interacting with clients, noting for each the type of information processing or learning style for which it might be effective or ineffective. For example, email may be very effective for a visual learner, but ineffective for communicating important information to a client with a strong auditory or kinesthetic preference. Be creative in identifying different approaches to client interaction.

5. How should an advisor design the office to help clients feel comfortable about sharing information? Describe how the office environment can convey an image of trust and professionalism.

6. Compare and contrast an experiential map, heuristic, and money script. Give examples of how each might influence the financial planning process. How might they influence the way a client interprets a financial planner's recommendations?

7. Identify and briefly describe the cues a financial planner might use to identify an emotionally stressed client.

8. List and explain the communication skills typically used to clarify a client's story. For whose benefit is the story told?

9. Develop a list of 10 expected or unexpected life changes or events that financial planners can help a client prepare for or respond to. Identify at least five emotions or feelings that might surround each change. Challenge yourself to be more creative and descriptive by listing something other than basic emotions (e.g., happy, sad, lost). Why might a list of feeling words be of value to a student or novice planner?

10. Explain why questions beginning with the word "why" can be problematic in planner-client communication. Are "why" questions more commonly used as level-I or level-II probes?

11. Identify and describe the three categories of prospective financial planning clients.

12. List five strategies for overcoming a client's resistance or objections to a recommendation.

13. Compare and contrast the communication skills of listening and silence.

14. Explain how communication skills influence the way a financial planning practice is marketed.

15. Identify three marketing strategies used by financial planners and describe them as servicing or prospecting, direct or indirect, and whether based on oral or written communication. Try to identify strategies that are not listed in Table 3.5.

Notes

1. As noted in Chapter 1, for simplicity most comments throughout this book reference the client in the singular, although the plurality of couples, partners, families, or other legal entities should not be ignored. The content of this chapter is equally useful with one or more clients, but communicating with more than one client at a given time increases complexity and challenges the planner's ability to employ strategies that are effective and engage each client. Furthermore, it sometimes becomes necessary to promote communication between the clients, as well as between clients and planner.

2. H. J. Geis, "Toward a Comprehensive Framework Unifying All Systems of Counseling," in John Vriend (ed.). *Counseling Effectively in Groups* (Englewood Cliffs, NJ: Educational Technology Publications, 1973), 15.

3. H. J. Geis, 12.

4. George Kinder and Susan Galvan, *Lighting the Torch* (Denver, CO: FPA Press, 2006).

5. International Coach Federation, *What is ICF?* Available at http://www.coachfederation.org/.

6. David Dubofsky and L Sussman, "The Changing Role of the Financial Planner Part 1: From Financial Analytics to Coaching and Life Planning," *Journal of Financial Planning* August (2009): 48–57.

7. D. R. Evans, M. T. Hearn, M. R. Uhlemann, and A. E. Ivey, *Essential Interviewing*. (Belmont, CA: Brooks/Cole, Cengage Learning, 2011), 1.

8. R. Sommers-Flanagan and J. Sommers-Flanagan, *Clinical Interviewing*, 4th ed. (New York: Wiley, 2009), 55.

9. Sommers-Flanagan and Sommers-Flanagan, *Clinical Interviewing*, 58.

10. Sommers-Flanagan and Sommers-Flanagan, *Clinical Interviewing*, 31–32.

11. J. E. Grable and S. L. Britt, "Assessing Client Stress and Why It Matters to Financial Advisors," *Journal of Financial Service Professionals* 3 (2012): 39–46.

12. S. Britt and J. Grable, "Your Office May Be a Stressor: Understand How the Physical Environment of Your Office Affects Financial Counseling Clients," *The Standard* 30 no. 2 (2012): 5, 13.

13. Sommers-Flanagan and Sommers-Flanagan, *Clinical Interviewing*, 34.

14. B. Klontz, R. Kahler, and T. Klontz, *Facilitating Financial Health* (Cincinnati, OH: National Underwriter Co., 2008), 14.

15. H. Weisinger, *The Emotionally Intelligent Financial Advisor* (Chicago: Dearborn, 2004).

16. Evans et al., *Essential Interviewing*, 103.

17. Charles J. Pulvino and Carol A. Pulvino, *Financial Counseling: A Strategic Approach*, 3rd ed. (Madison, WI: Instructional Enterprises, 2010).

18. Evans et al., *Essential Interviewing*, 60.

19. J. H. Rattiner, *Getting Started as a Financial Planner* (Princeton, NJ: Bloomberg Press, 2000), 255–257.

20. Janet Levaux, "Morgan Stanley Gives Advisors the OK for Twitter, LinkedIn," *AdvisorOne*. Available at http://www.advisorone.com/2012/06/26/morgan-stanley-gives-advisors-the-ok-for-twitter-l?utm_source=dailywire062612&utm_medium=enewsletter&utm_campaign=dailywire&t=life-planning-ltc&page=2.

Chapter 4

Decision Making

Learning Objectives

1. Explain the significance of understanding a decision and for studying decision making in the context of financial planning.

2. Describe and apply a general model of decision making.

3. Explain how decision-making rules can be applied in the decision-making process.

4. Understand and apply the traditional decision-making approach and probabilities, including the use of stochastic and deterministic modeling.

5. Explain the three themes that frame the scope of behavioral finance and cite behavioral finance biases common to each.

6. Recognize and explain how behavioral finance concepts can affect the decisions and choices made in the financial planning process.

7. Identify and explain threats to the decision-making process.

8. Summarize how uncertainty, intuition, and habits affect decision making.

153

Key Terms

Aversion to loss

Behavioral finance

Complacency

Decision

Decision making

Defensive avoidance

Deterministic model

Financial numeracy

Framing

Gambler's fallacy

Habit

Herding

Heuristics

Hot hand fallacy

House money

Ignoring the base rate

Illusion of validity

Intuition

Maximization

Mental accounting

Mental accounts

Objective probabilities

Optimization

Overconfidence bias

Panic reactions

Prospect theory

Regression to the mean

Regret avoidance

Representativeness

Satisficing

Stochastic modeling

Subjective probabilities

Traditional decision-making approach

WHAT IS A DECISION?

Financial planners—like medical, legal, and other professionals—are charged daily with making decisions with, or on behalf of, clients that will affect their lives—and perhaps even that of the professional. But the complexity of the relationships, the multitude of factors affecting the decisions, and the uncertainty surrounding choice outcomes make decision making a fundamental financial planning tool. In addition, the element of time underlies all financial planning decisions. For example, judgments regarding the choice and funding of retirement savings vehicles, although made today, can influence outcomes for decades into the future. Then there is the issue of the number of decision makers. A decision can involve one or many people and can affect the decision maker or others, immediately or in the future. Cumulatively, all of a financial planner's decisions determine whether a practice will be successful for the planner and the clients served.

But what is a decision? What is decision making? Superficially, these questions may seem silly because they are easy to answer. But the volumes written and numerous theories developed on this subject attest to their complexity. These questions have been approached in various ways, ranging from personal self-help books to complex statistical and computer modeling. A **decision** represents a choice, resolution, or conclusion arrived at after considering alternatives. If there are no options or choices to make, the need for a decision is eliminated. Similarly, engaging in behavior from **habit** averts conscious decision making because individuals select the same choice every time. To make a decision is synonymous with coming to a conclusion based on facts, emotions, assumptions, conjectures, interpretations, or some combination of these and other factors.

Decision making is the dynamic process of defining a problem or issue, identifying alternatives, clarifying the criteria on which the alternatives will be evaluated, reviewing the alternatives, and then making a choice. For some, decision making ends with the choice. Some decision theorists assert that decision making continues through the stage of acting on the choice and then evaluating both the choice and the process. Some authors writing about decision makers, the decision-making process, decisions, and the outcomes of decisions use evaluative terms like *good* and *bad*. Using these terms, good decisions lead to positive outcomes, and bad decisions lead to results that are less than optimal.

However, it is important to recognize that a good decision process can result in a bad outcome. Conversely, a bad decision process, randomly, can produce a good result. The problem is that humans often equate the success of the decision process with the outcome. This can sometimes lead to throwing out beneficial decision-making processes when an outcome was not the one originally desired, and to maintaining inadequate decision processes because, coincidentally, the outcome was the one desired. Without objective analysis of the decision process and the outcome, a harmful decision process might continue to be used until it fails, and then the error is glossed over by saying, "Who could have known?"

For example, financial planning decisions are sometimes made in a way that results in negative outcomes for client and planner. The results of a poor decision range from hurt feelings to the termination of the client-planner relationship. Flawed decisions can sometimes lead to professional reprimand and civil liability. Consider the case of a planner who decides, after careful deliberation, to borrow money from a client to cover cash flow deficits in the planning firm. This decision may seem like a good one. The planner wins by obtaining needed cash flow and the client wins by gaining a fair rate of return on a relatively low-risk loan.

On closer inspection, however, this decision is fraught with problems. First, the client-planner relationship becomes a creditor-debtor interaction, which places the planner in a financially compromising position. The CFP Board has concluded that this type of relationship is subject to review and reprimand. *Rule of Conduct 3.6* expressly forbids certificants from borrowing money from clients, with certain exceptions. This example illustrates that what may appear to be a simple decision is not always so straightforward or may lead to unanticipated outcomes.

There are several important reasons to study decision making in the context of financial planning. Based on concepts discussed in Chapters 1 and 2, it is important to recognize that decision making with, for, or on behalf of a client, can invoke a fiduciary or trustee relationship. As such, the planner has an ethical, professional, and legal responsibility to act in the best interest of the client. This is the first reason that knowledge of decision making is important. Second, professional or regulatory codes of conduct can further define professional responsibility. Both professional standards and fiduciary responsibilities require defensible decision-making practices. In the early 2000s, one financial services firm's advertising slogan summarized the decision-making process succinctly: "You cannot predict, but you can prepare." Third, sound decision-making processes lay the foundation for solid planning practices that prepare clients—to the extent possible—for the uncertainty of the future. Finally, well-conceptualized and documented decision-making practices also help planners construct a defensible position regarding the distinction between prediction, or management of client expectations, and preparation for uncertainty.

No decision-making framework can ever be expected to perfectly replicate the qualitative aspects of the behavioral process. Furthermore, the scope of this topic far exceeds what can be addressed in this chapter. But better understanding of the steps involved in decision making and increased awareness of some of the myriad factors that can affect it can yield new insights for planners and their clients.

A GENERALIZED MODEL OF DECISION MAKING

One reason people sometimes make faulty decisions is that they fail to use a standard model for decision making. A model can be quite helpful in illustrating the ideal steps for fully defining a problem, identifying alternatives and their potential consequences, and choosing an alternative that best utilizes resources relative to goal fulfillment. Although a model can be a useful tool, it may not be necessary to follow all of the steps prescribed for every decision or choice situation. Over millennia, humans have developed simplified rules for action, often based on habits. Consider a consumer's choice of soft drink when purchasing a fast food lunch. Most people choose a familiar course of action using habit as a mental shortcut that alleviates the need to process information routinely. Although often useful as a time-saving device, this use of mental shortcuts often leads to suboptimal outcomes. (The pitfalls associated with habit-based decisions are discussed later in this chapter.) Thus, financial planners generally find that following a better-defined decision-making process facilitates optimal outcomes. Following is a discussion based on a generalized model of decision making, shown in Figure 4.1, which can be applied in most decision situations, including choice dilemmas commonly encountered in the financial planning process.

Figure 4.1 A General Model of Decision Making

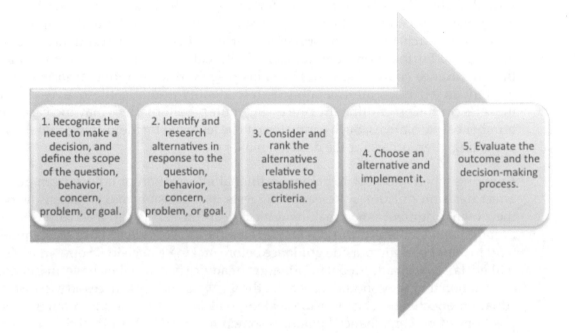

1. Recognize the need to make a decision, and define the scope of the question, behavior, concern, problem, or goal.

2. Identify and research alternatives in response to the question, behavior, concern, problem, or goal.

3. Consider and rank the alternatives relative to established criteria.

4. Choose an alternative and implement it.

5. Evaluate the outcome and the decision-making process.

Step 1: Recognize the need to make a decision and define the scope of the question, behavior, concern, problem, or goal. Every decision begins by recognizing the need to make a decision. This need may be prompted by a question, behavior, concern, problem, or goal. The issue may be threatening to the individual— a problem, or it may offer a new challenge or welcome change—an opportunity. The issue prompting the need for a decision must be evaluated to enable the decision maker to identify the issue and not simply its symptoms. Questions to ask during this step include: (a) Is the issue longstanding or is it a short-term event? (b) Is the issue self-correcting? (c) If nothing is done, will it be harmful? (d) If something is done, will it be beneficial?

Step 2: Identify and research alternatives in response to the question, behavior, concern, problem, or goal. At this stage of the decision-making process a decision maker must put experience, knowledge, assumptions, and expectations to work. Some issues have obvious alternatives, and others do not. Some decision makers prefer to identify all possible alternatives—even those reasonably considered beyond execution. Others limit the identification of alternatives to those that are feasible given the resources available and the subjective values, attitudes, or goals of the decision maker.

Assumptions regarding the problem and all alternatives must also be identified, their impact considered, and, if relevant, the probability of their occurrence assigned. For example, when deciding whether to fund a traditional IRA or a Roth IRA, one primary decision criterion is the tax implications for the current funding year versus the year of withdrawal. The assumption of a lower tax bracket during retirement is critically important to the benefit of tax deferral. If the decision maker cannot reasonably assume being in a lower tax bracket when the funds are withdrawn, a Roth IRA offers an immediate advantage over a traditional IRA, excluding other considerations.

The search for solutions and strategies may be intuitive or it can be done more formally. The method used to search for strategies depends on a person's knowledge, experience, and familiarity with an issue as well an individual's willingness to conduct a search for new information that might introduce additional alternatives or insights. Furthermore, the number of alternatives generated tends to vary with the importance of the decision. Decisions perceived to be more important typically warrant an extended information search to identify multiple alternatives. A decision maker's confusion or difficulty processing multiple alternatives may increase with the number of alternatives. Such confusion can be lessened by identifying a wide range of appealing alternatives for the decision maker.

Knowing when and how to gather additional information or advice from others can affect decision outcomes. Research suggests that decision makers often overweight their own judgment when making critical decisions.[1] This can lead to serious errors in judgment. Generally, those who perceive their level of expertise to be quite high tend to avoid seeking outside guidance before making a decision. Sometimes decision makers fail to seek additional information or advice because they have an internalized expectation that they should have all of the answers and tools necessary to assess their situation effectively. This decision-making bias is most pronounced among those in positions of power. Financial planners sometimes exhibit this proclivity because they do not want to appear lacking in financial knowledge or evaluation capacity.

This reliance on one's own professional judgment sometimes leads to critical errors in appraisal. Roszkowski and Grable found, for example, that financial planners do a particularly poor job of evaluating their clients' risk tolerance.[2] The results associated with the use of advisor-assessed risk appraisals as inputs into financial planning decisions, such as over- or underweighting certain asset classes in a portfolio, can be problematic. The key to managing overconfidence is to acknowledge that few people have the expertise needed to make a sound decision in every situation. Asking for advice and additional information is not only acceptable; it is sometimes a necessity.

Finally, time should be invested in thinking about the potential unintended consequences of a decision. The more significant the potential for a negative consequence, the more time and work should be put into developing alternatives. Questions to ask at this step include: (a) Is the decision maker guilty of paradigm paralysis or the inability to see or identify alternatives that do not agree with the decision maker's perspective? (b) Has the alternative search resulted in the repeated identification of the same or similar alternatives, suggesting that the search is exhaustive *or*, conversely, that the decision maker is not open to new ideas? (c) Do the alternatives identified truly address the problematic decision, and not merely the symptoms of the problem?

Step 3: Consider and rank alternatives relative to established criteria. In most cases, this is the most difficult step in the decision-making process. First, taking action at this step requires a decision maker to consider the criteria, both subjective and objective, that are important to a particular decision. Subjective factors include tastes, preferences, values, attitudes, beliefs, needs, wants, assumptions, and morals or ethics—all of which can influence the assessment of choices. Objective factors include the availability of resources, the costs and benefits associated with each alternative, the attributes or characteristics of each alternative, and when applicable, projections regarding the probability of the outcomes or assumptions.

Second, the decision maker must identify the most important criteria for the decision in question. Third, the alternatives must be ranked relative to the criteria set. Questions to ask at this step of the process include: (a) Are the decision-making criteria appropriately balanced between objective and subjective criteria? (b) Which criterion will have the greatest impact on this decision situation? (c) Which alternative is least costly or affords the greatest benefit? (d) Which alternative best matches the decision maker's values, goal, and available resources?

Step 4: Choose an alternative and implement it. Once the alternatives have been evaluated and ranked, a selection must be made. Often a choice must be made among several alternatives to arrive at an optimal course of action. Some choices result from conscious deliberation, whereas others stem from intuition and—on occasion—habit. **Intuition**, sometimes explained by the decision maker as "just knowing" or a "gut reaction," typically is not based on a conscious review of alternatives, but rather on an assumed broad-based comprehension of the situation and a realization of the alternative to be selected. An ideal choice is often impossible, because the decision maker does not, cannot, or will not have full knowledge of all alternatives, potential consequences, or the likelihood of any given consequence. In addition to being the optimal, well-conceived, or "best" choice, the alternative selected and its projected outcome should also reduce doubt and anxiety for the decision maker.

Once a course of action has been chosen, it is essential that it be implemented. Without implementation, a decision is nothing more than a desire. The choice of action may be positive, negative, or neutral (i.e., inaction). The timing of the action chosen may be determined by the urgency of the client's situation, the importance placed on the need to improve the situation, or the availability of resources to meet the need.

As part of this step, it is also important to identify evaluative criteria, or preliminary signals—ranging from the anecdotal to the catastrophic—that the decision maker will use to assess the success or failure of the alternative selected, as well as the decision process. Evaluative criteria should be a valid reflection of the decision and the decision maker and may be limited by the decision maker's knowledge, experience, and familiarity with the issue.

Questions to ask at this step of the process include: (a) was the choice of the alternative based primarily on intuition, fact, or a combination of both? (b) was the choice, the implementation, or the decision-making process affected by the decision maker's procrastination and/or by the decision maker's eagerness to make a decision? (c) were evaluative criteria identified that reflect both the objective and subjective issues that characterized this decision and its significance for the decision maker?

Step 5: Evaluate the outcome and the decision-making process. It is important to complete the decision-making process by assessing outcomes (positive, negative, or neutral) and making decision process adjustments by monitoring the process and outcomes associated with previous actions. Not only does the decision maker need to identify and rank the criteria used to evaluate outcomes, but the decision maker must also set a standard as a metaphorical yardstick to measure the outcome. Identifying appropriate standards for comparison at this step serves as a final check on the most significant objective and subjective evaluative criteria. Without an established standard that can be substantiated—based on intangible measures such as personal experience or satisfaction, or on fact-based knowledge—the process fails to be repeatable.

The use of a systematic decision-making process does not guarantee that all choices will result in optimal outcomes. Sometimes someone will make a bad decision or one with negative outcomes, and at other times a decision may lead to unknown or unanticipated consequences. As discussed earlier in this chapter, sometimes a good process can lead to a bad decision and at other times a bad process may lead to a good decision. The difference may not be directly associated with the decision-making process. Rather, outside events, unforeseen environmental changes, or simple bad timing can affect decision outcomes.

For the most part, each of these factors is beyond the decision maker's control. This is why financial planners should take the time to identify a process that can be applied consistently with the expectation of yielding a satisfactory decision. Thus, it is important to document each of the following: (a) the decision process; (b) the information search; (c) the criteria and assumptions considered; (d) the alternatives identified; (e) the rationale for the choice; and (f) the evaluative criteria identified to monitor the success of the choice or, if necessary, the need for a new decision. This type of information can be instrumental in the review of the decision outcome and process, or it can be helpful when facing a similar decision in the future.

Evaluating how effectively a particular systematic decision-making process works is important. Questions to ask when making an evaluation include: (a) what can be learned from this situation and the outcome achieved? (b) in hindsight, what information could have been useful and possibly changed either the decision-making process or the outcome? Was the information available but not included, or available but ignored? (c) how should the decision-making process change in the future, either in general or specifically, when applied to similar situations?

A simple example serves to illustrate the model shown in Figure 4.1. Consider a young professional who recognizes the need to save regularly for retirement through an available 403(b) plan. She undertakes an Internet search for investment product information related to the retirement plan. She obtains objective information on the returns, volatility, and risks of different mutual funds—all of which involve investment risk. Instead of taking on any market risk, the young professional chooses to invest all of her monthly retirement savings into a money market mutual fund based on the single criterion of safety of principal.

Although this choice significantly reduces the fear of loss associated with funds invested in the stock market, the risk of the inflationary erosion of purchasing power associated with low-yielding investments is not accounted for in this decision: she ignored or was unable to process information in a way that would have led to a better decision outcome. After decades of savings, funds will likely be insufficient to support her retirement goal. Her decision means either a significantly reduced standard of living in retirement, or continued full-time or part-time employment during what had originally been planned to be the retirement years.

DECISION RULES FOR CHOOSING AMONG ALTERNATIVES

Multiple decision-making rules can be used to facilitate the evaluation of alternatives when making a decision. The first strategy is called **maximization**, which involves choosing the outcome with the highest unadjusted result. This rule is based on the assumption that the best possible outcome from a set of alternatives will, in fact, occur. For example, if a client is given two choices with one offering a 10% return and another offering a 5% return, the maximization rule would have the client choose the 10% alternative. Obviously, this choice does not take into account the probability of success or qualitative client factors, such as risk tolerance, time frame, or experience. Day traders and other investors who attempt to time the market and chase returns often implement strategies based on a maximization rule.

Optimization is an alternative to the maximization approach. This technique can be used when all relevant goals, data, and resources are known and more than one alternative is available. Optimization simply requires a decision maker to choose the optimal course of action, or the one that will lead to the highest level of satisfaction. Choices grounded in optimization are based on the assumption that all alternatives are identified and feasible (given the goal, resources, and decision-making criteria), and the decision maker has the time and energy to evaluate and compare all alternatives. Financial planners and clients who use the optimization rule must take into account a wide range of quantitative as well as subjective data in an effort to identify the optimal choice among alternatives. Furthermore, the time and energy required for such an exhaustive review should not be overlooked when considering the use of this decision-making rule.

Satisficing, which originated in the 1950s with economist Herbert Simon, can be summarized by the question, "When is good, good enough?" For example, a client might need to reinvest proceeds from the sale of an investment immediately. The client may desire a security that offers both liquidity and relatively high returns. In any given market, these two attributes are hard to find, and there will always be uncertainty regarding the availability of such investments. A satisficing decision strategy would lead the client to choose the first best available security that met the need. Once the investment had been made, little additional research or security searching would occur even though further searching might lead to a better investment selection. In other words, when applying this rule, the objective is to satisfy as many criteria as possible while sacrificing other criteria. The identification and selection of the "good enough" alternative, per the criteria identified as most important, end the search.

Aside from the examples cited, how might these three decision-making rules influence the planner-client relationship? Consider that each of the rules or paradigms for viewing a decision establishes a unique framework that may be counter to that employed by the others involved. For example, if a client typically employs an optimizing approach, then the client will expect extensive evaluation of every possible alternative with a clear explanation of the planner's ultimate choice. The client will want to be fully convinced that the best option is the one recommended; however, the advisor may interpret the client's search for additional information as an effort to delay a decision or as reflecting little confidence in the advisor. Consequently, making a recommendation that satisfies only one or two client criteria (albeit the most important ones) will likely disappoint the optimizing client.

Conversely, a client using the satisficing approach could be overwhelmed by extensive analysis and the presentation of competing alternatives, and wonder "Why can't we just make a decision, given our preference for X and Y, and move on?" The maximizing client might also limit the information search and decision criteria, but care must be taken that the best choice is, in fact, based on the criteria most likely to result in long-term success.

Typically, the most difficult challenge facing financial planners during the decision-making process involves the evaluation of alternatives. Almost all of the decision-making approaches discussed in this chapter can be used to enhance product, service, and relationship evaluations. The assessment step is challenging because of the number of quantitative and qualitative factors that go into the assessment method. Furthermore, not every strategy lends itself to a single evaluation approach or to a defensible probability estimate.

So how does a financial planner or client evaluate solutions and strategies that are not easily measured statistically? Decision rules related to maximization, optimization, and satisficing certainly can be used. The problem with these evaluative tools is that they tend to be one dimensional and focused almost entirely on one outcome measure (e.g., increasing a client's satisfaction or maximizing returns). None of three standard evaluation tools takes into account the behavioral processes that individuals use when making decisions, nor do they account for full consideration of the objective, subjective, and qualitative factors that can influence the evaluative process. As an alternative, some decision theorists recommend using a more traditional approach to decision making, as described below.

THE TRADITIONAL APPROACH TO DECISION MAKING

The **traditional decision-making approach** has its roots in economics. In the world of economic decision making, individuals are assumed to be rational. It is also assumed that outcomes, or the likelihood of an alternative, can be estimated using probability. Under conditions of certainty, a decision maker is assumed to have full knowledge of all possible outcomes for any alternative considered. In a situation of certainty, any given outcome may not have a 100% chance of occurring, but the decision maker has a 100% chance of predicting the correct outcome.

For example, consider a weather report that predicts a 60% chance of rain, consistent with the assertion that any given outcome (rain) may not have a 100% chance of occurring. However, the outcome, as predicted by the individual hearing the weather report, is either 100% or 0%: it will either rain or not rain. Under conditions of uncertainty, the decision maker does not have reliable information regarding the probability of various outcomes associated with a given alternative. With uncertainty, the individual outcomes do not have a 100% chance of occurring, nor does the decision maker have a 100% chance of correct prediction. Risk differs from uncertainty in that risk is represented by the personal or economic loss associated with a choice, whereas uncertainty is simply the failure to make the right choice regardless of gain or loss.

As described, the traditional decision-making process relies on probabilities to arrive at a solution. A financial planner can apply two types of probability when using this approach: objective or subjective. **Objective probabilities** are known with some certainty, based on experience or experiments, or the result of research or study using large samples. Mortality probabilities are one example of an objective probability, as are other actuarial data such as number of accidents, weather-related injuries, and long-term care claims trends.

Subjective probabilities are based on a person's belief or best guess regarding the likelihood of an event actually occurring. For example, a market pundit's prediction might be based on history repeating itself. When someone says something like, "This year the stock market will end up higher, because 75% of the time when January is up, the market ends the year up," they are estimating a subjective probability. Conversely, another expert might conclude that "The market will be down, because of X, Y and Z, although history would predict a different outcome."

It is important to understand the basis of predictions. Both are subjective judgments, based on objective data that support the conclusions, but they are judgments that may or may not be supported by objective probability. Evaluation of financial planning strategies that use the traditional decision-making approach works best when probabilities are objective rather than subjective. Examples include evaluating insurance solutions where the probability of accidents, theft, and death are relatively well known.

It is possible to value an outcome objectively so that a decision maker can choose the best solution to a problem using the traditional decision-making approach. The best way to understand this methodology is with an example. Assume that a financial planner is faced with a decision to reallocate a client's portfolio. Based on professional judgment, the financial planner concludes that there are two scenarios. In the first scenario, the planner can choose to do nothing. In this case, the planner estimates that the year-end value of the portfolio will be $110,000. In the second scenario, the planner reallocates the portfolio to 80% stocks and 20% bonds. If successful, the portfolio will be worth $125,000 at year's end. If unsuccessful, the value of the portfolio value will drop to $85,000. The financial planner, who has many years of experience, believes that if the portfolio is reallocated the chance of success is 75% and the chance of failure is 25%. Should the planner reallocate the portfolio or leave it as it is?

A traditional decision-making approach can be used to answer this question. An easy way to do this is to summarize the information in a table. Table 4.1 illustrates how reallocating the portfolio results in a higher expected outcome compared to maintaining the current portfolio. The weighted return associated with achieving success ($125,000 × 75%) plus the weighted return of failure ($85,000 × 25%) is $115,000. This probability-weighted return is greater than the guaranteed return of $110,000 available in the first scenario. Thus, someone using the traditional decision-making approach would choose to reallocate the portfolio. (Note that if the probability of success versus failure was 50/50 this decision-making approach would indicate holding the current portfolio.)

Table 4.1 Traditional Decision-Making Approach

Scenario	Ending Value	Probability	Calculation	Outcome
Maintain current portfolio	$110,000	100%	$110,000 x 100%	$110,000
			TOTAL	**$110,000**
Reallocate portfolio	A. $125,000	A. 75%	$125,000 x 75%	$93,750
	B. $85,000	B. 25%	$85,000 x 25%	$21,250
			TOTAL	**$115,000**

A relatively new branch of traditional decision-making theory is known as **stochastic modeling**. A stochastic model is one in which the inputs are randomized within a certain range so that the model can account for variations and the timing of returns. Essentially, stochastic models are mathematical projections that account for multiple variables (e.g., both mean and standard deviation). A stochastic model can be compared to a **deterministic model**, where inputs are static.[3] Deterministic models are mathematical projections that account for only one variable (e.g., return). Hence, deterministic models must use averages, which do not account for the fluctuation or timing of returns.

Consider the situation of a planner who wants to evaluate a potential retirement savings strategy for a client. Using a standard deterministic modeling technique, the planner would base the evaluation on the average rate of return of each asset class corresponding to the projected client portfolio. If the portfolio historically returned 9% on average, the planner could conclude that approximately 50% of the time the client would earn returns greater than 9%, and 50% of the time the client would earn less than 9%. In either case, the probability of achieving 9% remains constant across the evaluation period because the input is static.

Proponents of stochastic modeling argue that using only one variable (e.g., average annual rate of return over x years) as an input to arrive at a probability estimate can result in misleading or potentially erroneous solutions. Consequently, stochastic modeling instead takes the actual distribution of returns over the period and uses this data to run hundreds or thousands of iterations to arrive at returns with specific probability estimates attached. In other words, a stochastic model can more accurately tell a planner the probability of actually earning 9.00% over time based on historical data. Using a stochastic modeling procedure, the probability of achieving a straight-line 9.00% return (as assumed in the deterministic model) is in reality less than 50% and, depending on the standard deviation of the distribution, it could be much less.

The most common stochastic model is based on a normal distribution of one standard deviation from the mean. This model graphs the 85% probability line and the 15% probability line to illustrate that approximately 70% of the time predicted results will fall between the upper and lower limits. Planners find this useful because they can tell the client that 85% of the time the value under the projected scenario will be equal to or greater than the lower limit value. Obviously, this is much more conclusive than telling the client that there is a 50/50 chance of meeting or exceeding a certain value.

The results of stochastic modeling—one example of which is called *Monte Carlo Simulation*—can provide very useful inputs for the traditional decision-making process. Recognizing that the probabilities generated are based entirely on past returns of similar securities, and that past performance is no guarantee of future returns, a stochastic model can produce a range of expected rates of return with corresponding probabilities. Output from a stochastic model can be presented graphically.

As shown in Figure 4.2, the results of thousands of scenarios can be plotted so that the midpoint of a diamond represents a 50/50 probability of successfully meeting an investment objective. Potential deviations from that point can then be plotted with the probabilities of over- or underachieving a particular investment target graphically demonstrated. This type of graphic presentation is useful as a tool illustrating how 70% of the time returns should fall between very high and very low extremes, both of which could occur 15% of the time.

Figure 4.2 Graphical Representation of the Output of a Stochastic Model

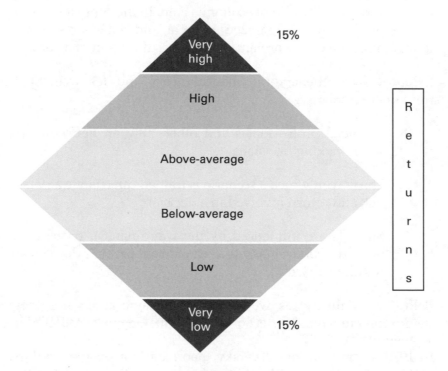

The traditional decision-making approach coupled with new stochastic modeling techniques offers financial planners a useful way to evaluate some—but certainly not all—financial planning strategies or recommendations. Unfortunately, not all strategies lend themselves to arriving at objective probabilities. The majority of financial planning techniques do not allow probability modeling. Consider strategies related to funding retirement through a 401(k) plan or a Roth IRA. What are the probabilities of success using either solution? Financial planners will most likely be willing to give estimates, but such approximations will be subjective rather than objective. Using the traditional decision-making process to evaluate these types of solutions and strategies, employing only subjective probabilities, is problematic at best—and dangerous at worst.

The traditional decision-making approach works quite well when the probability of outcomes can be estimated with some degree of reliability and in cases where outcomes can be quantified. Unfortunately for financial planners, very few decision outcomes can be quantified that precisely; and even when estimates can be made, the probabilities assigned to different events tend to be biased. Evidence of this fact can be found in another approach to decision making, behavioral finance, which is introduced below.

THE BEHAVIORAL FINANCE APPROACH TO DECISION MAKING

Daniel Kahneman and the late Amos Tversky introduced the concept known as **prospect theory** in 1979, and many regard this as the establishment of the serious study of behavioral finance. However, the origins of behavioral finance can be traced back to the mid-1950s.[4] **Behavioral finance** attempts to bridge the gap between the solely economic model of utility maximization and the more psychological model of value. According to the classic "economic person" theory, the concept of internal motivation is based on the condition of economic gain. In the context of this theory, when given a choice, people use an organized, rational, and stable system of preferences designed to maximize the utility or value received as the result of a choice.

In a review of behavioral finance theory and research, Shefrin identified three fundamental themes:

1. Financial professionals and others rely on **heuristics** (i.e., simplified rules) when making decisions.

2. The way in which a scenario is framed can change a person's perception of the risk and return involved in a decision.

3. Markets are influenced by the way financial professionals and their clients make decisions; markets are inefficient because decisions are based, in part, on cognitive biases.[5]

Below, each theme, as well as other behavioral finance themes that have been determined to have an effect on decision making, is considered in greater detail.

In 1979, Kahneman and Tversky theorized that people exhibit certain biases when making decisions, resulting in the formation of heuristics.[6] In the context of prospect theory, decision making occurs as a two-step process.[7] The first step involves editing, which is defined as organizing and formulating decision alternatives, or what are known as *prospects*. The editing stage requires that prospects be defined and compared to a reference point. Kahneman and Tversky argued that this framing action results in decisions being defined as either gains or losses.

The second stage of decision making deals with choice evaluation. This is where the decision maker assesses edited prospects and chooses the option that provides the highest outcome value. The theory proposes a decision valuation function comprising three factors: (1) reference dependence; (2) diminishing sensitivity; and (3) loss aversion. Once a valuation has been made, the decision maker is assumed to rank multiple outcomes via a decision weight, which is similar to a probability estimate. At this stage of decision making, biases enter and alter judgments regarding choices. Essentially, prospect theory suggests that decision makers tend to overweight low probability events while underweighting more probable events.

The preeminent bias is that people tend to avoid risk—more precisely, the kind of risk experienced when the outcome of an event is uncertain. When an event has multiple possible outcomes, each separate outcome has a probability, or a range of probabilities, that it will happen; the higher the likelihood, the higher the probability. However, the number of variables becomes overwhelming when attempting to calculate a probability when there are many possible outcomes, each affected by multiple factors.

To deal with these complexities, people use experiential knowledge to reduce the probability equations into simpler judgments. This experiential or common sense knowledge results in mental shortcuts known as heuristics and can lead to the development of heuristic tools. An example of a commonly used heuristic tool, or general rule of practice, for retirement planning is the following equation:

100 – Client's Age = Percentage of the Portfolio in Equities

With increasing longevity and concerns about retirees outliving their assets, the equation was later adapted to the following:

110 or 120 – Client's Age = Percentage of the Portfolio in Equities

This straightforward formula simplifies portfolio development by replacing a client's personal situation, goals, time horizon, risk tolerance, attitudes, expectations, and risk capacity with a single assumption. The formula assumes that as a client ages, there is less tolerance for financial risk. Note, however, that there is no convincing empirical research to suggest that age alone causes people to become less risk tolerant.[8] Instead, tolerance for risk is more closely linked with a client's income, net worth, education, and financial knowledge than it is directly correlated with age.[9]

Consequently, although heuristics may be widely accepted, the blending of judgment and fact actually results in more subjective probabilities being assigned to the various outcomes of a choice; it does not, however, guarantee an optimal or accurate prediction of outcome. In other words, as subjectivity increases, accuracy (at least theoretically) declines.

In addition to the problem of the misconception of chance, Tversky and Kahneman identified several other reasons that heuristics and representativeness might also fail to capture true probabilities. People apply heuristic judgments based on how well the current situation represents a situation with which they are familiar. This idea is known as **representativeness** (or in a social context, as a *stereotype*). The more representative the current situation is to the referent situation, the greater the confidence the individual has in the validity of the outcome. Unfortunately, this type of flawed thinking leads to a second cause of heuristic failure: frequency of occurrence or the relative frequency that the event will occur in a large sample. Simply because one situation mimics another does not necessarily mean that the outcomes will be identical or frequently occurring. A third threat is called the **illusion of validity**. The preceding asset allocation illustration is a case in point on how a formula can give the illusion of validity because on the surface the heuristic tool seems reasonable

Although heuristics offer some distinct benefits to decision makers, heuristic processing can inadvertently bias the decision-making process. To compensate, the decision maker should consciously challenge the heuristics involved—especially when making decisions of significant importance. Simplified decision rules and the natural tendency to observe patterns and extrapolate might be successful in some situations, but they have limited validity for most decision-making situations.

The role of heuristics in the decision-making process can be quite significant. But, according to Shefrin (and others), what is less well known is how the **framing** of a question, case, or scenario can influence the way in which a person arrives at a decision.[10] Framing can occur when the decision maker frames the context of the choice by considering the possible outcomes from a particular paradigm or perspective representative of a set of norms, habits, or personal characteristics.

Framing can also occur when a provider of information frames or alters the context of the information in such a way as to influence the decision maker. Consequently, decision framing can be altered by the formulation of the problem or the context of possible outcomes. This use of information in a misleading context is readily seen when quoting a short passage from the Bible. Unless the decision maker has complete and unbiased information, the representativeness of the situation, or in this example the meaning of the quote, it could be altered to suit the speaker's purposes. Therefore, changing the context has the potential to alter predictability and the subsequent accuracy of the decision maker.

Framing is possibly the most apparent when analyzing issues of risk. Consider the following scenario:

Please choose between the following two alternatives:

    A. Take a sure loss of $750; or

    B. Take a 75% chance that you will lose $1,000 and have a 25% chance of losing nothing.

Now consider this alternative:

Please choose between the following two alternatives:

    A. Take a sure gain of $750; or

    B. Take a 75% chance that you will gain $1,000 and have a 25% chance of gaining nothing.

Nearly all people choose answer B in the first scenario and answer A in the second scenario. Traditional decision-making theory and traditional economic theory suggest that the same answer should be chosen in both scenarios. In other words, individuals should exhibit consistent risk choices. This is true because the mathematical outcomes of each question are identical. However, behavioral decision-making theory illustrates that framing a question in terms of a known guaranteed loss (the first scenario) leads people to take risks and gamble by choosing alternative B. When the same question is framed so that the decision maker can walk away with a guaranteed gain, the gamble is the less likely choice.

What does this mean in terms of decision theory? First, people tend to have a strong **aversion to loss**. People dislike losing significantly more than they like winning. Put another way, the attraction of winning is not as strong as the aversion to losing. Second, people are not rational (as defined in traditional economic theory) when it comes to making certain decisions. For example, consider the frequent practice of not acknowledging an investment loss by asserting that a paper loss in a stock is not a loss until the stock is actually sold. This tendency is particularly true when it comes to making decisions about money. These two observations offer evidence that traditional economic decision-making theory may not be as applicable to financial scenarios as once thought. Taking into account both the planner's and the client's cognitive biases appears to be one way to improve financial decisions.

A concept related to framing is the notion of **financial numeracy**, which is defined as a person's ability to process mathematical and probabilistic data.[11] It is assumed, especially among financial planners, that access to timely, high-quality data leads to better decision making. This is generally true, but an overreliance on numbers can sometimes lead to decision biases. Some clients can be influenced by the way a scenario is framed. For example, clients tend to perceive the riskiness of a situation as less when the event is described in a probabilistic manner, such as, "You have a 10% chance of losing money." When an event is described in a frequency format, such as "10 out of 100 clients lose money," clients often attribute more risk to the situation.

Peters noted that those with high financial numeracy are less affected by framing issues. A problem arises when those with high numeracy become overly dependent on the analysis of numbers and data. This can lead to less rational decision processes. Consider the way in which Wall Street firms relied on complex mathematical tools and techniques to control the risks associated with collateralized mortgages in the mid- to late-2000s. Although it is true that those with high financial numeracy make better overall decisions, they sometimes fail to use common sense when evaluating a situation that has potentially large negative outcomes. Financial planners can help their less numerate clients by (a) reducing the number of alternatives from which to choose when making a decision; (b) attaching labels, such as "excellent" or "risky" to numbers; and (c) relying on visual charts, tables, and figures to communicate mathematical concepts. Consistently using such tools with clients can facilitate better decision making.

Refer back to Figure 4.1, which illustrates the traditional decision-making approach. Decision makers uneasy about selecting the choice to reallocate assets based on the mathematical outcome may be experiencing a behavioral bias called **regret avoidance**. In the reallocation example discussed earlier, recall that the portfolio was projected with 100% certainty to equal $110,000. With reallocation, there was the possibility of actually losing value in the portfolio. People who exhibit regret avoidance make decisions that will minimize the negative effect of making a bad or wrong decision. In other words, they will either stick with the status quo or avoid making the decision to reallocate the portfolio. If they do reallocate, it is likely that they will be uncomfortable with their decision. If the client, rather than the planner, makes the decision, the financial planner can expect regular phone calls, text messages, and emails inquiring about the exact market value of the portfolio. There is also a high probability that at the first market decline the client will want to return to the original portfolio allocation.

As noted earlier, traditional decision-making approaches require individuals to assign relatively precise probabilities to events and outcomes. Most financial planners believe that they are very good at predicting outcomes with financial data.[12] However, the evidence suggests otherwise. Consider the now-famous prediction presented below:

> The closing price of the Dow Jones Industrial Average was 40 in 1896. By the end of 1998 the Dow stood at 9,181. Because the Dow is a price-weighted average, dividends are not shown in the closing value of the Dow. Pick a range of possible returns where you are 90% certain that the Dow would have closed had dividends been reinvested and included in the closing price.[13]

Nearly all respondents—financial planners included—chose ranges such as 9,000 to 18,000 or 9,000 to 36,000. Few people even estimated that the real value of the Dow would have been 652,230 with dividends at year end 1998! This example illustrates how traditional decision-making theory can lead to significant errors in action. People have a tendency to be overly optimistic in their own ability to predict the future. In fact, everyone is subject to psychological biases that tend to influence the way they view the world and make decisions.

How overconfident is the average person? Very overconfident, indeed. Ask 100 people to rate themselves compared to other drivers on the road in terms of what kind of driver they are (i.e., average, below-average, or above-average), and most will likely offer some interesting information about overconfidence.[14] Statistically, one-third of respondents should answer average, another third below average, and the final third above average. However, in reality it is likely that well over 75% of respondents will rate themselves above-average drivers. How is this possible? People overestimate their own abilities and underestimate the abilities of others, and this almost always leads to overconfidence and a tendency to take risks when caution should be foremost.

People become overconfident for a number of reasons. Investors in particular equate knowledge with control. Individuals who are subject to **overconfidence bias** believe that they can control random events simply by obtaining more knowledge of and familiarity with a situation. In other words, overconfident investors believe that a risky decision can be controlled through a combination of superior knowledge, familiarity with a situation, and active involvement in the implementation of a decision. Again, however, history suggests otherwise.

Overconfident investors tend to trade too much and earn lower returns than other investors because of increased tax liability and commissions. Overconfident investors are also more likely to subject themselves to substantially riskier decisions because they underestimate the probability of failure and overestimate the probability of success.

Making money during bull markets may be perceived as easy, and overconfident investors may continue to make the same mistakes during a bear market, but with significantly different outcomes. And because of overestimating returns, overconfident investors may not save enough to reach their goals.

For example, consider the often-cited 2003 and 2011 updates of the longitudinal *Quantitative Analysis of Investor Behavior* (QAIB) study by DALBAR, an independent research group. The original study revealed that the average equity mutual fund investor earned 2.57% annually, less than the comparable inflation rate of 3.14% and significantly less than the S&P 500 average annual earnings of 12.2% over the 19-year period ending in 2003.[15] DALBAR updated their research to include the 20-year period ending in 2010. During this time, the broad equity markets returned approximately 9% annually; however, equity investors averaged only slightly more than 4%. DALBAR observed that investor fear and greed motivate poorly timed buying at market upturns and selling on market downturns. One of the hallmarks of behavioral finance theory is the concept of **mental accounting**. Consider the following story, told by Belsky and Gilovich:

> By the third day of their honeymoon in Las Vegas, the newlyweds had lost their $1,000 gambling allowance. That night in bed, the groom noticed a glowing object on the dresser. Upon closer inspection, he realized it was a $5 chip they had saved as a souvenir. Strangely, the number 17 was flashing on the chip's face. Taking this as an omen, he donned his green bathrobe and rushed down to the roulette tables, where he placed the $5 chip on the square marked 17. Sure enough, the ball hit 17 and a 35-to-1 bet paid $175. He let his winnings ride, and once again the little ball landed on 17, paying $6,125. And so it went, until the lucky groom was about to wager $7.5 million. Unfortunately the floor manager intervened, claiming that the casino didn't have the money to pay should 17 hit again. Undaunted, the groom taxied to a better-financed casino downtown. Once again he bet it all on 17—and once again it hit, paying more than $262 million. Ecstatic, he let his millions ride—only to lose it all when the ball fell on 18. Broke and dejected, the groom walked the several miles back to his hotel.
>
> 'Where were you?' Asked his bride as he entered their room.
>
> 'Playing roulette.'
>
> 'How did you do?'
>
> 'Not bad. I lost five dollars.'[16]

What does this have to do with decision making? Actually, quite a bit; because this story illustrates how people tend to separate and categorize money into different **mental accounts**. Did the man in the green robe lose $5 or did he lose $262 million? If you answered $5 it is likely that you, too, rely on mental accounts as a way to manage your money and resources. Some people believe in something called **house money**. The man in the green robe mentally placed the $5 chip into one account and the earnings on the bets in a second account. This cognitive bias allows gamblers and investors to operate under the illusion of controlling their losses because they feel that losing money in the house money account is not really losing. In effect, using mental accounts is one way that people reduce the feeling of regret associated with gambling and investment losses.

Nearly everyone uses mental accounting in some form or other. It helps explain why some people hold high account balances in low-interest savings accounts while simultaneously maintaining an outstanding credit card balance. Although this is illogical, it can be explained by the fact that some individuals view cash in a liquid emergency fund as one account and their liability on a credit card as another account. In general, few people manage their entire available resources with a global perspective. Understanding how mental accounting can influence financial planning decisions is one way to evaluate a solution to a financial question or concern. It can also be useful to explore the concept of mental accounting with clients. Helping a client who is heavily influenced by mental accounting objectively understand this concept could lead to a necessary behavioral change or even motivate a client to accomplish other goals.

For example, individuals frequently identify "buckets" of money, or money earmarked for a particular purpose. Common examples include "This is my fun money, or my speculative fund," and "This is my 'safe' money, or the kids' education fund." Frequently, however, the risk taken with each individual bucket, when added together, exceeds the total risk ascribed to the client's situation or total portfolio. In other words, the mental accounting for each bucket or goal allowed the individual to exceed— perhaps even dangerously— the previously identified *comfortable* level of aggregate risk exposure.

Gamblers often believe that success is due after a run of bad luck. They believe that a series of independent trials with the same outcome will soon be followed by the opposite outcome. According to Shefrin in his review of behavioral finance theory and research, the **gambler's fallacy** arises from the very poor understanding people have about the outcomes of independent, random events. The example most widely used to validate the gambler's fallacy is the coin toss. Suppose that an unbiased coin is flipped three times and each time the coin lands on heads: as of the third flip, heads has occurred 100% of the time. Therefore, if a gambler had to bet $100 on the next toss, which side of the coin should be chosen? This is a trick question because the gambler should recognize that the next toss is an independent event, unrelated to the last three tosses. The gambler should have no preference between heads or tails (if the coin is honest).

However, most people will choose tails anyway. This is the concept of "They're due (to lose or win)," meaning that an individual actually has a sense of regression to the mean, but not a clear understanding of the probability of each independent event. People mistakenly believe that because even odds exist for both heads and tails, the moving average should closely reflect actual probability in both the short- and long-term. The idea that regression to the mean happens on a self-correcting, continual basis leads people to believe in the gambler's fallacy.

The **hot hand fallacy** is another cognitive bias to which many people succumb. People often interpret accidental success as the result of skill (i.e., don't confuse a rising stock market with being an expert investor!) and are, therefore, overconfident regarding their own abilities. Investors, money managers, advisors, and analysts are particularly overconfident in their ability to outperform the market because of their perceived level of knowledge; however, most fail to do so. Increasing levels of confidence frequently show no correlation with greater success—hence the term, "It is better to be lucky than good."

For example, suppose that a basketball coach is designing a play and that one player must be chosen to take the final shot. There are 10 seconds left in the game and the team is down by a basket. The star player, who is a lifetime 65% shooter, is only three for 10 tonight having missed several easy shots. Another veteran player, who has a 45% shooting percentage, has hit the last 10 shots attempted. For whom should the coach design the final shot? Although open for subjective argument, the coach should give the ball to the star player who has averaged 65% over the season. In this example, a basketball player with a "hot hand" is no more likely to make his next shot than at any other time.[17] However, most people will choose the player with the hot hand. Again, wherever independent events are concerned (i.e., shooting a basketball, flipping a coin, or selecting a stock), people are prone to overestimate the representativeness of the situation and assume that they have additional valid information.

In both the gambler's fallacy and the hot hand fallacy, financial planners and their clients fail to account fully for the fact that independent trials regress to a mean, or they assume that the regression happens continuously. **Regression to the mean** is a statistical phenomenon pertaining to numerical data in which abnormal results tend to be followed by more average results, or they at least average out over a large number of attempts. In other words, extreme results in one direction are averaged out by equal extremes in the opposite direction.

People tend to focus on specific elements of information (e.g., a percentage) and extrapolate well into the future based on what happened in the recent past. Unfortunately, this does not take into account the tendency of events, scores, and market returns to revert to their averages. For instance, suppose a stock is selling for a price-to-earnings ratio of 35 when similar stocks in the same industry are selling for a price-to-earnings ratio of 20, the historical mean for the industry. Over time an investor should expect the first stock to decline in value relative to other stocks in the industry. To assume otherwise is to discount statistical probability.

Regression to the mean is one example of how statistics can be misconstrued; sometimes, however, statistical probabilities are simply unknown or ignored. Kahneman and Tversky posed the following scenario to many people over the years, but few answered the question correctly:

> Steve, 37-year-old American, has been described by a former neighbor as follows: "Steve is very shy and withdrawn, invariably helpful, but with little interest in people of the social world. A meek and tidy soul, he has a need for order and structure and a passion for detail." Which occupation is Steve currently more likely to have: a salesman or a librarian?

If common assumptions are made about the character traits of librarians, and the commonalities between Steve and the average librarian are compared, the predicted outcome is that Steve is a librarian. Unfortunately, people do not generally consider the fact that according to the Bureau of Labor Statistics there are more than 15 million salespeople in America and there are only 180,000 librarians. Therefore, regardless of Steve's character traits, he is 83 times more likely to be a salesman. This tendency to disregard the overall likelihood of a certain outcome is known as **ignoring the base rate**.[18]

One of the financial outcomes associated with ignoring the base rate is momentum investing, a technique that can drive markets ever higher or lower than a rational model would predict. In the fall of 1987, the United States stock market crashed, falling nearly 25% and scaring away investors for nearly two years. Investors opted instead for bank accounts or bonds because of the perception of relative safety attached to these investments. This *flight to quality*, as it has become known, occurred because investors and their advisors failed to remember that the base rate indicated that stocks outperform bonds. Therefore, had they considered history rather than recent past events, they would have recognized that the risk in the stock market had been reduced by the crash, not increased. For example, a review of market returns for 1987 reveals that the market was actually up that year in spite of the significant correction—an interesting but overlooked fact, given that many investors left the market.

The other cause of momentum investing stems from the fact that that nearly all investors suffer from a behavioral trait called **herding**, the tendency of animals—including people—to group together for protection. People realize that if they are going to be wrong, they would rather be wrong in a group; conversely, if the group is correct, people do not want to be left behind. As described by John Maynard Keynes, "Investors may be quite willing to take the risk of being wrong in the company of others, while being much more reluctant to take the risk of being right alone."[19] In other words, people are comfortable investing in speculative stocks and investments because everyone else is doing so.

This herding effect can cause a stock price to gain momentum. Generally, the price momentum is upward, but herding instincts can drive prices down as well. Other applications of herding extend to the often-quoted "keeping up with the Joneses" as a rationale for consumer spending and debt or the tendency of young adults to "opt out" of health insurance because "We're all healthy."

In summary, behavioral finance blends the disciplines of finance and psychology into an explanation of human behavior that stands in stark contrast to traditional economic theory. Behavioral finance theory is premised on the assumptions that when making investment and financial decisions:

- Few people act in consistently rational ways.

- They cannot accurately predict the consequences of their choices.

- They are loss-averse and feel regret when outcomes are not as anticipated.

- And perhaps most importantly, they can be influenced by contextual changes in the presentation of information.

Furthermore, advocates of behavioral finance theory believe that people use mental shortcuts when making decisions and are often subject to cognitive biases and misplaced confidence in their abilities to anticipate outcomes. In addition, the misinterpretation of statistics and knowledge inference can be problematic when trying to make good financial decisions.

What does this mean for financial planners and their clients? For some clients, biases result in inaction. Other clients may be prone to seemingly irrational actions, but upon further consideration they can be persuaded to stay the course with the original plan. This discussion has introduced only some of the most widely acknowledged concepts related to behavioral finance theory and is in no way comprehensive. However, it illustrates how biases can significantly influence the decision processes of planners and clients. Understanding these biases provides the student and novice planner a rich new perspective for interpreting their own decision-making strategies as well as those of clients.

THREATS TO THE DECISION-MAKING PROCESS

Financial planners face a myriad of decisions daily. Some are inconsequential and others can change a client's life for better or worse. Most people, financial planners included, tend to make decisions using rules that they have learned or acquired over time (i.e., heuristic processing). The question is whether the use of heuristics as a decision-making shortcut is effective. The use of heuristics is a fact of life; thus, it is important to understand when simple rules can work well and when they can lead to critical errors. When it comes to making decisions that have a low cost or little consequence, decision heuristics offer an effective way to arrive at a conclusion. However, the use of heuristics to solve more complex problems can lead to problematic outcomes. Excessive dependence on heuristics should, at the very least, call into question the method used to make a decision.

Given this, why are heuristic models so widespread? One reason is that people ordinarily are not exposed to generalized decision-making models, whereas they are exposed to heuristic models on a daily basis. Think about advertisements on television. Most—if not all—provide viewers with simplified rules for decision making. If someone has a cold they are told to simply take a particular medication. Little explanation is given as to why or what the consequences might be. It is interesting to note that selling products and services via heuristic models seems to work. People constantly look for simple solutions to what are often difficult problems.

Wheeler and Janis have identified three additional factors that can result in seriously negative decision outcomes: complacency; defensive avoidance; and panic decision making.[20] **Complacency** occurs when a person either cannot or chooses not to see approaching danger. Sometimes a person cannot see that a dangerous situation is occurring or believes that an event is more likely to happen to someone else. Common examples of complacency include an individual who fails to adopt healthier lifestyle practices (e.g., exercise, balanced diet, stress reduction) or a person who fails to take cover on a golf course during a thunderstorm. Complacency can also occur when opportunities are passed up. Consider the financial planner who chooses not to interview a recent graduate from a college financial planning program because the planner does not want to risk hiring someone with no experience. In effect, the planner has missed an opportunity. The planner may hire someone with experience, but that experience could be costly in terms of salary, benefits, and the direct and indirect costs of training and retraining the individual to the firm's planning practices and procedures. Passing up the opportunity to hire a recent college graduate means that the planner might miss out on cutting-edge knowledge the graduate can bring to the practice, a willingness to learn and use the planner's techniques (no retraining required), and a higher level of enthusiasm and gratitude for a career-entry opportunity.

Defensive avoidance refers to situations where a person acknowledges a danger but tends to deny its importance or the potential role of individual responsibility to lessen the danger. The old adage about how buggy makers failed to appreciate the competitive risk posed by automobiles illustrates defensive avoidance. Some financial planners engage in defensive avoidance when it comes to preparing a succession plan for their firms. As the average age of planners increases, the number of planners who will leave the profession also increases. What will happen to clients as planners either retire or pass away? How will retired planners draw income from their practices without a succession plan? Both of these questions are worth asking, but few planners have attempted to answer them.

Procrastination is a symptom of defensive avoidance,[21] and it may explain the lack of succession planning by many planners. Procrastination occurs whenever someone feels that the likelihood of a threat is minimal or too far in the future to plan for. Clients can also suffer from procrastination. The lack of plan implementation is most closely associated with defensive avoidance and procrastination.

The third threat to the decision-making process is a person's likelihood to engage in **panic reactions**. Panic occurs when people are faced with a threat that they believe is too urgent to solve using the decision-making process. Panic situations related to financial planning include a sudden decline in the stock market, the bankruptcy of a large firm, the death of a loved one, or job loss. All of these events can be both emotionally and physiologically highly stimulating events, which can lead a person to frenzied searches for solutions or action.

This response, in very simple terms, is the same fight-or-flight syndrome that is a natural response of the human brain and body. It once did and still does protect humans from physical danger (i.e., a charging woolly mammoth or the city bus that seemingly appeared from nowhere). But the fear of significant financial loss, job loss, or other financial threats can prompt the same hormonal and physiological response that unconsciously demands humans to take protective action. This often leads to minimal evaluation of a situation and a response or possibly even multiple courses of action being undertaken simultaneously. Implementation may be swift with little follow-through or effort to sustain action. Panic almost always leads to negative outcomes. Irrational responses replace rational responses.

Think about the person, whom we will call Joe, who wakes up one morning to find that the stock market is in free fall. Commentators and stock market pundits are on television hinting that the current market drop will be the next 1929, 1987, 2001, and 2008. Panic has already set in on Wall Street and at this moment Joe senses a threat. Immediately, he runs through his options. He never anticipated such a serious market drop. He has no plan to account for this or to guide him through the decision-making process.

Joe senses that time is short and that he must make a decision. Should he sell now or later? He is definitely not complacent, nor is he engaging in defensive avoidance. Instead, Joe is panicked. Not sure exactly what to do, he logs onto the Internet. Within three minutes he has liquidated his stock holdings and moved to cash. Joe is relieved—for now. A day or two later, Joe thinks through his decision. Was it really best to sell in the midst of a downturn? Almost all of his assets were invested for retirement—in 20 years. As he checks the market returns, he is disappointed to learn that the market has corrected and is now only 2% below record highs. Suddenly Joe realizes that he missed a grand opportunity to invest new money at low prices. He also realizes that someone else took advantage of the situation, and he did not. Someone else used a disciplined decision-making approach and made money. Joe did neither.

Heuristics, complacency, defensive avoidance, and panic are all threats to decision making and an individual's ability to make a proactive decision. But perhaps the biggest threat to decision making is the failure to appreciate its significance. Joe's example, and others throughout this chapter, illustrate the importance of understanding the decision-making process, as well as the spoken and unspoken (and too often, unrecognized) influences affecting the way people make decisions. Regardless of the scope of their assets, most clients have limited resources, but unlimited wants and needs. It is always easier to spend more—no matter how many zeros are attached to the number that defines "more." It is unlikely that all client goals can ever be achieved, and even less likely that all alternatives can—or even should—be considered. The dilemma facing financial planners often comes down to the simplest of questions: which recommendation should be given to meet a client's goal? Without a process that balances the qualitative and the quantitative, the objective and the subjective, and the conscious and the unconscious to arrive at a conclusion, it is likely that the planner and client will face a disappointing outcome.

CHAPTER SUMMARY

This chapter attempts to fill a void in financial planning decision making. The objective is not to offer students or advisors an assortment of labels to attach to themselves or to clients. A generalized decision-making model was presented to illustrate how decisions can be reached in a logical and practical manner. For example, for the client who is "stuck" and refuses to move forward, a simple exercise of sequentially discussing the decision-making process could help the planner and client achieve new awareness and insight into the client's reservations.

Understanding behavioral finance concepts and how they can influence a decision maker's approach to problems and the selection of alternatives can help the planner and client explore an issue more astutely; furthermore, it could facilitate awareness of cognitive biases or other threats to decision making, because neither advisors nor clients are exempt from such influences. Integrating the logic of a standard approach with what sometimes appears to be illogical behavioral influences should afford new insights into the planner-client relationship. Like other fundamental financial planning skills, continued study, training, and experience will make systematic decision making a more comfortable tool for planners to incorporate into daily practice.

Learning Outcomes

1. A decision requires a conscious choice from alternatives that have been assessed, whereas a habit is an almost unconscious dependence on routine selection of the same choice. Financial planners and their clients can benefit from studying decision making for several reaons. First is the ability to fully satisfy the fiduciary or trustee relationship by ensuring that both planner and client are truly making decisions and not simply resorting to habitual actions that could limit financial success. Second, the repeated use of a recognized and documented decision-making process provides a defensible explanation against any allegations stemming from failure to act as a fiduciary or to demonstrate ethical conduct. Third, financial planning is built on numerous decisions, so sound decision-making methods are essential to sound planning practices. Fourth, planners strive to help clients prepare for and weather uncertainty. Extreme care is necessary to help clients realize that preparation is not prediction, an important distinction when motivating client action and managing client expectations.

2. Decision making is a dynamic process that involves defining a problem or issue, identifying a set of alternatives, clarifying the criteria on which the alternatives will be evaluated, reviewing the alternatives, and making a choice. A five-step generalized model of decision making can be used to guide choices. The process begins by recognizing the need to make a decision. This is followed by identifying and researching alternatives in response to the question, behavior, concern, problem, or goal. Alternatives should then be considered and ranked according to established criteria. An alternative should then be chosen and implemented. The process ends with an evaluation of the outcome and the decision having been implemented. Evaluation of the decision-making steps is important for empowering the decision maker to improve the application of individual steps, or to practice incorporating steps that might otherwise be overlooked.

3. Several decision-making rules can be applied in the decision-making process. Decision makers who use a maximization approach choose alternatives where the choice provides the highest unadjusted outcome. Optimization relies on a thorough analysis of all relevant goals, data, and resources and then choosing the alternative that lead to the highest level of satisfaction. Some decision makers use a satisficing procedure. In this approach, the first alternative that meets a specific set of criteria is chosen. Although each of these approaches offers a way to reach a decision, each also tends to be one-dimensional, with little emphasis placed on subjective and qualitative factors that can affect the evaluation process.

4. The traditional decision-making approach is premised on the economic principle of rationality. Based on this underlying premise, some financial decisions and related outcomes can be defined using objective probabilities. At other times, subjective probabilities derived from personal beliefs, experiences, and guesses can be used to guide decisions. A probability-weighted decision analysis technique, using either objective or subjective probability, provides a way to rank alternatives. Alternatively, stochastic models have gained acceptance as decision-making tools. These models use inputs such as rate-of-return and standard deviation data, to randomize outcomes to account for variations and the timing of returns. When probabilities are known with some degree of accuracy, traditional decision-making and stochastic modeling approaches work quite well.

5. Alternatives to the traditional decision-making process have existed for many years, but the development of prospect theory in 1979 brought behavioral finance to the attention of the financial planning community. Behavioral finance theorists argue that people are not always rational when making decisions, and quite often objective probabilities are unknown. As such, people do not always act consistently or maximize utility (i.e., satisfaction) when making decisions, which are driven by three themes in the context of behavioral finance: (a) people rely on mental shortcuts, called *heuristics*, when choosing among alternatives; (b) the way in which alternatives are framed influences choice decisions; and (c) the markets are generally inefficient because decision makers exhibit consistent cognitive biases.

6. Cognitive biases associated with heuristics are representativeness and the illusion of validity. Financial numeracy is one example of how the ability to process mathematical and probabilistic data—part of how a problem or issue is framed to the client—can affect the result. Examples of cognitive biases that can influence decision making include mental accounting, the hot hand fallacy, and herding.

7. Behavioral finance, or cognitive biases such as representativeness, the illusion of validity, aversion to loss, regret avoidance, overconfidence bias, mental accounting, herding, and the gambler's fallacy, influence the ways people make choices. Regret avoidance and the fact that the impact of loss is stronger than the impact of gain encourage complacency and failure to act, whether to rebalance a portfolio, sell a security, or even to make a major purchase or take a vacation because the status quo is good enough. Because of mental accounting, some income (e.g., bonus, tip, or commission) may be viewed as free money that can be freely spent, whereas other income is the foundation of all living expenses. Herding encourages clients to sell at the wrong time: when the market is declining and everyone else is selling to avoid loss. In fact, the exact opposite is the best advice: buy when the market is down, because individual share prices are, too.

8. Some decisions are inconsequential, and others have far-reaching implications. It is, therefore, important to understand threats to the decision-making process. In additional to behavioral biases that tend to threaten the decision-making process, complacency, defensive avoidance, and panic reactions compromise the ways in which people arrive at decisions. Complacency occurs when someone cannot or will not recognize and deal with an approaching danger. Defensive avoidance occurs when danger is recognized, but the danger is mentally minimized and/or denied. Panic reactions occur most often when someone is faced with a threat that is both urgent and serious. When panic sets in, traditional decision-making processes are put aside and replaced with emotion-driven actions based on the fight-or-flight syndrome. Any or all of these reactions can seriously limit how well decisions are made in practice.

9. Financial analyses and recommendations are seldom easy. The process involved in identifying a set of alternatives, clarifying the criteria on which the alternatives will be evaluated, reviewing the alternatives, and making a choice is cognitively difficult. This is one reason some financial professionals and many financial planning clientele fall into a persistent decision-making trap that involves making choices based on intuition and habit. As described in this chapter, the use of heuristics is one way people attempt to make difficult decisions fit into easily recognized choice rules. Sometimes heuristics are effective, but simplified decisions

based on intuition and habit frequently lead to unbalanced and simplistic choices. Financial planners are encouraged, whenever possible, to utilize and document a more precise model of decision making.

Chapter Resources

Books

Ariely, Dan. *Predictably Irrational: The Hidden Forces That Shape Our Decisions*. New York: HarperCollins, 2008.

Ariely, Dan. *The Upside of Irrationality*. New York: HarperCollins, 2010.

Kahneman, D., P. Slovic, and A. Tversky (Eds.). *Judgment under Uncertainty: Heuristics and Biases*. Cambridge, England: Cambridge University Press, 1999.

Lennick, D. with K. Jordan. *Financial Intelligence: How to Make Smart, Values-based Decisions with Your Money and Your Life*. Denver, CO: FPA Press, 2010.

Peterson, Richard L. *Inside the Investor's Brain: The Power of Mind over Money*. Hoboken, NJ: John Wiley & Sons, 2007.

Plous, S. *The Psychology of Judgment and Decision Making*. New York: McGraw-Hill, 1993.

Shefrin, H. *Beyond Greed and Fear: Understanding Behavioral Finance and the Psychology of Investing*. Boston: Harvard Business School Press, 2000.

Zweig, J. *Your Money and Your Brain: How the New Science of Neuroeconomics Can Help Make You Rich*. New York: Simon & Schuster, 2007.

Journals

Advances in Decision Sciences

Decision Sciences

Journal of Behavioral Finance

Journal of Financial Counseling and Planning

Journal of Financial Therapy

Judgment and Decision Making

Organizational Behavior and Human Decision Processes

Theory and Decision

Internet Resources

Academy of Behavioral Finance & Economics (http://www.aobf.org/index.htm).

Research Laboratory for Behavioral Finance (http://www.befinlab.com/index.html).

Paper Links (http://www.behaviouralfinance.net/).

Discussion Questions

1. Explain and illustrate the five steps of the decision-making process using a financial planning question, behavior, concern, problem, or goal. Be sure to identify as many alternatives as possible and clearly define your criteria set. How does the identification of alternatives change when approached from the perspective of all possible alternatives versus only feasible alternatives?

2. Using a financial planning question, behavior, concern, problem, or goal, explain how the choice of alternatives would vary when applying a maximizing, optimizing, or satisficing decision rule. What are the advantages and disadvantages of each rule?

3. Why is it important for financial advisors to understand, follow, and evaluate a decision-making process? Why is it important to conduct an evaluation of the decision outcome as well as the decision-making process?

4. What is the difference between objective and subjective probabilities? Identify five to eight financial planning questions, behaviors, concerns, problems, or goals for which objective probabilities can be applied to the alternatives.

5. Based on the table below, employ the traditional decision-making approach to determine which of the investments should be chosen if the most important decision criterion is to maximize the likelihood of receiving the highest return over a 10-year period.

Rate of Return on Investment	Future Value of $1,000 Invested for 10 Years	Probability That Rate of Return Will Be Achieved
12%	$3,105.85	50%
9%	$2,367.36	75%
5%	$1628.89	99%

6. Explain the difference between stochastic modeling and deterministic modeling. What is the benefit of knowing the probability of earning $x\%$ to planner and client?

7. Explain the three fundamental themes commonly associated with behavioral finance. How do they influence financial planning?

8. Make a list of 5–10 heuristics that you use to simplify decisions in your own life. What are the advantages and disadvantages of relying on heuristics, personally or professionally?

9. What does the conclusion that people dislike losing more than they like winning imply for financial planners who manage client investment assets?

10. Explain how behavioral finance merges two opposing theoretical views. Define representativeness and explain its significance in behavioral finance.

11. Identify and explain the three cognitive biases that you think are most prevalent in financial decision making. Then identify the three that you think are the most difficult to grasp or apply to actual decisions. Why?

12. Identify two relatively important decisions that you made recently, and then analyze your decision-making style. Did you follow the general model of decision making? What decision rules, if any, were used? Did you use heuristics or other behavioral finance concepts? Why are values, ethics, and other personal perceptions or attitudes an important part of the decision-making process?

13. How do herding and panic reactions support the view that decision makers can affect markets, thus supporting the claim that markets are inefficient?

14. How might the five-step decision-making process be applied to diffuse the negative effects of heuristics, complacency, defensive avoidance, or panic reactions? For each threat, which step in the process is likely the most important for the decision maker to consider fully?

15. Explain the four threats to decision making. Create an example to illustrate each.

Notes

1. 1. K. E. See, E. W. Morrison, N. B. Rothman, and J. B. Soll, "The Detrimental Effects of Power on Confidence, Advice Taking, and Accuracy," *Organizational Behavior and Human Decision Processes* 116, no. 2 (2011): 272–85.

2. M. J. Roszkowski and J. Grable, "Estimating Risk Tolerance: The Degree of Accuracy and the Paramorphic Representation of the Estimate," *Journal of Financial Counseling and Planning* 16 (2005): 29–47.

3. G. G. Kautt, *Stochastic Modeling: The New Way to Predict Your Financial Future* (Fairfax, VA: Monitor Publishing, 2001).

4. D. Kahneman and A. Tversky, "Prospect Theory: An Analysis of Decision under Risk," *Ecometrica* XVLII (1979): 263–291.

5. H. Shefrin, Beyond Greed and Fear: Understanding Behavioral Finance and the Psychology of Investing (Boston: Harvard Business School Press, 2000).

6. D. Kahneman and A. Tversky, "Judgment under Uncertainty: Heuristics and Biases," *Science* 185, no. 4157 (1974): 1124–1131.

7. J. J. Xiao, M W. Ford, and J. Kim, "Consumer Financial Behavior: An Interdisciplinary Review of Selected Theories and Research," *Family & Consumer Sciences Research Journal* 39 (2011): 399–414.

8. H. Wang and S. Hanna, "Does Risk Tolerance Decrease with Age?" *Journal of Financial Counseling and Planning* 8, no. 2 (1997): 27–31.

9. J. E. Grable, "Risk tolerance," in *Advances in Consumer Financial Behavior Research*, ed., J. J. Xiao (New York: Springer Publishing in conjunction with TCAI, University of Arizona, 2008), 1–20.

10. A beneficial source for behavioral decision-making theory and application can be found in D. E. Bell, H. Raiffa, and A. Tversky, eds., *Decision Making: Descriptive, Normative, and Prescriptive Interactions* (Cambridge, England: Cambridge University Press, 1998).

11. E. Peters, "Beyond Comprehension: The Role of Numeracy in Judgments and Decisions," *Current Directions in Psychological Science* 21 (2012): 31–35.

12. M. J. Roszkowski and J. Grable, "Estimating Risk Tolerance: The Degree of Accuracy and the Paramorphic Representation of the Estimate," *Journal of Financial Counseling and Planning* 16, no. 2 (2005): 29-47.

13. J. R. Nofsinger, *Investment Madness: How Psychology Affects Your Investing—and What to Do about It* (New York: Prentice-Hall, 2001).

14. H. A. Deery, "Hazard and Risk Perception among Young Novice Drivers," *Journal of Safety Research* 30 (1999): 225–236.

15. DALBAR, Inc. (2003). The DALBAR study shows that market-chasing mutual fund investors earn less than inflation. Data originally retrieved at www.dalbarinc.com/content/printerfriendly.asp?page=2003071601 on 11/21/05. Data updated from information published by American Century Funds (http://americancenturyblog.com/2011/07/lessons-from-investor-behavior-studies-better-to-have-patience-and-a-plan/).

16. G. Belsky and T. Gilovich, *Why Smart People Make Big Money Mistakes—and How to Correct Them*, (New York: Fireside, 2000).

17. For a more detailed description of the hot hand fallacy and the specific basketball example used in the original study, see T. Gilovich, R. Vallone, and A. Tversky, "The Hot Hand in Basketball: On the Misperception of Random Sequences," *Cognitive Psychology* 17 (1985): 295–314.

18. An excellent summary of this and other heuristics based on the work or Daniel Kahneman and Amos Tversky can be found in D. Kahneman, P. Slovic, and A. Tversky, eds., *Judgment under Uncertainty: Heuristics and Biases* (Cambridge, England: Cambridge University Press, 1999).

19. John Maynard Keynes, *The General Theory of Employment, Interest, and Money.* Available at http://www.marxists.org/reference/subject/economics/keynes/general-theory/.

20. D. D. Wheeler and I. L. Janis, *A Practical Guide for Making Decisions* (New York: Free Press, 1980).

21. D. Bouckenooghe, K. Vanderheyden, S. Mestdagh, and S. V. Laethem, "Cognitive Motivation Correlates of Coping Style in Decisional Conflict," *The Journal of Psychology* 141 (2007): 605–625.

PART III: The Systematic Process of Financial Planning

Chapter 5

An Overview

Learning Objectives

1. Identify and explain the six steps in the systematic financial planning process.

2. Define and characterize professional judgment in financial planning using the criteria of stakeholders, setting, problem framing, problem resolution, and standards of practice.

3. Explain the conceptual model of professional judgment in the development of a financial plan.

4. Differentiate between a goal orientation to planning and a cash flow orientation to planning—both of which must be integrated for a proactive, sustainable plan.

Key Terms

Cash flow orientation to planning

CFP Board Code of Ethics and Professional Responsibility

CFP Board Financial Planning Practice Standards

CFP Board Rules of Conduct

CFP Board Standards of Professional Conduct

FPA Code of Ethics

Goal orientation to planning

NAPFA Code of Ethics

NAPFA Standards of Membership and Affiliation

Problem framing and problem resolution

Professional judgment

Qualitative data

Quantitative data

Setting

Stakeholders

Standards of practice

Systematic financial planning process

Figure 5.1 The Systematic Financial Planning Process

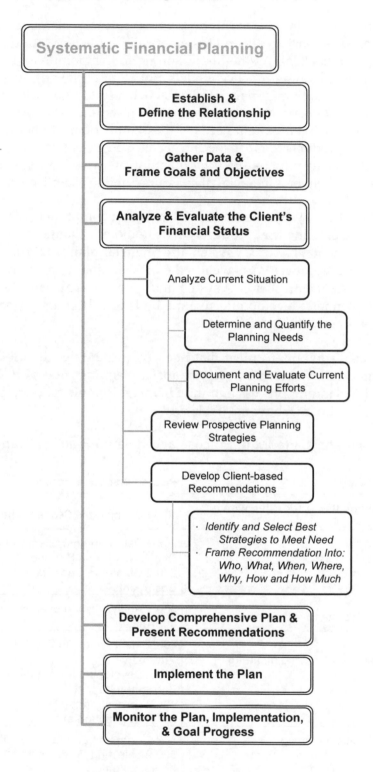

189

THE SYSTEMATIC FINANCIAL PLANNING PROCESS

The underlying premise of this book is that financial planning can be improved when the process is consistently and systematically applied to produce a financial plan to be delivered to a client. As the discussion up to this point has shown, there is a variety of financial planning practice models; not all financial advisors write comprehensive financial plans. Some financial planners choose to work on a per-project basis or to write a single-focus, or modular, plan when writing a comprehensive plan is beyond the scope of what the client needs or the planner offers. Other financial planners focus on selling products to meet specific needs. Contingent on their business models, such planners may conduct a financial planning analysis but not prepare a plan, whereas others may deliver a financial plan as a method to establish product needs.

Whether the final deliverable or outcome is a comprehensive plan, a modular plan, or the sale of a financial product, what should not change in any of these situations is the fundamental *process*. A **systematic financial planning process** is needed to guide the analytic approach to as well as the presentation, implementation, and monitoring of plan results with clients. A systematic approach is also needed to help students and novice planners develop effective methods to collect and apply the necessary client information.

This book attempts to meet that need by presenting, describing, and illustrating a systematic, almost step-by-step, financial planning process based on the recognized financial planning process and the **Financial Planning Practice Standards** promoted by the CFP Board, shown in Table 5.1.[1]

Table 5.1 CFP Board Financial Planning Process and Related Practice Standards

Financial Planning Process	Related Practice Standard
1. Establishing and defining the relationship with a client	100-1 Defining the Scope of the Engagement
2. Gathering client data	200-1 Determining a Client's Personal and Financial Goals, Needs and Priorities 200-2 Obtaining Quantitative Information and Documents
3. Analyzing and evaluating the client's financial status	300-1 Analyzing and Evaluating the Client's Information
4. Developing and presenting financial planning recommendations	400-1 Identifying and Evaluating Financial Planning Alternative(s) 400-2 Developing the Financial Planning Recommendation(s) 400-3 Presenting the Financial Planning Recommendation(s)
5. Implementing the financial planning recommendations	500-1 Agreeing on Implementation Responsibilities 500-2 Selecting Products and Services for Implementation
6. Monitoring	600-1 Defining Monitoring Responsibilities

Source: Reprinted from http://www.cfp.net/Learn/Standards.asp by permission of the CFP® Board of Standards.

Table 5.1 illustrates how the general six-step financial planning process delineated by the CFP Board can be expanded to provide systematic guidance. Although the systematic financial planning process is intended for the use of planners to develop a comprehensive plan, the process applies equally to those who write modular financial plans or simply want to conduct a systematic and defensible analysis of the suitability of a client investment or an investment-based insurance product. The systematic process described in Figure 5.1 refers to developing, implementing, and monitoring the *plan*; the CFP Board process and practice standards refer to developing, presenting, and implementing *recommendations*.

The explanation of Practice Standard 400-2, Developing the Financial Planning Recommendation(s), states that "a recommendation may be an independent action or a combination of actions which may need to be implemented collectively."[2] The systematic financial planning process presented in this book assumes that this "combination of actions"—in other words, a plan—is the ideal, holistic outcome of the process. The next three chapters describe the process necessary to develop, implement, and monitor such a plan. Following is a brief overview of each step illustrated in Figure 5.1.

Step 1: Establish and Define the Relationship

The process begins by establishing and defining the planner-client relationship. A planner's actions at this stage of the process include initiating the relationship with potential clients (by referral or marketing strategies), meeting with prospective clients, and formalizing the scope of the planner-client engagement.

Step 2: Gather Data and Frame Goals and Objectives

Once the initial step of establishing and defining the client relationship has been taken, the process proceeds by gathering client data to help frame goals and objectives. The data gathered can encompass a broad range of information, contingent on the scope of the financial planning engagement. A client's financial dreams, goals, fears, current financial situation, behavioral tendencies, attitudes, and personal traits may all be included. Assessments at this stage of the process can be both **quantitative** (e.g., factual, pertaining to the client's family, health, employment, or financial status) and **qualitative** (e.g., the personal and social dimensions of the client, including personality, interests, attitudes, and values), depending on the nature of the planning to be done. The desired outcome of this step in the process is the framing of complete, direct, and measurable client goals. For a goal to be measurable, it must be anchored in time and have a probable and realistic cost and funding strategy.

Step 3: Analyze and Evaluate the Client's Financial Status

Many view the step of analyzing and evaluating a client's financial situation as the essence of financial planning. The realities of a client's income and expenses, net worth, financial products owned, and financial strategies employed to date are scrutinized at this stage. Viewed narrowly, this step is fact-based and solution-oriented. But central to this step is a perspective that goes beyond the present factual situation to a larger, and perhaps more multifaceted, view of the client and the client's financial future.

This exploration should have occurred in Step 2, Gather Data and Frame Goals and Objectives, and it should have identified issues that could influence the analysis and planning that occur during this third step of the process. Too often at this step the solution-focused planner over-emphasizes quantitative analysis to the exclusion of the *person* for whom the plan is being designed. It is essential that a planner consider a client's goals and related planning assumptions during this analysis. Only by knowing a client's specific goals and using the assumptions agreed upon with the client can a financial planner anticipate, determine, and quantify planning needs.

As illustrated in Figure 5.1, the three primary substeps involved in analyzing and evaluating a client's financial status include

1. analyzing the current situation;

2. reviewing prospective planning strategies; and

3. developing client-based recommendations.

These steps might be summarized as *first*, "know your client," and *second*, consider the universe of strategies for meeting that client's needs. Then, using professional judgment, the advisor should match the client's situation with the strategies available to formulate client-specific recommendations that have the greatest likelihood of successfully satisfying the client's goals.

The first substep—analyzing the client's current financial situation—is further delineated to focus on identifying and reviewing planning needs and on the planning efforts currently in place. This means that a thorough review of the qualitative and quantitative data ought to be undertaken to describe the client's financial situation fully. The planner must focus on the current situation but also use the information gained to anticipate present *and* future planning issues. Personal financial products and strategies that are currently in place, whether implemented by the client or in consultation with another financial services professional, must also be evaluated. Outcomes associated with this step include quantifying the client's financial strengths and weaknesses, documenting areas where the situation can be strengthened, and identifying opportunities for future planning.

The second substep involves reviewing prospective financial planning strategies that can be used to meet a client's needs. This might be thought of as brainstorming or reviewing the universe of strategies or possible solutions that could apply to a client's situation.The financial planner develops client-based recommendations from this thorough review of strategies.

The third substep requires a planner to identify, select, and potentially combine the best strategies to meet a client's needs. The result is a series of concise recommendations designed to optimize the client's financial situation and lead to goal achievement. As shown in the model, seven key questions must be addressed whenever a recommendation is made:

1. Who should implement the recommendation?

2. What should be done?

3. When should the recommendation be implemented?

4. Where should the recommendation be put into place?

5. Why should the recommendation be implemented? Why is it important to the client's financial future?

6. How should implementation take place?

7. How much should be purchased, saved, invested to implement the recommendation?

Without adequate consideration of these seven questions, it is likely that a recommendation will not be as complete as necessary for full client acceptance and implementation. Without implementation, even the very best recommendations will result in unprotected client needs or unfulfilled client aspirations.

Step 3 can also be viewed as the essence of financial planning because this step incorporates the comprehensive dimension of the planning process. This step, and the repetition of the substeps, must be completed for each of the following core content planning areas:

- Current financial situation

- Income tax planning

- Risk management (i.e., life, health, disability, long-term care, property and liability, and other insurance needs)

- Investment planning and management

- Retirement planning

- Education planning or other special needs planning (e.g., expensive purchase, second home, future support for a special-needs family member, charitable giving, etc.)

- Estate planning

By the conclusion of this step, the financial planner has prepared client-based recommendations representing the various planning components that now must be developed into a comprehensive financial plan.

Step 4: Develop a Comprehensive Plan and Present Recommendations

Developing a comprehensive plan requires a planner to integrate and prioritize recommendations for a client. It may be impossible for a client to implement all recommendations immediately, because the list may be long and recommendations may compete for funding. Consequently, tracking the use of discretionary cash flow and changes in net worth is critical at this step in the planning process.

The plan may require that the implementation of recommendations be staggered over time. Funding priorities usually center on the recommendations that most closely match a client's goals or that provide protection from the greatest perceived risk of loss. Complementary recommendations or those that can be used to meet more than one goal may also emerge as priorities. For instance, recommending that a client fund a Roth IRA may serve the dual goals of saving for retirement and a child's educational expenses. In the simplest sense, the plan must provide a realistic and workable road map for the actions needed, immediately and in the future, to afford the client the greatest likelihood of protecting and growing assets.

Step 5: Implement the Plan

The fifth step in the process calls for the client and planner to implement the recommendations. Depending on the planner-client engagement, the financial planner can assume responsibility for this, or the implementation can be directed or completed by the client.

Step 6: Monitor the Plan, Implementation, and Goal Progress

Sometimes it is easy to lose track of why a comprehensive financial plan was written. The real reason clients' need a comprehensive financial plan is to ensure that their short-, intermediate-, and long-term financial goals are met. Only by looking at how each component of a client's financial life fits together can a full picture of financial threats and opportunities be drawn. Furthermore, client outcomes must constantly be tracked and monitored to truly know whether the client is on target to meet goals. Thus, it should be obvious that the sixth and final step in the financial planning process is critically important. Ongoing monitoring and client interaction enable a planner to determine the client's progress toward goals as well as responses to changes in the client's economic or personal life. Continued monitoring also offers financial planners an opportunity to add value to the planner-client relationship by helping the client respond to a situation and feel in control.

PROFESSIONAL JUDGMENT: FROM PROCESS TO PRACTICE

Professional judgment is assumed to be central to the practice of any profession. A review of the literature describing professional judgment from professions such as accounting, medicine, and education reveals terms like "expertise," "advanced level of competence," "integrity, objectivity, and independence," "advanced level of expertise," "expertise that goes beyond competence," "fairness," and "compliance with regulations and guidelines."

But what does professional judgment really mean, and how does it bridge the *process* of financial planning with the *practice* of financial planning? As do many other professional disciplines, financial planning relies on professional judgment. In the explanation of Practice Standard 400-1, Identifying and Evaluating Financial Planning Alternative(s), the CFP Board uses the phrase "the subjective nature of exercising professional judgment."[3] Similarly, in Rule 4, Obligations to Prospective Clients and Clients, the CFP Board *Rules of Conduct* 4.4 states, "a certificant shall exercise reasonable and prudent professional judgment in providing professional services to clients."[4]

Writing from the perspective of a broad array of professions, Facione in Facione, Facione, and Giancarlo defined **professional judgment** as:

> [A] goal-oriented decision-making or problem-solving process carried out in the interest of one's client wherein one gives reasoned consideration to relevant information, criteria, methods, context, principles, policies and resources.[5]

Although this definition offers some insight, the significance of professional judgment in the practice and governance of financial planning warrants a fuller explanation, such as might be found in the literature of other professional disciplines. Facione, Facione, and Giancarlo offer a framework of four general characteristics of professional judgment: (1) Analyzing the interests of **stakeholders;** (2) **setting;** (3) **problem framing and problem resolution;** and (4) abiding by **standards of practice**.[6] Considered from the context of the expectations for professional judgment in other disciplines (e.g., medicine, psychology, accounting, education, or law), the Facione, Facione, and Giancarlo framework is very applicable to financial planning. The examples that follow are not meant to be exhaustive or definitive; rather, they are offered as illustrations of professional judgment to help students and planners develop a richer definition of this important concept.

Stakeholders

A universal tenet for all professions is acting in the best interest of the client, the primary stakeholder. To do so in the context of financial planning requires not only the planner's complete engagement, but also that the client be actively involved in and fully informed of all aspects of the professional relationship. The client should be fully informed of the proposed recommendations (including the products and procedures) available to achieve the financial objectives and, whenever appropriate, should be offered alternatives. Furthermore, the planner has a responsibility to fully disclose, explain, and educate the client on the logic supporting the recommendations.

Safeguarding the confidentiality of client information is yet another way to act in the best interest of the client as primary stakeholder. For example, protecting the confidentiality of client data is one of the principles included in the **CFP Board of Standards** *Code of Ethics and Professional Responsibility* (http://www.cfp.net/learn/codeofethics.asp) and the **NAPFA** (http://www.napfa.org/about/CodeofEthics.asp) and **FPA** (http://www.fpanet.org/AboutFPA/CodeofEthics/) *Code of Ethics* statements.

Secondary stakeholders (based on the Facione, Facione, and Giancarlo framework) are other individuals or groups who may be favorably or adversely affected by the outcome of the professional relationship dedicated to maximizing the client's interests. Secondary stakeholders include the planner, the planner's employer or partners (if applicable), and the client's family. Recognizing conflicts of interest and heeding professional ethics are central to making professional judgments involving multiple stakeholders. For example, the decision to offer a lower fee structure to attract a large client could benefit the client and still bring in a large portfolio and future revenue stream for the firm. However, the fee structure must cover all the costs involved so that it does not adversely affect the firm, its employees, or other clients. Furthermore, the planner must be reasonably competent and capable of delivering the investment management services offered to the larger client base with no reduction in quality.

Some financial planners might regard the preceding situation as merely a subtle—perhaps even insignificant—conflict of interest. A more straightforward conflict of interest where multiple stakeholders could be affected is the potential conflict between a planner's desire to make money and a client's need to receive high-quality, cost-effective solutions. Such a conflict could be manifested by churning (or other sales practices designed to increase commissions) or by inconsistent fee setting (e.g., higher rates for some clients and lower for other clients) to increase revenue. Both practices could signify questionable professional judgment on the planner's part, either because they do not fully consider all stakeholders, they are unethical, or they are illegal.

The impact of planning recommendations and client choices about long-term care insurance, umbrella insurance, estate planning options, and large (perhaps even extravagant) purchases can demonstrate another dilemma of professional judgment for advisors. In some situations the financial planner may need to take into account the interests of secondary stakeholders in addition to those of the primary stakeholder (i.e., the client) when making recommendations. For example, the interests of a beneficiary named in a will might be considered in the planning process. Secondary stakeholders—children or other family members who may in the future question the judgment of the advisor in failing to prudently plan for asset enhancement or potential expenses, such as nursing home care—might need to be accounted for. (Conversely, the argument could be made that children who subsequently question an advisor's judgment in prudently planning for potential expenses are co-opting an issue that is rightfully the client's.) Situations like this may ultimately result in charges of professional malpractice or malfeasance and demonstrate that a challenge to professional judgment does not necessarily have to come from an adversely affected primary stakeholder.

Not all financial planners agree that secondary stakeholders' interests must influence recommendations. It is also possible that an individual whom one planner considers a secondary stakeholder may be defined as a primary stakeholder by another planner. For example, a child questioning the judgment of an advisor in prudently planning for the potential expenses associated with providing care for an elderly parent could be interpreted as an offshoot of a primary stakeholder issue. However, if the parents have decided to spend their assets for their own enjoyment, to the detriment of a child's inheritance, that is the parents' (as the primary stakeholders) prerogative. A planner representing the children's interest in protecting the inheritance would fail to maximize the interests of the primary stakeholder. As long as the task of spending down assets can be accomplished reasonably and prudently, some financial planners would question whether it is the planner's professional duty or obligation even to attempt to represent the children's interests.

This matter of stakeholder interests cannot simply be distilled to questions of "who is paying the bill for the service" or "who is the primary beneficiary of the advice." Consider two primary reasons for seeking the advice of a planning professional: college planning and estate planning. In both cases it is easy to see that the true beneficiary of the advice is not the one paying for it.

What is important, as these examples illustrate, is a commitment to the principles of professional ethics and behavior and an awareness of *normative principles*, or accepted practice standards within the profession. Even more important in the context of professional judgment is a willingness to think and to critically evaluate the issue, the decision, and the potential ramifications for all of the people or groups with an interest in the outcome of the plan. These are the stakeholders.

Setting

Setting refers to the characteristics or dimensions of the problem or decision that a professional must address on behalf of a stakeholder or client. In describing settings, Facione, Facione, and Giancarlo identify seven dimensions.[7] However they note that, when taking into account the interactions among the individual dyads or the two ends of each scale, there is the potential for 49 (or 7^2) different kinds of decisions or problems a professional might encounter—not to mention all the interim points along each scale. The explanation of the seven dimensions offers some useful criteria for characterizing professional judgment in financial planning:

1. *High*-stakes decisions to *low*-stakes problems or issues

2. *Time-constrained* issues to decisions that are *time unconstrained*

3. *Novel* problems/decisions to issues that are *very familiar* to the professional

4. *Unexpected* problems/issues to decisions that are *planned*

5. Issues that require *specialized knowledge* to problems requiring *knowledge commonly shared* by the community of professionals

6. Issues that can be handled *solely by the professional* to problems that require *collaboration with other professionals*

7. *Routine*, commonly addressed problems in the profession to an *unusual* situation that rarely occurs

These descriptors suggest a variety of financial planning situations that expand and contextualize professional judgment and practice. For example, imagine Figure 5.2 as a "slider" scale on an interactive Web page. Estate and tax planning issues for a high-net-worth client with multinational assets might represent an unusual situation requiring the collaboration of a planner, accountant, attorney, interpreter, or even a professional in another country. A high-stakes and time-sensitive situation might arise suddenly in response to a life event. Or a situation with less urgent time constraints could be proactively planned for. Planning for a child's education shortly after the child is born might be characterized as a routine issue with relatively low stakes and no immediate time pressure. But a buy-out offer in advance of an employer relocation plan might require immediate action and involve very high stakes for an executive. To characterize the setting fully, each dimension must be considered. The "sliders" move across the seven scales in what may appear to be a random pattern, but this is a very useful tool for identifying the different dimensions of a setting.

Figure 5.2 7^2 or Infinite Possibilities for Characterizing the Setting

Many Decisions, Problems of Issues to Consider...

Low stakes	High stakes
Time constrained	Time unconstrained
Novel	Very familiar
Unexpected	Planned
Specialized knowledge	Knowledge commonly shared
Solely by the professional	Collaboration with other professionals
Routine	Unusual

When exercising professional judgment, planners must be sensitive to a client's setting; however, they must also recognize that they may be influenced by their own settings. An inexperienced planner might view each client with a sense of urgency and time pressure that an older, more established planner would not feel. Planners with dissimilar business models and methods of compensation could attribute different characteristics to a setting in the same client situation.

This is not to say that planners are not always acting in the best interest of the client; they simply may approach client situations with different expectations and points of view. Consider the preceding executive buy-out offer example, except this time approach it from the planner's setting. If asked to manage all of the funds from the buy-out along with the retirement funds, a planner practicing under the assets under management model might view this situation with a greater sense of urgency than a planner working on a retainer basis.

These examples illustrate several important considerations about exercising professional judgment in financial planning. First, the characteristics or dimensions of the setting may or may not be the same for the client and the planner. The client might view a routine issue for the planner such as a mortgage refinance or an IRA conversion as high stakes and challenging because the client has no experience with such things. A different planning issue might be considered very important by both the planner and the client, demanding the immediate attention of the advisor.

Second, for many financial planning issues, the setting can be further defined by the advisor's business practice model. The scope of the client engagement as well as the products, services, and expertise the planner offers may define the setting or indicate the need to collaborate with other professionals. Planners who offer tax preparation services have specialized knowledge to apply to a client situation, whereas another planner with limited tax expertise will have to refer the client to another professional or perhaps collaborate with that professional to fully resolve the client's issue.

Third, and perhaps most importantly, when exercising professional judgment, planners must be careful to reflect on how the setting for stakeholders *and* themselves can affect the financial planning process. For example, both advisor and client attitudes can influence the process. The emotional response of a client who is feeling particularly vulnerable or stressed by a financial issue can change the typical advisor-client interaction. By recognizing the significance of the client's attitudes, the skilled advisor can appropriately adapt the planning and decision-making processes to address the client's concerns. Likewise, advisors must monitor their own attitudes and emotional responses to economic, market, or client situations to ensure that the setting is not unduly influencing their decisions.

Finally, the multidimensional criteria that define the setting suggest the need for multifaceted, case-based education for planners. The critical thinking skills needed to enhance professional judgment suggest that planners must build and maintain technical competency concurrently with client-centered planning approaches sensitive to the client's setting or situation. In fact, Facione, Facione, and Giancarlo assert that

> education, in contrast to training, does not require covering every possibility. Education implies preparing professionals with the content knowledge, reasoning skills, and habits of mind necessary to make whatever kinds of judgments might be required.[8]

In summary, the setting encapsalates both the *facts* and the *feelings* that characterize a problem or decision that a client, or stakeholder, has brought to the planner for assistance. In the context of professional judgment, it is important to exercise a "willingness to think" and not jump to conclusions, apply stereotypes, or provide a quick answer. Professional judgment demands that planners critically evaluate a problem or decision from multiple perspectives to fully comprehend the scope of the issue and its significance to stakeholders, and that they continually enhance their expertise to do so.

Problem Framing and Problem Resolution

The difference between problem framing and problem resolution is fundamental to the definition of professional judgment, whether a layman's or a professional's. Problem resolution, represented by some baseline professional competence, is expected of the novice. True acumen at problem framing comes only from broad-based experience that alerts the professional to critical situational data and key patterns within the data that lead to problem identification *and* resolution. Facione, Facione, and Giancarlo assert that professional judgment, as characterized by problem framing, may hinge on the nuances of "problem identification, interpretation, differentiation, and diagnosis,"[9] which closely parallel the steps in the financial planning process.

Applied to financial planning, problem framing focuses on a planner's ability to use knowledge and experience to discern an ill-defined or complex situation, gain the information necessary, and then generate potential planning solutions. The planner should skillfully build the planner-client relationship to gain information from the client, using both verbal and nonverbal cues. Professional judgment requires a balanced perspective that considers not only all relevant quantitative and qualitative data, but also the details of the situation, or setting, as well as its broader scope. In fact, the CFP Board, in explaining Practice Standard 400-1, Identifying and Evaluating Financial Planning Alternative(s), states that "alternatives identified by the practitioner may differ from those of other practitioners or advisers, illustrating the subjective nature of exercising professional judgment."[10]

Defining the scope of the planner-client engagement, carefully selecting products and services as well as possible alternatives—all consistent with the client situation—is another example of problem framing. The planner has an obligation to limit the engagement to the boundaries of his or her personal expertise, or to seek the assistance of other professionals when necessary. Furthermore, decisions and recommendations should bear some resemblance to those of other advisors under similar circumstances. In reference to Practice Standard 500-2, Selecting Products and Services for Implementation, the CFP Board notes that

> The financial planning practitioner uses professional judgment in selecting the products and services that are in the client's interest. Professional judgment incorporates both qualitative and quantitative information.[11]

Whereas the dimension of stakeholders focuses on *people* and the dimension of setting focuses on the *facts and feelings* surrounding a client's situation, the dimension of problem framing and problem resolution continues the process through *diagnosis and resolution* of the client issue. The need to build the expertise to surpass basic problem resolution to arrive at the more expert level of problem framing is critical to professional judgment. Beyond the "willingness to think,"[12] professional judgment involves the willingness to continue to learn so that the advisor can adeptly diagnose a client situation and suggest viable, effective recommendations. Continuing education requirements to maintain memberships, credentials, and licensing both underscore and support this need.

Standards of Practice

In defining standards of practice, Facione, Facione, and Giancarlo suggest that there are really several "layers" or dimensions of standards of practice that may be used to assess professional judgment.[13] First are the obvious criteria that the action or resolution satisfies the objective effectively and efficiently. The third layer defines the action as legal, ethical, and culturally acceptable. Between these micro- and macro-layers is a second layer, represented by *codes of conduct* and *standards of practice* unique to the profession used to establish when, where, or how judgments are made, as summarized in Table 5.2. Also important to this discussion is the question of who has the right to impose these standards or to determine whether they have been met.

Table 5.2 The Three Levels of Standards of Practice

Dimensions	Level	Judges
Legally, ethically, culturally responsible resolution	Level 3	Representatives of society, culture (e.g., NASAA, NAIC, SEC, FINRA)
Resolution is consistent with professional codes of conduct and standards of practice	Level 2	Credentialing, designation, and membership organizations
Effective, efficient resolution	Level 1	Advisor/client

In the first layer, or dimension, it seems reasonable that the planner and the client should be the judges of effectiveness. Additionally, standards of practice, such as those promulgated by the CFP Board as well other informally recognized "best practice standards," focus attention on the probable consequences and effectiveness of proposed planning recommendations. For example, questions to consider might include:

- Is the recommended product or service a cost-effective alternative with a relatively high probability of success for the client? Have the method of compensation and any potential conflicts of interest regarding compensation been disclosed, if applicable?

- Is the plan built on mutually agreeable, valid assumptions representative of the legal, tax, and broader economic environment?

- Does the plan allow for readjustment or product or service changes in response to changing situations?

- Are the client alternatives and proposed recommendations consistent with ethical professional conduct? Have any potential conflicts of interest been appropriately and clearly disclosed to the client?

- Are the alternatives and proposed recommendations posed to the client socially and culturally acceptable? Financial decisions surrounding divorce, estate planning, and distribution of assets are just a few examples of decisions that carry strong social, cultural, or religious implications for the planner-client relationship.

The opposite end of the spectrum—the third layer of standards—represents a larger, more macro, social and cultural view, as shown in Table 5.2. Therefore it seems reasonable that society at large, particularly the consumers of financial planning services, could determine—and expect—standards of practice consistent with societal mores or norms. For financial planning, designated representatives of the society, such as state and federal securities and insurance regulators (e.g., NASAA, NAIC, SEC) and other self-regulatory organizations (e.g., FINRA), are sanctioned to make judgments about prudent business practices and to express those judgments in a socially powerful context. As a result, legal, regulatory, and other compliance standards govern various responsibilities and actions of financial advisors contingent on their business model and the services or products delivered, as explained more fully in Chapter 2.

Increasing this ambiguity is the in-between layer of standards that Facione, Facione, and Giancarlo assert is unique to the profession. In financial planning, credentialing and membership organizations also define acceptable standards of practice. In combination, the *Code of Ethics and Professional Responsibility*, the *Rules of Conduct*, and the *Financial Planning Practice Standards* make up what the Board refers to as its *Standards of Professional Conduct*. Referred to as the *Standards*, these documents and their doctrines represent the standards of ethical conduct for CFP® professionals. Similarly, **NAPFA** membership or affiliation is contingent on meeting and abiding by the **Standards of Membership and Affiliation**,[14] which include: adherence to the NAPFA definition of a fee-only financial planner; prohibition of certain ownership interests and employment relationships; compliance with NAPFA standards and industry regulations; and prompt notification to NAPFA of certain disciplinary and legal events. These criteria define the *required* practice standards, as well as the business model for NAPFA members, and set parameters for both that are distinct from the CFP Board *Financial Planning Practice Standards* or *Rules of Conduct and Professional Responsibility*.

Despite these differences in business practice methods, both organizations as well as the FPA share the principles of objectivity, competence, fairness, integrity, confidentiality, and professionalism in their *Code of Ethics* statements. In fact, the FPA adopted the CFP Board *Code of Ethics and Professional Responsibility* and asserts that "All FPA members are asked to commit to this Code, CFP® certificants and non-CFP certificants alike."[15]

These principles help define the standard of practice for financial advisors affiliated with these credentialing and membership organizations—principles that are common to other financial services organizations as well as other professions. Furthermore, these principles reflect the macro (i.e., social or cultural) view of actions that are legally, ethically, and culturally acceptable.

Therefore, the concept of standards of practice as a characteristic of professional judgment goes beyond simple adherence to the typical codes of conduct or practice standards common to most disciplines, including financial planning. For example, full and accurate documentation of the planning process, as well as all efforts to implement the plan (when applicable) should be maintained as part of standards of practice. Documentation extends beyond that required for all legal, regulatory, and compliance requirements to the larger professional responsibility of full accountability, transparency, and the transfer of information to other stakeholders consistent with confidentiality policies. Rule 3 of the CFP Board *Rules of Conduct* regarding Prospective Client and Client Information and Property states:

> A certificant shall treat information as confidential except as required in response to proper legal process; as necessitated by obligations to a certificant's employer or partners; as required to defend against charges of wrongdoing; in connection with a civil dispute; or as needed to perform the services.[16]

Finally, both the client and society at large, when judging the effectiveness of the financial planning relationship, would expect private client information to remain confidential. Furthermore, the 1999 Gramm-Leach-Bliley Act and subsequent SEC rulings mandate that any firm with access to private and confidential client data must disclose in a privacy statement how the data will be used and safeguarded.

At issue for the future of financial planning are the acceptance of consistent and broadly applicable financial planning standards of practice to guide the profession and clarification regarding whom should be sanctioned to make such judgments— in other words, the second and third dimensions of standards of practice as defined by Facione, Facione, and Giancarlo. Most would agree that procedures and protocols typically applicable to particular client situations might not be applicable to financial planning because of the need to match recommendations and products to unique client situations and the prevailing economic, legal, and tax environment. This subjective aspect of professional judgment is further defined by the business practice model of the advisor and (1) standards of care and fiduciary responsibility and (2) the commitment to transparency and full disclosure of compensation and potential conflicts of interest.

Just as problem framing and problem resolution focus on the diagnosis and resolution of client or stakeholder issues, standards of practice focus broadly on the *methods* employed to serve the client. Specifically, standards of practice are judged on their effectiveness, their representation of normative and prudent practices within the profession, and whether society approves them as ethically or legally acceptable. In other words, did it work and was it the right thing to do? Ponzi schemes are an effective investment recommendation for initial investors who receive high returns, but after nearly 100 years of use, Ponzi schemes are still not considered the right thing to do.

From Process to Practice

Considered from the Facione, Facione, and Giancarlo framework, it is easy to see why everyone tries *but no one really succeeds* in defining professional judgment. But the real value of the framework is to call attention to the multidimensional characteristics of stakeholders, setting, problem framing, problem resolution, and standards of practice that define professional judgment. Although many overriding principles apply to any profession, professional judgment is contextualized by an individual's professional pursuit and hinges upon professional skepticism (i.e., a willingness to reflect and self-correct in pursuit of professional excellence). Professional judgment challenges advisors not to become complacent with their modes of operation or the adequacy of advice. Nonetheless, the trap of "paralyzing perfectionism" (i.e., the fear of making the wrong decision) can result in inaction. The confidence to proceed can be gained from a fuller understanding and consistent application of the systematic financial planning process and methodology.

PROFESSIONAL JUDGMENT IN THE DEVELOPMENT OF A FINANCIAL PLAN

What might be considered the core of financial planning occurs when a planner—or team of planners—proceeds from identifying strategies potentially useful to a client to the integration of those strategies, stated as recommendations, within a plan. This complex, dynamic process is a cognitive challenge that demands knowledge regarding which pieces of data (qualitative and quantitative) to consider as well as how to evaluate and apply them in planning and decision making. This aspect of the process as well as the plan must be tailored to the client's values and goals.

The process must be *efficient* to attain accurate and complete data, to interrelate and analyze the data, and to identify the best use of the planner's and the client's resources. But the process must also be *effective* to focus on the most important data to produce a plan that offers the greatest probability of success in an environment where few, if any, factors can truly be controlled. Few things are harder to predict than the whims of human nature, the stock market, or the global economy—all of which are likely to contribute to the perceived success or failure of the financial planning effort.

A question was raised earlier in this chapter: "How does professional judgment bridge the *process* of finanical planning with the *practice* of financial planning?" The conceptual model of Professional Judgment in Plan Development (Figure 5.3) attempts to answer that question. A conceptual model is an abstract representation of the relationship among the most important components of a process, phenomenon, or event.

Figure 5.3 Professional Judgment throughout the Development of a Financial Plan

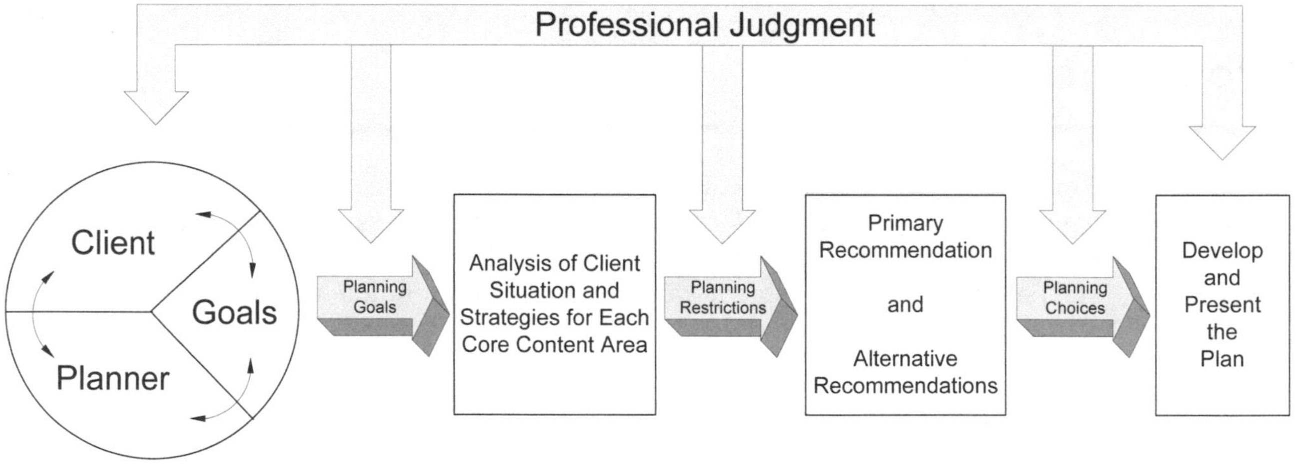

A conceptual model attempts to capture information by focusing on (1) the identification of critical elements, and (2) the relationships among those elements. Representing only the essentials, conceptual models should be simple but also broad enough to be generalized to a variety of "realities" explained by the model. As such, models are useful to planners who offer financial products, modular plans focused on one issue within a core content planning area, or comprehensive plans involving multiple goals.

As Figure 5.3 illustrates, professional judgment is integral to the financial planning process from the initial identification of planning goals to the development and presentation of a comprehensive plan. The following questions are intended to help integrate professional judgment throughout the financial planning process.

- Who are the stakeholders to consider when a planner and a remarried couple are identifying the goals of their financial plan?

- How will the unique experiences and attitudes of this remarried couple shape the development of planning goals that are mutually agreeable to the couple and the planner?

- How might the setting or scope of the issues to be addressed vary across the seven dimensions? And how might the facts and feelings of the planner and the couple differ individually for each of the seven dimensions?

- How might the attitudes and experiences of a remarried couple uniquely contribute to the problem framing and problem resolution that the planner must consider when analyzing the situation and developing strategies?

- How might the planner's business model, the couple's values, or standards of practice establish planning restrictions that may define, or frame, the recommendations?

- Similarly, how might those same factors influence the planning choices resulting in the recommendations that comprise the plan?

- Finally, what practice standards are likely to remain constant across clients, regardless of client household dynamics?

Professional judgment should be the foundation for the application of the systematic financial planning process, as well as the evolving planner-client relationship.

Another aspect of the integration of professional judgment into the systematic process of financial planning can be found in two recognized standards of practice that ground the financial planning process: **goal orientation** and **cash flow orientation**. Both are hallmarks of a successful plan, yet neither can fully protect a client from the eventualities of life. Attention to cash flow (which may include discretionary income as well as other available assets) ensures, but cannot guarantee, that the client will be able to afford the goals. Goal orientation ensures that the plan is consistent with a client's values, needs, and desires—both now and in the future—because as one goal is accomplished, a new goal may be identified and new recommendations initiated.

Attention to cash flow ensures that the pursuit of any single goal does not expose the client to unwarranted risk or leave the client completely unprepared to withstand unexpected negative financial consequences. In fact, it can be argued that the primary purpose of financial planning is to maximize and stabilize cash flow across the client's planning period. Yet, there is an equally valid argument that it is the goal orientation of financial planning that provides the framework and motivation for sustained client commitment. Thus, by its very nature, financial planning is circular because it attempts to respond to the client's "circles of life"—none of which can be fully anticipated, but which are the focus of life and financial planning.

CHAPTER SUMMARY

This chapter introduced the six-step systematic financial planning process. The process was characterized as grounded in the planner-client relationship, controlled by the professional judgment of the advisor, and based on the dual but integrated perspectives of the goal orientation and cash flow orientation to planning. The four dimensions of stakeholders, setting, problem framing and problem resolution, and standards of practice offer a useful approach to characterizing and contextualizing professional judgment within financial planning. Critical to the understanding of professional judgment in financial planning is a commitment to consider these dimensions broadly throughout the planning process, albeit influenced by the advisor's business practice model and the subjectivity of professional judgment.

Learning Outcomes

1. The essence of the six-step financial planning process can be condensed into the following:

   • Establish a personal and professional relationship.

   • Collect data to profile the client's situation and goals.

   • Use the data to assess the client's situation and develop recommendations.

   • Formulate and present a plan.

   • Set the plan in motion.

   • Continue to evaluate the client's situation, the plan, and goal progress.

2. Professional judgment is a multifaceted problem-solving and decision-making process that provides a context, or framework, for professional practice in the service of clients.

3. Professional judgment is characterized by:

   • stakeholders, or individuals, who are affected by or influence the financial planner's decisions;

   • setting, or the problem, issue, or decision that the financial planner must address with the client. The setting is charaterized by multiple features, or parameters, that can complicate the problem.

- problem framing and problem resolution, which represent different levels of a financial planner's capability to conduct the multifaceted problem solving and decision making needed to serve the client. Problem resolution reflects a baseline competency of service, and problem framing incorporates knowledge and experience to discern the nuances of unclear or complex client issues.

- practice standards, or "best practices, " which are measured by their *effectiveness* in meeting a client's need; their *representativeness* of normative practices supported by member or credentialing organizations within the profession; and their *endorsement* by society as morally, ethically, culturally, and legally acceptable.

4. Professional judgment can and should be the underlying framework for conducting the problem-solving and decision-making processes throughout each of the six steps in the financial planning process.

5. Financial plans, like children, need to be given "roots and wings." Financial plans must be *rooted* in the cash flow orientation of planning to ensure that funding is available to make the plan actionable and sustainable. Likewise, financial plans must have *wings*, or clearly articulated goals, to give the plan direction and to motivate the client to act. A goal orientation to planning provides the roots to sustain a client's commitment to the plan.

Chapter Resources

Certified Financial Planner Board of Standards, Inc. (www.CFP.net).

Financial Planning Association (www.fpanet.org).

National Association of Personal Financial Advisors (www.napfa.org).

Discussion Questions

1. List the steps and substeps in the systematic financial planning process. How might the application of the process, or progression through the steps, differ when developing a modular rather than a comprehensive plan?

2. When developing a client-based recommendation, what seven key questions should be addressed? What might happen if these seven questions are not given adequate consideration?

3. List the core content planning areas that should be included in a comprehensive plan. For each core content area, give an example of how at least three of the seven key questions might be answered in the development of a recommendation.

4. Using online or other dictionaries, review the definitions of *profession, professional,* and *judgment.* Which aspects of these terms relate to Facione's definition of professional judgment? Explain why a succinct defintion may not adequately define professional judgment.

5. Using online or other dictionaries, review the definitions of *profession, professional,* and *judgment.* What aspects of these definitions relate to, or could serve as a foundation for, the four characteristics of professional judgment?

6. How does the identification of the primary and secondary stakeholder differ if the financial advisor has a fiduciary responsibility to the client? To the advisor's employer?

7. How do the seven dimensions of setting influence the type of decisions a financial planner might face when working with clients? Provide an example of a client issue or situation to illustrate each dimension.

8. Describe the difference between problem framing and problem resolution. Illustrate this difference by using a financial planning example from one of the core content planning areas.

9. How might problem framing and problem resolution vary with the expertise or experience of the advisor? Explain the interaction between the complexity of a setting and problem resolution.

10. List and describe the three layers or dimensions of standards of practice that could apply to financial planning. For each, give an example of a judgment or measure that could be applied to determine the outcome of the standard of practice.

11. This chapter states:

    > Most would agree that specifically defined procedures and protocols that typically apply to a particular client situation may not be applicable to financial planning because of the need to individually match recommendations and products to a unique client situation and the prevailing economic, legal, and tax environment.

    Complete Question 10, above, from the perspective of another profession, such as medicine, law, accounting, theology, education, etc. How does the uniqueness of the client situation for the profession chosen compare to that of financial planning?

12. Five questions, based on standards of practice, were suggested to evaluate the effectiveness of a financial planning recommendation. Where do the key concepts from each of these questions intersect with the six-step financial planning process? In other words, what actions in each step(s) help to ensure that the standards of practice are not violated?

13. Using the four characteristics of professional judgment, explain how they contextualize or establish parameters for the six-step financial planning process shown in Figure 5.1.

14. Describe the two fundamental issues that ground the financial planning process. Why are these perspectives on planning both unique and integrative?

Notes

1. Certified Financial Planner Board of Standards, Inc., *CFP Board's Standards of Professional Conduct.* Available at http://www.cfp.net/Downloads/2010Standards.pdf, p. 15 or http://www.cfp.net/learn/standards.asp/.

2. CFP Board, *Standards of Professional Conduct*, p. 23, or http://www.cfp.net/learn/standards400.asp.

3. CFP Board, *Standards of Professional Conduct*, p. 22, or http://www.cfp.net/learn/standards400.asp.

4. CFP Board, *Standards of Professional Conduct*, p. 11, or http://www.cfp.net/learn/rulesofconduct.asp#4.

5. P. A. Facione, N. C. Facione, and C. A. F. Giancarlo, *Professional Judgment and the Disposition of Critical Thinking* (Millbrae, CA: The California Academic Press, 1997), 3. Available at http://www.insightassessment.com/CT-Resources/Independent-Critical-Thinking-Research/pdf-file/Professional-Judgment-and-the-Disposition-Toward-Critical-Thinking-PDF/(language)/eng-US, p. 3.

6. Facione, Facione, and Giancarlo, *Professional Judgment and Critical Thinking*, 3–4.

7. Facione, Facione, and Giancarlo, *Professional Judgment and Critical Thinking*, 3–4.

8. Facione, Facione, and Giancarlo, *Professional Judgment and Critical Thinking*, 4–5.

9. Facione, Facione, and Giancarlo, *Professional Judgment and Critical Thinking*, 4.

10. CFP Board, *Standards of Professional Conduct*, p. 22, or http://www.cfp.net/learn/standards400.asp.

11. CFP Board, *Standards of Professional Conduct*, p. 26, or http://www.cfp.net/learn/standards500.asp.

12. Facione, Facione, and Giancarlo, *Professional Judgment and Critical Thinking*, 2.

13. Facione, Facione, and Giancarlo, *Professional Judgment and Critical Thinking*, 4.

14. National Association of Personal Financial Advisors, *Our Standards.* Available at http://www.napfa.org/membership/OurStandards.asp.

15. Financial Planning Association, *Code of Ethics.* Available at http://www.fpanet.org/AboutFPA/CodeofEthics/.

16. CFP Board, *Standards of Professional Conduct*, p. 10, or http://www.cfp.net/learn/rulesofconduct.asp#3.

Chapter 6

Framing the Relationship, the Situation, and the Goals

Learning Objectives

1. List and explain the purpose of the documents provided to clients during the first step of the financial planning process.

2. Identify the fundamental outcomes of the first step of the systematic financial planning process.

3. Explain and apply the CFP Board requirements for ethical professsional conduct relative to Step 1 of the systematic financial planning process.

4. Explain the categories of client data that a planner should collect to understand a client's situation.

5. Describe the discovery process and how it relates to situational factors, life planning, or money scripts.

6. Define *financial risk tolerance* and explain its importance in financial planning decisions.

7. Explain the different ways client data may be collected and the cautions to consider.

8. Describe a Client Intake Form and its purpose.

9. Describe the focused interview between planner and client.

10. Explain what it means to frame client goals and objectives.

11. Explain SMART goals and their relationship to the client's wants, needs, life cycle events, and life transitions.

12. Demonstrate use of the goal-ranking form.

13. Explain and apply the CFP Board requirements for ethical professsional conduct relative to Step 2 of the systematic financial planning process.

Key Terms

Attitudes and beliefs	Life planning
Client Intake Form	Life transition
Conceptual model	Money scripts
Data collection questionnaire	Needs
Discovery process	Objective
Financial coaching	Personality
Financial therapist	Privacy statement
Frame	Risk tolerance
Focused interview	Temperament
Goal	Transference
Help-seeking behavior	Values
Investment policy statement	Wants
Life cycle event	

Figure 6.1 The Systematic Financial Planning Process

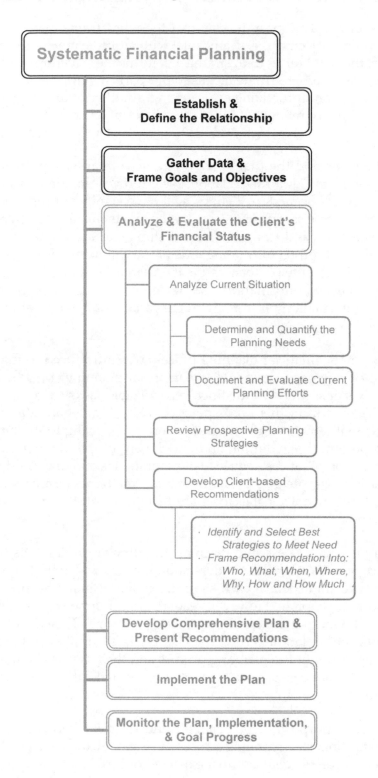

FRAMING: THE WIDE-ANGLE VIEW VS. THE MICROSCOPIC VIEW

A check of the dictionary reveals that the word *frame* may be used as a noun or a verb, or as an adjective (i.e., frameable) with multiple meanings. As a noun, a common usage of the word refers to the frame that forms the structure of a building (e.g., timber or steel). As a verb, to frame means to put parts together, as in framing a house, or in the abstract, conceptualizing or designing. Another noun usage refers to a paradigm, view, or frame of reference. All of these definitions are relevant to financial planning goals and objectives, which provide the core structure or frame for a financial plan.

Both the goals and the plan must be framed—that is, put together, conceptualized, or designed—through the collaborative efforts of the planner and the client. How a goal is viewed, framed, or defined will have significant repercussions for both. The planning process is grounded on the engagement and relationship that a planner and client forge, and from that relationship goals are framed and data are gathered. Recall also that problem framing, one of the characteristics of professional judgment discussed in Chapter 5 focuses on the planner's wisdom in assessing a situation, gathering needed information, and developing plausible planning solutions. Finally, for more information on framing in the context of behavioral finance, see Chapter 4, Decision Making.

The systematic financial planning process was introduced in the previous chapter as a frame of reference, or model, for financial planning. In proceeding through each of the six steps, there are distinct, recognizable tasks to complete and decisions to make. Viewed from this linear perspective, a "stage-gate" (to borrow a production management term) must be passed before progressing to the next step. These stage-gates represent the evolution and enrichment of the planner-client relationship, the planning process, and a sequence of planning tasks that should be completed before progressing to the next step. This systematic method, or process, ensures that a client's personal and financial objectives are being met by the most effective and efficient means possible.

Simplifying the process into discrete steps to be examined, as through the lens of a microscope, fosters greater understanding of the tasks, decisions, and minutiae that must be accomplished in each step; this is the primary purpose of this chapter and the next two chapters. However, readers are cautioned not to overlook the fact that, although financial planning is systematic—in terms of the development of a plan and the continuing relationship with a client— it is not always linear. The wide-angle, long-range view of the planning process and the advisor-client relationship provides a much different perspective than when the details of each planning step are viewed in isolation.

A secondary purpose of this chapter and the next two chapters is to consider the systematic financial planning process in relation to the CFP Board explanation of the ethical professsional conduct expected of certificants and registrants. Recall from Chapter 2 that the *Code of Ethics*, the *Rules of Conduct*, and the *Financial Planning Practice Standards* make up what the CFP Board calls its **Standards of Professional Conduct**. Referred to as the *Standards*, these doctrines represent the standards of ethical conduct for CFP® professionals that are enforced by the CFP Board through the Disciplinary and Ethics Commission. Additionally, the CFP Board integrates the most applicable individual *Codes of Ethics* and *Rules of Conduct* in the explanation of each *Practice Standard* in the *Standards of Professional Conduct*. The integration of these guidelines is discussed in this chapter and the next two chapters following the explanation of each step in the systematic financial planning process.

In summary, Chapters 6, 7, and 8 offer an in-depth explanation of the steps of the systematic financial planning process. Once each step is described, the CFP Standards for ethical conduct are explained to provide a context for the accomplishment of each step. Then, with this important scope and regulatory background, the personal financial planning process is personalized through the experience of working with a financial planner as told from the perspectives of Tom and Nyla Kim. Let's begin with Step 1.

STEP 1: ESTABLISH AND DEFINE THE RELATIONSHIP

The planner-client relationship is almost always initiated by the client. Whether a planner's marketing efforts motivate a client or the client seeks out the planner independently or as the result of a referral, a decision has been made—to consider engaging the planner's services. Clients are, in the end, responsible for accepting the opportunity to meet with an advisor. However, once the initial **help-seeking behavior** (defined as the act of seeking assistance) has occurred, the task of further establishing the planner-client relationship shifts primarily to the financial planner.

Step 1, *establish and define the relationship*, is seemingly simple: meet the client, define the planning services, and sign the contract. The relationship is defined and established. But accomplishing this objective is complicated by the need to integrate professional, disclosure, and contractual responsibilities, required in the execution of Step 1, with the initiation of a personal relationship. While fulfilling the legal obligations the planner must also lay the foundation for a trusting and personal advisor-client relationship. Based on these initial interactions that characterize this intersection of the *business* and the *personal* relationships, the client and the advisor must decide whether they are well-matched to continue a financial planning relationship—however the scope of that relationship is defined.

It would seem to be good business practice and to reflect sound professional judgment to routinely profile for potential clients one's business and the products or services offered. Similarly, it would seem reasonable for most clients to have questions before signing a contract. Certainly concerns raised by the Madoff incident, and other questionable practices of financial product and service providers, have given consumers reason to be cautious. As an analogy, consider the following criteria that profile a home floor cleaning company—a business relationship that does not require the sharing of personal client information but does require access to a client's home.

- *Company name and contact information*: LGK Floor Services (referred to as LGK). Name and contact information for employee.

- *Scope of products/services offered/provided*: Does LGK clean only carpet or multiple types of flooring surfaces (i.e., hardwood, cork, ceramic tile)? Is the contract for the entire house, or are à la cart services available to clean selected rooms and/or flooring surfaces?

- *Responsibilities of each party*: Will LGK or the client move the furniture before and after the cleaning? What is the client expected to do before LGK arrives? What level of care will LGK employees take while cleaning? How will employees conduct themselves on the job? Will LGK employees respect the privacy of clients while in their home? Will the employees secure the home to keep it safe and protected?

- *Other professionals who may be involved*: Will LGK involve others to move furniture? Clean specific types of floor surfaces? Provide specialized services such as sterilizing the bath or laundry room floor? Or will other providers assist with other aspects of the cleaning contract? If other professionals are used, how will this direclty, or indirectly, affect the cost of the service?

- *Compensation*: What will the cleaning service cost? Does the fee include cleaning products and labor? Are there additional, or hidden, fees that will be identified later? Does the fee vary by type of cleaning products used or services provided? What is the accepted, or expected, method of payment?

- *Time frame*: How long will it take LGK to complete the cleaning? Does the contract cover whole-house service? One cleaning of selected rooms? Three cleanings in an annual contract? Can the contract be renewed, or is a new contract necessary?

- *Dispute resolution*: How does the client amend or terminate the contract? If the client is dissatisfied with the staff or services provided, what procedures are available to settle disputes? To resolve complaints? To compensate for any damage that occurs?

The criteria that profile a tangible but personal consumer service, such as home floor cleaning in this example, are equally applicable to establishing and defining a relationship for delivering intangible but very personal financial planning products or services to a client. In fact, these same factors have been codified in the disclosure documents that are provided to clients to help them better understand the delivery of financial planning services. As summarized in Table 6.1, disclosure documents, for different purposes, may be necessary to meet regulatory requirements or to comply with best practices within the profession. A discussion of each follows, but for more information on the regulatory requirements for these documents, see Chapter 2. For more information on the inclusion of the documents in the financial plan, see Chapter 9.

As shown in Table 6.1, the financial planner is responsible for educating clients about products or services offered within the scope of the financial planning process. In addition to an explanation of the responsibilities and obligations of both parties, clients should expect a financial advisor to disclose conflicts of interest, compensation arrangements, the length of the agreement period, and the products or services to be provided. For example, the CFP Board, through its professional *Rules of Conduct* and model disclosure documents, established the expectation that disclosure applies not only to those practicing as Registered Investment Advisers (RIAs) but to all CFP Board certificants, regardless of how they are compensated. SEC and state regulatory disclosure rules require all RIAs to distribute Part II of Form ADV to clients and prospective clients. Similar requirements have been proposed for retail investment brokers.

Table 6.1 Select Documents Used to Define and Establish the Financial Planning Relationship

Disclosure Documents	Purpose	Why Provided
Proprietary Disclosure Statement	To disclose: • Contact information • Description of services to be provided, including • Responsibilities and obligations of each party and • Identification of other professionals who may be involved • Sources of compensation • Conflicts of interest • Any other information material to the relationship	To comply with CFP Board Rules of Conduct; for examples see • Form OPS, Other Professional Services • Form FPD, Financial Planning Disclosure Sample • Form FPDA, Financial Planning Disclosure & Agreement Sample Available at http://www.cfp.net/Downloads/CFP_Board_Sample_Disclosure_Forms.pdf Or, to meet proposed FINRA Regulatory Notice 10-54, Concept Proposal to Require a Disclosure Statement for Retail Investors at or Before Commencing a Business Relationship proposed in October 2010. For more information, see: http://www.finra.org/Industry/Regulation/Notices/2010/P122362
Form ADV Part 2	The 19 items required to be disclosed in the brochure include the information shown above. For more information on Form ADV Part 2, see http://www.sec.gov/divisions/investment/iard/formadv-part2-0710.pdf. To review Form ADV Part 1 or Part 2 for a registered adviser at the Investment Adviser Public Disclosure (IAPD), see http://www.adviserinfo.sec.gov/IAPD/Content/Search/iapd_Search.aspx.	To comply with SEC or state regulatory disclosure requirements for clients of registered investment advisers. Must be provided to prospective clients (orally or in writing) before or at the time the relationship is established. Notice of updates to the brochure, access to the brochure, or delivery of the updated brochure must be provided to all continuing clients within 120 days of the end of the adviser's fiscal year.
Privacy Statement	Written notice describing the privacy policies and practices to protect the nonpublic private information of customers of brokers, planners, and other investment professionals. For more information, see http://www.sec.gov/	To comply with the Gramm-Leach-Bliley Act of 1999 and SEC Regulation S-P. Must be provided no later than when the relationship is established (i.e., at contract signed) and at least once annually for the duration of the relationship.
Investment Policy Statement	Written statement documenting the mutually agreed upon practices and policies for investing, or managing, the client's assets.	To comply with best practices when working with individual investors; required for trusts, foundations, endowments, and retirement accounts. Useful to document investment practices consistent with the fiduciary standards of an investment adviser registered with the SEC or state regulatory authority or for others to document prudent investment practices.

Contractual Documents		
Engagement Letter May also be called a: • Service Agreement • Management Agreement • Financial Planning Agreement • "Third-party"/ Custodian Agreement • Advisory Agreement	To establish the contractual relationship between an advisor and a client. Although the scope of the contract varies with an advisor's business model, minimal information includes: • Contact information • Description of the services/products to be provided, including the responsibilities and obligations of each party • Time frame for the agreement • Compensation for the services • Other material information related to the relationship, such as, but not limited to: • Arbitration as a method for settling disputes arising from the contract or a breach of contract • Assignment of the contract • Methods for amending or terminating the agreement	To comply with CFP Board Rules of Conduct. To establish a signed, legally binding contract to govern the offer of services and/or products by the advisor and the acceptance of the services and/or products by the client. Initiation of new contracts will vary with the business model and contract stipulations of the advisor.

As a part of the explanation of the financial planning services or products, it is important to outline both the planner's and the client's responsibilities. It is important for clients to understand that they play an essential role in making the planner-client relationship an effective and trustful one. It is appropriate for financial planners to expect clients to fully engage in the process, once explained by the planner, and that clients will provide data and documents in as complete and timely a manner as possible. It is impractical to conduct either modular or comprehensive planning if there is doubt about the validity of client data. Furthermore, issues related to trust should be discussed at the beginning of the financial planning process. This is important to promote the sharing of client information, as well as to establish some relationship boundaries, such as the need for a planner to be persistent if the client does not respond in a timely manner.

Whenever a planner attempts to establish trust with a client and these efforts are met with client resistance, the planner should take steps to reestablish client expectations and obligations. Financial planners must feel comfortable working with clients, and confident that their recommendations reflect the client's true wishes, concerns, and financial goals. Likewise, clients should feel comfortable in the relationship and be assured that the recommendations made are, in fact, in their best interest. This can best be accomplished when clients are truthful, responsive, and open to suggestions and when advisors fully disclose material information about their products and services as well as any potential conflicts of interest.

SEC instructions for the development of Part 2 of Form ADV, the Uniform Application for Investment Adviser Registration, state

> As a fiduciary, you also must seek to avoid conflicts of interest with your clients, and, at a minimum, make full disclosure of all material conflicts of interest between you and your clients that could affect the advisory relationship. This obligation requires that you provide the client with sufficiently specific facts so that the client is able to understand the conflicts of interests you have and the business practices in which you engage, and can give the informed consent to such conflicts or practices or reject them. To satisfy this obligation, you therefore may have to disclose to *clients* information not specifically required by Part 2 of Form ADV or in more detail than the brochure items might otherwise require.[1]

The actual definition of a conflict of interest varies and reflects the nexus of the business model and ethics of the advisor. As described above, the SEC requires an adviser to alert clients to any particular advantages that may be available to the adviser as a result of the choices made in the scope of working with the client. Such choices could relate to products, services, providers, the advisor's employer, or other business or personal relationships that may exist or come into existence during the course of serving the client. Likewise, the CFP Board, through the *Rules of Conduct*, established a similar requirement for certificants to disclose any conflicts of interest that could materially affect the relationship.

Consider a situation where a financial planner serves on a voluntary board of directors for a charitable organization. It would be appropriate for the planner to disclose this information generally, but also specifically to a prospective client who works for the charitable organization. There may be situations in which a planner will learn something considered private but that may also affect the client. Disclosing such information to the client would conflict with the advisor's board position. Before engaging the client in a professional capacity, it would be essential to disclose, and have the client acknowledge receipt in writing, the planner's role on the board. Not only would such a disclosure lessen the possibility of misplaced expectations, but full disclosure would also contribute to greater client trust.

For some disclosures, however, such as the **privacy statement** that explains the planner's use or dissemination of private client information, it is wise to receive written confirmation of disclosure to clients. It is a good idea to have clients sign a form indicating that they not only received the disclosure but also read it. Some advisors incorporate verification of receipt of the privacy statement and Form ADV Part 2, or updates, into the annual contract.

Today's litigious environment suggests that financial planners—even those whose investment advice is secondary to their planning activities—should use an **investment policy statement** (IPS) to disclose and document professional expectations for the management and investment of client assets. The IPS integrates investment performance in the context of risk tolerance, risk capacity, investment philosophy, and investment methods to establish parameters for the actual investment strategies used. Practicing full disclosure with a client-signed IPS is prudent because it establishes a mutually agreed-upon standard of conduct while reducing the possibility of a future lawsuit brought by a client who claims misrepresentation or poor performance. For more information on the IPS, see Chapter 9.

After full disclosure of all information that defines the planner-client relationship, the relationship should be cemented by means of a contract. As shown in Table 6.1, the name of the contractual agreement varies, as does the scope of information included. However, the contract should clearly delineate the services and/or products to be provided, the responsibilities and obligations of the client and the planner in delivering those products/services, the time frame for delivery, and their cost. As in the floor care example, the contract could provide for delivery of a financial plan (i.e., a one-time cleaning service), delivery of a plan and selected implementation strategies over the course of a year (i.e., selected rooms cleaned x times over a year), or delivery of planning and implementation services integrated with other money management, insurance, or tax specialists (i.e., whole-house floor cleaning with coordination of other floor care professionals).

Establishing and defining the planner-client relationship—the first step in the financial planning process—is often overlooked as important but fundamentally routine. Sometimes the routine nature of providing clients with disclosure documentation leads to complacency. This tendency should be combated. Long-term planner-client relationships are grounded, in large part, on the initial discussions between a planner and a client. Setting expectations, disclosing relevant information, and revealing real and potential conflicts of interest are sure ways to build trust and commitment with clients and to establish a solid foundation—as well as a contract—for continuing the planning process.

Finally, it is important to consider the time frame for conducting Step 1 of the systematic financial planning process. As discussed in Chapter 2 and summarized in Table 6.1, compliance requirements dictate the delivery of some disclosure documents at the initial client meeting or no later than the meeting when the contract is signed. Because of differences in practice models, the delivery of the disclosure documents and contract may occur in one meeting, or with other practice models several meetings may occur, after the delivery of the disclosure documents but before the contract is initiated. Similarly, the delivery of the IPS is more likely to be dictated by an advisor's business model and client services. For example, if an advisor's planning approach typically begins with the transfer of assets to the firm for management, then the IPS will be provided with other initial documents. But if the advisor's planning approach is to develop a plan, after which the client can choose to contract for investment management services, then another contract would be initiated and the IPS would be developed to govern the related services.

Although establishing and defining the relationship is the first step in the financial planning process, students and novice planners are cautioned that this step is never really completed because of the need (1) to continually foster the trust on which the client-planner relationship was initially established and (2) to continually maintain the legal relationship by providing disclosure documents and new contracts.

Step 1 and the CFP Board Standards of Ethical Conduct

The CFP Board integration of Practice Standard 100-1: Defining the Scope of the Engagement with the most applicable *Code of Ethics* and *Rules of Conduct* is shown in Appendix 6A. The Principle of Fairness, as it pertains to professional relationships and the disclosure of conflicts of interest, and the Principle of Diligence in providing professional services were identified by the Board as particularly relevant to the first step of the process. Four *Rules of Conduct* related to defining the relationship and disclosing information to prospective and current clients establish the expectations for professional conduct. Note that *Rules of Conduct* 1.2, 1.3, and 2.2 assert that if the "services include financial planning or material elements of financial planning," then the required disclosure and agreement information should be disclosed in writing.

Specifically, *Rule of Conduct* 1.2 addresses the need to explain to a client the six-step financial planning process, the methods of compensation, and the terms for offering proprietary products or involving other third-party providers. This information may be conveyed orally, but if it is provided in a written format, certificants are required to encourage the client to review the materials. The requirements of the "Agreement" between the advisor and client is defined by *Rule of Conduct 1.3*, and the Board notes that other disclosure documents required for compliance with state or federal law or a self-regulatory organization, such as Form ADV required by the SEC, will satisfy this rule. This latter statement regarding other disclosure documents also is repeated with *Rule of Conduct* 2.2 regarding disclosures about compensation, conflicts of interest, and any information about the certificant or the certificant's employer that might affect the client's decision to enage the certificant.

It is notable that the Board chose to associate all *Rules of Conduct* related to Rule 1: Defining the Relationship with the Prospective Client or Client and Rule 2: Information Disclosed To Prospective Clients and Clients with Practice Standard 100-1: Defining the Scope of the Engagement and Step 1 of establishing and defining the relationship with the client *except* one rule -- *Rule of Conduct 1.4*. This rule requires the certificant to place the interests of the client first, and if the certificant is providing financial planning or material elements of financial planning, then the duty of care of a fiduciary is required. As defined by the Board, this is "one who acts in utmost good faith, in a manner he or she reasonably believes to be in the best interest of the client."[2] *Rule of Conduct 1.4* is identified by the Board as particularly relevant to Steps 2, 3, and 5 of the process.

STEP 2: GATHER DATA AND FRAME GOALS AND OBJECTIVES

The second step in the planning process involves collecting information and identifying client goals. Client information can be obtained from data collection questionnaires, client and planner interviews, and original source documents provided by the client. Some planners provide a data collection package, by mail or electronically, to prospective clients before the first meeting. In such cases, clients independently complete and return the forms prior to the meeting or bring them to the meeting. Secure, encrypted Web sites allow clients and planners to complete the forms together electronically from different locations. A more traditional method employs joint form completion, with the client and planner filling out the data collection forms in the planner's office. However, not all financial planning practitioners use, or approve, of the latter method.

When the "data gathering meeting" focuses primarily on compiling financial data, the discussion is often excessively focused on quantitative data to the exclusion of effective qualitative information gathering about the client's values, goals, dreams, beliefs, and risk tolerance. Increasingly, best practice planning models suggest that clients should be encouraged to complete data forms independently. Then the forms can be reviewed during the data gathering meeting to ensure both parties' full understanding, but quantitative data collection is not the focus of the meeting. Regardless of the method(s) utilized, the objective is for the planner to gather vital financial and personal information—both quantitative and qualitative—that encourages discussion. Once the forms are complete, the client and planner mutually agree on the client's goals, objectives, and assumptions to guide the planning process.

But a client rarely states a goal in the form of a statement such as, "We need $55,000 for Susie's college expenses." Instead, a client might state a general goal like, "We want to provide Susie with a college education." Note that either statement can be problematic for the planner attempting to fully understand and quantify the client's goal. For example, the $55,000 cost of education will probably be significantly higher in the future, dependending on the assumed rate of inflationary increases and the length of time until the funds are needed. Also, the client may not have fully considered the range of costs attributable to different types of educational institutions or the most appropriate choice for Susie.

So which assumptions are valid for this situation? It is up to the planner, in conjunction with the client, to quantify this cost and determine the best means to achieve the education goal without sacrificing the client's other goals. From here the planner and client can determine together the goals and assumptions upon which the plan will be developed. There are two very important outcomes of these initial meetings: (1) the establishment of trust between both parties; and (2) the exploration and collection of information to help the planner understand the client and the client's financial situation.

Although factually accurate, this brief summary of Step 2 ignores the nuances of this important foundational step in the planning process. Because of the significance of this step and the variety of approaches used in practice, this discussion focuses on the abstract and practical implications of four fundamental questions:

1. Which client data are collected?

2. How does a planner use the data?

3. How are the data collected?

4. What does it mean to frame goals and objectives?

Which Data Are Collected?

Time is a valuable commodity for clients and planners. Yet planners must somehow find a way to gain enough information to fully understand the client, diagnose the situation, and generate a workable plan that is acceptable to a client—and do so effectively and efficiently. And, if that conundrum is not sufficiently perplexing, realize that most people consider talking about money culturally unacceptable. For too many, any talk about money is laden with emotional undertones that may reflect explicit memories (good or bad) or an implicit uneasiness that defies explanation. It is not hard to understand why many planners prefer the safety of products to the psyche of clients, but increasingly planners are considering both. To be effective, the student or novice planner must understand which data to consider and why they might be useful. Then, to be efficient, the student or novice planner must be armed with a Client Intake Form or questionnaire and other relevant assessments that will garner the needed insights.

A conceptual model of the types of client information typically collected by planners is presented in Figure 6.2. Recall that a **conceptual model** is an abstraction of reality, or an attempt to explain the relationship among the key elements of a phenomenon, event, or process. Four influential client factors have been identified as descriptive of a client and the client's situation, including:

1.   temperament and personality;

2.   attitudes, beliefs and behaviors;

3.   financial knowledge and experience; and

4.   socioeconomic descriptors.

Figure 6.2 Situational Factors: A Key to Understanding the Client

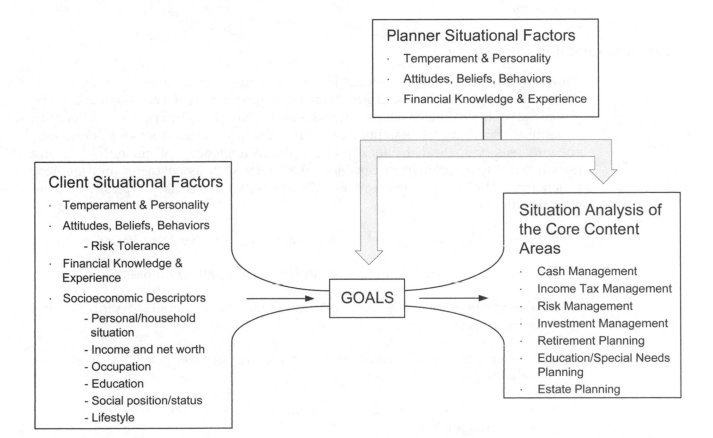

Similarly, temperament, personality, attitudes, beliefs, behaviors, and financial knowledge and experience characterize the planner—both as an individual and as a professional. As shown in Figure 6.2, goals are a direct consequence of the client's situation, but they are also influenced by the planner. Goals are considered in light of each of the core content planning areas, but they are still influenced by the client's and planner's situational factors.

For example, a client's household situation, lifestyle, and occupation could suggest a need for additional life insurance based on the planner's attitudes, financial knowledge, and experience with other, similar clients. The client may have come to the planner with the goal of purchasing more life insurance. Or the client may never have considered this need, which was revealed only when the advisor analyzed the situation. But the client's attitudes about insurance and risk will influence the final purchase decision, as will the advisor's personality, assertiveness, or conscientiousness in educating and motivating the client about this need.

As Figure 6.2 illustrates, client situational factors yield the data for framing a client's goals and subsequently for analzing the client's financial situation in each of the core content planning areas. A client's situational information is shaped and interpreted—directly or indirectly—by a planner's temperament, personality, attitudes, beliefs, and financial knowledge and experience. Certainly, not all planners measure or directly consider all four client situational factors, but increasingly planners are expanding the scope of information used to become familiar with the client situation and build trust with clients. Following are an explanation of each of the situational factors and examples of how planners are collecting client data in the day-to-day operation of their firms.

Temperament and Personality

Temperament is commonly defined by mood or disposition. It is generally agreed that it reflects inherited, cross-cultural traits that appear early in childhood and shape personality. Dimensions of temperament focus on characteristics such as emotionality, sociability, sensitivity, adaptability, distractibility, persistence, and activity. **Personality** encompasses both the behavioral and emotional tendencies of an individual and goes beyond temperament to consider other traits such as character and intellect. Psychologists believe that there are five dimensions of personality, typically referred to as the "Big Five":

1. *Extraversion*—exemplified by being energetic, assertive, talkative, or outgoing.

2. *Agreeableness*—represented by indications of sympathy, kindness, and affection.

3. *Conscientiousness*—described as being organized, thorough, disciplined, and achievement-oriented.

4. *Neuroticism*—characterized by being moody, anxious, tense, or displaying other unpleasant emotions.

5. *Openness to new experiences*—exemplified by having numerous interests and being imaginative.

Understanding the dimensions of temperament and personality can provide advisors useful insights into a client's life decisions and actions, including the client's relationships with others *and* with money. For example, clients with a high degree of neuroticism may be more difficult to work with and require more planner and staff time. Clients with a low degree of conscientiousness could need more motivation to remain engaged in the financial planning process. Similarly, temperament and personality can help explain emotional responses to market or economic activity, such as requests to abandon the plan and go to a concentrated position (e.g., cash, gold, or silver). Clients with stronger traits of persistence or conscientiousness may recognize that market downturns are a normal occurrence when working toward a long-term goal (e.g., retirement), and "stick to the plan."

For example, some planners and clients liquidated assets to a majority (or even 100%) cash position following the events of September 11, 2001, or after Lehman Brothers failed in October 2008. Perhaps this was an understandable risk-averse reaction to the situation. Or it could have been a costly decision, which in retrospect, might have been avoided. Part of a planner's role in understanding a client's temperament and personality is to help the client make the best decision for the immediate situation *and* the long term goals of a plan.

An increasing number of financial planners are turning to personality profiling as a way to better understand their clients and facilitate communication. Other planners view the administration and interpretation of personality or temperament tests as beyond the range of their professional competence, and they outsource such profiling to other professionals. The planner then reviews the results and incorporates this information into the planning process.

The services of a financial therapist may also be sought. **Financial therapists** combine their expertise in traditional psychotherapy or treating emotional or behavior disorders with specialized knowledge about the factors that influence financial behavior. According to Maton, Maton, and Martin,[3] some advisors (1) collaborate with a financial therapist throughout the financial planning process, but others only (2) collaborate with the financial therapist in the initial data-gathering meetings to gain a richer understanding of the client. Other advisors may only (3) refer a client to a financial therapist if problematic money attitudes or behaviors are identified, just as an advisor might make a professional referral to a tax or estate specialist.

Some psychologists, for example, Katherin Gurney, Olivia Mellon, and more recently Ted and Brad Klontz, have popularized the intersection of money and personality via books and other assessment tools. A few have developed distinct profiles of different money personalities, such as Gurney's *hunters and high rollers*[4] and Mellon's *money amassers* and *hoarders*[5]—a few examples of their many profiles. Klontz, Kahler, and Klontz suggest that **money scripts**, which they define as "unconscious beliefs people hold about money, often unexplored and only partially true [that] are formed in childhood,"[6] may have a significant effect on adult money behaviors. They offer exercises for exploring money scripts as well as other issues related to money disorders (e.g., compulsive spending or hoarding) and problematic money behaviors (e.g., overspending or underspending). Klontz, Kahler, and Klontz describe their approach,

financial coaching, as a range of advisory services that is neither traditional financial planning nor traditional therapy. Financial coaching methods, founded on "advice, encouragement and information,"[7] help clients achieve their goals by understanding more about their beliefs and behaviors—especially those that may be self-destructive or can sabotage a financial plan.

Attitudes, Beliefs, and Behaviors

Attitudes, beliefs, and behaviors are interrelated concepts in that attitudes and beliefs are thought to affect behavior. Simply put, thoughts and feelings affect action. Shared attitudes, beliefs, and values that charaterize a group are said to reflect the culture of a society or a smaller group, such as the *corporate culture* of IBM or Google. Conversely, personal attitudes, beliefs, and values emanate from the cultural, social, and religious experiences of an individual. **Attitudes** often reflect an individual's views, opinions, desires, choices, purposes, or values. Although *belief* can have different meanings, in psychology **beliefs** are recognized as a type of attitude, because they reflect an interpretation, expectation, or claim about some aspect of life. **Values** represent strongly held attitudes and beliefs that indicate an individual's perception of what is right or desirable. Values are said to reflect an individual's fundamental interpretation of life or its meaning; as such, they have a significant influence on personal goals and choices.

Attitudes, beliefs, and values are considered distinct from temperament and personality because it is theorized that attitudes and beliefs potentially change over time, particularly as a result of experience. On the other hand, values are thought to remain consistent over the life cycle, although the priority of individual values may change over time. Attitudes, beliefs, and values have far-reaching implications for clients and their financial plans. For example, consider some of these expressions about money, all of which may reflect deeply held attitudes or beliefs:

- "Money is the root of all evil."

- "Pinch a penny until it screams."

- "Money doesn't grow on trees."

- "Blood money."

- "It takes money to know money."

- "I feel like a million bucks."

- "Born with a silver spoon in her mouth."

Similarly, consider the characteristics often freely associated with money (e.g., power, self-worth, independence, freedom, reward, or happiness) that reflect attitudes, beliefs, and values that directly or indirectly affect financial practices.

It should be noted, however, that the effect of attitudes on financial behavior is much more pervasive than merely the attitudes, beliefs, and values associated with money, poverty, or wealth. Consider the following examples:

- A parent who wants to "teach" the value of independence by refusing to pay for four years of a child's college education, although the parent is fully capable of paying the expense.

- A blue collar worker who diligently saves for retirement, becomes a millionaire, and chooses to continue working, or who makes a large charitable gift, rather than "enjoying life's luxuries" and spending the savings.

- A couple with an annual income of $750,000 who save little and continually increase their debt in pursuit of the "good life."

In each case, the behavior may be viewed on a continuum ranging from rational to irrational—contingent on the attitudes, beliefs, values, and experiential map of the individual making the assessment. Although making a judgment may be a natural human reaction, the financial advisor's role is limited to understanding why and how an individual's attitudes, beliefs, and values affect financial decisions *and* to helping clients identify and understand why and how these attitudes, beliefs, and values influence their lives. Showing the client empathy (not necessarily agreement) while exploring these topics is important for building trust. Equally important is an open mind to avoid judging a client's attitudes, beliefs, values, or goals, assuming that they do not violate the planner's ethical code.

The importance attributed to attitudes, beliefs, and values—both in shaping the client's relationship with money and the client's goals—gave rise to two related developments. The first was the adoption of **life planning** as part of financial planning. Although the definition and scope of financial life planning as actually practiced by advisors vary, the focus of financial life planning is to ground the financial plan in the life—past, present, and future—of the client. In short, financial life planning integrates financial planning and life planning. Exploring a client's attitudes, beliefs, and values can then encompass the emotional, experiential, and spiritual issues that influence not only the use of money, but also the goals that frame a meaningful life for the client.

The scope of the questions and methods that can be involved in this holistic exploration have resulted in this portion of the data collection process being called **discovery**, or referred to as the *discovery meetings*. This second development, or focus on discovery, further validates the significance of the individual, not merely the financial situation, as the focus of financial planning.

Specialized approaches, such as those promoted by George Kinder,[8] Mitch Anthony,[9] Roy Diliberto,[10] and Carol Anderson,[11] for example, offer planners training as well as interview questions and other assessment tools for helping clients gain an increased understanding of financial and life planning. Childhood memories about money and its use; family experiences and money practices (both family of origin and current houshold); feelings and perceptions about money (both positive and painful); and values and attitudes associated with money are themes of life planning discovery. It is important to note that life planning is, foremost, about helping clients understand *their* relationship with money. Although this may seem counterintuitive, the fundamental purpose is to "discover" attitudes, beliefs, values, and behaviors (or what Klontz, Kahler, and Klontz refer to as *money scripts*, discussed earlier) that directly—or indirectly—affect a client's decision making and could, therefore, contribute to the success or failure of any financial planning recommendations. The planner can then apply the insights that emerge to the planning relationship. Kinder, one of the founders of the life planning concept, is recognized for the following questions (asked in order), which help clients explore what he calls "a life worth living":

1. "If you had all the money you needed, what would you do with your life?"

2. "If you had only five to ten years to live, but would be in good health the entire time, what would your life look like?"

3. "If you knew you were going to die tomorrow, what did you miss? What did you not get to do? Who did you not get to be?"[12]

Although some planners might argue that these questions are beyond the scope of any client conversation they wish to have or are capable of managing, other advisors are incorporating some combination of these methods to discover a client's cognitive, emotional, spiritual, and behavioral relationship with money. Whereas the approaches used and methods employed may vary, in each case the objective is to gain a deeper understanding of the client.

Professional judgment cautions the advisor not to generalize, not to judge a client, and not to exceed professional expertise in the services offered. Each of these cautions applies when an advisor considers the best practices to understand how temperament, personality, attitudes, beliefs, and values shape a client's unique money map, as defined in Chapter 3. But it is equally important to keep two points in perspective. First, the advisor is seeking information to help a client succeed in accomplishing the goals that frame the financial plan. The objective is to inform the process and benefit the client. Second, there are opportunities for advisors to develop skills, use resources developed by other experts, or collaborate with other professionals.

Some planners choose to collaborate because they fear exceeding their own expertise, and others use professional referrals for issues that might jeopardize a plan. Although building expertise in this area requires further study or collaboration with an expert, appreciating the importance of these situaional factors is an important first step. Shifting from a client experience based on one or more separate *transactions*, typically to sell a product, to a client experience based on *transformation* of the client's financial situation and relationship with money could have a significant impact on the practice of financial planning in the future.

Risk tolerance. Financial **risk tolerance** is defined as the maximum amount of risk a client is comfortable accepting in a financial situation. Research suggests that risk tolerance is a personal characteristic or attitude that can change depending on the situation being faced or the activity in question. Risk tolerance, and its counterpart *risk aversion*, is a complicated and elusive concept typically measured on a continuum that reflects the *attitude* to accept risk and the *capacity* to withstand any potential losses stemming from the risk. Financial risk tolerance affects a wide range of financial decisions beyond its application to investments, where it is typically considered. A client's risk tolerance may also affect decisions concerning type of mortgage, a comfortable debt level, the amount of an emergency fund, the choice of insurance coverage, or an estate planning strategy. One person may view a financial choice such as an interest-only mortgage as highly risky, yet it would be perfectly acceptable to another.

Considered in the context of investment management choices, risk tolerance centers on a client's perceived feelings, reactions, or level of comfort with decreases in investment values. A client with a high level of risk tolerance can be expected to take greater risks and act with less information than someone with a lower risk tolerance. Individuals with high levels of risk tolerance generally require a greater likelihood of gain, tolerate more uncertainty, and require less information about the performance of an investment. Highly risk-tolerant individuals accept volatile events, but less risk-tolerant individuals require certainty. What appears speculative to one client may seem like prudent hedging to another. Anecdotal evidence from market downturns over the last decade suggest that a meaningful way to help clients understand their own risk tolerance is to discuss potential losses in actual amounts rather than in statistical (i.e., standard deviation) or more general terms.

Although client attitudes about financial well-being, economic trends, or market returns can also be queried, a client's attitude toward financial risk is typically considered the most important because it represents the juncture of the *need to understand the client* for the purposes of client-centered financial planning with the *need to document the client's risk tolerance* for regulatory compliance. For example, most planners accept the practice of using interview-based assessments to profile client attitudes, beliefs, and values, although some may use standardized personality profiles, as mentioned earlier. However, questionnaires tend to be the norm for risk tolerance evaluation because they produce a documented assessment of risk tolerance for regulatory purposes.

Some planners use self-developed measures of risk tolerance, but caution is recommended to ensure that they meet all compliance requirements. Other planners infer risk tolerance from available client information; however, it is recommended that any attempt to measure risk tolerance be directed to a specific activity. For example, using a client's willingness to engage in risky physical behaviors (e.g., sky diving, skiing, hockey) as a proxy for taking risks in financial situations could lack validity. Some planners use scales included in financial planning software or provided by their broker-dealer or custodian, and others purchase psychometric tests from independent firms, such as *FinaMetrica*.[13] Regardless of the method or combination of methods used, it is important for an assessment instrument to be valid—that is, the scale should measure what it purports to measure. A thirteen-item financial risk tolerance scale that has been shown to offer practitioners a reasonable level of validity and reliability is included in Appendix A: Assessing Your Financial Risk Tolerance. The scale can be used to broadly assess a client's propensity to take investment and financial risks.[14]

Financial Knowledge and Experience

Financial knowledge and experience may represent the most extreme difference between planner and client; both parties bring a range of knowledge and experience to the planning engagement—but at different levels. Professional judgment constrains the planner not to recommend products or services that are beyond the boundaries of the client's knowledge, experience, or capacity for loss. Inevitably though, some recommendations almost certainly present the need for products or services about which a client lacks experience or knowledge. In such cases, it becomes even more important to educate the client about the risks and benefits of that product or service. This precaution will not only satisfy the planner's responsibility for client education, but also help the planner overcome potential client objections.

A client's financial knowledge and previous financial experience may influence initial goal choices, recommendations proffered by a planner, and subsequent client reactions. The planning process offers advisors the opportunity to assess and build clients' knowledge as a foundation for making more fact-based, rational decisions. In the role of educator, the advisor has an opportunity to use the planning process and other forms of client communication to increase a client's financial knowledge and foster independence of thought and decision making.

Socioeconomic Descriptors

Socioeconomic descriptors represent a broad range of characteristics, typically quantitative, that describe a client. While these are typically the easiest data to collect and interpret, bear in mind that clients may not always be totally forthright. Categories of information include the demographic profile of the client's household, including relevant medical history or other factors that may influence the client's goals; financial data (e.g., income, assets, liabilities, insurance protection; and a description of the client's lifestyle, or what might be referred to as social position or status). The latter category may include travel, hobbies, collectibles, leisure activities, personal property, or real estate that supports the client's lifestyle.

How Do Planners Use the Data?

The client and planner enter a planning relationship with unique characteristics of temperament, personality, attitudes, and beliefs, and with financial knowledge and experience that shape the planning process. Some simple examples may help illustrate their impact on the planning process:

- Some clients may cry, scream, or yell in response to a life event, a change in the stock market, or an advisor's recommendation, whereas others will calmly discuss the situation. For some clients, a downturn in the stock market or other financial difficulty will represent a temporary setback, but others will claim the loss as personal and it pervades everything they attempt to do. A client's attitude may be demonstrated by an emotionally charged statement such as, "I knew this would happen to *me*!" rather than by exhibiting a calm, logical application of knowledge of the investment market and economic cycles to the situation at hand.

- Some clients make a decision on a whim, readily accepting a planner's recommendations; others nitpick and challenge the planner until fully convinced that every last detail has been carefully considered from every angle.

- The financial lives of some clients are perennially disorganized. Such clients may be easily distracted from their financial plan by the latest "hot" market sector, financial warnings in the media, or the whim to purchase a currently popular "adult toy." Meanwhile, other clients remain focused on the plan and diligent in reaching specified goals.

As discussed earlier, risk tolerance (or the client's comfort with risk) is an attitude typically linked with investment or portfolio management choices; but it can also affect other financial decisions, such as type of mortgage, comfortable debt or emergency fund level, choice of insurance products and levels of coverage, or estate planning strategies. For example, a risk-tolerant individual may not willingly purchase insurance or may purchase lower amounts of coverage because of their preference to gamble by risking a potential loss, and instead spend the money on goals perceived to be more worthwhile. The risk-averse client, who may expect and fear loss, could have a tendency to purchase larger amounts of insurance for the assumed protection offered.

Considered in light of portfolio management choices, risk tolerance centers on a client's perceived feelings, reactions, or level of comfort with losses in investment value. Without specific training, a planner's experience could be the best guide for working with the range of temperaments, personalities, and attitudes that clients exhibit. The more a planner knows about a client, the greater the chances of developing a plan that will accommodate the client's unique situation.

Temperament, personality, attitudes, beliefs, financial knowledge, and experience characterize a client; the same is true for the planner. These factors shape a planner's relationship with a client, the mitigating effect of the planner, and consequently the style of planning. A planner's role is to collect and objectively process client data. However, two limitations must be acknowledged. First, regardless of all efforts to function as an objective, independent professional, the planner is confined to some extent by personal temperament, personality, attitudes, beliefs, values, financial knowledge, and experience. These "filters" directly and indirectly affect the planning process. Although this may be equally true of other professionals, it is more apparent in planners because of the personal nature of the planning relationship and the need to divulge very private information. Second, planners are privileged to only the information about the *individual* and the situation that a client is willing to share. Clients may withhold information, either knowingly from lack of trust, or unknowingly because the information is thought to be irrelevant or was overlooked. Without a client's full disclosure, planners are unable to suggest optimal solutions.

Ideally, crafting client goals and objectives, analyzing a situation, and developing recommendations should be based on objectivity rather than subjective inference. Planners must be careful to minimize the effect of personal feelings, interpretive judgments, and opinions that develop or evolve during the planning relationship. Although such insights may be significant to the planning relationship, it is important that interpretations be confirmed with the client for validity. Furthermore, it is incumbent on planners to make every attempt to encourage clients to divulge as much information as can be useful in the planning engagement. As professionals, advisors must fully acknowledge the limitations of their own expertise or other paradigms that could adversely affect or bias the client-planner relationship. Steps should be taken to compensate for or override such issues within the professional relationship.

How Are the Data Collected?

As noted earlier, client data typically are collected through some combination of original source documents (e.g., bank, investment, loan or retirement plan statements), a client questionnaire, and one or a series of planner-client interviews. However, students and novice planners are cautioned about the limitations of and problems associated with these data collection methods. Once provided by the client, original source documents or copies thereof are conveniently available to the planner; but extreme care must be taken to safeguard these documents and the client's privacy. The utility of the questionnaire will be limited by its ease of use, clarity, and applicability to the client. It is important that neither the questionnaire nor the interviews overwhelm a client or cause undue time commitments.

The accuracy of the data is important, and care must be taken to ensure, to the extent possible, that a client is being candid and forthright. It is not unusual for clients to choose not to disclose all information, to procrastinate on providing the information requested, or to provide answers that are more socially acceptable or what the planner expects. Later, when the planner-client relationship is stronger, when, for example, couple/partner dynamics or client trust issues are discussed and resolved, clients may suddenly disclose additional information. A client's schedule may preclude immediate attention to researching or collecting data, or other clients' lack of knowledge or feelings of financial anxiety may cause delay.

Regardless of the reasons for failing to provide the requested information, planners and staff must be supportive but firm in their reminders to clients. Additional, or new, information could subtantially change the whole perspective on a client's situation. Thus, it is important to develop a system for collecting, organizing, and managing data throughout the planning process and for safeguarding them in the future. But it is equally important that the system respond to individual client needs.

To summarize, the importance of client data collection is reflected in the following objectives:

- To allow a planner to gain a more complete and nuanced understanding of a client;

- To measure a client's financial risk tolerance;

- To empower planner and client to clarify goals and set realistic expectations for planning outcomes; and

- To provide the information needed for a planner to diagnose a situation and identify the most appropriate recommendations given a client's resources and personal and financial situation.

Supporting Documents

Several different forms can be used to collect, verify possession, and track the flow of the original source documents or third-party information used in the planning process. Both planner and client can use the form shown in Exhibit 6.1 to track the flow of original documents between parties. A planner can duplicate and modify the supporting documents column to verify or record their receipt—or later, return—to the client, as shown in Exhibit 6.1. This form could include a signature line for the planning staff or client to verify the transfer. Clients may also be asked to sign documents authorizing the planner to obtain, on their behalf, private client information from other financial service advisors or professionals such as bank or trust officers, an attorney, an accountant, an investment advisor, an insurance professional, or an employer. Information requests should be limited to what is necessary to analyze the client's situation or to develop planning recommendations.

Every effort should be made to scan or copy the documents so that the originals can be returned to the client quickly. These documents are used to verify information already provided by the client and to provide technical information to the planner that may be beyond the scope of the client's knowledge. Tracking forms can be completed for the household by adding individual lines or other details to each category, as applicable, for each spouse or partner. Alternatively, an individual form may be completed for each individual.

Exhibit 6.1 Client Supporting Document Tracking Form

Client Supporting Document Tracking Form

Date Requested from Client	Date Received from Client	Date Returned to Client	Supporting Document (for Client 1, Client 2, and joint accounts, as applicable)
			Latest Bank Statement(s)
			Latest Investment Account Statement(s)
			Loan Statement(s) (e.g., real estate 1, real estate 2, car 1, car 2, boat/motorcycle/ATV/Recreational Vehicle, furniture/appliances, student loan(s), etc.)
			Real Estate Deed, Deed of Trust, and HUD-1: Summary of Closing Costs
			Latest Credit Card and/or Department Store Credit Statement(s)
			Federal and State Tax Returns for the Last Three Years
			All Insurance Policies (e.g., life, disability, health, homeowners, automobile, umbrella, etc.)
			Any Current Budget or Record of Spending
			Most Recent Paycheck Stub(s)
			Employee Benefit Statement(s)
			Employee Retirement Plan Statement(s)
			Other Retirement Plan Statement(s)
			Summary of the Retirement Plan Description
			Wills, Trusts, or Other Estate Planning Documents
			Other:
			Other:

The Client Intake Form

Although not all financial planners actually use a formal **Client Intake Form** or **data collection questionnaire**, the benefits of such a form are too important to be overlooked. Because the task of gathering data can be somewhat subjective, it is a good policy to complete an objective data collection questionnaire with each client. To the extent that it is completed with accuracy and candor, a well-designed form or questionnaire is a tool that helps capture a client's qualitative and quantitative information.

From a purely practical point of view, a Client Intake Form reduces professional liability. Without a well-defined and consistently applied data collection method, a client, family member, or legal entity could make a future claim that a planner's recommendation did not match the client's situation, goals, or engagement with the planner. Planners who document—objectively and definitively—a client's responses will be in a better position to defend themselves against claims of professional misconduct. Finally, a questionnaire can help pinpoint a client's financial strengths and weaknesses as well as attitudes or expectations that could contribute to, or hinder, a successful planner-client relationship.

Whenever a client engages the services of a financial planner there is the possibility that the client will begin to over-identify with or, in some cases, reject the planner and the advice provided. This is referred to as **transference**. According to Klontz, Kahler, and Klontz, "transference occurs when clients' reactions to the facilitator are unconsciously affected by the unfinished business from their pasts, and their feelings are transferred to the facilitator."[15] Transference occurs unconsciously, as a client responds to a planner based on experiences with someone else from the client's life. Klontz and his associates recommend that financial planners reduce transference by asking clients, early in the financial planning process, to talk about their previous experience working with other financial advisors. Discovery meetings may reveal other individuals who had a significant influence on a client's financial life. Clarifying misunderstandings based on a client's preconceived expectations is an effective way to lessen transference.

In summary, using a client data gathering questionnaire provides a framework for summarizing a client's goals, attitudes, income, expenditures, assets, and liabilities, all of which are needed to write a comprehensive plan. More importantly, it introduces the discussion of other issues, fears, or concerns beyond merely the data collected on the interview form.

Data Gathering Tip: Share Completed Forms with Clients?

It is unnecessary to share completed forms with clients. Some planners include a copy of the completed questionnaire as an appendix to the final plan, but this is certainly not a universal practice. The completed form and future data revisions can also be made available to planner and client by means of a secure, electronic "file box"—a value-added service that some planners provide to encourage clients to collect, update, and securely store their financial documents. Access to selected file box information, or planner-provided reports (i.e., gain/loss statements, fee statements, or personal property inventories) may also be granted to other professionals, such as the client's accountant or attorney, to facilitate their work with the client and planner.

The data collection questionnaire shown in Appendix B: Client Intake Form offers one way to gather client information. Note that this form is designed to be completed by the client, but it could be adapted for use in a planner-guided interview. Each section of the form is summarized below:

Section 1. Confidential Client Data. It is essential that a planner know basic demographic information about the client as well as client contact data. It is important to have items such as name, nickname (if any), address, phone numbers, birth date, and Social Security number in a client file. This type of information is generally needed whenever investment or insurance products are purchased, and it is less burdensome to ask a client once rather than several times for this basic information.

Section 2. Family Considerations. This section of the form allows clients to share information about immediate or extended family. Such information is useful for tax and estate planning issues and may offer insights into a client's goals—spoken and unspoken.

Sections 3 and 3a. Employment Status. Employment status and income reporting are summarized in this section of the data collection form. Note that retirees are given their own subsection to answer income questions.

Section 4. Leisure Activities. It is important to note how a client spends leisure time. Leisure activities usually cost money and having a client identify hobbies and activities allows a planner to double-check the accuracy of the client's budget. For instance, if the budget does not account for leisure activities, this could indicate that the client is not fully accounting for all expenditures. Discussing these activities also allows the planner and client to connect on a personal level that transcends the focus on income and expenses and that offers insights into client dreams or goals that might affect the financial planning process.

Section 5. Goals and Objectives. Goals are the basis of financial planning. This section of the form allows a client to identify and rank personal and financial goals. The assignment of time horizons for realizing goals and depleting funding helps the planner and client establish more realistic expectations.

Section 6. Insurance Information. This section of the form provides the information necessary for the planner to conduct a thorough insurance analysis. Information is collected regarding the client's life, disability, health, long-term care, property, and liability insurance coverage. Note that the page for each type of insurance allows for the entry of multiple policies to meet the needs of different client or household situations.

Section 7. Asset Information. Helping clients manage their assets is an important aspect of financial planning. This section of the form documents ownership of taxable and tax-deferred assets. The additional information requested focuses on current value, cost basis, and growth rate; contribution schedule; ownership or titling of the asset; the purpose assigned to the asset; and the proposed use of the asset upon the owner's death. Some caution is warranted regarding the client's designation of the purpose and use of assets, although this approach is commonly used in financial planning.

As noted in Chapter 4, the behavioral finance concept of mental accounting can lead to faulty decision making. Consequently, planners need to be cautious about accepting the client's assignment of assets, but at the same time they should exercise professional judgment that is sensitive to a client's views and maximizes client interests. The second part of this section tells planners how assets are currently allocated across different broad market sectors. Section 7 may challenge the average client and oblige the client to provide investment or other statements for the planner's review and summary of the necessary information.

Section 8. Personal and Business Assets. This section summarizes the client's tangible personal assets and business assets, if applicable. Consistent with Section 7, additional information requested focuses on current value, purchase price, and growth rate; ownership or titling; and the proposed use of these assets upon the owner's death.

Section 9. Debts and Liablities. This section documents a client's personal debt situation, including the outstanding amount of any liability, the origination date, monthly payment, fixed or variable interest rate, rate of interest, duration of the loan, the person(s) liable, and planned disposition upon the client's death. Sections 7, 8, and 9 provide data for the planner to complete a net worth statement.

Section 10. Monthly Expenses. In this section, the client calculates annual expenditures to assist the planner with the creation of an income and expense statement.

Section 11. Investment Attitudes. These 10 questions provide a snapshot of the client's investment risk preferences and attitudes, values, and expectations about investing. Although the obvious objective is to engage the client in completing the form, a broader objective of this exercise is to promote conversation to increase a planner's knowledge of the client and to encourage discussion of mutually agreed-upon planning assumptions.

Section 12. Attitude Assessment. This section continues the attitudinal assessment. Clients are asked to reflect on the economy as well as their personal finance knowledge. Self-assessment questions focus attention on the client's satisfaction with his job, income, and overall financial situation. Responses to these items can serve as a foundation for formulating client goals and establishing assumptions to guide the planning process. (*Scoring note:* Lower levels of satisfaction may indicate a need for more planner-client discussion about the financial situation. Also, research suggests that low levels of self-assessed financial knowledge are positively correlated with lower levels of financial risk tolerance.)

Section 13. Retirement and Estate Planning. Answers to questions in this section are designed to help planners quickly identify potential retirement or estate planning concerns. The checklist can be used to spot weaknesses in a client's financial situation or areas where financial improvements can be made.

Section 14. Additional Advisors. This section of the data collection form identifies other financial professionals with whom the client has worked and asks the client to reflect on satisfaction with these relationships. The information obtained can help the planner understand why a client is seeking help, provide insights into the client's motives or expectations, and identify other professionals who might be involved in plan implementation.

Section 15. Expectations. The final item queries the client on the expected primary outcome of the planner-client engagement.

Just as no tool, technique, or strategy is appropriate for every client or client situation, the Client Intake Form provided in Appendix B is not necessarily right for every client situation. It may be too comprehensive for planners working on an as-needed basis or on single-issue plans, although selected sections could still be useful and exposure to the form could alert a client to future planning issues. Planners often use specialized data collection forms for targeted client situations, such as small business owners or retirement and employee benefit plan participants. Others use forms coordinated with professional software packages to facilitate data entry. Finally, for planners affiliated with product providers, a proprietary client data form may be required to ensure regulatory compliance. After gaining experience, advisors may edit the forms provided or design their own questionnaires and forms to be used in addition to the proprietary forms mandated by product providers or regulatory agencies.

Guided Planner-Client Interviews

Meaningful exploration of a client's financial situation (and its many nuances, described earlier in this chapter) does not typically occur through a *conversation*, which usually involves an exchange of information, such as facts, opinions, and feelings. The same information can be solicited through what is often casually referred to as an *interview*, but an interview is actually defined as a conversation with a purpose. Planners who work with clients to jointly complete, or subsequently review, client intake forms have a purpose: to collect accurate factual data. So to expand that preliminary exchange into the realm of goals, attitudes, values, dreams, concerns, or fears surrounding money, or the role of money in a client's life, may necessitate entering into such a conversation with a purpose—an interview.

A **focused interview** is an excellent way to explore a client's feelings, experiences, perceptions, attitudes, views, or knowledge. The concept of a semistandardized—or focused—interview is borrowed from social science research, where a set of questions guides the interview, but the interviewer may adapt the sequence of the questions, the wording, and follow-up probes and interviewer responses. The interview is focused on learning about a client's map, defined by feelings, experiences, views, or knowledge, whereas a standardized interview would be formally structured, like the Client Intake Form, to collect specific quantitative data.

Approaching a client meeting as an interview should not inadvertently change the tone or formality of the exchange. Instead, preparation for the discussion can increase a planner's confidence, encourage more in-depth understanding of the topic and the client's perspectives and motives, and build the planner-client relationship. But to be effective, the financial advisor must consider several issues:

1. An issue-oriented, topical list or set of questions must be carefully planned to serve as a framework or guide for the interview. Although digressions to other topics may occur, the framework ensures that important topics are not overlooked. Furthermore, with repeated use, a planner can gain experience from typical client responses and refine the questions.

2. Although planned in advance, the questions must allow for adaptation with regard to the level of language, word choice, or sequence of questioning to best match the client and the situation. This contributes to an air of informality and allows a planner to more effectively mirror the client. However, caution must be exercised when using licensed discovery tools or assessments, where the planner is prohibited from changing or adapting copyrighted materials.

3. The client should be encouraged to share information, feelings, perceptions, and observations openly and freely.

4. Open-ended, nonjudgmental questions that respect the sensitivity of a topic should be used. It is important to fully consider the meaning of the question *and* its impact. For example, what may appear to be a straightforward question, "Do you gamble?" may not solicit as truthful a response as "About how many times a week/month do you think that you gamble?" (Similar questions could be designed for arguments about money, going over the limit on a credit card, providing funds to a relative or friend, etc.) Questions beginning with *why* should also be avoided.

5. Follow-up questions and verbal or nonverbal reinforcements should be used as necessary to encourage clients to elaborate or offer fuller explanations. Simple questions (e.g., "Can you tell me more about that experience?" or "How did that happen?" or "Earlier you mentioned X; can you tell me more about that?") or simple statements (e.g., "Um-hum" or "I understand" or "Tell me more") are not only encouraging, but they will not bias the response. Nonverbal cues (e.g., eye contact, posture, expressions such as a smile, a nod, or silence) may all encourage a client to continue talking and to reflect on the situation.

6. Rapport, which is characterized by trust or positive feelings, is important to a successful interview. It can be encouraged by identifying common interests or, within the confines of the professional relationship, sharing personal information.

7. With the consent of the client, a planner must identify an efficient and effective strategy for capturing and summarizing data for future use. Some planners record or videotape the meeting, whether it is held in person or by telephone,

and they transcribe the important data. A planner can take notes during the meeting, if it can be done without creating a distraction. Another option is for a paraplanner or other client services staff member to take notes during the meeting. However, it is very important that the notetaker be respectful of the sensitivity of a topic and the emotional responses of clients, who may be upset by efforts to record their story. Alternatively, a planner can summarize information immediately following the meeting. This method can be problematic—a high-quality, in-depth interview will produce more detailed information than virtually anyone could entirely recall and accurately record after the interview. (For more information on planner-client communication strategies, see Chapter 3.)

Consequently, planner-client conversations conducted for the purpose of data gathering in the context of a guided interview can benefit the relationship and offer new opportunities to increase a planner's expertise. Consider, for example, the following questions from the *Journal of Financial Planning*, which Ross Levin reports using with clients to explore needs, wants, accomplishments, and future goals (personal and financial) that might be motivating an individual:

1. "What financial things do you currently have that you appreciate the most?"

2. "What are some things that you set out to obtain and have done so?"

3. "If you were to look back over your life today, what, financially, will you have been most grateful for accomplishing?"

4. "What are you most proud of financially?"[16]

These questions, although scripted, are a good example of the type used for a focused interview.

But where can students or novice planners get targeted questions for different planning issues in the first place? Industry literature, continuing education and specialized training opportunities, and conversations with experienced advisors are all good sources of targeted, useful questions. Increased familiarity with typical client goals and life cycle events, as well as client motives and reactions, can provide the background for developing additional questions and responses. Although the ability to guide a client skillfully through the preceding questions goes beyond the fundamental skills for conducting a focused interview, training and experience are invaluable for mastering different methods of client data collection.

What Does It Mean to Frame Goals and Objectives?

Goals are sometimes defined as dreams that become reality. This simple definition suggests that if the idea, or the ideal, can be made real, then something happened between the idea of the goal and its accomplishment. For most people, motivated or purposeful action is needed to pursue and accomplish a goal.

Depending on the issue being considered, a goal can range from abstract to concrete. In Chapter 1 a **goal** was defined as a more global statement of a client's personal or financial purpose, while an **objective** was defined as a more discrete financial target that supports a goal. For example, a client may state that he or she desires a "comfortable retirement," but it is only through further discussion and clarification that the planner might discern the definitive objective of accumulating $1.65 million by the age of 65 to support 30 years of retirement income. Blanchard coined the acronym "SMART" to describe goals that are

- **S**pecific;

- **M**easurable;

- **A**ttainable;

- **R**ealistic; and

- **T**rackable.[17]

This type of analysis offers planners a useful guideline for working with clients and can easily facilitate discussions on assumptions and expectations appropriate for the planning situation and the goal in question. (Framing SMART goals also facilitates consideration of the seven questions that must be answered in any well-written recommendation.)

Many times a planner, through the discovery process with a client, will uncover a goal that the client was either uncomfortable listing, could not fully articulate, or simply thought was out of reach. Such insights increase a planner's understanding of the client and help the planner discover nuances and subtle priorities among the client's goals. Planners should not look at each goal in isolation. Goals may be independent, interrelated, or interdependent. And the best solution for one goal may have a deleterious effect on another goal. For interrelated goals, the first goal may need to be fulfilled as a precursor to fulfilling the second goal. The idea of a personal goal hierarchy or ranking is commonly accepted, as is the duration of the time available to fund the goal. Typically, goals are categorized by a time line for accomplishment, such as:

- *Short-term*: less than two years.

- *Intermediate-term*: requiring from two to 10 years.

- *Long-term*: requiring more than 10 years.

Exact specifications for the goals may range from a few months to multiple years or even decades. Recognizing and examining the relationships among the client's goals provides a deeper understanding of the client situation. The communication required to fully identify and frame goals can sometimes be challenging. Nonetheless, the outcome of these efforts is essential to preparing feasible, actionable, client-oriented recommendations.

In financial planning, much attention is focused on goals—especially those that are socially acceptable or supported by tax policy (e.g., accumulating funds for retirement or education expenses). But from a broader perspective, it is also important to consider the *origin* of a client's goals. Although clients' goals can be framed or defined in limitless ways, they basically emanate from (1) wants and needs, (2) life cycle events, and (3) life transitions. Wants and needs are differentiated by their significance, with **wants** described as desires or pleasures while **needs** are required to sustain life. The interpretation of wants and needs varies widely across the spectrum of income or wealth.

Life cycle events represent typical biological, socioeconomic, or sociocultural events that occur over the life span of an individual or household. Anthony defines goals as what a client would like to have, do, or be during life, while a **life transition** represents a change or transition currently faced or expected to occur in the near future.[18] Using this definition, life transition might represent a life cycle event or a random occurrence (e.g., the diagnosis of a chronic disease). Clients may identify a new goal, modify existing goals, or change the hierarchy of the goals as a result of a perceived want or need, life cycle event, or life transition.

The preceding categories for classifying goals are not necessarily mutually exclusive. For example, a divorce might result from an unfulfilled personal need, or be viewed as a life cycle event or a life transition. Rebuilding a vacation home following a hurricane could be viewed as a need (i.e., to receive the insurance reimbursement), a want (i.e., to continue family memories), or a life transition resulting from the change to the household as a result of the property damage. Examples of selected needs, wants, life cycle events, and life transitions are shown in Table 6.2; for additional examples see Section 5 of the Client Intake Form in Appendix B. Table 6.2 could be adapted into a form to be completed by the client or into questions to be used during discovery. Either way, a very productive discussion could ensue, whether between a client and planner, or perhaps more importantly, between a couple or partners, who may never have considered these issues.

Two significant questions typically emerge after data have been collected and reviewed. Should client financial goals be ranked? And if so, how? Answers to these questions range from easy to complex. In situations where a client is able to prioritize goals, the answer can be relatively straightforward. But in cases where a client has several equally important but somewhat conflicting goals, answering the question becomes significantly more problematic. Of course the ranking of goals may not be an issue if sufficient funding is available; however, this is rarely the case for most clients.

Table 6.2 Examples of Client Needs, Wants, Life Cycle Events, and Life Transitions

	Need	Want	Life Cycle Event	Life Transition
Selling/buying/starting a business	√	√		
Vacation/travel		√		
Second home/vacation home		√		
Change in marital status (formation, dissolution, widowed)		√	√	√
Military service or deployment				√
Having children or grandchildren		√	√	√
Signing up for Social Security and Medicare			√	√
Change in employment	√	√		√
Children entering or graduating from college			√	√
Hobbies/leisure activities		√	√	
Risk management protection	√			
Funding for education expenses	√	√	√	
Leaving a legacy (for family, charity, community, etc.)		√	√	
Caring for parents			√	√
New car every x years		√		
Boat/motorcycle		√		
Family celebration (wedding, anniversary, reunion, Bar/Bat Mitzvah, second honeymoon)		√	√	√
Death of family member or friend			√	√
Disability of friend			√	√
Receipt of a large settlement				
Pool, spa, tennis court or other home improvement		√		
Moving parents to a care facility			√	√
Financial independence (freedom, security, etc.)	√	√	√	
Financial gift for a family member or friend		√	√	
Funding for retirement	√	√	√	√
Debt reduction or elimination	√	√		

Exhibit 6.2 illustrates one way to prioritize and rank a client's financial goals. The logic behind this table is rooted in goal-based decision-making theory, which suggests that goals can be prioritized to allow a decision maker to choose the most important goal to achieve. In principle, once this goal is reached, or at least fully funded, the next highest-ranking goal would be dealt with, and the process would continue until all goals were either accounted for or a client's resources were depleted. This is one approach, but there are alternatives for ranking and funding goals that exceed the funding available. Exhibit 6.2 provides a definition and a scoring methodology for

each goal-ranking item. In effect, multiple goals can be compared using these items, with a total score generated for each goal. The goal with the highest total score would be ranked number one; the next highest-scoring goal would be ranked number two, and so on.

Exhibit 6.2 Goal Ranking Form

Goal Ranking Form

What is the goal?

Goal Feature	Explanation	Scale	Score
		Total possible score range (9 – 33)	
Emotional Importance	How important is this goal to the client's personal well—being?	Low Medium High	1 2 3
Financial Importance	How important is this goal to the client's financial situation?	Low Medium High	1 2 3
Need/Want	Does the client define this goal as a need or a want?	Want Need	0 2
How Many Ways Can the Goal Be Achieved?	Are there many alternatives to achieve the goal or just a few ways to satisfy goal?	Many Ways Few Ways Limited Ways	1 2 3
How Many Times Goal Could be Achieved?	Is the goal recurring or is funding the goal a one-time event?	Often Limited One-Time	1 2 3
Likelihood of Goal Accomplishment	What is the probability or likelihood that the goal will be achieved?	Low Moderate High	1 2 3
Time Horizon for Funding the Goal	When is the funding for the goal needed?	More than 10 years Between 2 and 10 years Within 2 years Within 3 months	1 2 3 4
Is a Delay possible?	Can the target date for goal realization be delayed?	Yes Maybe No	1 2 3
Time Horizon for Depleting the Goal Funding	For how many years must the funding for the goal last?	Within 3 months Within 2 years Between 2 and 10 years More than 10 years	1 2 3 4
Financial Impact of Goal Failure	How serious are the financial consequences for the client if the goal is not achieved?	Minor Serious Devastating	1 3 5
Total Score			

Source: Adapted from Slade, S. (1994). *Goal-Based Decision Making: An Interpersonal Model.* Lawrence Erlbaum Associates, Inc., Publishers. NJ: Hillsdale.

A word of caution is in order. Because goals can be ranked does not necessarily mean that the highest-ranking goal should be dealt with first. Client goals and objectives and the resulting recommendations can be moderated by a planner's knowledge of a client's situational factors. Goals and recommendations may then be subject to further refinement based on the planner's own financial planning knowledge and experience as well as other descriptive factors. These issues are amplified in the following case example.

Data Gathering Tip: The Importance of Specifically Recording Client Goals

It is always good practice to take client information—no matter how it is provided—and put it into a format for practical use. It is unlikely that a client will ever arrive in a planner's office with goals specifically outlined and ranked. Most clients have a general idea of what they would like to accomplish, but few will be able to define their goals precisely during a first meeting. It takes energy, intuition, and persuasion to coax goals and objectives from a client. Recording a client's goals and objectives, as understood by a planner, is a good way to develop a checklist for further discussion. Furthermore, realistically framing, articulating, and ranking goals can occur only as the client's "dreams" are brought into perspective by the analytical and technical knowledge of the planner. A thoughtful and honest interchange between client and planner is needed to arrive at the final goals for a plan—and everyone must realize that both the goals and the plan are subject to changing circumstances and the vagaries of the future.

Step 2 and the CFP Board Standards of Ethical Conduct

Step 2: Gather Data and Frame Goals and Objectives in the systematic financial planning process corresponds to the CFP Board Practice Standards 200 Series: Gathering Client Data. The CFP Board integration of Practice Standards 200-1 and 200-2 with the most applicable *Code of Ethics* and *Rules of Conduct* is shown in Appendix 6A.2. These two practice standards address the collection of qualitative and quantitative data necessary (1) to identify and mutually agree on the client's personal and financial goals, needs and priorities and (2) to fulfill the certificant's obligations as defined by the agreement and/or to conduct financial planning *prior* to making or implementing any recommendations.

The Principle of Diligence in providing professional services is identified as particularly relevant to this aspect of the process. Diligence is explained by timely and thorough client services, as well as the appropriate planning for and supervision of the professional services provided the client. It is important to consider the broad scope of this principle, particularly for planning for and supervising the professional services provided, across all steps of the financial planning process. The Board specifically relates this principle to all steps in the financial planning process.

As shown in Appendix 6B, the same three *Rules of Conduct* apply to both 200 Series Practice Standards. *Rule 3.3* focuses on the importance of obtaining all information needed, and when not available to inform the prospective client or clients of "any and all material deficiencies."[19] The other two *Rules of Conduct* focus on the CFP certificant's obligation to the prospective client or client to exercise professional judgment in providing professional services, as explained in *Rule 4.4* and to only make or implement suitable recommendations in the best interest of the client, *and* when providing financial planning or material elements of financial planning to act as a fiduciary, as explained in *Rule 4.5*. As defined earlier in this chapter, the Board defines a fiduciary as acting in a manner reasonably believed to be in the best interests of the client.

From Process to Practice

The vignette that follows introduces the Kims, a young professional couple with an 8-year-old daughter named Azalea, and their financial planner, Jane. Their story, which recounts their financial planning experience, will continue from Chapter 6 through Chapter 8. In this first section, the Kims recall the events that characterize Steps 1 and 2 of the financial planning process for them.

Tom and Nyla asked Jane on the way out of her office, "Are we done?" "Not quite," Jane said, "But we have made a lot of progress this year." Tom and Nyla Kim had just completed their first annual check-up and monitoring meeting with Jane, their financial planner. The meeting did not go at all as the Kims had expected. There were no questionnaires to complete, no forms to fill out, no disclosure agreements to sign; in fact, neither of them had even picked up a pen. "Wow," Tom mused as they headed for the car, "Did we make it?"

As Tom and Nyla drove home, they began to reflect on Jane's final comment. They had made a lot of progress, but there had also been a lot of hard work, soul searching, prioritizing of their goals, budgeting of their income, attending several meetings, and participating in several phone calls with Jane over the course of a little more than a year.

Tom and Nyla initially met with Jane after a recommendation from a friend who was also one of Jane's clients. Their friend explained that Jane, a graduate of a college financial planning program, was a fee-based comprehensive financial planner who worked with young professional clients who wanted to establish strong, long-term planning relationships. They went to Jane for what they now call "the first of our financial physicals. We wanted to know that we were financially healthy and that there weren't any problems looming on the horizon," Tom recollected.

In the beginning, Tom and Nyla both felt unsure about their financial future. They had often thought about seeing a professional, but they did not know where to go, whom to ask, how to begin—or what to expect. They felt sure that their lack of a clearly defined direction and limited assets meant that professional help was out of their reach. However, when they initially met with Jane, her approach was just what they needed. She did not spend much time on the financial aspects of their life; instead she asked some thought-provoking questions, such as "Where do you see yourselves financially in 10 years?" and "How did you come to be where you are now?"

She also took the time to explain what financial planning was really about, how they would work together, and what they would do over the course of a year—if Tom and Nyla decided to become her clients. Jane explained the typical fees for developing a comprehensive plan. And, she asked Tom and Nyla what questions they had, which she willingly answered. In fact, she gave them several documents—disclosures and a privacy statement to take home.

Near the end of the meeting, Jane asked a final question: "What would a successful financial planning outcome look like (and feel like) one year from now? Five years from now?" At the end of that discussion, Jane said, "If you think I can help you achieve that, let me know and I will prepare and send a letter of engagement, or contract, for you to sign and return." Tom and Nyla left Jane's office without an answer to her question, "If you think I can help you achieve that...." But after a week of pondering their future and the potential cost/benefit of Jane's services, they decided to commit the time, effort, and money to their future and called Jane's office.

Once the Kims had returned their signed agreement, they received an email with several attachments or "fact-finder" questionnaires, called the Client Intake Form (to complete jointly), the Goal Ranking Form (to completely individually and jointly), and the Risk Tolerance Assessment (to complete individually). The completed forms and originals or copies of several other financial documents were to be returned to the office a few days before their next meeting. But to the Kims, the most important thing Jane said in her follow-up phone call was that she would be available to help if they started to feel overwhelmed by the forms. "It is a lot of work," she said, "but totally worth it." Some clients look back at the Client Intake Form several years later and take pride in how far they have come. It is like throwing another log on the fire. Most people get re-energized because they see progress and want to make even more." With that, the Kims started their financial planning relationship with Jane—that was about a year ago.

Two weeks after their introductory meeting, the Kims had completed the intake form and brought the requested documents back to Jane's office for what she called a *discovery meeting*. Again, they were surprised at how relaxed Jane was about their prospects. Although they had talked with her and her staff several times over the phone about getting assistance with the forms, they were very happy to see that she was still so upbeat. They had been afraid that with all of their questions and their obvious lack of financial knowledge, Jane might have decided not to work with them.

Tom recalled that as Jane meticulously reviewed the intake form and their other financial documents, she paid particular attention to the Goals and Objectives section as she began asking questions. These were not questions that made them feel uneasy or that implied they had not done the right things thus far—just questions. For example, "How do you feel about providing funding for your daughter's college?" and "Will you be staying with family on your proposed international vacation?" Exhibit 6.3 shows an example of the Goals and Objectives section of the Client Intake Form as completed by Tom and Nyla Kim.

Exhibit 6.3 Goals and Objectives Form for Tom and Nyla Kim

Goals/Objectives (Tom & Nyla Kim) Personal	Importance Level (0-5)	Time Horizon to Begin	Time Horizon to Complete
Becoming more financially knowledgeable	3	Now	
Improving recordkeeping methods	0		
Starting a family	0		
Advancing in current career	4	Now	
Changing careers	0		
Returning to college	0		
Caring for parents	2	15 years	Unknown
Retiring early	3	25 years	Unknown
Traveling extensively in retirement	0		
Other:			
Other:			
Financial			
Reducing revolving debt	5	Now	Unknown
Increasing periodic savings	3	Now	
Reducing taxes	1		
Evaluating insurance needs	3	Soon	
Increasing investment diversification	1		
Increasing investment return	2	Now	
Starting a small business	0		
Saving for children's education	5	Now	10 years
Purchasing a vehicle	0		
Saving for the down payment on a home	0		
Purchasing a home	0		
Investing an inheritance	0		
Saving for retirement	5	Now	25 years
Giving to charity	2	5 years	Unknown
Transferring estate assets	0		
Other: Vacation	4	Now	2 years
Other:			
Other:			

Nyla remembered being really impressed by the questions that Jane asked and the fact that she seemed genuinely interested—as if she was really paying attention to their lives and not just their money. Jane had explained that her additional questions helped her get a better picture of her clients—to learn about their values, goals, attitudes, and even their family health histories as a background for understanding what was important in their lives and their financial plan. As the discussion focused on their goals, Jane reviewed the Kims' completed Summary Goal Ranking Form. Jane's original instructions said that the Kims could individually complete a form for each goal and then come to a consensus, or that they could simply discuss each goal and complete the scoring. Either way, Jane needed their summary form. Exhibit 6.4 provides an example of the Goal Ranking Form completed by the Kims (after several hours of discussion) for three of their goals.

Exhibit 6.4 Summary Goal Ranking Form for Tom and Nyla Kim

What is the goal?		Azalea's Education		Retirement		Vacation Trip	
Goal Feature	**Scale**						
Emotional importance	(1–3)	High	3	Low	1	High	3
Financial importance	(1–3)	Medium	2	High	3	Low	1
Want/need	(0/2)	Need	2	Need	2	Want	0
How many ways can the goal be achieved?	(1–3)	Few	2	Many	1	Few	2
How many times can the goal be achieved?	(1–3)	One-Time	3	One-Time	3	Limited	2
Likelihood of accomplishment	(1–3)	High	3	Moderate	2	Low	1
Time horizon for funding	(1–4)	Between two and ten years	2	More than ten years	1	Within two years	3
Is a delay possible?	(1–3)	No	3	Yes	1	Maybe	2
Time Horizon for Depleting the Funding	(1–4)	Between two and ten years	3	More than ten years	4	Within three months	1
Financial impact of goal failure	(1–5)	Serious	3	Devastating	5	Minor	1
Total Possible Range	**(9–33)**						
	Total Score		26		23		16

Source: Adapted from Slade, S. (1994). *Goal-Based Decision Making: An Interpersonal Model.* Hillsdale, NJ: Lawrence Erlbaum Associates, Inc., Publishers.

Nyla recalled how difficult it was to complete the form, and although the total scores were very close for each goal, Nyla and Tom remembered that discussing each goal and ranking each item had been very helpful. Each of their goals was very important to them. Ever since Azalea was born, they had talked about wanting to at least partially pay for her to go to college—or whatever form of education she chose. When they discussed the possibility of not taking the international trip, Tom quickly reminded her of the promise "to go on a honeymoon someday even if we have to take the kids." Furthermore, they were pleased that Jane, even with her extensive financial knowledge, did not presume to know their desires or arbitrarily rank the goals and proceed with the plan development without their input.

Overall, Tom and Nyla remembered the discovery and goal-setting process as emotionally difficult but informative. Ultimately, they were both very pleased with the relationship they had established with their new financial planner. They recalled leaving the second meeting feeling as if they had shared their life story with Jane—with the unexpected benefit that they had actually learned some new things about each other after more than twelve years of marriage. They had three goals for their future, and Jane had left them with the impression that they weren't just dreams—they could be goals!

CHAPTER SUMMARY

The establishment of the client engagement sets the parameters for the breadth of information to be gathered about a client situation. But the depth of information gathered about client situational factors provides the background for the upcoming client situational analysis, whether it is completed for a single issue, a core content planning area in a modular plan, or for a comprehensive financial plan. As a result of Step 1, the advisor and client will have initiated a trust-based professional relationship and contractual agreement. That agreement and the necessary disclosures will more fully define and characterize the scope of the engagement.

The Client Intake Form and guidelines for conducting a focused interview were introduced as methods for gathering quantitative and qualitative data. Through these efforts a planner comes to know and understand the client and the planning needs. By the end of Step 2, Gather Data and Frame Goals and Objectives, the advisor and client should have identified mutually agreeable, clearly defined goals and objectives. The scope of the planner-client engagement (from Step 1) and the planner-client relationship and goals (forged from Step 2) serve as a foundation for the continuation of the financial planning process.

Learning Outcomes

1. Documents provided in Step 1 serve two purposes: to disclose the scope of the business relationship (e.g., disclosure, privacy, and investment management policies, if the latter are applicable) and to formalize the relationship with a contract.

2. Three fundamental outcomes result from Step 1, Establish and Define the Relationship. First, the foundation is laid for a longer-term trust-based relationship. Second, the client and advisor agree on the personal and professional obligations and responsibilities expected within the relationship. Third, a contractual obligation with all requisite regulatory and compliance

requirements establishes the legal relationship between the planner and client. It is important to note that these outcomes may result from one or several advisor-client meetings.

3. The CFP Board *Code of Ethics* Principles of Fairness and Diligence are particularly important when conducting Step 1 of the systematic financial planning process. The *Rules of Conduct* reflect the importance of mutually agreed upon services that are guided by a full disclosure of the financial planning process, a clearly defined agreement, and disclosures (e.g., compensation, conflicnts of interest, and expertise) that support an informed decision by the client or prospective client.

4. Both quantitative and qualitative data are collected to help a planner understand a client's situation. Quantitative data represent socioeconomic descriptors that explain *factual* aspects of a client's financial life, such as income, net worth, and other data targeted to each of the core content areas. Qualitative data reflect *behavioral* aspects of a client's life—and financial life—because the two are intertwined. Through the discovery process, advisors learn about a client's temperament and personality; attitudes, beliefs, values, and behaviors; and financial knowledge and experience. The qualitative information is *factually* accurate, truthfully portraying the client. But the methods used to collect and confirm the qualitative data are quite different from those used to collect and confirm *factual*, quantitative data.

5. The discovery process refers to the use of focused interviews or other assessments that advisors use to collect primarily qualitative, situational information about a client. The focus is on the client's temperament and personality; attitudes, beliefs, values, and behaviors; and financial knowledge and experience as well as goals and objectives—all of which explain the client's financial situation. Because of the increased focus on a client's life, not solely finances, advisors are incorporating questions and other discovery tools that identify life planning issues or money scripts. Discovering the emotional, experiential, and spiritual issues that influence the use of money and the goals that frame a meaningful life for the client is one example of life planning. Discovering money scripts, or typically unconscious beliefs that significantly shape a client's use of money or choice of goals, is another example.

6. A client's ease or level of comfort, with accepting risk in a financial situation is reflected in the financial risk tolerance attitude. One common way to think of this is, "Are you ok if the value of your portfolio decreases to $X, given the riskiness, or volatility, of the portfolio?" Although risk tolerance is always a factor in investment decisions, a client's acceptance of risk has implications for financial decisions across all of the core content planning areas.

7. Clients may complete forms (on paper or electronically), submit original source documents, agree to planner access or inquiries to third-party providers, and/or respond in face-to-face, telephone, or other electronic meetings. It is essential to show respect for the client and the advisor-client relationship; to ensure the accuracy of the data and objectivity when working with the client and the data; and foremost, to maintain confidentiality and protect the privacy of the data.

8. The Client Intake Form is only one method among a variety of approaches that advisors use to collect client data. A standardized form ensures that needed information is available for

analyzing the client's situation and it reduces professional liability by documenting the scope of data used to profile the client situation. A systematic data collection process is an important step in providing consistent and defensible financial planning services for all clients.

9. A focused interview might be thought of as an in-depth conversation with a *purpose* guided by a set of questions, typically open-ended. The interview is designed to encourage an in-depth understanding of the client and the client's motives and perspectives. The interview should build rapport to encourage an open, free sharing of information that will enable the planner and client to more fully comprehend planning needs and goals.

10. To frame, or conceptualize, client goals and objectives requires both the planner and the client to fully appreciate the attitudes, values, motives, needs, wants, life cyle events, and life transitions that exemplify the client's situation. Goals reflect a broader personal or financial purpose, which can be further defined by a specific financial target, or objective, which supports the goal. Achieving the objective(s) leads to goal accomplishment, which typically gives way to framing another goal and set of objectives.

11. Clients' lives and the goals they pursue are defined and characterized by wants, needs, life cycle events, and life transitions. Clients differentiate desires from essentials when considering wants and needs, respectively. Both life cycle events (sociocultural, socioeconomic, or biological) and life transitions (changes) reflect life stages that clients are either experiencing or anticipate in the future. Considering these dimensions in the context of a SMART goal helps planners and clients identify the (1) most important, or meaningful, goals to pursue—the destination, and (2) the requirements to facilitate goal progress—the road map. Stating a goal so that it is specific, measurable, attainable, realistic, and trackable also requires attention to the questions of who, what, when, where, why, how, and how much. A good map can mean a more efficient but still enjoyable trip!

12. If clients' lives and the goals they pursue are defined and characterized by wants, needs, life cycle events, and life transitions, then competition among these goals and objectives is to be expected. The goal ranking form provides a standardized, numeric scale to rank competing goals—whether by an individual, a couple, partners, or a family—to decide whether or when a goal should be pursued. Despite the client's ranking, in some cases it may be necessary for the advisor's professional judgment to prevail to ensure that a client's best interests are served.

13. The CFP Board Practice Standards 200 Series: Gathering Client Data corresponds to Step 2 of the systematic financial planning process. The focus is on the need to collect the required qualitative and quantitative data to mutually define the client's goals and priorities and to satisfy the scope of the engagement *before* any recommendations are made or implemented. This step should be distinguished by the Principle of Diligence, or the timely and thorough planning for and supervision of the services rendered. *Rules of Conduct* focus on the significance of collecting the necessary client information, exercising prudent professional judgment, and ensuring that recommendations are in the best interest of the client and, when applicable, consistent with a fiduciary duty of care.

Chapter Resources

Assessing Your Financial Risk Tolerance (http://www.rce.rutgers.edu/money/riskquiz/default. asp).

Certified Financial Planner Board of Standards, Inc. (www.cfp.net).

Financial Therapy Association (http://financialtherapyassociation.org/).

FinaMetrica® (www.finametrica.com).

Investment Adviser Registration Depository (http://www.iard.com/).

Money Harmony (http://moneyharmony.com/).

MoneyMax® Personality Profile (http://kathleengurney.com/).

Money Quotient® Putting Money in the Context of Life™ (http://moneyquotient.org/).

The Kinder Institute of Life Planning (http://www.kinderinstitute.com/index.html).

The Financial Life Planning Institute (http://www.flpinc.com/).

U.S. Securities and Exchange Commission (www.sec.gov).

Your Mental Wealth™ (http://www.yourmentalwealth.com/).

Anthony, M. *Your Clients for Life: The Definitive Guide to Becoming a Successful Financial Planner.* Chicago, IL: Dearborn Financial Publishing, 2002.

Bradley, Susan, and Mary Martin. *Sudden Money: Managing a Financial Windfall.* New York: John Wiley & Sons, 2000.

Diliberto, R. T. *Financial Planning—The Next Step: A Practical Approach to Merging Your Clients' Money with Their Lives.* Denver, CO: FPA Press, 2006.

Kay, M. *The Business of Life.* Sunnyvale, CA: Advisor Press, 2010.

Kinder, G. *Seven Stages of Money Maturity: Understanding the Spirit and Value of Money in your Life.* New York: Dell Publishing, 2000.

Kinder, G., and S. Galvan. *Lighting the Torch: The Kinder Method™ of Life Planning.* Denver, CO: FPA Press, 2006.

Klontz, B., R. Kahler, and T. Klontz. *Facilitating Financial Health: Tools for Financial Planners, Coaches, and Therapists.* Cincinnati, OH: National Underwriter Company, 2008.

Klontz, B., and T. Klontz. *Mind over Money: Overcoming the Money Disorders That Threaten Our Financial Health.* New York: Crown Business, 2009.

Schott, J. W., and J. Arbeiter. *Mind over Money: Match Your Personality to a Winning Financial Strategy.* New York: Little Brown & Co., 2000.

Discussion Questions

1. List the seven criteria to profile a business. Explain how each specifically relates to the CFP Board *Rules of Conduct*. For each, give examples of the questions that a client might ask or the information that a planner might disclose to establish and define the relationship.

2. Match the criteria listed above to the documents that are typically provided to clients. What is the purpose of each document?

3. How does the concept of help-seeking behavior fit with financial planning, financial therapy, financial coaching, life planning, and money scripts?

4. Although not truly a linear process, how do the outcomes from Step 1 serve as a foundation for the activities and outcomes of Step 2?

5. What kinds of client information are encompassed in the exploration of client situational factors? Identify the four types of factors, list five examples of each, and explain how each might affect the planning process and, therefore, be important for the advisor to consider. Why are the situational factors that describe a planner also important?

6. Why is it important for a financial planner to know whether a client is currently working with another financial professional, such as an attorney, accountant, or enrolled agent?

7. How might the financial planning attitudes and practices of a risk-tolerant client vary from those of a risk-averse client? Consider multiple attitudes and practices beyond those associated with investments. How can these insights inform the planning process for planner and client? How can these heuristics, or stereotypes, negatively affect the planning process?

8. Identify at least five original source docments that an advisor may wish to review. For each, identify why the document would be wanted and the information to be gained.

9. What is a focused interview? How is it similar and dissimilar from a conversation? Why are verbal and nonverbal communication important aspects of a focused interview?

10. Why is a goal stated as "to live life with a relatively high level of financial satisfaction" not very useful in terms of practical financial planning analysis? What might a SMART objective state in support of such a goal?

11. Answer the sample focused interview questions from Kinder or Levin. How might your answers differ from the answers given by your spouse, partner, or close friend? How might these differences affect your financial choices?

12. What are the benefits of using a formal Client Intake Form? Review the form and identify: (1) data that you suspect will be most difficult for the average client to provide; and (2) data that you were surprised to see requested. For each answer, explain why.

13. Review the definitions of needs, wants, life cycle events, and life transitions. Identify examples of each, noting those that might not be mutually exclusive. Try to identify examples that are not shown in Table 6.2.

14. According to goal-based decision-making theory, how might goals be prioritized to allow an advisor and client to choose the most important goal(s)? What criteria contribute to this ranking?

15. Explain how privacy and the protection of client data are important concepts in both Step 1 and Step 2 of the systematic financial planning process. Using the *CFP Board's Standards of Professional Conduct* (available at: http://www.cfp.net/Downloads/2010Standards.pdf), identify the relevant *Code of Ethics* principle(s) and the *Rules of Conduct* that govern privacy and the protection of client data.

Notes

1. Securities and Exchange Commission, Form ADV (Paper Version), *Uniform Application for Investment Adviser Registration.* Available at http://www.sec.gov/divisions/investment/iard/formadv-part2-0710.pdf, pp. 1–2.

2. Certified Financial Planner Board of Standards, Inc., *CFP Board's Standards of Professional Conduct.* Available at http://www.cfp.net/Downloads/2010Standards.pdf, p. 4.

3. C. C. Maton, M. Maton, and W. M. Martin, "Collaborating with a Financial Therapist: The Why, Who, What and How," *Journal of Financial Planning* 23, no. 2 (2010): 62–70.

4. K. Gurney, *Your Money Personality: What It Is and How You Can Profit From It* (New York: Doubleday, 1988). Revised under the same title, 2009, Financial Psychology Corporation, Sarasota, FL.

5. O. Mellan, *Money Harmony: Resolving Money Conflicts in Your Life and Relationships* (New York: Walker & Co., 1994).

6. B. Klontz, R. Kahler, and T. Klontz, *Facilitating Financial Health* (Cincinnati, OH: National Underwriter Co., 2008), 14.

7. Klontz, Kahler, and Klontz, *Facilitating Financial Health*, 9.

8. G. Kinder, *Seven Stages of Money Maturity: Understanding the Spirit and Value of Money in Your Life* (New York: Dell Publishing, 1999).

9. M. Anthony, *Your Clients for Life: The Definitive Guide to Becoming a Successful Financial Planner* (Chicago, IL: Dearborn Financial Publishing, 2002).

10. R. D. Diliberto, *Financial Planning—The Next Step, A Practical Guide to Merging Your Clients' Money with Their Lives* (Denver, CO: Financial Planning Association Press, 2006).

11. Carol Anderson, MoneyQuotient® Putting Money in the Context of Life. Available at http://moneyquotient.org/.

12. G. Kinder and S. E. Galvan, *Lighting the Torch: The Kinder Method™ of Life Planning.* (Denver, CO: Financial Planning Association Press, 2006), 77–78.

13. FinaMetrica Pty Limited, *FinaMetrica*, Sydney, Australia. Available at http://www.riskprofiling.com/home.

14. J. E. Grable and R. H. Lytton, "Financial Risk Tolerance Revisited: The Development of a Risk Assessment Instrument," Financial Services Review 8, no. 3 (1999): 163–181.

15. Klontz, Kahler, and Klontz, *Facilitating Financial Health*, 190.

16. R. Levin, "When Everything You Have *Is* Enough," *Journal of Financial Planning* 16, no. 2 (2003): 35.

17. K. Blanchard, P. Zigarmi, and D. Zigarmi, *Leadership and The One Minute Manager: Increasing Effectiveness Through Situational Leadership* (New York: William Morrow & Co., 1985).

18. M. Anthony, *Life Transitions Profile*. Financial Life Planning Institute (2004) at http://www.financialifeplanning.com/ under the FLP Tools Preview tab.

19. Certified Financial Planner Board of Standards, Inc., *CFP Board's Standards of Professional Conduct*. Available at http://www.cfp.net/Downloads/2010Standards.pdf, p.10. ffff1f1.

Step 1 – Establish and Define the Relationship

CFP Board Practice Standards 100 Series: Establishing and Defining the Relationship with the Client

100-1: Defining the Scope of the Engagement
The financial planning practitioner and the client shall mutually define the scope of the engagement before any financial planning service is provided.

CFP Board Code of Ethics	CFP Board Rules of Conduct

Principle 4 - Fairness
 	
Principle 7 – Diligence
	1. Defining the Relationship with the Prospective Client or Client
	
	1.1 The certificant and the prospective client or client shall mutually agree upon the services to be provided by the certificant.
	
	1.2 If the certificant's services include financial planning or material elements of financial planning, prior to entering into an agreement, the certificant shall provide written information or discuss with the prospective client or client the following:
	
	    a. The obligations and responsibilities of each party under the agreement with respect to:
	
	          i. Defining goals, needs and objectives,
	
	          ii. Gathering and providing appropriate data,
	
	          iii. Examining the result of the current course of action without changes,
	
	          iv. The formulation of any recommended actions,
	
	          v. Implementation responsibilities, and
	
	          vi. Monitoring responsibilities.
	
	    b. Compensation that any party to the agreement or any legal affiliate to a party to the agreement will or could receive under the terms of the agreement; and factors or terms that determine costs, how decisions benefit the certificant and the relative benefit to the certificant.
	
	    c. Terms under which the agreement permits the certificant to offer proprietary products.
	
	    d. Terms under which the certificant will use other entities to meet any of the agreement's obligations.
	
	If the certificant provides the above information in writing, the certificant shall encourage the prospective client or client to review the information and offer to answer any questions that the prospective client or client may have.

Step 1 – Establish and Define the Relationship (continued)

CFP Board Practice Standards 100 Series: Establishing and Defining the Relationship with the Client

100-1: Defining the Scope of the Engagement
The financial planning practitioner and the client shall mutually define the scope of the engagement before any financial planning service is provided.

CFP Board Code of Ethics	CFP Board Rules of Conduct

Principle 4 - Fairness
 	
 Principle 7 – Diligence
	1.3 If the services include financial planning or material elements of financial planning, the certificant or the certificant's employer shall enter into a written agreement governing the financial planning services ("Agreement"). The Agreement shall specify:
	
	 a. The parties to the Agreement,
	
	 b. The date of the Agreement and its duration,
	
	 c. How and on what terms each party can terminate the Agreement, and
	
	 d. The services to be provided as part of the Agreement.
	
	 The Agreement may consist of multiple written documents. Written documentation that includes the items above and is used by a certificant or certificant's employer in compliance with state or federal law, or the rules or regulations of any applicable self-regulatory organization, such as the Securities and Exchange Commission's Form ADV or other disclosure documents, shall satisfy the requirements of this Rule.
	
	 2. Information Disclosed To Prospective Clients and Clients
	
	 2.2 A certificant shall disclose to a prospective client or client the following information:
	
	 a. An accurate and understandable description of the compensation arrangements being offered. This description must include:
	
	     i. Information related to costs and compensation to the certificant and/or the certificant's employer, and
	
	     ii. Terms under which the certificant and/or the certificant's employer may receive any other sources of compensation, and if so, what the sources of these payments are and on what they are based.
	
	 b. A general summary of likely conflicts of interest between the client and the certificant, the certificant's employer or any affiliates or third parties, including, but not limited to, information about any familial, contractual or agency relationship of the certificant or the certificant's employer that has a potential to materially affect the relationship.
	
	 c. Any information about the certificant or the certificant's employer that could reasonably be expected to materially affect the client's decision to engage the certificant that the client might reasonably want to know in establishing the scope and nature of the relationship, including but not limited to information about the certificant's areas of expertise.
	
	 d. Contact information for the certificant and, if applicable, the certificant's employer.
	
	 e. If the services include financial planning or material elements of financial planning, these disclosures must be in writing. The written disclosures may consist of multiple written documents. Written disclosures used by a certificant or certificant's employer that includes the items listed above, and are used in compliance with state or federal laws, or the rules or requirements of any applicable self-regulatory organization, such as the Securities and Exchange Commission's Form ADV or other disclosure documents, shall satisfy the requirements of this Rule.
	
	 The certificant shall timely disclose to the client any material changes to the above information.

Source: Certified Financial Planner Board of Standards, Inc., *CFP Board's Standards of Professional Conduct.* Available at http://www.cfp. net/Downloads/2010Standards.pdf, pp. 6, 7, 9, 10, and 16; or at http://www.cfp.net/learn/ethics.asp#intro.

Step 2 – Gather Data and Frame Goals and Objectives

CFP Board Practice Standards 200 Series: Gathering Client Data

200-1: Determining a Client's Personal and Financial Goals, Needs and Priorities
The financial planning practitioner and the client shall mutually define the client's personal and financial goals, needs and priorities that are relevant to the scope of the engagement before any recommendation is made and/or implemented.

CFP Board Code of Ethics	CFP Board Rules of Conduct
Principle 7 – Diligence	**3. Prospective Client and Client Information and Property** **3.3** A certificant shall obtain the information necessary to fulfill his or her obligations. If a certificant cannot obtain the necessary information, the certificant shall inform the prospective client or client of any and all material deficiencies. **4. Obligations to Prospective Clients and Clients** **4.4** A certificant shall exercise reasonable and prudent professional judgment in providing professional services to clients. **4.5** In addition to the requirements of Rule 1.4, a certificant shall make and/or implement only recommendations that are suitable for the client. *Note Reference to Rule 1.4 Above:* 1. Defining the Relationship with the Prospective Client or Client **1.4** A certificant shall at all times place the interest of the client ahead of his or her own. When the certificant provides financial planning or material elements of financial planning, the certificant owes to the client the duty of care of a fiduciary as defined by CFP Board.

Step 2 – Gather Data and Frame Goals and Objectives (continued)	
CFP Board Practice Standards 200 Series: Gathering Client Data **200-2: Obtaining Quantitative Information and Documents** The financial planning practitioner shall obtain sufficient quantitative information and documents about a client relevant to the scope of the engagement before any recommendation is made and/or implemented.	
Principle 7 – Diligence	**3. Prospective Client and Client Information and Property** **3.3** A certificant shall obtain the information necessary to fulfill his or her obligations. If a certificant cannot obtain the necessary information, the certificant shall inform the prospective client or client of any and all material deficiencies. **4. Obligations to Prospective Clients and Clients** **4.4** A certificant shall exercise reasonable and prudent professional judgment in providing professional services to clients. **4.5** In addition to the requirements of Rule 1.4, a certificant shall make and/or implement only recommendations that are suitable for the client. ***Note Reference to Rule 1.4 Above:*** **1. Defining the Relationship with the Prospective Client or Client** **1.4** A certificant shall at all times place the interest of the client ahead of his or her own. When the certificant provides financial planning or material elements of financial planning, the certificant owes to the client the duty of care of a fiduciary as defined by CFP Board.

Source: Certified Financial Planner Board of Standards, Inc., *CFP Board's Standards of Professional Conduct*. Available at http://www.cfp.net/Downloads/2010Standards.pdf, pp. 7, 9, 10, 11, 18, and 19; or at http://www.cfp.net/learn/ethics.asp#intro.

Chapter 7

Analyzing the Situation and Developing a Plan

Learning Objectives

1. Explain how to analyze a client's current situation.

2. Identify information needed to determine and quantify planning needs, document planning assumptions, and document and evaluate current planning efforts for each of the core financial planning content areas.

3. Understand the role of potential products and strategies within the analysis of a client's current situation and be able to provide an example of a product, product strategy, or procedural strategy for each of the core financial planning content areas.

4. Explain and apply the CFP Board requirements for ethical professional conduct relative to Step 3 of the systematic financial planning process.

5. Explain how a financial plan is developed.

6. Explain, apply, and defend the options available to a planner and client when the costs of funding all recommendations exceed available discretionary cash flow or other assets.

7. Explain the implementation actions and their impact on discretionary income, net worth, or both.

8. Identify and demonstrate planner practices important to the successful presentation of a plan to a client.

9. Explain and apply CFP Board requirements for ethical professional conduct relative to Step 4 of the systematic financial planning process.

10. Differentiate between holistic judgment, the systematic approach, and triangulation when analyzing a client situation and developing a plan.

Key Terms

Actionable recommendation

Assumptions

Cash flow orientation, or cash flow-based planning

Discretionary cash flow (DCF)

Goal orientation, or goal-based planning

Holistic judgment

Impact analysis

Procedural strategy

Product strategy

Systematic approach to planning

Triangulation

Figure 7.1 The Systematic Financial Planning Process

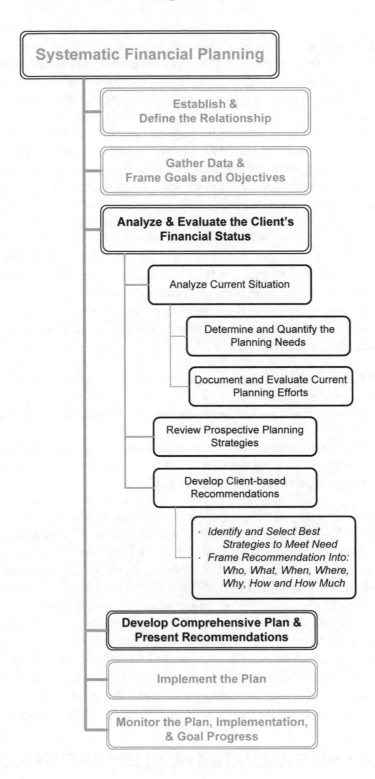

PROFESSIONAL JUDGMENT: THE "BLACK BOX" OF FINANCIAL PLANNING

Nearly all financial planners agree that developing a list of potential financial planning strategies to address a specific client issue is a relatively straightforward process. Some planners gravitate toward simple, easy-to-understand strategies. Others use their knowledge and experience to create more complex strategies that address multiple goals (e.g., funding a § 529 plan with the maximum five-year allowable contributions to reduce the taxable estate while gaining income tax benefits). The identification of strategies is grounded in knowledge of the products and procedures surrounding the core financial planning content areas. Difficulty in strategizing can occur when a planner is forced to narrow a list of potentially workable strategies into one or more recommendations. This process may become more difficult as a planner integrates multiple recommendations into a workable plan, and even more frustrating if the cost of funding all of the recommendations exceeds the funds identified. In fact, the process actually goes beyond product knowledge into the realm of analytical thinking, problem solving, synthesis, and inference. Students and novice planners may struggle with the questions of "How does it happen?" or "What is the process for moving from strategies to the selection of a recommendation or multiple integrated recommendations that make up a plan?" Too often, experienced planners offer little or no explanation, such as:

"I just know....it comes to me as I think about the client and the options."

"Most of the time I agree with the plan produced by the software."

On the other hand, some planners are honest enough to admit that, "For some clients I really struggle with plan development. There just never seems to be an easy answer. Other times, the pieces just fall into place."

Similar to Chapter 6, this chapter has three purposes. Using the analogy of a microscope, the first is to continue the examination of the tasks and decisions that must be accomplished in the next two steps of the systematic financial planning process: Step 3, Analyze and Evaluate the Client's Financial Status; and Step 4, Develop the Comprehensive Plan and Present the Recommendations. This chapter explores what happens inside the "black box" of developing the plan, or what some planners refer to as professional judgment, expertise, or intuition. A second purpose is to consider these steps relative to the CFP Board explanation of the financial planning process and the ethical professional conduct expected of certificants and registrants. Third, this chapter uses this background on the scope of the steps and expectations for ethical professional conduct to continue recounting the experiences of Tom and Nyla Kim working with their financial planner Jane through Steps 3 and 4.

STEP 3: ANALYZE AND EVALUATE THE CLIENT'S FINANCIAL STATUS

It may take years of study and experience to fully comprehend the nuances and complexities of thoroughly analyzing and evaluating a client's situation. This process is a financial planning conundrum built on facts known about the client, inferences gleaned from the planner-client relationship and the discovery process, and assumptions that should be mutually agreed upon by planner and client. It is, simply put, the application of professional judgment in the assessment and diagnosis of a client's financial situation, followed by a review of available alternatives. Then, in conjunction with the client, a course of action that offers the best risk-adjusted probability of success is identified. As illustrated in Figure 7.1, Step 3: Analyze and Evaluate the Client's Financial Status is a multilayered step consisting of three substeps: (1) Analyze the Current Situation; (2) Review Prospective Planning Strategies; and (3) Develop Client-based Recommendations.

Analyze the Current Situation

Analysis of a client's current situation requires a planner to review and distill all of the information collected about a client's situation in the context of the marketplace— the tax; economic; and political, legal, or regulatory environment. This analysis, summarized in Appendix 7A, is designed to answer four questions for each core content area:

1. *What is the client's planning need?* The determination, or qualification, of the planning need is based on an advisor's familiarity with the client's situation. Quantitative and qualitative data are considered, such as income replacement needs, the time horizon for a goal, family health history, occupational hazards, and attitudes. This investigation focuses on current *known* needs as well as any client information that might suggest *unknown* needs, current or future. For example, a 45-year-old client may not currently need long-term care insurance but may be strongly committed to purchasing a policy anyway because of a potential future need driven by a family history of Alzheimer's disease. Planning needs can be identified by the client or planner.

2. *What assumptions are relevant to the client's planning need?* **Assumptions** are inferences based on premises, reasoned conclusions, facts, or circumstantial evidence that affects a client's planning need and the quantification of that need. Assumptions must be fully disclosed, mutually agreed upon, and realistic. The latter two points are particularly important because the assumptions must be consistent with professional practice standards as well as the client's tolerance for risk matched to a particular goal.

   Although assumptions can be referred to as global, working, or goal-specific, assumptions really can be classified as relating to (1) a core content planning area or (2) the client. For example, historical stock market returns, recent inflationary increases in the cost of higher education, and average skilled nursing home costs are supported by factual data that can be stated as an assumption and included in the quantification of the client's need. Although factual data are available, and experts may be commenting on future trends, an assumption must be made because no one knows what the future value will be, and many issues clients face require planning for the future. These examples of core content assumptions, and many others, reflect the current known facts and the projected marketplace as well as the tax, economic, political, legal, or regulatory environment.

   Some assumptions reflect a client's personal situation and, although based in fact, are really mere conjecture (e.g., the assumed need for long-term care insurance, the likelihood of a child receiving college scholarships or fellowships, or life span projections). Other assumptions require a planner and client to make projections regarding both the marketplace and the client. For example, there are two considerations when projecting an assumption on a client's future marginal tax rate. First, how will the tax rate structure potentially change in the future? Will the top tax rate be high, as was the 70% rate during the Carter administration, or low, like the 31% during the first Bush administration?[1] Second, will the client's nominal income likely be higher, lower, or the same? Answers to these questions help determine the most accurate tax rate assumption to include in the analysis. And, like all assumptions, over time it may be necessary to update them to reflect changes in the marketplace pertaining to the core content areas or the client's life.

Carefully selecting and documenting key planning assumptions is an important element in the planning process. The CFP Board explains that an advisor must utilize client-specified, mutually agreed-upon, and/or other reasonable (1) personal and (2) economic assumptions when conducting the analysis, as explained in the Practice Standards 300 Series: Analyzing and Evaluating the Client's Information.

3. *Can the client's planning need be quantified?* Technical expertise, computations, and other analytical tools are used (where applicable) to objectively analyze and quantify a client's need. For some core content planning areas, such as estimating life insurance needs, several recognized approaches may be available and supported by different software applications. The quantification of other needs (e.g., the need for long-term care insurance protection) may be far harder to defend and to consider multiple, seemingly unrelated amounts, such as the client's projected net worth and daily benefit amount.

4. *How is the planning need currently being met?* The planner must document the planning efforts currently in place to meet the need, or the absence of any efforts on the part of the client to attempt to address the need. Then, a thorough and objective assessment of the products and strategies currently in use must be completed to project the likelihood of achieving the goal. Results of this evaluation may reveal needed changes or they may validate the client's approach and the fact that no changes are warranted. (For more information on some standard benchmarks that can be used to evaluate insurance and investment products, see Appendix C.)

Whereas the need to answer these four questions applies to each core content area, the data sources considered and the analytics completed may be quite different. Because of its importance and complexity, the substep Analyze the Current Situation must be individually and systematically applied to each of the core content planning areas, as summarized in Appendix 7A. A thorough exploration of the analysis surrounding each of these four questions is too extensive for consideration here; however, Appendix 7A should offer students and novice planners some useful insights into how these analyses could be conducted. For more information on the analytical approaches used with each core content planning area, see the companion book, *The Case Approach to Financial Planning: Bridging the Gap between Theory and Practice*, Second Edition.

Increased awareness of issues to consider in the analysis of a client's current situation can inform and frame the data gathering that occurs in Step 2 of the systematic financial planning process. For example, as shown in Appendix 7A, insurance needs must be evaluated against certain client risk classification factors because these risk factors determine the need for, availability of, and cost of insurance. Although planners are not expected to be knowledgeable of a specific company's underwriting methods, a general knowledge of the factors to be considered is critical to effective data gathering and planning. In reviewing a client's characteristic hazards and risks, planners should consider the following factors:

- **Lifestyle**

    - Using tobacco, alcohol, or drugs

    - Convictions for reckless driving, driving under the influence of alcohol or drugs, or receiving multiple speeding tickets

    - Participating in sensation-seeking activities, including ultralight flying, scuba diving, or mountain climbing

    - Personal character or household financial situation

- **Occupation**

    - Working in a hazardous profession or occupation

    - Piloting commercial, private, or military aircraft

- **Medical condition or history**

    - Gender, age, height, and weight

    - Family medical history

Individuals who, because of any of these factors, have a higher-than-standard mortality are considered substandard risks for privately purchased life insurance. These same factors can also affect cost, availability, or the need for other types of insurance. Depending upon the company, client insurability factors could result in the denial of a policy application, increased policy costs, or the inclusion of riders that control coverage. Insurance planning in particular exemplifies the need for a broad-based exploration of a client's situational factors, such as the lifestyle, personal, attitudinal, and socioeconomic profile that comprise Step 2: Gather Data and Frame Goals and Objectives. Gathering the client data needed for a thorough and defensible evaluation of a client's situation, whether for the purposes of a single-issue analysis, to support a product sale, or to complete a comprehensive plan, may appear intrusive, but it is, in fact, the foundation of the planner's future with that client. Throughout the planning process, the planner or planning team must demonstrate genuine empathy toward the client and support for the client's goals balanced with rigorous analytical skills.

At this juncture in the planning process, based on the data gathered and the analysis of the client's current situation, the planner has an arsenal of useful information to begin to answer the seven critical questions of who, what, when, where, why, how, and how much that guide the systematic financial planning process, as outlined below:

- Insights into the client's temperament, personality, motivations, money scripts, risk tolerance, financial knowledge, experience, and perceived level of financial success up to this point. A planner can begin to answer the questions of *who* and *why* as well as the questions *for whom, what,* and *how.*

- Clear, mutually agreed-upon definitions of the client's goals and desired outcomes for the planning process. The planner can begin to answer the questions of *why, what, when,* and *for whom.*

- For each of the core content planning areas—cash flow management, income taxes, risk management (e.g., life, health, disability, long-term care, property and liability), investments, education or other special needs planning, retirement planning, and estate planning, the planner can begin to answer *why, what, when, where, how,* and *how much* based on the following results:

  - Quantitative data analyses built on mutually agreed-upon core content and personal assumptions conducted independently and systematically for each of the core content planning areas;

  - Qualitative and household needs assessment to identify potential individual, lifestyle, life event, or other factors that might affect the client in any of the core content planning areas;

  - The planner's knowledge and professional insights regarding any factors that might impact the client in any of the core content areas, including issues, problems, or concerns beyond the client's awareness;

  - The planner's and/or client's scan of the legislative, tax, political, and economic environmental factors both now and pending that might affect the implementation of the plan, either immediately or in the future; and

  - The planner's consultation or collaboration with other professionals.

Review Prospective Planning Strategies

Once the analysis of the situation is complete, the advisor should have a clear understanding of the issues to be addressed and thus should be ready to proceed to the next substep, Review Prospective Planning Strategies. This substep of the analysis of a client's situation focuses on identifying possible strategies or available alternatives to meet the client's needs and goals. With the results of the quantitative and qualitative analysis complete, the planner can begin to fully answer the strategy, recommendation, and implementation questions of *why, what, when, where, how much, how,* and *by whom.*

Strategies reflect an advisor's technical competence, or the universe of possible solutions that might be applicable to a client's situation. Simply put, strategies are the "Rolodex" of answers that a planner must identify and then apply to a client's situation (or at least eliminate as an option) until the process yields a limited number of viable alternatives for each core content planning area considered. Strategies can be categorized as product or procedural. A **product strategy** reflects the use of a specific type of product or product feature to meet a planning goal or need.

A summary of some of the most widely used financial planning products and select product features matched to each of the core content planning areas is provided in Appendix 7B. For example, a § 1035 exchange is shown as a service used by financial planners to implement a tax-free annuity, endowment, life insurance, or qualified long-term care contact exchange. In Appendix 7B, a § 1035 exchange is shown to be useful in five core financial planning content areas: (1) tax planning; (2) risk management planning; (3) investment planning; (4) retirement planning; and (5) estate planning. Note that the specific relationships among the products, services, and core content areas are somewhat fluid—meaning that although a relationship may be indicated in the table, the actual role of a product or feature could be different for each client.

A **procedural strategy** emphasizes a process, service, or type of ownership rather than a specific product. Select examples of procedural strategies are shown in Table 7.1 and are grouped not by individual core content planning areas, but under three broader categories of planning for client earnings (i.e., cash management and income taxes), planning for risk protection, and planning for growth and distribution of assets (i.e., education, retirement, and estate). Notice that procedural strategies may be applicable across several core content planning areas, as was true with the products.

This almost uncountable combination of products and procedural strategies intensifies the complexity of planning across all of the core content planning areas. This complexity forces the profession to demand competence of individuals and firms; some firms achieve this by means of ensembles of specialized professionals or through referrals to construct a team matched to a client's needs. This complexity is also the reason for lifelong learning and continuing education requirements.

Examples of product and procedural strategies matched to each of the core content planning areas are shown in Table 7.2. Note that the product strategies focus on a financial product or type of tax-advantaged account (e.g., § 529 plan or IRA), and the procedural strategies focus on a feature, action, or assumption that affects the planning process. All of these product and procedural strategy tables are intended to serve as a summary—not as a comprehensive list—to help students or novice planners develop their Rolodex of strategies.

Table 7.1 Select Examples of Procedural Strategies

Procedural Strategies to Plan for Client Earnings

- "Substitute" the cash value of a life insurance policy as a supplement to cash reserves in an emergency fund.
- Pay off unsecured debt with assets earning a lower after-tax rate of return.
- Maximize long-term capital gains by holding assets for more than one year.
- Donate appreciated assets to charity.
- Compare taxable and tax-free interest on a taxable equivalent-yield basis.

Procedural Strategies to Plan for Client Risk Protection

- When adding property and casualty coverage, be sure to consider increasing deductibles to lower the premium.
- When comparison shopping for life insurance, ask about the break points or bands because increasing the coverage could actually reduce the premium.
- Use COBRA to bridge employment termination or continue group health coverage for dependents.
- Bundle homeowners and personal auto policies to reduce annual premiums.
- When risks are high, include a disability waiver in insurance policies so premium payments will continue.

Procedural Strategies to Plan for the Growth and Distribution of Assets

- Change assumptions to better meet the funding goal for education (i.e., level of support, risk/return, college inflation rate) or retirement (i.e., income replacement ratio, risk/return, life expectancy), but recognize the disadvantages and costs, personal and financial, associated with these changes.
- Allocate additional resources to the goal (i.e., education or retirement).
- Understand Social Security eligibility rules to optimize benefits.
- Consider an IRA conversion.
- Make complete and appropriate use of property transfer law by using beneficiary designations.

Table 7.2 Select Examples of Corresponding Product and Procedural Strategies

Financial Planning Core Content Area	Sample Product Strategy	Sample Procedural Strategy
Financial situation	Assuming the client is not subject to the alternative minimum tax (AMT), use a home equity loan to pay off high-interest debt or to finance a needed purchase, such as a new auto.	In consultation with the client, identify expenses that could be reduced or eliminated to free up cash flow for meeting other recommendations, which are mutually agreed to be more important.
Income tax planning	Purchase tax-managed mutual funds to reduce capital gain and dividend income.	Reduce tax liability by holding the accounts for more than one year to qualify for long-term capital gains rather than pay the higher short-term capital gains rates.
Life insurance planning	Choose a declining-term policy to meet decreasing needs as children mature.	If estate taxation is not at issue, make some life insurance benefits payable to the estate to ensure liquidity.
Health insurance planning	Choose a high-deductible health plan (HDHP) and fund a health savings account (HSA).	If a member of the household is self-employed, consider having that person purchase and pay for a policy to utilize self-employment deductibility of 50% of premiums.
Disability insurance planning	If cost difference is not great, purchase individual disability policy to avoid income tax on any policy benefits.	Match a short-term disability benefit period with a long-term disability elimination period to ensure no gap in benefits.
Long-term care (LTC) insurance planning	Purchase a joint LTC policy that utilizes a shared pool of benefits.	Consider an adaptable policy, or policies, that provide coverage for the continuum of care from home to an assisted living facility and progresses, if necessary, to a skilled nursing facility.
Property & liability insurance planning	Purchase a personal auto policy (PAP) with minimum split-limit coverage of 100/300/100.	Separate children's potential liability claims from parents' assets by having the children purchase their own auto policy.
Investment & asset management planning	Purchase ETFs or mutual funds, based on the advantages and disadvantages relative to the individual client, to diversify the portfolio.	Increase portfolio rates of return by reallocating the portfolio more aggressively and then following a periodic schedule of rebalancing to maintain the allocation.
Education planning	Fund a § 529 plan.	Title education assets in parents' name to increase the flexibility of distribution and use of assets.
Retirement planning	Balance funding of tax-deferred and IRA accounts (as available) to maximize employer matching funds while planning for future projected tax implications.	Plan to work part-time in the active post-retirement years to supplement income.
Estate planning	For a high-net-worth household, establish an A/B, or marital bypass, trust to provide for the spouse and beneficiaries and reduce estate taxes for the second to die.	Start or increase annual gifting and charitable giving to reduce the gross estate, thereby avoiding or reducing estate taxes and/or probate fees.

Initially, the ability to identify multiple strategies in response to identified planning needs appears to be highly correlated with a planner's experience and expertise. Recall that professional judgment, as well as professional ethical conduct expectations, such as those established by the CFP Board discussed later in this chapter constrain a planner to offer services within the purview of acknowledged expertise, to seek the collaboration of other professionals, or to refer the client to other professionals when the client's issues surpass the advisor's expertise. Like everyone else, financial planners become accustomed to using certain strategies or products or focusing on particular patterns of information.

The development of two to four alternative recommendations is becoming common practice; equally common is the practice of planners falling back on using the same old strategies they have used for years. A planner may turn to such heuristics, or favored solutions, when working with a client. The biggest problem with this approach is that the financial planning industry (and, more specifically, the products and regulations) are almost constantly changing. These changes create additional opportunities for both planner and client, but they also create confusion.

While commonly used strategies or products can increase a planner's efficiency and promote depth of knowledge in a diverse universe of products, they may or may not yield the best outcome for a client. Professional judgment and ethical practice standards, for example from the CFP Board, suggest that advisors acknowledge any limitations, prejudices, or other relationships that could adversely affect or bias the planner-client relationship. Furthermore, advisors are encouraged to continually apply some professional skepticism to compensate for, or override, such issues.

A primary source of confusion for planners today is that they have so many—almost too many—sources of information to consider. As Figure 7.2 suggests, there could be as many as eight factors, with multiple data points, that influence the generation of client-specific strategies. The five factors on or above the horizontal axis characterize the planner and client and, for the most part, represent a planner's inferences, gleaned from available data and interactions with the client. Note that assumptions appear directly across from planning goals and objectives to represent the significance of this relationship.

Of the three factors below the horizontal axis, all represent factual information that can also serve as the basis of assumptions (e.g., a client's projected life span or tax bracket in retirement). In sum, the integration of the facts, inferences, and assumptions adds to the complexity of identifying client-specific strategies. Some financial planning firms control the types of strategies, products, and recommendations that can be used. For example, it is not uncommon for planning firms to restrict the number and types of securities that may be used (known as an "approved investment list" or a broker-dealer's authorized products), or the type of insurance products that may be offered to a client. These limitations, based on established criteria to screen for performance or due diligence, can make the identification of strategies less complicated, but they can also limit a planner's creativity in designing unique strategies to meet a client's needs. These issues, as well as other regulatory or compliance issues, make a planner's business model a significant consideration in identifying and evaluating strategies.

Figure 7.2 Factors Affecting a Planner's Strategy and Recommendation Development

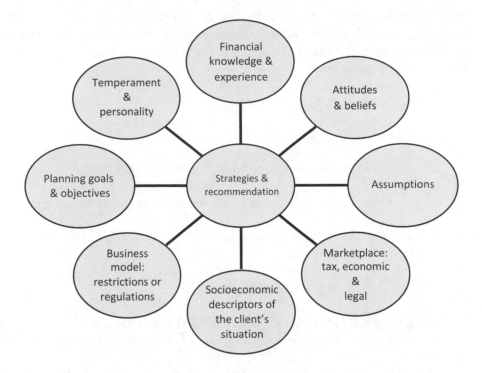

Develop Client-based Recommendations

With strategies identified, a planner can begin to formulate recommendations. Strategies may need to be altered or combined as the planner deliberates the advantages and disadvantages of each potential recommendation and considers the probable outcomes and effects on the client's situation. As the planner attempts to align the recommendations with a client's goal(s), the total cost of the recommendations must be compared to the available cash flow or other available assets for funding recommendations. Consider the example of an investment recommendation to fund a future goal (e.g., retirement, education, a vacation home) based on a product strategy of an actively managed mutual fund. Facts and assumptions are at issue as the advisor considers increasing the anticipated rate of return (an assumption) in an attempt to limit or reduce the present value cost (a fact). Another relevant assumption, the client's risk tolerance for the goal, must be incorporated. This assumption influences portfolio allocation and projected returns as well as the client's potential comfort with, and commitment to, the recommendation if risk tolerance is exceeded.

The process of separating, distilling, and integrating client situational factors, planner factors, and strategies results in the development of one or more client-based actionable recommendations representing the scope of the planning engagement (i.e., the responsibilities of all parties as established in the engagement agreement). An **actionable recommendation** answers the seven fundamental questions of who, what, when, where, why, how, and how much that are the consistent focus of the systematic financial planning process. Furthermore, an actionable recommendation is one that a client can afford to implement. This is true whether the advisor is developing a comprehensive plan or a modular plan targeted to either a single issue or the entire core financial planning content area. Recommendations should offer clients cost-effective, adaptable alternatives. Contingent on the scope of the engagement and the degree of specificity implied by that arrangement, recommendations should address the seven key questions:

1. *Who* should implement the recommendation?

2. *What* should be done?

3. *When* should the recommendation be implemented?

4. *Where* should the client, or other party, implement the recommendation?

5. *Why* should the recommendation be implemented? Why is it important to the client's financial future?

6. *How* should implementation take place?

7. *How much* should be purchased, saved, or invested to implement the recommendation? Specifically, what is the cost of the recommendation?

The significance of considering each of these questions in the development of the recommendations should not be overlooked. These questions may seem too simplistic to be meaningful, or answering all seven may seem unnecessary. But routine use of this simple rubric for framing recommendations can be a powerful tool for two reasons. First, careful consideration of the questions helps advisors reconsider the logic of each recommendation and the consistency with a client's goals and situation. Second, the rubric helps advisors meticulously consider and articulate the funding and other implementation issues critical to sound plan development and motivated client action.

Financial planners ought to provide reasonable and actionable answers to these seven questions for each recommendation. However, the importance of working with a client to arrive at mutually agreeable, realistic recommendations that comprise the final plan must be considered. Care should be taken that the sheer amount of money or time required to implement recommendations does not overwhelm the client. Although lifestyle changes may be necessary to fund a plan, the advisor must work with the client to identify recommendations that will motivate the client to take action because of the pride or personal satisfaction that result. As for the components of the comprehensive plan, it is essential that the recommendations generated in Step 3 from the analysis of the client situation be thoroughly grounded in the client's goals and values, discovered in Step 2.

Step 3 and the CFP Board Standards of Ethical Conduct

Step 3: Analyze and Evaluate the Client's Financial Status, as presented in the systematic financial planning process shown in Figure 7.1, includes both the CFP Board Practice Standards 300 Series: Analyzing and Evaluating the Client's Information and two of the three Practice Standards from the 400 Series. Similar to the first substep in Step 3, Analyze the Current Situation, Practice Standard 300-1 asserts that a practitioner must analyze the data to understand the client situation and ascertain whether "the client's goals, needs and priorities can be met by the client's resources and current course of action."[2] The second substep of Step 3, defined as Review Prospective Planning Strategies, aligns with Practice Standard 400-1: Identifying and Evaluating Financial Planning Alternative(s). Similarly, the third substep, Develop Client-based Recommendations, parallels Practice Standard 400-2: Developing the Financial Planning Recommendations. The Board summarizes the latter two standards with the questions, "What is possible?" and "What is recommended?" respectively, for Practice Standards 400-1 and 400-2.

As shown in Table 7.3, the ethical principles of Objectivity, Competence, and Diligence are identified as particularly relevant to all three of these practice standards, whereas the Principle of Professionalism is cited with both of the 400-Series practice standards. The Principle of Objectivity focuses on honesty and impartiality; the Board cautions certificants not to compromise their professional or ethical judgment but to maintain the integrity and objectivity of their work. Competence demands the commitment to maintain and update professional knowledge and skills, as well as the wisdom to collaborate with other professionals and to refer clients to other professionals when clients' needs are not well matched to the certificant's competence. Certainly these are important traits when analyzing a client's needs as well as when identifying potential strategies to form recommendations.

To provide services diligently, certificants are required to act in a "reasonably prompt and thorough manner, including the proper planning for, and supervision of, the rendering of professional services."[3] The Principle of Professionalism extends beyond the ethical responsibilities of treating the client with dignity and courtesy, to applying the same standards to relationships with other professionals and others involved in business-related activities. Certificants are encouraged to work with other certificants to promote the public image of the financial planning profession and to advance the quality of services—perhaps a warning not to criticize the services of the client's other advisors.

Table 7.3 Step 3: Analyze and Evaluate the Client's Financial Status

Step 3—Analyze and Evaluate the Client's Financial Situation	
CFP Board Practice Standards 300 Series: Analyzing and Evaluating the Client's Financial Status **300-1: Analyzing and Evaluating the Client's Information** A financial planning practitioner shall analyze the information to gain an understanding of the client's financial situation and then evaluate to what extent the client's goals, needs and priorities can be met by the client's resources and current course of action. Gathering Client Data	
CFP Board Code of Ethics	**CFP Board Rules of Conduct**
Principle 2 – Objectivity Principle 3 – Competence Principle 7 – Diligence	**1. Defining the Relationship with the Prospective Client or Client** **1.4** A certificant shall at all times place the interest of the client ahead of his or her own. When the certificant provides financial planning or material elements of financial planning, the certificant owes to the client the duty of care of a fiduciary as defined by CFP Board. **4. Obligations to Prospective Clients and Clients** **4.1** A certificant shall treat prospective clients and clients fairly and provide professional services with integrity and objectivity. **4.4** A certificant shall exercise reasonable and prudent professional judgment in providing professional services to clients. **4.5** In addition to the requirements of Rule 1.4, a certificant shall make and/or implement only recommendations that are suitable for the client.
CFP Board Practice Standards 400 Series: Developing and Presenting the Financial Planning Recommendation(s) **400-1: Identifying and Evaluating Financial Planning Alternative(s)** The financial planning practitioner shall consider sufficient and relevant alternatives to the client's current course of action in an effort to reasonably meet the client's goals, needs and priorities.	
Principle 2 – Objectivity Principle 3 – Competence Principle 6 – Professionalism Principle 7 – Diligence	**1. Defining the Relationship with the Prospective Client or Client** **1.4** A certificant shall at all times place the interest of the client ahead of his or her own. When the certificant provides financial planning or material elements of financial planning, the certificant owes to the client the duty of care of a fiduciary as defined by CFP Board. **4. Obligations to Prospective Clients and Clients** **4.1** A certificant shall treat prospective clients and clients fairly and provide professional services with integrity and objectivity. **4.5** In addition to the requirements of Rule 1.4, a certificant shall make and/or implement only recommendations that are suitable for the client.

CFP Board Practice Standards 400 Series: Developing and Presenting the Financial Planning Recommendation(s)

400-2: Developing the Financial Planning Recommendation(s)

The financial planning practitioner shall develop the recommendation(s) based on the selected alternative(s) and the current course of action in an effort to reasonably meet the client's goals, needs and priorities.

Principle 2 – Objectivity Principle 3 – Competence Principle 6 – Professionalism Principle 7 – Diligence	**2. Information Disclosed To Prospective Clients and Clients** **2.1** A certificant shall not communicate, directly or indirectly, to clients or prospective clients any false or misleading information directly or indirectly related to the certificant's professional qualifications or services. A certificant shall not mislead any parties about the potential benefits of the certificant's service. A certificant shall not fail to disclose or otherwise omit facts where that disclosure is necessary to avoid misleading clients. **4. Obligations to Prospective Clients and Clients** **4.1** A certificant shall treat prospective clients and clients fairly and provide professional services with integrity and objectivity. **4.4** A certificant shall exercise reasonable and prudent professional judgment in providing professional services to clients. **4.5** In addition to the requirements of Rule 1.4, a certificant shall make and/or implement only recommendations that are suitable for the client.

Source: Certified Financial Planner Board of Standards, Inc., *CFP Board's Standards of Professional Conduct*. Available at http://www.cfp.net/Downloads/2010Standards.pdf, pp. 6, 7, 9, 11, and 21–23; or at http://www.cfp.net/learn/ethics. asp#intro. Reprinted with permission.

Aside from *Rule of Conduct 2.1*, which the Board matches only to Practice Standard 400-2: Developing the Financial Planning Recommendations, Step 3 in the financial planning process and the corresponding three practice standards share four other rules of conduct. *Rule of Conduct 2.1* prohibits communicating any false or misleading information about professional qualifications or services to a client or prospective client either directly or by failure to disclose. When applied to client recommendations, the admonition not to mislead clients about the potential benefits of the services is very important and applies both to the commission of providing false or misleading information as well as the omission of information that would more clearly and fairly inform the client about the financial professional and the services offered.

Rule 1.4 asserts that the interests of the client must be placed before the interests of the certificant, and if financial planning or material elements of financial planning are provided by the certificant, a fiduciary duty of care is required. Subsequently, *Rule 4.5*, which is cited relative to all three standards of practice—analyzing the client's information, identifying financial planning alternatives, and developing the recommendations—establishes that "in addition to the requirements of *Rule 1.4*, a certificant shall make and/or implement only recommendations that are suitable for the client."[4]

As a corollary of the ethical principles of Objectivity, Competence, Diligence, and Professionalism, *Rule of Conduct 4.1* requires certificants to exercise fairness with both prospective and current clients, and to exhibit integrity and objectivity in the delivery of professional services. This rule applies when analyzing and evaluating a client's information (300-1), when identifying and evaluating alternatives (400-1), and when developing recommendations (400-2). Finally, *Rule of Conduct 4.4* calls for reasonable and prudent professional judgment, especially as applied to the analysis and evaluation of client information and the development of planning recommendations.

STEP 4: DEVELOP THE COMPREHENSIVE PLAN AND PRESENT THE RECOMMENDATIONS

Well-designed financial plans are characterized by thoughtful analyses, logical consistency, thoroughness, clarity of purpose, and feasible, client-centered recommendations. This is true regardless of the style, format, scope, or length of the documents (i.e., comprehensive or modular) provided to the client. For example, each recommendation should be clearly supported by the analysis of the situation and the criteria used to prioritize alternative strategies. The analysis should consider multiple aspects of the client situation and be based on reasonable assumptions acceptable to both planner and client. This is equally true for recommendations that support product sales. If the rationale for the recommendation is not clearly supported, the logical inconsistency will be apparent. This will confuse the client and may call into question the viability of the entire plan.

Thoroughness is represented by the comprehensiveness of the analysis, the number of alternatives considered, and the recommendations identified. Caution is warranted, however, in the way alternative recommendations are presented to clients. Client involvement in decision making is important, but care must be taken to tailor the presentation of alternatives so that it does not overwhelm the client or suggest bias on the part of the planner. (A biased presentation could leave the client feeling manipulated and inadequately informed.) A clear focus on the best interest of the client and a thorough understanding of what is important to the client, coupled with the integration of the recommendations into a goal-based workable plan, strongly support clarity of purpose. Furthermore, clarity of purpose in reflecting the client's situation is important in the design and feasibility of the implementation steps. For example, if simplicity of implementation is an issue, this factor should be a primary consideration in the choice of recommendations. If the client has a tendency to procrastinate, the implementation plan must compensate for this trait and incorporate strategies to avert potential oversights. If the client wishes to delegate most, if not all, responsibilities to the planner, then other issues such as cost-effective and efficient delivery of services must be considered. Finally, the plan should project—but not promise—the potential outcomes and consequences of each recommendation.

In summary, both the plan and its presentation to the client must be logically consistent throughout. A well-designed plan is the foundation of an effective presentation to the client. Such plans and presentations are easier for clients to understand and are more likely to motivate client action. But how are well-designed plans developed? What happens in the black box when developing a financial plan?

Developing the Financial Plan

The foundation for plan development is the constantly evolving and developing relationship between planner and client. This interaction results in the identification of client values, attitudes, and goals that ground the financial planning process. Such mutually agreed-upon goals, in conjunction with information about a client's situation, serve as the foundation for the analysis of each core content area and the identification of potential strategies. The integration of applicable strategies, available resources (discretionary cash flow, short-term or liquid savings, and other assets), and knowledge of the client situation results in client-based, actionable recommendations that are the output of Step 3 and building blocks of the integrated plan. The more closely the plan is matched to the client's needs and priorities, the greater the likelihood that the client will take action and continue the engagement with the planner.

Recall from Chapter 5 that there are two recognized standards of practice that ground the financial planning process: **cash flow orientation** and **goal orientation**. Both are hallmarks of a successful plan and, ideally, are integrated into the plan, but for some planner-client engagements one approach might take priority over the other without disadvantaging the client. In fact, it may be the client's preference.

Attention to cash flow ensures that the pursuit of any one goal does not expose a client to unwarranted risk or leave the client completely unprepared to withstand unexpected negative financial consequences. For many clients, cash flow must dominate the planning process, with attention focused primarily on the affordability of the plan and the prioritization of recommendations most critical to meeting the client's planning needs—both now and in the future. In fact, it can be argued that the primary purpose of financial planning is to maximize and stabilize cash flow across the client's planning period. But there is an equally valid argument that the goal orientation of financial planning provides a framework and motivation for sustained client commitment.

A goal orientation to planning ensures that a plan is consistent with the client's values, desires, and planning needs—both now and in the future—because as one goal is accomplished, a new goal can be identified and new recommendations initiated. This approach is broadly applicable as a planning tenet. But for some clients with sufficient cash flow, attention may rest primarily on accomplishing specific goals, because within reason, cash flow to meet living expenses or fund any other recommendations is not an issue. Thus, planning efforts are focused on accomplishing only select goals, with little attention directed to other core content planning issues—except to ensure that the client's current efforts are sufficient to avert problems. This type of goal-based planning might be more closely associated with wealth management services, where the primary focus is on wealth accumulation and distribution rather than cash flow maximization.

Although it may be easy to assume that only wealthy clients have the luxury to choose a goal-based planning approach, the choice is not based solely on income or net worth. Both planners and clients prefer the goal-based approach, either as the result of attitude, temperament, or personality, or because they reason that such detailed cash flow-based planning, particularly over a number of years, is built on so many assumptions that without constant updates the plan is of limited value. From the goal-based planning perspective, one is motivated by achieving particular goals and the focus is on the end result; everything else—and the associated expense—is simply constrained by the resources remaining. Simply put, these clients live on what is left over after the primary goal has been funded and accounted for in the plan.

For other advisors and clients, cash flow-based planning, despite the range of assumptions, is indisputably the only way to plan. They prefer a comprehensive approach, with periodic reviews and updates. Although cash flow may be sufficient, these clients are more comfortable with a comprehensive approach and annual tracking system that establish spending and saving guidelines. Many clients assert that this method gives them the freedom to spend however they want within the plan. Simply put, these clients live in concert with their spending and saving/investing needs.

In Step 4, the development of the plan, the fundamental philosophy of goal-based or cash flow-based planning intersects with three critical issues that guide the development of a comprehensive plan:

1. Given the client's planning needs or goals, have all recommendations been identified and a preliminary priority assigned?

2. Given the client's planning needs or goals, what are the effects or consequences, potentially beneficial or detrimental, that could result from implementing or failing to implement the proposed recommendations?

3. Given the client's planning needs, are all proposed recommendations affordable from available discretionary cash flow, short-term or liquid savings, or other assets?

Answering these questions with confidence is a complex and intellectually challenging exercise that truly represents the professional judgment—of both *financial planning* and the *client*—gained from study and experience. And, at some level, all three questions must be answered to ensure that the resulting plan is both appropriate for a client's goals and feasible given the resources available and risks faced. But the fundamental philosophy or approach of the plan is also established at this step of the financial planning process. The first two questions are central to the goal-based orientation to planning, whereas the third question is central to cash flow-based planning.

Whereas students and novice planners may be proficient at calculating the amount needed to fund retirement and the periodic savings needed—a commonly cited objective of goal-based planning—it may be more challenging to project other results that must be considered for different strategies. For example, funding an employer-sponsored plan such as a 401(k) may yield a match and reduce annual income taxes. Conversely, funding a Roth IRA offers no free money or reduction in income taxes, but it could provide a wider range of less expensive investment vehicles. Both have the potential to increase net worth. As this example illustrates, recommendations are not made in a vacuum, nor do the actions projected from implementing recommendations occur independently. Implementing one recommendation tends to have a ripple effect throughout a client's financial plan, as illustrated in Table 7.4.

Table 7.4 Typical Recommendations with Multiple Effects on a Client's Financial Situation

Recommendation	Potential Result
Refinance mortgage (results will vary depending on whether closing costs are/are not included or if cash is/is not taken)	1. Changes cash flow 2. Changes net worth[a] 3. Changes tax liability
Restructure debt	1. Changes cash flow 2. Changes net worth 3. Changes tax liability
Change federal tax withholding	1. Changes cash flow
Change state tax withholding	1. Changes cash flow
Reallocate nonqualified portfolio assets	1. Changes cash flow (only if earnings are not reinvested) 2. Changes net worth[b] 3. Changes tax liability
Liquidate nonqualified portfolio assets	1. Changes cash flow (only if earnings are not reinvested) 2. Possibly changes net worth, depending on how the assets are used [b] 3. Changes tax liability
Increase retirement savings	1. Changes cash flow 2. Changes net worth 3. Changes tax liability 4. Changes estate tax situation
Purchase additional life insurance	1. Changes cash flow 2. Possibly changes net worth, depending on type of insurance 3. Changes estate tax situation
Retitle assets	1. Changes cash flow 2. Changes net worth 3. Changes tax liability 4. Changes estate tax situation
Begin gift strategies	1. Changes cash flow 2. Changes net worth 3. Changes tax liability 4. Changes estate tax situation

[a] Assuming closing costs are paid from assets rather than current income
[b] Transaction costs or sales charges may apply

Because of this, it is important for planners to incorporate an **impact analysis** as part of the planning process. Although integration across core financial planning content areas is beyond the scope of engagement of an advisor focused on single-issue analysis, the importance of impact analysis should not be overlooked. Projecting the integration of all recommendations via impact analysis gives the advisor a much richer perspective on the logic and assumptions upon which a plan is based. It also helps confirm that a client has enough discretionary cash flow and assets to fully fund, and continue funding, all recommendations. In other words, impact analysis can be an important consideration in responding to the three preceding questions.

A Comprehensive Planning Checklist and an Impact Analysis Form, part of the systematic financial planning methodology, are presented later in this chapter. These forms can help the student or novice planner fully integrate the recommendations of a plan and identify any issues that might have been overlooked.

In summary, the development of a comprehensive plan, ideally, is the culmination and integration of both the cash flow and goal orientation to planning. Although comprehensive plans are more complex, the synthesis of goals and funding strategies applies to both comprehensive and targeted (or modular) plans. The same is true of analysis in support of product sales, because a client must be convinced that a product fulfills a recognized need or goal *and* is worthy of funding. Despite the fact that goal-based planning places much less emphasis on comprehensive planning for cash flows and limits cash flow planning to specific goal projections, it is nonetheless essential that planners fully understand the significance of cash flow planning and its many implications in the development of a feasible, client-focused plan.

Affordability—The Heart of Cash Flow-based Planning

Discretionary cash flow (DCF) is the income that remains at the end of the planning period (e.g., an average month or a year) after all expenses have been met. Critical to this definition is the definition of *expenses*. Some planners and clients define expenses as those minimally required or necessary to support a chosen standard of living. However, clients may choose to define expenses more broadly and could, in fact, be spending excess funds over which they have discretion. In that case, the client could either choose not to spend or could reasonably reduce spending in lieu of other goals.

In reality, the determination of DCF can vary with a client's income, values, and lifestyle, but initially it represents the periodic cash flow available to a planner for funding goals (e.g., retirement) or purchasing products (e.g., insurance). If projected funding from DCF or other client assets (i.e., savings, investments) is insufficient, both planner and client may face an "either/or" situation. Then the planner, on the basis of knowledge of the client situation or working directly with the client, must conduct a cost-benefit analysis to determine the best use of available funds relative to the "ideal" recommendations proposed. Although creative options may be available, generally planners and clients are limited to considering one or more of the options illustrated in Figure 7.3.

Figure 7.3 Options for Funding Recommendations

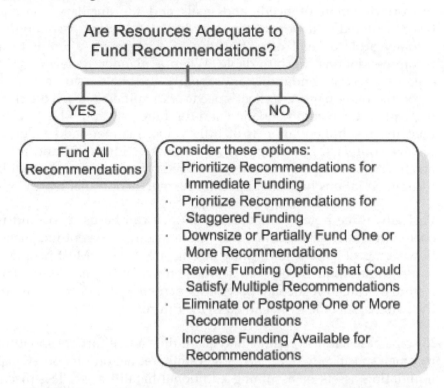

- Fully fund the most important recommendation in support of the goal determined by planner and client, then prioritize the other recommendations and corresponding goals or planning needs and apply the remaining funds.

- Agree to fund all recommendations, but stagger implementation over a reasonable period of time that does not adversely affect the client's financial situation. This approach assumes that other assets will become available to facilitate future funding—as the result of an inflow of income, assets, or the completion of funding a goal—thus freeing money to be redirected to another goal(s).

- Reconsider the recommendations and "downsize," or reduce, one or more of the suggested funding alternatives so that all recommendations receive some funding.

- Review mutually exclusive recommendations that could be integrated and achieved through another multipurpose planning product or procedure (e.g., a Roth IRA or life insurance).

- Prioritize recommendations and goals, fund those that are most important, and eliminate or postpone others.

- Increase discretionary cash flow or available funding for all or some of the recommendations by reducing spending (e.g., for goods, services, or interest on debt) or by earning more (e.g., by increasing personal income, liquidating assets, or reallocating other assets for higher earnings).

Notice that funding alternatives align with plan development questions regarding the prioritization of needs and goals and the ancillary consequences that must be considered. However, the last bullet, although seemingly straightforward, actually adds a level of complexity to a planner's attempt to ascertain whether recommendations are affordable. When a planner reviews various strategies and organizes recommendations, affordability must be considered. No matter how well a recommendation meets a client's needs or identified goals, if the client cannot afford to implement the recommendation and fund lifestyle and other saving/investing goals, then the recommendation is of little value. Planners add value by helping clients resolve conflicts between goals, which may be idealized, and the needs that signify an affordable alternative. Cash flow-based planning grounds itself in the tenet that all recommendations have an impact on current income, net worth, or both.

Basically, three potential sources of money can be used to fund recommendations: current income, past income, and future income. Current income is self-explanatory; however, past income and future income are less so. Most people know past income as *assets* and future income as *liabilities*. From a purely economic standpoint, assets are a store of value for income previously earned and invested; liabilities are a claim on the value of income to be earned in the future.

In some cases, much planner and client time and effort are spent maximizing current income, specifically DCF, by suggesting reductions in other expenses. However, liquidating assets or assuming additional liabilities is a less-discussed approach to maximizing available income in the present period. One potential reason for this is that reductions in periodic expenses yield a *recurring* source of funding, whereas liquidating an asset or assuming a new liability yields only a *one-time increase* in available funds. For example, reducing a client's discretionary spending on holiday gifts or travel may yield an annual increase of $5,000 in funds available for other goals, but redeeming a $5,000 certificate of deposit can be done only once.

As another example, if a planner is making a recommendation that a client increase a monthly credit card payment to pay off a debt more quickly, it is most likely to be adopted successfully if planner and client can identify and reduce an annually occurring expense to offset the increased payment. But if the planner is recommending that the client completely pay off the credit card balance, it might be better to (1) find an asset that could be liquidated or (2) assume a new liability that offers a lower interest rate or potential tax advantages. Therefore, once a planner has identified all potential funding sources, it is the planner and client's responsibility to mutually agree on the alternative that best matches the frequency of the funding need and offers more positive than negative consequences across all core content areas.

As previously mentioned, every recommendation affects discretionary income, net worth, or both. Generally speaking, nine potential financial impacts are associated with implementing a recommendation.

1. Reducing discretionary income to fund current expenses has no impact on net worth. Example: purchasing a term life insurance policy.

2. Reducing discretionary income to repay liabilities decreases liabilities and therefore increases net worth. Example: increasing the monthly payment on a home mortgage.

3. Reducing discretionary income to purchase assets increases assets and net worth. Example: increasing contribution to an employer-sponsored retirement plan.

4. Liquidating assets to fund current expenses decreases assets and therefore decreases net worth. Example: selling a mutual fund to pay federal income taxes.

5. Assuming new liabilities to fund current expenses increases liabilities and therefore decreases net worth. Example: purchasing groceries or other basic necessities with a credit card instead of managing spending to pay for current expenses from current income.

6. Liquidating assets to repay liabilities decreases both assets and liabilities and therefore has no impact on net worth. Example: redeeming a CD to repay a credit card balance.

7. Assuming new liabilities to purchase new assets increases both assets and liabilities and therefore has no immediate impact on net worth. Example: purchasing a car with an auto loan.

8. Reallocating assets has no impact on net worth but has a potential impact on cash flow as a result of changes in periodic distributions or tax liabilities. Example: selling a mutual fund in a nonqualified account to fund a Roth IRA.

9. Restructuring (or consolidating) liabilities has no impact on net worth but has a potential impact on cash flow as the result of changes in monthly payment, interest expense, or tax liabilities. Example: securing a home equity line of credit to repay an auto loan or credit card.

Each of these implementation actions and their effect on cash flow and net worth are shown in Table 7.5. These are generally expected trends because there can be no guarantee that an asset will always appreciate, thereby increasing net worth, or depreciate, although many do. All associated purchase, sales, or carrying (interest) costs and any capital gains or loss taxes are ignored in these general trend statements.

Table 7.5 Summary of the Cash Flow or Net Worth Impact of Implementing Recommendations

Possible Financial Impact of Actions to Implement a Recommendation	Impact on Cash Flow	Impact on Net Worth
Reduces discretionary income to fund current expenses	↓	None
Reduces discretionary income to repay liabilities	↓	↑
Reduces discretionary income to purchase assets	↓	↑
Liquidates assets to fund current expenses	↑	↓
Assumes new liabilities to fund current expenses	↑ (current) ↓ (future)	↓
Liquidates assets to repay liabilities	↑(future)	None
Assumes new liabilities to purchase new assets	↑ (current) ↓ (future)	None
Reallocates assets	↑ or ↓	None*
Restructures liabilities	↑ or ↓	None**

* Although this action would have no direct impact on net worth, there is the potential financial impact of fees associated with the sale/purchase of assets for the reallocation of assets. Generally, these costs are negligible but they should not be overlooked in the analysis of this option.

** Fees could be associated with establishing new accounts to restructure liabilities. Generally, these costs are negligible, but they should not be overlooked in the analysis of this option.

In summary, up to this point the planner has considered different options for funding recommendations, such as funding the most important recommendation, eliminating recommendations, or increasing the funding available. The planner has also considered the impact of different funding actions on net worth and DCF. From these two perspectives and knowledge of the client's personality, temperament, values, goals, and priorities, the planner develops a plan. The following example illustrates in greater detail the impact on cash flow and net worth that could occur as the result of some fairly typical recommendations.

As a part of the first meeting for their plan presentation, the financial planner surprised Elsa and Nils Henriksen with her evaluation of their situation and her recommendations. Although they knew they had been relying on their credit cards, and the balance had continued to creep up, recognizing that their annual spending was $2,100 more than their income was a shock. But the planner proposed three recommendations to maximize their DCF and optimize their credit usage in preparation for other recommendations, which were postponed.

First, the planner proposed that they refinance their home mortgage to take advantage of lower interest rates and consolidate their consumer debt. She explained that by consolidating their credit card balance in a new first mortgage they could eliminate $12,500 in credit card balances and their monthly credit card payments of $550.

Additionally, given the low mortgage rates, they would reduce their monthly mortgage payment from $979 for their current 30-year, 6.5% APR mortgage with an original balance of $155,000 to a new payment of $879 per month. The new 20-year, 5.00% APR mortgage would have a beginning balance of $133,284, requiring three more years of payments than the 17 years remaining on the old mortgage with a balance of $120,784. The planner also explained that, although the mortgage did not include any discount points, total fees associated with the loan would be about $2,600, and that Elsa and Nils should pay the closing costs out of their available savings.

The planner went on to explain that before she made this recommendation she had reviewed their previous income tax forms. She wanted to be sure that they would not be subject to the AMT because their new mortgage would include both acquisition debt and equity debt, when the latter was not used for home improvement. Furthermore, her analysis revealed that this approach yielded savings significant enough to justify rolling the credit card debt into the new mortgage.

Second, she suggested that Nils reduce the annual funding of his Roth IRA by $2,000 and increase his 401(k) plan contribution by $4,000 to maximize the 50% employer match. She explained that this would reduce their current annual income tax liability by about $500, assuming that they remained in the 25% marginal tax bracket, and that the employer match more than compensated for the increased tax liability because withdrawals from the 401(k) plan would be taxable, whereas withdrawals from the Roth would not. In their earlier meetings, the planner and the Henriksons had mutually agreed that they did not expect a higher marginal tax bracket in retirement because of significantly lower income.

Finally, the planner recommended that Elsa redeem a $10,380 CD, pay off the remaining $9,327 balance of her auto loan, and place the remainder in savings to offset closing costs. The planner reasoned that Elsa had sufficient emergency savings, had not identified a specific goal-based purpose for the CD money, and the CD did not offer any needed liquidity advantages. It was earning only $10 a month at a rate of 1.25% APR while Elsa's auto loan payment was $350 per month at a rate of 3.90% APR. From all perspectives, eliminating the debt and freeing up $350 each month for other financial needs made financial sense; Elsa agreed.

To summarize these recommendations, their planner developed a tracking form; an excerpt is shown in Exhibit 7.1 to help her confirm that sufficient cash flow, savings, and assets were available to implement the recommendations. The Available Cash Flow and Other Assets Tracker Form could also be easily modified during their meeting to demonstrate the different alternatives considered. Once finalized, the form can be used to document the information for the planning staff or to communicate the costs of individual recommendations—and the entire plan—to a client. Note that the Henriksons' Tracker Form begins with their original discretionary cash flow of negative $2,100 per year and their original net worth of $180,130.

Exhibit 7.1 Available Cash Flow and Other Assets Tracker Form

Annual Cash Flow and Other Assets Tracker

Recommendation	(Cost)/ Benefit	Frequency (single / annual)	Discretionary Cash Flow	Running Balances			
				Monetary Assets[a]	Other Assets[b]	Liabilities[c]	Net Worth
	Beginning Balances		($2,100)	$20,280	$321,500	$161,650	$180,130
Payment savings from mortgage refinance	$1,200	A	$1,200	$0	$0	$0	$0
			($900)	$20,280	$321,500	$161,650	$180,130
Pay mortgage closing costs	($2,600)	S	$0	($2,600)	$0	$0	($2,600)
			($900)	$17,680	$321,500	$161,650	$177,530
Take cash from home equity	$12,500	S	$0	$12,500	$0	$12,500	$0
			($900)	$30,180	$321,500	$174,150	$177,530
Pay off credit card debt	($12,500)	S	$0	($12,500)	$0	($12,500)	$0
			($900)	$17,680	$321,500	$161,650	$177,530
Payment savings from paying off credit cards	$6,600	A	$6,600	$0	$0	$0	$0
			$5,700	$17,680	$321,500	$161,650	$177,530
Change retirement contribution to 401(k)	($2,000)	A	($2,000)	$0	$2,000	$0	$2,000
			$3,700	$17,680	$323,500	$161,650	$179,530
Reduction in tax consequence	$500	A	$500	$0	$0	$0	$0
			$4,200	$17,680	$323,500	$161,650	$179,530
Redeem CD	$10,380	S	$0	($10,380)	$0	$0	($10,380)
			$4,200	$7,300	$323,500	$161,650	$169,150
Pay off auto loan with CD proceeds	($9,327)	S	$0	$1,053	$0	($9,327)	$10,380
			$4,200	$8,353	$323,500	$152,323	$179,530
Payment savings from paying off auto loan	$4,200	A	$4,200	$0	$0	$0	$0
			$8,400	$8,353	$323,500	$152,323	$179,530
	Aggregate Change		*$10,500*	*($11,927)*	*$2,000*	*($9,327)*	*($600)*
	Final Balances		*$8,400*	*$8,353*	*$323,500*	*$152,323*	*$179,530*

[a] Monetary assets include Elsa's CD ($10,380), their checking account ($5,700), and an emergency fund ($4,200).

[b] Other assets include their cars ($24,000 and $14,500), home ($210,000), and retirement funds ($73,000).

[c] Liabilities include their auto loans ($19,039 and $9,327), credit cards ($12,500) and home mortgage ($120,784).

When Nils and Elsa reviewed the Tracker Form, they were surprised that such seemingly simple recommendations had such a profound effect on their cash flow and a marginal effect on net worth. With only a couple of relatively modest steps, they were able to increase their annual discretionary cash flow by $10,500. This change turned a $2,100 shortfall into an $8,400 surplus, and all of this happened with only a $600 reduction in net worth. Although this all seemed very simple, they also reflected on a comment that their planner had made, that "no recommendation has only one consequence." In fact, the single decision to refinance their home seemed to have several effects. There were two changes in cash flow because of the payment they eliminated by paying off their credit card and the reduction in monthly mortgage payment from refinancing. There was also a reduction in their net worth due to paying the closing costs for the refinance from monetary assets.

Although this section of the plan and the planner's proposal seemed quite reasonable to Nils and Elsa, there was still work to be done. They needed the resolve to discontinue the spending patterns that had gotten them into $12,500 of credit card debt. With the planner's help, they had some insightful discussions during the discovery meetings, which led to other discussions during the plan presentation meeting regarding conflicting goals (some of which were perhaps a bit lavish) and what their income and investments could support. The planner had been instrumental in helping them recognize these issues, and in making suggestions about how Nils and Elsa could compromise on their plans for retirement. To the Henriksons' surprise, their planner had deftly managed their disagreements as well as the numbers reported on their Tracker Form.

The planner—in the roles of counselor, educator, advisor, and mediator—can offer explanations to assist clients like Nils and Elsa with the decisions necessary to adopt and implement a plan. Working with or on behalf of clients, planners must resolve the issue of competing recommendations in light of the same analysis that supported the development of the original recommendations (e.g., the multifaceted analysis of the client's current situation, the marketplace scan, and consultation with other professionals, if warranted). In exercising professional judgment, a planner must decide whether personal issues or modifications to client attitudes or behaviors can be addressed by the planner's skills and experience or whether referral to a money therapist or other professional is needed. Ultimately, this stage of the planning process should end with a realistic plan for achieving a client's financial and life goals, and lay the foundation for a potentially long-term planner-client relationship.

As noted earlier, a well-designed financial plan reflects thoughtful analysis, logical consistency, thoroughness, clarity of purpose, and feasible, client-centered recommendations. A feasible plan should also include annual fees or a retainer, if applicable, for plan development. As explained in Chapter 1, financial planners, depending on their business model, are paid for products, services, or advice delivered in different ways. But a final consideration in the development of the plan and its associated funding is the planner's payment—which should not be overlooked.

The Plan—Modular or Comprehensive

Chapter 9 thoroughly explores the components and stylistic elements of a financial plan as a deliverable product and the outcome of the financial planning process. However, in the context of considering how to integrate multiple recommendations into a plan, it is worthwhile to briefly consider how to convey this information to a client. One of the challenges facing planners who write comprehensive financial plans is how to account for the integrative nature of recommendations, implementation, and monitoring within the plan. Analysis, recommendations, and projected outcomes must be completely integrated into each individual section of the plan as well as across all core content planning areas. The following ideas might be helpful:

- Describe the current situation for each core content area as though no other recommendations have been made or implemented.

- Present all recommendations in a core content section (e.g., the retirement planning section) on the basis of the current situation analysis.

- Describe alternatives or various outcomes in client circumstances where a recommendation in one core content area is based on the implementation of a recommendation in a different core content area. For example, show alternative recommendations and alternative outcomes when education funding is done with or without gifting from the grandparents.

- Conclude the plan by illustrating a client's projected situation (i.e., income and expenses, net worth, and income tax projections) one or more years in the future, assuming that all recommendations have been implemented.

This last point requires certain client data to be reanalyzed and recalculated. Minimally, the following information should be recalculated to project the client's financial situation after one year (or some other time frame) that assumes the recommendations have been implemented:

- Available discretionary cash flow;

- Net worth balance;

- Income tax situation; and

- Estate tax situation (when applicable).

Recalculating these measures to reflect projected outcomes is another way to motivate clients. For instance, if a client can be shown that refinancing debt, reallocating portfolio assets, purchasing additional forms of insurance, and implementing other recommendations will result in positive outcomes, it is more likely that the client will take action. Revised cash flow, net worth, income tax, and estate tax projections can be included within a plan as a separate section or in an appendix, perhaps titled *Key Financial Measures in 200X*, to reflect the projected status one year hence. Some financial planners incorporate future projections (tabular or graphic) for each core content planning area in each section of the plan. Different time frames, coordinated to individual goals or planning needs, would be used to project the short-, intermediate-, or long-term impact on the client's future of a successfully implemented recommendation(s).

Both approaches help the client grasp how recommendations are integrated into a plan, and to grasp the potential impact of financial planning. However, it is extremely important that any projections be accompanied by appropriate disclaimers (e.g., "past performance is no guarantee of future returns," "all projections are based on historical data, which may not be reflected in future returns," or "projections are hypothetical") to avoid misleading the client or giving the impression of "promised" returns or outcomes. Professional disclaimers (e.g., "please consult your tax professional to confirm all projections" or "please consult your attorney for estate planning advice and document preparation") should also be included.

Presenting the Plan

If Starbucks thought that *connecting with the customers* was important enough to develop and deliver a board game to 8,000 managers for training its baristas, then consider the importance of a connection between financial advisors and clients when presenting a financial plan.[5] Much of the planner-client relationship discussed so far was forged through exploration of the client situation, which grounded the goals and informed the planning process. Regardless of the planner's business model, the presentation of the plan is an opportunity to "close the deal" with the client. Whether spoken or implied, the planner is *selling* something—from the obvious (e.g., a product or service) to something more subtle (e.g., client education or advice on a recommended change in a client's attitudes or behaviors). Good presentations are the outcome of training and experience, but a few simple reminders can help a student or novice planner present a plan clearly and consistently. For additional information on communication techniques, dealing with client emotions, and overcoming client resistance, review Chapter 3.

1. **Be genuinely warm, open, and welcoming**. Although planners and clients can sometimes develop personal friendships or interact socially, most advisors prefer to maintain an exclusively professional relationship with the client when dealing with financial planning issues. Nevertheless, the significance of the planner-client connection cannot be overstated. The topics addressed in the plan are of utmost importance to the client and can trigger a range of emotions (e.g., delight, guilt, regret, embarrassment, or shame). It is equally important that a planner address such concerns in a respectful, nonjudgmental way. In this situation, acting like a reassuring friend—by effectively reading and conveying verbal and nonverbal cues—is probably more important than actually being a friend. Using the client's name, asking about the client's family, career, hobbies or other interests—in other words, generally encouraging the sharing of information—are all ways to build a connection.

2. **Practice being an effective communicator.** Smile, nod, lean, and listen—with both eyes and ears—for words and feelings. Good salespeople listen more than they talk. Recognize that most communication occurs not through words, but by the use of paralanguage (i.e., rate, tone, volume of speech), body language (i.e., face, eyes, gestures), and space. Matching messages to a client's preferred information processing and communication style will lead to more meaningful client interactions and ensure that the advisor is tuned in to the client's needs and goals, spoken or otherwise. The use of pictures, charts, and graphs is recommended, especially for visual communicators, but it is important to attempt to connect using all three information processing styles.

3. **Practice empathy**. Financial planners are often called *advisors,* but many unwittingly ignore the universal fact that people do not accept advice, on any topic, unless they are first convinced that: (1) the other party is truly

listening; and (2) the other party is genuinely concerned and committed. Empathy validates the client and sends the message, "You are important and I understand."

4. **Make a confident, competent impression by being prepared**. This idea applies to the office environment as well as the planner. The meeting area should be clean and arranged to facilitate the presentation and discussion of the plan. The office, staff, and planner should present an image that represents the firm but that is also appropriately matched to the client. The plan and other supporting documents should be neatly prepared and organized for the presentation, as should any documents that might require a signature. Both plan and presentation should be free of errors and have an attractive and professional appearance that also represents the image of the firm. The presentation should use a font size and style that is easily legible to all viewers. If presentation equipment is to be used, the equipment and the presentation should be checked to ensure that everything is working properly. Finally, the planner should be familiar with the plan and the analysis upon which it was built so that explanations are clear and the planner can comfortably address any questions. A good joke is lost in bad delivery; the same goes for a financial plan.

5. **To the extent possible, involve the client**. Some clients lack the time, interest, or willingness to be fully engaged in the planning and implementation process. Other clients are seeking financial education, confirmation, reassurance, or simply direction. In fact, contingent on the business model of the planner and the products or services provided, the balance of independence/dependence is a defining characteristic of the planner-client relationship. By engaging a client in the planning and decision-making process, the planner is more likely to garner commitment followed by action. Put simply, the client "buys in" and takes ownership with the planner. Advisors who appear to be approachable and knowledgeable, regardless of their target demographic, are likely to be more successful than those who proudly assert their knowledge or position. An advisor's language is an obvious example; be careful to match word choice, terms, and acronyms to ones that are comfortable for the client. "Big words" and jargon may sound professional, but overuse can show a lack of professionalism.

6. **Plan the message and anticipate the response.** Planners should be mentally and emotionally prepared for the meeting, having given thought to the message to be delivered and possible client reactions. The presentation must summarize all stages of the planning process and present recommendations in such a way that the client can adequately judge the merits of the plan. Making the effort to educate the client by means of the plan itself, with any supporting documents, or during the presentation can be an important value-added service. The presentation should not be scripted, and it is important that it be logical and well organized. It should encourage the client to read the plan, but provide enough information to fully inform the client about the situation analysis and the recommendations proposed. Logical organization also reduces the likelihood of overwhelming a client with data and charts.

Detail is important only up to a point, contingent on the temperament and personality of the client.

7. **Motivate action with thorough, clearly defined, manageable steps**. Morrow relates a very important analogy to keep in mind.[6] He asks planners to imagine going to a medical clinic for a diagnosis, only to have the personnel respond that life-saving efforts will require that 10 courses of treatment be undertaken at the same time. The patient would likely be in shock. But this is exactly what most planners, especially those who write comprehensive financial plans, often do. They show clients 10 to 20 problems and provide 10 to 20 solutions, including alternatives. Clients feel overwhelmed and apathetic, which can result in a lack of action.

The communication rule that should be used to overcome client inaction involves summarizing the results of the analysis in simple, logical, and straightforward terms. A summary table, "To-do List," or timeline accompanied by crisp narrative should be provided in the plan. Recommendations should be prioritized to match a client's goals and objectives. It may be helpful to list the most important recommendations in bold type, followed by secondary recommendations. In this way, the client can better grasp, both intellectually and fiscally, the importance of the recommendations.

8. **Time it right**. It is important that sufficient time be allowed for a full presentation and exploration of the plan. Correctly judging the amount of time is subject to a client's demographic profile (e.g., age, education, family), personality, temperament, lifestyle, and personal finance knowledge and experience. Explaining even a simple plan can be a lengthy process. It is essential that an advisor read a client's body language and other communication cues to gauge and adjust the tempo of the presentation. Gender, cultural, and ethnic differences in communication should also be considered. For example, males typically have a "bottom line, get to the point" approach, while women are typically more interested in the details and relationships.

9. **Expect small changes**. It may be unrealistic to expect a client to commit immediately to implementing more than a few recommendations, if any. The very nature of comprehensive planning implies that a multitude of interrelated and integrated issues be considered concurrently. Often this level of analysis is too much for a client to absorb in one meeting. It is reasonable to gain client affirmation on one or two implementation policies during the presentation meeting, but clients should not be pressured into making a large number of decisions. Instead, specific follow-up dates should be established. Communication can continue electronically or by phone, or it might be necessary to schedule additional meetings in the following weeks or months. Building planner-client trust and rapport will expand the relationship and the potential for change. Implementation of plan recommendations is most closely tied to a planner's ability to communicate a sense of accomplishment, value, and goal achievement.

10. **Do not make promises.** Regardless of the sophistication of the analysis or the expertise of the planner, under the best of circumstances a financial plan is nothing more than an educated supposition. A well-developed plan built on valid personal and economic assumptions can help the client *prepare* for the unknown with realistic expectations, but it will not help the planner or client *predict* the unknown. To build a trusting relationship, clients and planners are best served by unbiased presentations that acknowledge that tax, legislative, economic, and/or personal life-changing events can positively or negatively affect planning projections. For this reason alone, a long-term relationship with periodic reviews and adjustments offers clients the greatest likelihood of reaching financial goals. The subject of the next chapter is how to maintain and foster that relationship by implementing and monitoring the plan.

Step 4 and the CFP Board Standards of Ethical Conduct

Step 4: Develop the Comprehensive Plan and Present the Recommendations, as presented in the systematic financial planning process, corresponds to only one CFP Board Practice Standard, 400-3: Presenting the Financial Planning Recommendations. Recall that the other two Practice Standards from the 400 Series, Practice Standard 400-1: Identifying and Evaluating Financial Planning Alternative(s) and Practice Standard 400-2: Developing the Financial Planning Recommendations, were discussed earlier in Step 3.

The ethical Principles of Integrity, Objectivity, and Professionalism are identified as particularly relevant to this practice standard, as shown in Table 7.6. This is the only Practice Standard where the Board specifically relates the Principle of Integrity. Integrity is the first of the seven principles identified in the *Code of Ethics*, and the Board declares that personal integrity is the ultimate source of a client's trust in an advisor. Despite allowances for error or differences of opinion, the Board states that "integrity demands honesty and candor, which must not be subordinated to personal gain and advantage."[7]

Although integrity is expected throughout the financial planning process, during the presentation of recommendations advisors have the distinct advantage of presumed knowledge, expertise, and trust, which can be misused to mislead clients. This principle correlates with *Rule of Conduct 2.1*, which prohibits certificants from communicating or failing to communicate any information that is false or misleading regarding the professional's qualifications, services offered, or the potential benefit of those services. A corollary to this rule and principles is *Rule 4.1*, which requires certificants to treat current and potential clients fairly and to "provide professional services with integrity and objectivity."[8] As shown in Table 7.6, two other *Rules of Conduct* under *Rule 4. Obligations to Prospective Clients and Clients* admonish certificants to practice prudent professional judgment (*Rule 4.4*) and to make or implement only recommendations suitable for the client (*Rule 4.5*).

Table 7.6 Develop the Comprehensive Plan and Present Recommendations

Step 4 – Develop the Comprehensive Plan and Present Recommendations	
CFP Board Practice Standards 400 Series: Developing and Presenting the Financial Planning Recommendation(s) **400-3: Presenting the Financial Planning Recommendation(s)** The financial planning practitioner shall communicate the recommendation(s) in a manner and to an extent reasonably necessary to assist the client in making an informed decision.	
CFP Board Code of Ethics	**CFP Board Rules of Conduct**
Principle 1 – Integrity Principle 2 – Objectivity Principle 6 – Professionalism	**2. Information Disclosed to Prospective Clients and Clients** **2.1** A certificant shall not communicate, directly or indirectly, to clients or prospective clients any false or misleading information directly or indirectly related to the certificant's professional qualifications or services. A certificant shall not mislead any parties about the potential benefits of the certificant's service. A certificant shall not fail to disclose or otherwise omit facts where that disclosure is necessary to avoid misleading clients. **4. Obligations to Prospective Clients and Clients** **4.1** A certificant shall treat prospective clients and clients fairly and provide professional services with integrity and objectivity. **4.4** A certificant shall exercise reasonable and prudent professional judgment in providing professional services to clients. **4.5** In addition to the requirements of Rule 1.4, a certificant shall make and/or implement only recommendations that are suitable for the client.

Source: Certified Financial Planner Board of Standards, Inc., *CFP Board's Standards of Professional Conduct*. Available at http://www.cfp.net/Downloads/2010Standards.pdf, pp. 6, 7, 9, 10, 11, and 23; or at http://www.cfp.net/learn/ethics.asp#intro. Reprinted with permission.

"THINKING OUTSIDE THE BOX"

Conceptualizing a financial plan may require a great deal of cognitive and emotional energy, a task further complicated by the complexity of financial planning issues and personal challenges posed by the client. To exercise prudent professional judgment suggests that a planner must fully engage in the process, consider all data and information, and arrive at a reasonable solution clearly supported by the data. But professional judgment also requires a planner to maintain and practice an attitude of inquisitiveness, skepticism, or what is commonly described as "playing devil's advocate." This sort of focused inquiry and "gentle debate" on the part of the planner does not occur in isolation. In reality, planners work in group practices where expertise can be shared. Other planners—through formal or informal networks, often facilitated by professional associations—rely on colleagues for advice, counsel, or knowledge on how to deal with a new, complex, or unique client or client situation.

The term *paradigm* is used to describe a viewpoint, perspective, or distinct way of thinking. It is what some call "the pair of glasses through which the world is viewed." Change the glasses, and the view of the world changes. This section introduces several paradigms for thinking about professional judgment or the conceptualization of a financial plan.

Holistic Judgments

The similarities are striking between how financial planners and other professionals, as "expert practitioners," arrive at conclusions and diagnoses. Expert status is typically accorded those who have completed a lengthy educational process and gained significant on-the-job experience that enables them to demonstrate outstanding problem-solving abilities. Professionals pride themselves on being able to make holistic judgments in response to the cognitively challenging and information-rich situations encountered in daily professional practice. Ruscio defined **holistic judgments** as those based not on independent consideration of data separately or additively, but on each piece of information considered in light of all other available data.[9] In other words, the possible interactions among all pieces of data must be considered—or as Ruscio said, "everything influences everything else" in a complex whole. In a review of the research on the accuracy of holistic judgments (i.e., physicians, medical pathologists, mental health clinicians, weather forecasters, mechanics, venture capitalists, auditors, and financial advisors), Roszkowski and Grable observed that experts were generally not reliable or accurate in their holistic judgments, although this varied by profession.[10] Professionals who utilized more fact-based information and depended less on subjective human preferences, tendencies, and conditions demonstrated greater accuracy.

Many financial planners use a form of holistic judgment to generate client recommendations. This approach is premised on the idea that the planner has a thorough knowledge of the client and the client's situation, including client attitudinal and behavioral factors. After making observations about the strengths and weaknesses inherent in a situation, financial planners who use a holistic approach then compare their observations and conclusions against what they know about a client's circumstances. Although a planner may use heuristics, or mental shortcuts, to simplify the inputs used to make a decision or design a recommendation, the actual process involved in making a holistic judgment can be subjective and difficult to measure. The success of the judgment can be affected by the patterns of information observed about the client, or the emphasis placed on those patterns.

This is not to say, however, that holistic methods of arriving at client recommendations are totally inadequate. Research has shown that training may be more highly correlated with the accuracy and effectiveness of judgments than experience, and that judgments are more likely to improve in situations where feedback on performance is available and can be considered in future decision making or problem solving. More experienced planners rely on a combination of training, background, knowledge, and temperament to craft recommendations. It is possible that students and novice financial planners could benefit from training that:

- Focuses attention on the most germane information in the client situation (i.e., the most important patterns of information); and

- Provides feedback that enables students not only to judge the merits of alternative approaches but also to incorporate that knowledge into future scenarios.

The Systematic Approach

Too often students look for one correct answer. Unfortunately, financial planning does not always lend itself to a single correct response. As acknowledged by the CFP Board, multiple solutions may enable a client to reach a goal (e.g., the Practice Standards 400 Series), an example of subjective professional judgment. Different financial planners can address client situations in numerous ways. Some recommendations may be equally effective; others can be dismissed as ill-conceived or simply less likely to result in successful goal attainment. It is important for students and practitioners to thoroughly review the methodologies they used to guide the progression from strategies and recommendations to final plan.

The **systematic approach to planning** promotes repeated use of planning forms to guide and document the planning process. Because this approach is very methodical and organized, systematic planning tools can help students and novice planners:

- Organize what may initially appear to be an overwhelming mass of data and analysis into a manageable format;

- Focus attention on critical planning needs;

- Focus attention on problems or issues that might entail research or consultation with other professionals;

- Focus attention on issues or questions that require additional input from the client;

- Recognize the need for creative alternatives to achieve client goals; and

- Gain confidence that relevant issues have not been overlooked and that decisions and advice are based on sound analysis and professional judgment.

The Summary Goal Ranking Form (discussed in Chapter 6 and illustrated in Exhibit 6.2 and Exhibit 6.4), the Comprehensive Planning Checklist, the Planning Recommendation Form, and the Recommendation Impact Form are four such planning tools. Some financial planners find systematic tools and techniques quite useful for framing a methodology to "attack" the issues of a client's situation. Others might conclude that such tools limit creativity and are cumbersome or repetitive to apply. But consistent use can build the skills necessary to analyze, apply, and synthesize client data into an integrated plan.

The Comprehensive Planning Checklist in Appendix 7C challenges advisors to carefully consider key questions related to each of the core content planning areas. Although these questions may not offer a comprehensive or sophisticated analysis of every client situation, the form provides a framework for reviewing and summarizing a client's individual circumstances. An initial negative response to any question should prompt the planner to reconsider the need for additional preparatory work. Any positive answers to the question "Is a recommendation needed?" should help planners initially identify and summarize the parameters of a client's planning situation. Finally, the section of the checklist addressing cross-planning analysis helps focus on problem solving on fundamental interactions, represented by the "⇔" symbol. As noted earlier, it is impossible to encapsulate a process as broad and dynamic as financial planning in a simple form; this limitation cannot be overlooked. However, the form does offer the advantage of focusing attention on the most common patterns of interaction to consider, whether developing a single-issue or a comprehensive plan.

The Planning Recommendation Form (Exhibit 7.2) helps planners focus on the essential issues to include in an actionable recommendation. This useful planning tool summarizes the answers to the seven critical questions of *who, what, when, where, why, how,* and *how much* into one simple format for communicating information to the planning staff and the client.

Possibly one of the most beneficial uses of this form is to document the titling of assets. Titling may be one of the more overlooked aspects of a financial plan; however, it is also one of the most important, because ownership implies control. There are four primary forms of ownership: (1) individual; (2) joint (i.e., joint tenants with right of survivorship, tenants in common, or tenants in the entirety); (3) custodial; and (4) trust. Individual ownership or any form of joint ownership should be carefully reviewed for its impact on other aspects of the plan or the transfer wishes of the owner(s). Custodial ownership is extremely common in retirement and other tax-qualified accounts where the custodian plays a key role in reporting and control. The trust form of ownership is used primarily for asset transfer purposes or for minors (who cannot legally own assets in most states). Planning for the eventual distribution or transfer of assets can have far-reaching ramifications regarding how they should be held. The Planning Recommendation Form also prompts the planner and client to identify a beneficiary, or contingent beneficiary, as applicable. Keeping track of ownership is a crucial part of tax planning and estate planning. In this regard the Planning Recommendation Form (Exhibit 7.2) offers an additional benefit: to help the planner fully consider the integration of the proposed recommendation with other core content planning areas.

Initially, the Planning Recommendation Form is simply a tool for planners to summarize and cost out potential recommendations to meet client goals. Issues related to how much a recommendation will cost and the potential benefits associated with recommendations can also be addressed. As the plan develops, it may be necessary to combine, sort, and rank recommendations from other core content planning areas, and the forms are a means to quickly summarize the costs and benefits of each recommendation.

Exhibit 7.2 Planning Recommendation Form

Planning Recommendation Form

Financial Planning Content Area	Life Insurance			
Client Goal	Maximize Life Insurance Protection			
Recommendation No.		**Priority (1–6) lowest to highest:**		
Projected/Target Value ($)				

Product Profile

Type				
Duration				
Provider				
Funding Cost per Period ($)				
Maintenance Cost per Period ($)				
Current Income Tax Status	Tax-qualified		Taxable	
Projected Rate of Return				
Major Policy Provisions				

Procedural Factors

Implement by Whom	Planner		Client	
Implementation Date or Time Frame				
Implementation Procedure				

Ownership Factors

Owner(s)				
Form of Ownership				
Insured(s)				
Custodial Account	Yes		No	
Custodian				
In Trust For (ITF)	Yes		No	
Transfer On Death (TOD)	Yes		No	
Beneficiary(ies)				
Contingent Beneficiary(ies)				

Proposed Benefit

The Recommendation Impact Form (Exhibit 7.3) offers a final opportunity to verify that no potential interactions among the recommendations have been overlooked. This form is completed as each recommendation is finalized. Should cash flow or other assets be insufficient to fund all recommendations, completing the Recommendation Impact Form might help a planner identify mutually exclusive recommendations that could be integrated and achieved through another "multipurpose" planning product or procedure. The forms might also help the student or novice planner *complicate* the planning process—not in the sense of making it more difficult, but in the sense of more broadly informing it.

By seriously considering the impact of each recommendation on other core content planning areas, the planner may gain new insights into a client situation that otherwise could have been overlooked. Likewise, if the advisor cannot reasonably and knowledgeably assess the impact of recommendations, more research or consultation with other professionals may be warranted. Thus, the systematic approach, which can be justifiably criticized for stifling creativity, might actually encourage a broader depth and range of thinking. Ultimately, it is important that a consistent approach be used to rank and order strategies and recommendations in a way that is comfortable for the advisor. But to be effective, whatever approach is chosen must encourage the professional freedom—and responsibility—to shift paradigms when analyzing and reviewing a client's situation.

Triangulation

The term *triangulation* is usually associated with military practices, navigation, and mapmaking, all of which are based on multiple celestial or terrestrial references. The term also refers to a social science research method designed to improve the validity or accuracy of research findings. In its simplest form, **triangulation** refers to study, exploration, or examination from multiple (typically three) perspectives. In research, these perspectives might refer to multiple data sources or data collection methods, multiple theories of explanation, multiple researchers, multiple methods of conducting the research, or some combination of these research activities.

Consider for a moment the obvious parallels with financial planning. Client data range from confirmed facts to perhaps unconfirmed assumptions or observations. Advisors working independently or in teams, representing different business models and product or service orientations, approach a client situation from very different vantage points and offer diverse explanations and solutions. Yet all are focused on *helping clients achieve multiple financial goals and objectives through the application and integration of synergistic personal finance strategies.* Although researchers and financial planners—through their various modes of professional practice—can arrive at alternative explanations of the same situation, both are motivated by the need for accuracy. Triangulation offers another method for pursuing accuracy and exploring the interactions among the data considered.

Exhibit 7.3 Recommendation Impact Form

Recommendation Impact Form

Recommendation:

Recommendation No.						
Planner Decision	Accept		Reject		Modify	
Client Decision	Accept		Reject		Modify	

Financial Impact

Annual impact on cash-flow ($)	
Immediate impact on net worth ($)	

Planning Issue	Degree of Significance				Notes
	Major	Modest	Minor	None	
Financial situation—cash management					
Tax planning					
Life insurance planning					
Health insurance planning					
Disability insurance planning					
LTC insurance planning					
Property and liability insurance planning					
Investment planning					
Education or other special needs planning					
Retirement planning					
Estate planning					
Other planning need					
Other planning need					

In this context, the multiple perspectives might refer to multiple client data sources or data collection methods (e.g., client-provided, planner-observed, planner-and-client confirmed); multiple strategies, recommendations, or financial products; multiple planning team members or collaboration with other professionals (e.g., accountants, attorneys, investment or money managers, product providers); multiple methods of conducting quantitative analysis of the client situation; or some combination of these planning activities. The list that follows, although by no means exhaustive, offers examples of how triangulation might be used to enrich or expand an advisor's perspective:

- *Data or information.* The plan is built on quantitative and qualitative data collected from the client and from independently generated analytical or diagnostic results and mutually agreed-upon assumptions. What is the most effective method for collecting client data? What types of analysis should be considered as most appropriate for the client situation? How might a client's fundamental motives, values, morals, or ethics affect the interpretation and acceptance of the planner's mathematical computations and logical explanations?

- *Stakeholders.* How would the client, the planner, other members of the client's household, or other professionals react to the recommendation? How would the recommendation serve their interests? How might fees, commissions, other methods of compensation, or other costs influence the choice? How might another professional identify, interpret, differentiate, and diagnose the same client situation? What biases, if any, could affect the planner's perspective on this client situation?

- *Competing goals or recommendations.* Is protection of the future income stream the foremost objective? What are the projected short- and long-term implications of the recommendation on the client's assets? What is the client's net worth? How do planner, client, or the two in combination, weigh the wants and needs identified in the planning situation?

Which Approach Is Best?

Triangulation has been used throughout this chapter to demonstrate and explain the essence of the systematic financial planning process by offering new ways to consider the process from multiple perspectives. Holistic judgment assumes that all of the data interrelationships known about a client situation are considered in plan development. The systematic approach strips away much of the "noise" in the data and initially focuses attention on the core content planning issues of the client situation. Both approaches have recognized advantages and disadvantages. Triangulation builds on both approaches and serves as a solid reminder that no recommendation should be left to intuition, good intention, or stark fact. The use of this method challenges planners to triangulate three sources of evidence or information upon which to build a sound justification for any conclusion or recommendation. Recall that professional judgment is the application of knowledge balanced with the willingness to always review, question, or evaluate a solution.

From Process to Practice

The vignette that follows continues to explore the experiences of the Kims with their financial planner, Jane. Recall that the Kims are on the way home from their first annual checkup and monitoring meeting. This installment includes the Kims' and Jane's reflections, as they offer their insights into their "real life" experiences with Steps 3 and 4—from both sides of the desk.

Looking back on their first meetings with Jane, Tom could now jokingly reminisce with Nyla about how difficult it was, initially, to verbalize and prioritize their goals.

"With two women, you can't get a word in, and planning for the future is harder than I could ever have imagined. Should we worry about our retirement or Azalea's education? Should we give her a good education and hope for the best in retirement? You know what they say, 'Be good to your kids, they'll pick your nursing home'... but saving for it all is a HUGE challenge!"

Nyla's promotion, which occurred just a few months before their first meeting with Jane, had meant an annual increase of $6,900 in after-tax income. Based on the Kims' responses on the Client Intake Form, the Summary Goal Ranking Form, and the discussion during their second meeting, focused on data- gathering and discovery, the Kims and Jane were able to rank their financial goals as follows:

1. Partially fund Azalea's education through savings over the next 10 years.

2. Increase annual funding so both Tom and Nyla can retire in 25 years.

3. Save for an international vacation in two years to visit extended family.

The Kims finally had a direction for their future! And they had no doubt that with Jane's help, they could do it all.

But the third meeting (called the *plan presentation meeting*) quickly eliminated all of their bravado. It was a bit of a shock to learn that none of their plans would work, at least not according to Jane. Tom reminisced to Nyla, "It was getting tough to handle. We thought we had done fairly well. We knew we could do better, that is why we sought out Jane, but it was very hard to hear Jane present her findings."

"No, it wasn't all 'hearts and flowers,' nor was it all 'dollars and cents' leading up to the plan development," commented Nyla. She remembered that on top of their own predetermined goals, Jane had also added some recommendations based on the Recommendation Planning Checklist that she had completed. Jane shared the Recommendation Planning Checklist (Exhibit 7.4) with the Kims to help them learn more about some of the standard "checkpoints" for measuring their financial status. Jane had made the analogy that the checklist results and other financial ratios and analyses reported in the plan were comparable to checking height, weight, blood pressure, and cholesterol to measure physical health. In both cases, standards of measurement are matched to the individual situation. It turned out the Kims were not as financially healthy as they thought.

Exhibit 7.4 Recommendation Planning Checksheet for Tom and Nyla Kim

Abbreviated Comprehensive Planning Checklist*

Cash Flow Analysis to Maximize Client Discretionary Cash Flow			Recommendation Needed?	
1. Has planner verified that the client is able and willing to proactively save money on a regular basis?	Yes	*No*	Yes	*No*
2. Have debt reduction or debt restructuring alternatives been reviewed?	*Yes*	No	*Yes*	No

Insurance Analyses to Limit Client's Household Risk Exposures			Recommendation Needed?	
3. Has a life insurance analysis been conducted?	*Yes*	No	*Yes*	No
4. Has a disability insurance analysis been conducted?	*Yes*	No	*Yes*	No
5. Has a long-term care (LTC) insurance analysis been conducted?	Yes	*No*	Yes	*No*
6. Has a health insurance analysis been conducted?	*Yes*	No	Yes	*No*
7. Has a property, casualty, and liability insurance analysis been conducted?	*Yes*	No	Yes	*No*
8. Are there other client specific risk management issues to consider?	Yes	*No*	Yes	*No*

Investment Planning Analyses to Maximize Client Return			Recommendation Needed?	
9. Has an investment funding goal been identified?	*Yes*	No	*Yes*	No
10. Is the client on track to meet the targeted amount and date?	Yes	*No*	*Yes*	No
11. Other client-specific investment planning issues to consider?	Yes	*No*	Yes	*No*

Education or Special Needs Planning Analyses to Maximize Client Return			Recommendation Needed?	
12. Has an education funding goal been identified?	*Yes*	No	*Yes*	No
13. Is the client on track to meet the targeted amount and date?	Yes	*No*	*Yes*	No
14. Are asset allocation and the investments suitable given the client's time horizon, risk tolerance, and other assumptions?	Yes	*No*	*Yes*	No
15. Is the client fully benefiting from tax-advantaged accounts?	Yes	*No*	*Yes*	No
16. Other client specific education planning issues to consider?	Yes	*No*	Yes	*No*

Retirement Planning Analyses to Maximize Client Return			Recommendation Needed?	
17. Has a retirement funding goal been identified?	*Yes*	No	*Yes*	No
18. Is the client on track to meet the targeted amount and date?	Yes	*No*	*Yes*	No
19. Are asset allocation and investments suitable given the client's time horizon, risk tolerance, and other assumptions?	*Yes*	No	*Yes*	No
20. Is the client fully benefiting from tax-advantaged accounts?	*Yes*	No	Yes	*No*
21. Are other retirement funds available?	*Yes*	No	*Yes*	No
22. Are there other client specific retirement planning issues to consider?	Yes	*No*	Yes	*No*

Abbreviated Comprehensive Planning Checklist* (cont'd)

Cross Planning Analyses: Have the Following Interactions Been Considered?			Recommendation Needed?	
23. Net worth ⇔ insurance?	*Yes*	No	Yes	*No*
24. Life insurance ⇔ estate planning?	*Yes*	No	*Yes*	No
25. Education funding ⇔ income tax planning?	*Yes*	No	*Yes*	No

*For illustrative purposes selected questions are not shown, although the analysis was comprehensive.

Note: The Kims' answers are indicated by ***bold italic*** type.

Tom recalled being very impressed by all of the effort that Jane had obviously put into analyzing each area of their financial life. It was evident that she truly had been listening to their concerns. She seemed to be making every effort to conduct their financial physical and develop a plan for their future in a manner that reflected their financial and life goals. As a result, Jane had made the following recommendations:

1. Pay off credit card debt with cash assets.

2. Purchase a $250,000 term life insurance policy for Nyla.

3. Purchase long-term, 70% income replacement disability coverage for Tom.

But the bad news came with Jane's explanation that even with Nyla's raise, they did not have enough DCF or other assets to fully fund all of *their* goals and *her* recommendations concurrently. During her analysis, Jane had calculated the reduction in DCF (i.e., the total cost to implement all recommendations) to be $13,100 over the upcoming 12 months. Tom remembered that this was a much larger amount than the $6,900 available from Nyla's raise. "Where are we going to come up with the additional money?" he remembered thinking. "Does this mean we have to give up everything we enjoy and go back to the way we lived when we were first married and living on only one income?"

As Tom and Nyla continued their conversation in the car, they recalled how they each felt frustrated and more than a little annoyed that Jane would recommend more goals, knowing that they did not have sufficient funds to meet their own priorities. However, as that meeting continued, Jane sensed the Kims' frustration and encouraged them to discuss their sense of dissatisfaction as well as their other questions as they reviewed the draft of their financial plan.

Next, Jane explained each section of the Kims' plan—even those sections where they were on track and no changes were needed. Tom recalled, "I was relieved to know that at least we were doing some things right!" She also explained each of the approaches used to calculate the amounts of insurance Tom and Nyla needed. Then Jane explained how she had calculated education and retirement costs, the assumptions she had considered, and how the projected rate of return, asset allocations, and investments had been matched appropriately with their goals and risk tolerance. Tom and Nyla recalled feeling overwhelmed by all of the information, but they were still confident that there was some balance of good and bad news. They were convinced that Jane was a knowledgeable professional, but they were very glad that they would have the draft of their plan and all of her analyses to study more carefully at home. Most of all, they were amazed at how patient Jane had been in explaining charts and graphs and answering their questions.

Tom and Nyla recalled feeling some combination of naïveté, stupidity, and embarrassment that their plan for how to use the $6,900 salary increase could be so wrong. But Jane quickly reminded them of what Nyla had said: "We didn't really know how to determine the cost of the goals, so we took most of the raise and allocated it as best we could." Before proceeding further, Jane had revisited the underlying planning assumptions and analyses to help them understand why some of the recommendations seemed so different from their initial suggestions. Her assumptions, which they had mutually agreed on, and the analyses were accurate and representative of the Kims' wishes. This helped Nyla cope with the decisions, but it was little consolation to Tom. The initial suggestions and results of Jane's analysis are shown below:

1. Accumulate $40,000 over the next 10 years to partially fund a four-year public college education for Azalea.

    Kims' suggested annual reduction in discretionary cash flow = $2,200

    Jane's suggested annual reduction in discretionary cash flow = $3,000

    Number of years = 10

2. Increase annual funding so both Tom and Nyla could retire in 25 years.

    Kims' suggested annual reduction in discretionary cash flow = $1,700

    Jane's suggested annual reduction in discretionary cash flow = $4,000

    Number of years = 25

3. Save for an international vacation in two years to visit extended family.

    Kims' suggested annual reduction in discretionary cash flow = $3,000

    Jane's suggested annual reduction in discretionary cash flow = $3,600

    Number of years = 2

4. Pay off $4,000 in credit card debt with current assets.

    Annual reduction in discretionary cash flow = $0

    Number of years = 0

5. Purchase a $250,000, 20-year guaranteed renewable term life insurance policy for Nyla.

Annual reduction in discretionary cash flow = $300 (based on quotes received)

Number of years = 20

6. Purchase a long-term, own-occupation, 70% income-replacement disability policy for Tom.

Annual reduction in discretionary cash flow = $1,800 (based on quotes received)

Number of years = 10 or more

Tom mused, "I almost fell over when Jane started talking about spending, really saving, more than $10 grand this year to reach our goals." "In fact," Nyla interjected, "there was not enough cash flow remaining to fully fund either the trip or retirement at the level Jane believed necessary, if we saved for Azalea's education." Nyla and Tom both recalled that hearing this was a deflating surprise, but they trusted Jane that if $3,000 was really necessary, then that is what they would do.

Jane had explained as she continued presenting the draft of the Kims' plan that in her professional opinion, funding all of their investment goals without regard to their insurance shortfalls could leave them susceptible to unwanted income reductions that, in the event of a death or disability, could undo all of their efforts to save for future goals. Nyla remembers Jane explaining that "goal funding should follow a logical pattern. First, financial protection needs should be funded." This was why Jane recommended that Tom and Nyla strengthen their insurance protection. Paying off credit card debt and building additional short-term savings with the diverted funds were also financial necessities.

Tom recalled that with Nyla's new salary they felt more comfortable about saving, but they had never thought about insurance. Furthermore, they had not considered that Nyla's income now made up a much more significant portion of total household income. For Nyla not to have life insurance could create an undue hardship on Tom and Azalea, should something happen to Nyla. Tom and Nyla remembered thinking that the choices among funding Azalea's college, taking her to meet extended family, and protecting their lifestyle by purchasing life insurance were ones that they had never even considered. Nor did they feel prepared to make that choice. Jane explained to them that it could be very hard emotionally to delay or even let go of a goal, but that they had some choices to make.

After some discussion, and having received Tom and Nyla's general consent to pursue all six recommendations, Jane promised to work out the details and send them specific alternatives that Tom and Nyla could study. At their next meeting, they would make final choices about how to implement their plan. "But the *really* good news is," Jane said, "you can take care of those credit card balances you hate so much without compromising our other goals and still save some money. That much we all agree on!"

Nyla also remembered how Jane had outlined possible alternatives to help resolve the cash flow shortage and fund all six goals (the three that they had for themselves and the three that Jane suggested). Each alternative, and the Kims' initial reaction, is shown below:

A. *Alternative*: Postpone the projected retirement date; this would allow them to reduce the current funding requirement or delay funding it altogether until after their trip.

   Reaction: Based on their discussions on the time value of money, Tom and Nyla knew this suggestion did not take full advantage of their money working for them.

B. *Alternative*: Reduce the *ideal* amount dedicated to funding retirement with the intent of increasing funding after the trip.

   Reaction: Tom and Nyla agreed this could be a viable compromise.

C. *Alternative*: Reevaluate and discuss the current rate of return on their retirement and education assets to see whether increasing the return assumption could offset funding and any cash flow shortage.

   Reaction: Jane had cautioned that this should be done very prudently and only as a last resort because increasing expected returns typically increases risk. This increased risk could cause the Kims to abandon the plan or create regulatory issues for Jane. Tom and Nyla reasoned that this might not be the best alternative.

D. *Alternative*: Reduce current expenditures and use this cash flow to fund the retirement goal or to pay for one or more of the insurance premiums.

   Reaction: Some reductions were possible, because Tom was convinced that everyone could reduce some expenses. But they reasoned that their lifestyle was not extravagant, so any reductions would yield minimal savings.

E. *Alternative*: Postpone the vacation to allow more time to accumulate the necessary savings.

   Reaction: Not really what they wanted to do.

F. *Alternative:* Continue to self-insure for some or all projected insurance needs.

   Reaction: Tom and Nyla realized this really was not a good choice given Jane's needs assessment, including multiple approaches to calculating Nyla's life insurance needs and supporting explanations regarding why life and disability insurance were needed.

Nyla remembered how relieved she was when Jane had suggested that fourth meeting to finalize the plan and its implementation; she and Tom were too overwhelmed with facts, figures, and alternatives to make a decision at that time. Nyla remembered thinking that Jane must have really had her work cut out for her. "All of those dreams and needs, but so little money to realize them," she recalled thinking to herself as she and Tom left Jane's office with the draft of their plan that day. Then she realized that, although Jane had commented at the end of the meeting that "they would work something out," it was really up to Tom and her to make the decisions. As scary as that seemed, though, she knew that Jane would be involved to guide their next steps.

Today, almost a year later, as Tom and Nyla continued their drive home, Jane was still involved and the future did not look so scary. In fact, they were regaining some of the bravado they had lost in that plan presentation meeting!

* * * * * * * * * *

As Jane watched Tom and Nyla Kim walk to their car following their first annual checkup and monitoring meeting, she recalled how far their planner-client relationship had come in a little more than one year. She was also quite pleased, as were they, with the progress they had made. But, Jane recalled as she watched the Kims drive away, getting there had presented challenges, particularly as she had developed the plan.

About a year ago, after completing the data-gathering meeting with the Kims and an analysis of their current financial situation for all core financial planning content areas, Jane knew that she was facing a challenge. Jane, Tom, and Nyla had identified three goals that the Kims were committed to accomplishing. But Jane's initial "gut reactions" to the Kims' financial situation were confirmed by her systematic risk management analyses: Nyla's life insurance coverage was woefully low, and Tom had no long-term disability insurance.

Now Jane was faced with identifying potential strategies to achieve their goals for education, retirement, leisure, and risk management—not to mention paying off the outstanding $4,000 of credit card debt to pay for the heat pump replacement. Fortunately, in addition to the projected $6,900 increase in after-tax salary for Nyla, the Kims' balance sheet revealed some good news: their emergency fund savings were $4,000 more than the amount Jane thought necessary given the Kims' stable careers and financial situation. Their remaining investment assets were already devoted to funding either college or retirement.

As Jane proceeded to plan development, she knew she had to rank the recommendations in order of funding priority. One alternative was to simply accept the allocations proposed by the Kims and fund each of their three goals accordingly. Using this approach, the Kims had enough money to fund all of their goals, but not in the preferred time frame or in a manner consistent with their risk tolerance or other assumptions they had discussed. This made Jane feel uncomfortable about the likelihood of the Kims achieving their goals, even if they diverted some of the international vacation money to other needs. Furthermore, in Jane's opinion, it would be foolhardy to move forward with funding the Kims' financial goals without first making sure that they were covered in case of a financial loss, which meant buying insurance—yet another annual expense for the foreseeable future.

Tom and Nyla had consistently ranked funding Azalea's education as their top priority, although they ranked retirement funding as a close second. So Jane started with the one thing she was sure the Kims wanted—Azalea's college funding. She reviewed Tom and Nyla's risk tolerance, the parameters of their education goal, other available strategies, and then she started to write her recommendation:

To establish an AnyState College Savings Plan with a Real-life Mutual Fund Company age-based account with monthly funding of $250 to accumulate a projected $40,000 to partially fund the cost of a four-year public college education for Azalea beginning in 2022.

To supplement the recommendation, Jane completed the Education Planning Recommendation Form (Exhibit 7.5). As alternatives, Jane repeated the analyses assuming that the Kims (1) continued funding their taxable mutual fund account, or (2) funded a Roth IRA with the idea that the funds could be withdrawn for Azalea's education, if necessary. (The completed Education Planning Section of the Kims' plan is shown in Appendix D). The Kims had mentioned that there *might* be an inheritance. Lots of things could change in 10 years!

Jane would have preferred that the Kims consider funding a lower-cost education goal and using some of that cash flow to fund retirement; so the Roth IRA could be a good option. But, at least initially, she felt that it was more important to meet the Kims' primary goal of dedicating funding to Azalea's education. However, given the total cost they projected for a public four-year institution, the time horizon, and the amount of their current savings in a taxable mutual fund account, the $2,200 Tom and Nyla had wanted to save annually was simply not enough.

Exhibit 7.5 Education Planning Recommendation Form for Tom and Nyla Kim

Planning Recommendation Form

Financial Planning Content Area	Education planning			
Client Goal	Funding for Azalea's college expenses			
Recommendation No.	1	**Priority (1–6) lowest to highest:**		6
Projected/Target Value ($)	$40,000			

Product Profile

Type	§ 529 account		
Duration	14 years		
Provider	Real-life Mutual Fund Company		
Funding Cost per Period ($)	$250 per month		
Maintenance Cost per Period ($)	$25 set-up fee (one time only)		
Current Income Tax Status	Tax-qualified	X	Taxable
Projected Rate of Return	Variable (8.0% for first 7 years)		
Major Policy Provisions	None		

Procedural Factors

Implementation by Whom		Planner			Client	X
Implementation Date or Time Frame	Within next 60 days					
Implementation Procedure	We will provide you with the appropriate forms to complete. Upon completion, mail the forms and your check to Real-life Mutual Fund Company. We will monitor account progress for funding adequacy, risk/return objectives, and all other investment aspects of the account.					

Ownership Factors

Owner(s)	Tom Kim					
Form of Ownership	Individual, but as allowed in the plan, Nyla will be designated as the successor on the account					
Insured(s)	NA					
Custodial Account		Yes	X		No	
Custodian	Any State					
In Trust For (ITF)		Yes			No	X
Transfer On Death (TOD)		Yes			No	X
Beneficiary(ies)	Azalea Kim					
Contingent Beneficiary(ies)	NA					

Proposed Benefit

	By using a § 529 Plan, you will benefit from tax-deferred growth as well as tax-free withdrawals (restrictions apply). Furthermore, we have agreed to maintain a fairly passive approach and this plan has several age-based portfolios that will adjust the asset allocation, thereby reducing account volatility as Azalea approaches college age. However, the plan selected also offers a static account (i.e., one that allows the owner to control asset allocation) so that additional risk/return adjustments can be made.

Jane's analysis revealed that the projected annual cost of funding their $40,000 education goal would be nearly $3,000—if all cost and return assumptions held true. Given Tom and Nyla's desire to fund the account on a monthly basis, they actually needed only a monthly payment of $220 to achieve their goal. But because the account Jane was recommending required a minimum additional payment of $250, she felt that this was a reasonable trade-off. She finalized this analysis for inclusion in the Kims' plan.

This left Jane with $3,900 in DCF to fund their other goals and insurance needs. Unfortunately, this was not enough money. Fully funding the education goal could significantly affect other core content planning areas that the Kims wanted to address. To confirm her thoughts, and to provide documentation for the Kims' plan, Jane completed the Recommendation Impact Form, as shown in Exhibit 7.6.

Exhibit 7.6 Recommendation Impact Form for Tom and Nyla Kim

Recommendation Impact Form

Recommendation: Increase education funding for Azalea's college to $250 per month contributed to the AnyState College Savings Plan with Real-life Mutual Fund Company.

Recommendation No.	1					
Planner Decision	Accept	X	Reject		Modify	
Client Decision	Accept	X	Reject		Modify	

Financial Impact

Annual impact on cash flow ($)	$3,000 Reduction
Immediate impact on net worth ($)	$0

Planning Issue	Degree of Significance				Notes
	Major	Modest	Minor	None	
Financial situation— cash management	X				Review automatic investment plan possibilities with client.
Tax planning			X		State income tax deduction might be available.
Life insurance planning		X			Funding the education goal will impact the ability to purchase life insurance.
Health insurance planning				X	
Disability and long-term care insurance planning		X			Funding the education goal will impact the ability to purchase long-term disability insurance.
Property and liability insurance planning				X	
Investment planning	X				Funding the education goal will impact the ability to fund the vacation goal.
Education or other special needs planning	X				Select age-based portfolios to reduce management time.
Retirement planning			X		Funding the education goal might impact the ability to fully fund the retirement goal.
Estate planning			X		Per plan requirements, Nyla will be designated as the account owner in the event of Tom's death.

With this recommendation complete, Jane decided that the best interests of the Kims could be served by proceeding with all of the goals and needs identified. She knew this would take some creative planning, with perhaps multiple scenarios for the Kims to consider, but it seemed to be the best approach.

She felt that Tom and Nyla might not agree with her prioritization of recommendations should she proceed with a comprehensive plan. She knew from working with other clients that sometimes people do not appreciate the immediate need to protect income by funding life and disability coverage. She realized that if the insurance policies were not funded there would be excess cash flow available to fund the Kims' other goals; yet they would still be underinsured.

This meant that Jane had to help the Kims make some tough decisions about their financial goals, dreams, and realities. One alternative was to tell Tom and Nyla that the international vacation was out of the question. This was, in Jane's opinion, a financial want, not a need. But Jane realized that this was not a decision that she could, or should, make. Jane knew that a workable and sustainable plan had to reflect the clients' wishes, situational factors, and financial goals balanced with the money available and the advisor's professional judgment. She realized that Tom and Nyla placed a great deal of personal value on the vacation. In terms of lifestyle choices, she suspected they would be willing to sacrifice some current pleasure for long-term well-being—but only up to a point. Canceling all funding for a family vacation, especially of this significance, was beyond that limit in Jane's opinion.

With Jane settled on following through on all six recommendations, she had to decide how to finish the Kims' plan. Rather than developing multiple series of formal recommendations, which might overwhelm her clients and complicate decision making, she decided to outline some integrated alternatives that the Kims could study. All of the analyses of the financial situation, income tax, risk management, investment management, retirement, and estate planning sections of the plan were complete. A discussion of that much of the plan and a review of the alternative scenarios for meeting the Kims' needs would be more than enough to discuss at their third, or plan presentation, meeting. With that, Jane started to brainstorm how to turn $10,900 of available funds into $12,700 of needs and goals.

CHAPTER SUMMARY

Following the systematic financial planning process described in this chapter is one way to develop the skills necessary to conduct a comprehensive analysis of a client's situation for the purposes of a product sale or the development of a comprehensive or modular financial plan. Following the black box analogy, a step-by-step process is fully explained with the objective that important information not be overlooked or overweighed in the decision-making process. Analysis in each core content planning area of the client's current situation, using both quantitative and qualitative data, leverages an advisor's professional judgment while accounting for a client's financial and life goals. The analysis of the situation should quantify a client's financial strengths and weaknesses and identify areas where the situation could be improved and any potential short-term or future opportunities for planning. After a review of possible strategies, individual recommendations are developed and, once finalized, integrated into an affordable comprehensive financial plan that is presented to the client. Finally, ideas for "thinking outside the box" by using holistic judgment, the systematic method, or triangulation are presented to illustrate and integrate how professional judgment can be applied in response to the question, "How does it happen?"

Learning Outcomes

1. Analysis of a client's current situation focuses on identification of the client's planning needs, quantification of the client's planning needs (when applicable), and identification and review of the strategies currently in place to meet planning needs. The analysis of each core content planning area is predicated on realistic, defensible assumptions that are mutually agreed upon by advisor and client. The identification of needs incorporates all of those previously identified by the client as well as current and future needs identified by the planner.

2. The scope of information required to analyze each core content planning area of a client's financial status is broad and deep. Quantitative and qualitative data as well as legislative, tax, political, and economic environmental factors that could affect a client's current or future situation are collected. Information on lifestyle, occupation, medical history, temperament, attitudes, values, goals, financial knowledge and experience, and data gleaned from discovery meetings and data collection efforts are considered relative to each core content area. Additionally, mutually agreed-upon personal and core content area assumptions must be clearly identified to guide analysis. Finally, all data are analyzed to begin to answer the seven questions of who, what, when, where, how, and how much that are critical to Steps 3 through 6 of the systematic financial planning process.

3. Savings, insurance, and investment products and their unique characteristics are the focus of product strategies, which may be limited to one (i.e., a Coverdale Education Savings Account) core content planning area or applicable to several (i.e., an index mutual fund). Procedural strategies focus on a process, assumption, service, or type of titling or ownership. A *product strategy* to fund a specific § 529 savings plan could be modified by *procedural strategies* related to plan investments, funding strategies, or the assumptions on which the analysis of the cost of education and funding needs is based. Examples provided in this chapter help students and novice planners expand their catalog of products and product and procedural strategies.

4. Step 3: Analyze and Evaluate the Client's Financial Status, as presented in the systematic financial planning process, encompasses CFP Board Practice Standards from both the 300 and 400 Series. Together these three Practice Standards parallel the three substeps of Step 3, as explained in this chapter. The ethical Principles of Objectivity, Competence, and Diligence are identified as particularly relevant to all three of these Practice Standards, whereas the Principle of Professionalism is cited with both 400-Series Practice Standards related to financial planning alternatives and recommendations. The *Rules of Conduct* require professionals (1) to be forthright with clients regarding professional qualifications; (2) to place the interests of clients first, and when applicable to provide a fiduciary standard of care; (3) to recommend or implement only suitable recommendations; (4) to exhibit fairness, integrity, and objectivity; and (5) to exercise professional judgment. Together, the *Code of Ethics* and the *Rules of Conduct*

promote unbiased ethical professional conduct when analyzing a client situation and recommending actions that are suitably matched to a client and in the client's best interest.

5. Ideally, the development of a comprehensive plan is the culmination and integration of the cash flow orientation to planning and the goal orientation to planning. From these foundations, a planner must ascertain that all necessary recommendations are identified and prioritized, that their potential effects have been considered, and, finally, that they are affordable. Several forms are introduced to facilitate this analysis and the development of logically consistent, thorough, clear, and feasible plans.

6. Few clients have sufficient income or assets to fully fund all of their goals or planning needs. Several options are available to planner and client, and they can be grouped around the themes of scope, timing, and funding. The scope and timing of recommendations focuses on funding the most important one(s) immediately, staggering their funding based on priority, eliminating or postponing others, and reducing or only partially funding some recommendations. Clients also have the option to increase funding or "substitute" for funding by choosing alternatives that satisfy multiple recommendations. Investing in a Roth IRA or a 401(k) plan funds the retirement goal. But if necessary, funds can be withdrawn without penalty (taxes may be due) from the Roth account *or* a 401(k) loan can be used to fund education. Although tax-advantaged accounts are preferred, a nonqualified account offers flexibility for funding or supplementing the funding of different goals.

7. Some recommendations (e.g., changing a beneficiary or titling an account as POD or TOD) can be implemented for free, but typically this is not the case. Most implementation actions precipitate a change in discretionary income, net worth, or both—either immediately or in the future. As shown in Table 7.5, some actions cause an inverse change in cash flow and net worth, whereas other actions affect cash flow but have no measurable effect on net worth. Understanding these relationships and their implications for the client can help a planner and client consider multiple factors when choosing the most effective recommendation(s).

8. The successful presentation of a plan to a client is built on knowledge of the plan (the analysis, the product and procedural strategies that form the recommendations, and the methods for implementation and monitoring) and the client (what will bring pride, satisfaction, or meaning to a client's life). Without this fundamental knowledge, confidence and trust in the advisor-client planning process other techniques are likely to be ineffective. However, recommended guidelines for successful presentations focus on empathetic, engaging communication skills; the timing of the presentation; implementation that is respectful of the client; and realistic planner and client expectations with regard to outcomes.

9. Step 4: Develop the Comprehensive Plan and Present the Recommendations, as presented in the systematic financial planning process, corresponds to only one CFP Board Practice Standard: 400-3: Presenting the Financial Planning Recommendations. The ethical Principles of Integrity, Objectivity, and Professionalism are identified as particularly relevant when making honest, candid presentations to clients that do not take advantage of the trust-based advisor-client relationship. This is the only Practice Standard where the Board specifically addresses the Principle of Integrity. The *Rules of Conduct* establish requirements for transparency in

communicating professional qualifications and client benefits: to provide services with integrity and objectivity; to practice sensible professional judgment; and to limit services to recommendations that are suitable for the client.

10 Holistic judgment requires a professional to develop the knowledge, intuition, and critical thinking skills to propose resolutions or make decisions based on a wide-ranging survey of the problem or issue. The systematic approach to planning promotes the repeated use of planning forms and protocols to guide and document the planning process. Repeated use of the method results in the development of the professional, or holistic, judgment that no longer requires dependence on forms, except when facing an unusual or complex scenario. Triangulation requires a planner to continually challenge a proposed resolution or decision from different—typically three—perspectives. All three approaches are useful when analyzing a client situation and developing a plan, because they promote the critical thinking, evaluation, and synthesis skills necessary to develop a comprehensive, integrated plan matched to client needs.

Chapter Resources

CFP Board's Standards of Professional Conduct. Available at http://www.cfp.net/Downloads/2010Standards.pdf.

Freedman, M. S. *Oversold and Underserved: A Financial Planner's Guidebook to Effectively Serving The Mass Affluent.* Denver, CO: FPA Press, 2008.

Richards, C. *The Behavior Gap: Simple Ways to Stop Doing Dumb Things with Money.* New York: Portfolio/Penguin, 2012.

Discussion Questions

1. Analysis of the client's current situation involves four substeps. Explain and apply each step to a specific retirement goal that you identify. Be sure to identify both core content planning and client-specific assumptions.

2. How do the seven questions of who, what, when, where, why, how, and how much guide the analysis of the current situation, the review of prospective strategies, and the development of recommendations?

3. Identify three to five corresponding product and procedural strategies.

4. Using the *CFP Board's Standards of Professional Conduct*, available at http://www.cfp.net/Downloads/2010Standards.pdf or http://www.cfp.net/learn/rulesofconduct.asp review *Code of*

Conduct Rule 4.2, explain this rule in the context of the complexity of products, product strategies, and procedural strategies. How does "thinking outside of the box" relate to the requirement for competency and the *Code of Ethics* Principle of Competency?

5. Why is it important that financial planners be aware of their own limitations and planning prejudices when developing financial planning solutions for a client?

6. For a financial planning goal of your choice, identify one to two specific example of each of the factors shown in Figure 7.2 and explain how those factors influence strategies (both product and procedural) and the resultant recommendation.

7. Based on the seven questions that all financial planning recommendations address, write a recommendation for a client goal or need of your choice. Complete the Planning Recommendation Form (Exhibit 7.2) and identify the information that answers the seven questions. How could the answer to the "who" question apply to the planner, the client, neither, or both?

8. Explain the five characteristics that describe a well-designed financial plan.

9. Why should a financial advisor conduct an impact analysis as part of the transition from formulation of recommendations to development of a comprehensive plan? Explain the benefit of the Recommendation Impact Form (Exhibit 7.6) to Jane and the Kims.

10. What issues or considerations must be integrated into the development of a comprehensive plan? Compare and contrast this to the development of a modular plan.

11. `Why is it important to consider the affordability of a recommendation from the perspectives of alternative options for funding the recommendation and the impact of that action on DCF and net worth?

12. List and summarize the five most important strategies for making an effective plan presentation. Defend your choice of those strategies. Why are communication techniques so important when presenting a plan?

13. What interactions might be identified through cross-planning analysis? Provide an example of an interaction and explain how it might affect a client's situation and planning outcome. What might have been the outcome had the interaction been ignored?

14. Explain CFP Board expectations for ethical conduct when presenting financial planning recommendations or a plan to a client.

15. Define triangulation. What purpose does it serve when conceptualizing financial recommendations? How else might it be useful throughout the financial planning process?

Notes

1.   The Tax Foundation. *Federal Individual Income Tax Rates History, Nominal Dollars*, Income Years 1913–2011. Available at http://taxfoundation.org/sites/taxfoundation.org/files/docs/fed_individual_rate_history_ nominal%26adjusted-20110909.pdf.

2.   Certified Financial Planner Board of Standards, Inc., *CFP Board's Standards of Professional Conduct*. Available at http:// www.cfp.net/Downloads/2010Standards.pdf, p. 21; or at http://www.cfp.net/learn/standards300.asp.

3.   *CFP Board, Standards of Professional Conduct*, p. 7; or at http://www.cfp.net/learn/codeofethics.asp.

4.   *CFP Board, Standards of Professional Conduct*, p. 11; or at http://www.cfp.net/learn/rulesofconduct.asp.

5.   *Business Week*, "At Your Service: Therapy with Your Latte? It's My Job," *Business Week* (October 24, 2005): 16.

6.   E. P. Morrow, "Presenting the Financial Plan," *Financial Planning* (October, 2001): 176.

7.   *CFP Board, Standards of Professional Conduct*. Available at http://www.cfp.net/Downloads/2010Standards.pdf, p. 6; or at http://www.cfp.net/learn/codeofethics.asp.

8.   *CFP Board, Standards of Professional Conduct*. Available at http://www.cfp.net/Downloads/2010Standards.pdf, p. 11; or at http://www.cfp.net/learn/rulesofconduct.asp.

9.   J. Ruscio, "Holistic Judgment in Clinical Practice," *The Scientific Review of Mental Health Practice* 2 (1): Available at http://www.srmhp.org/0201/holistic.html.

10. M. J. Roszkowski and J. Grable "Estimating Risk Tolerance: The Degree of Accuracy and the Paramorphic Representations of the Estimate." *Financial Counseling and Planning* 16, No. 1 (2005): 29–47.

Select Examples of Issues Analyzed in the Client's Situation in Each of the Core Financial Planning Content Areas

Financial Planning Core Content Area	Determine Planning Needs	Document Current Planning Assumptions	Quantify Planning Needs	Document and Evaluate Current Planning Efforts

Cash flow planning or "financial situation"	• Attitudes about debt
	• Availability of emergency fund
	• Goal commitment
	• Potential career, income, and/or asset changes
		• Interest rate changes
		• Asset and liability acquisition
		• Job security
			• Review of
			  o income statement
			  o balance sheet
			  o financial ratios
			  o net worth
			  o short- and long-term debt
				• Uses of debt
				• Discretionary cash flow
				• Cash management system
				• Current/future financial needs and goals

Income tax planning	• Attitudes about tax
	  o tax payments
	  o charitable giving
	  o tax reduction strategies
	  o audits
		• Marginal tax bracket
		• AMT triggers
		• Changes in the tax code
			• Project current tax liability
			• Identify possible implications from other planning issues
				• Review past tax returns
				• Review current employer withholdings or estimated tax payments

Financial Planning Core Content Area	Determine Planning Needs	Document Current Planning Assumptions	Quantify Planning Needs	Document and Evaluate Current Planning Efforts

Life insurance planning	• Need for
	  o dependent income
	  o liability mitigation
	  o small business continuation
	  o estate planning
	  o charitable giving
	• Potential beneficiaries
		• Client's life span (age at death)
		• Spouse or other financial dependents' life spans
			• Human life value approach
			• Capital retention approach
			• Income retention approach
			• Income multiplier approach
			• Needs analysis approach
				• Amount of current coverage
				• Product review
				  o provider quality/rating
				  o fees and expenses
				  o past performance
				• Annual price per thousand
				• Ownership and beneficiary designations

Health insurance planning	• Family health status
	• Pre-existing conditions
	• Couple/partner issues
	• Self-employment issues
		• Life cycle events
		  o young adult
		  o retirement
		  o Medicare/Medigap
		• Health care inflation rate
		• Family health history
			• Savings to meet deductibles or copays
			• Stop-loss limit
			• Coverage limits
				• Employer-provided
				• Individual or group policy
				• Product review
				  o provider quality/rating
				  o cost
				  o amount of coverage

Disability insurance planning	• Leave available
	  o medical
	  o personal/vacation
	• Savings available
	• Partner/spouse income
	• Risk tolerance
	• Occupation
	• Caregiver availability
	• Self-employment issues
	• Occupational hazards
		• Projected
		  o severity
		  o length
		• Eligibility for Social Security disability benefits
		• Family Medical Leave Act eligibility
			• Short-term need
			• Long-term need
			• Need during any gap in coverage
				• Employer-provided
				• Individual or group policy
				• Tax status of benefits
				• Product review
				  o provider quality/rating
				  o fees and expenses
				  o amount of coverage
				  o definition of disability

Financial Planning Core Content Area	Determine Planning Needs	Document Current Planning Assumptions	Quantify Planning Needs	Document and Evaluate Current Planning Efforts

Long-term care insurance planning	• Current or family health history
	• Attitudes
	  o care giving
	  o caregivers
	  o charitable giving
	• Lifestyle choices
	• Occupational hazards
		• Health care inflation rate
		• Family health history
		• Client's life span (age at death)
		• Spouse or other financial dependents' life spans
		• Care preferences and providers
			• Review current and projected net worth
			  o < $250,000
			  o $250,000–$1.5M
			  o > $1.5 M
				• Employer-provided
				• Individual or group policy
				• Long-term care or hybrid product
				• Product review
				  o provider quality/ rating
				  o fees and expenses
				  o amount of coverage

Property & liability insurance planning	• Maximum, probable, and typical loss exposure
	• Extended replacement cost endorsement
	• Building code upgrade endorsement
	• Other endorsements
		• Real and/or personal asset acquisition
		• Replacement cost
		• 80% coverage rule
			• Assets—real and financial
			• Location of property
			• Potential liability exposure
			• Need for
			  o GAP
			  o endorsements, riders, extensions
			  o excess liability
				• Excess liability/ umbrella coverage
				• Coverage needs matched to assets
				• Deductible amounts
				• Product review:
				  o provider quality/ rating
				  o cost
				  o amount of coverage

Investment & asset management planning	• Risk tolerance
	• Knowledge and experience
	• Time horizon
	• Risk capacity
	• Satisfaction with investments
		• Expectations of market conditions
		  o interest rate changes
		  o inflation rate
		  o financial markets
		  o currency valuation
		• Marginal tax bracket
		• Projected returns
			• Current and projected cost of goals
			• Required rates of return
			• Asset allocation
				• Asset allocation and portfolio statistics relative to index
				• Sensitivity analysis
				• Rebalancing
				• Product review
				  o provider quality/ rating
				  o fees and expenses
				  o past performance

Financial Planning Core Content Area	Determine Planning Needs	Document Current Planning Assumptions	Quantify Planning Needs	Document and Evaluate Current Planning Efforts
Education planning	• Projected education needs— grade school, secondary, or post-secondary (technical, college, graduate/ professional) • Attitudes (who pays for post-secondary costs, access to funds, control of funds, etc.)	• Duration of education; time to completion • Education inflation rate • Financial aid availability and cost • Access to academic, athletic, or other scholarships	• Estimate future education costs	• Current taxable and tax-advantaged accounts • Investments • Asset allocation • Asset ownership
Retirement planning	• Early, typical, delayed retirement • Early and post-retirement lifestyle • Retirement issues (e.g., attitudes, health, employment, etc.)	• Eligibility for Social Security disability and/ or retirement benefits • Life span, years in retirement • Retirement lifestyle	• Asset allocation • Capital depletion approach • Capital preservation approach • Inflation-adjusted approach	• Projected need vs. savings • Investment types • Use of employer-provided retirement accounts • Other qualified and nonqualified accounts • Beneficiary designations

Estate planning	• Estate tax attitudes
	 • Family and charitable gifting attitudes
	 • Small business continuation
	 • Legacy issues
	 • Guardianship appointment for children or other financial dependents
	 • Recent family changes (e.g., birth, death, marriage, divorce, etc.)
		• Client's life span (age at death)
		 • Spouse or other financial dependents' life spans
		 • Changes in tax code
			• Projected taxable estate value
			 • Use of unlimited marital transfer
				• Current estate planning documents
				   ○ wills
				   ○ letters of instruction
				   ○ power of attorney
				   ○ advance medical directives
				 • Ownership issues
				 • Trusts (living and testamentary)
				 • Gifting

Products and Product Features for Identifying Strategies

Product or Product Feature	Potential Role of Product or Service in the Financial Planning Process X = Product or Service Impact in Core Planning Content Area						
	Financial Situation Planning	Income Tax Planning	Risk Management	Investment Planning	Education Planning	Retirement Planning	Estate Planning
§ 1035 Exchange		X	X	X		X	X
§ 2503 (b) & (c) accounts		X		X	X		X
§ 529 Plan					X		X
Advance medical directive (AMD)			X				X
Alternative investments		X		X			
Annual gifting	X	X		X	X		X
Annuities							
Fixed	X	X	X	X	X	X	X
Variable	X	X	X	X	X	X	X
Bonds							
Corporate				X			
Government agency		X		X			
Junk				X			
Municipal		X		X			
Treasury		X		X			

Product or Product Feature	Potential Role of Product or Service in the Financial Planning Process — X = Product or Service Impact in Core Planning Content Area						
	Financial Situation Planning	Income Tax Planning	Risk Management	Investment Planning	Education Planning	Retirement Planning	Estate Planning
Buy/sell agreement	X	X	X			X	X
Certificate of deposit (CD)	X	X		X		X	
COBRA provision			X				
Collectibles			X	X			
Commodities		X		X			
Coverdell Education Savings Account		X			X		X
Credit cards	X						
Critical illness insurance			X				
Disability insurance		X	X			X	
Donor-advised fund		X					X
Family limited partnership		X					X
Flexible spending account (FSA)							
Dependent care	X	X					
Health care	X	X	X				
Hard assets				X			
Health insurance			X				
Health savings account (HSA)	X	X	X			X	
High-deductible health plan (HDHP)	X		X				
Home equity line of credit	X	X					
Home equity loan	X	X					
Homestead exemption			X				X
Individual retirement account (IRA)							
Roth		X		X	X	X	
Traditional		X		X	X	X	
Letter of last instructions							X
Life insurance							
Term			X				X
Universal			X				X
Variable			X	X			X

Product or Product Feature	Potential Role of Product or Service in the Financial Planning Process						
	X = Product or Service Impact in Core Planning Content Area						
	Financial Situation Planning	Income Tax Planning	Risk Management	Investment Planning	Education Planning	Retirement Planning	Estate Planning
Variable universal life (VUL)			X	X	X	X	X
Whole-life/cash value			X				X
Life settlement	X	X	X				X
Living will							X
Long-term care (LTC) insurance							
LTC	X		X			X	X
LTC with life hybrid	X		X			X	X
LTC with annuity hybrid	X		X			X	X
Medicaid			X			X	X
Medical savings account (MSA)		X	X	X			
Medicare			X			X	
Medigap insurance			X			X	
Money market deposit accounts (MMDA)	X			X			
Mortgages							
Conventional	X	X					
Interest-only	X	X					
Refinance	X	X		X			
Reverse mortgage	X	X		X		X	X
Shared appreciation	X	X		X			
Mutual funds							
Bond	X	X		X			
Commodity				X			
Foreign/global/international				X			
Money market	X			X			
Real estate				X			
Stock				X			
Nonqualified retirement plan		X				X	
Options and futures				X			
Pooled-income fund		X				X	X

Product or Product Feature	Potential Role of Product or Service in the Financial Planning Process X = Product or Service Impact in Core Planning Content Area						
	Financial Situation Planning	Income Tax Planning	Risk Management	Investment Planning	Education Planning	Retirement Planning	Estate Planning
Power of attorney (POA)							
Durable POA	X						X
General POA	X						X
Medical POA	X						X
Property & casualty insurance							
Boat insurance			X				
Personal automobile insurance			X				
Earthquake insurance			X				
Flood insurance			X				
Guaranteed auto protection (GAP) insurance			X				
Homeowner's insurance			X				
Personal articles policy			X				
Personal automobile insurance			X				
Umbrella, or excess liability, insurance			X				
Qualified retirement plan		X		X		X	
Real estate		X		X		X	
Real estate investment trusts (REITs)							
Savings account	X			X			
Savings bonds (E/EE/H/I)[1]		X		X	X		
Scholarships and grants		X			X		
Social Security benefits							
Retirement		X		X		X	
Survivor/disability		X	X	X		X	
Stock							
Domestic			X			X	
Foreign			X			X	

Product or Product Feature	Potential Role of Product or Service in the Financial Planning Process X = Product or Service Impact in Core Planning Content Area						
	Financial Situation Planning	Income Tax Planning	Risk Management	Investment Planning	Education Planning	Retirement Planning	Estate Planning
Stock Options							
Incentive stock options		X		X		X	
Nonqualified stock options		X		X		X	
Qualified stock options		X		X		X	
Tax credits	X	X			X		X
Titling							
Payable on death (POD)		X					X
Transfer on death (TOD)		X		X			X
Trust							
A/B trust		X					X
Charitable lead trust		X					X
Charitable remainder annuity trust (CRAT)	X	X				X	X
Charitable remainder unitrust (CRUT)	X	X				X	X
Grantor retained annuity trust (GRAT)	X	X					X
Grantor retained unitrust (GRUT)	X	X					X
Irrevocable trust		X					X
Irrevocable life insurance trust (ILIT)			X				X
Intervivos or living trust		X					X
Qualified personal residence trust (Q-PRT)	X	X				X	X
Qualified terminal interest property (Q-TIP) trust	X	X					X
Revocable or living trust		X					X
Spousal limited access trust (SLAT)	X	X					X
Testamentary trust		X					X
Uniform Gifts to Minors Account Act (UGMA) account		X		X	X		X
Uniform Transfers to Minors Act account (UTMA)		X		X	X		X

Product or Product Feature	Potential Role of Product or Service in the Financial Planning Process X = Product or Service Impact in Core Planning Content Area						
	Financial Situation Planning	Income Tax Planning	Risk Management	Investment Planning	Education Planning	Retirement Planning	Estate Planning
Unsecured line of credit	X	X					
Viatical settlement			X				X
Will							X

1. The U.S. Department of the Treasury, Bureau of Public Debt, no longer issues Series E, Series HH, and Patriot Bonds; however, these bonds are still held by the investing public.

Comprehensive Planning Checklist

Comprehensive Planning Checklist for _____

Cash Flow Analysis to Maximize Client's Discretionary Cash Flow			Recommendation Needed?	
1. Has planner reviewed financial ratios and compared them to benchmarks?	Yes	No	Yes	No
2. Have steps been taken to designate savings or other assets for use as an emergency fund or source of emergency income?	Yes	No	Yes	No
3. Has planner reviewed client budget or income and expense statement for possible expense reductions?	Yes	No	Yes	No
4. Has planner verified that the client is able and willing to proactively save money on a regular basis?	Yes	No	Yes	No
5. Have debt reduction or debt restructuring alternatives been reviewed?	Yes	No	Yes	No
6. Have mortgage refinancing alternatives been reviewed?	Yes	No	Yes	No
7. Are there other client-specific cash management issues to consider?	Yes	No	Yes	No

Tax Analysis to Minimize Taxes and Maximize Client's Discretionary Cash Flow			Recommendation Needed?	
8. Have tax projections for 1, 3, or 5 years been done to guide the planning process?	Yes	No	Yes	No
9. Has client income tax withholding been matched to tax liability?	Yes	No	Yes	No
10. Has client FICA withholding been matched to FICA liabilities?	Yes	No	Yes	No
11. Has planner reviewed client's tax situation to ensure that other tax-reduction opportunities have not been overlooked?	Yes	No	Yes	No
12. Is the client currently subject to the AMT? Have projections been made for the next 1, 3, or 5 years?	Yes	No	Yes	No

13. Has planner checked to determine whether client is maximizing tax-reducing insurance alternatives?				
a. Health flexible spending account?	Yes	No	Yes	No
b. Dependent care flexible spending account?	Yes	No	Yes	No
c. Employer provided life, health, disability, or LTC benefits?	Yes	No	Yes	No
d. Any other § 125 cafeteria plan benefits?	Yes	No	Yes	No
14. Are there other client-specific tax management issues to consider?	Yes	No	Yes	No

Insurance Analysis to Limit Client's Household Risk Exposures			Recommendation Needed?	
15. Has a life insurance analysis been conducted?	Yes	No	Yes	No
16. Has a disability insurance analysis been conducted?	Yes	No	Yes	No
17. Has a long-term care (LTC) insurance analysis been conducted?	Yes	No	Yes	No
18. Has a health insurance analysis been conducted?	Yes	No	Yes	No
19. Has a property, casualty, and liability insurance analysis been conducted?	Yes	No	Yes	No
20. Are there other client-specific risk management issues to consider?	Yes	No	Yes	No

Investment Planning Analysis to Maximize Client's Return			Recommendation Needed?	
21. Has an investment funding goal been identified?	Yes	No	Yes	No
22. Is the client on track to meet the targeted amount and date?	Yes	No	Yes	No
23. Are asset allocation and investments suitable given the client's time horizon, risk tolerance, and other assumptions?	Yes	No	Yes	No
24. Is the client fully benefiting from tax-advantaged investments?	Yes	No	Yes	No
25. Are there other client-specific investment planning issues to consider?	Yes	No	Yes	No

Education or Special Needs Planning Analysis to Maximize Client's Return			Recommendation Needed?	
26. Has an education funding goal been identified?	Yes	No	Yes	No
27. Is the client on track to meet the targeted amount and date?	Yes	No	Yes	No
28. Are asset allocation and investments suitable given the client's time horizon, risk tolerance, and other assumptions?	Yes	No	Yes	No
29. Is the client fully benefiting from tax-advantaged accounts?	Yes	No	Yes	No
30. Are there other client-specific education planning issues to consider?	Yes	No	Yes	No
31. Has a special needs funding goal(s) been identified? Is the client on track to meet the targeted amount(s) and date(s)?	Yes	No	Yes	No

32. Are asset allocation and investments suitable given the client's time horizon, risk tolerance, and other assumptions?	Yes	No	Yes	No
33. Are there other client-specific special needs planning issues to consider?	Yes	No	Yes	No

Retirement Planning Analysis to Maximize Client's Return			**Recommendation Needed?**	
34. Has a retirement funding goal been identified?	Yes	No	Yes	No
35. Is the client on track to meet the targeted amount and date?	Yes	No	Yes	No
36. Are asset allocation and investments suitable given the client's time horizon, risk tolerance, and other assumptions?	Yes	No	Yes	No
37. Is the client fully benefiting from any available match?	Yes	No	Yes	No
38. Is the client fully benefiting from tax-advantaged accounts?				
39. Are other retirement funds available?	Yes	No	Yes	No
40. Are there other client-specific retirement planning issues to consider?	Yes	No	Yes	No

Estate Planning Analysis to Minimize Estate Taxes and Ensure Client's Final Wishes			**Recommendation Needed?**	
41. Has the client begun giving assets to dependents, other family members, or charity?	Yes	No	Yes	No
42. Are documents in place to distribute property and provide for dependents, heirs, or charities?	Yes	No	Yes	No
43. Have steps been taken to minimize probate, estate, or inheritance taxes?	Yes	No	Yes	No
44. Have steps been taken to minimize settlement costs, including legal and accounting fees?	Yes	No	Yes	No
45. Are funds available, or plans in place, for the payment of estate taxes and settlement expenses?	Yes	No	Yes	No
46. Are documents in place to guide incapacitation or other end-of-life decisions?	Yes	No	Yes	No
47. Are documents in place to care for, or name guardians for, children or other financial dependents?	Yes	No	Yes	No
48. Are documents in place to care for a pet, if applicable?	Yes	No	Yes	No
49. Has a letter of last instructions been prepared to provide for the distribution of personal and digital assets (i.e. accounts, music, pictures, etc.) as well as other final wishes?	Yes	No	Yes	No
50. Are there other client-specific estate planning issues to consider?	Yes	No	Yes	No

Cross-planning Analysis: Have the Following Interactions Been Considered?			Recommendation Needed?	
51. Net worth ⇔ insurance?	Yes	No	Yes	No
52. Income taxes ⇔ insurance?				
a. Health flexible spending accounts?	Yes	No	Yes	No
b. Dependent care flexible spending accounts?	Yes	No	Yes	No
c. Employer-provided life, health, disability, and LTC benefits?	Yes	No	Yes	No
53. Income taxes ⇔ mortgage refinance?	Yes	No	Yes	No
54. Life insurance ⇔ estate planning?	Yes	No	Yes	No
55. Life/LTC hybrid ⇔ life insurance?	Yes	No	Yes	No
56. LTC ⇔ estate planning?	Yes	No	Yes	No
57. Education funding ⇔ estate planning?	Yes	No	Yes	No
58. Education funding ⇔ income tax planning?	Yes	No	Yes	No
59. Investment planning ⇔ income tax planning?	Yes	No	Yes	No
60. Retirement planning ⇔ income tax planning?	Yes	No	Yes	No

Chapter 8

Implementing and Monitoring the Plan

Learning Objectives

1. Describe the scope of responsibilities involved in plan implementation.

2. Know the use and purpose of professional referrals.

3. Recognize and explain the significance of timing on plan implementation and client motivation.

4. Identify strategies that can be used to motivate client action.

5. Demonstrate how to use an Implementation Checklist.

6. Explain and apply the CFP Board requirements for ethical professsional conduct relative to Step 5 of the systematic financial planning process.

7. Describe the scope of responsibilities involved in monitoring the plan.

8. Explain why monitoring is such an important step in the financial planning process.

9. Explain and apply the CFP Board requirements for ethical professsional conduct relative to Step 6 of the systematic financial planning process.

10. Explain how financial planning may appear to be a linear process, but it is really a recursive or circular process when applied to a discreet core content area, comprehensive plan development, and the maintainence of the planner-client relationship over time.

Key Terms

Fee disclosure

Fiduciary liability

Implementation

Implementation Checklist

Liability release form or waiver

Monitoring

Referral network

Strategic alliance

To-do list

Figure 8.1 The Systematic Financial Planning Process

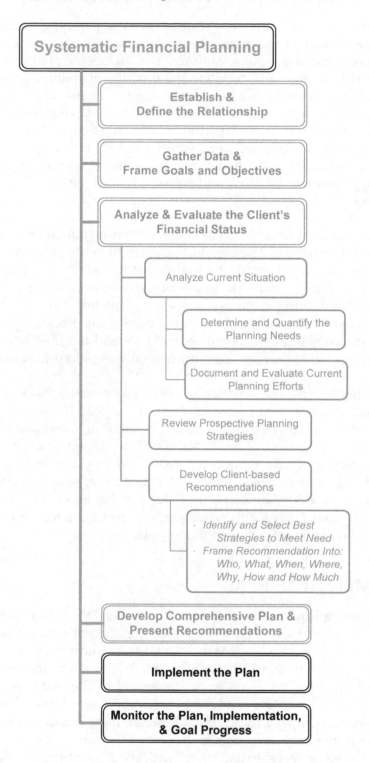

INTEGRATIVE IMPLEMENTATION AND MONITORING

In response to the question, "What is financial planning?" Chapter 1 introduced the idea that financial planning is a profession, a process, and a product. Subsequent chapters have more fully explored how financial planning can be framed as a deliverable *service*—advice on life and financial planning issues, or a *product*—discrete financial instruments or a modular or comprehensive financial plan. Consistent with this variety is an assortment of business models and compensation methods. The three preceding chapters are built on the premise that financial planning could, and should, be guided by a systematic process or method. However, the diversity of business models and deliverables that comprise financial planning is perhaps most evident in Step 5: Implement the Plan, and Step 6: Monitor the Plan, Implementation, and Goal Progress.

It is easy to think that simply because a recommendation has been made that, first, it will be implemented, and second, it will result in the outcomes anticipated. Although this may be true, it would be imprudent to believe that clients always implement recommendations and that an advisor's recommendations always work according to plan. Monitoring client outcomes is one method to ensure that recommendations actually work to help clients meet financial goals. Recall that the implementation of every recommendation should be explicitly and thoroughly explained as part of the plan presented to the client before any implementation efforts are actually undertaken.

As the final chapter in the discussion of the systematic financial planning process, this chapter serves several purposes. First, it explores the responsibilities and activities accomplished in Steps 5 and 6 of the systematic financial planning process, illustrated in Figure 8.1. Second, it reviews the CFP Board explanation of these steps and the ethical professsional conduct expected. Third, this chapter introduces the concept that this process is recursive, despite the fact that the systematic financial planning process is illustrated and, in some instances, described as linear. Finally, the chapter concludes with Tom and Nyla Kim's reflections on implementaion and monitoring after their first annual review meeting with their planner Jane.

STEP 5: IMPLEMENT THE PLAN

Implementation means putting a recommendation into action. Offering realistic recommendations is essential for meeting a client's financial goals and objectives. Without a thorough, defensible, and easily understood description of how each recommendation should be implemented, it is likely that some clients will fail to implement them—or even to be convinced of the need or appropriateness of the recommendations. Some advisors argue that providing clients with a reasonable implementation plan could, in fact, be the most important part of a financial plan. Often, implementation entails buying a product from the advisor or another professional or transferring assets, with the help of the advisor, to a new custodian to then be managed by the advisor. For other planners, and their chosen business model, selling a specific product or managing assets is simply not part of the service offered to clients. Some planners sell only their advice, after which the client must take responsibility for implementing the advisor's recommendations. Although the definition of implementation may appear straightforward—putting a recommendation into action—the complexity of business models can make the actions involved quite dissimilar, even when implementing the same recommendation for different clients.

The CFP Board requires CFP® certificants to work with clients to establish mutually agreed-upon implementation responsibilities. According to the CFP Board's explanation of Practice Standard 500-1: Agreeing on Implementation Responsibilities, the client is:

> ...responsible for accepting or rejecting recommendations and for retaining and/or delegating implementation responsibilities. The financial planning practitioner and the client shall mutually agree on the services, if any, to be provided by the practitioner. The scope of the engagement, as originally defined, may need to be modified. The practitioner's responsibilities may include, but are not limited to the following:
>
> - Identifying activities necessary for implementation;
>
> - Determining the division of activities between the practitioner and the client;
>
> - Referring to other professionals;
>
> - Coordinating with other professionals;
>
> - Sharing information as authorized; and
>
> - Selecting and securing products and/or services.[1]

The complexities and range of responsibilities involved in the execution of Step 5 provide additional support for why it is so important that every recommendation fully answer the seven questions *who, what, when, where, why, how,* and *how much.* Attention to these questions provides a standard protocol to ensure that recommendations are well conceived and that Steps 3 through 6 of the planning process are well integrated. With a reliable framework as guide, attention can be turned to how these questions frame the implementation of a plan.

Who Should Implement the Recommendation? What Should Be Done? Where Should It Be Done?

Once a planner ensures that a client approves of a plan, the implementation step begins. A recommendation is only as good as the planner's, client's, or other professionals' ability to implement the recommendation effectively, whether working together or independently. In the simplest terms, *who* will do *what,* and *where* should it be done? Plan implementation approaches vary among planners and perhaps even among clients served by the same planner depending on the planner's business model and the products or services offered. Some advisors assume most, if not all, responsibility for carrying out the various aspects of a plan (assuming such authority is granted) and request little assistance from the client. Other planners educate or assist, but the client has primary responsibility for executing some or all of the recommendations.

Some recommendations may require clients to work with professionals with whom they have existing relationships (e.g., insurance agent, broker, banker), and other recommendations require the forging of new relationships. Planners often consider themselves the hub of a wagon wheel as they facilitate plan implementation in collaboration with the client and multiple other parties (e.g., the client's accountant, attorney, trust administrator, or personal assistant).

Professional referrals have a considerable impact on the way some financial planning recommendations are implemented. For example, unless a financial planner is also a licensed attorney, the planner cannot draft legal documents or qualified retirement plan documents. In some instances, even as a licensed attorney the advisor may be limited by broker-dealer or other employer restrictions from "practicing law." Consequently, if there is a need for new or revised legal documents, a planner's role may be to:

- make the recommendation and let the client take responsibility for engaging an attorney, whether an existing or new professional relationship;

- provide the client with a list of qualified attorneys whose practice and personality match the client's needs, based on the advisor's broader knowledge of the client's situation and professional colleagues; or

- refer the client to an attorney within the advisor's referral network or strategic alliance.

Contingent on the planner-client-attorney relationship, the planner could serve as an intermediary between the client and the attorney primarily to facilitate the conversation. For example, the planner knows and can quickly share relevant information that might be useful to the attorney. Conversely, the planner's knowledge can be a source of questions that will benefit and inform the client, who may not know what to ask the attorney or might feel uncomfortable doing so.

A **referral network**—a more informal network for making client referrals, or a **strategic alliance**—a more structured collaboration among allied professionals to serve clients, are often used to facilitate plan implementation. Although the number and mixture of professionals varies, typical examples include certified public accountants (CPAs), enrolled agents (EAs), attorneys (e.g., estate planning, divorce, personal injury), trust officers, charitable giving specialists, brokers, money/wealth managers, insurance professionals, psychologists, money therapists, and mortgage or real estate brokers. Providing easy and convenient access to a professional is one way to help a client move from recognizing that action is needed to actually implementing recommendations. If referrals are made, clients must be notified if fees or other forms of compensation are shared among the planner and the referred professionals. The CFP Board explanation of this practice standard states that:

> If there are conflicts of interest, sources of compensation or material relationships with other professionals or advisers that have not been previously disclosed, such conflicts, sources or relationships shall be disclosed at this time.

> When referring the client to other professionals or advisers, the financial planning practitioner shall indicate the basis on which the practitioner believes the other professional or adviser may be qualified.[2]

Professional referral networks are one way to benefit both clients and their advisors, so long as there is full **fee disclosure**, coupled with full disclosure of any conflicts of interest (e.g., Accountant A is part of the network, Accountant B is not). The planner benefits from increased revenues from shared clients, but more importantly both planner and clients benefit from a group of like-minded professionals who can collaborate and contribute to the mission of serving clients well. Each professional can play an important role in helping clients implement financial planning recommendations, because both advisor and client are assured of the provider's professionalism in meeting client objectives.

In conjunction with the question of *who* are the issues of *what* and *where*. The latter may refer, literally, to the place a client must go to access a product or service recommendation (e.g., URL, mailing address). *What* represents the variety of traditional insurance, investment, retirement, and other ancillary financial planning products and services that emanate from the strategies identified in Step 3 to a wide range of "concierge" services. Some planners provide high-net-worth clients a variety of time- and money-saving services (e.g., to shop and negotiate for transportation or mortgages, or to handle routine bill payment for themselves or other extended family members).

What in this instance may also refer to the client information that can be shared with other professionals? This will depend on the scope of the agreement and the disclosure agreements signed by the client authorizing the advisor to act on the client's behalf. In some instances the client may be the go-between among all of the financial service providers; in other cases the client will sign a disclosure document that allows the financial planner to contact other providers (e.g., tax preparer, lawyer, trust administrator) directly. This can be done simply for convenience, or to reduce delays in plan implementation for a client who is frequently unavailable. Situations like this require the utmost care and trust in the planner-client relationship and the boundaries of such authority must be clearly documented.

Some core content planning areas offer unique implementation challenges that requir careful coordination of responsibilities and attention to the details of *who*, *what*, and *where*. For example, without follow-through an advisor's recommendation to establish a trust may not be fully and successfully executed for the benefit of the client. Bear in mind that the scope of the attorney's work is most likely limited to the preparation of the trust documents. Thus, from the attorney's perspective, the transfer of assets to fund the trust is the client's esponsibility. However, the client may lack the knowledge or time to complete the transfer. Consequently, to avoid a lapse in execution, the planner may have to provide full instructions to the client to facilitate the process or act on behalf of the client to effect the transfer. In either case, someone must be knowledgeable of and responsible for the details necessary to accomplish the advisor's recommendation: to establish and properly fund the trust to accomplish the client's goal. The actual implementation process is contingent on the advisor's expertise, the business model, and the scope of the planner-client engagement.

A more common example, such as implementing health insurance recommendations, presents another challenge. Generally, a planner can execute—or at least facilitate—implementation with most forms of insurance; but because most health insurance plans are employer-provided group health plans, a planner may have limited or no access to them. To further complicate the situation, coverage changes are generally limited to an annual open-enrollment period, unless specific exceptions apply. Consequently, the planner's role may be to urge the client to inform the planner of any company policy changes; to remind the client (by postcard, email, or telephone call) to make necessary changes during the open-enrollment period, or in some cases, to actually implement the change for the client assuming the planner has client-authorized access to the client's accounts.

As these scenarios illustrate, the actual implementation process is contingent on several factors, including the advisor's business model, the advisor's expertise, and the client's expectations. Perhaps most important is the advisor's responsibility, per the agreement, to assist and motivate the client to *act in the client's best interest*.

Why Should It Be Done? When Should the Recommendation Take Place?

Regardless of an advisor's range of products or services or whether the client is solely or partly responsible for implementing recommendations, ultimately implementation rests with the client. Although it is often assumed that clients acting in their own best interest will put plans into action, this is not always the case. The implementation issues of *why* and *when* can be inextricably intertwined. Regardless of the reason for inaction, lack of implementation is the single greatest deterrent to achieving financial goals. Thus, it is imperative that planners take steps to examine, and in some cases supervise or facilitate, the timeliness and progress of client implementation if such responsibilities are part of their business plan and the agreed-upon engagement with the client.

One of an advisor's primary goals is to use the plan and the plan presentation effectively to educate the client on two subjects: (1) *why* the recommendations are viable solutions to the client's concerns; and (2) *when* implementation should occur to best meet the client's objectives in a timely manner. Just because a client pays for a plan, it does not mean the client is motivated to take action. Both the plan and the presentation should clearly communicate to the client that without proper implementation, the capacity to reach long-term financial goals is jeopardized. Therefore, it is essential that a financial planner adopt a proactive position regarding plan implementation.

Two methods to convey differences in implementation to a client are a two-by-two matrix and a timeline. The two-by-two matrix divides goals into four categories. This can be a useful tool for educating and motivating clients regarding timelines that the advisor takes for granted. But it is important that clients realize and commit—both intellectually and personally—to the complexities of implementation. It is equally important to acknowledge that the implementation of a recommendation and the satisfaction of the goal may occur in different time frames, as outlined below:

1. Immediate implementation and immediate completion (e.g., purchasing a single-premium life insurance policy);

2. Immediate implementation and delayed completion (e.g., purchasing a whole-life policy that requires premium payments for decades);

3. Delayed implementation and immediate completion (e.g., using proceeds from a 401(k) liquidation to purchase a guaranteed fixed annuity); or

4. Delayed implementation and delayed completion (e.g., purchasing a hybrid long-term care and life insurance policy between ages 50 and 55).

The meaning of *immediate* or *delayed implementation* is fairly obvious; however, it is not completely transparent. Writing a will, for instance, is a goal that can be immediately completed, regardless of delays in implementation, as clients often postpone action on this recommendation. The idea of immediate completion is that there is very little or no continuous action required to achieve the desired result; it is basically "one and done." Once the initial action has occurred, the recommendation or goal is realized. However, client or marketplace changes could prompt a review or revision of the goal, for example, the need to rewrite or add a codicil to a will. If periodic or continuous action and/or monitoring is needed, then the goal should be categorized as a delayed completion goal. Typically these goals require more commitment and effort on the part of both client and planner to bring to fruition. Figure 8.2 shows a sample matrix that can be used to classify recommendations.

Figure 8.2 Recommendation and Goal Classification Matrix

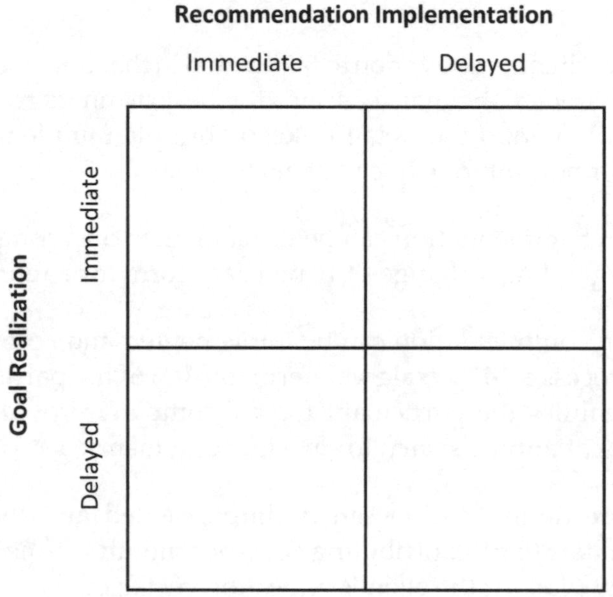

Another method to illustrate some of the complexities surrounding the timing (*when*) of implementation is a timeline. The old adage, "A picture is worth a thousand words," is especially apt for clients who process information visually. For kinesthetic learners, collaborating with an advisor to build the timeline can be a valuable exercise, as discussed in Chapter 3. Exhibit 8.1 graphically demonstrates the concepts of immediate and delayed implementation and offers examples of how goals can be satisfied over different time horizons.

Exhibit 8.1 Recommendation Implementation Timeline

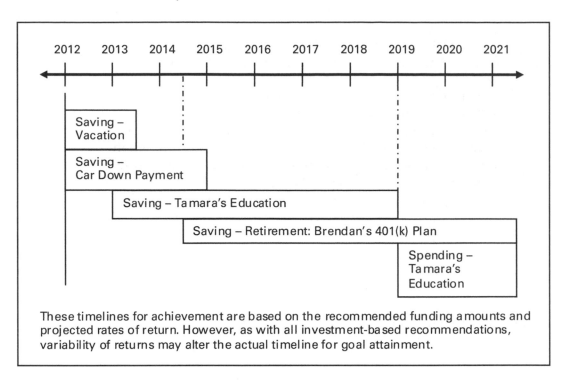

These timelines for achievement are based on the recommended funding amounts and projected rates of return. However, as with all investment-based recommendations, variability of returns may alter the actual timeline for goal attainment.

Maintaining clients' motivation to take action in the short-term as well as over the longer term is a characteristic that separates the best planners from the rest. Furthermore, it takes careful attention to detail to keep both plan implementation and outcomes on track. It is important to help clients realize that:

- a recommendation can be implemented and completed almost immediately (e.g., filing a change-of-beneficiary form for a retirement account);

- a recommendation can be implemented and completed within *60 days* (e.g., process a 401(k) salary deferral of 10% of the participant's gross salary, which qualifies the participant for the company-provided match of an additional 3% of annual salary, to save for retirement);

- a recommendation can be implemented and the goal satisfied within *60 months* (e.g., contributing $500 per month for the next five years to fund a § 529 plan for the client's education costs); or

- a series of recommendations can be implemented over *60 years* or more (e.g., to fund and distribute retirement savings).

An advisor's technical and analytical skills are instrumental in explaining *when* and *why* to a client, but those same skills do not necessarily prepare the advisor to understand or help the client understand *why* the client is choosing *not* to implement. Recall that temperament, personality, beliefs, and attitudes are significant influences in a client's financial life. Some clients will begin to implement recommendations immediately without any nudging based on the belief that they will be rewarded by their progress, the perception of increased control over their financial situation, or other intrinsic or extrinsic factors. Other clients may know logically *why* they should implement, but emotional or other barriers regarding *when* may be the greatest deterrent. These clients may have the desire to implement but postpone taking action for any number of reasons, including:

- procrastination;

- avoidance of difficult or uncomfortable issues and decisions (e.g., estate planning, beneficiary designations, gifting);

- money scripts that interfere with financial progress;

- competition with other life arenas;

- lack of time, knowledge, organization, or commitment to the plan's benefits; or

- simply forgetting to follow through.

One way to motivate action involves a planner collaborating with a client's other advisors (e.g., tax professional, attorney) in an effort to continually reinforce that specific actions are necessary to reach financial goals and objectives (e.g., development of legal documents, filing taxes, or funding retirement accounts). Frequent informal communication with clients (e.g., social media, newsletters, or client appreciation events) and formal periodic review meetings to discuss progress are a second, often simple way to motivate action. Calling clients occasionally to confirm that implementation has occurred and meeting periodically with clients can also increase a client's commitment and offer opportunities to safely and empathically explore the issues that are blocking client progress. Notes of congratulations and recognition for implementation and goal achievement also may work well with some clients.

Most influential of all may be framing all of these efforts in the context of how the client can benefit from implementation and its impact on client goal achievement. To help clients put their attitudes and money scripts, competing spending habits, or procrastination into perspective, an advisor should confront the client with the question, "How would you feel if _____ is not accomplished?" However, because of the potentially emotionally charged response (e.g., shame, embarrassment, defeat), this approach should be used with care and reserved for strong, trusting client-planner relationships.

Sometimes a client must confront a significantly negative consequence to fully convey the importance of *when* and *why* implementation should occur. For instance, if the client chooses a course of action that could jeopardize his or her future financial situation or raise questions about the professional judgment of the planner, a **liability release form** or **waiver** of liability signed by the client might be considered. Likewise, if the client elects to take actions contrary to the advice and guidance of the planner, or if the client does not implement recommendations in a timely manner, the planner could ask the client to sign a waiver of liability. When presented with a liability release form that protects the advisor from future legal challenges, the client may fully comprehend the magnitude of the consciously chosen action or inaction.

But caution must be used when exercising this practice. A liability waiver should be used only when the client's conscious refusal or inaction could jeopardize the client's future financial situation or even raise questions about the professional judgment of the planner. Asking a client to sign a liability release because funds are unavailable or prioritized to meet other goals or planning needs must be done judiciously, relative to the individual client situation. Such a request without good cause could be interpreted, at best, as insulting or rude, and at worst, could damage the advisor-client relationship. A liability release form protects the advisor from future suitability or legal challenges from the client or other primary stakeholders for professional malpractice or malfeasance.

An increasing emphasis on fiduciary relationships and the encouragement of the judicious exercise of professional judgment when serving clients have heightened planner concern about **fiduciary liability** and the potential for civil suits over professional negligence. The client's signature on a liability release or waiver acknowledges that a planner made a recommendation that was declined by the client, and thus relieves the planner of further responsibility. Recall the earlier discussion of primary and secondary stakeholders (e.g., the client's spouse or children) who might, for example, question the planner's exercise of fiduciary duty to the client when long-term care insurance was not proposed, despite a family history of Alzheimer's disease. When working with clients to implement recommendations initially and subsequently in the monitoring step of the process, it is important to document all advisor or staff communication with the client clearly and accurately. Documentation of repeated efforts to convince a client to implement a recommendation, and well as other notes regarding the client's plans and wishes, could provide important evidence of the planner's professional judgment in the future.

In summary, efforts to motivate client action, and to fully explain *when* and *why* the recommendation is important to the client's financial future, can be equally important for the protection of the client and the planner. However, the decision rests with the client and must be consistent with the client's priorities, values, and beliefs.

In extreme situations a planner may resort to terminating the planner-client relationship unless client action is taken to implement specific recommendations. However, this approach also must be exercised with caution. Some advisors might suggest that a client would be better served by another advisor whom they may recommend. Obvious attempts to force a client to take action could be viewed as a conflict of interest *even if the action is in the best interest of the client*. This is especially true in situations where the action would result in increased commissions or other planner compensation.

How Should Implementation Take Place? How Much Should Be Purchased, Saved, or Invested to Implement a Recommendation?

Beyond the complex dilemma of deciphering client motivation are the final two implementation issues: *how* and *how much*. Often the best answers to these practical— and perhaps technical— issues are convenience and cost. These queries may appear simplistic, given the range of business models, recommendations, products, and services involved, but cost and convenience are important regardless of how implementation is handled. The following list offers some simple strategies that may help clients adopt new financial management practices:

- specific **to-do lists** (as shown in Exhibit 8.2) or timelines that clearly explain the *how* and *how much* for each recommendation; these lists can help planner and client divide what may appear to be an overwhelming list into manageable tasks that can be tracked easily;

- cash management tactics (e.g., electronic transfers, asset management [sweep account] or electronic access to bank or investment account information; online or phone applications for tracking spending and cash flow) that simplify how recommendations are put into practice;

- "low-maintenance" investment products such as index mutual funds, electronically traded funds, other passively managed investments, or age-based portfolios for use by clients with little or no need for continuing advisor support; and

- when applicable to the planner-client engagement, periodic meetings with the planner to facilitate plan implementation.

One of the most effective ways to motivate client action involves systematically summarizing recommendations so that implementation can be accomplished easily. The use of an **Implementation Checklist** in each core financial planning content area, whether in a modular or comprehensive plan, is recommended. However, inclusive checklists for the entire plan or for certain segments of time are also useful. For example, a client with goal implementation staggered across time or goals with staggered or changing funding schedules might best be served by having one checklist for each of several six-month periods. And in some instances, a single comprehensive form may be sufficient for a simple plan.

Exhibit 8.2 To-do List

This to-do list reflects the recommendations presented in your plan.
Don't hesitate to call our office for clarification or assistance with any actions recommended.

IMMEDIATE ACTION

☑ Visit a financial planning firm to get a road map for achieving your life goals.

☐ Pay off all credit card balances of $7,800 with money from the inheritance.

☐ Adam, contact the Human Resources/Personnel Department of your school district and increase retirement contributions by $180 biweekly. Acquire a copy of the beneficiary designation for your plan and send it to our office.

WITHIN 3 MONTHS

☐ Complete the paperwork with our office to roll over your 401(k) from your previous employer to a Traditional IRA.

☐ Have your attorney update your wills, draft a durable power of attorney, and establish a YourState advance directive. Provide our office with copies.

☐ Contact your corporate benefits provider online to determine the cost of increasing your group term coverage by an additional $300,000. Compare the premium to the low-load, direct-purchase online quote provided by our office. Complete the transaction to increase coverage. Provide our office with a copy of the beneficiary designation form.

WITHIN 6 MONTHS

☐ Use your tax refund to help build your cash reserve or emergency fund.

☐ Complete a comprehensive household inventory, including digital records. Meet with your insurance agent to review coverage for needed endorsements, riders, or extensions. Add an umbrella or excess-liability policy for $1.5 million.

A blank Implementation Checklist is shown in Exhibit 8.3, and completed forms for Tom and Nyla Kim are shown later in the chapter. An Implementation Checklist bridges the gap between tracking the financial implications of a plan and summarizing the information needed to describe and implement each recommendation. It provides an answer to the seven critical questions that a recommendation should address to facilitate implementation: *who, what, when, where, why, how,* and *how much*. As such, the Implementation Checklist provides an abridged plan that can be updated easily and serve as a useful reference for planning staff and client—during both implementation and monitoring.

Exhibit 8.3 Implementation Checklist

Recommendations

What	Who	When	Where	Why	How	Annual Cash Flow Impact (How Much)	Immediate Net Worth Impact (How Much)
Total impact of recommendations on cash flow and net worth							
Annual discretionary cash flow after recommendation implementation							
Net worth after recommendation implementation							

Financial planners are often adept at answering *how much*, but frequently they are much less comfortable with helping clients address fears and concerns associated with *how*. The results of the analysis of the client's goals, built on defensible assumptions and sound analytical approaches, will yield an answer to the question of *how much should be purchased, saved, or invested*. The planner's technical knowledge and the Implementation Checklist can provide clients with concise implementation instructions for *how* to put the recommendations into action.

Note, however, that fears and concerns about *how* might have a more significant impact on the client than even an experienced advisor initially recognizes. Explicitly, the client may be apprehensive about having insufficient financial knowledge, experience, or perseverance to implement the plans. Implicitly, the client's experiential map or attitudes about money may be a source of anxiety. What an advisor might interpret as reluctance to implement may actually be the client's lack of confidence to implement— regardless of the amount of income available or the logical benefit to the client. At this juncture of the financial planning process, advisor sensitivity to the impact of such client situational factors is an important first step toward acquiring the skill and confidence to explore these issues with clients. Such efforts to fully understand and respect a client's issues or money scripts contribute to a more trusting planner-client relationship.

Managing client expectations is another area of concern to planners. Too often a client assumes that if a plan is perfectly executed, the planner's recommendations will result in a perfect outcome. But the client may not fully understand that the planner: built the recommendation on the best (but imperfect) information available at the time; used professional judgment to determine the best (but not foolproof) course of action; and framed both actions and expected outcomes on the basis of mutually agreed-upon assumptions (some of which could ultimately prove invalid). Some of the assumptions originated with the client (e.g., the fact that the child was a highly talented musician and, therefore, would surely receive an academic scholarship). Other assumptions originated from historical data (e.g., the commonly accepted assumption of a future 7% annual increase in the average annual tuition at four-year colleges).

Managing client expectations during plan implementation and monitoring hinges on three important concepts. First, the client must acknowledge that the plan is based on the information given the planner; consequently, withholding relevant information, giving "socially acceptable" answers, or otherwise knowingly or unknowingly misleading the advisor will not result in a sound plan. Second, the client must be fully informed of the function and formulation of hypothetical projections in the financial planning process. Care must be taken not to overstate an outcome, regardless of a planner's confidence in it. Third, the client must be educated about financial trends and economic issues to provide a valid and reliable context for gauging plan results. The latter can be accomplished via planner-client interactions, such as periodic monitoring meetings, newsletters, or Web site postings. These also provide an opportunity for the advisor to continue to assist and motivate the client to *act in the client's best interest*.

Step 5 and the CFP Board Standards of Ethical Conduct

Step 5 of the systematic financial planning process, Implement the Plan, corresponds to the Practice Standard 500 Series: Implementing the Financial Planning Recommendations. As shown in Appendix 8A.1, this step and the 500 Series includes Practice Standard 500-1: Agreeing on Implementation Responsibilities and 500-2: Seeking Products and Services for Implementation.

Five of the seven principles in the *Code of Ethics* are particularly relevant to this step and these practice standards. They include Competence (500-1 only), Objectivity (500-2 only), Fairness, Professionalism, and Diligence. Certainly it is easy to see how competence is significant when Practice Standard 500-1 states that the "practitioner and the client shall mutually agree on the implementation responsibilities consistent with the scope of engagement."[3] In reference to establishing the scope of engagement, the Board states that competence means practicing with knowledge and skill but "also includes the wisdom to recognize the limitations of that knowledge and when consultation with other professionals is appropriate or referral to other professionals necessary."[4]

Thus, to satisfy these requirements to advise the client, an advisor must acquire and maintain professional expertise but also know the limits of that expertise and the time to involve other professionals. Similarly, when complying with 500-2 to select appropriate products and services consistent with the needs, goals, and priorities of the client, it would seem necessary for the practitioner to demonstrate the Principle of Objectivity. In this critical step of providing financial planning advice, services, or products to clients, the three other Principles of Fairness, Professionalism, and Diligence remind practitioners to act conscientiously with honesty, dignity, and courtesy.

Both Practice Standards share several of the same *Rules of Conduct.* When a certificant is providing financial planning services or material elements of financial planning, *Rule 1.2* addresses the responsibility to define the relationship with the client either by discussing or providing in writing a description of the financial planning process, compensation, the terms for offering proprietary products, and the terms for using other providers to fulfill any part of the agreement. *Rule 2.2* is also a disclosure rule regarding compensation, conflicts of interest (including familial, contractual, agency or employer information), information about the certificant's employer and expertise, and the certificant's and/or employer's contact information. Both of these disclosure rules apply to the 500-1 standard on implementation responsibilities and the 500-2 standard on the selection of products and services to implement. Two other rules require certificants to provide professional services with integrity and objectivity, *Rule 4.1*, and with reasonable professional judgment, *Rule 4.4*.

The CFP Board identified two additional rules as applicable only to Practice Standard 500-2: Seeking Products and Services for Implementation: First, to always place the interests of the client ahead of the certificants, and when providing financial planning or material elements of financial planning to provide the client the "duty of care of a fiduciary as defined by CFP Board."[5] As shown in Appendix 8.1, this is *Rule 1.4*, which is subsequently referenced in *Rule 4.5*, which requires that in addition to placing the client's interests first, only recommendations suitable for the client are to be made or implemented. This second rule completes the balance of service in that the client's interests must be placed first and only recommendations suitable for the client should be offered, and when applicable the fiduciary standard of care, or what is in the *best interest* of the client, must be expected.

STEP 6: MONITOR THE PLAN, IMPLEMENTATION, AND GOAL PROGRESS

The sixth and final step in the systematic financial planning process involves ongoing **monitoring** of:

- the *plan* as a malleable element of the client's life that is responsive to the client's changing situation and goals;

- the *effectiveness of the plan* as a comprehensive approach for meeting the client's needs in the current regulatory, economic, tax, and market environment;

- the *implementation* of the recommendations to date;

- the viability of the *products and services* incorporated in the implementation and their continued usefulness to meet the client's needs; and

- the *outcomes* associated with the recommendations and progress toward goal achievement.

It is important to recognize that monitoring incorporates periodic evaluation and ongoing monitoring of some products and services, such as investment management services. The review of product performance and returns, company ratings of providers, risk levels, expenses, and the need for portfolio rebalancing are only a few examples of the ongoing monitoring that must be done relative to original assumptions. But the extent of these monitoring activities—whether periodic or ongoing—varies with an advisor's business model and agreed-upon engagement with the client.

CFP Board practice standards state:

> If engaged for monitoring services, the practitioner shall make a reasonable effort to define and communicate to the client those monitoring activities the practitioner is able and willing to provide. By explaining what is to be monitored, the frequency of monitoring, and the communication method, the client is more likely to understand the monitoring service to be provided by the practitioner.
>
> The monitoring process may reveal the need to reinitiate steps of the financial planning process. The current scope of the engagement may need to be modified.[6]

However it is done, this last step in the financial planning process is important for several reasons.

First, monitoring compels a planner to stay in touch with a client. Periodic contact from the planner can motivate a client to continue to take action to meet financial goals and objectives, which can benefit the client's financial situation and benefit the advisor from a continuous revenue stream and possibly client referrals. Annual plan reviews are typical, but the frequency and extent of reviews varies with the client-planner relationship. Conducting annual reviews of changes in a client's situation as well as issues related to each of the core content planning areas may seem redundant—or even intrusive in some cases.

But it is important to remember that a comprehensive financial plan must be built on a thorough knowledge of the client that extends beyond changes in gross income to a broader exploration of other issues that can have an impact on current and anticipated lifestyle decisions. Proactive planners try to anticipate their clients' changing needs when appropriate and facilitate dialogue to identify potential responses. It is equally important to encourage clients to proactively initiate reviews or changes in the plan in response to upcoming needs (e.g., planning in anticipation of a divorce; a marriage, with or without a prenuptial agreement; or the birth of a child).

Second, periodic monitoring of a client's situation ensures that previous recommendations and products remain appropriate and useful for the client. The periodic monitoring step of the process begins with a review of the client's current situation and original planning assumptions and goals. Both client and planner may be sharing information on the client's current situation, consistent with the scope of the engagement. For example, the advisor typically provides an update on investment account values. Significant changes in the client's situation may require a reevaluation of the client's planning needs or priorities, including an analysis of the client's situation, the identification of new strategies, and the development and presentation of recommendations. Depending on the extent of the changes, new recommendations may be needed for an isolated goal or core content planning area, or for several goals integrated across multiple areas of the plan.

For example, over time, most if not all assumptions used in an initial education funding analysis change. College costs have risen substantially over the past 20 years. Although it is often a good idea to assume that similar increases in college expenses will continue in the future, it is possible to overfund educational needs if actual cost increases are lower than anticipated. On the other hand, as the time horizon for funding college costs gets closer, it may be easier to assess the validity of assumptions about financial aid, scholarships, support from other family members, or the type of educational program selected. If costs are not monitored relative to funding accumulation, a client's plan may fall short or exceed education expense needs.

Not all factors that need to be monitored and reviewed are quantitative; client aspirations should also be assessed periodically. Two examples illustrate this point. Consider a family that started saving early with the intention of funding 100% of a child's college costs. Over time the child excelled at the arts, athletics, or academics, and by the time the child was a teenager it was apparent that college costs could be covered through a combination of grants and scholarships. In this case, the need for continued education funding significantly diminishes. Or consider a family that intended to fund only a portion of a child's educational costs. Later, after receiving a large inheritance, the parents decide to use the money to fully fund four years of a moderately priced college education.

Both of these examples illustrate how a family's attitudes and capacity to fund college expenses or other goals can change dramatically. It is essential, therefore, that a planner who is engaged on a long-term basis with a client monitor both quantitative data and qualitative or situational life issues. Whereas underfunding a goal may seem more problematic than overfunding a goal, both can create uncertainty and stress for clients. Underfunding causes planner and client to reconsider the priority of the goal and the altenatives availble. The significance of overfunding is the opportunity cost, or previous opportunities lost, because of the commitment to goal funding.

Periodic monitoring also allows for the review of products for which ongoing monitoring is unnecessary or is not provided by the advisor. During monitoring, product reviews are conducted for purposes similar to those in Step 3 (i.e., to evaluate the client's current planning efforts). Criteria to consider include product and provider performance, product and provider ratings, fees and expenses, and other features unique to the product in question. (For more information on standard benchmarks that can be used to evaluate insurance and investment products, see Appendix C.) Finally, periodic reviews give the advisor an opportunity to continue educating the client and to manage client expectations regarding the performance of savings, investments, or investment-based insurance products.

Monitoring investment planning issues, regardless of the goal in question, can be considered from two perspectives: client and market specific. Planner action may be needed if any change is noted in relation to a client's goals, the time horizon for meeting a goal, risk tolerance, investment attitudes, economic expectations, or risk capacity (e.g., reduced income, a reduction in net worth). Changes in any factor that would have influenced the initial development of the portfolio are the same triggers that suggest the need for a review or change in an existing portfolio. Although a client's financial situation may not have changed, the economic environment may have changed significantly. With ongoing investment management services, the planner should be continuously responsive to market changes. However, if management services are not ongoing, any economic changes or anticipated adjustments to the economic situation are cues that a more thorough review and portfolio analysis are needed. Furthermore, periodic rebalancing of the portfolio is necessary to maintain the targeted asset allocation.

Insurance policy provisions and exclusions should also be reviewed periodically. If an option to purchase additional insurance without proof of insurability was included in the original plan recommendation, the exercise right provision needs to be evaluated on a regular basis. Although this option was initially postponed, the situation may now warrant an increase in the client's coverage through the exercise clause. Over the course of a year, a client's health situation (or expected health circumstances) can change dramatically. Financial circumstances can also change. The recommendation to self-insure for some or all of the client's long-term care needs may no longer make sense for a client whose asset values have collapsed in a bear market. Conversely, a client's need for coverage may be lessened in the event of receiving a large inheritance. The status of an insurance company's financial strength, ratings, and product ratings as well as policy provisions and exclusions should also be monitored at least annually.

It is also important to review any changes that may have occurred in employer-sponsored insurance or retirement plans. Sometimes clients are unaware of changes in employee benefit plans or fail to fully consider the implications of changes. Conducting ongoing audits of employer-provided benefits documentation or encouraging clients to voluntarily provide this information when they receive it could protect a client from the loss of future benefits, allow the client to take advantage of timely changes, or in extreme cases, necessitate a privately purchased policy or benefits through a spouse's or partner's employer.

Third, monitoring keeps planner and client on track to make time-sensitive changes or implement recommendations that were delayed until a future date (e.g., redirecting funds from a § 529 plan to retirement savings because the college savings goal has been met). Time-sensitive changes can also be precipitated by the marketplace (e.g., economic, tax, legal, or regulatory environment), the client's personal situation, or the availability of new planning products and strategies. These changes could necessitate both macro-level changes (e.g., revising a plan to accommodate divorce, remarriage, or career change) and micro-level changes (e.g., revising the amounts contributed for select investments; revising the asset allocation strategy; funding a new Roth 401(k); replacing a poorly performing mutual fund; or buying a previously unavailable product). Without consistent monitoring, a client's plan can inadvertently become obsolete, and an obsolete plan defeats the purpose of proactive planning.

Fourth, monitoring provides an emotional outlet for advisors and clients—the opportunity to celebrate what has been accomplished or to commiserate during market downturns. Despite the professionalism required of planner-client relationships, often there is a genuine personal relationship and mutual concern for the well-being of planner and client. Monitoring activities foster that relationship and provide an opportunity for clients to express appreciation that the advisor "made it possible" or for the advisor to express appreciation to the client for the continued professional relationship and client referrals. Conversely, during market downturns when clients are facing portfolio losses, perhaps accompanied by a range of emotions such as anger, defeat, and grief, advisor-client meetings are very important. They provide an opportunity to educate clients and proactively help them adapt to a situation by postponing retirement or adjusting other goals.

Obviously, some aspects of the monitoring step of the financial planning process pertain only to planners who are soliciting an ongoing relationship—for services, products, or servicing products—with their clients. Consequently, the process described as *monitoring* can vary widely. Some advisors are consistently involved with their clients, offering counsel on how to achieve financial and life goals. This kind of relationship is not necessarily characteristic of any business model; nor is it always consistent with a client's expectations. For planners who conduct their practices according to a medical model (i.e., with a treat-as-needed approach), or for those doing modular plans, monitoring may be beyond the scope of the planner-client engagement. The planner may not have an opportunity to follow up with a client in these business models because implementation and monitoring are the responsibility of the client, who may or may not re-engage the advisor to review and evaluate progress.

In a more sales-based or product-delivery model, service may not include monitoring the situation once a product is sold. Monitoring may be limited to periodic reviews of the client's progress on a multiyear schedule, or infrequent communication urging the client to come in for a review. Nevertheless, periodic client communication (e.g., a newsletter, periodic postings to a Web site, or targeted personal communication) can be a good reminder for future services or referrals—both of which are extremely important to a planner's success.

Thus, it is important to recognize that an advisor's business model and the scope of the agreed-upon planner-client relationship generally set the parameters for monitoring. This is particularly evident when the question of *who* will do the monitoring (either periodic or ongoing) is considered. Monitoring can be the responsibility of:

- the client;

- the planner, or the planner in conjunction with other product or service providers (recall the idea of the planner as the hub of a wheel that coordinates implementation and monitoring and the CFP Board expectation that professionals will "provide reasonable and prudent professional supervision or direction to any subordinate or third party to whom the certificant assigns responsibility for any client services.");[7]

- a variety of product or service providers with no coordination; or

- no one.

No monitoring of the implementation or success of proposed recommendations is inconsistent with the intent of the financial planning process. Unfortunately, though, it is a reality. For the greatest likelihood of client success, a financial plan must be responsive to change. The plan must mature in concert with the client and life cycle progression just as it must be responsive to unforeseen events or the need for different products or services. On any given day, clients might call about a job loss, a promotion, an inheritance, or a profoundly disabling accident or stroke; the list of possibilities is endless. During the monitoring stage a good planner can really demonstrate the value-added benefit of the planner-client relationship. But for this to occur, both the personal and business relationships of planner and client must support such a trust-based exchange.

Step 6 and the CFP Board Standards of Ethical Conduct

Practice Standard 600-1: Defining Monitoring Responsibilities aligns with Step 6 of the systematic financial planning process, Monitor the Plan, Implementation, and Goal Progress. The CFP Board states that monitoring responsibilities should be defined by both practitioner and client.

Only one principle, Diligence, is identified by the Board as critical to this practice standard and the corresponding *Rules of Conduct*. Recall that diligence refers to providing services promptly and thoroughly, but of particular relevance to this step is the "proper planning for, and supervision of, the rendering of professional services."[8] This latter expectation relates to the systematic planning discussions about the periodic or ongoing (depending on the advisor's business model) *effectiveness of the plan* for meeting the client's needs; the *implementation* of the recommendations to date; the viability and usefulness of the *products and services* implemented; and the *outcomes* associated with the recommendations and progress toward goal achievement.

As shown in Table 8.1, *Rules of Conduct* address the advisor's relationship with the client, the information and property of the client, and obligations to the client. *Rule 1.2* addresses the certificant's responsibility to define the relationship with the client, either by discussing or providing in writing a description of the six-step financial planning process; compensation, including factors that determine costs and how decisions might benefit the certificant; the terms for proprietary products; and the terms for using "other entities to meet any of the agreement's obligations."[9] *Rule 1.2* applies when the certificant is providing financial planning services or material elements of financial planning.

Table 8.1 Monitor the Plan, Implementation, and Goal Progress

Step 6— Monitor the Plan, Implementation & Goal Progress

CFP Board Practice Standards 600 Series: Monitoring

600-1: Defining Monitoring Responsibilities
The financial planning practitioner and client shall mutually define monitoring responsibilities.

CFP Board Code of Ethics	CFP Board Rules of Conduct

Principle 7 – Diligence	**1. Defining the Relationship with the Prospective Client or Client**
	
	1.2 If the certificant's services include financial planning or material elements of financial planning, prior to entering into an agreement, the certificant shall provide written information or discuss with the prospective client or client the following:
	
	    a. The obligations and responsibilities of each party under the agreement with respect to:
	
	        i. Defining goals, needs and objectives,
	
	        ii. Gathering and providing appropriate data,
	
	        iii. Examining the result of the current course of action without changes,
	
	        iv. The formulation of any recommended actions,
	
	        v. Implementation responsibilities, and
	
	        vi. Monitoring responsibilities.
	
	    b. Compensation that any party to the agreement or any legal affiliate to a party to the agreement will or could receive under the terms of the agreement; and factors or terms that determine costs, how decisions benefit the certificant and the relative benefit to the certificant.
	
	    c. Terms under which the agreement permits the certificant to offer proprietary products.
	
	    d. Terms under which the certificant will use other entities to meet any of the agreement's obligations.
	
	If the certificant provides the above information in writing, the certificant shall encourage the prospective client or client to review the information and offer to answer any questions that the prospective client or client may have.
	
	3. Prospective Client and Client Information and Property
	
	3.3 A certificant shall obtain the information necessary to fulfill his or her obligations. If a certificant cannot obtain the necessary information, the certificant shall inform the prospective client or client of any and all material deficiencies.
	
	3.4 A certificant shall clearly identify the assets, if any, over which the certificant will take custody, exercise investment discretion, or exercise supervision.
	
	4. Obligations to Prospective Clients and Clients
	
	4.1 A certificant shall treat prospective clients and clients fairly and provide professional services with integrity and objectivity.

Source: Certified Financial Planner Board of Standards, Inc., CFP Board's Standards of Professional Conduct. Available at http://www.cfp.net/Downloads/2010Standards.pdf, pp. 7, 9–11, and 27; or http://www.cfp.net/learn/ethics.asp#intro. Reprinted with permission.

Rule 3.3 instructs certificants to obtain the client information needed to fulfill obligations and inform the client of any deficiencies. As explained in *Rule 3.4*, certificants must clearly identify any assets for which they take custody or exercise investment discretion or supervision. Certainly these responsibilities would be ongoing, depending on the scope of the monitoring agreement, and they could necessitate changes in investment allocations or holdings. However, *Rule 4.1* admonishes certificants to treat clients with fairness, integrity, and objectivity, which precludes investment changes that benefit only the advisor.

FINANCIAL PLANNING IS RECURSIVE

The seeming simplicity of implementation (i.e., buy the product or service) and monitoring (i.e., check on the success of the product or service and any changes in the client's life) masks a number of complications that are both predicated on, and complicated by, the different business models and deliverables that comprise the practice of financial planning. Adding to the complexity is the fact that implementation and monitoring encompass time spans ranging from immediately after plan presentation to months, years, or even decades in the future. Other real challenges are the fact that recommendations are not implemented in a controlled environment; the implementation of one recommendation does not occur in isolation; and monitoring can range from consistent to none. Implementing one recommendation tends to have a ripple effect on a client's financial life, which can be anticipated by the advisor but cannot be forecast; neither can the client's life. The impact analysis considered and projected as part of plan development in Step 4 may now be the client's reality, which should be apparent because of the implementation and monitoring done to date.

Figure 8.3 provides a simple illustration of the integrative nature of plan implementation and monitoring. The process is actually circular, beginning with a recommendation. Once a recommendation has been implemented, a change in the client's situation will occur. Whether this change produces the intended consequences is something to be monitored over time. Future financial planning recommendations should then be based on how well a client is progressing toward meeting the original financial goals or new financial goals that may have evolved.

Figure 8.3 The Integrative Nature of Plan Implementation and Monitoring

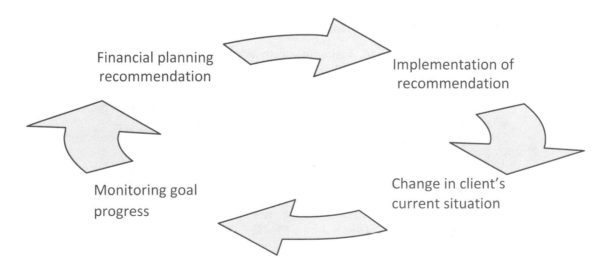

Financial planning recommendation

Implementation of recommendation

Change in client's current situation

Monitoring goal progress

Although Figure 8.3 can be applied to one—or more than one—recommendation related to a single goal, comprehensive planning typically involves multiple goals representing different core content areas. Although the illustrations of the systematic financial planning process suggest that financial planning is linear—and in many ways it is—in reality the entire planning process is circular, both from the initial development of the plan as well as throughout the entire advisor-client planning relationship. Consider the following.

An integrated, comprehensive plan is built on recommendations that evolve from multiple strategies originating from the core content planning areas. Strategies lead to recommendations, which lead to a plan—a very simplified 1-, 2-, 3-step process. But the process can also be recursive (from the Latin "running back") in that finalizing the plan might require the planner to "run back" to analyze competing recommendations, strategies, or other information to formulate the most affordable plan likely to satisfy the client's goals. What appeared initially to be the best recommendation may subsequently have to be abandoned considered relative to other planning restrictions or choices. Ultimately, every financial plan evolves from the linear—yet more often recursive, or iterative—process shown in Figure 8.4.

Figure 8.4 The Spiraling Professional Judgment and Planner-Client Relationship

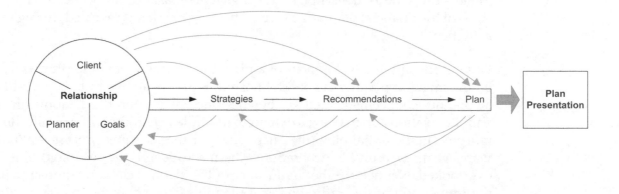

To illustrate this model, consider a couple for whom an advisor has identfied multiple potential strategies to save for education costs, fund retirement, and provide needed life insurance coverage to protect future income so these and other client goals can be funded. These strategies are matched to the clients' values, goals, and situation, and are represented in the model as the first set of arrows. But if the costs of competing strategies exceed the couple's available discretionary income, the strategies will not result in recommendations (the forward arrow from strategy to recommendation), and the planner must "circle back" (the backward arrow) to fundamental client goals and values to reassess and formulate another approach.

The process then begins again, with perhaps a decision to reduce the originally planned funding for education or retirement or both, to allow funding for the needed life insurance or yet another competing goal. Through multiple iterations of the process such as in this example, the most effective and efficient strategies are identified and integrated into a comprehensive plan. The process continues for as long as the planner-client relationship exists and to the extent that the process is within the scope of the agreed-upon (or, in some cases, what may be the renegotiated) planner-client engagement.

But the same recursive process is equally applicable after the plan is finalized, as suggested by Figure 8.3, or the circular and integrative nature of the latter two steps of the systematic financial planning process shown in Figure 8.1. Circling back to develop a new recommendation, if not isolated to a single goal, might actually require the planner to return to the client's goals, and potentially even the discovery process with the client, to ascertain a new direction(s). This circling back, or recursive flow, of the planning process could be in response to a change in the economic, tax, legal, or regulatory environment or in response to a need, want, life cycle event, or life transition experienced by the client.

The continuing evolution of the planner-client engagement and relationship must respond to changes, events, and transitions in the client's life. Whether goals are achieved or abandoned, the planner and client must "run back" and consider the impact on an individual goal as well as other aspects of the client's financial situation. In summary, the recursive process, whether applied to a single goal or multiple goals, allows the planning process to be adaptive and responsive to the client's changing planning needs. In fact, the CFP Board acknowledges there may be a need to return to Step 1 to modify the scope of the engagement as a result of the need to "reinitiate steps of the financial planning process" because of what is revealed during monitoring activities.

Beyond the initial development of a plan, the financial planning process, as reflected by the ongoing planner-client relationship, is also recursive or circular. Although not all planner-client engagements or business models support this relationship, many do, and the relationship may even extend to multiple generations of a family. But whether reflected in the initial plan (the micro level) or the planning process that ensues over many years or multiple generations (the macro level), the recursive trait cannot be overlooked. Neither can the significance of the planner-client relationship. It becomes the foundation of the entire financial planning process as the maturing of the trust-based relationship and the ensuing discovery process continue to reveal the goals that give direction to the plan. Carl Richards, a certified financial planner, argues that, "Financial plans are worthless, but the *process* of financial *planning* is vital."[10]

From Process to Practice

The vignette that follows continutes to explore the experiences of the Kims with their financial planner Jane. This installment includes reflections by the Kims and Jane as they offer some insights into their "real-life" experiences with Steps 5 and 6—from both sides of the desk.

As Tom and Nyla continued their trip home from their first annual check-up and monitoring meeting, they laughed, wondering that Jane had even worked with them in the first place! But after four meetings to get them started, they reasoned that she had too much invested not to see them through the process. But today's meeting had confirmed their initial impressions: it had all been worth it.

Recalling that fateful implementation meeting, Tom and Nyla remembered how Jane's normally upbeat demeanor had been uncharacteristically serious. She told them that she was willing to compromise her desires to protect their current and future financial position and would do everything she could to help them realize their goals—*if* they were fully willing to accept the possible consequences of postponing the insurance purchases. They remembered her saying that "finding a meeting point amidst the fundamental disconnect between the needs that *I* have identified and the goals that *you* have identified is a huge part of what financial planning is all about."

But to everyone's surprise, after evaluating Jane's different alternatives for funding, downsizing, and staggering the implementation of the recommendations, the puzzle about what to do quickly fell into place. By the end of the initial meeting, they had decided on a plan for the next year, broken into six-month time frames. The Implementation Checklist for the first six months is shown in Exhibit 8.4. Jane had everything she needed to complete the plan with formal recommendations, and the Kims had everything they needed to take responsibility for plan implementation.

Although putting the plan in place had been a bit challenging for everyone, implementing it could not have been easier. Jane's idea to stagger the implementation had been a great approach for several reasons. First, it allowed Tom and Nyla to immediately make progress but did not involve too much time or effort on their part. Jane's Implementation Checklist had certainly expedited the establishment of the § 529 plan and the savings plan for the trip. The purchase of Nyla's life insurance was soon complete, as well—all because the details were there.

Second, postponing the increase in their retirement savings by only six months turned out to be a very reasonable compromise, as shown in the Implementation Checklist in Exhibit 8.5. Tom and Nyla knew there should be opportunities to continually and gradually increase this funding. With the promise of Jane's careful attention to the plan in the future, they were confident that they could still consider retirement in 25 years. They also rationalized that when Azalea became independent, they could significantly increase their retirement savings.

Exhibit 8.4 Implementation Checklist for Tom and Nyla Kim, Months 1–6

Tom and Nyla Kim's Implementation Checklist (Months 1–6)

Recommendation (What)	Who	When	Where	Why	How	Annual Cash Flow Impact (How Much)	Immediate Net Worth Impact (How Much)
Pay off $4,000 in combined credit card balances.	Tom and Nyla	Immediately	Service Bank, Nichols, Guarantee National	This action will eliminate high-interest debt by using liquid, low-interest assets to increase your cash flow.	Use additional funds (beyond the projected need for an emergency fund) in your money market account.	+$600	None
Establish a § 529 plan for Azalea's college funding.	Tom, Nyla, and Jane	Within one month	Real-life Mutual Fund Company	§ 529 plans have the benefit of tax-deferred growth as well as tax-free withdrawals (restrictions apply).	Complete the provided forms and mail them to Real-life Mutual Fund Company. Begin with monthly contributions of $250.	–$3,000 (dependent upon availability of tax deductions)	None
Save $300/month for international vacation using a savings account at a local bank.	Tom and Nyla	Within one month	First Local Bank	Beginning to fund the trip will help reinforce your commitment to the goal.	Open a savings account specifically dedicated to this goal; when the money market deposit account (MMDA) minimum balance has been achieved, transfer the balance.	–$3,600	None
Purchase a $250,000, 20-yr. term life policy.	Nyla	Month 1	Online Life Insurance, Inc.	Life insurance will help protect your family in the event of your death.	Online forms are available. Our office will assist with their completion, if needed.	–$300 (count 5/6 toward year 1)	None
Total impact of recommendations on current "planning year" cash flow and net worth						**–$6,250**	**$0**
Annual discretionary cash flow after recommendation implementation						**$650**	
Net worth after recommendation implementation						**$147,800**	

Exhibit 8.5 Implementation Checklist for Tom and Nyla Kim, Months 7–12

Tom and Nyla Kim's Implementation Checklist

(Months 7–12)

Recommendation (What)	Who	When	Where	Why	How	Annual Cash Flow Impact (How Much)	Immediate Net Worth Impact (How Much)
Review "trip" savings account balance to see if MMDA minimum is met.	Tom and Nyla	Ongoing	First Local Bank	Transferring balance to higher-yielding account will increase returns.	Contact bank to transfer the balance (if minimum balance has been achieved).	None	None
Increase contribution to tax-qualified retirement accounts.	Nyla	Month 7	Your employer's Human Resources Dept.	Using a salary deferral plan to save for retirement, you decrease current tax liability and your savings will grow tax-deferred. This also allows you to reallocate your investments without incurring tax liability.	Visit your HR Department and increase your salary deferral from 4% to 5%.	–$400 (count ½ toward year 1)	None
Increase contribution to tax-qualified retirement accounts	Tom	Month 7	Your employer's Human Resources Dept.		Visit your HR Department and increase your salary deferral from 5% to 7%.	–$960 (count ½ toward year 1)	None
Additional impact of recommendations on current "planning year" cash flow and net worth						**–$680**	**$0**
Total impact of recommendations on current "planning year" cash flow and net worth							**–$6,930**
Annual discretionary cash flow after recommendation implementation							**–$30**
Net worth after recommendation implementation							$147,800

Third, although they knew they were taking a significant risk by postponing Tom's disability insurance for a year, given their other demands and the importance of the timing of their trip, they decided they were willing to take that risk. The flexibility of Tom's career and the low risk of their lifestyle were significant considerations, despite the fact that they admitted that some accidents could spell the end of their dreams and dramatically change their future and their finances. But in the end, they reasoned that the value of their memories from the trip could not be discounted so easily and the desire to visit aging family members took precedence. Their trip account value was steadily increasing, as was their excitement. Although they knew their international vacation was still more than a year away, they had already started planning an itinerary. Everything they had learned from planning their finances with Jane had made them strong proponents of planning ahead.

Today, the results of their first annual check-up and monitoring meeting further confirmed that view. According to Jane, everything was on course and only minor modifications had to be implemented. She recommended that Tom and Nyla automate their § 529 plan monthly contributions as a convenience. She also recommended that they rebalance Tom's retirement account because of recent out-performance in selected areas of the market. Because Nyla's retirement plan custodian had added some new mutual funds, Jane also wanted to change the asset allocation of Nyla's retirement account. With Tom and Nyla's approval, Jane agreed to prepare a new Implementation Checklist to explain the details, as shown in Exhibit 8.6. After a lighthearted and then serious discussion of the Kims' personal and financial situation, the first annual check-up and monitoring meeting was over. No questionnaires to complete, no forms to fill out, no disclosure agreements to sign, no hard decisions to make; in fact, neither of them had even picked up a pen!

Exhibit 8.6 Implementation Checklist for Tom and Nyla Kim, Months 13–24

Tom and Nyla Kim's Implementation Checklist

(Months 13–24)*

Recommendation (What)	Who	When	Where	Why	How	Annual Cash Flow Impact (How Much)	Immediate Net Worth Impact (How Much)
Continue funding $ 529 plan for Azalea's college funding.	Tom and Nyla	Ongoing	Real-life Mutual Fund Company			–$3,000 (dependent upon availability of tax deductions)	None
Reduce trip savings amount to $175/ month.	Tom and Nyla	Month 13	First Local Bank	Given amount invested in Year 1, goal can still be attained with reduced level.	Reduce amount of monthly savings from $300 to $175.	–$2,100	None
Maintain contribution to tax-qualified retirement accounts.	Nyla	Month 13	Your employer's Human Resources Dept.			–$400	None
Maintain contribution to tax-qualified retirement accounts.	Tom	Month 13	Your employer's Human Resources Dept.			–$960	None
Purchase a 70% income replacement long-term disability policy.	Tom	Month 13	Insure Your Life, Inc.	Disability insurance will replace some of your income in case you become disabled.	Contact Mr. Mathers at the local Insure Your Life office.	–$1,800	None

Exhibit 8.6 Implementation Checklist for Tom and Nyla Kim, Months 13–24 (cont'd)

Action	Who	When	Where	Why	How		
Pay life policy premium.	Nyla	Month 15	Online Life Ins., Inc.	Life insurance will help protect your family in the event of your death.	Mail check to Online Life Ins., Inc.	-$300	None
Total impact of recommendations on next "planning year" cash flow and net worth						-$8,560	$0
Total additional impact of recommendations on next "planning year" cash flow and net worth							$1,630
Annual discretionary cash flow after recommendation implementation							-$1,660**
Net worth after recommendation implementation							$147,800

*This list is for informational purposes only; we will review your progress at your annual check-up and make any adjustments at that time.

** Given your historical annual salary increases, this shortfall should be covered by your projected after-tax raise during months 13–24. The annual expense projections and funding alternatives can be adjusted, if necessary, at the annual check-up and monitoring meeting.

* * * * * * * * * *

As Jane watched Tom and Nyla Kim walk to their car following their first annual check-up and monitoring meeting, she recalled how far their planner-client relationship had come in a little more than one year. She knew they had laid a foundation for the future.

Returning to her office, Jane mused that the Kims might turn out to be her best clients—not because of the fees for her services, but because with clients like them she would need no advertising. They were very complimentary of the newsletters she sent and reportedly recommended Jane and her new online calculators to all of their friends!

After a year of working together, Jane and the Kims had finally admitted some of their frustrations along the way, but they had also acknowledged that the final plan was consistent with the values and attitudes of all parties. Jane knew she had a strong preference for funding recommendations that she defined as a *need* rather than a *want*; however, in this case she realized how important it was to balance ideals against what she perceived to be a very strong client aspiration (i.e., a vacation to strengthen family ties). Another planner, working with the same clients, might have discounted the Kims' vacation goal in favor of increased retirement funding or the immediate need to purchase insurance protection. But Jane was confident that she and the Kims had accomplished what she thought financial planning was all about—the merger of a client's goals, available cash flow and assets, and the advisor's professional judgment into a synergistic plan for the future.

CHAPTER SUMMARY

A financial plan has been called a road map to a client's future. Just as following a map enables a traveler to reach a destination, implementing and monitoring in the financial planning process keep both planner and client on course. In some instances, a financial planner can control all aspects of implementation; in other cases, a planner can only prompt a client to take action. What is necessary is for the client to commit to and act on recommendations in a timely manner, because without proper implementation a financial plan will yield few benefits for the client.

Similarly, a map is useless if the traveler never consults it. In the end, the implementation of plan recommendations depends most on a planner's ability to communicate the value (financially and personally) of the products or services, the real potential for goal achievement, and the methods for their accomplishment. The importance of monitoring should not be overlooked in the financial planning process. In fact, plan monitoring, conducted via ongoing assessments of products and services leveraged against a revised assessment of a client's situation, is the primary way successful advisors provide service to clients over time. Monitoring will almost always result in future opportunities to serve a client through product delivery, services, or consultation. The circular nature of the planning process is evident in the interplay of Steps 5 and 6. But the entire planning process is recursive, whether considered in a discrete core content area, in comprehensive plan development, or in the maintainence of the planner-client relationship over time.

Learning Outcomes

1. In combination, the CFP Board description of the scope of six possible responsibilities involved in plan implementation, and the systematic process focus on the seven key questions to guide monitoring explain Step 6. Recall that implementation responsibilities must be mutually agreed upon, thereby answering the questions of *what* and *who*. Identifying the activities necessary for implementation involves answering the questions of *what* activities, *why* the selected activities are necessary, and *how* the activities will or should be done. Determining the division of activities among the parties and referring to other professionals answers the questions of *who*, *why*, and *where*, although other details may also be relevant. Coordinating with other professionals and sharing information addresses *why* there is a need to know, *what* and *how much* information should be shared, *how* and *when* it should be shared, as well as with *whom* it should be shared. Selecting and securing products and services suitable for the client requires consideration of *what* products and services and *why* they are suitable and matched to the client.

2. Professional referrals and strategic alliances, when practiced with full disclosure to the client regarding any fees exchanged or other conflicts of interest, have the potential to benefit both client and planner. The client benefits from the diversity of talents and expertise assembled to respond to the client's specific needs. The client also benefits from efficient implementation and effective service from a group of collaborating professionals. The planner benefits from providing the best products and services possible, which results in satisfied clients and long-term relationships. Referrals from clients and the other professionals involved in the referral network are an additional benefit to the client.

3. Despite contracting for a plan and participating in the planning process, clients face several different roadblocks (i.e., procrastination, emotional issues, competition from everyday life, lack of follow-through) that can limit progress on implementation. These issues are compounded by the complexity and confusion surrounding immediate and delayed implementation, as illustrated in the Implementation Matrix and the fact that the timeline for "completing" the implementation of recommendations can range from almost immediately to decades into the future. A consistent, supportive, and empathetic relationship with a planner cannot overcome all of these issues, but it can help keep clients on track—regardless of their motivation or the pitfalls they encounter.

4. Both positive and negative reinforcement can be used to keep clients on track, because without action the plan offers the client no protection from the risks identified and no progress toward the goals chosen. Supportive networks of professionals to facilitate progress, frequent communication from the planner, and positive rewards (e.g., notes, recognition) for client progress or the completion of tasks can be important to motivate ongoing client action or behavioral change. More punitive advisor actions include frank client discussions about feelings and emotions associated with failure to achieve a goal or satisfy a recommendation, as well as asking the client to sign a liability release form. Finally, if all attempts to motivate client action are unsuccessful, planners can terminate, or fire, the clients.

5. An Implementation Checklist can be used for each core financial planning content area, as an inclusive checklist for the entire plan, or for specific segments of time. For example, a client with goal implementation staggered across time or goals with staggered or changing funding schedules might best be served by having one checklist for each of several six-month periods. The Implementation Checklist summarizes significant details of implementation while simultaneously tracking the financial impact of any actions on discretionary cash flow and net worth.

6. The 500 Series of Practice Standards, Implementing the Recommendations, includes Practice Standard 500-1: Agreeing on Implementation Responsibilities and 500-2: Seeking Products and Services for Implementation—both of which correspond to Step 5: Implement the Plan in the systematic financial planning model. Five of the seven principles in the *Code of Ethics*, including Competence (500-1 only), Objectivity (500-2 only), Fairness, Professionalism, and Diligence are particularly relevant to this step and these practice standards. The *Rules of Conduct* mandate:

    *   full disclosure to clients (*Rule 1.2* and *2.2*);

    *   the provision of professional services with integrity and objectivity (*Rule 4.1*);

    *   the exercise of reasonable professional judgment (*Rule 4.4*);

    *   the commitment to place the client's interests first, and when applicable to act as a fiduciary (*Rule 1.4*); and

    *   to suggest or implement only recommendations in the best interest of the client (*Rule 4.5*).

7. Just as financial planning focuses on the intersection of a client's personal and financial life, so does Step 6 (as the name implies), Monitor the Plan, Implementation, and Goal Progress. Foremost, the plan as a whole must be matched to the client and changes that have occurred in the client's life; this is equally applicable to the time span since the planning relationship began or since the last review meeting. Next, the plan must be matched to the current regulatory, economic, tax, and market environment. Again, this is equally applicable to the period since the planning relationship began or the last review meeting. Finally, it is important to monitor (1) whether implementation is on track or there are actions that should be changed, stopped or started; (2) the effectiveness of the products and services to meet the client's needs and whether changes are needed; and (3) the results of the planning efforts and goal progress. Monitoring activities can vary widely because of the possible range of responsibilities and differences in the business models of financial professionals. The CFP Board requires that certificants work with clients to mutually agree on monitoring responsibilities.

8. Monitoring is an important but often overlooked step in the financial planning process. It is valuable because it (1) promotes communication, which is beneficial to the advisor-client relationship; (2) requires an assessment of the recommended products and services; (3) provides an opportunity to make time-sensitive changes and implement delayed recommendations; and (4) provides an emotional outlet for celebrating and commiserating that can enrich the advisor-client relationship.

9. Only one principle, Diligence, is identified by the Board as critical to Practice Standard 600-1: Defining Monitoring Responsibilities, which aligns with Step 6: Monitor the Plan, Implementation, and Goal Progress. Diligence refers to providing services promptly and thoroughly, as well as properly planning for, supervising, and rendering professional services. Four related *Rules of Conduct* relate to disclosure (when providing financial planning or material elements of financial planning), the acquisition of information needed to fulfill the engagement, and treating clients with fairness, integrity, and objectivity. *Rule 3.4* establishes the need to identify any assets for which the professional has custody or exercises discretion or supervision. Certainly important to this step are disclosure of services included and compensation for monitoring, the need for up-to-date information to provide these services, and the ongoing professional treatment of clients. A typical example of monitoring services is investment management, but care must be taken when identifying assets over which an advisor has access or control.

10. Illustrations of the systematic financial planning process suggest that financial planning is linear—and in many ways it is. But in reality the entire planning process is recursive, or circular. In its simplest sense, an implemented recommendation results in a change in a client's situation, which through monitoring can lead to necessary changes in products or services or the identification of a new goal. This circular response in Steps 5 and 6, when applied to a discrete goal, can entail reconsideration or a return to earlier steps as the foundation of a response. The integrtion of these actions in each core content area into an ever-evolving plan means that advisor-client efforts can be simultaneous and ongoing in multiple steps of the process across various goals or needs.

Figure 8.3 attempts to illustrate this phenomenon, as advisor and client are forced to "run back" to change the engagement in Step 1; revisit goals, money scripts, or priorities in Step 2; and conduct a new analysis because of revised assumptions in Step 3, which could lead to new recommendations that must be integrated into a new plan. Similarly, life events and the ensuing emotions can challenge the advisor-client planning relationship to "recyle" through the steps as they strive to confront challenges. Thus, over time, the planning process for a discrete core content area, the development of a comprehensive plan, or the maintainence of the planner-client relationship is actually a recursive process.

Chapter Resources

CFP Board's Standards of Professional Conduct (http://www.cfp.net/Downloads/2010Standards.pdf).

Diliberto, Roy T. *Financial Planning—The Next Step: A Practical Approach to Merging Your Clients' Money with Their Lives*. Denver, CO: FPA Press, 2006.

Freedman, M. S. *Oversold and Underserved: A Financial Planner's Guidebook to Effectively Serving the Mass Affluent*. Denver, CO: FPA Press, 2008.

Richards, C. *The Behavior Gap: Simple Ways to Stop Doing Dumb Things with Money.* New York: Portfolio/Penguin, 2012.

Discussion Questions

1. Who is involved in implementation and monitoring? Identify the parties and explain their role in implementation, monitoring, or both Steps 5 and 6. Despite the diversity of who is involved, if the advisor is a CFP® certificant, what one ethical conduct standard must be met?

2. How can a referral network benefit client and planner? What disclosures, if any, are necessary? Be sure to consult the *CFP Board's Standards of Professional Conduct* at http://www.cfp.net/ Downloads/2010Standards.pdf or http://www.cfp.net/learn/rulesofconduct.asp and http:// www.cfp.net/learn/standards500.asp.

3. Why is the concept of time, or the consideration of when to implement or when a goal is satisfied, so important for a client to appreciate?

4. Identify and explain the reasons that clients fail to implement, despite initiating the planning process. How can providing a client with a to-do list or timeline improve the likelihood that a client will implement plan recommendations?

5. Identify approaches a financial planner can use to motivate a client to implement the plan, either for actions the client is solely responsible for or for actions to be completed with the advisor or other financial professional.

6. In what circumstances might a financial planner have a client sign a liability release or waiver? What is the purpose of this form? What cautions are warranted so that the potential for a long-term planner-client relationship is not threatened by the opinions and actions of both parties?

7. Review the Implementation Checklists developed for the Kims. Do you agree that the checklists serve as an abridged plan? If you were Tom and Nyla, would you know what you needed to do? What is the purpose of the Implementation Checklist?

8. Why is it important to manage a client's expectations during implementation and monitoring? How can this be accomplished? How does managing a client's expectations relate to CFP Board expectations for ethical conduct?

9. Five of the seven principles in the CFP Board *Code of Ethics* are deemed particularly relevant to the Practice Standards 500 Series. Identify and explain these principles. Why do you think this step in the process is assumed to be problematic regarding expectations for ethical conduct?

10. List the five objectives of monitoring and cite at least three "real-life" client examples to illustrate each objective. How is monitoring the plan different from monitoring an isolated recommendation?

11. Explain why monitoring is so important to a successful outcome for client and planner. For each reason cited, identify a "real-life situation" to exemplify its benefit to the client, the planner, both, or the planner-client relationship.

12. Mutually agreed-upon client and core content assumptions are an important part of Step 3: Analyze and Evaluate the Client's Situation. Assumptions are based on data collected in Step 2. Explain the role of assumptions in Steps 5 and 6.

13. The seven questions of *who, what, when, where, why, how,* and *how much* provide guidance for the systematic financial planning process when framing recommendations in Step 4 and for plan implementation in Step 5. Based on the Kims' three goals to fund education, manage risk to promote financial security, and save for retirement, answer the seven questions as applied to monitoring two of the Kims' goals.

14. The CFP Board acknowledges that monitoring can reveal the need to reinitiate steps of the financial planning process, which could lead to a modification in the advisor-client engagement. Why is the development of a comprehensive financial plan more likely to be a recursive, not a linear, process? Is this equally true for a targeted or modular plan?

15. Describe how failing to implement and monitor plan recommendations can jeopardize a client's financial well-being. Give at least two examples of each—failing to implement and failing to monitor.

Notes

1. Certified Financial Planner Board of Standards, Inc., *CFP Board's Standards of Professional Conduct.* Available at http://www.cfp.net/Downloads/2010Standards.pdf, p. 25 or http://www.cfp.net/learn/standards500.asp.

2. CFP Board, *Standards of Professional Conduct*, p. 25.

3. CFP Board, *Standards of Professional Conduct*, p. 25.

4. CFP Board, *Standards of Professional Conduct*, p. 6 or http://www.cfp.net/learn/codeofethics.asp.

5. CFP Board, *Standards of Professional Conduct*, p. 9 or http://www.cfp.net/learn/rulesofconduct.asp.

6. CFP Board, *Standards of Professional Conduct*, p. 27 or http://www.cfp.net/learn/standards600.asp.

7. CFP Board, *Standards of Professional Conduct*, p. 11 or http://www.cfp.net/learn/rulesofconduct.asp.

8. CFP Board, *Standards of Professional Conduct*, p. 7 or http://www.cfp.net/learn/codeofethics.asp.

9. CFP Board, *Standards of Professional Conduct*, p. 9 or http://www.cfp.net/learn/rulesofconduct.asp.

10. C. Richards, The Behavior Gap: *Simple Ways to Stop Doing Dumb Things with Money* (New York: Portfolio/Penguin. 2012), 96.

Step 5—Implement the Plan

Step 5—Implement the Plan

Practice Standards 500 Series: Implementing the Financial Planning Recommendation(s):

500-1: Agreeing on Implementation Responsibilities
The financial planning practitioner and the client shall mutually agree on the implementation responsibilities consistent with the scope of the engagement.

CFP Board Code of Ethics	CFP Board Rules of Conduct

Principle 3 – Competence
 	
Principle 4 – Fairness
 	
Principle 6 – Professionalism
 	
Principle 7 – Diligence
	1. Defining the Relationship with the Prospective Client or Client
	
	1.2 If the certificant's services include financial planning or material elements of financial planning, prior to entering into an agreement, the certificant shall provide written information or discuss with the prospective client or client the following:
	
	a. The obligations and responsibilities of each party under the agreement with respect to:
	
	    i. Defining goals, needs and objectives,
	
	    ii. Gathering and providing appropriate data,
	
	    iii. Examining the result of the current course of action without changes,
	
	    iv. The formulation of any recommended actions,
	
	    v. Implementation responsibilities, and
	
	    vi. Monitoring responsibilities.
	
	b. Compensation that any party to the agreement or any legal affiliate to a party to the agreement will or could receive under the terms of the agreement; and factors or terms that determine costs, how decisions benefit the certificant and the relative benefit to the certificant.
	
	c. Terms under which the agreement permits the certificant to offer proprietary products.
	
	d. Terms under which the certificant will use other entities to meet any of the agreement's obligations.
	
	If the certificant provides the above information in writing, the certificant shall encourage the prospective client or client to review the information and offer to answer any questions that the prospective client or client may have.
	
	2. Information Disclosed To Prospective Clients and Clients

Step 5—Implement the Plan (cont'd)

Practice Standards 500 Series: Implementing the Financial Planning Recommendation(s):

500-1: Agreeing on Implementation Responsibilities
The financial planning practitioner and the client shall mutually agree on the implementation responsibilities consistent with the scope of the engagement.

CFP Board Code of Ethics	CFP Board Rules of Conduct

Principle 3 – Competence
 	
Principle 4 – Fairness
 	
Principle 6 – Professionalism
 	
Principle 7 – Diligence
	2.2 A certificant shall disclose to a prospective client or client the following information:
	
	a. An accurate and understandable description of the compensation arrangements being offered. This description must include:
	
	    i. Information related to costs and compensation to the certificant and/or the certificant's employer, and
	
	    ii. Terms under which the certificant and/or the certificant's employer may receive any other sources of compensation, and if so, what the sources of these payments are and on what they are based.
	
	b. A general summary of likely conflicts of interest between the client and the certificant, the certificant's employer or any affiliates or third parties, including, but not limited to, information about any familial, contractual or agency relationship of the certificant or the certificant's employer that has a potential to materially affect the relationship.
	
	c. Any information about the certificant or the certificant's employer that could reasonably be expected to materially affect the client's decision to engage the certificant that the client might reasonably want to know in establishing the scope and nature of the relationship, including but not limited to information about the certificant's areas of expertise.
	
	d. Contact information for the certificant and, if applicable, the certificant's employer.
	
	e. If the services include financial planning or material elements of financial planning, these disclosures must be in writing. The written disclosures may consist of multiple written documents. Written disclosures used by a certificant or certificant's employer that includes the items listed above, and are used in compliance with state or federal laws, or the rules or requirements of any applicable self-regulatory organization, such as the Securities and Exchange Commission's Form ADV or other disclosure documents, shall satisfy the requirements of this Rule.
	
	The certificant shall timely disclose to the client any material changes to the above information.
	
	4. Obligations to Prospective Clients and Clients
	
	4.1 A certificant shall treat prospective clients and clients fairly and provide professional services with integrity and objectivity.
	
	4.4 A certificant shall exercise reasonable and prudent professional judgment in providing professional services to clients.

500-2: Selecting Products and Services for Implementation

The financial planning practitioner shall select appropriate products and services that are consistent with the client's goals, needs and priorities.

Principle 2 – Objectivity	**1. Defining the Relationship with the Prospective Client or Client**
	1.2 If the certificant's services include financial planning or material elements of financial planning, prior to entering into an agreement, the certificant shall provide written information or discuss with the prospective client or client the following:
Principle 4 – Fairness	
Principle 6 – Professionalism	e. The obligations and responsibilities of each party under the agreement with respect to:
Principle 7 – Diligence	i. Defining goals, needs and objectives,
	ii. Gathering and providing appropriate data,
	iii. Examining the result of the current course of action without changes,
	iv. The formulation of any recommended actions,
	v. Implementation responsibilities, and
	vi. Monitoring responsibilities.
	f. Compensation that any party to the agreement or any legal affiliate to a party to the agreement will or could receive under the terms of the agreement; and factors or terms that determine costs, how decisions benefit the certificant and the relative benefit to the certificant.
	g. Terms under which the agreement permits the certificant to offer proprietary products.
	h. Terms under which the certificant will use other entities to meet any of the agreement's obligations.
	If the certificant provides the above information in writing, the certificant shall encourage the prospective client or client to review the information and offer to answer any questions that the prospective client or client may have.
	1.4 A certificant shall at all times place the interest of the client ahead of his or her own. When the certificant provides financial planning or material elements of financial planning, the certificant owes to the client the duty of care of a fiduciary as defined by CFP Board.
	2. Information Disclosed To Prospective Clients and Clients

500-2: Selecting Products and Services for Implementation
The financial planning practitioner shall select appropriate products and services that are consistent with the client's goals, needs and priorities.

Principle 2 – Objectivity
 	
Principle 4 – Fairness
 	
Principle 6 – Professionalism
 	
Principle 7 – Diligence
	2.2 A certificant shall disclose to a prospective client or client the following information:
	
	a. An accurate and understandable description of the compensation arrangements being offered. This description must include:
	
	   i. Information related to costs and compensation to the certificant and/or the certificant's employer, and
	
	   ii. Terms under which the certificant and/or the certificant's employer may receive any other sources of compensation, and if so, what the sources of these payments are and on what they are based.
	
	b. A general summary of likely conflicts of interest between the client and the certificant, the certificant's employer or any affiliates or third parties, including, but not limited to, information about any familial, contractual or agency relationship of the certificant or the certificant's employer that has a potential to materially affect the relationship.
	
	c. Any information about the certificant or the certificant's employer that could reasonably be expected to materially affect the client's decision to engage the certificant that the client might reasonably want to know in establishing the scope and nature of the relationship, including but not limited to information about the certificant's areas of expertise.
	
	d. Contact information for the certificant and, if applicable, the certificant's employer.
	
	e. If the services include financial planning or material elements of financial planning, these disclosures must be in writing. The written disclosures may consist of multiple written documents. Written disclosures used by a certificant or certificant's employer that includes the items listed above, and are used in compliance with state or federal laws, or the rules or requirements of any applicable self-regulatory organization, such as the Securities and Exchange Commission's Form ADV or other disclosure documents, shall satisfy the requirements of this Rule.
	
	The certificant shall timely disclose to the client any material changes to the above information.
	
	4. Obligations to Prospective Clients and Clients
	
	4.1 A certificant shall treat prospective clients and clients fairly and provide professional services with integrity and objectivity.
	
	4.4 A certificant shall exercise reasonable and prudent professional judgment in providing professional services to clients.
	
	4.5 In addition to the requirements of Rule 1.4, a certificant shall make and/or implement only recommendations that are suitable for the client.

Source: Certified Financial Planner Board of Standards, Inc., CFP Board's Standards of Professional Conduct. Available at http://www.cfp.net/Downloads/2010Standards.pdf, pp. 6–7, 9–11, 25–26; or http://www.cfp.net/learn/ethics.asp#intro. Reprinted with permission.

PART IV: The Product of Financial Planning

Chapter 9—Writing a Financial Plan

Developing a Financial Planning Product: Writing a Financial Plan

Learning Objectives

1. Understand and explain the purpose of the financial plan.

2. Explain how information processing style preferences influence the effectiveness of a financial plan or other client communications.

3. Identify the factors that contribute to writing style and voice in a financial plan.

4. Identify and apply fundamental guidelines for crafting a well-written financial plan.

5. Construct an outline for a comprehensive financial plan.

6. Identify and explain the purpose of each component (optional or required) and how it corresponds to the six steps in the systematic financial planning process.

7. Construct and explain an outline for writing a client-specific core content section within a plan.

8. Evaluate a financial plan using a Financial Plan Review Checklist.

Key Terms

Acceptance letter

Actionable recommendation

Active voice

Auditory learning style

CFP Board Code of Ethics and Professional
    Responsibility

Client engagement letter

Code of ethics

Executive summary

First person voice

Impersonal voice

Implementation checklist

Information processing style

Investment performance disclaimers

Investment policy statement

Kinesthetic learning style

Living document

Mission statement

Observations

Personal voice

Pre-scripted material

Privacy statement

Second person voice

Statement of principles

Third person voice

Vision statement

Visual learning style

Voice

Writing style

WHAT IS A FINANCIAL PLAN?

As discussed throughout this book, financial planning can involve the delivery of financial products, financial services, financial advice, and in some instances, personal advice to help a client achieve life goals. The systematic financial planning process guides the collection and analysis of client data as well as the presentation, implementation, and monitoring of financial planning results. The CFP Board, in explaining Practice Standard 400-2, Developing the Financial Planning Recommendation(s), states that "a recommendation may be an independent action or a combination of actions which may need to be implemented collectively."[1] The systematic financial planning process presented in this book assumes that this *collective combination of actions*—in other words, the plan—is the ideal, holistic outcome of the process. In other words, the plan is the product or tangible outcome of the process, as described in Step 4, but the plan is also a summation of Steps 1 through 6. As described later in this chapter, the plan is really only a means to communicate to the client the financial planning process as applied to the client's unique situation.

And although the process may be guided by the sytematic financial planning method, in reality the manifestation of both the process and the plan can vary from one advisor to another. For example, a plan can range from a brief summary, perhaps even as short as the handouts from a PowerPoint presentation, to a document of 100 pages or more. Some plans may be bound as a permanent record of the recommendations made—a book frozen in time. Other plans are living documents in a binder where pages can be removed or added, so that the plan is responsive to changing recommendations matched to the client's changing life, and financial, situation. Electronic media make the plan even more adaptable and offer a "green" alternative to the printed page. Regardless of format, in most cases, the common element is a *written* document.

Writing a comprehensive financial plan can be an intimidating task, especially for those who have never undertaken an analysis and writing project that can easily exceed 100 pages. Many novice financial planners find making the leap from writing client reports, letters, brochures, or a few pages of client review to drafting a financial plan to be overwhelming. Many students question why they must *write* a comprehensive plan, when expectations for the product, or plan, and the software output for writing a plan vary so widely. But actually writing a financial plan is the best way to practice the process and to assess one's ability to successfully complete, integrate, and sythesize the discrete components of the financial planning process. For many students and novice planners, their first plan is their first opportunity to fully understand the entire process by practicing their skills and gauging their competence.

In actuality, writing a plan does not have to be onerous if a few simple tenets are followed: know your audience; know your information procesing style; and know your message. First and perhaps most important is the adage "know your audience." For some clients, a two-page executive summary and a thorough plan presentation or conversation with a planner may be sufficient. Other clients may want a longer document that thoroughly details the analysis and projections, which they can read and consult later. The format and length of the plan must fit the needs of the client *and* the planner. Second, it is equally important that advisors know themselves as well as their clients. Financial planners must understand their own preferred learning and information processing style as a foundation for interacting with clients, whether orally or in writing. Third, a workable outline of the message should make the time and energy devoted to crafting a plan more efficient. Because both the process and the plan are guided by the systematic financial planning process, key questions to ask include:

- Does the plan capture the client's situation and reflect the values, goals, needs, and desires of the client? Does the plan communicate a thorough understanding of the client's priorities?

- Can the client clearly and easily comprehend the analyses, recommendations, and implementation required both now and in the future? This question is important, regardless of who is doing the implementation. Even if a client delegates all of the implementation to the planner, the methods and projected outcomes must be transparent.

- Does the plan communicate the expert wisdom and best advice of the advisor? In light of currently available information, is the plan workable and able to achieve the desired outcomes? Can the recommendations be funded in a manner consistent with the client's values and lifestyle, and that strikes a balance between living today and planning for tomorrow?

- Does the plan, and the advisor's presentation, encourage the client to take action? The answer to this question is important to both advisor and client. Most advisors want to grow, or minimally sustain, their businesses. A client's situation will not change without a proactive response to the plan. In other words, success—as defined in many ways by both parties— is contingent on action.

- Does the plan meet standards consistent with the firm's business model and other regulatory requirements?

If the answer to these questions is yes, it is likely that the financial plan was effectively written, regardless of its format or length. With the repeated use of these three tenets, plan writing will become less daunting and allow the student or novice to focus more on building the professional judgment to conceptualize a plan matched to a client's needs. Planning the writing also becomes more efficient with experience. For example, plan sections that seem to be effective with most clients, or that provide basic client education, can be repeated almost verbatim in future plans, whereas sections that are client specific may need to be revised as the planner crafts plans that address different client situations and challenges. Practicing a sport makes players better as they develop "muscle memory" for the required response. Likewise, practice in writing more plans has the added benefit of making the planning process and the ability to communicate the process easier.

To assist students and novice planners in answering the question, "What is a financial plan?" this chapter presents an outline for writing a detailed, comprehensive financial plan. This approach is considered from the contexts of writing style and voice; plan style and format; and the key messages of a financial plan. Although the chapter is written from the perspective of a longer plan, the principles for conveying the fundamental message of the plan apply regardless of the style, format, or length of the plan.

WRITING STYLE AND VOICE

Writing a comprehensive financial plan is the optimal way to systematically describe a client's needs, wants, desires, and goals within the context of a reasonable approach to making those dreams become reality. The challenges associated with writing an effective plan lie hidden in the nuances of that statement. Writing plans, or even purchasing software to do much of the writing, requires a planner to identify and develop a personal **writing style**. Style is nothing more than a distinctive approach that is used consistently to communicate. Norman Mailer, the Pulitzer Prize-winning author, stated that writing style is a reflection of the author.[2] The good news is that a financial planner need not be Norman Mailer to write a good plan. All that is necessary is to follow some essential writing guidelines grounded on one fundamental premise: know your audience—or in this case, know your client.

A useful starting point in determining one's writing style is revisiting the learning and information processing style comparisons presented in Chapter 3. The three primary modes of processing information or experiences are visual, auditory, and kinesthetic. Although the theory and applications surrounding this topic are quite complex and worthy of more study, the simple approach of processing information through the eyes, ears, experiences, actions, or feelings can help guide a planner's communication approach with clients.

Individuals who prefer the **visual learning style** will find that pictures, graphs, charts, and other visual aids are helpful adjuncts to the written word when reviewing complex issues. Hearing information may offer only temporary insight for visual learners. On the other hand, clients who prefer the **auditory learning style** will quickly and easily grasp even the most complex issues without ever looking at a written plan; consequently, for these clients talking with the planner is critical. The **kinesthetic**, or experiential, **learning style** requires the client to experience or engage with the content of a plan. Internet-based calculators, software simulations, or well-defined "to-do lists" for plan implementation may appeal to this type of learner, as well as experiences that challenge the client to project feelings associated with scenarios.

Clearly, not every communication exchange can match clients' preferred information processing style, and everyone uses all three styles regardless of their dominant preference. But recognition of these styles can increase communication effectiveness and challenge planners to creatively adapt the various forms of client communication, including financial plans, to appeal to all styles of learners.

Before writing a single word of a financial plan, it is important for financial planners to recognize their own dominant **information processing style**—the way they prefer to receive information. Financial planners tend to write plans based on the assumption that their clients process information the same way they do. However, one approach, by itself, seldom meets the learning needs of most clients. Instead, each planner should attempt to balance aspects of all preferred information processing styles by employing a variety of methods for client communication.

For example, planners who are kinesthetic learners should make an effort to be more inclusive in their writing style by incorporating visual features. Some communication may, of necessity, require a dominant presentation approach; but one communication method should not dominate all forms of client interaction on a routine basis. This ensures that that all learners are "getting the message" because the visual, auditory, and kinesthetic needs of all clients are being met (at least to the extent possible). Employing a combination of learning methods also helps a client feel "understood" by the planner. Augmenting text with visual components, such as color, graphics, and font styles that are tastefully repeated throughout the plan increases visual interest.

In addition to writing style, the second most important consideration is the **voice** to be conveyed in the plan. Voice, or the image of the writer and his or her message, is conveyed through the (a) point of view or perspective of the author; (b) choice and use of pronouns; and (c) choice of active or passive verb forms. As background for these issues, first consider the voices that a planner might need to invoke:

- A knowledgeable expert with technical expertise

- An objective professional serving in a fiduciary role

- A trusted confidante and friend

- A counselor, coach, referee, challenger, or educator

- A business person or service provider with good customer relationship skills

- A trusted family friend

- A motivator and "voice of reason" for financial issues

Although it is neither possible nor necessary to convey all of these voices in a written plan, both the plan and the voice used should project an appropriate image of the planner and the planning firm.

The point of view or perspective chosen by a writer can be described as impersonal or personal. The **impersonal voice** is businesslike—objective, serious, fact-based, and devoid of any consideration of the experiences, feelings, or opinions of the author or the reader. In contrast, the **personal voice** communicates a more private or personalized message that employs pronouns that directly address and involve the reader. Consistent with these points of view is the idea of "person" and the use of the first, second, or third person voice. The **first person voice**, where the author is the speaker, provides a direct, personal account by using the term *I*. With the **second person voice**, the author as speaker directly addresses the reader by using the word *you*. For the **third person voice**, the author provides a more objective or distanced explanation, but pronouns (if used) may be in the subjective or objective case. Table 9.1 summarizes the accepted use of singular and plural pronouns when used in the subjective, objective, or possessive voice. Some authors choose the impersonal voice and the gender-neutral pronoun *one*, which can be used as a third person substitute for a first person pronoun (e.g., I, we, me), or in the possessive form, as in the example, "It is important to perfect one's writing style."

Table 9.1 Subjective, Objective, and Possessive Case Usage

Case	Singular Usage	Plural Usage
Subject or Subjective		
First person	I	We
Second person	You	You
Third person	She or he	The
Object or Objective		
First person	Me	Us
Second person	You	You
Third person	Her or him	Them
Possessive		
First person	My	Our
Second person	Your	Your
Third person	Her or his	Their

First and second person plural possessive usage is the most common style used in writing a financial plan. For example, it is conventional to state something like, "*Our* firm prides itself in meeting *your* financial goals." Some financial planners prefer to use a subjective plural pronoun style such as, "*We* believe that *you* will meet your goals by 2018." In some cases, financial planners use first person plural subjective pronouns to describe themselves, but then they use the first names of their clients in the plan. For example, a plan might state, "Jim and Mary, *we* recommend that a $250,000 policy be purchased for your disabled son Todd." Or consider the contrasting, more impersonal statement, "It is recommended that *one* purchase a $250,000 policy."

Generally, first person singular should be avoided unless the financial planner is truly a one-person firm or maintains very intimate personal relationships with his or her clientele. The excessive use of *I* (i.e., repeatedly saying, "I recommend," "I conclude," etc.) could be interpreted by clients as a form of arrogance on the part of the planner. Occasionally the overuse of *I* can set an adversarial tone, although this is almost never the planner's intent. If a plural usage is selected, then use of the singular should be avoided. However, it is likely that the plan will switch between subjective and possessive pronouns when appropriate.

The choice and use of active or passive verb forms is the third factor that contributes to voice. The **active voice** is recommended because it results in shorter, more forceful and direct sentences. Consider the following examples of the active and passive voice:

> "Based on the recommendation, a $1 million term policy was purchased by Yogini."

> "Based on the recommendation, Yogini purchased a $1 million term policy."

Use the active voice unless the object of the action or verb is more important than the subject or person doing the action. Note how the first sentence emphasizes the $1 million term policy, whereas the second sentence shifts the emphasis to Yogini. The choice of the active voice also makes the voice of the plan more personal.

The selection of point of view, pronoun and case usage, and active or passive verb usage depends entirely on the stylistic effect or voice each financial planner prefers to use. A plural possessive approach presents a more objective and slightly more impersonal image. Consistent with this style, a planner might use more passive sentences or the gender-neutral pronoun *one*. On the other hand, a more active style that incorporates pronouns with first names will make a plan read more informally, but also more personally.

Once chosen, the overall voice should be consistent throughout the plan. However, there may be subtle shifts between the elements of a plan that provide definitions or explanations to educate the client and the sections that reflect how a client's goals and assumptions influenced a recommendation. Attention to voice will help planners develop a consistent style that does not jolt the client between "hard core" facts versus a message that conveys a sincere understanding of the client's needs. Attention to the voice used to make observations and recommendations is also extremely important. The planner is the expert, but it is important to temper the role of expert with the roles of coach, educator, and friend.

PLAN STYLE AND FORMAT

Many details go into designing and writing a financial plan. Each distinct element is important and should not be overlooked. Factors such as how the plan is bound, the type of paper used, the use of fonts and color, and the mix of text and graphics all play a role in how the final plan will look, feel, and read. General formatting issues need to be considered carefully (e.g., how much text in relation to the number of graphs, charts, or tables). There is no universal answer, or even a typical recommendation, except to "know your audience."

A well-designed plan lends credence to a planner's recommendations—both literally and figuratively. For example, if a financial planner deals primarily with engineers and other professionals who tend to be highly analytical and well educated, plans may tend to emphasize detailed, mathematical explanations of the analysis over text or graphic summaries. Such clients may spend more time studying an abbreviated summary of the plan and examining the *exact* details of spreadsheets included in the appendix rather than reading the plan itself. Conversely, other clients may only glance through the appendix or simply ignore "all those pages of numbers." A planner who works with a clientele that is not as interested in the mathematical analysis may want to emphasize graphic displays that summarize and interpret plan projections and content over written text or spreadsheets filled with data. Regardless of client type, a planner should use the plan as an education tool, but the scope of the educational effort should be tailored to client needs.

It is equally important to spend time ensuring that each written plan is attractive and well organized. It is natural for clients to link the quality of analysis with the quality of presentation. Clients generally assume that planners who spend time on presentation details are more likely to also have spent time on analytical details and a carefully developed plan. Thus, formatting is an important aspect of an effective financial plan. Remember: anything that can assist a client in accessing and interpreting a plan enhances the probability that the client will buy into the ideas presented and, most importantly, ultimately implement the recommendations. Following are some basic rules to increase the effectiveness of a plan:

1. A functional format with easy-to-read fonts is advisable. At a minimum, an 11- or 12-point black font in either Times New Roman or Arial is recommended. Font sizes or styles can be altered to separate sections or designate headings, but it is important to remain consistent from section to section if different fonts or font sizes are used.

2. Consistency in formatting, writing style, and voice from one plan section to another is important. Clients expect uniformity in presentation, and the best way to achieve this is to choose a format and writing style and stick with it.

3. The mix between black-and-white and color within a plan is a major formatting issue. The use of color appeals to those who prefer to process information visually. Color also adds a sense of vitality and attractiveness to a plan that can otherwise be thought of as technical or impenetrable.

4. The choice of plan cover is also important. Some financial planners prefer to use a loose-leaf binder to organize a plan. This is a good choice for those who see a plan as a **living document** that will be added to on a frequent basis. Other planners prefer to actually bind the plan. This approach makes a plan look and feel more like a book, which presents an image of utmost professionalism. However, some planners and clients may interpret a bound plan as being inflexible in purpose and use. Still other financial planners use punch-hole binding methods or spiral binding. The choice of binding is an individual decision matched to the plan. However, a spiral-bound plan with a plastic sheet cover will impart a different feel than the same plan bound in a faux-leather binder.

5. Check and recheck the plan! Financial planners are encouraged to take extra time to edit all material within a plan for errors, omissions, and grammar. *How* something is said may be as important, or even more important, than *what* is said. Also carefully check all facts and numbers for accuracy throughout the plan.

6. Each core content section within a comprehensive financial plan should stand alone if read separately, explaining purpose, assumptions, analysis, recommendations, implementation, and monitoring, just as a targeted, or modular, plan should culminate with implementation and monitoring advice. This means that a client should be able to read a section on education planning, for example, and understand the (a) goal and current situation, (b) the analysis conducted, (c) the recommendations made, and (d) the methods for implementing and monitoring the recommendations in the future.

7. Needless to say, plans must be well written. Planners should avoid technical jargon and financial planning acronyms. Technically complicated topics and terms should be simplified and defined. There is no point in trying to impress

a client with technical jargon; in fact, this practice can make the plan seem more impersonal. Keep it simple, but whenever appropriate, use the text, or accompanying background articles, to educate the client. Supplement the text information with a glossary of terms or other supporting education articles in the appendices.

8. Write as if the plan were a financial road map rather than a corporate or household financial report. The plan should reasonably follow the financial planning process. This means that a logical progression from planning goals and objectives, the definition of terms, a current situation assessment and analysis, recommendations, and plan implementation and monitoring should be incorporated.

9. Use a combination of pre-scripted and client-specific information. Approximately half of any written plan can consist of **pre-scripted material** (e.g., explanations of core content topics within the plan, the definitions of terms, and explanations of financial products and strategies). Although it is true that, for instance, definitions in a plan may be exactly the same for every client, this does not mean that recommendations can be universally applied among clientele. Recommendations and implementation strategies may be similar, but it is important that each recommendation in a plan be matched to the client's unique goals, objectives, and situation. Recommendation and implementation plans should always reflect a client's personal circumstances, existing market conditions, laws and regulations, and the current state of the economy.

10. Document, document, document! Footnotes should be used to authenticate material in the plan referenced from other sources. The use of references suggests that the planner is well-read, which may enhance the planner's professional image. Also use footnotes or another referencing system to help the client easily locate supporting spreadsheet or software results in plan appendices.

COMPONENTS OF A FINANCIAL PLAN

Sometimes students and novice financial planners think of the written plan as the end product rather than the means to help a client reach financial goals and objectives. A well-written financial plan provides a client with a dynamic financial road map to enhanced financial wellness. By its very nature, a well-written comprehensive plan is integrative, realistic, and synergistic. A plan is *integrative* if one section builds upon or links with another section. The same is also true of a single-issue, or modular, plan, except the progression from analysis of the current situation to recommendation is limited to only one planning topic, whereas a comprehensive plan addresses a broader array of topics. In a comprehensive plan, the effects of one recommendation must be considered relative to the outcomes of another recommendation. Both the analysis and recommendations of modular and comprehensive plans must be realistic for a client's situation, the mutually agreed-upon assumptions, and the legal and economic environment.

The writing process allows a planner to combine multiple strategies and client solutions into one integrated presentation. A *realistic* plan is one that can be implemented with or without the assistance of a financial planner. A well-written plan is also *synergistic* if, when read as a complete plan, the whole is greater than the sum of the individual parts. In other words, an effective plan is one that provides a financial life road map for a client. The road map, when presented in its entirety, provides more information than simply looking at each piece of a person's financial situation separately.

Continuing with the road map analogy, it is equally important for plan writers to have a workable outline to guide the progression and development of a plan. To proceed without an outline that has been perfected to match the way a planner or firm serves clients is analogous to beginning a cross-country trip without a map. But the broad variation of planning services among providers is also evident in the plans produced. For example, the Letter to Client and the Copy of the Client Engagement Letter, or some of the information included, may not be applicable for advisors who are delivering a financial plan only as a way to establish product needs. Certainly, including these documents when a planner is actually in a continuing financial planning engagement may be helpful, but it may not be applicable when the financial plan is ancillary to a product sale. Although the applicability or sequencing of some components of a plan may vary, many financial planners follow a general outline similar to that shown in Exhibit 9.1 Following is a description of each plan component and a discussion of the purpose or reason for including the component in a comprehensive plan.

Exhibit 9.1 Comprehensive Financial Plan Outline

I. Cover Page

II. Letter to Client

II. Copy of the Original Client Engagement Letter

IV. Table of Contents

V. Other Introductory Materials *(optional)*

    a. Mission/vision statement

    b. Statement of principles or core values

    c. Ethics statement

    d. Privacy statement

    e. Investment policy statement *(or may appear in the section describing the investments for each client goal, such as retirement, education, etc.)*

VI. Client Profile, Summary of Goals and Assumptions *(general or global assumptions or all assumptions if not included in each core content planning section)*

VII. Executive Summary *or* Observations and Recommendations

VIII. Individual Core Content Planning Sections

    a. Cash flow analysis

    b. Net worth analysis

    c. Tax analysis

    d. Insurance/risk management analysis

        i. Life insurance

        ii. Health and disability insurance

        iii. Long-term care insurance

        iv. Property and liability insurance

        v. Umbrella or excess liability insurance

        vi. Other insurance needs

    e. Investment analysis

    f. Retirement analysis

    g. Estate planning analysis

    h. Specialized analyses

        i. Educational funding

        ii. Planning for special needs

        iii. Refinancing scenarios

        Saving for special objectives

IX. Implementation and Monitoring Section *(specific information should appear in each individual core content planning section)*

X. Client Acceptance Letter or Client Engagement Letter *(if not included earlier)*

XI. Appendices

    a. Calculations and projections

    b. Educational materials

I. Cover Page

It is important for a financial plan to have a well-designed cover page. The cover is the first detail a client will see, and as such, the cover provides a first impression of the quality and content of the plan itself. Typically, a cover page includes the firm logo (if applicable) and the following information:

- firm name and address;

- the planner's name;

- a brief firm or planner vision statement;

- a phrase such as "A Comprehensive Financial Plan Prepared for [Client's Name]";

- the term *confidential* clearly indicated;

- any applicable disclosure statements as required; and

- the date of the plan.

II. Letter to Client

A cover letter serves many purposes depending on the type of planner-client relationship or the business practice model used. One purpose may be to reintroduce the planner and the firm to the client. Another is to reiterate the planner's commitment to helping the client achieve financial objectives. The process used to develop the plan may be briefly reviewed. The planner's or firm's core values or commitment to client relationships may also be restated. Consistent with that message, the letter may outline the future relationship between the firm and the client, if applicable, such as the:

- timing of periodic reviews;

- expected client preparation for review meetings (e.g., updating the client information form by mail or online);

- provision of quarterly reports or other client updates;

- availability of the planner or other staff for client assistance;

- mailing of newsletters; or

- access to other services provided by the firm.

Another purpose that a cover letter may serve, such as when the planner and client do not have an ongoing relationship, is simply to convey specific required information. In such situations, the cover letter may include compliance or legal disclosure statements. Some advisors feel that these disclosures carry a stronger message when they are included in a more personal cover letter addressed to the client. Other advisors believe that the importance of compliance matters warrants omitting the Letter to Client altogether and including disclosures on a separate disclaimer page in the Introductory Materials section to reduce the likelihood that these messages will be overlooked.

Whichever format is used, compliance messages are typically reiterated in the plan after having been initially introduced in the client engagement letter (if applicable to the planner-client relationship). Compliance statements can relate to the planner's role in ensuring the confidentiality of the client's data, and in some cases they can even extend to protecting the confidentiality of the planning relationship. **Investment performance disclaimers** (e.g., "Past performance is no guarantee of future returns" or "All projections are based on historical data, which may not be reflected in future returns") can be included in the cover letter. Additional disclaimers regarding relationships with other financial professionals may also be needed. For example, the client may be reminded that "Prior to implementing the advice provided in this report, please confirm suggestions with your tax professional or attorney." Or, "Although we may offer tax or estate planning advice in this plan, we are not licensed tax professionals or attorneys. Please confirm our suggestions with your tax professional or attorney." It is wise to also include these disclaimers in select core content planning sections as relevant. The planner should date and sign the letter. Some advisors include a statement for the client to sign to acknowledge that the letter was read and that any questions were explained.

III. Copy of the Original Client Engagement Letter

A **client engagement letter** outlines the responsibilities and duties of the financial planner and the client. Although this may sound similar to the cover letter, there is a distinct difference. The client engagement letter, when applicable to a planner-client relationship, is contractual, whereas in most cases the cover letter is simply informational. As shown in Appendix 9A.1, the client signs the client engagement letter, although some versions require signatures from both client and planner. The client is agreeing to the services and costs explained and engaging the planner to provide the products or services outlined. As noted previously, compliance and disclaimer messages about performance and professional expertise can appear in the cover letter, the engagement letter, or elsewhere in the plan. Special attention should also be given to informing the client that all analyses and recommendations are based on information provided by the client. The engagement letter can also outline the components of the financial plan.

If the engagement letter is completed before the plan is developed, it may not appear in the written plan document, or a copy can be included simply for informational purposes. Note that some planners require that clients sign and return the letter before plan delivery to confirm the scope of the agreed-upon services. This letter can also be found at the end of the plan, as noted in the plan outline shown in Exhibit 9.1.

Because the letter of engagement establishes the contractual arrangement between advisor and client, it is important that the letter (or contract) include the following:

- Contact information for the firm and advisor;

- A description of the services/products to be provided, including the responsibilities and obligations of each party;

- A time frame for the agreement and the provision of services/products (e.g., client reviews and evaluations);

- Compensation for the services/products; and

- Other material information related to the relationship, such as, but not limited to:

  - Arbitration as a method for settling disputes arising from the contract or breach of contract;

- Assignment of the contract; and
- Methods for amending or terminating the agreement.

The scope of the contract will vary with the advisor's business model; however, the preceding are considered essential elements of an engagement letter. See Chapters 1 and 6 for more information on disclosures. The engagement letter may also be referred to as the financial planning, advisory, management, or service agreement.

This particular sample engagement letter clearly defines the scope of the relationship and outlines the rights and responsibilities of the interested parties when the engagement is limited to the delivery of a financial plan. However, other engagement letters could look substantially different depending on the scope of the planner-client relationship and the planner's business model. Notice that this letter mentions that commissions may be received by the advisor "if you request our assistance in directly making any financial acquisitions and decide to make purchases through us." In contrast, an advisor with a fee-only business model would likely state that the firm would not accept or receive any fees, commissions, or other forms of payment for investments or products recommended. If the implementation of planning recommendations is expected to happen in conjunction with the plan, then the engagement letter would include additional information about how, and by whom, implementation would occur. Additionally, if a financial planner provides a plan as part of an ongoing, perhaps retainer relationship, concierge services might be explained in the letter of engagement and would be available to the client as needed.

IV. Table of Contents

A table of contents helps the client navigate the financial plan by conveying its overall organization, the availability of supporting documents, and relevant page numbers. An increasing number of planners use a color coding scheme to identify sections within a plan, which are then coordinated with color coding in the table of contents. Some financial planners also use color-coded tabs to coordinate sections of a plan, with colored page numbers that correspond to the section font color in the table of contents. These are all good ideas, although care must be taken that these methods do not detract from the overall impression of the written document. Anything that will help a client read and understand the plan, seriously weigh the recommendations presented, and more importantly, implement the recommendations, is beneficial to both planner and client.

V. Other Introductory Materials

The inclusion of additional introductory materials (e.g., the firm's mission and vision statements, ethics statement, privacy statement, or client investment policy statement) provides a mechanism for fostering client confidence in the planner and the firm. Introductory materials (with the exception of the client-specific investment policy statement) do not generally change from one client to another. Although including these statements is optional, this should not be interpreted to mean that the information is not as valuable as material presented later. Because only the privacy statement is required by statute, the information in this section is provided solely to enhance the credibility of the planner. Inclusion of this information affords an opportunity to communicate or reinforce a planner's total commitment to the client. Because this information may have been included in a brochure, marketing or information packet, or other client communication provided earlier in the relationship, some planners choose not to include this introductory material (or if it is included, to summarize it in some way).

A planner's **mission statement** defines the strengths and expertise of the planner relative to the market segment that the planner or firm has chosen to serve. A planner's mission statement can be very simple. For example, a mission statement can be as straightforward as "Providing comprehensive financial planning services to middle-income clients." A mission statement is different than a **vision statement**, which typically summarizes a planner's ultimate aspirations and likely reflects some broadly defined values or principles that govern the operation of the business. Whereas a mission statement defines a target market or idealized goal for clients, a vision statement describes what efforts a planner or planning firm will make to accomplish the firm's mission. The mission and vision statements should resonate with the firm's clients and contribute to the clients' decision to choose the firm, as demonstrated by the following vision statement example:

> *We strive to bring our clients financial peace of mind. Our goal is to identify optimal recommendations to help guide clients in reaching their financial goals and objectives. We do this by building trusting, long-lasting client relationships that always focus on the best interests of our client—not our own. It is our highest aspiration to provide the best guidance and advice to help our clients consistently make sound financial decisions in pursuit of their hopes and dreams.*

The statement of values or principles that comprise the vision statement may reflect core firm values, such as customer service, teamwork, and professional expertise, as exemplified by the following statements excerpted from a student-developed **statement of principles** for a hypothetical firm:

- We expect a high level of customer service and customer satisfaction from our staff.

- We believe that planning through teamwork provides better service.

- We believe that expert knowledge in all financial areas is essential.

Increasing public concern over impropriety in the financial services industry has led some financial planners to include a code of ethics in the introductory section of a plan. Financial planners who are CFP Board certificants and registrants must adhere to **CFP Board *Code of Ethics and Professional Responsibility***. (For more information on the principles in the code see Chapter 2.) The FPA adopted the CFP Board *Code of Ethics and Professional Responsibility* (Code of Ethics) and asserts that "All FPA members are asked to commit to this Code, CFP® certificants and non-CFP certificants alike."[3]

A number of other professional planning associations and trade groups support a similar set of core values that should guide all business transactions. For example, NAPFA members and affiliates must abide by the Code of Ethics to maintain eligibility and good standing in NAPFA.

Finally, effective January 2005 (as explained in Chapter 2), advisers registered with the SEC (and also with most state securities agencies) were required to establish a code of ethics that established standards of conduct for the actions of advisory personnel and addressed any conflicts of interest in the personal trading practices of advisory personnel. The ruling stated that

> Many professional and trade organizations, such as the Financial Planning Association, the Association for Investment Management and Research, the Certified Financial Planner Board of Standards, the Investment Counsel Association of America, and the American Institute of Certified Public Accountants, have developed professional codes of ethics or model codes for their members' use.[4]

In summary, it is highly recommended—and in some cases mandated by law—that planners adopt and promote a **code of ethics**. Such adoption and adherence to the code does not require that the code be provided to clients, although many planners are choosing to make the code of ethics part of the plan or, at a minimum, a feature of the advisor's Web site or other client documents. Although including the ethics statement in the plan is optional, planners should adhere to and publish their commitment to an ethical code developed personally or in conjunction with a professional group.

It is not only prudent to include a **privacy statement** in a plan, in certain circumstances it is required by law. Federal legislation, the Gramm-Leach-Bliley Act of 1999, and the subsequent adoption of Regulation S-P by the SEC mandated that any firm that has access to private and confidential client data must disclose to each client how the firm will use and protect the data. In the case of financial planning firms, client data must remain totally confidential other than as required or allowed by law. Data should be shared only with members of the planning firm and regulators, or other financial professionals with appropriate disclosure and consent by the client.

A firm's privacy statement should communicate these policies to clients. A privacy statement is required to be distributed to clients at the initiation of the business relationship with subsequent annual privacy notice mailings. Although a privacy statement was likely provided before the financial plan was delivered, as required by law, some planners choose to include a statement in the plan as well. Furthermore, protecting the confidentiality of client data is one of the principles included in the CFP Board Code of Ethics as well as the FPA and NAPFA *Code of Ethics* statements.

An **investment policy statement** (IPS) is a written document signed by planner and client to acknowledge their agreement to the parameters guiding the investment or management of client funds. The IPS integrates the client's risk tolerance, risk capacity, investment philosophy, and planner-proposed investment methods to establish parameters for the actual investment strategies used. Because of the communication that transpires between planner and client during the development of a comprehensive IPS, it is possible the IPS was signed during the discovery process prior to the development of the plan. However, in some firms the plan may precede the IPS because the plan is developed as a foundation for establishing the kind of portfolio needed to maximize the likelihood of achieving client goals. For example, if an advisor's planning approach typically begins with the transfer of assets to the firm for management, then the IPS will be provided with the other initial documents. But if the advisor's planning approach is to develop the plan, after which the client can choose to contract for investment management services, then another contract would be initiated and the IPS developed to govern the related services.

The IPS is included because of its vital link to the planning process, and as a reminder to the client and planner of the importance of adhering to the guidelines established. If not included as an introductory document, an IPS can be incorporated into the investment planning section of the financial plan. Some advisors develop multiple investment policy statements individually matched to the investment management plan and aligned with different client goals. For example, two investment policy statements might be needed for managing retirement assets if the risk tolerance factors and acceptable investment management strategies are very different for spouses or partners. Regardless of the number of statements or where the IPS is situated in the written document, its inclusion is necessary to reduce financial planner liability through appropriate planning disclosure. Practicing full disclosure with a client-signed IPS is prudent because it establishes a mutually agreed-upon standard of conduct while reducing the possibility of a future lawsuit brought by a client who claims misrepresentation or poor performance.

As noted at the beginning of this section, the inclusion of these other introductory materials—the firm's mission and vision statements, an ethics statement, a privacy statement, or a client investment policy statement—is *optional*. However, as explained above, these documents are either required to be a part of the advisor's business plan or they represent best practice for presenting a positive image. In addition, the IPS, by documenting agreed-upon investment strategies, could limit an advisor's liability exposure.

VI. Client Profile, Summary of Goals, and Assumptions

The client profile typically (a) summarizes the demographic and socioeconomic profile of the client household, (b) lists the primary goals identified as a foundation for the planning process, and (c) reviews planner-client planning assumptions. Whereas a personal and household profile may seem redundant and unnecessary, it is still important to document this information as a final verification of basic client information such as names, addresses, employment data, the ages of all household members, and perhaps health status or other pertinent personal information. The statement of primary goals serves to clearly articulate and perhaps rank the goals identified by the planner and client. Because these goals not only serve as the foundation of the planning process but also strongly influence the choice of financial strategies to be implemented now or in the future, it is important that they be clearly defined.

Finally, one of the most important sections of a financial plan is a recapitulation of the planner's assumptions when writing the plan. It is important to note that, although called *assumptions*, this section may include *factual* information about the household or other planning issues as well as other situational information, as illustrated by the following list of education planning assumptions:

- Bradley will start college in the fall of 2020.

- A savings account earmarked for Bradley's college has an account balance of $5,384.

- Today, tuition, room, board, and fees at a state-supported 4-year institution total $16,500 per year.

- The tuition inflation rate is 7% per year, calculated on a calendar year basis.

- You are comfortable with a moderately aggressive risk allocation when investing for this goal, but you agree that the risk exposure will have to change as the time horizon for the goal shortens.

- Scholarships or other financial assistance is not anticipated for Bradley.

Facts and both client-specific and core content-specific assumptions serve as the basis for conducting this analysis and formulating recommendations by setting realistic parameters, or constraints, on the planning process. Although working assumptions, when used, generally appear in each section of the plan, it is also a good idea to summarize all assumptions at the beginning of the plan. This summary can be used as a reference during client meetings and as a tool to help clients understand the factors affecting an analysis. Finally, clearly delineating assumptions gives the client one last opportunity to validate or further clarify the planning situation.

VII. Executive Summary or Observations and Recommendations

The **executive summary** summarizes (a) key goals and objectives dealt with in the plan, (b) relevant assumptions, (c) the resulting recommendations, (d) the steps for implementation, and (e) the projected financial outcomes made possible by plan implementation. Many clients may never read an entire plan; instead, they might judge a planner's strategic approach after reading the executive summary. However, it may be necessary to revise the executive summary after presenting the plan to the client to accommodate mutually agreed-upon changes to recommendations, specific implementation strategies, or the timeline for implementation. An executive summary should include the following six elements:

1. Purpose of the plan;

2. Methods used to analyze the client situation;

3. Results of the analysis;

4. Recommendation(s);

5. Implementation strategies for action; and

6. Timeline for implementation.

The most common question about executive summaries involves how long a summary should be. The answer, unfortunately, is not easy to provide because it depends on the complexity of a client's objectives and the intricacy of the solutions offered. Usually, an executive summary can be written in one to three pages; however, a more complex plan might require five or more pages. An excerpt from an executive summary example is shown in Exhibit 9.2.

Exhibit 9.2 Sample Executive Summary

Executive Summary

The purpose of this comprehensive financial plan is to provide a framework for helping you reach your financial goals and objectives. The plan consists of a section for each of the following topical areas: financial situation; tax planning; insurance planning; retirement planning; education planning; and estate planning.

A comprehensive review of your financial situation was conducted using information you provided to our firm. Three primary financial goals were identified: (1) clarifying your financial situation as a recent widow; (2) funding retirement to begin at age 62; and (3) prefunding education costs for your twins, Jim and Gary.

Several financial strengths were identified during the analysis. It was determined that your net worth is excellent given your age and income level. You are also contributing 10% of your income to your firm's 401(k) plan, and you have an employe-provided own-occupation long-term disability policy. Your employment is secure, you plan to continue with this company until you retire, and your income is sufficient to meet projected expenses. You also are working with an attorney on a new estate plan.

Our analysis also indicates that four specific areas need immediate attention. First, you need to purchase an additional $500,000 in life insurance coverage. Second, to achieve retirement at age 62 you will need to save an additional $5,000 per year in a tax-advantaged Roth IRA. Third, tax withholdings ought to be reduced to increase annual discretionary cash flow and to better match your federal and state projected tax liability. Fourth, $130,000 should be allocated to a § 529 education funding plan to prefund college education costs for Jim and Gary. The following actions are recommended (additional details are provided later in the plan):

√   Purchase a $500,000, 20-year guaranteed-renewable term life insurance policy though the XYZ company.

- Date to be Completed: Within the next 30 to 45 days

√   Establish and fund a Roth IRA with $5,000 invested in the ABC Mutual Fund.

- Date to be Completed: Before the end of the calendar year

√   Adjust W-4 withholdings through your human resource department by claiming three exemptions.

- Date to be Completed: Within the next 60 to 90 days

√   Establish two Anystate-sponsored § 529 plans and prefund each with $65,000. We recommend using $130,000 of the proceeds from your late husband's employer-provided life insurance policy, which are currently held in ABC Money Market Account. The balance of ABC Money Market Account provides you an easily accessible emergency fund, as requested.

- Date to be Completed: Within the next 60 to 90 days

Some financial planners prefer to call this summary section "Observations and Recommendations," "Review of Recommendations," "Preview of Recommendations," or some other title that sounds less technical than "Executive Summary." The choice of terms is yet another reflection of the tone of voice that a planner or firm wishes to project through the written plan. Irrespective of the title chosen, the content should still include most if not all of the information included in the Executive Summary outline shown, or this section may be limited to some general observations about the client's situation followed by a listing of recommendations. The client's goals can serve as the organizational structure for observations and recommendations, or the observations and recommendations could be organized according to the individual core content planning sections.

The breadth and depth of information included in this section of the plan varies with the approach used to develop the entire written plan. For example, the message might progress from general to specific throughout the entire plan. A very general review of planning recommendations in the Executive Summary can provide a "big picture" description of the plan, followed by much more detailed information in each individual core content section. An "Action Plan," "To-do List," or timeline logically concludes the plan and summarizes and integrates the detailed information needed for plan implementation and monitoring.

Alternatively, this approach of progressing from general to specific can be used to provide the client a more detailed "snapshot" of the entire plan within the scope of the Executive Summary. If this section includes more detailed information as outlined above, the written narrative might not have to repeat this information in a later section of the plan, focusing solely on implementation and monitoring instead. However, if the "Observations and Recommendations" section includes a more general statement regarding recommendations, then more detailed implementation information is necessary at some other point(s) in the plan. In either case, the explanation of the analysis, where applicable, would be more fully developed in the core content section of the plan. The objective is not to repeat information needlessly, but to develop an approach that seems logical and easy for the planner to explain and the client to understand.

In some cases, a detailed Executive Summary may be the *only* written document provided to a client, in lieu of a more extensive plan. In this case, the Executive Summary might be accompanied by a summative Implementation Checklist for all recommendations. The Implementation Checklist was discussed in Chapter 8, and is again in the next section of this chapter.

VIII. Individual Core Content Planning Sections

The core elements of any financial plan consist of individual content sections, such as that the one shown in Appendix D: Education Planning: A Sample Section from the Kims' Comprehensive Plan. As the plan outline shown in Exhibit 9.1 indicates, comprehensive financial planning encompasses a number of critical areas including cash flow and net worth analysis, tax planning, insurance analysis and planning, retirement and estate planning, investment planning, and special needs planning, which can include education savings preparation. Because each client is unique, a comprehensive plan might also include sections devoted to charitable giving, trust management, long-term care planning, or family business continuation planning, in addition to other specialty topics. Such core content planning sections can educate clients on their current financial situation and motivate action where needed. It is extremely important that the format of each section be similar. Using a section outline is one way to ensure such consistency.

The outline in Exhibit 9.3 includes elements typically found in a core content section. This outline assumes that a client's background in personal finance is limited. Each section starts with a brief explanation of the topical area (e.g., life insurance planning or estate planning) and provides definitions of terms or explanations of products included in the discussion of that particular core content section. Once this section has been written for each core content area, it can be used again or easily adapted for use in other plans. In an effort to control the length of the introductory section, and to allow for greater flexibility in meeting the needs of individual clients, financial planners are increasingly using an appendix to provide articles that are particularly relevant to a client. This enables the planner to respond to a client's unique interests or to provide fundamental client education. Additionally, market reports, articles, newsletters, and financial calculators may also be made available on the planner's Web site to allow for timely updates and easy access.

Exhibit 9.3 Outline for Each Core Content Planning Section in a Plan

I. Overview of core content area and definitions

II. Restatement of planner-client assumptions

III. Review of the analysis of client's current situation

    1. Observations about the current situation

    2. Assessment of planning needs

    3. Assessment of current planning efforts

IV. Statement of financial planning recommendations (who, what, when, where, why, how, and how much)

V. Comparison of projected recommendation outcome(s) to the current situation

VI. Suggestions for alternative recommendations and outcome(s) where appropriate

VII. Plan implementation and monitoring procedures

    1. Explain the source of the cash flow or assets to be used to fund the recommendation

    2. Provide specific implementation advice

A review of planner or client assumptions used in the analysis or to guide the choice of recommendations should also be provided. Explanations of standard assumptions or other information included to educate the client about the assumptions also may be prudently duplicated from one plan to another. Careful disclosure of the assumptions offers several benefits. If a plan was based on reasonable and prudent assumptions that were matched to a client's situation and the information provided, it will be much more difficult to blame the planner for an unexpected outcome, or to make an allegation of failure to act with professional prudence. Clearly documenting the assumptions used helps a planner *manage* client expectations and establish a defensible approach to the planning process. Clients often seek a second opinion on important financial decisions. Financial planners who fail to document their key working assumptions often find that a competitor's calculations lead to different recommendations. Often, such divergence of analyses—and subsequent recommendations—is entirely attributable to the fact that different assumptions were used.

The tools and approaches used to analyze and quantify planning needs within each of the core content areas can be quite complicated and technical. Results from each analysis must then be compared with the planning efforts the client already has in place, assuming some strategies have been implemented. The challenge for the planner is to explain, thoroughly but succinctly, the analysis of the client's current situation in such a way as to educate and motivate the client. It is important for the planner to exhibit technical expertise in the plan, and to do so with a balanced approach that does not overwhelm or belittle the client. A combination of textual and graphical communication techniques should be employed to accomplish this. The use of graphs, charts, and tables is one way to illustrate analyses, compare products and planning strategies, and generally supplement written and verbal explanations. Spreadsheet or other software results can extend to several pages; some planners include them in the core content section, while others prefer to summarize the analysis there and place lengthy analytical results or output in an appendix at the end of the plan. If the latter approach is used, the plan must clearly note the availability of the results and direct the client to the corresponding documents.

Documenting all assumptions and analyses, makes it is easier to verify observations and recommendations. **Observations** are general statements about a client's financial situation that flow from a review and analysis of the client's situational data. It is not sufficient to say that the current financial situation is generally "good" or "bad." Rather, a planner must objectively and factually document how the situation is currently affecting or is likely to affect the client's goals and objectives.

Observations provide the perfect opportunity to add specificity to the written plan. They also provide an avenue for congratulating a client on past financial decisions and behaviors. Acknowledging a client's successful money management strategies is very important. Making supportive statements to the client balances recommendations that may be counter to the client's typical strategies or that in fact challenge the client to change some financial attitudes or behaviors. Consider the role of a coach who patiently and consistently offers praise for productive actions during the game and quickly takes action to curb behavior leading to fouls or penalties. In the role of financial coach, financial planners, too, must consistently offer balanced feedback.

Once the client's current situation has been described, financial planning recommendations are presented. Special attention should always be given to the careful crafting of recommendations, which help clients better understand what they must do to improve their financial situation. **Actionable recommendations** are clearly specified and affordable for the client to implement. Whether stated in text, reported in a Planning Recommendation Form (as shown in Exhibits 7.2 and 7.5 in Chapter 7) that is included in the plan, or communicated to the client using both methods, the recommendation must answer the seven fundamental questions of who, what, when, where, why, how, and how much.

In some cases, the answer to the question *who* may require the client to take action, whereas another recommendation might involve action on the part of a spouse, human resources professional, or another professional (e.g., an attorney or accountant). Fully knowing *what* the recommendation encompasses is critical to the client's comfort in taking action. This may hinge on the planner's ability to explain the planning process and the results of the analysis of the client's situation. *When* is particularly important because not all recommendations can or should be funded immediately. For instance, should the client implement a recommendation immediately or in five years? The choice can make a lasting difference in relation to client outcomes.

Clients need specific advice and guidance when answering the question of *where* a recommendation should be implemented. The answer to this question depends on the strategy and situation. Often a financial planner's firm will provide the best combination of products and services required for implementation. However, even if the planner's firm does not provide some of the products or services recommended, the firm is still likely to be involved in the process and should continue to be involved in future monitoring. *Why* can be answered by showing how the recommendation is based on a detailed analysis that leads to the fulfillment of a goal or objective. *How* and *how much* may seem repetitive, but it is important to be specific when noting both of these details to the client.

A financial planner ought to provide reasonable and actionable answers to all seven questions for each recommendation. However, the importance of working with the client to arrive at mutually agreeable, realistic recommendations must be considered. It is important to be flexible and willing to make changes in response to a client's input. Care also should be taken that the sheer amount of money or time initially required to implement the recommendations not overwhelm the client. As for the written plan as a whole, it is essential that the seven questions be answered clearly and specifically, as illustrated by the following:

> To reach your goal of accumulating an emergency fund equal to four months of current living expenses in your CIA Money Market Account, you need to automatically transfer, via bank draft, $150 from your checking account for the next 15 months. Cecillia, please initiate the request by calling Teresa Maldin at (555) 313-5555 within the next 30 days. She will have the paperwork ready for your signature to implement this recommendation. Or, if you have electronic banking access, you can initiate the monthly debit yourself without the assistance of Ms. Maldin.

If the situation warrants further exploration or the client seems reluctant to consider a recommendation, it may be helpful to compare the projected outcome—assuming the planner's recommendation is implemented—with the outcome should the client's current situation continue unchanged. Effective comparisons can have a dramatic impact on current and future client behavior. It is important when doing comparisons to clearly document the method used, to apply only disclosed client-planner assumptions, and most importantly, to conduct a fair comparison. All projections should be legitimate and conservative. Tables, charts, or graphs may be useful to illustrate these comparisons, as shown in Figure 9.1.

Figure 9.1 Sample Graph Comparing Projected Outcomes

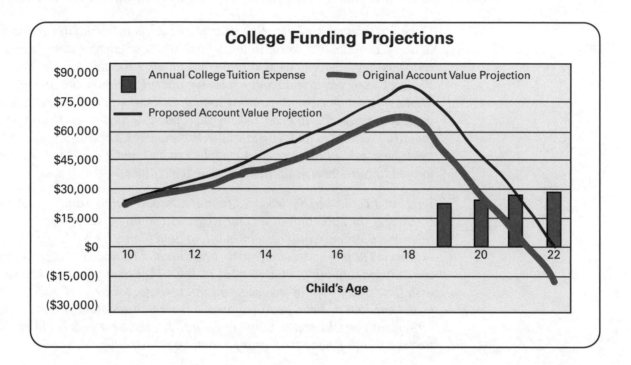

Depending on the planner-client engagement, it may be appropriate to provide one or more alternative recommendations. Alternative recommendations offer planners and clients choices for reaching client goals compared to other recommendations or to the current situation. Incorporating alternative recommendations can help a client choose the most appropriate path to goal achievement. Such an approach can more fully engage the client in the planning and implementation process. The planner should identify an optimal solution; it is likely that the majority of clients will accept the expert opinion without question. However, other clients may wish to be more fully involved in the planning process and the choice of alternative(s). It is important not to overwhelm the client with too many options or analyses. However, having data that supports various options can help educate a client and provide background information for making difficult choices, as illustrated by the following excerpt (without the referenced tables):

> *Doug and Nancy, we know that your ideal goal is to reach joint retirement on January 1, 2035, and to continue to fund 100% of current living expenses in retirement. We have discussed recommendations that will enable you to meet this goal; however, it will require some significant compromises in your current lifestyle, based on current planning assumptions. If you are unable to meet this goal, you would like to know whether it is possible for Nancy to fully retire on January 1, 2030 and for Doug to semi-retire and work as a consultant until 2035, when he would fully retire. To accomplish this second objective, it is important for you to consider two alternative recommendations.*
>
> *First, you could use the balances from the Jordon Value Fund, Quest Growth Fund, and the ARC Index Fund for retirement savings, as opposed to allocating these assets, as currently recommended, to fund Hannah's § 529 plan for college expenses. The projected balance in the accounts and Hannah's § 529 plan, without the additional funding, is illustrated in Table 11. Second, you could also divert cash flow away from other goals and living expenses to fund your retirement goal, as shown in Table 12. Along with our recommendations to reallocate your retirement portfolio and to invest in Roth IRAs, these changes could provide the necessary cash flow to fund your alternative retirement goal.*
>
> *These options also require you to reconsider your priorities and acceptable lifestyle compromises. Although these options might help you reach your retirement goal, it important to note that neither approach maximizes your overall financial planning situation. Both options require you to sacrifice other goals, such as fully funding Hannah's education, as a means to early retirement.*

As part of the explanation of each recommendation, some planners include a pro/con bullet list or a table listing the fundamental advantages and disadvantages of each recommendation. This serves to educate the client and to provide a record of the planner's evaluation of the situation relative to the client's specific situation. This discussion might focus solely on factual benefits and shortcomings of the proposed recommendation or it may also include factors that reflect the client's personal priorities or preferences. Factual data can easily be updated and prudently duplicated from one plan to another.

Finally, and perhaps most importantly, the implementation and monitoring strategies of each core content area should be explained. Carefully developed recommendations leave few questions about implementation procedures. However, a brief narrative or an Implementation Checklist or an implementation table, as in Table 9.2, can be used to fully address the implementation steps needed for each recommendation(s) posed in the core content sections of a written plan. As noted in the outline in Exhibit 9.3, the primary purpose of this discussion is to clarify the source of funds or assets to be dedicated or realigned to fund the recommendation. A secondary purpose is to describe any other details regarding the responsibility for plan implementation.

Table 9.2 Sample Implementation Table

Recommendation: Purchase a 20-year $1-million Term Life Insurance Policy	
Who:	Tony
What:	20-year annually renewable convertible term life insurance policy with Terry named as the owner and primary beneficiary
When:	Within the next 30–45 days
Where:	With your insurance professional or with an online provider that we can recommend for a comparison of premium costs
Why:	To ensure financial security for your family
How:	Consult your insurance professional or we can assist with an online provider. We will assist by discussing the underwriting issues, required application, and medical information.
How much:	$1 million based on the average of three standard methods to estimate life insurance need
Cash flow:	Estimated annual premium: $2,300

IX. Implementation and Monitoring Section

The implementation and monitoring section of a comprehensive financial plan can be thought of as the official summary of the written document. Not to be confused with the discussion of implementation and monitoring for each core content section, this section of the plan summarizes, integrates, and prioritizes all of the recommendations and actions required to implement the plan. Situations in which one recommendation affects other plan recommendations must be acknowledged and thoroughly explained. A narrative section, perhaps supported by data-based charts or other graphics, may be helpful to explain and illustrate alternatives. The Recommendation Impact Form might also be useful. The client's priorities and the planner's expertise must be integrated to prioritize the final methods that will be used to rank and fund each recommendation. For more straightforward situations where there are no or few competing recommendations, a simple to-do checklist or timeline can be presented to summarize the implementation process.

Three forms included in the systematic financial planning methodology are useful to explain this information to clients. The **Implementation Checklist** is an effective way to communicate fundamental information regarding implementation procedures and the projected impact of recommendations on discretionary cash flow (DCF), net worth, or both. The format can be used to document only implementation or both implementation and funding. As discussed in Chapter 8, the table format can be used to easily track multiple recommendations in support of one goal in one core content area. Or the information for all goals and recommendations can be combined into a comprehensive Implementation Checklist included in the Implementation and Monitoring Section of the plan. For an example of this, see Exhibits 8.4, 8.5 and 8.6, the Implementation Checklist for Tom and Nyla Kim in Chapter 8. These forms integrate recommendations by time frame; three forms illustrate the first two years of plan implementation. This versatile tool should be part of every plan, because it can effectively reduce or replace longer textual explanations.

The second form that may be helpful when funds are limited or the client is having difficulty committing to recommendations is the Recommendation Impact Form. Discussed and illustrated in Chapter 7 in Exhibits 7.3 and 7.6, the Recommendation Impact Form for Tom & Nyla Kim, this form can be used to facilitate client decision making. It is especially helpful for comparing the impact of emotionally favored recommendations when the objective significance on other core content areas is presented. The Recommendation Impact Form can be included in the plan only or provided to the client for specific, but not all, recommendations.

The Available Cash Flow and Other Assets Tracker Form is the third useful tool for communicating the effect of multiple recommendations on DCF and net worth. This form, also discussed and illustrated in Chapter 7 in Exhibit 7.1, is a valuable tool for communicating the details of a plan. It can also facilitate planner-client interaction and support client decision making, even during the presentation of the plan, by allowing the client to adjust the amounts allocated to different recommendations and immediately seeing the outcome. Tracking changes in DCF and net worth is one way to ensure that recommendations are actionable. Involving the client ensures that the client is fully informed about plan implementation and committed to taking action.

Whatever approach is chosen (forms, checklists, to-do lists, timelines, etc.) should match the planner's preferences, the planner's knowledge of the client , the client's information processing style, the complexity of the situation, and the variety of strategies and parties involved in putting the plan into action. This section offers the client another view—perhaps in conjunction with, or in place of, the "Executive Summary" or "Observations and Recommendations" section—that brings a multifaceted, perhaps complex, plan into a more manageable perspective.

The foremost purpose of the Implementation and Monitoring Section is to ensure that action occurs, regardless of the party responsible. Planner and client can use an effective implementation summary to orchestrate the plan in a timely manner. Furthermore, an effective monitoring summary can be used to guide future meetings with the client with respect to monitoring (a) plan implementation, including any delayed implementation strategies; (b) progress toward goals; and (c) needed changes in the plan resulting from changes in the economy, the market, the client's situation, or the client's goals. In other words, an effective monitoring summary promotes the iterative or recursive nature of the financial planning process.

X. Client Acceptance Letter or Client Engagement Letter

Depending on the business model followed, a letter formalizing the planner-client relationship can appear at the end of the plan. It is a prudent practice to ask clients to sign a letter accepting the financial plan as prepared and presented. Some financial planners refer to this as an acknowledgement of delivery. This letter may formalize the business agreement, but more importantly it verifies that the plan truly reflects the mutually agreed-upon assumptions on which the plan is based, as well as the goals identified by the client. Furthermore, the client's acceptance of the plan reiterates the point that the plan is based on the information provided by the client. Exhibit 9.4 is an example of an **acceptance letter**. This letter can be used in addition to the client engagement letter; or the client engagement letter can appear at the end rather than at the beginning of the plan. Again, depending on the business model followed, these letters can be used to formalize the business agreement, or they may be included only as a record of an earlier transaction or as confirmation that the plan reflects the client's current situation as presented to the advisor.

Exhibit 9.4 Sample Acceptance Letter

Mr. Jonathan T. Sample
111 East Avenue
Dayton, OH 45402-4300

Dear Jon and Annie:

Re: Acceptance of Your Financial Analysis

The planning process is an evolution that started with gathering information, comparing your planning assumptions and objectives, analyzing where you are headed, and defining the major problems or obstacles you might face.

Your plan contains recommendations for your consideration as well as a recommended Implementation Checklist.

However, at some point it is necessary to "freeze" the current plan and proceed with implementation follow-through.

If you are satisfied with the basic plan, please sign below and return a copy for our files. You might also call to schedule a session to begin plan implementation.

Plan accepted by: _____   Date: _____

Source: PracticeBuilder Financial, Financial Planning Consultants, Inc. 2507 N. Verity Parkway, P.O. Box 430, Middletown, OH 45042-0430. www.FinancialSoftware.com. Used with permission.

XI. Appendices

Appendices are almost always included in comprehensive financial plans. The purpose of appendices is to educate the client by supplementing, or expanding, the plan. As such, appendices typically include supporting printouts of all calculations or spreadsheets used in the analysis, copies or reprints of educational articles, or a glossary of key terms used in the plan.

Every calculation used in a financial plan should be documented. First, showing the calculations helps a client understand the mathematical framework of the plan. Second, sharing the calculation method increases the transparency of the analysis process. This reduces a planner's exposure to claims of unsuitability of the recommendations if the calculations are correct and the assumptions used in the calculations are the same as those listed in the plan. Presumably, the client already agreed to the assumptions before the plan was written. By using these assumptions it becomes difficult for a client to later claim that calculation inputs were unreasonable or incorrect.

It is important to note that some financial planners prefer to include all calculations, and any supplemental information, in each core content section of the plan. Using this method, a planner would incorporate not only basic income, expense, and DCF figures in the cash flow section of the plan, for example, but also a comprehensive income and expense statement and budget projection. Because of concerns about identity theft, the section might also include an explanation of the procedures used to secure a federally mandated free credit report or a summary of strategies to safeguard personal information.

The comprehensive financial plan outline shown in Exhibit 9.1 assumes that all complex calculations are grouped in an appendix. This approach reduces the level of complexity within each core content section by limiting the focus to the current situation, recommendations, and implementation. However, it is extremely important that footnotes or other references be used to clearly direct clients to specific pages in the appendix to illustrate how specific numbers were derived. Supplemental client information, such as that described above, also would appear in an appendix.

THE MESSAGE OF THE PLAN

Whether a planner writes comprehensive or modular plans or composes original drafts, uses reports from professional software packages, or combines the two, the real issue is not the plan, or its format, style, or length. What matters is the ability of the plan and the planner to communicate the planning process and to enable clients to take positive steps toward their financial future. It is important to note that the planning outline follows the sequential steps of the systematic financial planning process. The first five sections of the outline pertain to Step 1: Establish and Define the Relationship. Section VI: Client Profile, Summary of Goals and Assumptions captures the client data collected in Step 2: Gather Data and Frame Goals and Objectives.

Steps 3 and 4, which encompass analysis, identification of recommendations, and plan development, are reported in Section VIII: Individual Core Content Planning Sections. Exhibit 9.3, which outlines the proposed content for each core content planning area, closely follows the actions taken in these two steps. Although more detailed implementation and monitoring information may be provided in each core content area in Section VIII, the summary in Section IX parallels Steps 5: Implement the Plan and Step 6: Monitor the Plan, Implementation, and Goal Progress. From this perspective, seeing the plan as a representation of the process, planners can more easily adapt the style of their plans to match the needs and preferences of their clients.

It is widely acknowledged that almost all writers initially borrow and adapt a style from other successful authors. Although software-produced reports or plans might offer some advantages, many advisors still want the flexibility to adapt the plan to better match the needs of their practice or their clients. As noted earlier in this chapter, the general outline can be adapted in various ways to meet the needs of different planners and diverse business practice models. The outlines and examples provided illustrate just a few of the many ways that information can be presented to clients. As in almost all professional activities, this merely means that there are multiple ways to analyze and describe a situation. This is what is truly important: every financial planner must choose a format and style that he or she is comfortable with and expect that style to evolve over time as more plans are written and delivered to clients. Attention must be paid to the mundane issues of grammar, style, and readability. But the bigger issue of effectively communicating how the financial planning process was applied to the needs of the client also requires consideration. The plan and its presentation must send a message of competence, confidence, and collaboration that will foster trust in the advisor and empower the client to make knowledgeable decisions about the future. Checklists, such as the one in Exhibit 9.5, can also be used to review the plan to ensure that all critical issues are covered.

Finally, there is really only one way to truly become more proficient at the systematic process of planning and writing financial plans. This is true for those who want to begin writing financial plans and those who wish to improve the plans they write. The secret is deceptively simple—practice the craft of planning and writing!

CHAPTER SUMMARY

A well-crafted financial plan is one of the best tools for capturing the interest, trust, respect, and commitment of a client. A financial plan, whether comprehensive or modular, can systematically encompass the financial planning process and integrate the articulation of a client's needs, wants, desires, and goals with a realistic plan for reaching those goals. A written plan provides each client and the advisor with a synergistic financial road map to enhanced financial wellness. In addition to cementing a client relationship, standard materials can be used to establish consistent internal procedures for working with all clients. Many use this consistently applied procedure to distinguish a profession from an industry.

Exhibit 9.5 Financial Plan Review Checklist

Have the following actions been taken?	Yes	No
Has material been edited for color, font, and formatting consistency?		
Are header/footer messages, such as the firm's name or logo with the date of the plan, included?		
Is a carefully designed cover page with all required client information, disclosure information, plan date, and the word confidential used?		
Does the appearance of the plan, including the written word, reflect your professional image?		
Is a cover letter, engagement letter, or plan acceptance letter included?		
Is a detailed table of contents with page numbers included?		
Have the optional introductory materials been chosen and included?		
Is an executive summary included?		
Is a carefully compiled profile of the client included?		
Is there a summary of the client-specific goals, objectives, and planning assumptions?		
Is each of the required core content planning sections included?		
At a minimum, does each core content section address the situation (i.e., goal(s), assumptions, analysis, and interpretation), recommendations, and implementation?		
Is there a good balance between the text and the charts, graphs, and tables to summarize and illustrate the analysis? Have all charts, graphs, and tables been checked for accuracy?		
Is there an "Implementation Checklist," "To-do List," "Action Plan," timeline, or other explanation of the requirements and responsibilities for implementing and monitoring?		
Are the appendices clearly labeled and accurately referenced in the plan text by page number?		
Are all graphics, spreadsheets, or other supporting software results included?		
Have all coordinating plan and appendix page references been checked?		
Have all educational articles been included in the appendix?		
If a glossary of terms is provided, have all terms been included and defined?		

This chapter describes the features typically found in a well-written financial plan. Although these plan elements can be viewed as baseline concepts, not all sections may be applicable for all planner-client engagements or business models. It is also acknowledged that each planner or firm will develop its own "signature" plan outline, elements, style, and content standards, which best suit their needs and the needs of their clients, and that meet the compliance standards of their business model. However, following the recommendations in this chapter can help students and novice planners skillfully develop signature plans of their own, effectively matched to their clients' needs and preferences.

Learning Outcomes

1. The financial plan is a *product* or tangible outcome of the *service* of the financial planning process. But more important than the actual form of the plan (long or short, bound or unbound, etc.) is the intangible systematic financial planning process that the plan must communicate. A planner's competence, confidence in the plan and recommendations, and willingness to collaborate with a client are important messages the plan must convey. By regarding the plan as a representation of the process, planners can more easily adapt the signature style of their plans to accommodate their clients.

2. Clients and financial planners usually have a preferred method for processing information. Some people are visually oriented. Others are auditory learners, and some prefer an experiential or kinesthetic approach to learning. It is important to match the writing style of a plan to the information processing style of each client. For example, those who process information visually prefer charts, figures, and graphs. Kinesthetic information processors like to view analyses in detail. Learning about a client's processing style during the data-gathering stage of the financial planning process will help lead to a written plan that better meets client preferences and needs.

3. Writing style and voice are important factors to consider when composing a financial plan. Writing style refers to the approach used to communicate with clients. Similar to style, voice describes the point of view taken by a financial planner when writing the plan. The voice chosen can influence how clients view their planner—as technical expert, trusted confidante, counselor, objective fiduciary, friend, or motivator. The selection of a writing perspective, including the use of pronoun and case and passive versus active verbs, should be done purposely to best represent the needs of a financial planner's clientele.

4. This chapter identifies the following 10 fundamental guidelines for crafting a well-written financial plan:

    1. Use 11- or 12-point Times New Roman or Arial font.

    2. Be consistent with formatting, style, and voice.

    3. Make the plan visually interesting.

    4. Understand that a written financial plan is a living document that will change in the future; therefore, choose an appropriate binding method.

    5. Check and recheck the final written plan.

    6. Write each content section so that it can stand alone if read separately.

    7. Write simply and avoid technical jargon.

8. Consider the written plan a financial road map leading from definition to implementation.

9. Use a combination of pre-scripted and client-specific information.

10. Document, document, and document again all sources, assumptions, and supporting materials.

5. This chapter recommends an outline for a comprehensive financial plan. The outline includes components typically found in plans prepared by practicing financial planners. It is important to note that in some situations content can be removed, replaced, or relocated to meet the specific needs of a client's situation. As time goes by, each financial planner will develop his or her own plan-writing "signature" based on compliance standards and a business model. This means that the core outline described in this chapter, and the format of the plan, will likely be different for each planner as it is adapted over time.

6. Each written financial plan is a unique document, but at some level it should correspond to the financial planning process. As an outgrowth of Step 1: Establish and Define the Relationship, most financial plans include the following elements: (a) cover page; (b) letter to client; (c) client engagement letter; (d) table of contents; (e) other materials, including a vision and mission statement, code of ethics, privacy statement, and/or investment policy statement; and (f) a client acceptance letter. Financial planners should also consider including a client profile, summary of goals, and assumptions to report data collected in Step 2. A comprehensive financial plans should also contain individual core content sections related to cash flow and net worth planning, taxation, insurance, investing, retirement, estate planning, and special needs planning to report on the activities encompassed in Steps 3 and 4, analyzing the client situation and developing a plan. Steps 5 and 6 are reported in the individual core content sections and summarized in the Implementation and Monitoring section of the plan. The Executive Summary provides a summary of the planning process from goal setting to monitoring; its length is related to the depth of plan content.

7. Client-specific core content sections in the written plan include cash flow and net worth planning, tax planning, insurance analysis and planning, retirement and estate planning, investment planning, and special needs planning. It is important to follow a general outline within each section. The following outline, described in this chapter, is recommended:

I. Overview of core content area and definitions

II. Restatement of planner-client assumptions

III. Review of the analysis of client's current situation

1. Observations about the current situation

2. Assessment of planning needs

3. Assessment of current planning efforts

IV. Statement of financial planning recommendations (who, what, when, where, why, how, and how much)

V. Comparison of projected recommendation outcome(s) to the current situation

VI. Suggestions for alternative recommendations and outcome(s) where appropriate

VII. Plan implementation and monitoring procedures

1. Explain the source of the cash flow or assets to be used to fund the recommendation

2. Provide specific implementation advice

8. As discussed throughout this chapter, becoming a proficient financial plan writer requires practice. There are many ways to present information, describe recommendations, and prompt client action. Until someone gains sufficient experience and expertise in plan writing, it is useful to use a plan review checklist to evaluate a financial plan. A Financial Plan Review Checklist, such as the one shown in Exhibit 9.5, should be used to help ensure that all key elements associated with a comprehensive financial plan have been included in the final document. A checklist can also serve as a reminder to double-check all analyses and document resources, and to review the content and presentation one last time before handing the plan to a client.

Chapter Resources

CFP Board of Standards, Inc. (http://www.cfp.net).

Freedman, M. S. "Writing Your Clients' Financial Plan." Oversold and Underserved: A Financial Planner's Guidebook to Effectively Serving the Mass Affluent. *Denver, CO: FPA Press, 2008.*

RIA Compliance Consultants (http://www.ria-compliance-consultants.com/).

Discussion Questions

1. Describe and explain the purpose of a financial plan. Why is the message constant, regardless of the style, format, or length of the written document?

2. How do the preferred information processing styles of the planner and the client influence the writing style and format of a financial plan?

3. What factors contribute to a planner's voice in a financial plan? Why is this important? How does it relate to the idea that a plan should communicate competence, confidence, and collaboration?

4. Explain the five general principles to judge the effectiveness of a financial plan. How does each correspond to the steps of the systematic financial planning process?

5. Identify the four different disclaimers, or client warnings, typically included in a financial plan.

6. How do the purposes of the introductory client letter, the client engagement letter, and the client acceptance letter differ? Why might, or might not, these be included in the plan?

7. Identify the five documents that comprise the introductory materials of a plan. Explain the purpose of each and why it is included.

8. Why is it prudent for a planner to clearly identify and explain the assumptions used? Where might the assumptions appear in the plan?

9. Explain the content and purpose of the Executive Summary. How does the length and scope of the Executive Summary correspond to the format of a plan?

10. Using the outline in Exhibit 9.3, briefly outline the information needed to write the core content planning section for life insurance for a client of your choice.

11. What makes a recommendation actionable? How does the use of a Planning Recommendation Form, an implementation table, or an Implementation Checklist help both planner and client?

12. How does an effective monitoring summary support the recursive financial planning process?

13. Why are appendices included in a financial plan? Explain the information typically found there. Why might educational materials be included, and if not included in the appendices, where might they be found?

14. Review the 10 rules for increasing the effectiveness of a plan and the Plan Review Checklist in Exhibit 9.5. Choose five criteria and explain why you think they are most important for developing a plan that informs and motivates a client to take action.

15. Using Exhibits 9.3 and 9.5, critique the core content planning section in Appendix D.

Notes

1. Certified Financial Planner Board of Standards, Inc., *CFP Board's Standards of Professional Conduct*. Available at http://www.cfp.net/Downloads/2010Standards.pdf, p. 23; or at http://www.cfp.net/learn/standards400.asp.

2. N. Mailer, *The Spooky Art: Some Thoughts on Writing* (New York: Random House, 2003).

3. FPA, *Code of Ethics*. Available at http://www.fpanet.org/AboutFPA/CodeofEthics/.

4. U.S. Securities & Exchange Commission, *Investment Adviser Code of Ethics*. Available at http://www.sec.gov/rules/final/ia-2256.htm#P57_8433; see Footnote 6.

Client Engagement Letter

Mr. and Mrs. Jonathan T. Sample
111 East Avenue
Dayton, OH 45402-4300

Dear Jon and Annie:

Re: Financial Planning Engagement

This letter will confirm the terms of the financial services we will provide, per our recent conversation. You will furnish complete and up-to-date information on your personal circumstances and financial and investment objectives. We will make this task easier by providing information forms for you to complete and then clarifying the data in our interviews.

Once all your information is assembled, we will analyze your present financial situation. That analysis will include a review of your assets and liabilities, current and projected income, current insurance program, and investments.

We will provide written analyses and recommendations in the form of a financial review. Your written financial review will refer to such things as holding or selling securities and other assets; your projected income, cash flow, and tax consequences; and retirement, estate, and insurance planning.

Our recommendations will be based on the written data you provide and will include considerations of your stated personal, financial, and investment objectives, so please use care in providing the data. It is usually unnecessary for us to see your actual stock certificates, etc.

All information given to us and all recommendations and advice that we furnish you will be kept confidential and will not be disclosed to anyone, except as we may agree in writing or as may be required by law. You may later request that a copy of our plan be delivered to another professional advisor.

When you receive your written financial review, it will be your decision alone whether to implement the recommendations, either completely or in part. So there will be no future misunderstanding, you will pay a fee under this agreement for the written financial review alone, and this plan shall contain all of our financial services recommendations to you through the date of its delivery.

After you have evaluated your financial review, there are three aspects of follow-through:

1. Service Assistance

   This involves delivery of documents to, and conferences with, your other advisors as well as attention to the completion of forms and agreements to accomplish your objectives. There is no additional fee for this service.

2. Product Sales

   This involves your voluntary acquisition of investment, real estate, or insurance products to accomplish your objectives. This agreement and fee do not provide for any product-related activity.

3. Plan Implementation Assistance

   Implementation of any aspect of your plan via product acquisition is entirely at your discretion. We recognize that in many areas you will already have satisfactory business relationships, and we will assist you with them. However, if you request our assistance in making any financial acquisitions directly and decide to make purchases through us or our associates, we will receive commissions where commissions are due.

We emphasize that you are not obligated to make any purchases through our associates. You are free to select any brokerage firm, insurance or real estate agents, or other vendors that you desire for the implementation of product recommendations.

We are not authorized or qualified to give you legal advice or to prepare legal documents for you. You should consult your own attorney for these services.

We are not authorized or qualified to prepare or amend the filing of personal income, gift, or estate tax returns for you. You should consult your own accountant for these services.

We are not authorized or qualified to act as trustee, and acting upon the advice of your attorney, you should select appropriate individuals or trust companies to provide this service.

We regard the responsibility of preparing your written financial review as a very important personal relationship with you. So that you feel informed about dealing with us, we want you to have our brochure and a disclosure statement that describes our firm, its history, and our key personnel. Execution of this engagement letter acknowledges your receipt of this material.

Although we do not expect to ask anyone else to fulfill any of our responsibilities under this agreement, it may become necessary to do so. If such a situation should arise, we will obtain your prior written consent. Assignment will cancel this engagement.

If at any time you are dissatisfied with this agreement, you may cancel it. If you do so within five days of acceptance, you will receive a full refund. Thereafter, any fees that you have paid in advance will be charged for the time and effort we have devoted up until then, and the balance will be refunded.

Furthermore, you agree (as do we) that all controversies between us concerning any transaction or the construction, performance, or breach of this or any agreement between us, whether entered into prior to, on, or subsequent to this date, shall be determined by arbitration as permitted by law. Such arbitration shall be conducted in accordance with the Commercial Arbitration Rules of the American Arbitration Association then applicable. The award of the arbitrators or their majority shall be final and binding and not subject to review or appeal.

Because of changes in the tax laws or in your personal financial situation, you may wish to receive an annual update of your written financial review or a more frequent periodic review. These are available as a separate service of our firm. We feel that continued monitoring is essential to accomplish all of your objectives.

Our practice for this continued service is to charge 60% of the initial planning fee, commencing the first quarter of the next calendar year. Should you request our continued service and updated financial plan, we will bill you 15% of this year's fee on a quarterly basis commencing next January. In future years, this amount may be adjusted to meet changing circumstances.

Our fee for preparing your financial review is determined based on the anticipated work to be done. We appreciate that our clients wish to know the exact amount of the fee before retaining us. Because we cannot accurately determine that amount until learning about family and financial circumstances, it is our practice to establish the fee after an initial, no-obligation session.

One half of the fee is payable after the information-gathering interview and the remainder upon receipt of your financial review. The total fee for your financial review is $___.

If you understand the preceding terms and agree to them, please sign both copies of this letter and return one copy to us. You may include, or forward later, your deposit of one half of the initial fee.

We look forward to working with you for the achievement of your financial goals.

Understood and Agreed to by: _____

This _____, _____.

Source: PracticeBuilder Financial, Financial Planning Consultants, Inc., 2507 N. Verity Parkway, P.O. Box 430, Middletown, OH 45042-0430, www.FinancialSoftware.com. Used with permission.

PART V: Appendices

Appendix A—Assessing Your Financial Risk Tolerance

Appendix B—Client Intake Form

Appendix C—Financial Planning Benchmarks

Appendix D—Education Planning: A Sample Section from the Kim's Comprehensive Plan

Assessing Your Financial Risk Tolerance

Instructions: Circle your first response to each question. The response should be almost instinctive; in other words do not overthink your response.

1. In general, how would your best friend describe you as a risk taker?

    a. A real gambler

    b. Willing to take risks after completing adequate research

    c. Cautious

    d. A real risk avoider

2. You are on a TV game show and can choose one of the following. Which would you take?

    a. $1,000 in cash

    b. A 50% chance at winning $5,000

    c. A 25% chance at winning $10,000

    d. A 5% chance at winning $100,000

3. You have just finished saving for a "once-in-a-lifetime" vacation. Three weeks before you plan to leave, you lose your job. You would:

    a. Cancel the vacation

    b. Take a much more modest vacation

c. Go as scheduled, reasoning that you need the time to prepare for a job search

d. Extend your vacation because this might be your last chance to go first-class

4. If you unexpectedly received $20,000 to *invest*, what would you do?

a. Deposit it in a bank account, money market account, or an insured CD

b. Invest it in safe, high-quality bonds or bond mutual funds

c. Invest it in stocks or stock mutual funds

5. In terms of experience, how comfortable are you investing in stocks or stock mutual funds?

a. Not at all comfortable

b. Somewhat comfortable

c. Very comfortable

6. When you think of the word "risk," which of the following words comes to mind first?

a. Loss

b. Uncertainty

c. Opportunity

d. Thrill

7. Some experts are predicting that the prices of assets such as gold, jewels, collectibles, and real estate (hard assets) may increase in value; bond prices may fall. However, experts tend to agree that government bonds are relatively safe. Most of your investment assets are now in high-interest government bonds. What would you do?

a. Hold the bonds

b. Sell the bonds, put half the proceeds into money market accounts, and the other half into hard assets

c. Sell the bonds and put the total proceeds into hard assets

d. Sell the bonds, put all the money into hard assets, and borrow additional money to buy more

8. Given the best- and worst-case returns of the four investment choices below, which would you prefer?

a. $200 gain best case; $0 gain/loss worst case

b. $800 gain best case; $200 loss worst case

    c. $2,600 gain best case; $800 loss worst case

    d. $4,800 gain best case; $2,400 loss worst case

9. In addition to whatever you own, you have been given $1,000. You are now asked to choose between:

    a. A sure gain of $500

    b. A 50% chance to gain $1,000 and a 50% chance to gain nothing

10. In addition to whatever you own, you have been given $2,000. You are now asked to choose between:

    a. A sure loss of $500

    b. A 50% chance to lose $1,000 and a 50% chance to lose nothing

11. Suppose a relative left you an inheritance of $100,000, stipulating in the will that you invest ALL the money in ONE of the following choices. Which one would you select?

    a. A savings account or money market mutual fund

    b. A mutual fund that owns stocks and bonds

    c. A portfolio of 15 common stocks

    d. Commodities like gold, silver, and oil

12. If you had to invest $20,000, which of the following investment choices would you find most appealing?

    a. 60% in low-risk investments, 30% in medium-risk investments, 10% in high-risk investments

    b. 30% in low-risk investments, 40% in medium-risk investments, 30% in high-risk investments

    c. 10% in low-risk investments, 40% in medium-risk investments, 50% in high-risk investments

13. Your trusted friend and neighbor, an experienced geologist, is putting together a group of investors to fund an exploratory gold-mining venture. The venture could pay back 50 to 100 times the investment, if successful. If the mine is a bust, the entire investment is worthless. Your friend estimates the chance of success is only 20%. If you had the money, how much would you invest?

    a. Nothing

    b. One month's salary

    c. Three month's salary

    d. Six month's salary

SCORING
(Using the scale below, add the points for each response.)

1. a = 4; b = 3; c = 2; d = 1
2. a = 1; b = 2; c = 3; d = 4
3. a = 1; b = 2; c = 3; d = 4
4. a = 1; b = 2; c = 3
5. a = 1; b = 2; c = 3

6. a = 1; b = 2; c = 3; d = 4
7. a = 1; b = 2; c = 3; d = 4
8. a = 1; b = 2; c = 3; d = 4
9. a = 1; b = 3

10. a = 1; b = 3
11. a = 1; b = 2; c = 3; d = 4
12. a = 1; b = 2; c = 3
13. a = 1; b = 2; c = 3; d = 4

Scoring Instructions: Add the point values that correspond with your responses and compare the result to the scale below to determine your financial risk tolerance.

Score	Risk Tolerance Level
0–18	Low tolerance for risk
19–22	Below-average tolerance for risk
23–28	Average/moderate tolerance for risk
29–32	Above-average tolerance for risk
33–47	High tolerance for risk

Client Intake Form

Thank you for taking the time to complete this confidential client questionnaire. We realize it takes time and effort to retrieve the information requested. However, we are available to assist where needed and welcome your calls or emails. Please do not hesitate to contact us, or if it is easier for you, simply collect the insurance policies, financial statements, or other documents and return them with this form. Collecting this information is an important first step in our collaboration to develop a financial plan based on your financial and life goals. This is the *only* reason for asking for so much information. We look forward to learning more about your situation and working with you.

Section 1: Confidential Client Data

Personal Information

Client 1		Client 2	
Name		Name	
DOB		DOB	
SSN		SSN	

Contact Information

Client 1		Client 2	
Home phone		Home phone	
Mobile phone		Mobile phone	
Email		Email	
Home address		Home address	

Children (or Other Financial Dependents) Information

Name		DOB		Relationship		At home?	
Name		DOB		Relationship		At home?	
Name		DOB		Relationship		At home?	
Name		DOB		Relationship		At home?	
Name		DOB		Relationship		At home?	
Name		DOB		Relationship		At home?	

Section 2: Please tell us about your family. This information will give us a better understanding of who is affected by your financial decisions. (Please consider children and other financial dependents, including immediate and/or extended family.)

Are there any special considerations that relate to the future of your children—perhaps their future education or living conditions? *(Exceptionally bright? Special talents? Disabilities or special need? Prior marriages?)*

_____

_____

_____

_____

_____

_____

Is there anyone you are supporting now, or will be supporting in the future, whom you want to consider in your planning? If yes, please list below:

_____

_____

_____

_____

_____

_____

Are there any highly unusual aspects of your family situation that warrant additional consideration or special planning? If yes, please explain below:

_____

_____

_____

_____

_____

_____

Section 3: If you are currently employed, please tell us about your job below: (If retired, skip to Section 3a)

Employment Information

	Client 1	Client 2
Employer		
Occupation		
Work phone		
Work address		
Number of years employed		
Position		
Annual salary		
Annual bonuses/commissions		
Other earned income		
Do you anticipate employment changes?		
If so, when (date)?		
At what age do you plan to retire?		

If you were going to retire today, approximately how much annual after-tax income would you need to live comfortably? _____

Do you feel that you are on track to have enough income-generating assets to live comfortably in retirement?   *(Circle)*   Yes   No

If no, please explain. _____

_____

_____

Section 3a: If you are currently retired, please tell us about your current situation below:

Retirement Information		
	Client 1	**Client 2**
Number of years retired		
Annual Social Security income		
Annual pension income		
Annual income from annuities		
Annual income from investments		
Other annual income		

	Client 1	Client 2

Do you feel that your current income sufficient to meet your needs?   (*Circle*) Yes No   (*Circle*) Yes No

If no, please explain. _____

_____

_____

Do you anticipate working again?   (*Circle*) Yes No   (*Circle*) Yes No

If **yes**, please explain. _____

_____

_____

Section 4: Leisure activities are important to consider when planning your financial future. Please help us identify the activities that you enjoy by answering the questions below:

How do you use your leisure time? *(Outside organizations, activities, clubs, etc.)*

_____

_____

_____

_____

_____

_____

What other activities do you enjoy? *(Skydiving, long/short vacations, bridge, etc.)*

_____

_____

_____

_____

_____

_____

What activities would you like to begin in the future? *(Traveling, volunteering, etc.)*

_____

_____

_____

_____

_____

_____

Section 5: Please tell us what you consider to be your primary goals and objectives for the future.

Rank your goals/objectives using the following scale and time horizons. It is recommended that you complete this individually as well as jointly. Please do not discuss your responses until each client has been able to individually complete the form.

<table>
<tr><td colspan="2">**Importance Scale**</td><td>**Time Horizon**</td></tr>
<tr><td>0 – Not applicable at this time</td><td>3 – Important</td><td>S/T – 1–3 Years</td></tr>
<tr><td>1 – Not important</td><td>4 – Very important</td><td>I/T – 4–7 Years</td></tr>
<tr><td>2 – Somewhat important</td><td>5 – Crucial</td><td>L/T – 7+ Years</td></tr>
</table>

The generic goals provided below are typical examples for people throughout the lifecycle and are geared to assist us with goal setting.

Client 1 Goals / Objectives	Importance Level (0–5)	Time Horizon to Begin	Time Horizon to Complete
Personal			
Becoming more financially knowledgeable			
Improving recordkeeping methods			
Starting a family			
Advancing in current career			
Changing careers			
Returning to college			
Caring for parents			
Retiring early			
Traveling extensively in retirement			
Other:			
Other:			
Other:			
Financial			
Reducing revolving debt			
Increasing periodic savings			
Reducing taxes			
Evaluating insurance needs			
Increasing investment diversification			
Increasing investment returns			
Starting a small business			

Saving for children's education			
Purchasing a vehicle			
Saving for the down payment on a home			
Purchasing a home			
Investing an inheritance			
Saving for retirement			
Giving to charity			
Transferring estate assets			
Other:			
Other:			
Other:			

Client 2 Goals /Objectives	Importance Level (0–5)	Time Horizon to Begin	Time Horizon to Complete
Personal			
Becoming more financially knowledgeable			
Improving recordkeeping methods			
Starting a family			
Advancing in current career			
Changing careers			
Returning to college			
Caring for parents			
Retiring early			
Traveling extensively in retirement			
Other:			
Other:			
Other:			
Financial			
Reducing revolving debt			
Increasing periodic savings			
Reducing taxes			
Evaluating insurance needs			
Increasing investment diversification			
Increasing investment returns			
Starting a small business			
Saving for children's education			
Purchasing a vehicle			

Saving for the down payment on a home			
Purchasing a home			
Investing an inheritance			
Saving for retirement			
Giving to charity			
Transferring estate assets			
Other:			
Other:			
Other:			

Section 6: It is important to know the exact amount of your current insurance coverage to fully evaluate whether you are over-, under-, or adequately insured. Please provide the following information:

Life Insurance Information	Policy 1	Policy 2	Policy 3	Policy 4
Insurance company				
Policy owner				
Insured				
Beneficiary(ies), primary				
Beneficiary(ies), contingent				
Face value				
Group or individual policy				
Total annual premium cost				
Premiums paid (self or employer)				
Pretax or post-tax dollars				
Term or cash value policy				
If term, years remaining				
Policy Provisions				
Renewability[a]				
Inflation protection				
Declining value (term)				
If you have a cash value policy, please also provide the following information:				
Cash value				
Tax-equivalent rate of return				
Current dividend (if applicable)				
Current death benefit/face value				

[a] Renewability options include: annually renewable, guaranteed renewable, non-cancellable.

	Client 1	Client 2
Have you ever been turned down for life insurance?	*(Circle)* Yes No	*(Circle)* Yes No

If yes, what was the reason? _____

Disability Insurance Information	Policy 1	Policy 2	Policy 3	Policy 4
Insurance company				
Policy owner				
Insured				
Group or individual policy?				
Cost per year				
Premiums paid (self or employer)				
Pretax or post-tax dollars?				
Policy Provisions				
Type (short-term or long-term?)				
Disability definition[a]				
Waiting period (days)				
Benefit period (years)				
Total annual benefit				
Total benefit (life of policy)				

[a] Disability definitions include: any occupation, similar occupation, own occupation.

	Client 1	**Client 2**
Have you ever been turned down for disability insurance?	*(Circle)* Yes No	*(Circle)* Yes No

If yes, what was the reason? _____
_____

Do you anticipate any changes in the coverage or need for coverage for any of the policies listed above? _____
_____

Do you anticipate making changes to any of these policies that would alter any planning recommendation based on the preceding information? _____
_____

Health Insurance Information	Policy 1	Policy 2	Policy 3	Policy 4
Insurance company				
Policy owner				
Primary insured				
Group or individual policy?				
Cost per year				
Premiums paid (self or employer)				
Pretax or post-tax dollars?				
Policy Provisions				
Individual or family policy?				
Annual deductible amount				
Annual stop-loss limit ($)				
Lifetime maximum benefit				

	Client 1	**Client 2**
Have you ever been turned down for health insurance?	*(Circle)* Yes No	*(Circle)* Yes No

If yes, what was the reason? _____
_____
_____

Do you anticipate any changes in the coverage or need for coverage for any of the policies listed above? _____
_____

Do you anticipate making changes to any of these policies that would alter any planning recommendation based on the preceding information? _____
_____

Long-term Care Insurance Information	Policy 1	Policy 2	Policy 3	Policy 4
Insurance company				
Policy owner				
Primary insured				
Group or individual policy				
Cost per year				
Premiums paid (self or employer)				
Pretax or post-tax dollars?				
Policy Provisions				
Individual or joint policy?				
Elimination period				
Eligibility (number lost ADLs)				
Per-day benefit amount				
Lifetime maximum benefit				
Single or shared benefit pool				
Inflation rider (fixed or variable?)				
Inflation rider (simple or compound?)				

	Client 1	**Client 2**
Have you ever been turned down for long-term care insurance?	*(Circle)* Yes No	*(Circle)* Yes No

If yes, what was the reason? _____

_____

_____

Do you anticipate any changes in the coverage or need for coverage for any of the policies listed above? _____

_____

Do you anticipate making changes to any of these policies that would alter any planning recommendation based on the preceding information? _____

_____

Personal Automobile Insurance Information	Policy 1 / Vehicle 1	Policy 2 / Vehicle 2	Policy 3 / Vehicle 3	Policy 4 / Vehicle 4
Insurance company				
Policy owner				
Primary insured				
Other insured(s)				
Cost per year				
Liability Coverage				
Coverage per person				
Coverage per accident				
Property damage coverage				
Coverage per person (Uninsured/underinsured)				
Coverage Per Accident (Uninsured/underinsured)				
Property Damage Coverage (Uninsured/underinsured)				
Medical coverage per person				
Comprehensive and Collision Coverage				
Collision deductible				
Comprehensive deductible				
Uninsured/underinsured deductible				
Additional Coverage				
Towing/labor				
Rental reimbursement				

Homeowners/Renters Insurance Information	Policy 1	Policy 2	Policy 3	Policy 4
Insurance company				
Policy owner				
Property insured				
Cost per year				
Amount of dwelling coverage				
Deductible				
Amount of liability coverage				
Deductible/co-payment				
Special property endorsements				
Inflation rider				

	Client 1	**Client 2**

Have you ever been turned down for either
homeowners or auto insurance?

(Circle) Yes No   (Circle) Yes No

If yes, what was the reason? _____

_____

_____

_____

_____

_____

_____

	Client 1	**Client 2**

Have you ever been turned down for auto
insurance or had a policy cancelled?

(Circle) Yes No   (Circle) Yes No

If yes, what was the reason? _____

_____

_____

_____

_____

_____

_____

Do you anticipate any changes in the coverage or need for coverage for any of the policies listed
above? _____

_____

_____

_____

_____

Do you anticipate making changes to any of these policies, or the property covered, that would alter
any recommendations? _____

_____

_____

_____

_____

_____

Do you own, and have coverage for watercraft, motorcycle, RV, ATV or other off-road vehicle?
(Circle) Yes No

Additional Insurance:

	Client 1		Client 2	
	Coverage/Cost	Group or Individual?	Coverage/Cost	Group or Individual?
Umbrella liability	_____	_____	_____	_____
Professional liability	_____	_____	_____	_____
Errors & omissions	_____	_____	_____	_____

Is your primary residence currently covered by a state homestead exemption?   *(Circle)* Yes No Unknown

Have you ever been turned down for any other insurance product? *(Circle)* Yes No

If yes, what was the reason? _____
_____
_____
_____
_____
_____

Section 7: To better understand your current financial position, we need to review your available assets. Please tell us about your taxable and tax deferred assets.

Taxable Investment Assets*:	Ownership (Name or "Joint")	Current Value ($)	Cost Basis ($)	Current Annual Contribution ($) (if applicable)	Current Total Return (%)	Current Annual Yield (%)	Use Cash to Settle Estate? (Y/N)
		$	$	$			
		$	$	$			
		$	$	$			
		$	$	$			
		$	$	$			
		$	$	$			
		$	$	$			
		$	$	$			
		$	$	$			
		$	$	$			
		$	$	$			
		$	$	$			

* Taxable account examples include: checking; savings; certificates of deposit (CDs); money market mutual funds; money market deposit accounts; U.S. Savings Bonds; stocks; bonds; mutual funds; ETFs, direct or indirect real estate; precious metals and other.

Taxable Investment Assets* (cont'd):

Ownership (Name or "Joint")	Current Value ($)	Cost Basis ($)	Current Annual Contribution ($) (if applicable)	Current Total Return (%)	Current Annual Yield (%)	Use Cash to Settle Estate? (Y/N)
	$	$	$			
	$	$	$			
	$	$	$			
	$	$	$			
	$	$	$			
	$	$	$			
	$	$	$			
	$	$	$			
	$	$	$			
	$	$	$			
	$	$	$			
	$	$	$			
	$	$	$			
	$	$	$			

* Taxable account examples include: checking; savings; certificates of deposit (CDs); money market mutual funds; money market deposit accounts; U.S. Savings Bonds; stocks; bonds; mutual funds; ETFs, direct or indirect real estate; precious metals and other.

Tax-deferred Investment Assets*:

	Ownership	Current Value ($)	Cost Basis ($)	Current Annual Contribution ($) (if applicable)	Current Total Return (%)	Current Annual Yield (%)	Use Cash to Settle Estate? (Y/N)
		$	$	$			
		$	$	$			
		$	$	$			
		$	$	$			
		$	$	$			
		$	$	$			
		$	$	$			
		$	$	$			
		$	$	$			
		$	$	$			
		$	$	$			
		$	$	$			
		$	$	$			
		$	$	$			

* Examples of tax-deferred accounts include: 401(k); 403(b); 457; profit sharing; Keogh; Simple; SEP; traditional IRA; Roth IRA; 529 plans; Coverdell Education Savings Accounts (ESAs); fixed annuities; variable annuities; whole life; variable life; universal life; and variable universal life.

Tax-deferred Investment Assets* (cont'd):

	Ownership	Current Value ($)	Cost Basis ($)	Current Annual Contribution ($) (if applicable)	Current Total Return (%)	Current Annual Yield (%)	Use Cash to Settle Estate? (Y/N)
		$	$	$			
		$	$	$			
		$	$	$			
		$	$	$			
		$	$	$			
		$	$	$			
		$	$	$			
		$	$	$			
		$	$	$			
		$	$	$			
		$	$	$			
		$	$	$			
		$	$	$			
		$	$	$			

* Examples of tax-deferred accounts include: 401(k); 403(b); 457; profit sharing; Keogh; Simple; SEP; traditional IRA; Roth IRA; 529 plans; Coverdell Education Savings Accounts (ESAs); fixed annuities; variable annuities; whole life; universal life; variable life; universal life; and variable universal life.

Investment Asset Allocation (%):
Client 1
Optional, if this information is available.

(Please list accounts in same order as above.)

	Total Value ($)	Large-Cap	Mid-Cap	Small-Cap	Intl. Stock	Corp. Bonds	Govt. Bonds	High-Yield Bonds	Real Estate	Gold	Cash
Taxable	$										
	$										
	$										
	$										
	$										
	$										
	$										
Tax-deferred	$										
	$										
	$										
	$										
	$										
	$										
	$										

Investment Asset Allocation (%): Client 2

Optional, if this information is available.

(Please list accounts in same order as above.)

	Total Value ($)	Large-Cap	Mid-Cap	Small-Cap	Intl. Stock	Corp. Bonds	Govt. Bonds	High-Yield Bonds	Real Estate	Gold	Cash
Taxable	$										
	$										
	$										
	$										
	$										
	$										
	$										
	$										
	$										
	$										
Tax-deferred	$										
	$										
	$										
	$										
	$										
	$										

Section 8: We also need to learn about the types of personal assets you own. Use the following form to record your asset information:

Personal/Business Assets*	Ownership (Name or "Joint")	Purchase Price	Current Value	Appreciation Rate (if applicable)	Use Cash to Settle Estate? (Y/N)
		$	$		
		$	$		
		$	$		
		$	$		
		$	$		
		$	$		
		$	$		
		$	$		
		$	$		
		$	$		
		$	$		
		$	$		

* Suggestions for personal/business asset descriptions include: primary residence; secondary residence; vacation home; automobile; boat; motorcycle, ATV or RV; land; passive business interests; active business interests; and other.

Section 9: Now we would like to review your debts and liabilities. Use the following form to identify your financial liabilities:

Personal/Business Liabilities*	Person Liable (Name or "Joint")	Current Amount Owed ($)	Monthly Payment ($)**	Interest Rate (%)	Fixed or Variable	Origination Date	Maturity Date	To be Paid-off at Client's Death?
		$	$					
		$	$					
		$	$					
		$	$					
		$	$					
		$	$					
		$	$					
		$	$					
		$	$					
		$	$					
		$	$					
		$	$					

*Suggestions for personal/business liability descriptions include: primary residence; secondary residence; vacation home; automobile; boat, motorcycle, ATV, or RV; other consumer credit (e.g., credit cards, gas cards, store credit cards, etc.); student loans; land; passive business interests; active business interests; other.

**For credit card, gas card, or department store accounts, please indicate whether the monthly payment is the minimum monthly payment, an amount paid each month to reduce the balance, or the typical payment to pay the balance off in full each month.

Section 10: Please take a few minutes to indicate how much you spend on the following items on a monthly basis. If you are spending money on something not indicated, please add that item.

Housing

Mortgage/rent	$
Property taxes	$
Home repairs	$
Home insurance	$
Utilities	$
Telephone	$

Transportation

Auto payment	$
Auto insurance	$
Fuel	$
Maintenance	$
License	$
Parking/tolls	$
Bus/train	$

Taxes and Withholding

Federal income taxes	$
State & local taxes	$
FICA taxes	$
Other withholdings	$

Other Items

After-tax retirement	$
Other	$
Other	$
Other	$

Household/Personal

Groceries	$
Personal care	$
Clothing	$
Domestic help	$
Dependent care	$
Professional dues	$
Education	$
Allowances	$
Child care	$

Personal Insurance

Health insurance	$
Life insurance	$
Disability insurance	$
Long-term care	$
Medical/dental	$
Prescription drugs	$
Other	$

Savings

Pretax retirement	$
Roth IRA	$
Traditional IRA	$
Other savings	$
Emergency fund	$
Interest & dividends	$
Capital gains	$

Loan Payments

Credit card	$
Credit card	$
Installment loan	$
Installment loan	$
Other payment	$
Other payment	$

Alimony and Child Support

Alimony	$
Child support	$

Variable/Discretionary Expenses

Dining out	$
Bank charges	$
Recreation	$
Dues	$
Movies	$
Events	$
Hobbies	$
Vacation/travel	$
Gifts	$
Charitable giving	$
Laundry/dry cleaning	$
Other	$
Other	$
Miscellaneous	$
Miscellaneous	$

Section 11: Understanding your feelings toward investments can help us guide you when making investment choices. Please provide a response to each statement below that best matches your opinion today:

Client 1	Strongly Disagree	Disagree	Neutral	Agree	Strongly Agree
1. Keeping pace with inflation is important to me.					
2. I am comfortable borrowing money to make a financial investment.					
3. Diversification is important to investment success.					
4. The return I am making on my current investments is acceptable.					
5. I need to earn more spendable income from my investments.					
6. I am comfortable with the volatility I experience with my portfolio.					
7. Reducing the amount of taxes paid on my investments is a top priority.					
8. I am willing to risk being audited by the IRS in return for higher returns.					
9. I am willing to risk being audited by the IRS in return for paying less tax.					
10. My friends would tell you that I am a real risk taker.					

Client 2	Strongly Disagree	Disagree	Neutral	Agree	Strongly Agree
1. Keeping pace with inflation is important to me.					
2. I am comfortable borrowing money to make a financial investment.					
3. Diversification is important to investment success.					
4. The return I am making on my current investments is acceptable.					
5. I need to earn more spendable income from my investments.					
6. I am comfortable with the volatility I experience with my portfolio.					
7. Reducing the amount of taxes paid on my investments is a top priority.					
8. I am willing to risk being audited by the IRS in return for higher returns.					
9. I am willing to risk being audited by the IRS in return for paying less tax.					
10. My friends would tell you that I am a real risk taker.					

Section 12: We would also like to learn about your expectations regarding the future.

Client 1: Please provide your opinion of the following statements:

1. Over the next five years, do you expect the U.S. economy, as a whole, to perform better, worse, or about the same as it has over the past five years?

1	2	3	4	5	6	7	8	9	10
Perform worse				*Perform about the same*				*Perform better*	

2. How satisfied are you with your current level of income?

1	2	3	4	5	6	7	8	9	10
Lowest Level								*Highest Level*	

3. How satisfied are you with your present overall financial situation?

1	2	3	4	5	6	7	8	9	10
Lowest Level								*Highest Level*	

4. Overall, how satisfied are you with your current job or position?

1	2	3	4	5	6	7	8	9	10
Lowest Level								*Highest Level*	

5. Rate yourself on your level of knowledge about personal finance issues and investing.

1	2	3	4	5	6	7	8	9	10
Lowest Level								*Highest Level*	

Client 2: Please provide your opinion of the following statements:

1. Over the next five years, do you expect the U.S. economy, as a whole, to perform better, worse, or about the same as it has over the past five years?

1	2	3	4	5	6	7	8	9	10
Perform worse				*Perform about the same*				*Perform better*	

2. How satisfied are you with your current level of income?

1	2	3	4	5	6	7	8	9	10
Lowest Level								*Highest Level*	

3. How satisfied are you with your present overall financial situation?

1	2	3	4	5	6	7	8	9	10
Lowest Level								*Highest Level*	

4. Overall, how satisfied are you with your current job or position?

1	2	3	4	5	6	7	8	9	10
Lowest Level								*Highest Level*	

5. Rate yourself on your level of knowledge about personal finance issues and investing.

1	2	3	4	5	6	7	8	9	10
Lowest Level								*Highest Level*	

Section 13: One way that we can help you is by identifying specific areas in your financial life that need immediate attention. Take a few minutes to answer the following questions about retirement and estate planning.

Estate Planning Document Information	Client 1	Client 2
Do you have a will?		
If so, was it drafted more than five years ago?		
Do you have a living trust? If so, please list revocable or irrevocable.		
Do you have a living will?		
Do you have an advance medical directive (AMD)?		
Do you have a durable power of attorney? If so, please list by name.		
Have you named a health care proxy? If so, please list by name		
Are you or your spouse/partner named as the beneficiary of a trust?		
If so, from whom or where?		

Estate Planning Valuation Information	Client 1	Client 2
Do you or your partner expect to receive an inheritance?		
If so, when?		
Approximate value?		
Have you made any gifts to relatives?		
Have you received any gifts from relatives?		
Have you made substantial gifts to charities?		
Do you plan to make substantial gifts to charities in the future?		
If you or your spouse/partner were to die, would you pay off your mortgage?		
If you or your spouse/partner were to die, would you pay off your nonmortgage debt?		
If you or your spouse/partner were to die, would you fund your child's education goal?		
If you or your spouse/partner were to die, would you fund your retirement goal?		
Do you or your spouse/partner own real estate in a state other than your primary domicile?		

Section 14: It is possible that you either have worked with or are currently working with someone in the financial services profession. Please inform us of your existing advisors, so that we may coordinate advice when appropriate:

Do you have a CPA, accountant, enrolled agent, or tax preparer?   *(Circle)* Yes No

    If yes, who? _____

    How long have you worked with this person? _____

    Would you recommend this person to others? _____

    May we contact this person or firm directly on your behalf? _____

    If yes, an additional form must be signed granting this authorization.

Do you have an attorney or other person you depend on for legal advice?   *(Circle)* Yes No

    If yes, who? _____

    How long have you worked with this person? _____

    Would you recommend this person to others? _____

    May we contact this person or firm directly on your behalf? _____

    If yes, an additional form must be signed granting this authorization.

Do you have any other financial advisors?   *(Circle)* Yes No

    If yes, who? _____

    How long have you worked with this person? _____

    Would you recommend this person to others? _____

    May we contact this person or firm directly on your behalf? _____

    If yes, an additional form must be signed granting this authorization.

Are there any other financial professionals of whom we should be aware?   *(Circle)* Yes No

    If yes, who? _____

    How long have you worked with this person? _____

    Would you recommend this person to others? _____

    May we contact this person or firm directly on your behalf? _____

    If yes, an additional form must be signed granting this authorization.

Section 15: Summary

Is there any other information that you would like to share with us regarding your personal or financial situation?_____

_____

_____

_____

_____

_____

_____

What is the primary outcome that you expect when hiring us as your financial planning firm? What is the most important objective(s) that you wish to accomplish? _____

_____

_____

_____

_____

_____

_____

Again, thank you for taking the time to complete this confidential client questionnaire.

Welcome to our financial planning family!

We look forward to working with you.

Financial Planning Benchmarks

OVERVIEW

As noted in Chapters 7 and 8, planning assumptions are based on inferential knowledge that a planner either surmises from readily available information or concludes based on fact. Sometimes, a planner must rely strictly on fact. Because of the rapidly changing marketplace and regulatory environment of financial planning, data that clients may perceive to be factual are often accompanied by phrases such as "past performance does not guarantee future results" or similar disclaimers, which are offered to avoid misleading clients or guaranteeing results. Aside from fact, the next best evaluation measure is often a benchmark, which by definition is a widely accepted standard used for comparison. But care must be taken to ensure that the benchmark chosen is appropriate—that it correlates or is relevant to the data to which the benchmark is being compared. For benchmarks, advisors typically rely on third-party objective data or averages of data, typically historical, which serve as a proxy for facts. By using such benchmarks, advisors can defend professional judgment when:

- evaluating a client's previously selected planning strategies or products;

- recommending or selecting new or replacement strategies or products; or

- monitoring products previously recommended and currently in use.

Assumptions (often based on benchmarks) and benchmarks are important throughout the planning process. But caution is warranted—historical *fact* ceases to be factual when used as an assumption on which future projections are made. To clarify, when a planner uses a benchmark as a point of historical comparison on which to gauge the relative performance of a product, the past performance of both the benchmark and the product are documented facts that can be verified. However, when a planner uses historical product performance information as the basis for *projecting* future performance, the planner is now inferring, or making an assumption, based on historical fact. Hence, it is important to clearly disclose the projection as a fact-based forecast, not a guarantee about the future, by means of a disclaimer, such as the previously mentioned "Past performance does not guarantee future results." A word of caution: occasionally, either explicitly or implicitly, advisors overstate the persistence (or likelihood of continuation) of performance—a practice to be avoided.

PERSONAL FINANCIAL WELLNESS BENCHMARKS: RATIOS

It is said that consumers pay for three things—what they have already bought, what they are currently buying, and what they plan to buy. The trick to having more money is to remove just one thing from the pile of purchases. Unfortunately, recent history suggests that, given the dismal average savings rate, the one thing that individuals usually remove is what they plan to buy with future savings. Too often, past and present spending take precedence over saving for future spending, whether for an identified tangible goal (e.g., car, boat, trip) or an intangible future need (e.g., retirement income). Meeting living expenses and making all payments on time may not tell the whole story!

A financial ratio is used to help planner and client better understand a current financial position. Financial ratios provide a quantitative measure of a client's financial status compared to a benchmark. As such, ratios are used to identify and diagnose problems or issues not immediately evident from basic financial statements.

Financial planners do not agree about whether or how to use ratios as benchmarks to assess clients' financial health. These benchmarks—like any others, if taken out of context, misapplied, or incorrectly chosen—can offer helpful or misleading interpretations of a client's situation. However, if caution and professional judgment are exercised, ratios can provide an appropriate starting point for analysis. For example, the numbers on a client's financial statements generally tell a limited story, but by applying a series of financial ratios, further analysis of income and expense and net worth statements can yield useful insights.

Table C.1 presents nine commonly used financial ratios. The first two summarize a client's balance sheet data and offer a perspective on the relationship between asset and liability. The emergency fund ratio compares data from both financial statements, and the remaining six ratios summarize the client's income and expense statement and gauge how well current income meets savings and credit payment obligations.

Table C.1 Commonly Used Financial Ratios

Ratio	Formula	Benchmark
Current ratio	$$\frac{\text{Monetary assets}}{\text{Current liabilities}}$$	> 1.00
Debt ratio	$$\frac{\text{Total liabilities}}{\text{Total assets}}$$	< 40%
Emergency fund ratio	$$\frac{\text{Monetary assets}}{\text{Monthly living expenses}}$$	3–6 months
Savings ratio	$$\frac{\text{Personal savings and employer contributions}}{\text{Annual gross income}}$$	> 10%
Credit usage ratio	$$\frac{\text{Total credit used}}{\text{Total credit available}}$$	< 30%
Long-term debt coverage ratio	$$\frac{\text{Annual gross income}}{\text{Total annual long-term debt payments}}$$	> 2.50
Debt-to-income ratio	$$\frac{\text{Annual consumer credit payments}}{\text{Annual after-tax income}}$$	< 15%
"Front-end" mortgage ratio	$$\frac{\text{Annual mortgage (PITI*) payment}}{\text{Annual gross income}}$$	< 28%
"Back-end" mortgage ratio	$$\frac{\text{Annual mortgage (PITI*) and credit payments}}{\text{Annual gross income}}$$	< 36%

* Principal, interest, taxes, and insurance

The *current ratio* is a measure of client liquidity. This ratio determines whether sufficient monetary assets are currently available to pay off all outstanding short-term debts. The recommended minimum for the current ratio is a number greater than one, which means that if all current liabilities were paid, the client would still retain some monetary assets.

Clients often wonder whether they have too much debt. The *debt ratio* provides a guideline to help answer this question. In effect, this ratio shows the percentage of total assets financed by borrowing. Typically, a benchmark of 40% is used for this ratio. In other words, the typical client should strive to have no more than $4.00 in liability for every $10.00 in assets. As is true of most financial ratios, the interpretation of this benchmark is flexible, depending on the client's unique circumstances and stage in the life cycle. For example, clients in the earlier stages of their careers may not have much choice except to exceed the optimal percentage because of car loans, education loans, revolving credit accounts (for purchases such as furniture and appliances), and other household formation spending.

The *emergency fund ratio*, sometimes referred to as the *month's living expenses covered ratio*, is critically important because it indicates how long a client could live in a crisis situation without liquidating other assets or being forced into an unfavorable employment situation. A benchmark of three to six months of expenses is recommended. The rationale for having a range rather than a single value is based on a number of factors including job stability, the number of household earners, types and amount of available credit, current credit usage ratio, and current savings ratio. High unemployment and stock market declines over the past decade have increased concerns that the three- to six-month benchmark should be increased to perhaps 10 months. Additional issues for debate include the meaning of *living expenses*, as appropriately defined by the advisor and matched to a client's situation, and the choice of account(s) for depositing these emergency funds to compensate for inflation and liquidity risks.

One of the most important questions clients ask financial planners is, "Am I saving as much as I should?" The *savings ratio* can be used to answer this question. This ratio sums a client's personal savings and employer contributions to retirement plans, and then divides that figure by the client's annual gross income. A benchmark of 10% or greater is recommended. In other words, at least 10% of gross earnings should be saved annually. However, this ratio is highly subjective and should not be applied blindly; rather, great care should be taken to match a client's total savings need to the total goal funding need and stage of the life cycle.

The *credit usage ratio* is not only a factor in determining the adequacy of the emergency fund ratio; it is also one of the key factors in determining credit score. High credit usage, such as balances above 30% to 50% of the credit limit, is usually considered negative. This is because creditors may think more credit is being used than can readily be repaid.

The *long-term debt coverage ratio* reflects how many times a client can make debt payments based on current income. This formula can be calculated in several ways. A common method involves dividing annual gross income by total annual long-term debt payments. Examples of long-term debt payments include mortgage payments, automobile loan payments, student loan payments, or other debts that take more than a year to repay. If a client's monthly credit card payment is large enough that servicing the debt could take more then a year, this amount might also be included in the denominator of the formula. A long-term debt coverage ratio of at least 2.50 is recommended. The inverse of this formula tells an interesting story. The inverse of a long-term debt coverage ratio of 2.50 is .40. This means that a client should allocate no more than 40% of income to cover long-term debt payments.

Related to the long-term debt coverage ratio is the *debt-to-income ratio*, which measures the percentage of take - home pay, committed to consumer credit repayment (defined as all revolving and installment nonmortgage debts). A ratio of less than 10% of take-home, or disposable, income is optimal, although up to 15% is usually considered safe. A ratio of between 15% and 20% is generally considered questionable practice, and consumer debt repayments in excess of 20% of take-home pay are usually considered to be a serious problem. Because automatic payments, salary deferral retirement plans, and other employee benefits may further reduce after-tax disposable income, it is important that planners exercise care when calculating this ratio. However, the interpretation of this ratio is clear: when clients commit 15% to 20% (or more) of disposable income to consumer debt repayment; little is left for meeting all other financial obligations.

Lenders also use ratios as one measure to determine mortgage qualification. Variations of debt-to-income ratios, *mortgage qualification ratios* are used to determine how much of a client's annual gross income is used to pay for monthly mortgage and consumer debt payments. Two mortgage qualification ratios are widely used: the front-end ratio and the back-end ratio. The front-end ratio, or *mortgage debt service ratio*, is typically limited to 28% of gross income. This ratio compares the projected total mortgage payment for principal, interest, taxes, and insurance (PITI) to gross household income. The back-end ratio, or *debt repayment ratio*, is limited to 36% of gross income. This rule states that a client should pay no more than 36% of gross income on the projected mortgage PITI, plus other regular monthly consumer debt payments (e.g., credit cards, student loans, or automobiles). These qualification ratios are applied throughout the mortgage industry for conventional loans, although the range may vary by lender or type of loan. An important note: for a client to qualify for a *maximum* mortgage, the two ratios implicitly limit other consumer debt payments to 8% of gross income. This corresponds closely to the original debt-to-income ratio that recommends that consumer credit payments be limited to 10% of take-home income.

INSURANCE INDUSTRY BENCHMARKS: RATINGS

Often financial planners use third-party provider data or market data as a means of evaluation and comparison. Insurance company ratings are one example of a factor used to evaluate insurance policies currently held by a client or recommended by an advisor. Advisors compare the information available on a current or proposed policy provider with independent ratings information available from third-party evaluation services. Five firms currently assess the financial strength of insurance companies and rate overall company quality as measured by default risk. These third-party evaluators, along with their best and worst ratings, are summarized in Table C.2. In general, both planners and clients are encouraged to use insurance products from companies rated "A" or higher by the five rating agencies.

Table C.2 Insurance Company Ratings

Rating Agency	Best Rating	Worst Rating	Web Presence
A.M. Best	A++	F	www.ambest.com
Fitch	AAA	DDD	www.fitchratings.com
Moody's Investor Service	Aaa	C	www.moodys.com
Standard & Poor's	AAA	CC	www.standardandpoors.com
Weiss Ratings, Inc.	A+	F	www.weissratings.com

FIXED-INCOME BENCHMARKS: RATINGS

As reported in Table C.3, bonds are classified based on default risk (i.e., the probability that the issuing company will not be able to pay the principal as agreed). Ratings are particularly important to bond investors, but they also offer valuable insights into the bonds held by various mutual funds or pension funds. For clients with corporate or municipal bonds, ratings should be tracked to monitor potential rating and price changes.

Table C.3 Bond Rating Agencies and Descriptions

Investment-grade Bonds

Moody's	S&P	Fitch	Rating Description
Aaa	AAA	AAA	Highest investment bond rating
Aa	AA	AA	Very high investment grade rating
A	A	A	Medium investment grade rating
Baa	BBB	BBB	Lower investment grade rating

Speculative-grade Bonds—High Yield

Moody's	S&P	Fitch	Rating Description
Ba	BB	BB	Highest-grade junk bond
B	B	B	Speculative-grade junk bond
Caa	CCC	CCC	Low-grade junk bond
Ca	CC	CC	Default-grade junk bond
C	C	C	Issue that pays no interest
---	D	D	Issue in default

FINANCIAL MARKET BENCHMARKS: INDICES

Indices track the performance of a select group of equities, bonds, or in some specialized cases, equities and bonds. The news media typically report indices as indicators of general market conditions or movements, but indices are also useful as benchmarks or standards of measurement for an individual security or portfolio. For a meaningful comparison, it is important to select a benchmark that most closely matches both the type of security and the corresponding level of risk.

In addition to benchmarking individual assets, many advisors benchmark entire portfolios. To gauge overall portfolio performance, the returns for several indices reported over the same time period are matched proportionately to the assets in the portfolio. In other words, weighted average returns are compared based on the actual portfolio and the matching benchmarks for corresponding market sectors. Information to track the performance of most securities over time should be readily available, either free from the Internet or from the advisor's custodian, broker dealer, or other third-party source. Although numerous indices track different market segments (nationally, regionally, and internationally), some of the most commonly used indices are listed in Tables C.4 and C.5. However, it is important to note that a decision to purchase or sell a security should not be based solely on performance relative to the benchmark index; it should consider other aspects of the client's situation as well.

Table C.4 Most Widely Used Financial Market Indices (by Provider)

Company	General Market Segment	Most-quoted Index	Web Presence
Standard & Poor's	Stocks	Standard & Poor's 500	www.standardandpoors.com
NASDAQ[1]	Stocks	NASDAQ Composite	www.nasdaq.com
Russell	Stocks	Russell 2000	www.russell.com
Wilshire	Stocks & real estate	Wilshire 5000	www.wilshire.com
Dow Jones	Stocks	DJIA 30[2]	http://djindexes.com
Morgan Stanley	Stocks & bonds	MSCI EAFE[3]	www.msci.com
Barclay's	Bonds	U.S. Aggregate Bond	https://ecommerce.barcap.com

[1] National Association of Securities Dealers Automated Quotation System
[2] Dow Jones Industrial Average
[3] Morgan Stanley Capital, Inc., Europe, Australia and Far East

Table C.5 Select Widely Used Financial Market Indices

Market Sector	Corresponding Index by Provider			
	S&P/Barra	Russell	Morgan Stanley	Wilshire/DJ
All U.S. stocks	S&P Total Mkt	3000	Market 2500	Wilshire 5000
U.S. Equity (Size Segmented)				
Mega-cap	---	---	---	DJIA 30
Large-cap	S&P 500	1000	Large-cap 300	Wilshire 750
Mid-cap	S&P 400	Mid-cap	Mid-cap 450	Wilshire 500
Small-cap	S&P 600	2000	Small-cap 1750	Wilshire 1750
U.S. Equity (Style Segmented)				

Large Growth	Barra Growth	1000 Growth	---		Target Large Growth
Mid Growth	---	Mid-cap Growth	---		Target Large Value
Large Value	Barra Value	1000 Value	---		Target Mid-Growth
Mid Value	---	Mid-cap Value	---		Target Mid-Value
U.S. Equity (Sector Segmented)					
Consumer	S&P Consumer	---	---		---
Health Care	S&P Health Care	---	---		DJ Health Care
Utilities	S&P Utilities	---	---		---
Financials	S&P Financials	---	---		DJ Insurance
Technology	S&P Technology	---	---		DJ Telecom
International Equity (Region Segmented)					
World equity market	S&P Global 1200	---		AC World Index	---
International stocks (non-emerging market)	S&P 700	---		AC World Index (excluding U.S.)	DJ Developed Mkts
Emerging market stocks	IFCI	---		Emerging Markets	DJ Emerging Mkts
					DJ Latin Amer

Market Sector	Corresponding Index by Provider		
	S&P	**Wilshire/DJ**	**Barclay's**
All U.S. bonds	---	---	U.S. Universal
U.S. Treasury (Term Segmented)			
Long-term	BG Cantor U.S. T-bond	---	---
Intermediate	---	---	U.S. Treasury
Short-term	BG Cantor U.S. T-bill	---	---
TIPS	BG Cantor U.S. TIPS	---	U.S. Treasury TIPS
Corporate Debt (Quality Segmented)			
U.S. Investment Grade	---	---	U.S. Long Credit
U.S. High-Yield	---	---	U.S. Corp High-Yield
International (Region Segmented)			
World bond market	---	---	Multiverse
International bonds	Int'l Corp Bond	---	Global Aggregate
Emerging market bonds	---	---	Global Emerging Markets
Specialty			
Real Estate (REITS)	U.S. REIT	Wilshire RESI[1]	---
Global Real Estate	---	Global RESI	---
U.S. municipal bonds	Municipal Bond	---	U.S. Municipal
U.S. mortgage-backed	---	---	U.S. MBS

Notes

1.   Real Estate Securities Index.

Education Planning: A Sample Chapter from the Kims' Comprehensive Plan

The following education planning section of a financial plan is provided as an example intended for illustrative purposes only. Data and calculations are based on specific case assumptions, some of which are not shown in the illustration. The analysis, strategies, and recommendations are fictional and subject to alteration based on changes in assumptions.

Planning for Azalea's education is your primary goal. As we discussed, education expenses are very costly, but higher education is the gateway to opportunity. Like other financial goals, the key is to start saving early! You are already saving, sporadically, in a taxable account designated for Azalea's education. As background for this section, consider the latest available information from The College Board (http://www.collegeboard.org/) for the 2010–2011 academic year:

- The average cost of tuition, fees, and room and board was $16,140 and $28,130, respectively, for four-year in-state and out-of-state public schools, an average increase of 6.1% over the 2009–2010 academic year costs for in-state schools, and slightly higher than the 5.6% increase for out-of-state schools. Private school costs averaged $36,993 for an average annual 4.3% increase over the previous year's data.[1]

- Tuition and fees alone totaled $7,605 and $19,595 for in-state and out-of-state public schools, respectively. Tuition and fees were an average of $27,293 at private four-year institutions. These costs reflect average annual increases of 7.9%, 6.0%, and 4.5%, respectively, reflecting the trend for greater cost increases for public over private institutions.[2]

- Costs of education continue to outpace average cost-of-living increases. From academic years 2000–2001 to 2010–2011, published tuition and fee costs at public four-year institutions increased 5.6% more than the general inflation rate over the same period.[3]

- Also over that same time period, the cost of tuition and fees at public four-year institutions almost doubled to 5.6% compared to tuition and fees paid at four-year private institutions, where prices increased by 3.0%. These changes represent inflation-adjusted changes over the decade.[4]

- Private, institutional, federal, and state grants as well as federal and state tax credits and deductions cover approximately 33% of tuition, fees, room, and board costs for a private college and 27% of public college costs for four-year, full-time students.

- The Project on Student Debt estimated that two-thirds of the 2010 graduates of public and private nonprofit four-year institutions graduated with student loan debt. For those with debt, the average loan amount was $25,250—an average increase of 5% over the previous year.[5]

Finally, if financial aid is a consideration in your education goal planning, the account owner should be the parent and not the child. Financial aid formulas treat college assets in the parent's name more favorably than money saved in the child's name. For example, today, financial aid formulas typically include only 2.6% to 5.6% of parental assets (based on a sliding income scale and after certain allowances) versus as much as 20% of the child's assets.[6]

EDUCATION GOAL

The goal is to accumulate at least $40,000 toward funding the cost of a four-year public school education for Azalea beginning in 10 years.

ASSUMPTIONS

Based on our discussions and the information you provided, we have agreed to the following planning assumptions:

- Currently, $1,550 in a taxable mutual fund account, jointly owned by Tom and Nyla, is designated for Azalea's college expenses.

- You both own Roth IRA accounts with a combined *contribution* balance of nearly $100,000, which you agree could be withdrawn, if necessary, to fund Azalea's college expenses.

- For taxable account projections, the federal income tax rates on annual distributions are 15% on capital gains and 25% on nonqualified dividends and other income. It is assumed that no dividends are "qualified" for the lower income tax rate treatment.

- Tuition, fees, and room and board are estimated as $16,000 (in today's dollars) per year for a four-year public college.

- Azalea will begin college in 10 years, or in the fall of 2022.

- You wish to save for this goal through July 2022, the month before Azalea begins college.

- All planned future contributions will remain level during the funding period.

- College expenses will increase 5.5% annually.

- The stated risk tolerance for this goal is moderately aggressive.

- You want to maintain ownership of, and access to, the account.

- You prefer a dedicated account for Azalea's education.

- Scholarships will not be considered as a source of funding at this time.

- Azalea will be expected to contribute to her education funding through high school or college employment and personal savings.

ANALYSIS

Based on our discussions and the information you provided, the following three alternatives were analyzed to partially fund Azalea's education:

- Alternative 1: Continue funding the taxable account with a suggested constant annual end-of-year contribution of $2,200.

- Alternative 2: Establish a new § 529 plan account with fixed monthly contributions of $250 or a total of $3,000 per year. Distributions from this account are tax free if used exclusively for qualified education expenses.[7]

- Alternative 3: Fund a Roth IRA with fixed monthly contributions of $250 or a total of $3,000 per year, with the intention that the money could be withdrawn for Azalea's education. This account would generally be tax deferred rather than tax free even for qualified expenses, *unless only the contributions, and no earnings, are withdrawn.*

Finally, to provide consistent analysis across all scenarios, the same rate of return was used for all projections. Where applicable, the federal income tax rates on annual distributions are 15% on capital gains and 25% on nonqualified dividends and other income. It is assumed that no dividends are qualified for the lower income tax rate treatment. All state taxes are ignored in the analysis. Note also that if the tax-free account is used, then the taxable account—with the $1,550 balance—would be closed and the proceeds deposited into the tax-free account. Any taxes due upon liquidation of the taxable account (which should be a very small amount because of the size of the account) would be paid with outside funds to maintain an equivalent opening balance for either account.

Figure D.1 compares the tax-free account (the § 529 plan or the Roth IRA) and the taxable account for meeting your education goal funding. As shown in Figure D.1, the tax-free account would yield approximately $15,000 more than the taxable account at the beginning of the disbursement period because of the proposed differences in funding, $2,200 and $3,000, respectively, and taxation. (The spreadsheet documenting the results is shown on page xx of the plan Appendix).[8]

Figure D.1 Proposed Tax-deferred Account vs. Original Taxable Account

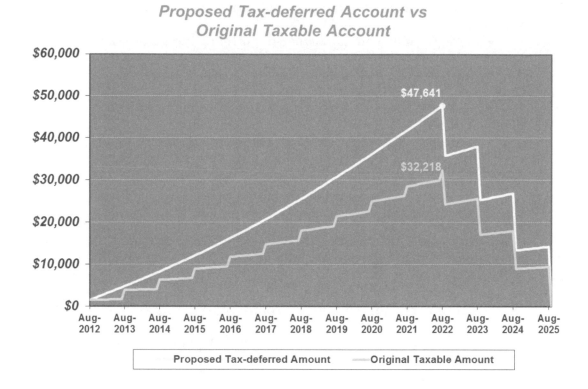

Alternative 1. Assuming you deposit $2,200 at the end of each year, Azalea's projected Year 1 college expenses of $27,300 would be underfunded by approximately $19,300 (≈$27,330 - $8,038) as shown in Figure D.2. This trend continues because the approach would provide less than one-third of the required amount for each year. As illustrated in Table D.1, this alternative yields an account balance of $32,218 when Azalea begins college. After accounting for the effects of continued compounding during her college years, this balance would allow for total withdrawals of $34,902, which, again, represents only one-third of the total cost of college. Results for all years are shown in Table D.1.

Figure D.2 Projected Taxable Account Annual Withdrawals

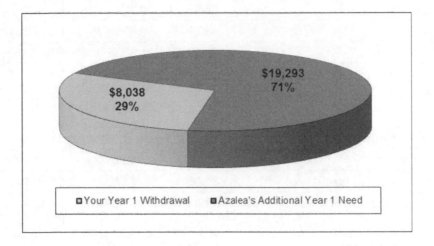

Table D.1. Education Planning Assumptions and Analysis Summary

College Begins	2022	Years until College	10
College Ends	2025	Total Years in College	4
Present Value Cost per Year	$16,000	Total Current Funding	$1,550
Annual Education Inflation Rate	5.50%		
Total Cost (future value dollars)	$118,675		
Annual Costs (future value dollars)	Year 1	Year 2	Year 3	Year 4
	$27,330	$28,833	$30,419	$32,092
Additional Periodic Funding:	Existing		Proposed	
Annual	$2,200		n/a	
Monthly	n/a		$250	
Assumed Nominal Rates of Return: (monthly compounding assumed in calculations)	Year 1-7	Year 8	Year 9	Year 10+
Total Return	8.00%	7.25%	6.75%	6.50%
Return from Capital Gain	6.00%	5.25%	4.25%	3.50%
Return from Dividend	2.00%	2.00%	2.50%	3.00%
Assumed Income Tax Rates:			
Capital Gains	15%		
Nonqualified Dividends or Income	25%[1]		

Education Planning Projections (Existing Taxable Account; $2,200/yr.)

Projections by Year	08/01/22	08/01/23	08/01/24	08/01/25
Account Values	$32,218	$25,475	$17,904	$9,438
Withdrawal Amounts	$8,038	$8,480	$8,946	$9,438
Percentage of Annual Expense Covered	29.5%	29.5%	29.5%	29.5%

Education Planning Projections (Proposed Tax-qualified Account; $250/mo.)

Projections by Year	08/01/22	08/01/23	08/01/24	08/01/25
Account Values (prior to withdraw)	$47,641	$37,908	$26,812	$14,223
Withdrawal Amounts	$12,113	$12,779	$13,482	$14,223
Percentage of Annual Expense Covered	44.3%	44.3%	44.3%	44.3%

1 To err on the side of safety, it is assumed that no dividends are "qualified" for purposes of determining after-tax returns. This should slightly understate the return and therefore understate the subsequent account balance. Actual after-tax returns should be higher because at least some of dividends distributed by most investment companies are "qualified." Your tax advisor will be better able to determine the exact amount of "qualified" dividends you receive.

Alternative 2. Increasing the funding to the equivalent of $3,000 per year, or contributions of $250 per month, to the § 529 plan account should cover more than 44% of the $27,300 of expenses for Year 1 as shown in Figure D.3. Results shown in Figure D.3 are based on the assumption that all § 529 plan distributions are made only for qualified education expenses, thereby qualifying the distributions as tax free. Again, see Table D.1 for the tax-qualified scenario for all years. Please note that in this scenario the account balance at the beginning of Azalea's college career has increased to $47,641. This increased balance would allow you to withdraw a total of $52,597 based on our return assumptions. Therefore, a manageable increase in savings of less than $70 per month, and the elimination of taxes (paid annually on earnings and capital gains taxes paid on withdrawal) yields an increase in available funding of more than $15,000 (≈$47,641 – $32,218) for Azalea's education.

Figure D.3 Projected Tax-free Account Annual Withdrawals

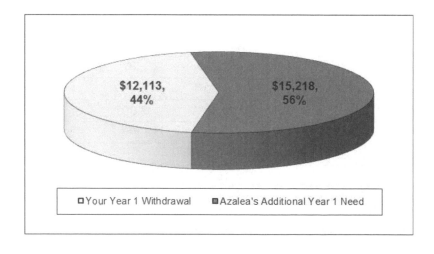

$12,113, 44% $15,218, 56%

☐ Your Year 1 Withdrawal   ■ Azalea's Additional Year 1 Need

Alternative 3. Results for Alternative 3, withdrawal of contributions from your existing Roth IRA accounts, assuming the equivalent of $3,000 of funding, would be the same as for Alternative 2. (Because both of you are currently fully funding each account, no additional funding is allowed.) Note that the federal income tax consequences for the § 529 plan and the Roth IRA would be the same, assuming both are used exclusively for qualified education expenses and total distributions from the Roth IRA do not exceed total contributions.

In our analysis, a total four-year distribution of $52,597, based on data in Table D.1, would not exceed the nearly $100,000 of contributions in the Roth accounts, ignoring all future contributions over the next 10 years. This is important because withdrawals from Roth IRAs are assumed to come out of your contributions first, and your contributions can always be withdrawn tax- and penalty-free. Even if it is used for qualifying education expenses, the "earnings" portion of a distribution from a Roth IRA is taxable, although the 10% additional tax penalty would not apply. State tax consequences for the earnings could vary; for simplicity they have been ignored in this analysis. (Please consult your tax advisor for a full explanation.)

Although the Roth IRA alternative could offer earnings and tax savings similar to the § 529 plan, invading the Roth contributions to fund Azalea's education has several negative consequences. Reducing the principal would not only reduce the account value by more than $52,000 over the four years of Azalea's college education, but it would also "rob" the account of all future earnings attributable to the $52,000.

Alternative 3 could be a viable contingency plan. But unless an extreme change in your household situation prohibits funding both your Roth IRA accounts *and* Azalea's education, trading your retirement income for Azalea's education is not advisable, nor is it consistent with the importance you place on both goals.

Summary of Alternatives

Our analysis, based on the assumptions, projects that Azalea's tuition, fees, and room and board for a four-year public school will cost $118,674 ($27,330 + 28,833 + 30,419 + 32,092), as shown in Table D.1. To meet your goal of saving $40,000 by the time Azalea enters college, funding of $250 per month will be required, assuming our tax and return projections are accurate. Table D.1 outlines all information on which calculations for both taxable and tax-deferred (potentially tax-free) account projections are based.

By increasing the level of funding, the account has the potential to grow to slightly less than $48,000—exceeding the $40,000 targeted amount. However, there is a better chance of achieving the goal by slightly overfunding the account. You have indicated that a $250-per-month commitment is not unreasonable given Nyla's recent salary increase. Note also that the projections are based on a continuous fixed contribution over the 10-year savings period, with no planned increases. Figure D.4 summarizes a comparison of how much money is projected to be available on an annual basis versus the annual projected college expense. (The spreadsheet documenting the results is shown on page xx of the plan Appendix.)[9] The available withdrawal from the account differs for each of the four years, as illustrated here and in Table D.1, to help keep pace with inflation. The higher account balance in the tax-deferred (and potentially tax-free) account, as compared to the taxable account, allows for more than $15,000 in additional disbursements over the life of the account.

Figure D.4 Available Account Withdrawals Compared to Annual Cost

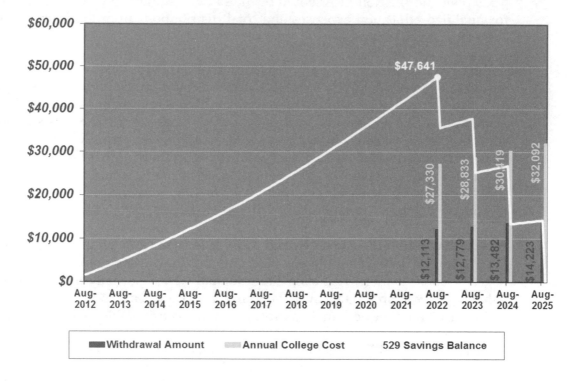

RECOMMENDATION AND IMPLEMENTATION

√   To establish an AnyState College Savings Plan with a Real-life Mutual Fund Company age-based account with monthly funding of $250 to accumulate a projected $40,000 to partially fund the cost of a four-year public college education for Azalea beginning in 2022.

With the AnyState College Savings Plan, we feel that the age-based portfolio is your best option. Because the asset allocation for the portfolio is coordinated with Azalea's time horizon for entering college, her portfolio will gradually shift from a riskier asset allocation to a more conservative one. As noted in Table D.1, rates of return are assumed to decrease in response to these changes. The age-based portfolio approach reduces the monitoring required by the owner; however, a static account (i.e., one that allows the owner to control asset allocation) is available so that additional risk/return adjustments can be made, if deemed necessary. In addition to automatic asset allocation adjustments, automatic periodic rebalancing of the portfolio is also available.

To fund this recommendation, liquidate the taxable account—with the $1,550 balance—and use the proceeds to open the § 529 plan. (Any income taxes due on the sale will be paid with other funds.) , Then deposit $250 per month from Nyla's salary increase (the minimum additional contribution accepted by this plan) beginning this month and continuing until July 2022—the month before Azalea starts college. We recommend an automatic debit from your checking account for convenience.

Additional funds may be contributed randomly throughout the year, should you or your extended family on friends wish to donate to the account on Azalea's behalf. In general, the maximum annual amount that can be given gift-tax free by any individual to the § 529 plan for Azalea is $13,000 (in 2012); however, a special provision allows a gift to the § 529 plan that exceeds the annual exclusion to be prorated over five years.

Our reasons for recommending the § 529 plan account are as follows:

- In addition to the previously mentioned federal tax advantages and the additional advantages described in the following section, Planning Tools and Other Background Information, you will be able to deduct up to $2,000 annually in account contributions from your AnyState taxable income. (Check with your tax advisor for details regarding this deduction.) [10]

- This account does not have an annual fee; however, a set-up fee will be due on account establishment.

- The taxable mutual fund account offers no tax advantages and does not provide automatic reallocation or rebalancing of the portfolio, as are available with the § 529 plan.

- The dual-purpose Roth IRA offers only tax-deferred growth, not tax-free distributions, unless distributions are limited to *contributions only* or are made after age 59½, death, or disability. Nor does it give you the desired dedicated account for Azalea's education. No state tax deductions apply for the Roth contributions. Furthermore, adjusting the portfolio to appropriately match the time horizon for the goal requires more active management. Typically, no account establishment fees apply, but nominal annual maintenance fees will be incurred. Also, withdrawals from this account reduce your savings for retirement.

Recommendation and implementation details are summarized in Exhibit D.1.

Exhibit D.1 Education Planning Recommendation Form for the Kim Family

Planning Recommendation Form

Financial Planning Content Area	Education planning
Client Goal	Funding for Azalea's college expenses

Recommendation No.	1	**Priority (1–6) lowest to highest:**	6
Projected/Target Value ($)	$40,000		

Product Profile

Type	§ 529 account
Duration	14 years
Provider	Real-life Mutual Fund Company
Funding Cost per Period ($)	$250 per month
Maintenance Cost per Period ($)	$25 set-up fee (one time only)

Current Income Tax Status	Tax-qualified	X	Taxable	

Projected Rate of Return	Variable (8.0% for first 7 years)
Major Policy Provisions	None

Procedural Factors

Implementation by Whom	Planner		Client	X

Implementation Date or Time Frame	Within next 60 days
Implementation Procedure	We will provide you with the appropriate forms to complete. Upon completion, mail the forms and your check to Real-life Mutual Fund Company. We will monitor account progress for funding adequacy, risk/return objectives, and all other investment aspects of the account.

Ownership Factors

Owner(s)	Tom Kim			
Form of Ownership	Individual, but as allowed in the plan, Nyla will be designated as the successor on the account			
Insured(s)	NA			
Custodial Account		Yes	X	No	
Custodian	Any State			
In Trust For (ITF)		Yes		No	X
Transfer On Death (TOD)		Yes		No	X
Beneficiary(ies)	Azalea Kim			
Contingent Beneficiary(ies)	NA			

Proposed Benefit	By using a § 529 Plan, you will benefit from tax-deferred growth as well as tax-free withdrawals (restrictions apply). Furthermore, we have agreed to maintain a fairly passive approach and this plan has several age-based portfolios that will adjust the asset allocation, thereby reducing account volatility as Azalea approaches college age. However, the plan selected also offers a static account (i.e., one that allows the owner to control asset allocation) so that additional risk/return adjustments can be made.

Finally, although this recommendation was based on the desire to simplify account management and monitoring, it will still be important to periodically review this education savings plan. Annual reviews help ensure that plan earnings are on target, and that adjustments are being made to reflect changes in your personal situation or to take advantage of changes in the economic, financial, legal, or tax marketplace. The integration of this recommendation and goal with other aspects of your financial life is summarized in the Exhibit D.2.

Exhibit D.2 Education Recommendation Impact Form for the Kim Family

Recommendation Impact Form

Recommendation: Increase education funding for Azalea's college to $250 per month contributed to the AnyState College Savings Plan with Real-life Mutual Fund Company.

Recommendation No.	1					
Planner Decision	Accept	X	Reject		Modify	
Client Decision	Accept	X	Reject		Modify	

Financial Impact

Annual impact on cash-flow ($)	$3,000 Reduction
Immediate impact on net worth ($)	$0

Planning Issue	Degree of Significance				Notes
	Major	Modest	Minor	None	
Financial Situation—Cash Management	X				Review automatic investment plan possibilities with client.
Tax Planning			X		State income tax deduction might be available.
Life Insurance Planning		X			Funding the education goal will impact the ability to purchase life insurance.
Health Insurance Planning				X	
Disability and Long-Term Care Insurance Planning		X			Funding the education goal will impact the ability to purchase long-term disability insurance.
Property and Liability Insurance Planning				X	
Investment Planning	X				Funding the education goal will impact the ability to fund the vacation goal.
Education or Other Special Needs Planning	X				Select age-based portfolios to reduce management time.
Retirement Planning			X		Funding the education goal might impact the ability to fully fund the retirement goal.
Estate Planning			X		Per plan requirements, Nyla will be designated as the account owner in the event of Tom's death.

PLANNING TOOLS AND OTHER BACKGROUND INFORMATION

Several tools can be used to save for Azalea's education. Following is a brief summary of the most commonly used options. A list of additional alternatives that could be considered and a review of the tax considerations are also provided.

Taxable Account (Current Funding Tool)

Tom and Nyla, you have been using a taxable mutual fund account to save for Azalea's education. A taxable account is simply an account (e.g., savings account, brokerage account) in your name(s) designated as savings for Azalea's education. Taxes are due on the earnings annually, and taxes are due on the capital gains when the assets are sold. Because this account has no specific planning or tax benefits, there are no annual or lifetime contribution limits.

Advantages

- There are numerous investment options (stocks, mutual funds, bonds, cash investments, etc.).

- The owner(s) controls the account and has unrestricted access and use of the account.

- There is no penalty for funds taken out for purposes other than education.

Disadvantages

- Earning and distributions are taxable in the year earned.

- Taxes will be due on any capital gains when account assets are sold.

- Because the owner can access the funds, it may be difficult to avoid the temptation of taking money out of the account for purposes other than Azalea's education.

- The account is included in the owner's gross estate, which could have estate tax implications.

- Diversification is harder to achieve because of minimum initial deposit requirements for some mutual funds.

§ 529 Plan (Proposed Funding Tool)

Established under § 529 of the Internal Revenue Code, § 529 plans are tax-advantaged accounts for paying qualified higher education expenses (i.e. tuition, fees, room and board, books, and supplies). Earnings grow tax free and qualified withdrawals are tax free. These plans have high contribution limits and other family members or friends can contribute to the account. It is important to note that there are two types of § 529 plans: prepaid tuition plans and college savings plans. With prepaid tuition plans, contributions are guaranteed to match the inflation rate of education costs, similar to paying tuition costs in advance. These plans are typically restricted to in-state institutions, so adjustments may be necessary for use out-of-state. With college savings plans, earnings are based on the performance of the market and mutual fund-type accounts.

Advantages

- Earnings grow tax free and qualified withdrawals are tax free.

- § 529 plans are considered assets of the parents for college financial aid purposes and reporting on the Free Application for Federal Student Aid (FAFSA). Effective in 2009–2010, a § 529 account owned by a dependent child, or by the child's custodian, must also be reported as a parental asset.

- The owner/contributor maintains control of the account (i.e., controls change of beneficiary, owner, distribution amount or frequency, or subaccount options).

- Contributions are not included in the contributor's gross estate because contributions to the account are treated as a completed gift.

- Contributions may be "front-loaded" (i.e., five years' worth of annual exclusion gifts may be made in a single year).

- § 529 plans have a high contribution limit (i.e., $300,000 or more per beneficiary), with no income phaseout.

- State income tax incentives (e.g., tax deductions or tax credits) may be available for contributions to your AnyState College Savings Plan and in some cases to out-of-state plans (consult your tax advisor for more information).

- There are no age or time restrictions on use of the asset.

Disadvantages

- There is a 10% penalty for early or nonqualified withdrawals, in addition to taxes on the earnings.

Custodial Accounts (UGMA/UTMA)

Under the Uniform Gift to Minors Act (UGMA) or the Uniform Transfers to Minors Act (UTMA), individuals can establish custodial accounts that are controlled by the custodian until a minor child reaches the age of majority (usually 18 or 21, as determined by state law). Like a taxable account, these accounts usually allow a broad range of investments and unlimited annual or lifetime contributions. However, funds placed in these accounts are considered an irrevocable gift. Thus, at the age of majority, the child will gain control of the account and have unrestricted use of its funds.

Advantages

- There are numerous investment options (cash, stocks, bonds, mutual funds, insurance, etc.), and real estate may be gifted to an UTMA account.

- Unlimited contributions are permitted.

Disadvantages

- The beneficiary (minor) gains control of the account at the age of majority.

- Income tax benefits are limited because of the "kiddie tax" law, which means the assets are essentially taxed at the parents' rate (consult your tax advisor for more information).

- These accounts are considered the property of the student for college financial aid purposes.

- Annual funding is limited to the tax-free gift threshold ($13,000 per person in 2012).

- The use of funds is restricted, for the benefit of the minor, before the beneficiary reaches the age of majority.

- The account is included in the custodian's gross estate (if the custodian was also the donor), which could have estate tax implications (consult your tax or legal advisor for more information).

Coverdell Education Savings Account

The Coverdell Education Savings Account (ESA) (formerly known as the Education IRA) is another tax-deferred (and potentially tax-free) account that can generally be distributed tax free if all funds are used for approved education expenses. These funds can be used for college expenses as well as elementary and secondary education savings. Other family members or friends may contribute to the account. However, contributions cannot exceed $2,000 per beneficiary per year for 2012. Furthermore, the $2,000 contribution amount may be limited by income level. Tom and Nyla, under the current law, you qualify to make the full $2,000 contribution.

It is also important to recognize that many of the benefits of Coverdell ESA accounts are scheduled to change when the Economic Growth and Tax Relief Reconciliation Act of 2001 "sunsets" at the end of 2012. Among the changes, three that could be important to you are a reduction in the annual contribution amount to $500; a restriction on contributing to both an ESA and a § 529 plan in the same year; and a restriction on claiming any education credit in the same year a tax-free withdrawal is made from a Coverdell ESA. Congress has previously extended the current ESA features, so these changes may not occur, but they should be monitored.

Advantages

- Earnings grow tax deferred and qualified withdrawals are tax free.

- There are numerous investment options (stocks, mutual funds, bonds, cash investments, etc.).

- Funds may be used for elementary, secondary, and higher education.

- Coverdell ESAs are considered the property of the parent(s) for college financial aid calculations and reporting on FAFSA, similar to § 529 plans, as noted above.

- Contributions are not included in the contributor's gross estate.

Disadvantages

- Contributions are limited to $2,000 per year per beneficiary (additional restrictions may apply), which may be insufficient to meet college costs.

- Contribution amounts may be phased out for those with higher incomes.

- There is a 10% penalty for early or nonqualified withdrawals, in addition to taxes on the earnings.

- Age restrictions apply; the assets must be deposited before age 18 and used by the account beneficiary before age 30, or rolled into the account of another eligible family member without penalty.

Other Funding Alternatives

Given the 10-year time horizon to save for Azalea's education, these options are not as relevant to your situation. However, the viability of any of these alternatives could be reconsidered in the future:

- Use Series EE and Series I Savings Bonds as savings tools. These bonds offer the benefit of tax-exempt earnings when used for qualified expenses assuming all rules are met and income does not exceed the phaseout for tax-exempt status. But earnings on these bonds are low.

- Use a home equity loan or 401(k) or other retirement account loan (if available).

- Use a Roth or traditional IRA to concurrently save for education and retirement. The 10% penalty does not apply to early withdrawals for qualified education expenses (i.e., tuition, fees, room and board, and equipment and supplies).

TAX CONSIDERATIONS

Nyla and Tom, federal income tax rules are certain to change before, and perhaps even while, Azalea is in college from 2022 to 2026. But understanding the tax implications, and monitoring them, may be helpful as you make choices on how to fund her education. In 2012, two federal income tax credits, a deduction for tuition and fees, and an adjustment for interest on education loans are available to those funding college education costs for themselves, a spouse, or dependents; phaseouts and income restrictions apply. Both of the credits can be coordinated with funds withdrawn from a Coverdell ESA or a § 529 plan, but tax-free withdrawals and credits cannot be applied to the same expenses. The two credits cannot be taken for the same child in the same year; the taxpayer must choose which credit to apply. Also, the credits may not be claimed for the same student in the same year, if the tuition and fees deduction is applied.

- The American Opportunity Tax Credit, projected to end in 2012, modified the Hope Credit to provide a credit of up to $2,500 per year for up to four years of a student's qualified higher education expenses. The Hope Credit offered a more limited credit of up to $1,800 for the first two years of qualified higher education.

- The Lifetime Learning Credit provides a credit of up to $2,000 per year for qualified higher education expenses or noncredit career advancement courses. This credit is available for an unlimited number of years.

- For those who do not qualify for the preceding credits, a deduction of up to $4,000 of qualified college tuition and related expenses may be available.

- Up to $2,500 of interest on education loans may qualify as an adjustment to income in the year paid, assuming all rules apply.

OTHER CONSIDERATIONS

In addition to the college savings vehicles mentioned above, we want you to be aware of some other important areas of financial assistance. Each college or university has its own financial aid system in place and will provide guidelines on application procedures.

- Scholarships

- Financial aid

- Pell grants

- Perkins loans and Stafford loans (subsidized and unsubsidized) available to students

- PLUS loans available to parents and others

Tom and Nyla, you may want to consider these and other options as the time approaches for Azalea to begin college. Her high school counseling department also may offer assistance on how to pursue financial aid.

ADDITIONAL INFORMATION

For further information visit the following:

The College Board (www.collegeboard.org).

FinAid! The SmartStudent™Guide to Financial Aid (www.finaid.org).

SallieMae (https://www.salliemae.com/).

Saving for College (www.savingforcollege.com).

Notes

1. The College Board, Advocacy and Policy Center, *Trends in College Pricing, 2010*. Available at http://trends.collegeboard.org/downloads/archives/CP_2010.pdf, p. 10.

2. College Board, *Trends in College Pricing*.

3. College Board, *Trends in College Pricing*, p. 3.

4. College Board, *Trends in College Pricing*, p. 13.

5. Institute for College Access & Success, The Project on Student Debt, *Student Debt and the Class of 2010*. Available at http://projectonstudentdebt.org/files/pub/classof2010.pdf, p. 1.

6. Savingforcollege.com. *Financial Aid Basics: Financial Aid and Your Savings*. Excerpted from Savingforcollege.com's *Family Guide to College Savings*, Available at http://www.savingforcollege.com/financial_aid_basics/financial_aid_and_your_savings.php .Joseph F. Hurley, *Family Guide to College Savings, 2011-2012* (Pittsford, NY: JFH Innovative), 66.

7. These expenses include tuition, fees, books, supplies, and equipment required for attendance at an *eligible* educational institution. Additional details about qualified expenses and eligible institutions can be found in IRS Publication 970 or discussed with your tax advisor.

8. Because this is only a sample extract of an actual plan, the referenced results are not included here, but they would be provided in an actual plan.

9. Because this is only a sample extract of an actual plan, the referenced results are not included here, but they would be provided in an actual plan.

10. Currently 34 states and the District of Columbia offer either state tax deductions or state tax credits to residents who invest in their home state's § 529 plan. For more information see http://www.finaid.org/savings/state529deductions.phtml.

Index